Dynamic Scheduling

With Microsoft® Project 2002
The Book By and For Professionals

Eric Uyttewaal, PMP
Vice President, Microsoft Project Certification
International Institute for Learning, Inc.

Published jointly by
J. Ross Publishing and International Institute for Learning

Copyright ©2003 by International Institute for Learning, Inc.

ISBN 1-932159-13-4

Printed and bound in the U.S.A. Printed on acid-free paper.

10 9 8 7 6 5 4 3 2
Library of Congress Cataloging-in-Publication Data
Uyttewaal, Eric.
   Dynamic scheduling with Microsoft Project 2002: the book by and for
   professionals / by Eric Uyttewaal.
   p. cm.
    ISBN 1-932159-13-4
   1. Microsoft Project. 2. Project management—Computer programs. I.
   Title
   HD69.P75U98 2003
   658.4'04'02855369—dc21

                                                    2003003797

Direct all inquiries to J. Ross Publishing, Inc., 6501 Park of Commerce Blvd., Suite 200, Boca Raton, Florida 33487.

Phone: (561) 869-3900
Fax: (561) 892-0700
Web: www.jrosspub.com

International Institute for Learning, Inc. (IIL)

The IIL Advantage

We provide the learning support needed to manage today's complex, global issues. We offer state-of-the-art training and consulting services in MS Project Certification, Project Management, Six Sigma and Theory of Constraints. IIL's experienced consultants and trainers are flexible and adaptable to meet your needs. IIL partners closely with clients to ensure that they achieve their business strategies. We help design, implement and maintain custom-tailored strategies that result in meaningful and measurable results. We create solutions that fit budget, schedule, business objectives and cultural needs. We have a learning solution that is just right for your unique needs and culture.

Many Methods of Learning

- **Traditional Classroom**
  Each year we schedule over one thousand live instructor-led sessions in major cities around the world. Chances are there is a course scheduled in a city near you.
- **Live eLearning**
  IIL offers a diverse curriculum of live, instructor-led classrooms via the Internet. Participants interact live with the instructor and fellow classmates. A cost-effective learning solution that eliminates the costs and hassles associated with travel and time away from work.
- **Online, On-Demand and Self-Paced Learning**
  IIL offers a variety of training courses that give you extraordinary content while learning at your own pace. Get world-class training when and where you need it.
- **Computer-Aided Simulation Learning**
  A growing number of our courses are utilizing computer-aided simulation. Learn by making critical decisions in a realistic and safe "virtual" business setting.
- **Onsite Learning and Corporate Solutions**
  More than 10,000 individuals a year are trained via courses that we deliver at locations specified by our clients. Such courses are custom-tailored for clients.
- **Worldwide Satellite Broadcasts**
  IIL is a pioneer in the production and delivery of live satellite learning broadcasts. Interact live with industry leaders, subject-matter gurus and respected CEOs.

For more information about IIL and to request a free copy of our catalogue, please visit www.iil.com, or contact Lori Milhaven at 212-515-5121 or Lori.Milhaven@iil.com.

Download Resource Center

Free value-added materials available from the Download Resource Center at:

www.jrosspub.com

At J. Ross Publishing we are committed to providing today's professional with practical, hands-on tools that enhance the learning experience and give readers an opportunity to apply what they have learned. That is why we offer free ancillary materials available for download on this book and all participating Web Added Value™ publications. These online resources may include interactive versions of material that appears in the book or supplemental templates, worksheets, models, plans, case studies, proposals, spreadsheets and assessment tools, among other things. Whenever you see the WAV™ symbol in any of our publications, it means bonus materials accompany the book and are available from the Web Added Value Download Resource Center at www.jrosspub.com.

Downloads available for *Dynamic Scheduling with Microsoft Project 2002* consist of quick reference tables with toolbar and keyboard shortcuts, answers to sample exam questions, about one hundred examples of certified schedules, filters to check the quality of your own schedule, and solution files for the Project 2002 exercises, plus a solutions manual for college instructors and professors.

Short Table of Contents

Long Table of Contents

Dedication

In Dutch:

Ik draag deze tweede editie op aan mijn dochter Maven. Maven, je was mijn inspiratie tot de eerste editie en nu ben je mijn inspiratie om de tweede editie het beste boek te maken dat ik kan.

Ik draag dit boek ook op aan Shelley. Shelley, terwijl jij onze tweede baby verwende in je buik, heb ik deze tweede editie geschreven. Zonder jouw geweldige steun zou het er nooit gekomen zijn. Tussen twee haakjes, hoeveel edities wil je nog?

In English:

To my daughter Maven. Maven, you were the inspiration for the first edition, and now you are the inspiration to make this edition the best I can.

To Shelley, while you were nurturing our second baby in your belly, I created the second edition. Without your marvelous support, it would never have been. By the way, how many editions do you still want?

List of Changes in This Edition

◆ All text has been reviewed and changed as necessary for the 2002 release of Microsoft Project. We did a complete re-write.

◆ The new features of MS Project are discussed throughout and indicated with a 2002 icon to make them easy to find.

◆ Project Server is added to this edition. People who are using Project 2002 in combination with Project Server will find the things they need to know in this book. People who are using Project 2002 as a standalone application will also find the things they need to know.

◆ The checklist of guidelines for valid and dynamic schedules in Chapter 13 has been researched, discussed and entirely re-written by our team of instructors. We now feel we have a solid checklist that candidates can use to create valid and dynamic models of their own projects. The checklist creates repeatability in project management processes, which can advance the project management maturity of individuals and their organizations. Also:

◇ The checklist items refer to the pages in the book where they are discussed in more detail and with procedural steps.

◇ The list comes with a corresponding set of filters and macros to perform the checks efficiently. The filters and macros are available for download at www.jrosspub.com.

◆ All learning objectives have been revised so as to truly capture the body of knowledge that participants are supposed to master in the Orange Belt of our certification curriculum.

◆ All project management stories and cartoons at the start of each chapter are new.

◆ Many review questions have been added to the end of each chapter.

◆ The index has three times more entries.

◆ This edition is written assuming that most readers are now using Windows 2000 or Windows XP. Some screen captures may differ depending on the operating system being used. The screen shots are made in Windows 2000.

Foreword

Finally, we have a book on MS Project written by a Project Management Professional! Over the years, I have been disappointed with books written on the scheduling software. Past books seem to have been written by non-practitioners using examples that were somewhat removed from real-world applications or examples that were so simplistic that the reader was left with a false impression of the true applications and capability of the software. This book, however, uses numerous practical examples from real-life projects. You will quickly discover that the author exhibits the necessary experience to give you the insights you need to manage your projects more effectively. In addition, this one book contains all of the necessary information to attain the Orange Belt certificate from the International Institute for Learning, Inc. (IIL).

This book will convince you that project management can be done more efficiently using software. Historically, PERT charts were hung in the war rooms of large project teams. These charts were excellent tools that provided insight into the downstream impacts of any changes made. Schedulers had to become skilled at identifying the impacts and the associated risks. This book is proof that project management can be made simpler by using Project 2002 and dynamic models of your project. The book has been enhanced from the previous edition by including more review questions at the end of each chapter so as to allow readers to measure their own progress. New tools are also included to allow the user a means of verifying the quality of their own schedules.

In terms of the Project Management Maturity model I have introduced, this book creates a common language (Level 1) that will help you to establish common processes for the scheduling of projects (Level 2). The summary chapter of the book contains *"guidelines for dynamic schedules"* that should be considered for the scheduling of your projects. These guidelines will help you move toward a singular methodology, the third level of the project management maturity model. The guidelines are universally applicable to projects of any size and in any industry. This is where the book has added value over the many books that have been published on scheduling in general and on MS Project in particular. It combines scheduling best practices with the how-to in Project 2002.

The scheduling guidelines are an integral part of the MS Project certification curriculum that IIL has put together. Many organizations are sending their project managers and schedulers to IIL's courses, and the guidelines have been embraced by several organizations. What seems to be evolving is a body of knowledge on scheduling with Project 2002. I recommend this book be used as a new standard on scheduling in the project management body of knowledge.

Harold Kerzner
Cleveland, Ohio

Acknowledgments

I would like to thank all the people I have had the pleasure of meeting during my MS Project courses and consulting. The discussions we had provided valuable input for this book. Many people have opened my eyes to remarkable insights. Where I remembered individuals, I have recognized them in this book. Unfortunately, I have forgotten where many thoughts and insights originated. To all of those who should have been mentioned, I apologize.

Some people were actively involved in creating this book and deserve special recognition. First of all I would like to thank the technical editors for their contributions to the accuracy of the text. Because of their help, I have used the word "we" throughout the book when making recommendations. The recommendations are really a culmination of experiences and insights from this team, most of whom are instructors at the International Institute for Learning, Inc. (IIL). Let me thank the technical editors personally here:

- ◆ Jeff Turner, Boeing, thank you for your insightful comments. Jeff also created the helpful illustrations on WBS (aircraft), Critical Path and slack calculation.
- ◆ Linda Lawlor, Senior Consultant, IIL, thank you for your eye for detail. I can always count on you to carefully review everything. Thanks for trying out the steps.
- ◆ Sheri Young, thank you for the improved words and formulations you sent me. You really made a difference in many places.
- ◆ Brian Kennemer, Microsoft Project MVP, QuantumPM, thank you for your sharp observations on technical accuracy. You made me think again in several places.
- ◆ Judith W. Firestone, MPM, PMP, Senior Manager, Project Management Office, CSC, thank you for your eye for detail and your perseverance in the last chapters when the time available got tight.
- ◆ Ken Massey, Microsoft Project Trainer and Consultant, IIL, thank you for your last-minute diligence and catching oversights.
- ◆ John Sullivan, Vice-President, Instructional Design, IIL, I wished you could have had more time to review the book, since the comments I received were right on.
- ◆ Ray Moore, Director, Amethyst Project Management Limited, UK, thank you for the international perspective and the quote you provided.
- ◆ Ron Gardiner, EVM Tools Support, Boeing Integrated Defense Systems, thank you for your sharp observations on consistency and technical accuracy.
- ◆ Ellen Lehnert, Senior Instructor, IIL, thank you for your recommendations on how to make this information easier to teach.
- ◆ Frank Walker, TWG Project Management, LLC, thank you for sharing your wealth of practical experiences with me, which enriched this book in several places.

- Thomas Sauerbrun, Senior Instructor, IIL, thank you for your remarks on keeping the book aligned with the PMBOK® Guide 2000.

In addition to the technical editors, the following people have been involved:
- Sandy Pearlman, Senior Editor, J. Ross Publishing, thank you for the final editing. You improved not only the English but also the format and the layout. You must have the eyes of a hawk since you even noticed if dots and commas were bolded or not.
- Paul Mason, thank you for the cartoons that illustrate many of the points made from an angle that always surprises. Whenever I received a batch of new sketches, you gave me some good laughs.
- Rina van Adrichem, thank you for creating many of the snapshots, for checking the consistency in words and formats, and for entering all the language edits.
- LaVerne Johnson, CEO of IIL, thanks for your confidence that this second edition would be worthwhile again.
- Drew Gierman, Publisher & VP of Sales, J. Ross Publishing Inc., thank you for your belief in the product and for your diligent organizing of everybody involved.

Many people sent in reviews of the book on Project 2000. I would like to mention these people here in alphabetical order. These reviews turned out to be very valuable when writing this edition on Project 2002:
- Mazin Altoumah, PWGSC, Federal Government, Canada
- Joe Bellows , MPUG - San Francisco Bay Area, USA
- Lawrence Darbonne, PMP, SI International, USA
- Alban DeBergevin, MPUG - Boston Metro, USA
- Laura DiLaura, MPUG - NYC-Metro, USA
- Chas Eddingfield, MPUG - Greater Cincinnati, USA
- Yvon Guillemette, EDS, Canada
- Dr. Carol Hartz, MPUG - Atlanta, USA
- Ken Jamison, MPUG - Western New York Chapter, USA
- Adrian Jenkins, Microsoft, USA
- Neil Kemp, MPUG - Ottawa, Canada
- Ger Maguire, MPUG - Ireland
- Mark Mazerolle, MDS - Nordion, Canada
- David Meadows, MPUG - Sydney, Australia
- Charlie Milstead, PMP, Coca Cola Enterprises, USA
- Andy Orrock, On-Line Strategies, USA
- Linda Plummer, MPUG-Phoenix, USA
- Corine Porter, CGI Group, Canada
- Tom Sippl, MPUG - Orange County Chapter, USA
- Peter Slinn, Alcatel, Canada

- Karel Swinnen, EDS, Belgium
- Ricardo Viana Vargas, MPUG - Brazil
- Chris Vandersluis, HMS Software, Canada
- Mark van Onna, The Netherlands
- Larry Wentzel, Tribune CoOpportunity Center, USA
- Laura Williams, MPUG - Southeast Louisiana, USA
- Kevin Yamamoto, PWGSC, Federal Government, Canada

Thanks to all these people. They ensured that this textbook on Project 2002 would be even better than the previous edition.

Last but not least, thanks to you, the reader, for buying this book. If you have any comments or suggestions, please contact me by e-mail at EricU@iil.com.

Introduction

Microsoft Project 2002

Microsoft Project is a tool that helps you plan, control and communicate your project. This software can help you create Gantt Charts, network diagrams, resource histograms, and budgets. It will provide reports tailored to your needs and allow you to depict the progress of your project. The strengths of the software are:

◆ The ease of use and flexibility in scheduling and rescheduling

◆ The user-friendly reporting features
   With Project 2002 you can extract almost any information from the project database and present it in a concise report.

◆ Team collaboration features, as embodied in Project Server, help the project manager to communicate with dispersed team members using web browsers

Project 2002 is a powerful tool and, like other tools, requires knowledge and skill to use correctly. The software is not a magic bean that will grow a successful project by itself. Experience has taught me that a successful project results from the combination of sound project management knowledge and a skilled and committed project team that is equipped with the right tools.

What Is New in Project 2002?

◆ The major new feature in Project 2002 is the *Project Guides*. Project Guides are like wizards that guide you through an involved process. The Project Guides are entirely customizable for your organization. You can incorporate your own terminology, methodology and processes in them. Project Guides help new project managers to get up and running quickly.

◆ The *Assign Resources* dialog has been revamped. It now enables you to check the availability of a resource before assigning it. This has huge potential in that you can prevent over-allocations. The dialog now also has filters to find the right resource, and you can add resources from your address list or active directory. It features a new field, called *Request/Demand*, which allows you to indicate if you really want the resource on the task or if the resource can be substituted in scenario analysis done with Project Server.

 ◆ MS Project is now more helpful than ever in keeping your schedule up-to-date. It can automatically reschedule the *Actual Durations* to before the status date and the *Remaining Durations* to after the status date. This will decrease the time you spend keeping your schedule up-to-date when you are busy already.

 ◆ Other than that, there are many small improvements in the interface. Some of the remarkable ones are:

◇ **Tools, Import Outlook Tasks** allows you to import task from MS Outlook.

◇ There are now three levels in the timescale, thus allowing you to display the fiscal year next to the calendar year.

◇ You can print row and column totals in the views.

◇ You can update your schedule with a **Physical % Complete**.

◇ Smart Tags help you enter the data in the proper way by asking for clarification.

◇ The `Delete` key deletes cells again instead of rows.

Last but not least, Project Server is new in Project 2002.

Project Server

Project Server is the greatly enhanced web-based product for MS Project. It was formerly called *Project Central*.

Project Server facilitates the communication between the project manager and other project stakeholders:

◆ The project manager can easily send out time sheets and status report forms for team members to fill in, collect them back and then transfer the data into the project file.

◆ Team members can access their task lists, time sheets and status reports to fill in.

◆ Executives can see their portfolio of projects and develop what-if scenarios.

◆ Clients, suppliers, banks, government agencies, unions or other stakeholders can also be given access to certain project or resource data.

The project manager needs MS Project, whereas other stakeholders only need *Internet Explorer* and a *Microsoft Project Web Access* license. Project Server makes MS Project, MS Outlook, Internet Explorer, SQL Server and Web Server communicate with each other.

However, Project Server is more than a postal service. Below is a complete list of the benefits you can enjoy by using Project Server:

◆ Standardization across the enterprise:
Project Server allows standardization of templates, options, views and fields. Project Server allows you to create an enterprise-wide resource pool of thousands of people. In previous versions of MS Project, you typically could not go over a few hundred resources in the shared resource pool. MS Project got progressively slower as you added more resources.

◆ Modeling of portfolios of projects and integrated program schedules:
Project Server also allows the organization to model their projects and resource needs in the longer term. It provides a flexible interface that allows you to slice and dice the project data and drill down into the supporting details. Executives and resource managers can thus make analyses to find answers to questions like:
◇ What are our resource needs in the longer term such that we can train existing or hire new employees in a timely manner? In general, resource availability is flexible as long as the need for the resource is about three months away.
◇ Can we take on another project given the resources we have? If not, when can we take it on? Or, if we were to take it on right now, how much would that cause our current projects to slip?

◆ Collaborating:
As a project manager you can collect input from team members, like new tasks, changes to the work day and vacation time. The Project Server interface is a two-way street:
◇ project data from the project manager to the team member, and
◇ personal data from the team member.

◆ Integrating project planning with personal planning:
◇ One single integrated to-do list of project and non-project tasks. The to-do list can be maintained in MS Outlook.
◇ You can synchronize the Outlook calendar with the resource calendar in Project 2002.
◇ You can make Project Server one of the views in MS Outlook such that team members only need to go to one place.

◆ Delegating tasks:
Project Server can accommodate large projects and more than two hierarchical levels of the project manager and his team members. There can be an intermediary level of team leaders. A team leader can delegate a task to one of his team members through the delegation feature.
The delegation feature can also be beneficial for matrix organizations.

◆ Reporting progress electronically in both hours worked and/or a narrative:
  ◇ Time sheets:
    The big benefit of electronic time sheets is one-time data entry. Project Server allows the time sheets to be filled in online or offline and the time sheets in Project Server can include project and non-project tasks. Project managers can send out reminders.
  ◇ Textual status reports:
    The project manager can send out freeform status reports or create template status reports that have the fields he expects to be narrated.

◆ Automatic updating of the project file:
  ◇ A project manager can create rules that allow updates from trusted sources to be processed automatically.
  ◇ The project manager can even choose to manage by exception using this feature; if certain thresholds are exceeded, the message is not processed automatically but called to his attention.

◆ Providing visibility of the project to other groups of stakeholders:
  ◇ The project office can create categories of target groups: team member, project manager, resource manager, and executive manager. Each category comes with a set of access rights.
  ◇ The project office can give access to certain projects through portfolios of projects.
  ◇ The project office can give viewing rights to certain data in the project database through custom views.

Is This Book for You?

This book is different from other books written on Project 2002. It not only shows you how to use MS Project, but also adds insights and experiences from real-life project management. This book teaches you how to manage projects using Project 2002.

The book is intended for the following target groups:

◆ Project managers who use Project 2002 on a day-to-day basis
  It is aimed at the novice to intermediate user of MS Project, but I am confident that advanced users will find it worthwhile. Advanced users may find better ways to do things, as well as best scheduling practices. Advanced users may discover better words to explain features to colleagues.

◆ People who schedule and manage a single project
  This book is used as the courseware in the "Managing a Single Project with

Project 2002" (Orange Belt) course at the International Institute for Learning (IIL). For the next levels in the certification curriculum, there is separate courseware. The Blue Belt focuses on managing multiple projects with MS Project and Project Server. The Black Belt course focuses on advanced resource modeling and customization of *Project Server*.

◆ Students and professors at colleges and universities
For professors and instructors, I have added review questions, a cradle-to-grave exercise project, trouble shooting exercises and case studies at the end of the chapters. In Appendix 1 at the end of the book you will find sample exam questions on Project 2002 similar to the questions used in the certification curriculum at the International Institute for Learning. Professors can get a solution manual at www.jrosspub.com .

What You Will Find in the Book

I will present the features to create project schedules efficiently and the features that create dynamic schedules. These are the features that will benefit you most in practice. At IIL we constantly ask course participants what features they use, why they use them and how. The book will give you guidance in how to run your projects in practice.

The book is aimed at the busy, practicing project manager who needs to get up to speed quickly. Many people have asked me for a good process to follow for creating schedules. The structure of the book matches the order of steps we recommend you take. The recommended process is as simple as following the *Short Table of Contents* of this book.

I have kept the text as succinct as possible. Less text is more, in my opinion, and the last thing I want is to waste your precious time by being verbose. I have inserted graphics throughout the text wherever I felt I could save words with an illustration. A picture is worth …

This book has an attitude. It is not just a description of the features of Project 2002. I will recommend certain features and I will argue against using some other features. An important criterion I use for my recommendations is that the schedule you build with Project 2002 should be a good schedule of your project. In our opinion, a good schedule is:

◆ **A model of the project**
A model is a deliberate but smart simplification of the complex reality of the project.

◆ **A valid model of the project**
A model is valid if it reflects the reality of your project and if it forecasts your project well.

◆ **A dynamic model of the project**
A dynamic model updates itself when a change is entered. When one change happens in your project, ideally you would have to update only one field in the model to have a valid representation of your project — again. Changes happen often during the execution of the project, when you also happen to be very busy. Therefore, a dynamic model is a tremendous help during project execution because it helps you keep the model alive. Hence the title of this book: *Dynamic Scheduling with Microsoft® Project 2002.*

Static schedules do not maintain themselves. Some features in MS Project are nice to have but create schedules that are hungry for maintenance. Therefore, I don't recommend features that continue to need attention. I have found the judicious application of features critical in using MS Project. I have tried to be objective in my assessment, and thousands of students have helped with that.

In this book we will focus on the two main configurations of MS Project currently in use: MS Project standalone and Project 2002 Professional used with *Project Server* (*enterprise mode*). We will devote less attention to using Project 2002 Standard with Project Server in the *workgroup mode*. The workgroup mode uses a subset of the features of enterprise mode.

What you will NOT find in this book is:

◆ This book does not explain all features of Project 2002. I have made a careful selection of features that will benefit users most when managing a single project. This book is not a complete reference on Project 2002.

◆ This book does not explain all there is to know about Project Server. It will only cover the basics of working with Project Server that project managers need to know.[1]

◆ The book does not discuss how to manage multiple projects with MS Project. You will not find in this book a discussion on managing integrated program schedules or portfolio management.

---

[1] IIL has separate classes on Project Server; the Blue Belt Professional and Black Belt Professional courses. See www.iil.com and follow the link *Microsoft Project*.

Now that you know that you are reading a book with an attitude, you may be interested in how the attitude came about.

Who Is the Author?

The author is a project management practitioner. Over the past 15 years I have managed many projects using MS Project and I have taught thousands of people in its use. The insights you will find in this book are a combination of the collective wisdom of our team at IIL and the clients we met in our work.

In September 1993, I became the first Canadian to be certified in MS Project by Microsoft. At that time, the current version was 3.0. When 4.0 came out, I recertified immediately. More eager than ever, I awaited the exam for Project 98 ... and waited ... and waited, but it was never released. I realized that I was probably not the only person who was looking for it. I also observed that practitioners and organizations needed a meaningful certification curriculum. In particular, those organizations that are setting up a *project office* need a thorough professional development curriculum. In the last few years, I have seen many project offices sprout up. I have helped several in formulating scheduling guidelines, and I decided to address the need for certification in the marketplace.

In 1998, I developed a certification curriculum in MS Project. I approached IIL to market it and was hired as Director, MS Project Certification. Since then we have held many certification classes in North America and in Europe. In these workshops, I have had the pleasure of working with some of the finest project managers.

The consulting and training I have done included people from a wide variety of sectors: information technology, telecommunications, banking, automotive, construction, manufacturing, pharmaceutical, international development and government. As a result, you will find a wide variety of examples in this book. It does not cater to one sector in particular.

The Project Management Institute (PMI) certified me as a Project Management Professional (PMP) in March of 1994. IIL promoted me to Vice-President, Microsoft Project Certification in December 2001. I am currently managing a team of fifteen instructors.

The Author's Perspective on Scheduling

In my years of consulting in organizations and training project managers, I have made some observations:

♦ Some large schedules I have seen did not have a Work Breakdown Structure (WBS). All tasks were on the first (and only) indentation level. Imagine that this book did not have a hierarchy of sections, chapters and paragraphs. A well-known automotive company used schedules like these. (Sorry, no names!) Organizations were not using the basic concept of logical and hierarchical Work Breakdown Structures. Such a schedule is difficult to explain to anyone who is not interested in the detail activities — like executives.

♦ Many schedules created by "experienced" project managers turned out to have only a few dependencies (links between tasks). Not surprisingly, those schedules had many schedule constraints that anchored the task bars to their dates. Constraints, however, made the schedule very rigid. Every time a change occurred, the entire schedule needed to be reviewed and updated before it depicted the project well again. Isn't this reminiscent of the time when we made schedules on paper to hang on our walls? Such schedules are nice charts of the project, but definitely are not useful dynamic models of the project. These people spend too much time on scheduling. And they are spending this time when they don't have a moment to spare — during project execution. Needless to say, these project managers aren't managing their projects as they could.

♦ Many organizations create schedules that are so complex that it takes weeks to understand them. I am always afraid to ask these project managers how long it took to create monsters like that. If the *model* of the project is as complex as or more complex than the reality itself, you do not have a better handle on the reality by modeling it. Modeling is, by its definition, simplifying the reality to get a better handle on it. Too many project managers seem to forget this. If you cannot explain your project schedule to your team, the schedule simply is too complex. If your team understands it, you get much more value from your schedule and scheduling efforts. If other stakeholders can also understand your schedule, even better.

♦ Many organizations invest in making schedules, but abandon them when the project execution starts. The chance that it will be abandoned increases with the complexity of the schedule and with the lack of dependencies or abundance of constraints. One aerospace company had never been able to keep its schedules alive. Only after they had one project manager trained in our program (sorry for this plug), this person managed to do that as a primer. Project managers tend to get very busy with fighting fires after the project kick-off. If you don't update your schedule, you don't have accurate forecasts of your project. You need constant forecasting to control your project. A dynamic schedule is easy to maintain and provides continuous forecasts.

◆ Many project managers often do not enter resources into MS Project. Even if they do, they often do not check if they over-allocated their resources. The schedule may show finish dates that executives like, which may result in swift approval, but when the workloads are leveled, it becomes painfully clear that the promised dates are not feasible. If you notice that deadlines are often not accomplished in your organization, a lack of modeling availability of resources and their workloads may very well be the cause of that.

◆ Any organization that shares its resources across projects but does not have a central, shared resource pool suffers from missed deadlines because of resource impacts across its projects. Many IT departments experience this. IT resources tend to be expensive and they are often shared across all projects. The individual schedules show date forecasts that executives liked. When the project execution starts, project managers start stealing each other's resources in order to meet their own deadlines. Doing so wrecks havoc with each other's deadlines. If the total workload of the resources has not been modeled across the projects, the dates shown by individual schedules may not be feasible at all. With *Project Server* you can set up an enterprise resource pool that can relegate this issue to the past.

◆ Last but not least, in 1994 The Standish Group published a report on the performance of IT projects.[2] They surveyed 365 IT managers representing 8,380 applications from many different industries. Only 1 in 8 projects was delivered successfully. In 1996, the number had improved to 1 in 4, because the shock wave of the first report led to quicker cancellation of dead-end projects. My personal conviction is that the project management concepts are solid and could successfully be applied to IT projects. My personal observation is that IT people, for some weird reason, are just not applying the principles of project management properly.
I admit, however, that in certain areas it is necessary to adjust the techniques used. One contribution this book will make in that respect is, for example, that most IT project managers will have to do a Resource Critical Path analysis instead of a Critical Path analysis since most are in a resource-constrained situation. This relatively new concept is explained in this book.

If you have been bothered by any of these observations, you should read this book cover to cover. This book will provide you with insights and techniques to address them.

---

[2] Chaos, The Standish Group International, 1994, Dennis, MA, page 2-7.

These observations on the current state-of-the-art in scheduling led me to believe a certification curriculum was much needed. Such a curriculum can elevate the skills of MS Project users to new heights and improve the accuracy of finish date forecasts. Other benefits would be more reasonable workloads, less burnout and more reliable long-term forecasts of resource needs. The cost of managing projects should decrease. The competitiveness of the organization should increase.

Why Do We Need Valid and Dynamic Schedules?

Most project managers create schedules to better forecast their projects. If the schedule is not valid, it does not produce reliable forecasts.

There are several reasons why we need schedules to be dynamic as well:

◆ Changes happen so frequently in projects that it is hard enough to keep up with them. If your schedule is not as dynamic as it can be, you will spend too much time keeping it alive. You will likely stop updating it sometime during project execution.

◆ Schedules of subprojects need to be dynamic *models* when you want to roll them up into a master schedule. Otherwise you will spend too much time making changes in the master schedule. When schedules are rolled up, problems become visible in the master schedule. Problems require making changes in the master schedule.

◆ In order to develop scenarios in MS Project and in Project Server using the modeler features, the schedules need to be dynamic. If there are too many constraints in the schedules, the portfolio modeler does not provide useful results.

◆ In order to do schedule simulation, you will need dynamic schedules. Monte Carlo schedule simulation is essential to provide more realistic forecasts to executives and clients.

In order to provide an evaluation instrument to determine if your organization produces valid and dynamic schedules, we have created a certification curriculum.

The Project 2002 Certification Curriculum

Three Levels of Certification

The curriculum consists of four levels. Each level is designed with a specific target group in mind (see the illustration below):[3]

◆ Microsoft Project 2002 Fundamentals (*White Belt*) for people who are new to MS Project

◆ Managing a Single Project with MS Project (*Orange Belt*) for project managers who use MS Project regularly

◆ Managing Multiple Projects with MS Project (*Blue Belt Standard*) or with Project Server (*Blue Belt Professional*) for project managers who manage multiple projects

◆ Masters Certificate in MS Project (*Black Belt Standard*) or Project Server (*Black Belt Professional*) for project office staff

In the Orange Belt workshop we bring people who make nice charts of their projects to the level of making dynamic *models* of their projects that produce valid forecasts. If a person is certified at the Orange Belt level, we guarantee their employer that the person has a demonstrated capability to create good schedules of their own projects. The Orange Belt is tailored to project managers and schedulers.

This book will cover all of the content presented in the Orange Belt level workshop as offered by IIL.

The Blue Belt is designed for people who manage multiple projects simultaneously. These people have successfully managed single projects and have ended up managing

---

[3] If you are interested in detailed topical outlines of the courses, visit www.iil.com and follow the link *Microsoft Project*.

multiple projects as a reward. They can be project managers, program managers, portfolio managers and resource managers, as well as staff working in a project office.

Notice that there are two alternative tracks at the Blue Belt level: Blue Belt Standard and Blue Belt Professional:

◆ In the Blue Belt Standard, we equip people with the know-how to integrate schedules into a master schedule with MS Project standalone. We teach tools and techniques to handle these large schedules. It is for people who use MS Project in a standalone fashion, typically using Project 2002 Standard edition.

◆ In the Blue Belt Professional, we equip project managers who have Project 2002 Professional how to work with *Project Server* to manage and control their projects.

The Black Belt level is targeted at people in the project office who want to make project management more efficient. They can lower the cost of managing projects by developing views and custom solutions on the foundation of MS Project (Black Belt Standard) or Project Server (Black Belt Professional). In other words, the Black Belt is for people who need to know everything about the tools.

The *American Council for Education* audited our curriculum in September 2001 and accredited it. People can get (elective) university credits with our certificates.

In 2002, *PMI* started to offer our Orange Belt workshop in its *Seminars World* offering. The *Project World* organization followed suit.

Also in 2002, *Microsoft* formally recognized our curriculum. If organizations want to become an *Enterprise Premier Partner* for MS Project, they need to have certified people on staff. People who are certified through the IIL curriculum qualify.

How Many Are Currently Certified?

As of December 31, 2002 there were 810 people certified at the Orange Belt level, 396 at the Blue Belt level and 73 at the Black Belt level. The curriculum has been very well received.

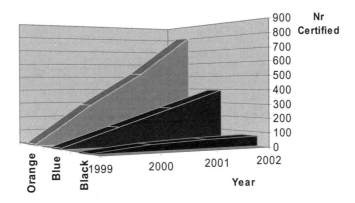

In 2001, the number for the Orange Belt was 521 and we reached 810 in the year 2002, which is regarded as a difficult year for training and certification. We expect to pick up the pace in 2003 and possibly double the number of people certified. We are attempting to set the standard in the marketplace for MS Project certification.

The following are some quotes from participants:

Orange Belt

Thank you, I LOVED the course!!
Caroline Robison, PMP

I want to thank you and all the trainers from IIL for some of the best training I have taken. David W. Weigel, New York State

The knowledge I have gained by taking this course has set me apart from other project managers. I now create dynamic schedules that work!
Dino Nosella, Project Manager, SAP Canada, Inc.

Since I completed the Orange Belt certification, other people in my company are now coming to me for advice and help in using MS Project.
Stephanie Ghingher, AEGON, USA

I found the online Orange Belt course one of the most effective and beneficial software courses I have ever taken. The focus on 'how to use the software to manage a project' was a refreshing contrast to the usual 'how to use the functions of this software'. Tommie G. Cayton, Ph.D., Assistant Director, Project Management

Blue Belt

This series will definitely get your organization on the right track in terms of project schedules. Chas Eddingfield, Project Controller, Cincinnati Insurance Company

Superb instruction and excellent course content. A must for even experienced MS Project users. Bill Reinhart, Project Manager, SBC/Ameritech, USA

I have managed projects for a number of years, but the course was of such high quality that I now feel the quality and accuracy of my project plans will be enhanced. Dave Kempster, Consultancy & Research Manager, Centrefile Limited, UK

We reviewed a number of training vendors when we determined who to send our folks to and the IIL courses are by far the best quality with regard to content and instruction. David Peeters, PMP, Sr. Project Management Consultant, Alliant Energy

Black Belt

The IIL MS Project Certification series should be required by every project manager who uses the product! Stephanie Iverson, Director Program Management, Marriott Vacation Club International, USA

Although there are millions of copies of MS Project sold, only a few thousand people really know how to use it. If you want to become a real 'master' user of MS Project, this is the class for you. Jacob Myers, Program Manager, Limited Technology Services, USA

This course focuses on teaching Project Managers how to use Microsoft Project to be more productive and proficient. It is extremely valuable. Len Maland, PMP, Senior Program Manager, HP Consulting & Integration Services, May 2002

We are currently experiencing a lot of interest in our certification curriculum not only from the United States, Canada and Europe, but also from China to Australia.

Overall, we attempt to create the body of knowledge for scheduling projects using MS Project.

What Are the Certification Requirements?

IIL does not provide certification at the White Belt level. The certification levels have a combination of knowledge and skill tests:

◆ The Orange Belt candidates must submit a schedule of their own project that meets the guidelines for good scheduling practices (a skill test). Many organizations use Orange Belt certification to ascertain that their people create good schedules that can be rolled up and used to do scenario development.

◆ The Blue Belt participants must pass a multiple-choice exam that covers the Orange Belt and the Blue Belt materials. The exam discriminates well between people who studied in preparation and those who didn't. Sample exam questions can be found on page 635 in Appendix 1: Certification Curriculum Sample Exam Questions. These sample questions only cover the Orange Belt content that is in this book.

◆ The Black Belt experts must do an assignment in which they plan, implement and report on a customization of MS Project (Black Belt Standard) and/or *Project Server* (Black Belt Professional). This is another skill test.

The blend of a knowledge test and two skill tests has proven to be very well liked by and beneficial for individuals and their organizations.

Qualifying Instructors

If you are working as an MS Project instructor, we would like to invite you to partner with us and offer this certification curriculum to your clients as well. IIL has started to license the certification services to partnering individuals and organizations. Please contact me at EricU@iil.com if this is of interest to you.

In order to maintain quality in the delivery of our certification curriculum, we select instructors based on several criteria:
◆ Candidates must have hands-on experience in managing projects.
◆ Candidates must be using MS Project on an almost daily basis.
◆ Candidates must have the Project Management Professional (PMP) designation by the PMI.
◆ Candidates must have earned credentials in training groups in MS Project.
◆ Candidates must be certified in MS Project in our certification curriculum on one level higher than the level they will be teaching in the curriculum.

A final criterion is that the candidate must go through a train-the-trainer session. If you are interested in becoming an instructor at IIL in this curriculum, please send me your resume at EricU@iil.com.

Consulting

In addition to training and certification services we offer consulting. We help people understand how tools like MS Project and Project Server can best be implemented in their organization. Not every organization is the same. The output of the consulting can take the shape of:

◆ Implementation of *Project Server*
Setting up the enterprise global options, views, codes and resource pool. Establishing the configuration of servers needed considering the usage within your organization.

◆ Creation of project management handbooks
A handbook is a document containing best practices, scheduling guidelines, methodology or project management framework specifically for your organization.

◆ Development of project templates
Templates can contain custom views, tables, filters and groups. Macros can be added if the basic functionality in MS Project does not support what is needed in your organization.

◆ Training and certification
After the tools are developed, people often need training in how to use them. We create or adapt the course material and train the project managers and schedulers. We provide certification to verify if people acquired the right skills.

◆ Coaching, mentoring and help desk
A final step is often to coach and mentor on the job or provide technical support. People tend to get stuck sometimes when they strike out on their own to model their projects. If so, we are here to help.

Give Us Your Feedback

You are the person who can make the next edition of this book better. Please give us your feedback.

If you have any questions or if you would like to discuss any recommendations we make in this book, don't hesitate to contact me at EricU@iil.com.

Thanks for choosing this product co-published by the International Institute for Learning, Inc. and J. Ross Publishing. And thank you for the time you will spend reading it. I hope you will find it well worth the effort!

Eric Uyttewaal, PMP
Vice-President, Microsoft Project Certification
International Institute for Learning
EricU@iil.com
www.iil.com

About This Book

Learning Objectives

The following are the learning objectives we aim to accomplish with this book. After reading this book you will:

◆ understand project management terminology

◆ be able to create a valid and dynamic model of your own project:
   ◇ choosing the options and creating the project calendar
   ◇ entering tasks, estimates, dependencies, constraints, resources and assignments

◆ know how to optimize the schedule to meet deadlines and budget restrictions while keeping the workloads of the resources within their availability

◆ be able to create reports and custom views for the project that meet the need of stakeholders

◆ know how to efficiently update the schedule when the project is running to continue to forecast the project finish date and cost

In general, you should feel very comfortable with Project 2002 after you finish reading this book. We will now outline the topics that will address these objectives.

Outline of This Book

First you initiate the project, then you plan it, and while you execute it, you control it. At

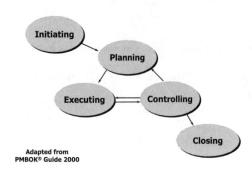

Adapted from
PMBOK® Guide 2000

the end, you close it out. The illustration to the left shows the five process groups as distinguished by the Project Management Institute (PMI) in the Guide to the Project Management Body of Knowledge (PMBOK®), 2000 Edition. We have used these five processes to structure the book. We treated creating the project plan as a mini-project in itself, and we mapped all the steps that you need to take to create a schedule for these processes. The result can be seen in the illustration below.

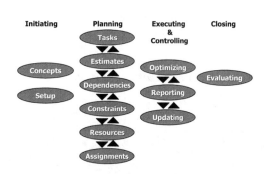

The illustration to the left provides an overview of the contents of this book. Each balloon is a chapter. The overview illustration will be shown at the start of every chapter to indicate where we are. It will pull us back into overview mode before we delve into the next topic.
In this book, we will follow the same sequential approach that we recommend you use when you model your project with Project 2002. We will now elaborate on each step (balloon) in the approach.

Initiating

Concepts (Chapter 1)

In this chapter we will explain some basic concepts of project management. Even though this book is not meant to be a project management theory book, we will provide as much as you need to utilize Project 2002 well.

In this chapter we will also explain the different purposes for using Project 2002. In this book, we will aim at accomplishing the most ambitious one — forecasting a project by building a dynamic model in Project 2002.

Setup (Chapter 2)

In this chapter we will introduce the Project 2002 interface. We will discuss file management, templates and creating a new project. Setting up a new project includes naming the project and entering the project start or finish date. We will invite you to think about the default settings that are active in Project 2002, because some important options need to be set at this stage before any tasks are entered. The project calendar for the project will be created.

Planning

In this section we will develop and enter all the schedule data into Project 2002. This step involves most of the effort in creating the schedule. There are six types of data that Project 2002 needs to create the schedule. We will discuss each of these in the next six chapters.

Tasks (Chapter 3)

Tasks answer the question: *What needs to be done?* The task list is developed from the Work Breakdown Structure (WBS). The structure can have several hierarchical levels as in an organizational chart. In Project 2002 the levels are called outline levels. This chapter will show how to create a structured task list and how to enter it into Project 2002. We will also discuss how to reorganize the task list by moving and copying.

Estimates (Chapter 4)

Estimates answer the question: *How long will the task take?* They can be made in business days (duration) or in person days (work). There are many factors to consider when estimating. We will provide a process in this chapter that will make estimating easier. We will also discuss the human side of estimating and the biases that occur in practice. We will suggest how to handle these biases.

Dependencies (Chapter 5)

Dependencies deal with the question: *In what sequence do the tasks have to be done and how will the tasks affect each other?* In this chapter we will explore this feature, which is important for creating dynamic schedules. Dependencies are the logical cause-and-effect relationships between tasks. Scheduling with project management software does not require that the user enter dates for each task, even though many people do so. By entering dependencies, as opposed to dates, you build a very powerful, dynamic model of the project. If you change the duration of one task, Project 2002 will reschedule all affected dependent tasks. Core secrets of dynamic schedules will be revealed in this chapter.

Constraints (Chapter 6)

Constraints are the answer to the question: *What time limitations are imposed on the schedule?* Constraints can be dates imposed on the project or promises made to meet certain dates. Constraints can also be used for restricting Project 2002's freedom to move task bars around in the timescale. In addition to constraints, we will also discuss the feature of deadlines. The Gantt Chart is finalized in this chapter, and we will show you how to create a printout of it.

Resources (Chapter 7)

Resources are the answer to: *Who will do the work?* Resources can be human resources, facilities, machines or materials. In this chapter we will discuss all these types of resources and how to enter them into Project 2002. We will conclude with how to print the list of resources.

Assignments (Chapter 8)

This last type of project data answers the question: *Who does what?* Multiple resources can be assigned to work on a task, and many tasks can be assigned to one resource.

Resources do the work and have to be assigned to the appropriate tasks. We will discuss the mechanics of assigning resources.

Project 2002 does its own thing when you work with assignments. Behind the screens it uses a formula with which it recalculates data you may have entered. We will explain the when and how and provide you with the insight to help you predict what Project 2002 will do. The goal of this chapter is to make Project 2002 work for you instead of you working for Project 2002. If you found that MS Project did not do what you wanted, this is the chapter to read.

Executing and Controlling

Optimizing the Schedule (Chapter 9)

After entering all the data, Project 2002 shows a schedule that ends before or after the project deadline. The schedule may be under or over the budget. The first draft of the schedule hardly ever meets time and cost constraints. Changes may have to be made to stay within the deadline and budget; this is called optimizing the schedule.

We will present three different approaches for optimizing schedules. You should choose the approach that best fits your own project.
◆ Optimizing for Time
◆ Optimizing for Time and Cost
◆ Optimizing for Time, Cost and Resources
Each approach also includes consideration of the scope and the quality.

In *Optimizing for Time* we will explain the Critical Path method briefly and show how to highlight the Critical Path in your schedule. Sometimes the Critical Path is fragmented, and we will show you how to make it complete from the start of the project to the end. We will then present many different ways in which you can reduce the duration of your project.

In *Optimizing for Time and Cost* we will make the optimization a bit more complex (or more interesting) by incorporating the cost dimension of projects. We will explore the methods available to bring down the cost without compromising too much on scope, quality or time.

Optimizing is more complex when you also want to ensure that the required resources are available and not overloaded with work. Over-allocating resources can compromise the scope of the project or the quality of the deliverables and will often lead to missing deadlines. In the section on *Optimizing for Time, Cost and Resources* we will address the issue of over-allocations by leveling the workloads. We will also introduce the new concept of a Resource-Critical Path, which appears like a regular Critical Path but also takes resource constraints into account. The Resource-Critical Path allows you to find the tasks that drive the finish date of the project. Thus, the Resource-Critical Path allows you to shorten a resource-constrained schedule, just as the Critical Path allows you to do this in other schedules.

After reading this chapter you will be ready to print and distribute the plan to stakeholders.

Reporting (Chapter 10)

In this chapter we will not change the data in the schedule; we will only adjust the appearance of the schedule. Views and reports can, for example, be used to communicate to resources what to do, what to deliver, when and with whom to cooperate. Filters hide certain tasks and display other tasks and can be used to provide the overview to executives — or the detail of a specific problem to the team members. Tables can be used to communicate certain data by inserting or deleting fields. The tasks or resources can be grouped by any commonalities found in the data. Formats can be applied to lead the eye of the reader to the important parts of the report.

The first prints of the project will be used to get the project approved. After that, project managers typically produce status reports periodically.

Updating (Chapter 11)

As soon as the project is approved, a baseline schedule is set based on the approved schedule. The baseline schedule serves as the standard of comparison to track progress. Progress information has to be entered into MS Project, which is known as *updating* the plan. Just like bookkeeping, this should be done on a regular basis. An updated schedule shows the actual performance compared to the baseline.

After updating, you need to establish whether another round of optimizing is needed in case there are progress slippages. During the execution phase of the project, status reports will support the decision making in and about the project, such as modifying the activities or approving the next phase.

During the executing and controlling phase of the project, many cycles will be made among the last three project management activities of optimizing, reporting and updating. Delivering a project involves many iterations of making progress (updating), monitoring the progress (reporting) and taking corrective actions (optimizing).

Closing

Evaluating (Chapter 12)

Evaluating your projects is the only way to become a better project manager. It can prevent you from running into the same traps with your next project. Looking back can also improve your skills in setting dependencies and estimating. These are the hardest skills to acquire as a project manager. It has been predicted that the most competitive organizations will be *learning organizations*.

It is important to take some time to look back and see what went well, what went wrong and why. In this chapter we will discuss what to evaluate in your project and why.

Summary (Chapter 13)

In this chapter you will find a summary of scheduling guidelines to create valid and dynamic schedules for your project, as discussed throughout the book. You can use this chapter as a handy reference to the appropriate pages if you need more explanation on specific topics.

The instructors at the International Institute for Learning use this checklist to certify course participants at the Orange Belt level in the certification curriculum. This book is the course material for the Orange Belt level in the curriculum.

Appendix 1: Certification Curriculum Sample Exam Questions

This appendix contains sample exam questions on Project 2002. These questions are representative of the exams we conduct in the certification curriculum at the International Institute for Learning. The questions pertain to the contents of this book, which corresponds to the Orange Belt level of certification. The real exam is taken at the end of the Blue Belt level and also includes the Blue Belt course materials on managing multiple projects. The answers to these sample questions are available for download at www.jrosspub.com.

Appendix 2: Certified Schedules Available For Download

This appendix has a list of about one hundred examples of excellent real-life schedules that were certified in the certification curriculum. You will find schedules from a wide variety of industries. The schedules are listed with the names of the people who created them and who allowed us to publish them. The schedules are available for download at www.jrosspub.com.

Exercises

You will find exercises at the end of each chapter. Several projects will be worked out step by step throughout the exercises to familiarize you with MS Project. There are four types of exercises:

◆ **Review**
These exercises are meant to consolidate the knowledge you gained in each chapter. These questions review the theoretical concepts.

◆ **Hands-on exercise project: The Relocation Project**
You can test yourself and see if you can create a schedule with Project 2002 on the *Relocation Project*. The Relocation Project is an office move that you will lead as the project manager. You will be moving about 100 co-workers to a new location that you have yet to find. The solutions to these exercises are available for download at www.jrosspub.com. These exercises are meant to provide a checkup to see if you also gained the skills with the knowledge.

◆ **Troubleshooting**
These exercises will help you understand some of the pitfalls in MS Project. These exercises help you prepare for providing technical support to other MS Project users. All the troubleshooting exercises are situations I have run into over the years of staring at people's schedules. We have reviewed thousands of schedules since we first started certifying schedules in 1999. The typical troubleshooting situation is one in which the schedule stubbornly refuses to do what you expect.

◆ **Case studies**
The case studies are meant to give an idea of what is going on in the practice of project management and, in particular, the implementation of MS Project. The case studies are real-life cases from our consulting experience. In all cases, I have disguised the organizations involved.

In Appendix 1, you can find sample exam questions as used in the certification curriculum at the International Institute for Learning. If you want to check if you answered the multiple-choice questions correctly, compare them to the answers available for download at www.jrosspub.com.

Professors can acquire a separate solutions manual that contains all the answers to the review questions, multiple-choice questions, troubleshooting exercises and discussions on the case studies. The solutions manual is available for download at www.jrosspub.com.

Conventions in This Book

Symbols and Text

 The light bulb shows a tip or recommendation to the user. It may be a time-saver or a way of achieving better project control information.

 An exclamation mark shows a warning to the user of Project 2002. Heeding the warnings may keep you out of trouble and avoid unexpected results, loss of data or quirks in Project 2002.

 The 2002 icon indicates that the feature is new in the *Project 2002* release, in both the *Project 2002 Standard* and the *Project 2002 Professional* edition. For people who are upgrading to Project 2002 and who want to focus on just the new features, this graphic is the thing to look for. If you have Project 2002 Professional, also look for the next icon.

 Indicates the new features you will only find in the Project 2002 Professional edition when used with *Project Server*.

File   Words in bold type can literally be found on your screen in Project 2002 — either as a menu item or as a label in a dialog box.

Quotes   Italicized words are literal references. These can be literal quotes from people, data you literally need to enter into Project 2002 or literal words from the index at the back of the book. The indexed keywords are italicized so you can find them easily in the text.

<file name>   Any text enclosed within smaller than (<) and greater than (>) signs is text that should not be taken literally, because it refers to other labels. For example, <file name> refers to the name of the current project file you have open. File names often show up in menu items or in dialog boxes.

Step Formulation

We have not used creativity in formulating the stepwise instructions; in fact, we have followed very rigid guidelines to be as clear and consistent as possible. It can be difficult enough to interpret technical books. These formulation guidelines are:

◆ For menu items, we used the verb "*Choose*". Example: Choose **File, Save As**; the **Save As** dialog appears.

◆ For the toolbars, we used the verb "*Click*" as in: Click **Open** 📂 on the **Standard** toolbar.

◆ For buttons in dialog boxes, we used the verb "*Click*" as in: Click 💾 Save .

◆ For tab pages in dialog boxes, we used the verb "*Click*" as in: Click **Advanced**

◆ For shortcut key combinations, we used the verb "*Press*":

◇ For a single keystroke: Press F2 .

◇ For two keystrokes: Hold down Alt and press F .

◇ For three keystrokes: Hold down Alt + Shift and press → .

◆ For entering text into the fields that have a name, we used "*Key in*" as in: Key in *Relocation* in the field **File Name**.

◆ For check boxes that are checked or not and where the user can choose one or more, we used the verb "*Check*" or "*Uncheck*" as in:
Check ☑ **Display Help on Startup**
Uncheck ☐ **Display Help on Startup**

◆ For radio buttons where the user has to choose one of many options, we used the verb "*Select*" as in: Select ⦿ **Automatic**.

◆ For lists with a label or screen tip, we used:
Select from the list **Insert Field** ID ▼ a column to be inserted.

We used the default toolbars when we wrote the text. In order to easily follow the steps, you may always want to display the full menus. You can do this by choosing **Tools, Customize, Toolbars**, clicking tab **Options** and checking ☑ **Always show full menus**.

Screen Snapshots and Illustrations

We used many illustrations in this book. Most illustrations show only a few tasks extracted from a larger schedule. This allowed us to keep the illustrations concise and to the point.

The procedural steps include dialog boxes inserted right at the places where you can expect to encounter them. This is to ensure that you are in the right dialog box before proceeding with the next step. Otherwise, you could easily get lost.

Where snapshots of MS Project views are shown, we have tried to show only the relevant portion of the screen.

We have annotated the snapshots with blue arrows, lines and callouts so you can easily find the option or field referred to in the text. The annotations often contain extra tips as well, so you may still find them worthwhile even though you understand the steps.

Meet the Cartoon Characters...

Throughout this book you will find little stories with cartoons. One of the main characters in these stories is Bob, a very dynamic and successful project manager. This is Bob (any resemblance to actual people is purely coincidental):

As you can see, the man is busy communicating in several different ways at the same time. The smile on his face radiates success. Notice the certificate on the wall.

The second project manager looks rather confused and overwhelmed. His name is Nob (any resemblance to actual people is, again, purely coincidental):

As you can see, Nob has not mastered the latest communication technology, which is epitomized by the way he uses the computer monitor. For him it is just a bulletin board for yellow stickies.

Bob and Nob will share their project adventures with us. You will find several stories and cartoons on their experiences. Each chapter typically starts with one. I hope you will enjoy them during this serious project management stuff as much as I did when I first saw them. Paul Mason created these wonderful cartoons.

For the cartoons, I needed a successful project manager and a loser. We discussed what their gender should be. There was no way we could come out unscathed by using both a male and a female. Was the successful project manager going to be a man and the loser a woman? Or was the loser going to be a man and the winner a woman? We realized it was a lose-lose situation, and eventually we decided to make both of them men. I apologize to those women who would have liked to see the successful project manager be female. However, the stories that come with the cartoons apply to both genders.

Throughout the book I will randomly use *he* or *she* in my examples.

Chapter 1 Concepts of Project Management

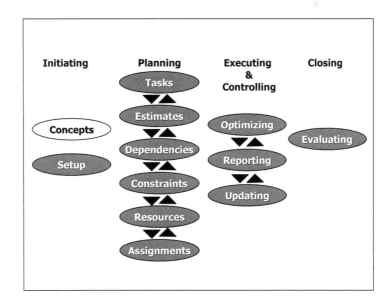

The first *Initiating* phase starts with the *concepts* of project management. The first step is making sure every stakeholder is clear on these concepts. Most concepts are straight from the Project Management Body of Knowledge (PMBOK®), 2000 Edition.

After reading this chapter you will:

◆ be aware of the Project Management Body of Knowledge (PMBOK®)
◆ understand how projects relate to programs and portfolios
◆ understand the concept of a schedule as a model of the real-world project
◆ be able to recognize and analyze the driving forces in projects
◆ be able to determine the purpose of a schedule you create
◆ know what project management software can do

Why Can't It Just Do What I Want It To?

Nob is in agony when Bob enters his cubicle. "What's wrong?" Bob asks. Nob perks up when Bob shows this interest and quickly assesses Bob as a possible source to help relieve some of his work pressures. Nob: "I was busy entering my estimates. I tried entering a work estimate of 20 person days here in the Work field, but when I do that MS Project changes the duration of the five-day task to ten days. I have just been fighting with the tool for hours. Why can't it just do … what I want it to?"

Bob sits down and says: "Let's see what is going on. Did you want to enter 20 days of effort on this task number 134? Let me try it … oh, I see. The duration changed indeed. You did not want the duration to change? Well, let's change the duration back to five days. Wow! That changed the work to ten days. What's going on here? Oh, I remember learning something about a task field called 'Type.' Supposedly, it allows you to control what MS Project recalculates. Let's first set the 'Type' to 'Fixed Duration' and then enter the work estimate again. See … it tells you now that you need four resources to work on the task. Do you have four resources?" Nob thinks and says, "No, I will only have three people for this task." Bob: "Okay, let's change the type to 'Fixed Work' and remove one resource. It now tells you that you will need almost seven business days to finish this task; does that sound right?"

"Yeah, I guess so!" Nob says, somewhat in awe of Bob's mastery of the tool.

Projects

A project is *a temporary endeavor undertaken to create a unique product, service or result*.[4] A project is the vehicle to create change. Project team members create unique deliverables. When the deliverables are ready, the project is over. A project team is a temporary organization within an existing organization.

A project has the following characteristics:
- It has a concrete objective or goal.
- The objective is a relatively new or unique challenge for the organization in the sense that it has not been done to those specifications before.
- The end date of the project is forecasted before the project begins. A project is temporary by definition.
- The project product is divisible into *deliverables*. The deliverables can be further broken down into concrete activities and tasks.
- A temporary team performs the activities in a project.

Some organizations have projects as their core of operations, like construction and consulting companies. In other companies, projects are often used to implement changes (like relocations and reorganizations) or for creating new systems (such as information and financial systems). The manager of today has, apart from his operational management, often one or more projects in progress as well. To manage any endeavors like these, Project 2002 can be a helpful tool to create a solid project plan and maintain it.

Examples of Projects

Below we will give many examples of projects from different industries.

- **Organizational change projects**
  - ◇ Implementing a new financial system
  - ◇ Implementing a Six Sigma quality system
  - ◇ Implementing supply chain management
  - ◇ Designing and implementing a project management methodology

---

[4] Guide to the PMBOK®, 2000 Edition, published by the PMI.

- ◇ Creating a Project Management Office (PMO)
- ◇ Office relocation project
- ◇ Business process re-engineering
- ◇ Designing and implementing a new job classification system

◆ **Regulations implementation projects**
- ◇ Projects to make changes to the manufacturing process in order to meet environmental standards
- ◇ Realizing equal opportunity in the workplace
- ◇ Airport security projects

◆ **Event projects**
- ◇ Conferences
- ◇ Writing the yearly financial report
- ◇ Creating a broadcast or press conference
- ◇ Formal presentation to investors

◆ **New product development**
- ◇ Developing a new pharmaceutical drug
- ◇ Developing new computer hardware

New product development typically involves Research and Development (R&D).

◆ **Information systems projects**
- ◇ Programming a desktop application
- ◇ Implementing a LAN or WAN
- ◇ Developing the company's e-commerce website

◆ **Construction projects**
- ◇ Designing and constructing buildings
- ◇ Designing and constructing new infrastructures like bridges and roads
- ◇ Construction of a new plant
- ◇ Assembly of a new manufacturing line

◆ **Education projects**
- ◇ Developing and pilot testing new courseware
- ◇ Organizing training workshops for different target groups across several sites

◆ **Maintenance-type projects**
Project managers who schedule maintenance projects often deal with many small projects or "jobs". Sometimes the maintenance project is huge and can stop an entire plant, as is the case when a condenser needs to be replaced in a coal-fueled power plant. Such a project can take up to five weeks during which operations are suspended. Thus the project needs to be planned carefully. Every day early or late has huge financial consequences.

Managing Multiple Projects

When you start to manage multiple projects, the projects can be similar projects or related subprojects. A program is a group of related subprojects that need to be managed in a coordinated way. There are often dependencies between the projects. The schedule is an *integrated program schedule*, and the term is *program management*. Projects can be integrated into programs for a variety of reasons:

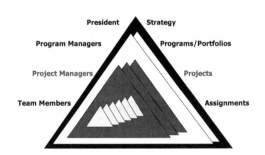

- ◆ a need for overall reporting on all projects: project portfolio management
- ◆ a need to model the logical impacts a project has on other projects: cross-project dependencies
- ◆ a need to monitor resource utilization when several projects share the same resources; when resources are shared, projects will impact each other through resource availability

A portfolio of projects consists of projects that support the strategy of the organization. Portfolios often are similar projects that use the same pool of resources. With *portfolio management* you optimize the mix of projects given the scarce resources of the organization.

This book will deal with managing a single project only and not address issues related to managing multiple projects.[5]

---

[5] The Blue Belt course is for people who manage multiple projects simultaneously with MS Project. Please visit www.iil.com and follow the link *Microsoft Project*.

Guide to the Project Management Body of Knowledge

The Project Management Institute (PMI) has issued the Guide to the Project Management Body of Knowledge, or PMBOK®. The PMBOK has become a global

Adapted from
PMBOK® Guide 2000

standard on project management. Each project has to deal with all nine knowledge areas as specified in the PMBOK (see the illustration on the left). This book is entirely based on and aligned with the 2000 Edition of the PMBOK published by the PMI.

The PMBOK® Guide 2000 describes project management as *"the application of knowledge, skills, tools and techniques to project activities in order to meet the project requirements."*

The Pulling Forces of a Project

All the areas in which project managers need to have knowledge and skills can also be seen as the areas that require attention from the project manager. The areas even pull the project in opposite directions and can be traded off against each other. The illustration on the left shows this.

MS Project isn't a tool to help you manage all of the areas. For example, Project 2002 does not have many features to manage the quality, risk and procurement side of projects. It does not capture data on risk events, quality standards or contracts.

The five areas that can be managed well, however, with Project 2002 are:
◆ *Scope*: what to accomplish
◆ *Time*: the deadline
◆ *Cost*: the budget
◆ *Resources*: availability (or capacity) and workloads of the resources

◆ *Communication*: information flow to and from project stakeholders. While Project 2002 provides many flexible reporting features, *Project Server* dramatically enhances real-time communication with project stakeholders. You can also create libraries of documents and link them to tasks or projects. Project Server is not a full-feature document management system. You can handle different versions of your MS Project schedule in Project Server, but not other types of documents. Comprehensive document management will arrive in future versions of *SharePoint Team Services* that comes with Project Server.

An important activity in *risk management* is to analyze adverse events and to rank and then manage them. Project 2002 alone is not suitable for this purpose. It can do some PERT analysis and, yes, there are add-ons that do Monte Carlo risk analysis. We will explain both of these in chapter 9 on optimizing, see page 359. Project Server has issue management features; Microsoft has started to address the *risk* area.

In project *procurement management* you want to create and track your contracts. There is no feature in Project 2002 that is designed to manage contracts, but what you can do is create links to contract documents (like MS Word files) using the hyperlink feature. Project 2002 and *Project Server* are not a procurement management system by themselves.

The area of *quality* can be managed only somewhat with Project 2002. Quality control activities can be scheduled but the tool, as it comes, does not capture quality standards of deliverables, for example. The application is not a *quality management* system.

We first have to ask ourselves why we are scheduling.

Why Do We Schedule?

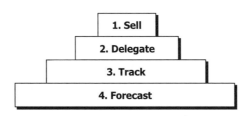

There are four reasons why people prepare schedules of their projects. The reasons can be ranked by level of challenge (least challenging first):

◆ **Sell**

Aspiring project managers want to sell upper management an idea in order to start a new project. A consulting firm may try to sell a new project to a client. The selling is supported by making the timing visible in a high-level but slick Gantt Chart and the cost visible in a budget. Selling requires the least amount of detail in your schedule and does not require the schedule to be dynamic. The result could be that you win the contract.

◆ **Delegate**

When you have a detailed Work Breakdown Structure (WBS) in MS Project, you can easily delegate by assigning activities to team members. When you have all the assignments, you can easily create to-do lists for each resource. The benefits are that everybody knows what to do and that there is a sense of direction in your project.

◆ **Track**

In order to track your project you enter the current status regularly into your MS Project schedule. The output of tracking is a status report. A status report shows how far the project has progressed. Tracking allows you to report to stakeholders what has been accomplished. Tracking has the benefit that you can learn from past mistakes. If you don't track, you will lack the facts to learn from. The main benefit is for future projects.

◆ **Forecast**

You can use MS Project to model your project in such a way that you forecast the project end date and total cost. You have to set the schedule up in such a way that it immediately shows what impact actual events have on the project end date and cost as you enter progress information. Forecasting also requires that you enter the progress in such a way that the forecasts are updated. The main benefit of forecasting is that you benefit from this immediately in your current project. You will have answers for:

◇ When will deliverables be available?
◇ On what dates will individual resources be needed?
◇ When will the project be done?
◇ What will the project cost?

The levels described above are listed in order of increasing challenge or difficulty. The farther down the list, the more ambitious you are with MS Project. Forecasting is the most ambitious goal you can have when using scheduling software. If you want to predict the outcome of your project, you have to set up your schedule in a particular way. For example, you have to use dependencies wherever applicable. We will provide you with all the guidelines to help you set up schedules that will give you this predictive power. The summary chapter of this book contains the complete checklist of guidelines. Forecasting is what most project managers aspire to accomplish with MS Project.

First, we need to deal with a well-known saying on project planning.

Dwight Was Right, But Is He Still?

"In preparing for battle, I have always found that plans are useless, but planning is indispensable."

President Dwight D. Eisenhower (1890-1969)

In the time in which President Dwight Eisenhower lived (1890-1969), project plans only existed on paper. Paper plans are static and therefore dead. They are a snapshot of the project and the project's vision of the future when the plan was written. A written plan printed on paper is a project-plan-of-the-past. At best, written plans are "*history-books-written-ahead-of-time*". In his time, Dwight was right.

With the advent of computers, we can now create plans that are alive and dynamic. Let's start thinking of a project plan as an online database that contains current status data and prediction algorithms. This project-plan-of-the-future has a model of your project that is up-to-date and that allows you to make forecasts for the future at any time during the life of the project.

The project-plan-of-the-future is a powerful tool for project managers. I like to think that, if Dwight was still alive, he would likely admit: "*In preparing for the global marketplace, I have found that planning is indispensable and that dynamic plans are the critical success factor*".

Scheduling Is Modeling

As a project manager you should attempt to create a model of your project situation, not just draw a chart that you hang on your wall and is nice to look at. Nice charts are very useful for selling purposes, but not for managing purposes. The differences between a *static chart* and a *dynamic model* of your project are:

◆ **A model is a simplified reality**
Architectural models are small three-dimensional versions of the final building.

Similarly, project models should be simple versions of a large and complex reality. Simplification is a very legitimate modeling activity.

◆ **A dynamic model has to be kept up-to-date**
A schedule that is not maintained is static and will be useless soon after it is made. Dynamic models are kept alive; otherwise they would not be dynamic.

◆ **A dynamic model needs to be responsive**
In order for schedules to be easily kept up-to-date, they need to be responsive. A responsive model updates itself as much as it can. Schedules can do this if they are created with as many dependencies as needed and as few fixed dates as possible. Fixed dates are known as *constraints* in MS Project.

◆ **A dynamic model has predictive power**
Schedules need to show the latest forecasts of the finish date and expenses of the project. Only then can a schedule truly be a powerful decision-support system for the project manager. It is nice to have a prediction that holds true in, let's say, 9 out of 10 cases. This requires the model to use empirical, actual data that are translated into forecasts using algorithms. An example of such an algorithm is the 15% rule on earned value from Fleming and Koppelman.[6] The 15% rule states that if you are 15% into your project, you should be able to predict the final cost of your project within a margin of plus or minus 10%.

◆ **A dynamic model needs to be accessible online and in real time**
Project Server is one example of a new class of business intelligence tools arriving in the marketplace that allow you to slice and dice the data any way you want. *Project Server* allows you to drill down into the project database to see supporting detail. These powerful and dynamic features are accessible through a user-friendly interface that executives can use to keep their finger on the pulse of their portfolio of projects. Executives can do their own analysis and what-if scenario development using data that are as up-to-date as data get (real-time data). But best of all, with its web-based access, no longer are project reports tied to regular reporting periods and static formats. They can be viewed at any time and from any place with intranet access.

In the chapters that follow, we will show you how to create a dynamic model of your projects — a model that meets all the criteria of a dynamic model as explained above.

---

[6] See their book *Earned Value Project Management*, PMI, 2000.

The next thing we will do is explore the field of forces that surrounds our project. This will help us model the important aspects of our project.

How Strong Are the Forces in My Project?

As we described in the previous paragraphs, scheduling treated as a modeling activity is supposed to simplify the reality of the project. One of the first things a project manager needs to do is find out how strong each of the forces is. Recognizing the dominant force and modeling the project accordingly will determine the success of the schedule early in the project life cycle. For example, if a nuclear power station has to be renovated, it is clear that the scope and the quality cannot be tampered with because of the immense consequences an error could or would have (see the illustration). Meeting the quality standards of the International Atomic Energy Agency will be a dominant force, even if this leads to higher than anticipated cost and/or a delay in the project.

Remodeling a Nuclear Power Station

For most projects, however, the dominant force is less obvious. Sometimes two forces are equally important. Therefore, a good question to ask before starting is: *Which force is dominant?* Or, if that question is difficult to answer, ask yourself first: *Which force is least dominant?*

Depending on whether scope, time, money, quality or resources is the dominant force, different schedules may be the result. If the deadline is very hard, you may want to enter it as a constraint into the model and schedule regular status meetings. If the deadline is soft, you may choose to let it float freely. If the budget is very tight, you want to model all expenses in detail. If the resource availability is very limited, you want to capture all workloads. If quality is the dominant force, you could add more testing tasks.

Project Management Software

In any project, the following seven questions are important:
1. *What needs to be done?* Deliverables and Tasks
2. *How long will it take?* Duration or Work Estimates
3. *In which order?*   Dependencies
4. *When must it happen?*   Constraints
5. *Who is going to do it?* Resources and Assignments
6. *When will it happen?*   Start and Finish Dates
7. *How much will it cost?* Rate Assignment Effort

The user will have to enter the answers to the first five questions, and Project 2002 will automatically answer the last two questions and create the schedule and the budget.

Notice that when you schedule electronically you hardly ever enter start or end dates for tasks. You enter durations and dependencies instead. The software then calculates the start and finish dates by itself based upon those durations and dependencies. A schedule with dependencies is flexible and "knows" how to update the other tasks automatically when preceding tasks are changed.

Based upon resource cost rates and assignments you entered, the software calculates the total cost, per deliverable and for the whole project. Project 2002 calculates a lot of data automatically.

Scheduling software is efficient in reporting. The software behaves like a database in that you can pull from the database data that focus on any kind of activity, any period or any resource you want. The type of information in a report can be changed as well, like scheduled dates or cost figures. Reports allow you to compare actual against planned progress.

Review Questions

1. What are the two main ways in which projects differ from other things such as programs, operations, task forces, committees, work groups and departments?

2. Are there organizations that never have any projects?

3. Are there organizations that have only projects?

4. What is the difference between project management and program management?

5. Which knowledge areas does the PMBOK cover?

6. What are the forces that pull at your project that you need to constantly trade off between as a project manager?

7. What are the strongest pulling forces in your current project? Or, what are the weakest pulling forces?

8. What are the differences between a *static chart* and a *dynamic model* of your project?

9. Why do you intend to create a schedule of your project? Is it for selling, delegating, tracking or forecasting purposes?

10. What is the difference between tracking a project and forecasting a project?

11. What data do you need to enter into MS Project to generate a schedule with which you can forecast your project?

Chapter 2 Setting Up a Project

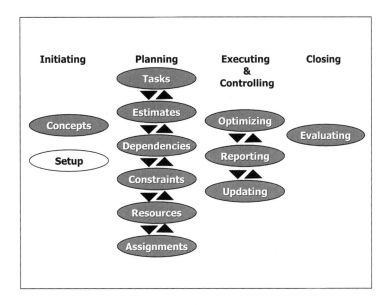

Now that we have reviewed the terminology, we are ready to set up a new project.

After reading this chapter you will:
- be familiar with the MS Project interface
- understand the structure of the relational database of MS Project
- be familiar with the file types MPP/MPT and the file Global.MPT
- know how to create and use a project template
- be familiar with the MS Project views
- be able to set up a new project and choose the appropriate options
- be able to create the project calendar and task calendars
- know the best practices for setting up new project schedules

"Have You Been Choked by a Template Lately?"

Nob: "Hey Bob, I opened up this template that our project office put together and I found 300 tasks in there! Do we really have to use them? What the heck were these guys thinking?"

Bob: "Well my friend, the project office didn't put them together for nothing!"

Nob: "But come on ... 300 tasks for a software modification project; that is ridiculous!"

Bob: "Listen man ... the templates are part of this expensive methodology our company purchased. You don't want to be seen throwing that money away!"

Nob: "Spending the money was not MY decision!"

Bob: "Why don't you comb through the templates and use whatever seems applicable and just delete the rest."

Nob: "You can't do that, can you?"

Bob: "Of course you can ... they just made these templates as reminders of everything that MIGHT be necessary in your project. If it is not applicable, it is not applicable! That is how I deal with these templates."

Nob: "I am not sure..."

Bob: "They made more templates than necessary on purpose because it is always easier to delete than to add!"

Nob: "How did you get so smart???"

Two Editions: Project 2002 Standard and Professional

MS Project now comes in two editions: Project 2002 Standard and Project 2002 Professional. Both editions of MS Project can be used with *Project Server*:

◆ If you use Project 2002 Standard, you are running Project Server in *Workgroup mode*. In workgroup mode you can use a limited number of features in Project Server, the features that were already present in Project Central (Project 2000), like time sheets and status reports.

◆ If you use Project 2002 Professional, you are running Project Server in *Enterprise mode*. In enterprise mode you can use all features in Project Server.

When working with project files there are differences between using Project 2002 with Project Server and using Project 2002 by itself (standalone). To distinguish, we will call it *MS Project standalone* when it is used by itself, i.e., without Project Server.

We will focus in this book on two main configurations currently in use: MS Project standalone and Project 2002 Professional used with Project Server. We will devote less attention to the workgroup mode.

Working with Files in Project 2002 Standalone

File Types

Project 2002 can store its data in project files and project template files among other file types. Project templates are like regular project files but with an added protection against accidental changes. Project templates are standardized schedules, and are used in organizations that run similar projects over and over, like construction companies.

Project files (.MPP) and project template files (.MPT) can contain:
◆ *Data*: tasks, estimates, dependencies, constraints, resources, assignments
◆ *Objects*: views, tables, filters, groups, fields, calendars, reports, forms, maps, toolbars (including the menu bar) and modules (Visual Basic)
◆ *Project-specific options*: relate to the project only and are stored in the individual project file

A special template exists, the default template file, called Global.MPT. It contains all the default objects. The *Menu Bar* and *Toolbars* in the Global.MPT are the active menu bar and toolbars accessible in MS Project. The *Global.MPT* is always open when Project 2002 is running. The *Global.MPT* exposes its objects that are ready to be used in new project files. The *Global.MPT* also contains the menu bar and the toolbars that are active for all your projects. It can have a custom menu bar, and custom toolbar objects, if desired.

The differences between a *project template* and the *Global.MPT* template are that:
◆ The *Global.MPT* cannot contain schedule data like tasks and dependencies.
◆ Only the menu bar in the *Global.MPT* is active.
◆ Only the toolbars in the *Global.MPT* are accessible through the menu items **View, Toolbars**.

The file extensions have been well thought out by Microsoft:
◆ A project file has an **.MPP** extension, which stands for **M**icrosoft **P**roject **P**roject.
◆ A template file has an **.MPT** extension, which stands for **M**icrosoft **P**roject **T**emplate. Project and template files can contain project data, as well as objects and options. You can view the objects in the Organizer by choosing **Tools, Organizer**.

Objects can be transferred from one file to another with the *Organizer* on the **Tools** menu.

When you migrate from Project 2000 to Project 2002, the first time you run Project 2002, you will be asked if you want to upgrade your Project 2000 *Global.MPT* to Project 2002:
◆ Automatically: All the objects in your Project 2000 *Global.MPT* will be transferred.
◆ Manually: You can transfer selected objects to your Project 2002 *Global.MPT*.
◆ Not at all: In this case you get the new and default Project 2002 *Global.MPT* installed.

The *global options* and the default project-specific options are stored in the *Windows Registry*.

Opening a Project File in Project 2002 Standalone

1. Choose **File, Open**; the **Open** dialog appears:

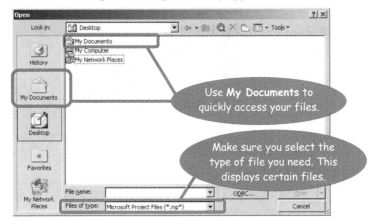

2. If the project is on a drive or directory other than the current one, select it from the list **Look in** at the top of the dialog.

3. Double-click on the name of the file to open.
   OR
   Single-click on the file name and click ⟨ Open ▾ ⟩.

Saving Changes in an Existing MPP File

1. Click **Save** 💾 on the **Standard** toolbar OR choose the menu items **File, Save**.

2. If your file exists already, the file on your hard disk will be updated with the changes.

Saving a New File with MS Project Standalone

1. If you save a schedule for the first time or if you opened the file read-only, you are prompted for a file name in the **Save As** dialog:

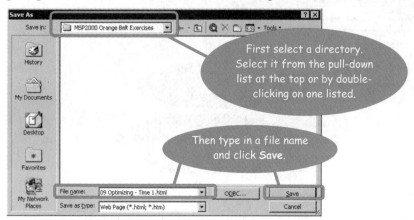

2. Click [Save]. Each project file will be saved with the extension **.MPP** unless specified otherwise.

Saving an MPP File in a New Directory or Under a New Name

1. Choose **File**, **Save As**; the **Save As** dialog appears (see above).

2. Select the drive and directory from the list **Save In** at the top of the dialog.

3. At the bottom of the dialog, type a name in the field:
   File Name: [_____▼].

4. Click [Save].

Closing a File

1. Choose **File, Close**. If you have made changes to the open project, MS Project will prompt you to save the changes. The **Microsoft Project** dialog appears:

2. To save changes, click [Yes]. If the project hasn't been saved before, the **Save As** dialog appears. Type a name for the project and choose a subdirectory.

To discard changes, click 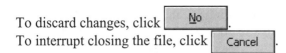 .
To interrupt closing the file, click Cancel .

Working with Files from the Project Server Database

MS Project as a Relational Database

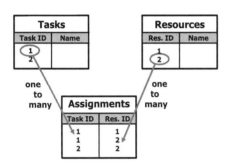

At first glance, Project 2002 bears a striking resemblance to a spreadsheet. It has columns and rows. However, instead of seeing it as a spreadsheet, we suggest you think of Project 2002 as a relational database. A relational database has several different tables that are related to each other through fields they have in common. In MS Project these are the ID fields.[7] You can see this in the illustration to the left.

There are three reasons for seeing the tool as a relational database:

1. **Three types of data**
   There are three distinct types of data in MS Project: tasks, resources and assignments. In one spreadsheet you typically monitor only one type of data.

2. **The data are relational by nature**
   The three types of data in MS Project are related. There are one-to-many relationships between these entities: one task can have many resources assigned and one resource can be assigned to more than one task.

3. **Each type of data has its own tables**
   Tasks can be found in task views and *resources* in resource views. *Assignments* do not have their own views. Assignments can be found in between the tasks in the *Task Usage* view or in between the resources in the *Resource Usage* view.

---

[7] In fact, the **Unique ID** fields, because the **ID** values are just row numbers that change as items are inserted or moved.

In fact, MS Project users can choose to store their projects in a database like MS Access or SQL Server instead of in MPP files. In a relational database you can see the data in

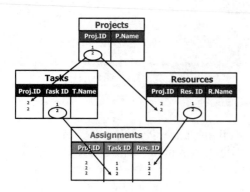

their own tables. If you use *Project Server*, you will store the projects in an SQL Server database.

The Project Server database has an extra table in which all projects are contained. The schema for the database is shown in the illustration. The projects table is where Project Server stores all the project-level data, like project name, project manager and project start and finish date, among others, for all projects in the database.

Entering an Account to Connect to the Project Server Database

When we discussed MS Project in standalone mode, the projects were stored as separate files on your file system. When you use *Project Server* the database contains the project schedules. There are no separate MPP files when you use Project Server in *Enterprise mode*. The *SQL Server* database contains all the projects. The Project Server administrator manages this database and the security, which determines who can read and write to each project in the database. This is done through Project Server accounts. After the Project Server administrator has set up an account for you as the project manager, you can configure Project 2002 in such a way that it uses the account to establish a connection between Project 2002 and Project Server.

1. In Project 2002 Professional, choose **Tools, Enterprise Options, Microsoft Project Server Accounts**. The **Microsoft Project Server Accounts** dialog appears.

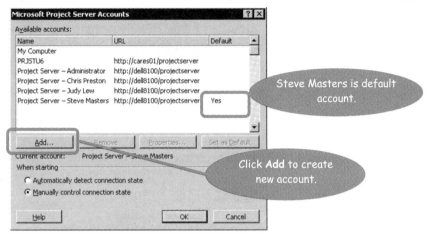

2. Click [**Add...**]; the **Account Properties** dialog appears:

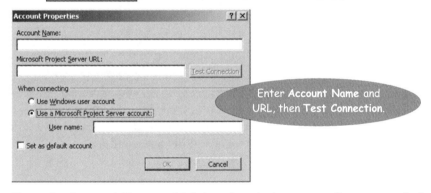

3. Enter the **Account Name**, which is a descriptive name of your own choice.

4. Enter the **Microsoft Project Server URL**; you have to enter in the following syntax:
   http://<server>//ProjectServer
   where <server> is the name (like DELL8100) or the IP address (like 63.118.100.55) of the computer on which Project Server is installed.

5. Under **When connecting**, select either
   ⊙ **Use Windows user account** or
   ⊙ **Use a Microsoft Project Server account** and enter the **User name**.

6. Click [OK] and you are back in the **Microsoft Project Server Accounts** dialog. You can select one of your accounts to be the default account and you can even select **Automatically detect connection state** if you don't want to be prompted any longer for which account to use. If you will always connect to Project Server and have only one Project Server account, you could select this.

7. Choose **File, Exit** to close MS Project.

Connecting to the Project Server Database

1. Restart Project 2002 Professional and the **Microsoft Project Server Accounts** dialog appears (if you selected ⦿ **Manually control connection state** in previous steps):

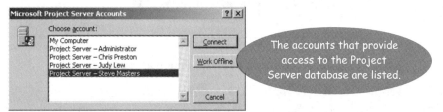

2. If you want to work with your file without a connection to the *Project Server* database, you can click [Work Offline]. This allows you to be productive on a laptop while on a plane or wherever you don't have access to the server computer. In order to have the project files accessible offline, you first need to copy them onto your laptop. Open the file you want to work on offline in Project 2002 and choose **File, Save offline**. When you come back, you choose **File, Save online**.

3. You need to identify yourself to the secure database by choosing an account. Double-click the account you want to use from the list.
OR

Select the account and click [Connect]. The **Microsoft Project Server Security Login** dialog appears.

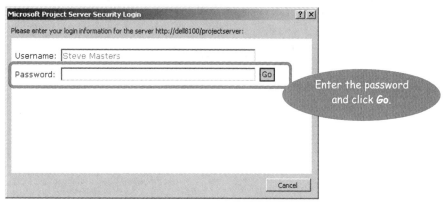

4. The account you chose will establish a connection to a Project Server database. Enter the password and click [Go] to open the connection.

Opening a Project File from the Project Server Database

You have to select the project from a list of projects in the database. When saving a project you have to give it a title under which you can retrieve it from the database.

1. Choose **File, Open** and the **Open from Microsoft Project Server** dialog will appear. It lists all projects you have access to in the Project Server database. The *Project Server* administrator sets access rights.

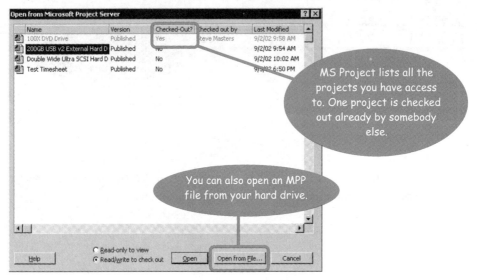

2. Select from the list with a single click the project to open.
    OR
    If you want to open an MPP file, click Open from File... and the same steps apply as when opening a project file in Project 2002 standalone.

3. Select whether you want to open the project:
    ⊙ **Read-only to view**: You will not be able to save changes.
    ⊙ **Read/write to check out**: You will be able to save changes if nobody else has the file checked out currently. Look at the column **Checked-Out?** to verify.

4. Click Open .

The steps for opening a project from the *Project Server* database are quite different from opening an MPP file from your file system. So are the steps for saving a new project to the database.

Saving a New Project to the Project Server Database

1. Choose **File, New** to create the file.

2. Choose **File, Save As** and the **Save to Microsoft Project Server** dialog appears:

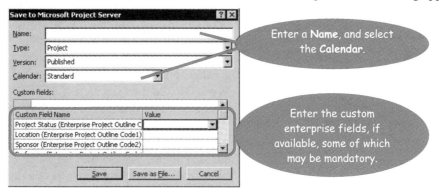

3. In the field **Name**, enter a descriptive name for the project that will be clear to other users of the database with many project files in it.

4. Under **Type**, select to save the project as a **Project** or as a **Template**.

5. Under **Version**, select the version identifier for this project. Project Server makes an important distinction between the *Published version* and other versions. The published version is the one that is the latest and active version.

6. Under **Calendar**, select one of your corporate calendars your project should be based on.

7. Under **Custom Field Name**, there can be one or more custom fields that allow, or even require, you to describe your project in more detail.

8. Click Save.

The steps for saving changes and closing files are similar for Project Server files and MPP files (MS Project standalone); choose **File, Save** and **File, Close**, respectively.

Project Templates

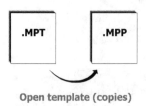

Open template (copies)

Project templates are useful as a quick-start on your project plan. If you run similar projects over and over again, templates are particularly useful. Templates can be created centrally to promote consistent Work Breakdown Structures, common options, standard resource names and the use of standard reports and project calendars. Templates are protected from accidental changes, so they will stay the same and can be used over and over again.

The way the templates are protected is simple. When you open a project template file, Project 2002 copies it; you never open the template file itself. When saving the template file, you will always be asked for a (new) file name. This way the templates are safe and can be used by many different people. Template files have the extension **.MPT**.

Using a Project Template

1. Choose **File, New…** as if you are opening a project file; a blank project file appears and the *task pane* on the left changes to **New Project**:

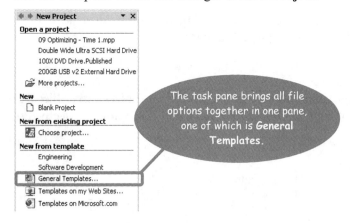

2. Click **General Templates** from the task pane and you will see the following dialog in MS Project used standalone:

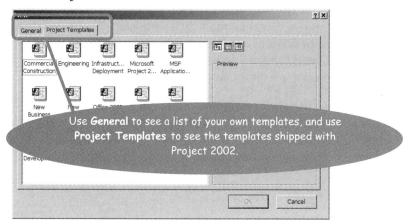

3. In Project 2002 Professional with *Project Server*, you will see an extra tab **Enterprise Templates** as in the dialog below:

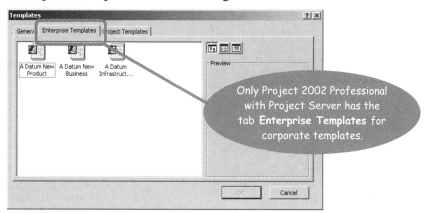

4. These tabs contain:

   ◇ Tab **General** lists the *user templates* you created yourself for your own purposes. General templates are stored in the directory as set in **Tools, Options, Save, User templates**. If you were to fill in a subdirectory under *Workgroup Templates*, you would see it appear as another tab in this dialog.

   ◇ Tab **Enterprise Templates** (only in Project 2002 Professional with *Project Server*) lists the enterprise templates used in your organization. Your organization may expect you to use these enterprise templates that were custom-made for you.

◇   Tab **Project Templates** lists templates shipped with Project 2002. It has ready-to-go templates for several industries. Enter *Templates included with Microsoft Project* in the *Answer Wizard* at the top right of your screen or in the help file and you will find an explanation of each template. These templates are stored in **C:\Program Files\Microsoft Office\Templates\1033** where 1033 reflects the English language and would be a different number for each language. You can add templates to or delete them from this directory.

5. Double-click on a template OR select one template and click [OK]; the template opens. The schedule appears with the options and project calendar set. There may be tasks, dependencies, estimates and generic resources that are assigned in the project template as well. There may be custom views and reports in the template.

The Project 2002 Interface

The Main Screen

We suggest that you open one of the project templates at this point to follow the instructions for navigating the Project 2002 interface. MS Project has many different screen areas that pop up when they are needed (and sometimes when they are not). In order for you to follow the procedural steps, I have labeled these different screen parts in the next snapshot:

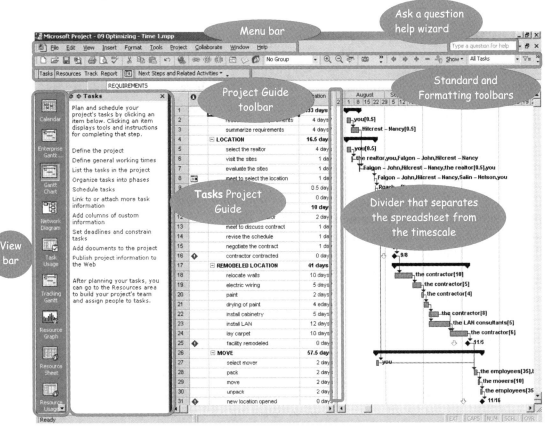

Working with the Menus

To choose a menu item, just click on it with the mouse OR hold down the ⌈Alt⌉ key and press the underscored character of the menu item.

Working with the Toolbar

Toolbars are a great shortcut to commonly used features. To invoke the action of the toolbar buttons, click with the left mouse button on the tool you need. If you are not sure which tool you need, place the mouse pointer on top of a button without clicking and a tool tip will remind you what the button does. An example of a tool tip for the 🐾-tool is: `Go To Selected Task`.

Each toolbar now has on the right-hand side an extra button ⌈▾⌉ or ⌈»⌉ (when there are tools currently invisible on the toolbar). This button allows you to customize your toolbar very quickly. You can also reset your toolbar to its original setting if you choose from its pull-down menu **Add or Remove Buttons, Customize**, click tab **Toolbars**, and click `Reset...`. Customizing the toolbar allows you to access features you use often with one click.

Working with the Task Pane

Project 2002 includes the new task pane feature from *Office XP*. The **New Project** task pane is similar to the **New Document** task pane in *Word XP* and the **New Workbook** task pane in *Excel XP*. Task panes provide a single list of related choices in a sidebar at the left of the main screen. You can display the **New Project** task pane by choosing **File, New**. The most recently used projects are listed. Using hyperlinks you can create a **Blank Project** or new projects from an existing project (**New from existing project**) or from templates (**New from template**).

Working with the View Bar

The view bar on the left is meant to quickly change views. To display or hide the view bar choose **View, View Bar** or right-click on the view bar and choose **View Bar**. You may see buttons for all views, if your screen is big enough (or your screen resolution is high enough).

Working with Scroll Bars

In Windows 2000 the scroll bar
looks like the illustration
to the right and
consists of three parts:

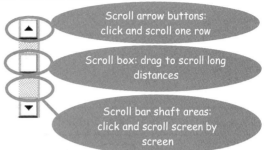

As you are dragging the timescale scroll boxes, you will see a yellow feedback box pop up that will tell you where you are. The vertical scroll box shows the ID number of the task you are browsing to:

```
ID:   4
Name: LOCATION
```

The horizontal scroll box tells you the date you are traveling to:

```
Aug 1 '01
```

Right-Mouse Clicks and Double-Clicks

For those who are right-handed, the right-mouse button (as opposed to the left-mouse button) under your middle finger can pop up shortcut menus that relate to a particular

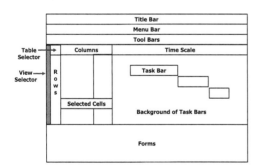

area. You can right-click on all the places that are labeled in the illustration. It is a stylized version of a Gantt Chart; you can make many more right-clicks in other views. Try them out instead of clicking yourself silly through the menus. Save your mouse muscles!

Alternatively, you can double-click in these places; this will take you to the most likely shortcut for that area and display a dialog box right away.

Moving Around in a Project

The following convention is used in the table: [Alt] + [→] means hold down [Alt] and press [→].

Move to	By keyboard	By mouse
Next row	[Enter ↵] or [↓]	Click
Next column	[Tab] or [→]	Click
Next minor time unit in the timescale	[Alt] + [→] or [Alt] + [←]	Click on an arrow button of the scroll bar [▶]
Next screen in timescale	[Alt] + [Page Up] or [Alt] + [Page Dn]	Click to the left or right of the scroll box [ ] in the horizontal scroll bar
The start date of the project	[Alt] + [Home]	Left align the scroll box [ ] in the horizontal scroll bar
The end date of the project	[Alt] + [End]	Right align the scroll box [ ] in the horizontal scroll bar
The first task of the project	[Control] + [Home]	Drag the vertical scroll box [ ] to the top
The last task of the project	[Control] + [End]	Drag the vertical scroll box [ ] to the bottom
A specific task, resource or date	[F5] OR [Control] + [F]	**Edit, Go To** OR **Edit, Find**
The other split window	[F6]	Click in the other split window to make it active
Move to a task bar in the timescale		Click **Go To Selected Task** 🔍 on the **Standard** toolbar

Moving Around in a Dialog Box

The following convention is used in the table: [Alt] + [Tab] means hold down [Alt] and press [Tab].

Action	By keyboard	By mouse
Move to next field in a dialog box	[Tab]	Click in the field
Previous field	[Shift] + [Tab]	
Move to any field in a form	[Alt] + press underlined letter of the field name	Click in the field
Increase or decrease value in a field	[Alt] + [↑] [Alt] + [↓]	Use the spin button
Move to next tab in the direction of the arrow	[Alt] + [↑] [Alt] + [↓] [Alt] + [←] [Alt] + [→]	Click on the tab

Selecting Data

The following convention is used in the table: [Alt] + [Tab] means hold down [Alt] and press [Tab].

Select	By keyboard	By mouse
A task	[Shift] + space bar	Click on the ID number of the task or click on its task bar in the timescale
An entire row or record	[Shift] + space bar	Click on a row heading
An entire column	[Control] + space bar	Click on a column heading

When you select an entire row as explained above, all the fields of a task (about 240!) are selected, even if they are not visible. It is important to select a task in its entirety before moving or copying it. Remember that MS Project is a relational database, as discussed on page 51.

Project 2002 Views

The view of a project is a predefined layout that presents the project from a certain angle. The fields in views allow you to enter, review or report your project.

View	Shows
Calendar	The tasks shown as bars on a calendar
Enterprise Gantt Chart	This view is essentially the same as the Gantt Chart unless this view was customized within your organization
Gantt Chart	The tasks over time, plus spreadsheet columns
Network Diagram	The network of dependencies between tasks (dependencies are shown as arrows)
Task Usage	The assigned resources by task and the effort over time
Tracking Gantt	The original (baseline) schedule and current schedule
Resource Graph	The workloads for resources in a bar chart format
Resource Sheet	The spreadsheet with resource information
Resource Usage	The assigned tasks by resource with the workloads over time

We will discuss each of these views on the pages that follow.

Calendar View

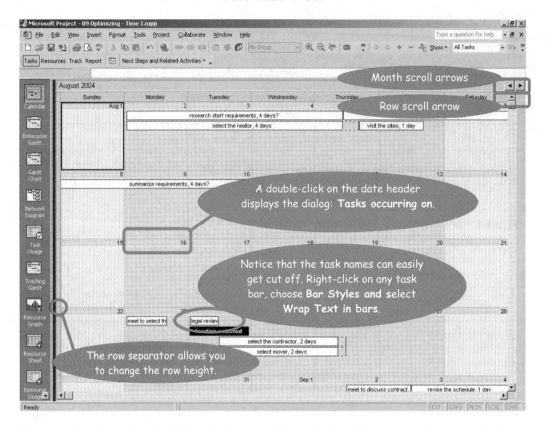

To apply the view, choose **View, Calendar**. The calendar view shows the schedule in a format that is similar to conventional calendars people hang on their walls. Everybody understands this type of layout. Not everybody understands Gantt Charts intuitively, in my experience. That is where this view adds value.

Notice that the *Calendar* view is different from the *Standard Project Calendar*. The calendar view, like the Gantt Chart, displays task bars, whereas the standard project calendar is used to define the working times and holidays.

To See All Tasks on a Day

The calendar view is not suitable for showing the entire schedule. As you can see in the snapshot below, not all task bars always show. This occurs if too many tasks take place on the same day. If there is too little room vertically, Project 2002 displays a down arrow in the date heading, as in the following snapshot:

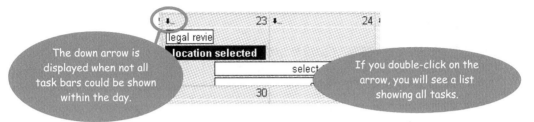

Point to the area where the down arrow is displayed and double-click; a list showing all the tasks on that day appears:

Notice the check mark in front of the tasks that were visible in the calendar view; the ones without a check mark were invisible!

To show all the task bars in the Calendar view, position your mouse pointer on any of the horizontal grid lines and double-click when you see the mouse pointer .

Because of the limited vertical space, we recommend you use this view to create to-do lists for resources. To-do lists typically have only one or two tasks per day and you will not likely run out of space. Furthermore, everybody will understand the Calendar view. We will explain and create a to-do list in the chapter 10 on reporting, see page 522.

To Create Tasks

Creating new tasks in this view is not recommended because the tasks end up at the end of the task list. You will still have to move them to the right place in the Work

Breakdown Structure in the Gantt Chart. If you insist, you can create new tasks by dragging the shape of a new task bar on the dates where you want it. Double-click on it to give it a task name. Notice that the task will have a constraint that is visible on the **Advanced** tab, and you should replace it with appropriate dependencies. Two strikes against this method.

To Edit the Data of a Task

1. Double-click on a task; the **Task Information** dialog appears:

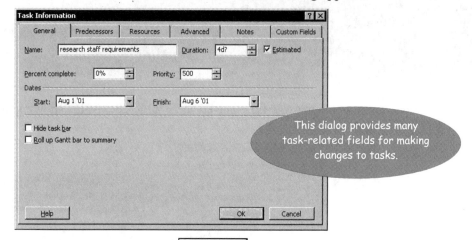

2. Make the changes, and click .

To Move Task Bars

 You can move task bars horizontally and vertically within a day or between days. Unless you stay within the same day, you are setting start-no-earlier-than constraints on the task. This happens just like in the Gantt Chart. Constraints are undesirable in schedules since they make schedules less dynamic. We recommend you proceed with care.

You can move a task bar by pointing to the border of a bar and dragging when you see the mouse pointer ✥.

Gantt Chart

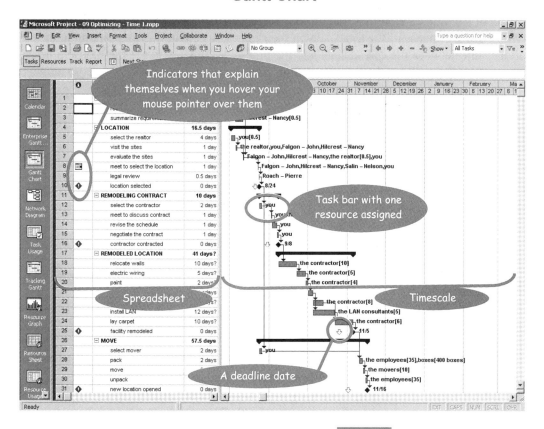

To apply the view, choose **View, Gantt Chart** or click in the *View Bar*.

The *Gantt Chart* shows tasks over time. The duration of each task is reflected in the width of its task bar. The Gantt Chart also shows the list of deliverables and tasks, which is commonly referred to as the Work Breakdown Structure (WBS). The WBS typically has a logical hierarchy of summary tasks with detail tasks indented beneath them.

The Gantt Chart is one of the best views to use when creating or modifying tasks in your project.

To See More Spreadsheet or Timescale

You can change the amount of the spreadsheet you see on the left of the screen and the length of the timescale on the right of your screen. Revealing more of the spreadsheet will be at the expense of the timescale on the right. You can do this by pointing to the divider line between the spreadsheet and the timescale. When you see the mouse pointer change to a ⟺, click and hold down to drag it to the desired position.

If you double-click on the divider, it will jump to the nearest split between two columns. This allows you to clean up the look of the view.

Collapsing and Expanding Levels

Click on the minus button ⊟ next to a summary task name to hide its detail tasks. Click the plus button ⊞ of a summary task to reveal its detail tasks.

Zooming the Timescale

To zoom the timescale in to smaller time units to see the details, click **Zoom In** ⊕ on the **Standard** toolbar.
To zoom the timescale out to larger time units to get an overview, click **Zoom Out** ⊖ on the **Standard** toolbar.

To fit the entire project timescale within the screen so you always see task bars when you are paging up or down, choose **View, Zoom** and select ⦿ **Entire Project**.

Finding the Task Bars

If you don't see any task bars in the Gantt timescale, the timescale is just displaying a time period when no tasks happen to be scheduled. If you put the horizontal scroll box at the extreme left on the scroll bar, you will always see the start date of the project. You can also press [Alt] + [Home] on the keyboard.

If you hold the left mouse button down on the scroll box in the horizontal scroll bar, it will tell you the exact date. It will include the year you currently have on your screen, which is handy in case the timescale does not reveal the year.

If you quickly want to see the task bar of a task, click on the task and then the tool **Go To Selected Task** 🔖 on the **Standard** toolbar.

Network Diagram

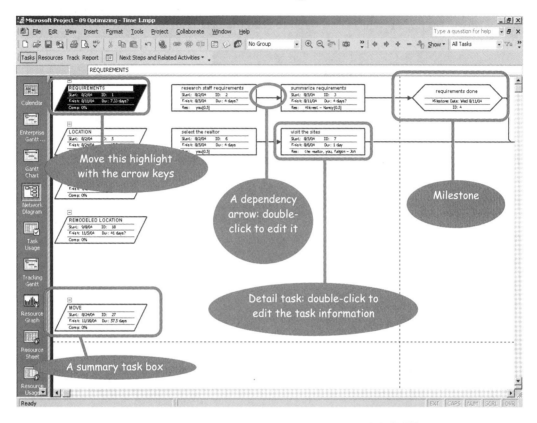

To apply the view, choose **View**, **Network Diagram** or click ![Network Diagram] on the *View Bar*.

The *Network Diagram* shows the network of dependencies between tasks. The dependencies are depicted as arrows. However, when you enter this view for the first time, you often don't see many, in which case you need to zoom out.

Click **Zoom Out** 🔍 on the **Standard** toolbar to see more task boxes and arrows. The text becomes illegible when zoomed out too far, but if you point the mouse pointer on a task, a screen tip pops up that allows you to read the task data. An example of such a screen tip is:

print	
Start: Thu 4/6/00	ID: 6
Finish: Fri 4/7/00	Dur: 2 days
Res:	

To zoom back in, use **Zoom In** 🔍 on the **Standard** toolbar.

By default, the Network Diagram displays the different types of tasks in boxes with distinct shapes:

◆ summary tasks in a parallelogram

◆ detail tasks in a rectangle

◆ milestones in a hexagon

The critical tasks have a red border instead of the (default) blue.

This view is typically used to check the logic in the network. To check the logic, just use the arrow keys on your keyboard to move the highlight from task to task. If the text is too small, keep your eyes on the *entry bar*. The entry bar will show the name of the task.

You can easily add and delete dependencies in this view. We will therefore discuss this view in more detail on page 206.

Task Usage

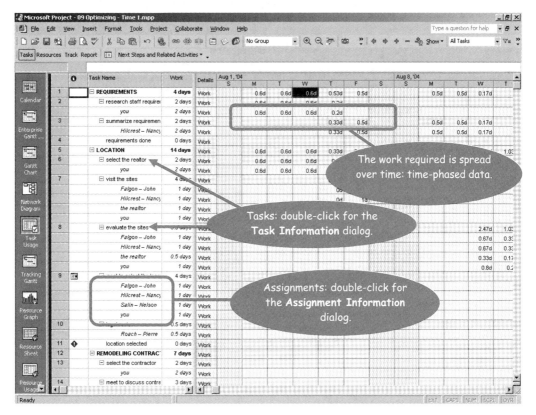

To apply the view, choose **View**, **Task Usage** or click [Task Usage] on the *View Bar*.

Notice how the *Task Usage* view shows the assignments in italicized type in between the tasks. Task Usage and Resource Usage are the only views that show the assignments as separate line items.

The timescale on the right shows how Project 2002 schedules the tasks and assignments. It shows the detailed numbers behind the task bars of the Gantt Chart. This view helps in understanding the Gantt Chart and troubleshooting it.

If you click **Zoom Out** 🔍 on the **Standard** toolbar, Project 2002 immediately calculates the totals for the new time unit. To zoom back in, use **Zoom In** 🔍.

You can report on the spread of the effort or cost across the life of the project with this view: a time-phased budget by activity. We will detail the steps on page 528.

Tracking Gantt

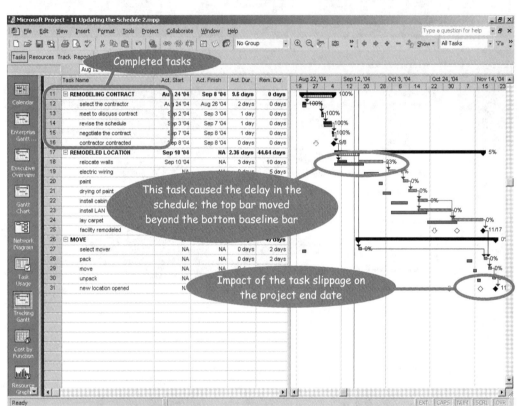

To apply the view, choose **View, Tracking Gantt** or click 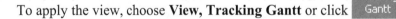 on the *View Bar*.

The *Tracking Gantt* view is used during the execution of the project to track the progress against the original schedule (the baseline). Notice that the task bars are split into two halves, a top half that represents the current schedule and a bottom half for the baseline. If you don't have a baseline in your schedule, it only shows thin task bars for the current schedule. We will discuss the use of this view extensively in chapter 11 on updating schedules, see page 555.

Resource Graph

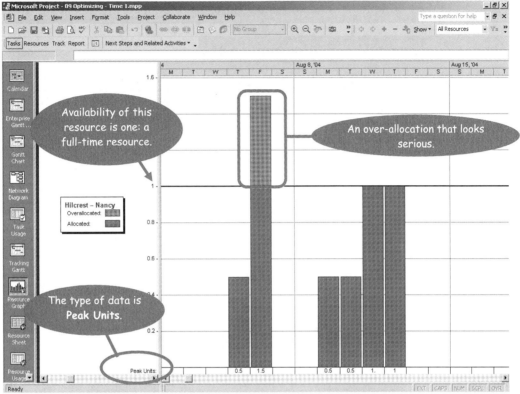

To apply the view, choose **View, Resource Graph** or click Resource Graph on the *View Bar*.

The *Resource Graph* shows bar charts of the workload over time for all resources.

If you don't see any bars, hold down `Alt` and press `Home` to jump to the project start date. If you still don't see any bars, use **Zoom Out** 🔍 on the **Standard** toolbar until you do.

By pressing `Page Dn` or by using the bottom left horizontal scroll bar you can browse from resource to resource.

Notice that the Resource Graph shows the **Peak Units** by default. Peak Units means that if you zoom out the timescale and go from days to weeks, the highest daily bar will be shown as the workload for the week. The more you zoom out, the more pessimistic the depiction of the workload becomes. You can change the Peak Units by choosing **Format, Details**. If you select **Work,** you will see the "real" totals of the work hours charted, OR right-click in the chart area and choose **Work** from the pop-up menu.

Resource Sheet

To apply the view, choose **View, Resource Sheet** or click [Resource Sheet] on the *View Bar*.

The *Resource Sheet* is used to enter the resources needed in a project. Resources can be human resources, facilities, machines and material resources.

Important fields in the Resource Sheet are:

◆ **Name**: Name of the resource.

◆ **Type**: You can indicate if a resource is a material resource or a resource that works on tasks.

◆ **Max.Units**: The maximum units represents the maximum availability of the resource to the project expressed in decimals or as a percentage depending on the setting in **Tools, Options,** tab **Schedule**, field **Show assignment units as**.

Resource Usage

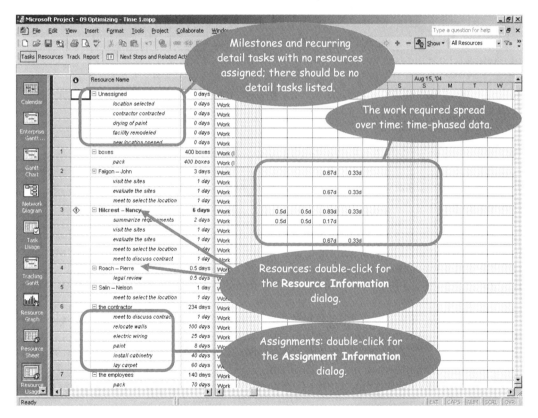

To apply the view, choose **View, Resource Usage** or click [Resource Usage] on the *View Bar*.

The *Resource Usage* view shows the amounts of work or cost over time. As in the Task Usage view, this view shows the assignments as separate line items in italics.

This view allows you to analyze the workloads and solve any over-allocations. We will discuss the how-to on page 411.

Navigating the Views

To Switch Views

Click the view on the view bar.
OR
Choose **View**; a check mark in front of one of the views means that it is the current view on your screen. Click on the view you want to switch to.
OR
If the view bar is not displayed, right-click on the blue bar at the left of your screen and select the view in the pop-up menu.

Single View Versus Combination View

A *single view* is a one-view screen. The views that appear on the previous pages are single views.

A *combination view* is a screen with two views. A combination view consists of a top and a bottom view. When switching a view when you have a combination view on, you first have to click on the view you want to switch out of. Then choose **View** and select the view you want to switch into or click on it in the view bar.

The bottom view only shows information pertaining to the tasks (or resources) selected in the top pane. This interaction between top and bottom view can be very useful for data entry with a sheet view in the top and a form view in the bottom. Form views allow you to enter detail information. The Task Entry view (**View, More Views, Task Entry**) is a combination view with the **Gantt Chart** in the top and the **Task Form** in the bottom (see the next snapshot).

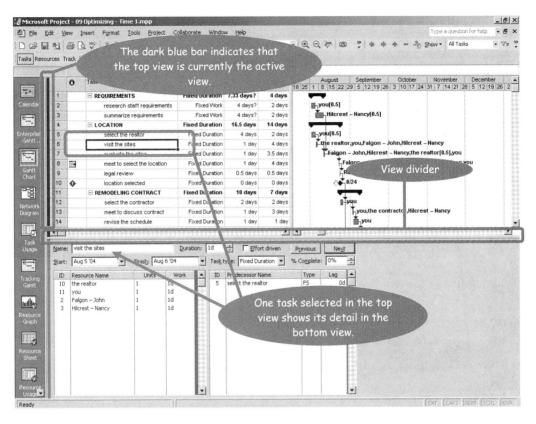

The **Task Entry** view allows you to enter detailed information on tasks. You can enter resource assignments and predecessors. The task you select in the top view, the **Gantt Chart**, is shown in detail in the bottom view, the **Task Form**. The top and bottom panes interact; whatever you select in the top is shown in more detail in the bottom. This makes combination views well suited for analysis of schedules:

◆ With a task view in the top and resource view in the bottom you can check assignments.

◆ With a resource view in the top and a task view in the bottom you can check over-allocations (**View, More Views, Resource Allocation**), as shown in the next snapshot.

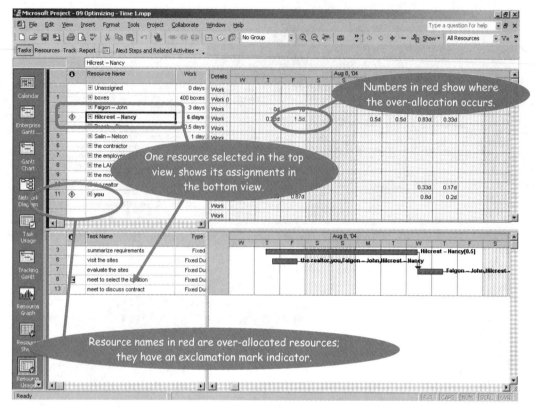

The **Resource Allocation** view has the **Resource Usage** in the top view and the **Leveling Gantt** view in the bottom. This combination view allows you to analyze and resolve over-allocations. The interaction between the top and bottom pane is such that the assignments on the task selected in the top are shown in detail in the bottom.

To Create a Combination View

You can create a custom combination view by splitting the window. Choose **Window, Split**.

Or you can point with the tip of the mouse pointer to the sliding window handle at the bottom right of your screen (the tiny little horizontal bar under the scroll down button).

The mouse pointer will become a double-headed arrow ⇕. Drag it up or double-click on it.

You will now see two views displayed, one in the top and one in the bottom. You can change the size of each view by pointing to the divider line between the views; the mouse pointer should change to ⇕. Hold down and drag when you see this mouse pointer.

To move the cursor between panes, press F6 or click in the other pane.

You can drag both the horizontal border and the vertical dividers at the same time. Put your mouse pointer on the intersection between the two divider lines:

Intersection between divider lines

You should see the mouse pointer ⤢. Drag the dividers to the sizes you need.

To Exchange One of the Views in a Combination View

1. Click on the view you want to exchange. This will make it the active view. You should see the blue vertical bar on the far left of the screen jump to the view you clicked in.

2. Choose **View** and select the view you want to apply.
OR
Click on the view in the view bar on the left side of your screen.

To Switch Back to a Single View

Drag the view divider line to the top or to the bottom using the mouse pointer ⇕, depending on which of the two views you want full-screen.
OR
Double-click on the view divider when you see the mouse pointer ⇕ .
OR
Choose **Window, Remove Split**.
OR
Hold down Shift, choose **View** and select another view.

Using Help

Help Index

1. Choose **Help**, **Contents and Index** to get a list of topics; the **Microsoft Project Help** dialog appears in its own window:

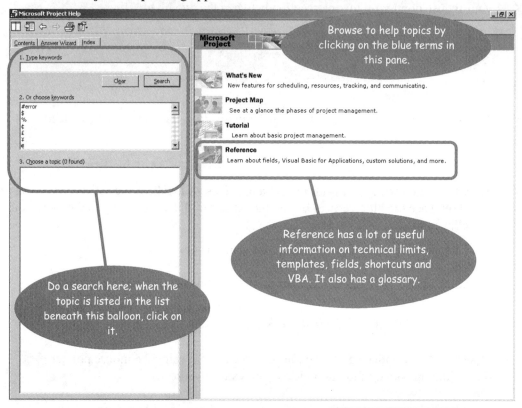

2. Click, for example, in the **Welcome!** screen on the item Reference to receive information on technical limits, fields, shortcuts, templates and the macro programming language (Visual Basic for Applications or VBA).

3. The terms with a blue solid underline (like Templates) are topics you can jump to by clicking on them. The blue terms without an underline (like Critical Path Method) are explained in a pop-up window, when you click on them.

To Search for Help Information

1. Choose **Help, Contents and Index**.

2. Click on the tab **Index**.

3. Type a word or phrase you want to search for in the field:
    1. Type Keywords

    The words that most closely match the text you type are immediately displayed in the list below as you are typing.

4. Double-click on a topic from the list: **2. Or choose keywords**

5. Single-click on an item in the bottom list: **3. Choose a Topic**; on the right-hand side you will now see the help text you asked for.

Help Texts about Screen Items

Hold down `Shift` and press `F1`; the mouse pointer has a question mark attached now. Click on the screen item you want to know more about.

Help with Scheduling: Planning Wizard

The Planning Wizard can help you find your way around MS Project. The Wizard gives you choices of things to do if there is any ambiguity. It presents choices to solve the problem.

Turn the Wizard on or off by choosing **Tools, Options, General** and (un)checking **Advice from Planning Wizard**.

Help When Making Changes: Smart Tags

Whenever you see a small graphical tag appear to the left of where you made changes to the schedule, you are given additional choices. These pop-ups are called *smart tags*. Smart tags ask for clarification when you can end up with unintended side effects. Depending on the situation, different smart tag graphics appear. Below you will find a table of them:

Graphic	Appears when
☒	You press ⌜Delete⌟ on a task name
◈	You change the duration, OR You change the work, OR You change the units, OR You add a resource to a task, or remove one, OR You change the start or finish date

An example of the choices you get when you increase a duration and click the smart tag is:

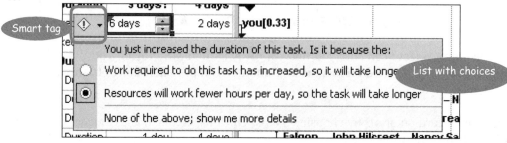

Help with Project Management

Project 2002 comes with a *project map* that can help you with the concepts of project management. You can find the steps to put a comprehensive project plan together by choosing **Help, Getting Started, Project Map**.

Help with the Technical Specs of Your Computer System

1. Choose **Help, About Microsoft Project**

2. Click ⌜ System Info... ⌟. If you are not sure if you have *Project 2002 Standard* or *Project 2002 Professional*, you can verify that in this dialog.

Setting Up a New Project Schedule

The process for preparing a new project schedule is:

1. Creating a new project file from a blank file
   OR
   from a project template see page 58.

2. Describing the project:
   ◇ **Project, Project Information**
   ◇ **File, Properties**

3. Setting the options:
   ◇ Date order
   ◇ **Tools, Options**
   ◇ **Tools, Level Resources...**

4. Setting the project calendar: **Tools, Change Working Time**
   ◇ Working hours
   ◇ Business days
   ◇ Holidays

Project 2002 includes a new toolbar called the *Project Guide*. The Project Guide provides a sidebar interface that acts like wizard interfaces; it holds the hand of new users and asks for information in the right order with a series of prompts. You can display the project guide toolbar by right-clicking on any toolbar and choosing **Project Guide**. The toolbar appears and looks like this:

Upon clicking Tasks , the sidebar changes to:

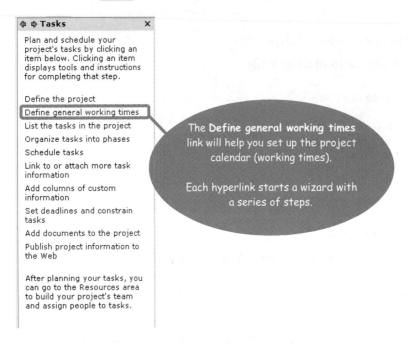

This sidebar now provides hyperlinks to perform certain functions, like **Define the project** and **Define general working times**. Clicking a hyperlink will start the wizard prompts.

The Project Guide wizards do not cover all the steps explained above and we will therefore discuss them in still more detail.

Creating a New Project File

Click **New** 🗋 on the **Standard** toolbar. This creates a blank project right away and displays the **Tasks** Project Guide.
OR
Choose **File, New**: a new project appears as well as the *task pane* on the left side of the screen. The task pane allows you to choose the basis for your new project. Your choices are:

◆ Under **Open a project**, the recently used files are shown.
◆ Under **New**, click **Blank Project** to create a fresh new project.
◆ Under **New from template**, click **General Templates** and the **Templates** dialog appears in which you can select a template.

 Choose to create the schedule from a blank project, or select one of the templates from the **Enterprise Templates** tab (available in Project 2002 Professional with *Project Server* only) or the **Project Templates** tab (project templates shipped with MS Project).

Describing the Project

1. Choose **Project, Project Information** and the **Project Information** dialog appears:

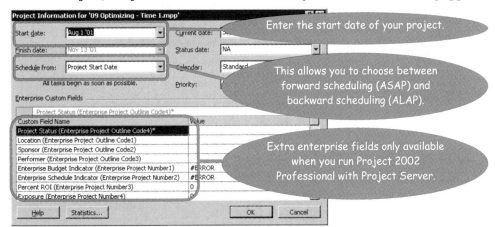

2. Enter basic project information in this dialog. There are two choices in the list **Schedule From**:

    ◇ **Project Start Date** (*scheduling forward*): Enter the **Start Date** and MS Project will schedule all tasks as soon as possible (ASAP) after the project start date.

After you have entered all the data, MS Project will show what the earliest finish date will be for the project.

◇ **Project Finish Date** (*scheduling backward*): Enter the **Finish Date** and MS Project will schedule all tasks as late as possible (ALAP) working backward from the project finish date. After you have entered all the data, MS Project will show what the target start date of the project should be.

The choice you make depends on what you know most certainly about your project: the start date or the finish date. Neither approach will prevent the common occurrence that the initial schedule is too long. You usually have to squeeze the project into the time frame that is available for the project. This makes the choice between entering the start or the finish date less important.

3. Choose **File, Properties** and the **<name of your project> Properties** dialog appears:

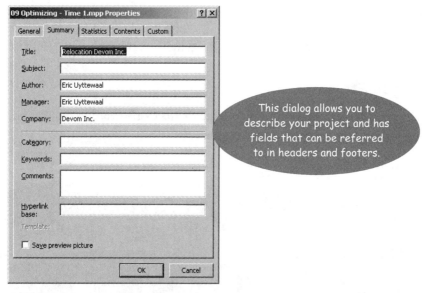

This dialog allows you to describe your project and has fields that can be referred to in headers and footers.

4. Click the tab **Summary** and enter in this dialog:
   ◇ the name of the project in the field **Title**,
   ◇ your name as the **Manager** or **Author** and
   ◇ the project objective or a description of the final project product in the **Comments** field.

5. Click OK .

The entries in the **File, Properties** dialog can be used in the headers and footers of each report you create by referring to them. They save time, particularly when an entry changes.

Setting the Options

The way Project 2002 operates is controlled by the settings in **Tools, Options**. The steps to change the options are:

1. Choose **Tools, Options…**; the **Options** dialog appears:

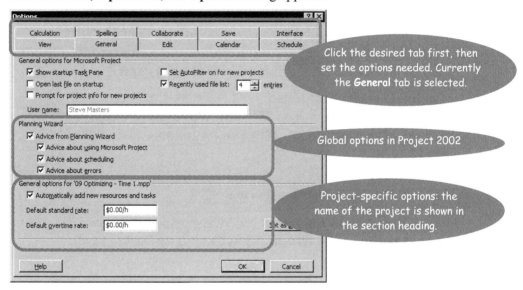

2. Select the category of options by clicking one of the tabs.

3. Set the options.

4. Click   OK   .

There are two types of options:

◆ *Global options* that take effect in all projects: These options are stored in the *Windows Registry*.

◆ *Project-specific options* that affect the active project only: You can recognize these because they start with a section divider showing the name of the project file. These options are stored in the project file (.MPP).

By clicking | Set as Default | you can make project-specific options the default for new projects. This button saves the project-specific options in the *Windows Registry* as well. When you create a blank new project, the Windows Registry is consulted. For existing project files, the project-specific options will not be overridden by clicking this button.

Setting the Date Order

The date order (ddmmyy or mmddyy) cannot be set inside Project 2002. You have to set it in the Windows *Control Panel*. This means that it will affect the date order in all of your Windows applications.

1. In Windows 2000, click | Start | and choose **Settings, Control Panel**.
    OR
    In Windows XP, click | start | and choose **Control Panel.**

2. The **Control Panel** folder appears:
    In Windows 2000 double-click on Regional Options .
    In Windows XP double-click on Regional and Language Options and click **Customize.**

3. Click the tab **Date** and select the date order from the list:
    In Windows 2000/XP: **Short Date Format** M/d/yy ▼.

4. Click | OK |; all lists in Project 2002 that provide choices for date formats will now only show items in the date order you chose in the Control Panel.

Options for a New Project

This table indicates the most important options we recommend you review at this point.

Tab	Set to
View	**Date Format:** `Mon 1/31/00` ▾
	To avoid confusion about dates in international projects, a date format should be chosen with the month spelled out, i.e., 31 Jan '00. Americans will interpret a date like 7-8-2000 as July 8, 2000. Europeans, South Americans and people from Québec, however, will interpret it as August 7th and think they have an extra month.
General	**User Name** [＿＿＿＿＿＿＿＿＿] Enter your name.
	☑ **Advice from Planning Wizard**
	Meant for novice users. Uncheck if the Wizard doesn't help you … or annoys you.
Calendar	**Hours per Day** `8.00` ▴▾
	MS Project uses this number to convert days entered in the **Duration** and **Work** fields into hours. This number should represent the hours worked by a *Full-Time Equivalent* (*FTE*) employee.
	Hours per Week `40.00` ▴▾
	MS Project uses this number to convert weeks into hours. If this number does not reflect your situation, the schedule will not be accurate. It should correspond to the **Hours per Day** setting.
	Days per Month `20` ▴▾
	MS Project uses this number to convert months into days. This number should reflect your situation.
	`Set as Default` Sets the calendar options entered above as the default settings for any new schedules you create. Your other existing schedules are not affected because this option is stored in the project file, as you can see in the label of the section divider **Calendar Options for <file name of the project>**.
Schedule	☑ **Show Scheduling Messages** will give helpful messages when it notices a problem in the schedule.
Calculation	⦿ **Automatic** will ensure that you see the effect of the last changes immediately. With the current speed of computers, the need for manual calculation is evaporating.

The **Calendar** option **Hours per Day** has to be decided upon first and cannot be changed without re-entering all durations. You have to specify how many work hours There are in a workday. If you start with the wrong number, MS Project will interpret the durations you enter incorrectly. It uses this setting to convert between time units. For example, if the **Hours per Day** is set to 8 hours and you enter a duration of 5 days, MS Project knows this equals 40 hours. If you then change the **Hours per Day** setting to 7h/d, MS Project changes the duration to 5.71 days (= 5 * 8 / 7). You must consider this option before entering data.

There is one way to keep the current durations without having to re-enter all durations again. Before changing the **Hours per Day** setting, copy all durations to one of the extra fields (**Text1** for example), change the **Hours per Day** and then copy the durations from the **Text1** field back into the **Duration** field.[8]

Most options we discuss in this chapter are global, which means that they apply to all your projects, existing and new. You can see this in the **Options** dialog box by reading the labels in the section dividers; on the **Schedule** tab it reads: **Schedule Options for Microsoft Project**.

Typically at the start of each chapter we will discuss the options relevant for that chapter.

----

[8] My colleague Linda Lawlor came up with this trick.

Leveling Option: Automatic or Manual

Workload leveling is changing the schedule in such a way that the workloads of the resources are within their availability at any given time. In the illustration below, you can see that on the left Harry has to work full-time on two tasks that are scheduled in

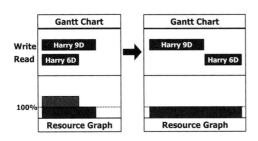

parallel. It causes a workload that exceeds his availability of 100%, which is called an *over-allocation*. The over-allocation was solved on the right by delaying the task *Read* until after *Write*. Delaying tasks is something MS Project can help you with; this is called *automatic leveling*. There are other ways to level the workloads; we will discuss them in Chapter 9 on optimizing, see page 359. These other ways can result in a shorter schedule, but require more effort from you as a scheduler.

1. Choose **Tools, Level Resources...**; the **Resource Leveling** dialog appears:

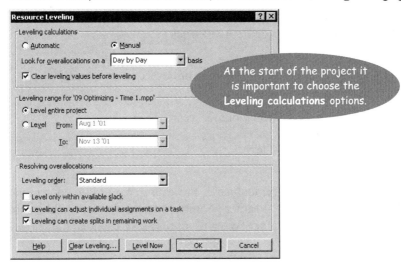

At the start of the project it is important to choose the **Leveling calculations** options.

2. At the top in **Leveling calculations**, select ⊙ **Manual**.

We recommend you use manual leveling at this time. If you select automatic leveling, MS Project will constantly make changes to your schedule as it tries to keep the workloads leveled. When we come to chapter 9 on optimizing schedules (see page 422), we will generate some scenarios using automatic leveling and discuss the dialog box in more detail. We will also explain methods to manually level workloads.

Setting the Project Calendar

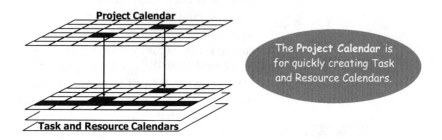

The **Tools, Change Working Time** dialog allows you to set the *project calendar*. The default project calendar is called *Standard*. On the project calendar you indicate:

◆ *Business days*
   Which days are working days in a regular workweek?

◆ Standard *working hours*
   What are the typical working hours for full-time project team members?

◆ National *holidays*
   What days are nonworking days throughout the year?

In addition to the project calendar there are:

◆ *Task calendars*
   These can be used to schedule individual tasks. For example, outdoor construction tasks can only take place when the weather permits. A task calendar could be created for all tasks affected by winter weather. We will discuss task calendars on page 139.

◆ *Resource calendars*
   These are calendars for each individual person. A resource calendar typically contains individual working days, hours and vacations. We will explain resource calendars on page 284.

The business days, working hours and national holidays of the project calendar will be transferred to all the task and resource calendars. The changes you make on the project calendar apply to every task and every resource in the project (unless you have overwritten those settings in the individual task or resource calendars). At this point we will only edit the project calendar; later we will create task calendars and resource calendars. On the resource calendars you can override the project calendar and individualize the business days, working hours and holidays for each resource. All tasks will be scheduled using the project calendar unless:

◆ they have their own task calendar, or
◆ they have resources assigned that have resource calendars.

In summary, the project calendar has two functions:

◆ It is a time-saving device to change all task calendars and resource calendars.
◆ It is used to schedule tasks without a task calendar or resources assigned.

One Project Guide has a wizard that prompts for the working times, hours per day, business days and holidays. You can access it by right-clicking on any toolbar and choosing **Project Guide**; a toolbar appears. Click the **Tasks** tool, the sidebar changes and one of the hyperlinks shown is **Define general working times**.

Hours per Day Option Versus Working Time

The following is very confusing to many people. If you change the number of hours per day in **Tools, Options, Calendar**, Project 2002 does not update the working times in the project calendar by itself. Project 2002 uses the hours per day option for conversion purposes only. When you enter a duration of *1w*, it will convert it to hours. If the setting in **Tools, Options** is 40h/w, then it knows that 1w = 40h.

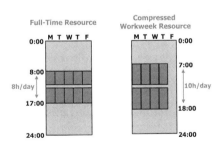

In the project calendar, you can indicate the regular working hours for a full-time resource. Project 2002 uses these settings to schedule the 40 hours of effort within the working hours. Forty hours of effort for a full-time resource will take 5 business days (Monday–Friday). Forty hours of effort for a compressed workweek resource who works 10 hours a day, will only need 4 business days (see the illustration). The conclusion is that the **Tools, Options Calendar, Hours per Day** setting needs to be aligned with the working hours in the project calendar.

Entering the Business Days

1. Choose **Tools, Change Working Time...**; the **Change Working Time** dialog appears:

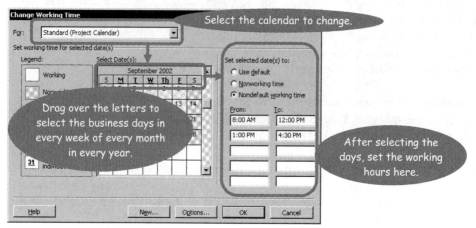

2. Select at the top of the dialog under:

For: Standard (Project Calendar)

the **Standard (Project Calendar)**, as this is the calendar that acts as the project calendar.

3. If the rest of the options in this dialog are grayed out, it likely is because you are using *Project Server* and are using one of the *Enterprise calendars*. Your project office is responsible for maintaining the enterprise calendars, not you. That is one less task for you!

4. If you have a Monday to Friday workweek, select the workdays of the week by dragging over the letters that stand for the days of the week. Click and hold down on the **M** for Monday and stop at the **F** for Friday: M T W Th F.

5. Select ⊙ **Use default**; this sets the days to working days with default working hours of **8:00 AM-12:00 PM** and **1:00 PM-5:00 PM**.

6. Click on the S for Saturday, then hold down Control and click on the S for Sunday and select ⊙ Nonworking time.

When you select the days by their letter at the top, you have selected "eternity"! The changes you make apply to those days in every week in every month and in every year!

Entering the Working Hours

1. Choose **Tools, Change Working Time…**; the **Change Working Time** dialog appears:

2. Select from the list: **For:** | Standard (Project Calendar) ▾ |;
   Standard (Project Calendar); this is the calendar that acts as the project calendar.

3. If the rest of the options in this dialog are grayed out, it likely is because you are using Project Server and are using one of the *Enterprise calendars*. Your project office is responsible for maintaining the enterprise calendars.

4. If you did not set the hours per day in **Tools, Options**, do this first by clicking | Options… |. Upon clicking | OK | you will be returned to this dialog.

5. Select the workdays Monday through Friday by dragging with the mouse from the **M** to the **F:** | M | T | W | Th | F |.

6. MS Project has a default calendar with 8 hours per day and working hours from 8:00 AM-12:00 PM and 1:00 PM-5:00 PM. For any diversion from these defaults, select⊙ **Nondefault working time**.

7. Type the normal work times into the boxes:
   From: To:
   | | | |
   The dates in the calendar now have a gray hatch pattern in the background and are **Edited working hours**.

8. Click | OK |
   OR
   select another calendar from the list and answer | Yes | to the prompt to save the changes.

Entering the Holidays

1. Choose **Tools, Change Working Time…**; the **Change Working Time** dialog appears.

2. Select at the top of the dialog under **For:** | Standard (Project Calendar) ▾ | the **Standard (Project Calendar)**, as this is the calendar that acts as the project calendar.

3. If the rest of the options in this dialog are grayed out, it likely is because you are using *Project Server* and are using one of the *Enterprise calendars*. Your project office is responsible for maintaining the enterprise calendars.

4. Take out your calendar to find the national or company holidays. Go to the first month in which there are holidays by clicking on the scroll arrows ▲ or ▼ (Windows 2000) or ⌃ or ⌄ (Windows XP) OR by pressing [Page Up] or [Page Dn]. To go faster, drag the scroll box ▢ (Windows 2000) or ▤ (Windows XP).

5. Select the holidays by dragging over them or by holding down [Control] and clicking and dragging over them.

6. Select ⊙ **Nonworking time**; the days are now gray, like the weekend days (nonworking). Repeat steps 3 and 4 for the rest of the holidays.

The holidays set in the project calendar are carried over to the individual resource calendars and task calendars.

Even if the project calendar is changed after resource calendars are created, the changes will show up automatically in the resource calendars.

The national holidays and the company holidays should be marked in the project calendar. Days should be marked as nonworking days if they apply to (almost) everybody involved in the project. These typically are either national holidays or company holidays. On *resource calendar*s the project calendar can still be overridden, and certain holidays can be set back to be working days for certain resources. Therefore the project calendar should merely be considered a time saver for creating and changing resource calendars.

The calendar information is saved in the project file. If you want to distribute a project calendar among colleagues, you have to transfer it via the Organizer (see page 180).

Checks on Setting Up a Project

Below you will find some checks to verify if you used the best practices when setting up a new project:

◆ Does the **File, Properties**, tab **General, Comments** field contain a description of the objective or final product of the project?
The description is visible as a **Note** on the project summary task. This criterion is mostly for schedule certification purposes; we need to have some background information on the project to properly evaluate the schedule.

◆ Do the working hours on the **Tools, Change Working Time, Standard (Project Calendar)** correspond to the **Tools, Options, Calendar, Hours per day**?
For example, working times of 8:00 AM-12:00 PM and 1:00 PM-5:00 PM are consistent with 8 hours per day and 40 hours per week. If the settings are inconsistent, your forecasts are either too optimistic or too pessimistic. Also, you will often see decimals in the task durations.
The quickest way to check consistency is by choosing **Tools, Change Working Time**. The ⎡ Options... ⎤ will take you directly to the **Tools, Options, Calendar** dialog. See page 93 for a way to make these two settings correspond.

Exercises

Review

1. Does MS Project function more like MS Excel or MS Access? Why?

2. What is the function of the *Global.MPT* file?

3. In which situations would you recommend the use of project templates?

4. What view would you use for:

	Recommended view
Entering tasks?	
Entering resources?	
Entering assignments?	
Checking the network logic?	
Viewing workloads?	
To-do lists?	

5. Why would you use a split view (combination view) in Project 2002?

6. What steps do you recommend as a process when creating a new project file?

7. How do the settings **Tools, Options, Calendar, Hours per day** and the **Tools, Change Working Time, Standard (Project Calendar)** relate to each other?

8. How can you change the default calendar, i.e., how can you edit the *Standard Project Calendar* in the *Global.MPT*?

Relocation Project — Scope Statement

You are put in charge of relocating your office. You have to find a new location and organize the move. The following is the scope statement created for the project. Your CEO has already signed the scope statement.

Scope Statement for the Relocation Project of DEVOM, Inc.
Project accounting code: MOVE001

The Business Need for the Relocation
DEVOM, Inc. is growing and needs larger facilities to accommodate the expanding workforce.

The Project Objectives
- To be moved and operational in the new location by November 1, 2004
- To stay within the available budget of $100,000 for labor cost
- To have an 80% satisfaction rate from the personnel for the new work environment

The Project Deliverables
- A project plan (including WBS, Network Diagram, Gantt Chart, budget, resource list and assignments)
- A new rented or leased location that has a maximum capacity of 150 work spaces
    - The location should be accessible to disabled people
    - The location should have parking facilities for at least 150 cars
    - The location should have modern work cubicles and an open workspace
- Contracts with the landlord, the general contractor and the moving company
- The physical move of people and equipment

The Project Constraints
- The work on the project is to be started no earlier than August 1, 2004
- The personnel have to be asked for input as to the location and facilities needed
- The disruption to the normal operations of DEVOM should be minimized and may not exceed a loss of 200 person days caused by the project
- Clients will have to be able to contact DEVOM at any time by phone, fax and e-mail
- The purchase of new materials and equipment shall be budgeted and approved separately
- The new location will be within the boundaries of the city and its suburbs
- The need for expansion is so urgent that the project has priority over normal operations
- Any changes to the project objectives will require the approval of the CEO

The Project Assumptions
◆ The market will continue to grow at the same rate
◆ The current furniture can be reused
◆ The current workstations can be reused
◆ The current LAN and servers will be replaced

Date: ………....................

Your signature   signature N.R. Salin:

                                                   NRSalin
....
Project Manager, Relocation Project   CEO, DEVOM, Inc.

You decide to make a project plan and to put the tasks into Project 2002 to keep track of them.

1. Fill in the date and sign the scope statement to take charge of this project.

2. Create a new MS Project file.

3. Set the start date for the project to *August 1, 2004*.

4. The title of the project is *Relocation Devom Inc.*

5. You are the responsible project manager; enter your own name under **Manager**.

6. Enter *Devom Inc.* under **Company**.

7. Save the file as *Relocation.MPP*.

Relocation Project — Tools, Options

Continue to work in the file *Relocation.MPP* and enter the options:

Page tab	Set to
Schedule	☑ *Show scheduling messages*
	Show assignment units as a: Decimal[9]
	Duration is entered in: Days
	Work is entered in: Days
	Default task type: Fixed Duration
	☐ *New tasks are effort driven*
	☑ *Tasks will always honor their constraint dates*
View	*Date Format: Jan 28 '02* [10]
General	*User name: <your name>* [11]
	☑ *Automatically add new resources and tasks*
Calculation	*Calculation mode:* ◉ *Automatic*
Calendar	*Hours per day: 7.5* [12]
	Hours per week: 37.5 [13]
	Days per month: 20

---

[9] In this project we will use mostly individual and group resources and will therefore use decimals rather than percentages.

[10] If you don't see *mmddyy* here, you could go to the Control Panel to change the date order.

[11] Enter your own name here instead of <your name>. This will allow you to refer to this field in the headers and footers of all reports you create.

[12] Enter this by typing instead of using the spin buttons.

[13] Same.

Relocation Project — The Project Calendar

Continue to work with your file *Relocation.MPP* and enter the following data:

1. Set the working hours on the **Standard (Project Calendar)** to:
    8:00 to *12:00* and
    13:00 to *16:30*

2. Take out your calendar and enter the national holidays for the months August, September and October in the **Standard (Project Calendar)**. If you want to achieve an exact match with the solution file, enter the national holidays of the United States:
    ◇ *Labor Day, September 6th, 2004*
    ◇ *Columbus Day, October 12th, 2004*
    ◇ *Veterans Day, November 11th, 2004*

3. Compare your file with the solution file *03 Entering Tasks.MPP* which is available for download at www.jrosspub.com.

Troubleshooting

Open the file *Wrong Hours per Day.MPP*, which is available for download at www.jrosspub.com. Correct the **Hours per day** setting in the **Tools, Options, Calendar** to 7 hours per day without affecting the durations.

Chapter 3 Entering Tasks

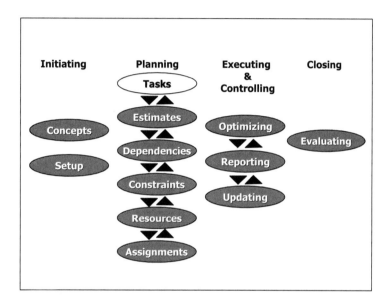

We have finished the *Initiating* phase and will now begin the *Planning* phase by entering *Tasks* (see the white balloon in the illustration). It starts with entering the deliverables. We recommend you enter the data in the order shown in this overview: first tasks, then estimates, dependencies, constraints, resources and assignments.

After reading this chapter you will:
◆ understand what a Work Breakdown Structure (WBS) is
◆ be able to create and change an indented WBS in MS Project
◆ be able to create summary tasks, detail tasks, milestones, split task bars, recurring tasks and overhead tasks
◆ be able to establish the right level of detail in the WBS
◆ know how to edit, copy and move tasks
◆ know about task calendars
◆ be able to check the WBS of the project schedule using scheduling best practices

Deliverables That Make a Difference

Bob has Monica in his office; she is one of his team members. They are discussing the WBS that Monica forwarded to Bob. After chit-chatting, Bob opens the serious part of the meeting with "Overall your plan looks really good, but I would like to have a look at the way you formulated your deliverables. Can we do that?" Monica nods and unfolds her schedule in front of Bob. Bob runs his finger along the WBS, stops at one item and asks, "Here is the planning phase and I don't see a deliverable in it. Isn't the deliverable here your *project plan*?" Monica nods again. "Can we replace the word 'planning' then with the words 'project plan'?" Monica shrugs her shoulders indifferently but asks, "Why do you find that important?" Bob answers: "It's important to me because now I know that I will get a project plan from you since you identified it as a deliverable in your WBS." "Oh, I see!" Monica says.

Bob runs his finger further down and stops at the element *subcontracting:* "What is your deliverable here?" he asks. "Well, the signed contracts, I suppose...," Monica replies. "Yes, I would think so. Can we replace the word *subcontracting* with the words *signed contracts*?" Bob suggests. "Sure, if you think that is important," Monica says.

Bob makes other changes like '*moving to new location*' to '*new and operational location*', '*marketing*' to '*30% increase in revenue*', '*renovation*' to '*renovated facility*', '*material procurement*' to '*procured materials*', '*developed prototype*' to '*prototype development*', and '*closing*' to '*customer approval*'.

Monica concludes: "You are pretty anal about this, aren't you?" "Yes, my dear," Bob says, "and I have found that anal retentiveness makes a world of difference in this case!"

Work Breakdown Structure

The task list in MS Project typically contains a logical grouping. By grouping the activities under deliverables, you can keep a better overview of the entire project. This grouping is known as the *Work Breakdown Structure* (*WBS*). The WBS is a breakdown of the project product into deliverables that defines the scope of the project.[14] Once you know the deliverables, you can then identify the activities to create those deliverables.

The WBS is the most important document in a project since all other project management documents need the WBS as input. Also, the WBS is the "*contract*" between the project manager and the customer. The WBS is the agreement between the project manager and upper management as the client of the project in an internal project. The illustration below shows a WBS for an aircraft manufacturer.

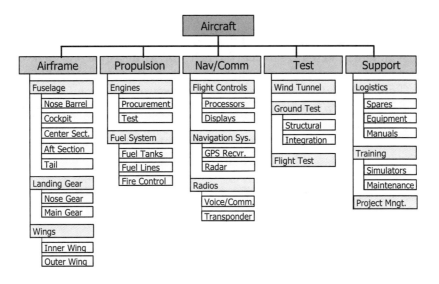

The WBS specifies explicitly what should be done. Implicitly it also specifies what should NOT be done. If the client requests output during project execution, the WBS

---

[14] See the PMBOK® Guide, 2000 Edition, published by the PMI.

should contain the output to be delivered. If it is not in the WBS, it is out of scope and you can then make a case to the client that the requested deliverable was not agreed upon. If it is not explicitly in (the WBS), it is implicitly out (of scope). This is the generally accepted project management practice.

In past projects you may have been forced by your client to deliver something that was never promised; this is commonly known as *scope creep*. From those projects you have probably learned to specify explicitly in the project plan which elements are out-of-scope. Otherwise you will continue to be burned by scope creep. If you expect any possible misunderstanding about the scope of the project, it is a good idea to also document the deliverables that you consider to be out of scope.

In Project 2002 you can capture the scope of the project in the **Task Name** column by creating an indented list of deliverables and tasks. Out-of-scope elements can be captured using the **Task Notes** on the **Standard** toolbar or in the **File, Properties, Summary** tab, **Comments** field. We recommend paying careful attention to clarifying what is in scope and what is out of scope.

Deliverables are tangible components of the project product that are handed over to the client during or at the end of the project. The deliverables are often broken down further into their components and eventually into tasks (activities). It is important to note that the PMBOK® Guide 2000 defines deliverables as: *Any measurable, tangible, verifiable outcome, result, or item that must be produced to complete a project or part of a project.*[15] In other words, a deliverable is not a deliverable if it is not *measurable* or *verifiable*. This means that by incorporating deliverables in the WBS and formulating them properly, you create verifiability in the project. You basically clarify what you are going to produce and ask your client to sign off on the WBS. You have now established how "*contract*" completion will be verified, which will decrease misunderstandings or disputes near the end of the project and the chance of litigation.

In the example, the WBS is shown as a chart, the WBS chart. MS Project does not have such a view, but *WBS-Chart*[16] is an add-on tool you can buy that will allow you to lay out the WBS in a graphic format. The graphic format is easy to read and understand for most people because it resembles an organizational chart.

---

[15] See the PMBOK® Guide, 2000 Edition, published by the PMI.

[16] WBS-Chart is available from Critical Tools, Inc. Please refer to www.CriticalTools.com.

Breaking Down into Phases or Deliverables?

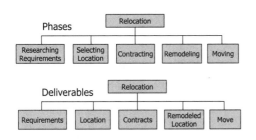

According to its definition a WBS is supposed to be deliverable-oriented. You may not be used to thinking in terms of deliverables, and sometimes it is difficult to identify the deliverables in a project. If you put some effort into finding the deliverables, you will be surprised to find them. Consider for example an office relocation project; *what are the deliverables in this project?* This is the question to think about. If you cannot identify deliverables, you can always divide a project into phases. Phases are distinct periods in the life of a project, a much vaguer concept than deliverables. Vagueness does not help us control projects. Phases are merely time-oriented groupings of tasks that do not necessarily provide verifiability. Many people tend to use phases because they like a chronological breakdown of the project. Establishing chronology is in essence sequencing and scheduling, which is a different project management activity than breaking down the work.

A WBS should be a logical breakdown, not a chronological breakdown. After the WBS is done, the sequencing and scheduling can start.

In small projects we recommend creating a deliverable-oriented WBS rather than a phase-oriented WBS. Particularly in IT project schedules, we find too often only phases and no deliverables. As per the PMI-definition, a WBS with only phases and activities without deliverables is <u>not</u> a WBS. A deliverable-oriented WBS is often clearer to all and has activities that are focused on producing components of the project product. Deliverables that create verifiability are often tangible and are easier to assign to teams. An office relocation project could be broken down into phases or into deliverables, as shown in the illustration above. In most projects, you can do either, and we then recommend using the deliverable-oriented breakdown rather than the phase-oriented breakdown.

Deliverables provide more direction to the team; they focus the team members better. Imagine you were made responsible for either "researching requirements" or for delivering the "list of requirements" in the office relocation project. The latter is a concrete deliverable; it is verifiable and therefore creates a firmer commitment. Imagine you are subcontracting out work; wouldn't you prefer to commit a subcontractor to delivering something rather than doing something without a specific end result?

Deliverables specify the end result better than phases. If you commit a subcontractor to a phase, you may end up with nothing because you did not ask for a deliverable.

Another reason to use a deliverable-oriented WBS is that deliverables make it easier to formulate milestones. Whenever a deliverable is ready, handed over or accepted, you could insert a milestone for the event. Examples of milestone names are *requirements summarized, report ready, preliminary design accepted* and *document delivered.*

Phases and Deliverables in Large Projects

In large projects you often see that the first breakdown level is phases, which are broken down into deliverables on the next level. The WBS then contains both phases and deliverables, with the deliverables on the lower level. This is also a deliverable-oriented breakdown because there are deliverables in the WBS. You don't need to do away with the phases specified in your project life cycle or methodology. You just have to add the deliverables to them as the next breakdown level to arrive at a "real" WBS, as shown in the next illustration:

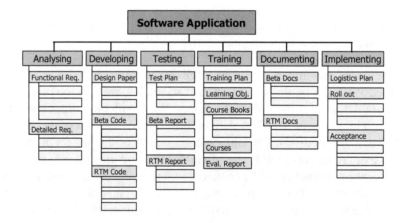

Breaking Down the Work

In the top-down approach, you enter the deliverables first and then you determine all the tasks needed to accomplish the deliverables. In the bottom-up approach, you brainstorm about all the tasks and then you group them under their deliverables. Each deliverable becomes a summary task.

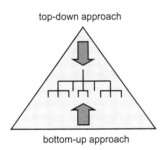

top-down approach

bottom-up approach

The two opposite approaches can lead to the same result. A person who is a novice at the type of project often prefers the bottom-up method. An experienced project manager usually takes the top-down approach. It requires experience to start from the top-down.

Either approach can be successful; there is no one best way. We recommend that if you used the top-down way to create the WBS, you use the bottom-up way to analyze the WBS to check on completeness and if the hierarchy is logical.

While breaking down the work, it is important to keep in mind that the WBS should be a *logical hierarchy*. This means that:
◆   There should be more than one level in the WBS.
◆   There should be no overlap between the phases, between the deliverables or between the activities.
◆   Each element should relate to all its higher level summary tasks.
◆   Subelements should fully comprise the work of their summary task.

The WBS is like an organizational chart in this respect. Each organization has multiple levels. You won't find one person in two different positions and you won't find subordinates who don't report to their boss.[17] Nobody should be left out of an organizational chart.

---

[17] Yes, I could think of some exceptions as well, but let's not get into that. The existence of 'exceptions' just confirms that there are rules.

However, a WBS should not follow the lines of an organization. Do not break down the work by functional group.[18] Eventually the deliverables will be assigned to functional groups in the *Responsibility Assignment Matrix*. This is a different project management activity than breaking down the work in the WBS.

From WBS Chart to WBS List

The WBS chart has to be converted to an indented list of tasks. The illustration below shows how the chart is converted to an indented list. The visual breakdown structure is rotated 90 degrees and the lower levels then become indentation levels. The add-on tool *WBS-Chart,* mentioned before, does this automatically for you.

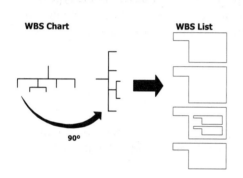

The Gantt Chart view or the Network Diagram view can be used for entering the tasks. You may find the Gantt Chart view the most comfortable window for creating the WBS, because you can create and see the levels of the breakdown structure. The hierarchical structure is shown through indentation of the tasks in the list. The farther indented to the right, the lower the level of the task, and the less important the item is. To switch to the Gantt Chart choose **View, Gantt Chart**.

---

[18] This important point was made by Frank Walker, TWG Project Management, LLC.

Choosing the Options

To set the options that relate to the WBS and tasks, choose **Tools, Options** and consider the following options:

Tab	Option
Schedule	**Default task type:** Most people enter the duration immediately and Project 2002 should not change it, unless required. We recommend setting it to **Fixed Duration** if you normally enter duration estimates.[19]
	☐ **New Tasks are effort driven** This option changes resource units on assignments; we recommend you turn it off. This option works the same as **Fixed Work** tasks and it is preferable to use that feature.
	Set as Default Sets the options above as the default setting for any new schedules you create. The existing schedules are not affected because these options are stored in the project files, as you can see in the section divider label **Scheduling Options for <file name of the project>**.

---

[19] The PMBOK® Guide, 2000 Edition, published by the PMI has *Activity Duration Estimating* as one of the core planning processes.

Categories of Tasks

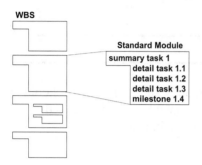

WBS

Standard Module

summary task 1
    detail task 1.1
    detail task 1.2
    detail task 1.3
    milestone 1.4

If you analyze an indented list of tasks, you will find that a standard building block or module recurs. The module consists of a summary task (the deliverable or phase) with subtasks (the detail tasks and a milestone). The summary task summarizes the cost, work and duration of all its detail tasks. That is where the name *Summary task* originates.[20] These standard modules can even be nested inside one another, thus creating the next indentation level, as the illustration shows.

Build your plan in a modular way and use the following standard module of tasks. Your WBS will consist of several of these standard modules:

Standard Module	Example
Summary task 1	REPORT
detail task 1.1	gather data
detail task 1.2	categorize data
detail task 1.3	write report
milestone 1.4	report ready

Please note that most schedulers indent the milestones on the same level as the detail tasks. The milestone relates to the deliverable, just like other detail tasks.

---

[20] The label "*summary task*" is not a very fortunate choice of words because a summary task is seldom a task (activity), but more likely a deliverable or phase. Better words would perhaps have been "*summary item*".

We will now discuss the categories of tasks in more detail:

◆ **Summary task**
To make a plan better understood by stakeholders, it is recommended that you group detail tasks and give each group a label that summarizes it. Summary tasks are often deliverables that give the list a logical and hierarchical structure.
MS Project will sum the costs and work from the detail tasks up to their summary tasks. MS Project summarizes the duration of the detail tasks as well, but not through addition. If tasks are scheduled in parallel, the summary task duration is not the sum of the durations of the detail tasks, but the time span in which those detail tasks happen. For example, suppose your project has two tasks scheduled in parallel. One task has a duration of 5 days, the other 8 days. The summary task of the project would indicate a duration of 8 days. MS Project calculates the summary duration and fills it in for each summary task. It is an enumerated field that you cannot change. MS Project "summarizes" the duration of the detail tasks; this is why it is called "*summary task*" instead of "*subtotal task*".

◆ **Detail tasks**
A detail task is any item that is <u>not</u> a summary task, in other words, any task that does not have lower level subtasks indented beneath it. *Detail Tasks* or *Activities* are the chunks of work that you would assign to resources. Detail tasks are by definition on the lowest level of the *WBS*.

◆ **Milestones**
A milestone is any important date in your schedule. Milestones are often evaluation points or critical points that executives and clients monitor. A milestone can be a date on which a deliverable has to be ready. A milestone has a zero duration; it is a point in time, an event and not an activity.[21] As a general rule of thumb, we recommend you enter at least one milestone for each deliverable. You insert one milestone among the detail tasks of each deliverable summary task. Also, most people will indent the milestone on the same level as the other detail tasks of the deliverable.

Even though as practitioners we make the distinction between summary tasks, detail tasks and milestones, MS Project simply expects that we enter all of these in the field called *Task Name* or *Task*. This misleads some people to think that you should only enter tasks in this field, and no phase, deliverable or milestone names.

---

[21] You can mark tasks with non-zero durations as "*milestones*" also. This creates hard-to-explain gaps between task bars in the timescale. We recommend you use *lag* on dependencies instead.

Styles of Task Bars

1 Summary Task
  1.1 Detail Task
  1.2 Detail Task
  1.3 Detail Task
  1.4 Milestone
2 Split Task Bars
3 Recurring Task
  3.1 Recurrence 1
  3.2 Recurrence 2
  3.3 Recurrence 3

Each category of task has a distinctive shape and color in the Gantt views. The illustration on the left shows the different task bar styles. You can change the shape and color of the task bars through the menu items **Format, Bar Styles**. The default appearance of the bars is shown here. MS Project has other types of tasks: split task bars and recurring tasks. In a split task bar the task has extra stop and resume dates. Recurring task bars have many splits that are not connected with dots. Their task bar styles are also shown in the illustration.

◆ *Summary task bar*
A summary task bar indicates its start and end point with small triangles. Notice that the summary task bar summarizes all its detail tasks and milestones. It starts when its first detail task starts and it ends when its last detail task or milestone ends.

◆ *Detail task bar*
A detail task bar is shown as a simple rectangular bar. A detail task is the lowest level of task in the WBS. The length of a detail task bar represents its estimated duration.

◆ *Milestone diamond*
Milestones appear as black diamonds and figure prominently in the Gantt Chart. Milestones have a zero duration.

◆ *Split task bars*
A split task bar has multiple parts connected by dots. The work on a split task bar is scheduled to be interrupted and resumed at a later date.[22] For example, when electricians wire a building, they have to come back to install the switch plates after the inspection. Another example is when a resource has to interrupt work on a task to attend a one-day meeting.

---

[22] The tool **Split Task** on the **Standard** toolbar should be called *split task bar*, because the tool really splits the *task bars* rather than *tasks*. If it were to split tasks, you would end up with multiple tasks.

◆ *Recurring task bars*
Recurring task bars have multiple parts that occur at a regular interval. Recurring tasks are useful to model things you do regularly, such as *team status meetings*, *schedule updates*, *change request reviews* and *status reports*. Recurring tasks are in fact summary tasks with detail tasks indented beneath.

Formulation of the WBS Elements

Attention needs to be paid to the wording you choose:

◆ *Summary task*
Summary tasks can be deliverables or phases. We recommend you use nouns for *deliverables*, for example *location* or *design*. You could insert an adjective in front of it and call it *new location* or *final design*. Adjectives can improve the measurability of deliverables, which is desirable.
If you use *phases*, use the imperfect tense (*-ing*). This tense best indicates that something is ongoing, which is typical of phases. Examples are *Researching* or *Remodeling*.

◆ *Detail tasks*
We recommend you use verbs for detail tasks. The preferred tense for the verb is the present tense (or imperative tense). The present tense indicates action, and that is exactly what you want because you will delegate the task to your team members. Examples are *contract the publisher*, *evaluate the alternatives* or *purchase equipment*. As you can see, detail tasks are like an order or a command. A resource assigned to the task will interpret it as a request or as an instruction which is what you want as the project manager.

◆ *Milestones*
Typically the milestone is formulated using the syntax:
< *deliverable*> <*past tense verb*>
where < *deliverable*> is a noun that describes the deliverable, and the <*past tense verb*> describes what happened to the deliverable at that point in time. The tense for the verb used in milestones is the past tense (perfect tense). Typical verbs for milestones are *delivered, accepted, completed, done, sent, shipped* and *finished*. Alternatively you could use the word *ready* to indicate completion, as in *report ready*. Or you could use the word *sign-off* as in *requirements sign-off*. Examples of milestones are *module completed, printer delivered* or *report accepted*.

◆ *Recurring tasks*
We recommend using plural nouns for recurring tasks, for example *team status meetings, meetings with client, meetings with sponsor, meetings with executives,*

schedule updates, *change request reviews* and *status reports*. The plural indicates there is more than one. Recurring tasks will become summary tasks. You could also use verbs to capture recurring tasks since, in essence, they are activities. Examples are: *review change requests* or *meet with team*. However, if there is a concrete deliverable resulting from the activity, we recommend you use a noun; for example, use *status reports* rather than *write status reports*.

When you apply these guidelines it is important that you apply them consistently throughout the entire WBS.

You may say to yourself, *I am not going to follow these guidelines. I will call the items whatever I want!* To those who take this attitude I would just like to say that if you follow these simple guidelines, you will ensure that your WBS will be clear to team members and any other stakeholders. Team members may not have been schooled in our profession of project management and therefore need this simplicity. Furthermore, your WBS will be the part of the project plan that you share first and most frequently with stakeholders. Make sure it is as clear as it can get. If you find yourself explaining it all the time, it is not (yet) a good communication piece. Ideally, a WBS should be self-explanatory. If needed, provide a legend of abbreviations with it. If a WBS is not self-explanatory, you could consider adding a *WBS dictionary*. A WBS dictionary provides a narrative explanation of each deliverable in the WBS, sometimes even certain tasks. In the WBS dictionary the requirements or acceptance criteria for the deliverables can be spelled out.

Sharper Formulation of Deliverables

The deliverables are supposed to create *measurability* and *verifiability* in the project plan. This is where project management becomes an art because capturing the deliverables in a few words so that they reflect their acceptance criteria is truly an art. At the International Institute for Learning we find that most schedules we receive for certification can be greatly improved in this respect. The challenge project managers face is aligning the expectations of all project stakeholders. A properly formulated WBS that is signed off on by all stakeholders is the best guarantee that alignment has been achieved. It can only be achieved when the deliverables are formulated as specifically as possible.

The following are examples of deliverables that we came across in real-life schedules (in the left column) and our suggestions for a tighter formulation (in the right column). In our view, the right-hand column gives deliverables that are easier to verify on completion:

Ambiguously formulated deliverable	Better verifiable, measurable deliverable
closing	*customer approval of the project product*
subcontracting	*signed contract*
moving to new location	*operational, new location*
higher revenue	*30% increase in revenue marketing*
renovation	*renovated facility*
planning	*project plan*
material procurement	*procured construction materials*
prototype development	*developed prototype*

The Right Level of Detail

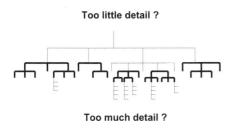

Too little detail ?

Too much detail ?

One of the biggest challenges in breaking down the work is finding the appropriate level of detail. The WBS should have neither too much detail nor too little! In the illustration, the right level is represented by the bold lines on the middle levels. Notice that they are not necessarily on one particular level in the WBS. If one deliverable is bigger, this deliverable ends up with extra levels, as you can see in the illustration. Finding the right level of detail for each deliverable is an art for the project manager.

Adding levels generally improves the accuracy of the estimates; however a larger WBS also requires more work from the project manager to maintain the schedule during project execution. At 7:00 PM you will probably go home instead of update your schedule if it will take another hour.

Below are some guidelines to follow to determine if you have found the right level of detail.[23]

Too Little Detail?

If you think you have a schedule that does not have enough detail levels, ask yourself the following questions while you go through your WBS:

◆ Is it clear how the deliverable will be created and what its criteria for acceptance are?

◆ Can I estimate the duration, effort and cost of the detail tasks?
  If you find estimating too hard without breaking them down into smaller tasks, you should break them down.

◆ Can I find the dependencies between the tasks?
  Each detail task will end up being a node in a network of dependencies. Dependencies are links between tasks that capture how they affect each other. Dependencies are an abstract concept; however finding the dependencies is easy once you have found the right level of detail.

◆ Can I assign the detail task to somebody?
  Eventually, we will assign each detail task to a resource, and if you can't assign it to an individual (or an organizational entity in large projects), you may have too little detail in the WBS.

We will discuss estimating, dependencies and assignments in later chapters.

Too Much Detail?

If you think you may have a WBS that is too detailed, ask yourself the following questions while you go through the list of tasks:

◆ Is this task necessary in the WBS?
  If it is not, get rid of it while you can. If you don't eliminate it now, you will be dragging it behind you until the end of the project.

◆ Is this task merely a reminder to myself?
  A WBS is not meant to be memory support. A WBS is supposed to capture tasks with significant effort involved. Reminders can be entered in the **Notes** field using **Task Notes** 📝 on the **Standard** toolbar.

---

[23] For more guidelines, see page 15 of the *Practice Standard for Work Breakdown Structures*, PMI, 2001.

◆ Is this task a to-do list item or a real task that will take significant effort?
If the items do not take much time or effort, you have not created a WBS but a checklist! Checklist items can be entered in the **Notes** field using **Task Notes** on the **Standard** toolbar.

◆ Will I continue to update all these detail tasks when I am busy during project execution?
If you think you may not be able to update the tasks during the execution phase, this is the time to remove them from the WBS or roll them up into a higher level task.

◆ Do I have at least two detail tasks for each summary task?
If you have only one detail task within a summary, you can leave it out since you are only restating what the summary task does. Each breakdown level should have at least two detail tasks. On average, each summary task has 5 to 7 detail tasks.

 We recommend keeping your schedule lean and mean! Only by doing so will you be able to keep it alive as a forecasting model during the hectic execution of the project.

Not Longer Than a Reporting Period

Detail task durations should never be longer than one reporting period.[24] If you report the status of your project every week, your reporting period is one week. If a detail task is longer than a reporting period, you may notice an out-of-control task only two reporting periods later. This simple rule allows you to ask your team at status time the very pointed question: *Is this task done now, or are we still working on it?* As a project manager you know that if a task is still in progress in two consecutive status meetings, there may be a bigger problem.

An exception to this rule is the *overhead tasks* that can stretch over the entire project duration (see page 132 for more information).

The 1%-10% Rule

There is another guideline. I call it the *1%-10% rule*. The duration of any detail task should be between a minimum and a maximum duration. The minimum duration is 1% of the project duration (rounded). The maximum is 10% of the project duration (rounded).

---

[24] Contribution from Frank Walker, TWG Project Management, LLC.

For example, if you have a project that you think will take 3 months, you can calculate the range for the right level of detail. Three months is about 60 business days. The minimum duration is 1% of 60 or 0.6 day; let's use half a day. Detail tasks should not be less than half a day. If they are smaller, you should lump them together into larger tasks. The maximum is 10% of 60 or 6 days; let's round it to one week. Detail tasks have to be one week or less in duration. You can find the project duration easily by choosing **Project, Project Information** and clicking Statistics... .

OR

In the **Duration** field of the project summary task, you can display the project summary task by choosing **Tools, Options, View,** ☑ **Show project summary task**. This task will appear at the top of the list as a task with ID number 0.

The beauty of this rule is that it can be applied to projects of any size. Other authors often suggest a maximum guideline of 40 or 80 hours for each work package. This absolute guideline is not universally applicable, because a fast-track, one-week project would not be helped by this guideline. We believe the 1%-10% rule has a more universal applicability.

There are some exceptions to which the 1%-10% rule should not be applied:
- *summary tasks*
- *overhead tasks* (*level of effort tasks*)
- *recurring detail tasks*
- *milestones*

Notice that the 1%-10% rule should only be applied to the durations and not to the work values (effort). If there is only one person assigned to most tasks, the work estimates should also be within 1%-10% of the total work of the project. If there are many part-time assignments or many multiple assignments per task, the boundaries for work estimates should be narrower or wider. In general, the minimum and maximum for work values are harder to indicate, which is why we stayed away from that.

Why Is the Right Level of Detail Important?

The rationale behind finding the right level of detail is to create enough checkpoints for monitoring and controlling the progress of the project. Systems theory tells us that we need feedback loops to control a process. In project management we need several feedback loops to control a project, and ten is the minimum number we recommend. This may seem like a lot, but it really isn't. We have to look at this from the perspective of the client or the executives. In the ten-period project shown in the illustration, the first status report normally becomes available halfway through the second period. If the report shows a problem, the client would suggest that an action must be taken. You will take the action in the rest of the second period, and you will likely see the results of this corrective action appear in the third period. The report on the third period becomes available in the fourth period. So problems in the first period will be corrected visibly for the client only in the fourth period. There is always a delay in determining the problem, taking action and seeing the result of the action. If you have ten *checkpoints,* clients really only have six or so *manage-points.* You need, therefore, a safe number of reporting periods. Ten periods seems to work in most projects as a minimum. Building in at least ten formal feedback loops seems like a good norm when communicating with clients and executives.

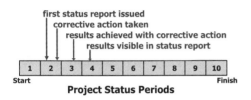

Clients and executives tend to get too nervous when you don't give them enough chances to make a difference in your project. As a result, they will start micro-managing you as the project manager.

Of course, successful project managers make sure they have at least 1000 manage-points. They know what the status of their project is at any time if they are in touch with their team. You can ask them the status 24 hours a day, 7 days a week. (Don't do this though!) Successful project managers continuously check up with their team and do much communication on the work floor. This increases the number of feedback loops dramatically and thus the chance for successful completion of the project. Successful project managers don't use their own status reports to find out what is happening in their project. And if they did, they wouldn't be successful.

Entering Tasks

We will discuss how to enter:
◆ Summary tasks (see below)
◆ Detail tasks (see below)
◆ Milestones (see next page)
◆ Split task bars (see page 129)
◆ Recurring tasks (see page 130)
◆ Overhead tasks (see page 132)

Entering Summary Tasks

For summary tasks you only need to enter the name since most other fields are calculated. These tasks summarize their subtasks in terms of duration, work and cost.

1. Choose **View, Gantt Chart**.

2. Click on the cell in the **Task Name** column where you want to enter the name of the summary task. A summary task typically is a deliverable (or a phase on the level above the deliverables).

3. Type the name of the summary task. It is preferably formulated using a noun. You can insert an adjective in front of it to reveal acceptance criteria for the deliverable. If the one adjective is not enough, use **Task Notes** 📝 on the **Standard** toolbar to add more explicit acceptance criteria.

4. Press ⌨ to go to the next task.

The name is normally the only thing you need to enter for summary tasks. A summary task will only start summarizing when tasks are indented beneath it, on the next row. At that time it will also get its characteristic task bar ▼━━━━━▼ .

Entering Detail Tasks

For detail tasks you typically enter the task name and the duration estimate. We will discuss estimating in more detail in the next chapter.

1. To insert a new row for a detail task, click on any cell in the row before which to insert a new task (row).

2.   Choose **Insert, New Task**, or press .

3.   Enter the **Task Name** and press [Tab] to go to its **Duration** field.

4.   Enter a **Duration** estimate and press [Enter ↵].

5.   If necessary, indent it under its summary task by clicking **Indent** [➡] on the **Format** toolbar OR **Outdent** [⬅] to outdent the task.

 We recommend you list the tasks in their chronological order as much as you can. Don't force this ranking though because you will always have difficulties with tasks that are meant to be done in parallel. In those cases, we recommend you let the logic of the breakdown structure prevail over the chronology of the tasks. Most projects have tasks that run in parallel. The more tasks you can do in parallel, the faster you will finish the project!

 Don't enter **Start** or **Finish** dates for detail tasks; this will automatically add schedule constraints to those tasks, which will make the schedule rigid. Let the task bars move freely, based upon their dependencies. This will be elaborated in chapter 5 on dependencies (see page 187) and chapter 6 on deadlines and constraints (see page 235).

Entering Milestones

For milestones, you typically first enter the name of the milestone, then you enter a zero in the duration field and finally you enter a deadline or constraint date where appropriate. You typically would insert one milestone for each deliverable. The milestone should capture an important event for the deliverable, like being *sent, approved* or *delivered*.

1.   In the **Gantt Chart**, click any cell of the task prior to which you want to insert a milestone.

2.   Press [Ins] and enter the name of the milestone in the **Task Name** field.

3.   Enter a **Duration** of 0 (zero). This will toggle the field **Milestone** from *No* to *Yes* behind the screen which marks the task as a milestone.

4.   If necessary, adjust the indentation level to the same level as the detail tasks above it by using the **Indent** [➡] and **Outdent** [⬅] tools on the **Format** toolbar.

5.   Click **Task Information** [📋] on the **Standard** toolbar or hold down [Shift] and press [F2]; the **Task Information** dialog appears.

6. Click the tab **Advanced**; the dialog should now look like:

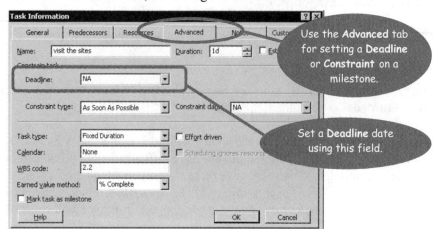

7. If you have a deadline, enter this target date in the field **Deadline** and press ⌷Enter⌷. The deadline shows up in the Gantt Chart timescale as a green ⇩. When the milestone is pushed past its deadline date, a red ◆ will appear in the **Indicators** column.
   OR
   Set a constraint under **Constraint Type** by selecting a type of constraint from the list. Enter a date under **Constraint Date**. A constraint will prevent the network of dependencies from changing the date of the milestone. Constraints can cause scheduling conflicts. We recommend you observe restraint in adding constraints since they tend to be maintenance-hungry.

See chapter 6 (on page 235) for an in-depth discussion of constraints and deadlines.

 There is also a **Mark task as milestone** feature in the **Task Information** dialog box. Click **Task Information** 🗒 on the **Standard** toolbar, and click the tab **Advanced**. This feature will change a regular detail task bar into a diamond. We recommend you don't use this, because it will shrink a task bar from 10 days into a 0-day diamond while keeping the 10-day duration. When dependencies stem from the task, it looks like there is a gap between this task and its linked task. The **Mark task as milestone** feature stores a *Yes* or *No* in the **Milestone** field. Instead of using **Mark task as milestone**, we recommend you use the field **Marked** or one of the extra **Flag** fields to handpick tasks that are important for reporting purposes.

Entering Split Task Bars

You can split any existing task bar into two or more parts or you can add a second task bar to an existing one. You can simply do the latter by drawing a second bar in the timescale to the right or to the left (but not before the project start date) of the existing task bar. Just click, hold down and drag to where you want the second part of the task bar.

To split an existing task bar into two parts:

1. Click **Split Task** ⊞ on the **Standard** toolbar; a yellow pop-up window appears and the mouse pointer now looks like: I⊩.

2. Point to a task bar and click and drag to where you want the split to start. The second part of the task bar splits itself off, and the new start and finish dates of this part appear in the yellow pop-up window when you release the mouse:

Task:	
Start:	Wed 4/5/00
Finish:	Sat 4/8/00

3. Drop it where you want it by releasing the mouse button; the task bar is now split into two parts. Notice that the two parts are connected by dots: ▬▬▬▬......▬▬▬

To remove a split, just drag the right-most part of the bar to the left and reconnect it to its original bar part.

Should we use split task bars?

◆ You cannot set dependencies on the start or the finish of the dotted split in the middle. You often create a split relative to other tasks in your schedule. Because of this, split task bars tend to be very maintenance-hungry in a schedule. We therefore recommend using them sparingly during the planning phase. During project execution, you will see enough split bars appear when you start updating your schedule with actual progress. This will happen when resources are reassigned temporarily, for example.

◆ Instead of splitting task bars, we recommend you split the task into multiple tasks (line items). For example, electricians cable a building, but after the inspection they have to come back to install the switch plates. You could do this with one task through splitting its task bar, but the schedule would be more dynamic if you split the task into two tasks: *pull cables* and *install switch plates.* Now you can set a dependency from the activity *inspect* to *install switch plates* task, and you have a fully dynamic model. (What was the title of this book again?)

Entering Recurring Tasks

Recurring tasks are tasks that take place repeatedly and regularly, for example every other week (biweekly) or monthly. Typical examples of recurring tasks are *status meetings* or *progress meetings*.

1. Choose **Insert, Recurring Task**; the **Recurring Task Information** dialog appears:

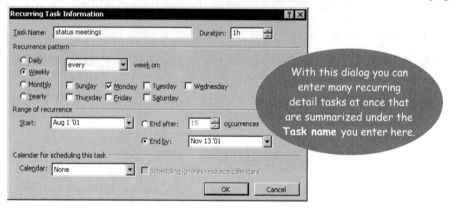

2. Type the name in the **Task Name** field.

3. Type the duration in the **Duration** field or use its ▲▼ to change the duration with pre-set increments.

4. Under **Recurrence Pattern** select the interval at which the task recurs; the dialog changes and presents appropriate choices.

5. Under **Range of recurrence** choose the period or the number of occurrences. Make sure that the status meetings or meetings with the client, sponsor or executive span the entire duration of the project.

6. Click [OK].

Some remarks about recurring tasks:

◆ Notice that recurring tasks are, in fact, a special kind of summary task, but have a different task bar than regular summary tasks. A recurring summary task bar displays all the task bars of its detail tasks.

◆ MS Project sets constraints on each recurring detail task that will keep them on their dates in the timescale. Even though we recommend against using constraints in schedules, there is nothing wrong with these constraints.

◆ If one occurrence accidentally falls on a national holiday (as entered in the project calendar), MS Project will prompt you for what to do with it: drop it or move it to the next business day.

◆ Notice that the duration of the recurring summary task has no meaning; it encompasses the entire period of its detail tasks.

◆ The number of recurrences for meetings may need to be adjusted several times when the project duration changes. We will therefore discuss an alternative way to capture overhead activities on page 132.

◆ The recurring detail tasks will not be included in the leveling process, because MS Project sets the field **Level Assignments** to *No* as a default. If you assign resources to the recurring detail tasks and level the workloads fully, you will still see slight over-allocations on the dates of the recurring tasks. To resolve this, use **Edit, Fill, Down** to enter *yes* in the field **Level Assignments** for all recurring detail tasks and level the workloads again. If you do this, you may see that the recurring detail tasks are rescheduled when you let MS Project level the workloads. You can prevent this by setting a very high **Priority** on the recurring detail tasks (1000). We will discuss leveling in more detail on page 411: Workload Leveling.

Three questions are important with regard to recurring tasks:

◆ When do you need recurring tasks?
Normally, recurring tasks are used for meetings, like status meetings. You could also use them for overhead tasks, but we will elaborate on those on page 132.

◆ Will you set dependencies on them?
Dependencies are only necessary when deliverables are due for a meeting and you want to capture that in the model. You can make the deliverables predecessors of the detail meeting task. In practice, we find that schedulers normally do not set dependencies on recurring tasks.

◆ Will you assign resources to them and level the workload?
Assigning resources is okay, but MS Project will not level recurring tasks by default!

Entering Overhead Tasks

Overhead tasks are tasks that are ongoing during the entire project, for example *project management*, *technical support* and *quality control*. You can enter overhead tasks by inserting long-duration tasks that extend over the duration of the project or by inserting recurring tasks. The table below provides pros and cons for each approach:

Long task bar	Recurring tasks
Easier to schedule with; you only need to remember one percentage to prevent over-allocations with other tasks.	Will cause over-allocations and will not allow automatic leveling unless **Level Assignment** is changed to **Yes** (is **No** by default) and **Priority** set to 1000.
Easy to maintain; when you extend them you don't need to renew their baseline and assign resources again.	When you extend them, you have to set a baseline on the new ones and assign resources.
Every time the project duration changes significantly, its duration needs to be adjusted.	Every time the project duration changes significantly, recurring detail tasks need to be added or removed.

As you can see from the table, we recommend entering overhead tasks as long-duration tasks rather than recurring tasks. Overhead tasks modeled as long task bars require less maintenance.

There is a way to prevent having to update the duration of the long task bar every time the project duration changes. Insert the overhead task on the first outline level. Insert a new summary task that will summarize the rest of the project detail tasks. Copy the duration from the new summary task, then paste link it into the duration field of the overhead task by choosing **Edit, Paste Special**, ⊙ **Paste link**. The duration of the overhead task updates itself automatically from now on and you don't need to constantly adjust it anymore when the project duration changes. Assign the project manager at 50% or 100% to the overhead task depending on how much time she spends managing the project. Set the task type to **Fixed Units**.

Now you have captured the overhead effort of your project in a way that is free of maintenance.

Creating an Outline

Outline Structure

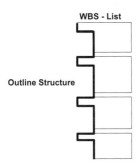

The logical hierarchy of the WBS is entered into MS Project as a list of tasks. The hierarchy of the chart is preserved through indentation in the list of tasks (see the illustration). The more to the left, and less indented, the more important the item is. The tasks on a lower level are indented to the right. The tasks on the lowest level are called *detail tasks*. Detail tasks do not have subtasks. Elements that do have lower level tasks are called *summary tasks*. Tasks can be promoted to a higher level by outdenting them or demoted by indenting them. Thus, an outline structure is created.

Purposes of the outline:

◆ Outlining makes the plan easier to read and understand. How can you eat a whole loaf of bread? Slice by slice or, in other words, deliverable by deliverable.

◆ Outlining generates extra aggregate information on the summary tasks. You can see immediately what a deliverable costs or how long a phase takes. For example, if you are a programmer and you have software features as your deliverable, executives can now see how much a feature costs and how many person hours are spent on it. Executives can easily make trade-off decisions with such a deliverable-oriented breakdown structure. These numbers are used when decisions have to be made on which feature will make it in this release of the software. MS Project automatically calculates the duration, cost and work fields in the summary tasks.

◆ Summary tasks can be collapsed and expanded on an as-needed basis, providing just enough detail to perform your analysis or to focus your reports. If you collapse the summary tasks, it provides an overview rather than details. Most CEOs like an overview of the phases or deliverables and would prefer to leave the detail tasks for you as the project manager.

Indenting a Series of Detail Tasks

Select the detail tasks by dragging anywhere over them in the spreadsheet.
Click **Indent** ⇨ on the **Formatting** toolbar.
OR

Hold down ⌊Alt⌋ + ⌊Shift⌋ and press ⌊→⌋.

After indenting, the summary task shows a duration that summarizes all its detail tasks.

Indenting a task cannot be done by inserting spaces in front of the task name. MS Project will not recognize this as a lower level subtask even though it may look right.

Indenting and Outdenting by Dragging

1. Select the tasks by dragging over them in the spreadsheet.

2. In the **Task Name** column, point to the first characters of the task name; the mouse pointer changes to a two-headed arrow: ↔. Make sure you see this arrow before proceeding (and not the ✛ mouse pointer).

3. Hold down and drag the task to the right for indenting or to the left for outdenting. A vertical gray line gives you feedback on which outline level it will end up on when you release the mouse.

4. Release the mouse button when the gray line appears at the right level of indentation.

Outdenting Tasks

1. Select the tasks by dragging in the spreadsheet.

2. Click **Outdent** ⬅ on the **Formatting** toolbar.
   OR

   Hold down ⌊Alt⌋ + ⌊Shift⌋ and press ⌊←⌋.

To Hide or Reveal Detail Tasks

Click the minus button ⊟ in front of the summary task name to hide its detail tasks.
OR

Select the summary task and hold down ⌊Alt⌋ + ⌊Shift⌋ and press ⌊-⌋.

The detail tasks can be displayed again by clicking the [+].
OR

Select the summary task and hold down [Alt] + [Shift] and press [+].

 If you use the numeric keypad on the keyboard, make sure the numbers lock (**Num Lock**) is off.

To Hide All Detail Tasks

1. Click on the heading of any column; the entire column should be highlighted now.

2. Click **Hide Subtasks** [−] on the **Formatting** toolbar. You should now only see the first outline level.

To Reveal the Next Level

Click on the title of any column and click **Show Subtasks** [+] on the **Formatting** toolbar.
OR
Click [**Show ▾**] on the **Formatting** toolbar, and select the next level down.

To Reveal a Certain Level

1. Click [**Show ▾**] on the **Formatting** toolbar.

2. Choose the level you want to see.

To Reveal All Levels

1. Click [**Show ▾**] on the **Formatting** toolbar; a list is displayed with different outline levels.

2. Select the top entry [⁺⁺] **All Subtasks**.

What You Do with a Parent, You Do with the Entire Family

When you manipulate summary tasks, you have to realize that what you do to a summary task affects all its detail tasks as well. If you delete a summary task, you are deleting its detail tasks as well. The same applies to cutting and copying (see page 139). If you indent a summary task, you indent the detail tasks as well.

Changing the WBS

Editing a Task Name

You can replace a task name by typing over it. If you need to make small editorial changes to correct a typo, you are better off editing the task name.

1. Press [F2]. The cursor blinks as a line in the cell, as in the following snapshot (which of course doesn't show the blinking): | write report | .
   OR
   Click once in the field and, after one second, click another time and a blinking insertion point will appear in the cell: | write report | .
   OR
   Click in the entry bar at the top of the screen; the cursor blinks as a vertical line:
   | X | ✓ | write report |

2. Move the cursor by clicking with the mouse or by using the arrow keys on the keyboard. Make the changes.

3. Press [Enter ↵] to finish the editing. The red-cross and green-check mark buttons in the entry bar should now disappear.

 If MS Project seems stuck and does not allow you to click on menu items, chances are that you are still in the middle of an editing process. Check if you see blinking insertion points or the red-cross and green-check mark buttons in the entry bar. Press [Enter ↵] or click on another cell to finish the editing. Now you can choose menu items again.

Inserting Multiple Tasks

We already discussed how to insert one task; you press [Ins]. Here we will discuss how to insert multiple tasks at once:

1. Point to the row heading before which you wish to insert multiple tasks, click and drag down to highlight as many rows as needed.

2. Press [Ins] and as many empty rows as you had selected are inserted.

If you insert tasks between linked tasks, MS Project may set dependencies automatically if the **Autolink** option is turned on. Choose **Tools, Options**, tab **Schedule** to verify if **Autolink inserted or moved tasks** has a check mark or not. Always check the dependencies after adding, copying or moving tasks (or turn **Autolink** off if you don't want MS Project to link and think for you).

Deleting Tasks

1. Select the tasks by dragging over their row headings.

2. Choose the menu items **Edit**, **Delete Task** OR press ⌦.

Notice that Microsoft has come around full circle in this release by having the ⌦ key delete cells instead of entire tasks (unless you selected row headings). I guess people were losing too much of their WBS without realizing it.

Copying or Moving Tasks

For copying or moving tasks it is important to select the entire task (including its fields that are hidden from view). If you want to copy or move the whole task, you have to select it by clicking on its row heading (the first column with the ID numbers and the gray color). This will highlight all the visible data of the task and select all 240-some fields of a task, including the ones that are not displayed.

The gray color tells you:
◆ that the column is locked,
◆ that it will not scroll off the screen,
◆ that its data cannot be edited and
◆ that you can select the entire task by clicking on it.

If the first column is not gray, you will have to lock the column first.

Locking the First Column of a Table

1. In the Gantt Chart, click on the menu items **View, Table: <name of the table>, More Tables**.

2. Click Edit... .

3. Check ☑ **Lock first column**.

4. Click [OK] and then [Apply].

5. If you now click on the locked title, the whole row is selected.

Copying Tasks

1. Select the tasks by dragging over the row headings with locked title by using the ➡ mouse pointer.

2. Release the mouse button; the tasks are now highlighted.

3. Hold down the [Control] key and click anywhere on the selected row headings with ➡. Drag the copied tasks to their new place; you should now see the mouse pointer ⧉,

   where the small plus sign indicates you are copying.
   OR
   Choose the menu items **Edit**, **Copy Task/Resource** or click ⧉ on the **Standard** toolbar. The task is now stored in the clipboard. Select the task before which you wish to insert, and choose **Edit**, **Paste** or click **Paste** ⧉ on the **Standard** toolbar.

Moving Tasks

1. Select the tasks by dragging over row headings using the ➡ mouse pointer.

2. Release the mouse button; the tasks are now highlighted.

3. Click and hold anywhere on the row headings of the selected tasks; you should now see the mouse pointer ⧉.

4. Drag the tasks to their new place; a horizontal gray line will indicate where the tasks will end up when you release the mouse.
   OR
   Click on the menu items **Edit**, **Cut Task/Resource** or click **Cut Cell** ✂ on the **Standard** toolbar. The tasks are now temporarily stored in the clipboard. Select the task before you wish to insert the cut ones and choose **Edit**, **Paste** or click **Paste** ⧉ on the **Standard** toolbar. Notice that MS Project creates new rows to accommodate the ones cut out.

To keep the dependencies as they are when moving tasks, choose **Tools, Options**, tab **Schedule** and deselect ☐ **Autolink inserted or moved tasks**. Perhaps you should make a habit of checking the dependencies after adding, copying or moving tasks unless you turn it off for all new projects by clicking [Set as Default] as well.

To Copy or Move a Summary Family

Select the summary task by clicking on its row heading. Hold the [Control] key down to copy. Click again and hold down to drag the summary task. Project 2002 will immediately highlight all its detail tasks and move or copy them as well.

If you use the clipboard instead, the detail tasks will also be copied or moved.

Using Task Calendars

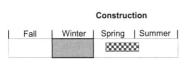

Project 2002 allows you to schedule tasks using *Task Calendars*. For example, in a construction project you could create a winter weather task calendar to schedule all outdoor construction activities affected by winter weather, as shown in the illustration. You can also use task calendars for scheduling testing in an expensive testing lab when you are only given certain windows of opportunity to use the lab. You can model those windows using a task calendar and assigning the task calendar to the test activity.

Task calendars are good for tasks to which you will not assign resources. If resources are assigned, the task will be scheduled based on the resource calendar (except with fixed duration tasks). Creating a task calendar for each individual task is not recommended; it would guarantee hardship when troubleshooting the schedule.

If there are conflicts between the calendars, the order of precedence seems to be:

1. Resource calendar
2. Task calendar
3. Project calendar

In other words, the resource calendar overrides the task calendar, which overrides the project calendar.

Creating a New Task Calendar

 Project 2002 Professional assumes that all calendars are created beforehand by project office staff for the project managers. As a result, you can only create new calendars if you have the right to open and change the **Enterprise Global** file by choosing **Tools, Enterprise Options, Open Enterprise Global**. Once you have this file open, the steps will be the same as for Project 2002 Standard:

1. Choose **Tools, Change Working Time**; the **Change Working Time** dialog appears:

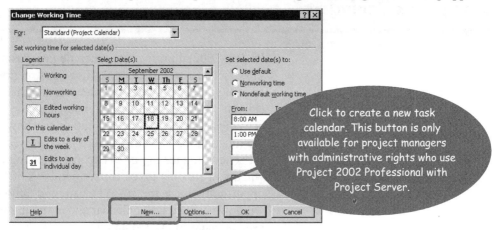

2. Select a base calendar that is closest to what you need for the new task calendar in:
For Standard (Project Calendar) ▾ .

3. Click New... at the bottom of the dialog; the **Create New Base Calendar** dialog appears:

4. Enter a descriptive name for the task calendar and select
⊙ **Create new base calendar** or
⊙ **Make a copy of** the calendar you selected under step 2 (that's the why of the step).

5. Click OK ; you have now created a new calendar.

6. Enter the change on the new task calendar and click OK when done.

Using a Task Calendar

Double-click on a task; the **Task Information** dialog appears. Click the **Advanced** tab, and select the task calendar under **Calendar**.

OR

1. In the Gantt Chart view, click on any cell in the column before which you wish to insert the **Task Calendar** column.

2. Choose **Insert, Column**; the **Column Definition** dialog appears:

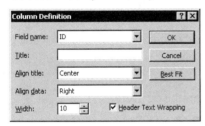

3. Select the item **Task Calendar** from the list **Field Name** and click OK.

4. Click in the **Task Calendar** field None of a task and select a task calendar from the list provided.

Checks on the WBS for Your Project

Below you will find a summary of the best practices for the WBS for your project:

◆   Is the WBS a deliverable-oriented breakdown structure? Are there deliverables in the WBS?
    Deliverables should be captured using nouns (perhaps with adjectives, but without verbs). Verbs change a deliverable into an activity. If there are no nouns in the WBS, we have to conclude that there are no deliverables.
    Alternatives for a deliverable-oriented breakdown are a phase-oriented breakdown or an organizational breakdown. From a project control perspective, these are less effective. See page 111 and the following for a detailed discussion on the proper orientation in a WBS.

◆   Is the list of deliverables complete?

◇ Are all expected deliverables explicitly included in the WBS? This should include the significant reporting items (e.g., monthly reports, test reports).

◇ Are out-of-scope deliverables that may be expected by the client explicitly excluded from the WBS? We recommend you capture exclusions in the **File, Properties,** tab **General, Comments** field.

◇ There are no unnecessary deliverables in the WBS.

◇ We recommend you include the project management deliverables and activities in the WBS. See page 132 for different ways of doing that.

◆ Does the WBS have a logical hierarchy?
If you don't have a logical hierarchy, you may report the wrong cost and duration by phase or by deliverable. You can check if the WBS is a logical hierarchy by expanding the outline structure level by level using the **Show** button on the **Formatting** toolbar.

◇ Is the WBS an indented list with multiple hierarchical levels instead of one long list?

◇ Are the phases, if present, on a higher level than the deliverables?

◇ Are the tasks, if present, on a lower level than the deliverables?

◇ Does each element logically relate to its summary tasks?

◇ Do the subtasks comprise all the work of their summary task?

◇ Does each summary task have at least two detail tasks?

◇ There should be no duplication of deliverables or overlap between the deliverables.

◇ Is the feature **Tools, Options, View, Project Summary Task** used instead of a physical project summary task? MS Project's project summary task has ID 0 (zero).

◆ Are the WBS elements properly formulated?

◇ Phases are formulated using the imperfect tense (-ing).

◇ Deliverables are formulated using a noun (perhaps with an adjective, but without a verb).

◇ Detail tasks are formulated using a present tense verb.

◇ Milestones are formulated using the noun of the deliverable and a verb in past or perfect tense. Instead of a verb, the words *ready, complete* or *sign-off* can be used.

◇ Are the names of the deliverables, tasks and milestones used consistently in the WBS?

◆ Are there enough milestones?
There are enough milestones when there is roughly one milestone for each deliverable. Milestone events typically capture when the deliverable is completed, approved, sent, signed-off, published or shipped, for example. You can check this by applying the standard filter **Milestones** and checking if most deliverables have a milestone.

◆ Does the WBS have the right level of detail?
There may be too few detail levels in the WBS:

◇ If you cannot estimate the duration or work on the detail tasks.

◇ If you have difficulties finding the dependencies between the detail tasks.

◇ If you often assign more than one resource per task.

◇ If there are detail tasks that are longer than a reporting period.

◇ If there are detail tasks with durations longer than 10% of the project duration (1%-10% rule). You can check this by applying the filter
1 IIL Level of Detail > 10% of Proj Dur....[25] You will be prompted to enter what 10% of the project duration is. You can find the project duration by looking at the **Duration** field of the project summary task. The filter will display all detail tasks that are longer than 10% of the project duration.
An exception to the 10% maximum is if you created long tasks to capture overhead effort, like *project management* or *technical support*.

There may be too many detail levels in the WBS:

◇ If you think there are too many levels or if you think the task list is too long.

◇ If you added checklist items or reminders into the task list. Transfer these to the **Notes** field.

◇ If you can't guarantee you will be able to update all detail tasks in the schedule during project execution.

◇ If there are tasks with durations shorter than 1% of the project duration (1%-10% rule). You can check this by applying the filter
1 IIL Level of Detail < 1% of Proj Dur...[26] You will be prompted to enter what 1% of the project duration is. You can find the project duration by looking at the

---

[25] This filter can be found in the file *Tools to check Orange Belt schedules.MPP*, which is available for download at www.jrosspub.com.

[26] This filter can be found in the file *Tools to check Orange Belt schedules.MPP*, which is available for download at www.jrosspub.com.

Duration field of the project summary task. The filter will display all detail tasks that are shorter than 1% of the project duration. Recurring detail tasks will not be displayed since they typically are short and are allowed to be shorter than 1%.

◆ Is the WBS clear to all project stakeholders?
Stakeholders like customers, suppliers, upper management, team members and support staff need to fully understand the WBS. If you, as a reviewer, don't understand it, chances are other stakeholders won't either.

◆ Project management overhead tasks, if present, should extend over the entire duration of the project. It does not make sense to stop managing the project halfway.

◇ Do the overhead tasks (like *project management*) extend over the entire duration of the project?

◇ Do the status meetings, as recurring tasks, continue over the entire duration of the project?

Exercises

Review

1. What is the definition of a WBS as per the PMBOK® Guide 2000 by the PMI?

2. What are the differences between a to-do list and a WBS?

3. You ask a person to manage a project. The objective of the project is to write a document. An author, an editor and a graphic artist are on the team. After a while, the person presents four different first-level breakdowns to you and asks you to choose one. Which one will you choose and why?
   ◆ First draft, final draft, final document
   ◆ Writing, editing, formatting, printing
   ◆ Draft text, edited text, final text, charts
   ◆ Table of contents, body of text, summary

4. Which of the following are proper formulations for deliverables? If you find the wording can be sharpened to improve verifiability, please enter your formulation:

	Your formulation of the deliverable
planning	
research phase	

	Your formulation of the deliverable
approved project plan	
pilot	
prototype	
module 36	
deliver code to Harry	

5. Which of the following are proper formulations for detail tasks? If you find the wording can be improved, please enter your formulation:

	Your formulation of the detail task
program module XT607	
print	
design of house	
writing proposal	

6. Which of the following are proper formulations for milestones? If you find the wording can be improved, please enter your formulation:

	Your formulation of the milestone
report ready	
project close	
design approved	
contract sign-off	

7. How do you know you have found the appropriate level of detail in your WBS? Why is finding the right level of detail important?

Relocation Project — Entering the WBS

1. Continue to work with your file *Relocation.MPP* or open the file
   03 Entering Tasks.MPP, which is available for download at www.jrosspub.com.

2. Check in **Tools, Options,** tab **Schedule**:
   - ◇ If the **Default task type** is set to **Fixed Duration**.
   - ◇ If the option ☐ **New tasks are effort-driven** is deselected.

3. Enter the WBS into Project 2002 as shown in the table below.[27]

4. Indent the detail tasks under their summary tasks. The summary tasks are the tasks with names in capital letters.

5. Compare your file with the solution file *04 Entering Estimates.MPP*, which is available for download at www.jrosspub.com.

   Below you will find the WBS for the Relocation Project.

ID	Task Name
1.	REQUIREMENTS
2.	research staff requirements
3.	summarize requirements
4.	LOCATION
5.	select the realtor
6.	visit the sites
7.	evaluate the sites
8.	meet to select the location
9.	legal review
10.	location selected
11.	REMODELING CONTRACT
12.	select the contractor
13.	meet to discuss contract

---

[27] Notice that capital letters are used here to indicate which tasks will eventually become summary tasks. MS Project displays the summary tasks in bold type to make them stand out by default. This will happen upon indenting tasks.

ID	Task Name
14.	*revise the schedule*
15.	*negotiate the contract*
16.	*contractor contracted*
17.	*REMODELED LOCATION*
18.	*relocate walls*
19.	*install electric wiring*
20.	*paint*
21.	*drying of paint*[28]
22.	*install cabinetry*
23.	*install LAN*
24.	*lay carpet*
25.	*facility remodeled*
26.	*MOVE*
27.	*select mover*
28.	*pack*
29.	*move*
30.	*unpack*
31.	*new location opened*

---

[28] You might wonder if *drying of paint* should be entered as a task because it happens by itself. I merely use it here to illustrate the use of an elapsed duration. Alternatively, you could enter it as lag on the dependency between *paint* and its successor.

Case Study: "My First Time ..."

Norm was proud but tense when he drove home from work. He was assigned to be the project manager on a project for the first time. He felt the assignment was recognition of his outstanding technical expertise. In the evening he would start breaking down the work. This project, though, was different than other projects he had worked on. He had an idea of what deliverables and activities would be needed, but was worried whether he knew or would find them all. He decided he wanted to stay ahead of his team and create a WBS so his team would be impressed. That night he worked very hard and lost some sleep over his WBS. The next day, he presented it and introduced it as "Here is what we are going to do..." His team was quick to point out that he forgot to incorporate the logistics, documentation and training components in his WBS.

Questions:

1. What do you think about Norm's decision to create a WBS by himself?

2. What led him to do it by himself?

3. Would you have done it by yourself if you were in his shoes? Why?

Troubleshooting

1. Open the file *My Schedule.MPP* that is available for download from the website www.jrosspub.com. Change the start date of a task. Why does the task bar not move in the time-scale?

2. Open the file *My Outline.MPP* that is available for download from the website www.jrosspub.com. Explain why the outline does not function as an outline with summary tasks that can be collapsed and expanded.

Chapter 4 Entering Estimates

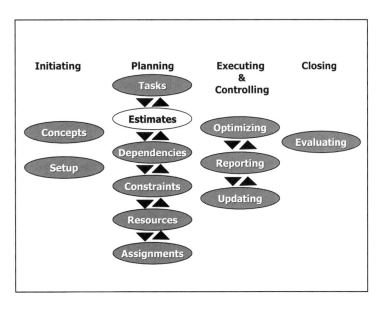

We have the Work Breakdown Structure including the activities (*Tasks*) entered into our project file. The next step is to enter the estimates as highlighted in the illustration above.

After reading this chapter you will:
◆ know a process for generating estimates
◆ know what duration and work/effort estimates are
◆ be able to enter duration and work estimates into MS Project
◆ understand how MS Project uses the formula D * U = W when assignments are made or changed
◆ be aware of the human tendencies when estimating
◆ be aware of difficulties in estimating
◆ know the techniques by which those difficulties can be addressed
◆ understand the rolling wave approach
◆ understand the difference between pure and gross work time estimates
◆ be able to check the estimates of the project schedule using scheduling best practices
◆ know how to enter, move and copy data efficiently

Deadly Dates

Nob is bouncing his views on estimating off Bob: "You know the thing I have noticed is that my team members always pad their estimates. Just last week, Brian told me he was really busy and would perhaps not meet his deadline. Since then I have caught him going for a nice long lunch and I heard him chat up a storm at the water fountain. I can't even think of all the times that I saw him goof off in or around his work cubicle. I made it very clear to him that he is holding up my project. He is on my critical path!"

Bob: "What kind of estimate did you ask for?"

Nob: "Well, the normal thing, you know ... I asked for a date he'd be ready!"

Bob: "A date ... !?"

Nob: "Yeah, a date; what's wrong with that?"

Bob: "Well, if you ask for dates, you can be certain that people will pad them."

Nob: "I don't understand that; what do you mean?"

Bob: "Well, it is like a negotiation, you know. If you ask for this date, they will ask for a later date. And when you agree, you basically have a verbal contract that implies that if they meet that date, you will not be able to criticize them in a performance review. People apply the CYA principle."

Nob: "Yeah, you don't need to explain that one to me..."

Bob: "I always ask for a work estimate. I ask them '*How many person days of effort do you need on this task?*' It's an easier question for team members because they don't need to think of how many hours they are tied up with other tasks or what their work hours will be over the next little while. MS Project will solve all of those problems much quicker and will tell me the date on which they will deliver."

What Are Estimates?

Estimates are predictions of how much time a task will take. The predictions can be made in terms of the duration of a task or in terms of the effort required to perform a task. The difference between duration and effort can easily be demonstrated with an example. If you have 3 carpenters working for 2 business days (duration), the effort is 3 * 2 = 6 person days of effort.

A duration estimate would be expressed in *business days* (working days), which will be the weekdays in most cases. A business day has 8 hours in MS Project by default. A duration estimate can be filled into the field **Duration**; the default time unit is **Days**. To enter a duration of five days (1 week), you could type:

◆ *5 days*
◆ *5d*
◆ *5*
◆ *1w*

Notice that MS Project displays it as *days* and not as *business days*. However, it will help you understand MS Project if you think of the duration as the number of business days.

An effort estimate would be expressed in *person days* or *person hours*. A person hour is one person working one full hour. The effort estimate is entered into the task-related field **Work** in Project 2002. The default time unit of the **Work** field is **Hours**. To enter work of 16 hours on a task, you could type:

◆ *16 hours*
◆ *16h*
◆ *16*
◆ *2d*

Notice that MS Project displays it as *hours* and not as *person hours*. It will help you understand Project 2002 if you think of the work as the number of person hours (person days) needed for a task.

Choosing the Options

Before entering the estimates, it is important to be aware of how Project 2002 will function. Choose **Tools, Options** to display the dialog with which you can change MS Project's behavior. We recommend you set or accept the following options.

Tab	Option
Schedule	**Duration is entered in:** Project 2002 will use this as the default time unit for the field **Duration**. With the default duration time unit set to *days*, you can type in *5* instead of *5d* to get 5 days. You don't need to type a *d* in the duration fields. Choose the unit that fits the majority of your inputs.
	Work is entered in: Same as above, but for the **Work** field.
	Default task type: Most people enter the duration immediately, and MS Project should not change it, unless required. We recommend setting it to **Fixed Duration** if you normally enter duration estimates rather than work (effort) estimates.[29]
	☐ **New Tasks are effort driven** When turned on, this option can change resource units on assignments; we recommend you turn it off. This option works similarly to the task type **Fixed Work**. We recommend you use the task type field instead of effort driven.
	Set as Default Sets the options above as the default setting for any new schedules you create. The existing schedules are not affected because these options are stored in the project files, as you can see in the section divider label **Scheduling Options for <file name of the project>**.

---

[29] The PMBOK® Guide, 2000 Edition, published by the PMI, has *Activity Duration Estimating* as one of the core planning processes.

Tab	Option
Edit	**Allow cell drag and drop** This allows you to move or copy the selected cells by dragging the selected area by its border. This option is global, as you can see from the label of the section divider **Edit Options for Microsoft Project**.
	View options for Time Units for **Minutes, Hours, Days, Weeks, Months,** and **Years** This allows you to change the way time units are shown in your project. The shorter you make the time unit, the more space you save. I set them habitually to the shortest label.

Difficult Situations

Estimating is one of the most difficult skills in project management. *"How do I estimate?"* is the question we are asked most often in our project management courses. Estimating is particularly difficult in the following situations:

◆ Entirely new tasks or tasks not done very often by the organization, like moving or implementing new hardware and software. For this type of task you need to buy some outside expertise and have these consultants help you plan the project.

◆ Tasks that have uncertain outcomes, like R&D-type tasks.

◆ When a team member is assigned who has little or no experience with estimating the tasks in his area of responsibility. Below we will discuss how to deal with inexperienced team members.

Estimating is difficult in projects because, by definition, projects are about doing new things or doing things in a new way. The first time you ask a new team member how long a task will take, the team member may be very reluctant to provide an answer. It is, however, more important that people start giving you their estimates than it is for those estimates to be very reliable. Estimating is a skill, and the only way to acquire a skill is by doing. That is how we learned to drive a car. After the person starts making estimates, he should check how good they were. As a project manager with experience in estimating, you can help in this process of continuous improvement. You should be a mentor for novice estimators. In chapter 11 we will explain how you can retain your original estimates in the baseline (see page 539).

In MS Project you can capture that you are not sure of the estimate. You can have the program treat an estimate like a *"guesstimate"*. You indicate that by adding a "?" to the entry. For example, enter "*3d?*" in the duration field if you are not entirely sure of the 3-day estimate. In its default settings, MS Project will add question marks to those duration cells filled in by the application.

Let's explore the human side of the estimating activity.

The Human Tendencies in Estimating

"I Can't Predict the Future!"

Often new team members have difficulty coming up with estimates. This is particularly true for team members who are new to the type of task to which they are assigned. This is very common because a fundamental characteristic of a project is that it is unique or is being done in a new way. So there is always improvisation and on-the-job learning in projects. What would happen if you filled in an estimate yourself when a team member states he cannot come up with one? If the team member is late with the task, he will simply say: "*I never told you it would be done in only five days!*" You have to get the estimate from the team member; he has to "own" it and then own up to it.

If a team member has difficulty producing estimates, one technique that often works is to ask for two or three estimates instead of one. It is after all easier to provide a range estimate than a single point estimate. The second estimate should be a pessimistic estimate: *What if many things went wrong; how long would it take then?* The person will soon consider disasters like *what if all resources go on strike* or *what if I get run over by a bus* or *what if the whole world crashes down*. You can tell the team member that *if those things happen, neither of you will be around, the project will not be needed any longer and you don't need to estimate anymore!* Have a good laugh about those extreme situations and move on with estimating. It is fine to think of those circumstances, but don't consider them in coming up with a pessimistic estimate.

You probably noticed that I suggest you ask the question: *What if MANY things went wrong; how long would it take then?* "Many things go wrong" is not the same as "everything goes wrong". Therefore, I tend to call it a "pessimistic" estimate rather than a "worst-case" estimate. Asking for the worst case will get people thinking of natural disasters and that sort of thing. The estimating becomes humorous and the process may lose credibility. Alternative questions to solicit for pessimistic estimates would be: *What is a safe estimate?* or *What would you feel confident you can achieve?*

You could even ask for a third estimate, an optimistic estimate: *What if many things go smoothly; how long would it take you then?* or *What would be an aggressive estimate?*

Asking for more than one estimate gives you a better idea of what to expect. It also helps you determine how much padding or buffer you need to apply to the duration estimate. With a three-point estimate you can even do a PERT analysis. Or you can apply Monte Carlo simulation to the schedule. We will discuss both starting on page 366.

In summary, when a team member feels insecure about an estimate:

◆ You ask for more than one estimate for the task: a pessimistic one and perhaps even an optimistic estimate.

◆ You pad the realistic estimate using the pessimistic estimate, such that you have a reasonable probability to realize the padded estimate.

◆ When the target date is not exactly met, you forgive the estimator. You use the padding you applied as the project manager to swiftly forgive. If you are not forgiving, the person may stop providing estimates. If you cannot get estimates from one of your resources, you are less likely to be successful as a project manager than if you get estimates that are less reliable. When you know the estimate is less reliable, you can pad it to create a reliable schedule.

◆ At the end of the project you sit down with the resources that were insecure about estimating and take a look at their original estimates and the factual actual. You help determine how they can improve their estimates the next time around. Evaluation serves as a learning opportunity to become a skilled estimator.

"I Am Always Off!"

People are optimistic or pessimistic by nature. Their personalities greatly affect their estimating. When you have a new team, it will be difficult to determine the optimism factor of the personalities that provide you with estimates. Asking for more than one estimate (optimistic, realistic and pessimistic) gives you a better understanding of the time risk of a task.

In my observation, people are consistent in their tendency to err toward pessimism or toward optimism. Once you have found out the tendencies of your team members, as a project manager you should be able to correct their estimates with a *personality factor*. You can determine someone's tendency by studying their track record of estimates and actuals realized. You can get a very quick impression if you look at a finished project file in the resource-related *Actual Work* field and compare it to the *Baseline Work* field.

If you divide the **Actual Work** by the resource's **Baseline Work**, you have calculated the person's personality factor. For example, if you find that Rich had 420 hours of actual work and 300 hours in his baseline, you know that from now on you should suggest a factor of 420 / 300 = 1.4 to him to make his work estimates more realistic. The beauty of this calculation is that the law of averages takes effect since the actual work and baseline work numbers are aggregated from all commitments the resource had in the project. The personality factors are fairly reliable.

If you get a date forecast from a young team member who you know is very optimistic, you can ask certain questions to make him realize that the estimate may be optimistic. Ask questions like:

◆ Is this estimate in terms of 100% fully focused work time or does it include the normal workday interruptions?
◆ Does it include continuing to answer your e-mail and voice mail?
◆ Do you have other ongoing responsibilities that will take time as well, like providing technical support, troubleshooting, attending meetings or training?
◆ Do you have any personal commitments or other work commitments that will take time out of your workday?

Together you may come to the conclusion that time needs to be added before entering the forecast into MS Project.

If the person tends to be pessimistic, you can ask questions that may lead to subtracting time. In any case, you should leave the final decision with the estimator; otherwise you take the ownership and responsibility away from the team member. The team member will not learn from discrepancies because "*It is not MY estimate!*" Also, the next time, the person may refuse to provide estimates to you since "*You are going to change them anyway!*" If you think the final estimate is still optimistic and you need an extra time buffer, you can always insert this elsewhere in your schedule.

"Can't You Do It?"

I have seen organizations get stuck in scheduling a project when they use estimates produced by people other than the people who do the work. Examples of people who tend to produce unsolicited "estimates" are:

◆ **Executives and upper management**: "*Can't you do it in two weeks?*"
Project managers all know the stress that occurs when executives impose their "estimates" on a project. Some executives will try to make you feel guilty in order to get you to commit to a crazy deadline. When executives make their guesstimates and impose them as committed dates, your unfortunate fate as a project manager is that they will also do your performance appraisal and you're put in a double-bind

position. Estimates from executives should be treated as targets, not as estimates. Enter these as deadlines in Project 2002 (see the discussion of deadlines on page 237).

◆ **Sales representatives**: "*The client gets what she wants.*"
Project managers all know the disastrous effects that occur when salespeople present their own "estimates" to the client without consultation. As a project manager you cannot win in such a situation. These "estimates" are not estimates; they are commitments to please the client and win a sale at the project manager's expense. All too often salespeople tell clients what they want to hear just to get the sale (and cash their commission).

Estimates from executives and salespeople often suffer from wishful thinking in an attempt to please the client and close the deal. As a project manager, you have to come to rely on the estimates of the resources on your team. If you feel the team estimate is high, you can always explore with the team members whether there are other, better, smarter ways of working. In an open discussion, it is often possible to decrease estimates with new ideas.

Now that we have discussed some of the human tendencies in estimating, let us explore how MS Project handles the estimates you enter.

The Difference Between Duration and Work

The *duration* of a task is the number of time units of working time the task will take. Duration is expressed in business hours or in business days, even though MS Project will just call it *hours* or *days*.

The *work* is the number of person hours or person days planned or spent on a task. Work is synonymous with *effort* in MS Project.

For example, one person who works for 2 *business days* (duration) delivers 2 *person days* of effort (work), or 2 painters who work for 3 business days (duration) to paint your house spend 6 person days of effort (work).

The business days are entered in the **Duration** field and the effort is entered in the **Work** field.

The Formula Behind the Screens

Project 2002 uses the formula: *Duration * Units = Work.*
- *Duration* is how many business days you have to finish the job.
- *Units* are how many resource units you have assigned to the task.
- *Work* is how many person days it will take.

The formula is meant to make your life easier, because you only have to provide two out of the three variables in the formula and MS Project will calculate the third one for you. However, if you are not aware of this formula, your life will be more complicated.

The first variable in the formula is a given in most project situations. It is the estimate you come up with. In most situation, you know the *duration* or *work*.

The second variable is the one to decide on: for example, when you know you have a 6 person day job, and you decide to assign 2 full-time people (2 * 100%) to it, MS Project can do the math for you and will calculate a duration of 3 days.

The third variable is calculated by MS Project to balance the equation and is automatically entered. MS Project tries to spare you calculating the value and entering it.

In summary, given the formula, we recommend you work like this:
- You estimate and enter the first value.
- You decide on the second value.
- You let Project 2002 calculate the third value.

If you override the third value that is calculated by MS Project and enter a different value, MS Project will recalculate the first or the second value you entered to keep the equation balanced. The field it will recalculate depends on the *Type* of task: fixed duration, fixed units or fixed work.

An Example of an Estimation

Let us assume you want to repaint one room in your house. You wonder on what date you could be done repainting the room; you need to know the number of calendar days this project will take.

Estimating the number of calendar days, however, is very difficult and you have to step back and try to estimate the number of workdays (business days) the job will take. Once you know the number of business days and on which day of the week you will start, you can convert the business days into calendar days.

Estimating in business days, however, may be difficult as well because you don't know how many resources will be available. You take another step back and decide to focus on an effort estimate. To estimate the effort (work), you realize you must look at parameters like area to be painted, the difference between the old and new color, the number of coats needed and what you will do with the wallpaper. After you have decided all of those factors, you figure it will take, let's say, 10 person days (see the illustration).

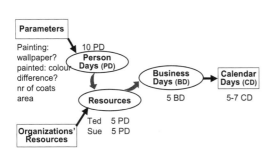

You still cannot say how many business days this requires because you have no firm commitments from family members or friends to help you. You ask around and you find that your significant other is willing to help and that you will share the workload. This means that both of you will take 5 person days of effort; 10 person days of effort can be delivered by 2 people in 5 business days.

If you start on Monday and you decide not to work on the weekend, you can have your house painted by Friday (5 business days and 5 calendar days). However, if you start on Tuesday, you will be done on Monday of the next week (5 business days but 7 calendar days). You now know what you wanted to know: the project end date.

The last conversion from business days to calendar days is taken care of by MS Project. Once you have filled in the project calendar, you can count on the eager and rapid cooperation of Project 2002. The challenge in estimating with MS Project lies in solving the puzzle of person days, resource units and business days. We will present a process for solving this puzzle.

A Process for Estimating

Estimating: Types of Tasks

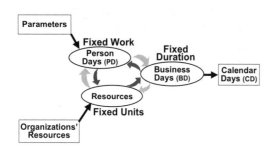

Eventually, you need to know the start date and the finish date of a task in order to fit it into the time line. To get to those dates, you need to find out the number of calendar days a job will take, as shown in the illustration. It is too difficult to estimate the number of calendar days. You will immediately get bogged down with questions like: *When will we start this task? If we start it on a Monday, it will take 2 calendar days, but if we start on a Friday, it will take 4 calendar days!* You don't want to deal with those issues at this point. You should instead try to estimate the number of business days and have Project 2002 do the conversion from business days to calendar days. The software does an excellent job of this once you have filled in the project calendar. We filled it in when we set up the project (see page 96).

In some situations it is possible to estimate the number of business days (or business hours) directly, for example for tasks like *meeting*, *training* and *presentation*. For a meeting you set the duration to, let's say, 2 business hours. Activities like these do not shorten in duration when you add more resources to them; on the contrary, meetings tend to take longer with more people attending.

For many other tasks, it is impossible to estimate the number of business days immediately. Those are the tasks for which it is important to know how many resources are available to do the work and how much effort it will take. You have to step back and estimate the amount of effort first. MS Project calls effort *Work*.

In order to estimate the work (effort) in person days, you may find that you have to look at the parameters of the job. For a programming job you can look at how many input screens the application will have. For a construction project you can look at how many cubic feet of concrete you will need to pour. For each job there are relevant parameters to consider. You may have to ask the client more questions.

Looking at the parameters of the job is important. Each industry has its own metrics to refine the estimates of a job. The construction industry has its quantity surveyors; they can tell exactly how much a brick wall will cost given the square footage and choice of brick. The software industry works with function point metrics. Once software estimators know the number of function points of an application to be built, they have their rough estimates. Dividing the function point total by 150 approximates the number of analysts, programmers and technicians they will need. Raising the function point total to the power of 0.4 gives a rough estimate of the time in months that the team will need.[30]

Once you have determined the amount of work, you have to decide how many resources will be assigned to the job. After that, you can usually determine how many business days the task will take (duration).

In our example, you estimate the amount of work first, then you decide on the number of resources and the number of business days is calculated as a result. This situation is called a *Fixed Work* task, because you estimate the work first. Note that only after durations have been calculated will the Gantt Chart make sense since the task bars in the Gantt Chart depict durations. The durations will be calculated when you assign resources to the task by entering the resource *units* of the formula.

What you estimate or decide first is entirely up to you and will depend on the situation. If you first determine the number of resource units, you have a *Fixed Units* task. If you first estimate the duration, you have a *Fixed Duration* task.

In any situation you will have to estimate the first variable, decide on the second and let MS Project calculate the third. The result: you will know the date the task will be done and the cost of it.

On the next pages we will discuss Fixed Work tasks and Fixed Duration tasks. The Fixed Units tasks are less common in the planning phase and we will postpone discussion of those to page 330. You need Fixed Units mostly when you make changes to assignments.

---

[30] These metrics were taken from *"Sizing Up Software"* by Capers Jones, *Scientific American*, December 1998.

If you don't intend to enter resources and assignments, you will have to estimate the durations for all tasks. Project 2002 needs durations to create the Gantt Chart. If you will assign resources eventually, you can use work estimates. We will not assign resources in this chapter and will discuss this in chapter 8, see page 315.

Preparing the Gantt Spreadsheet

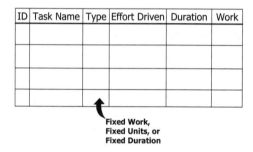

Fixed Work,
Fixed Units, or
Fixed Duration

Let us prepare the Gantt spreadsheet so we have the right fields to enter our estimates. The illustration on the left shows which fields we will insert. We recommend you insert them in the order shown in the spreadsheet of the Gantt Chart.

We need the following fields in the Gantt spreadsheet:
◆ **ID**
◆ **Task Name**
◆ **Type**: By setting the right task type, you tell MS Project to leave the estimate you enter alone. For example, if you estimate that a task will take 10 person days, you enter 10 days in the **Work** field and you set the task type to Fixed Work. The tool may (re)calculate the duration or the resource units needed, but never the Work when the task type is Fixed Work.
◆ **Duration**: To enter the duration for Fixed Duration tasks.
◆ **Work**: To enter the effort for Fixed Work tasks.

If you have the default **Entry** table displayed, you need to insert the fields **Type, Effort Driven** and **Work**:

1. Choose **View, Gantt Chart**.

2. Click anywhere in the column **Duration** and choose **Insert, Column**.
OR
Right-click on the **Duration** column heading and choose **Insert, Column...**; the
Column Definition dialog appears:

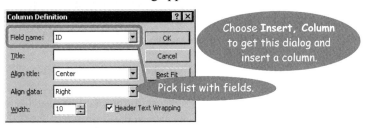

3. Select from the list **Field name** ID ▾ the item **Type** and click
OK .

4. Repeat steps 2 and 3 to insert the columns **Effort Driven** and **Work**.

5. Make sure you have the right default task type selected in **Tools, Options,
Schedule, Default Task Type**. This option determines the task type for new tasks
you create. Click OK . You are now ready to enter duration and work
estimates.

 If you started with the wrong default task type, you can change all tasks at once by
clicking on a column heading to select all tasks and clicking **Task Information** 📋 on
the **Standard** toolbar. Click the **Advanced** tab, select the right type from the list **Task
type** and click OK .

Fixed Work Tasks

A *fixed work task* is a task that has an amount of effort that is only dependent upon the technical requirements for the job. The amount of effort is not dependent upon the number of resources that will be assigned to the task or the working times (calendars).

Once you determine the amount of work, you will often find that your next step will be to establish how many resources will do the job, as shown with the black arrows in the illustration. When you know the work and the number of resource units, MS Project will derive the number of business days (duration).

In this chapter we will only give you the steps for entering work estimates. In chapter 8 we will explain how to assign resources to tasks, see page 315.

Once you know the amount of work (10 person days), you sometimes know in how many business days it needs to be done. Let's say you have only 4 business days for the task (duration). From this, Project 2002 can derive the number of resources you need (2.5).

1. Enter the name of the task in the field **Task Name**.

2. Press Tab ; the cursor moves to the field **Type**. (If you press Enter ↵, the cursor will move down to the next task.)

3. Select from the list Fixed Units ▼ the task type **Fixed Work**. Press Tab repeatedly to enter the **Work** field. Notice that Project 2002 entered a default duration of **1 day?**

4. Enter in the **Work** field 0 hrs ▲▼ the number of person hours you estimate the task will take. You only need to enter the number and MS Project will append "**hrs**". If the time unit is different, for example 3 weeks, you have to type "3w". In that case, Project 2002 needs the time unit abbreviation as well. Valid abbreviations are "m" for minutes, "h" for hours, "d" for days, "w" for weeks and "mo" for months.

5. Press Enter ↵ and then Home to position the cursor for the next task.

Fixed Duration Tasks

A *fixed duration task* is a task that has a duration that does not fluctuate with the number of resources assigned to it, or the working hours of those resources. Examples of tasks like these are *status meeting, training on methodology, back up computer system* or *drying of paint.* Tasks tend to have a fixed duration when you assign many resources to them (meeting, training) or none (back up computer system, drying of paint).

For Fixed Duration tasks you enter the duration first. A task such as *meeting* is a prime example of a fixed duration task, because you decide the duration up front. Then you can decide how much effort you are willing to spend in the meeting and enter the work as shown with the black arrows in the illustration. Or you can decide who you will invite to the meeting and assign the number of units. Once you have assigned the number of resource units, MS Project will calculate the total amount of work.

1. Enter the name of the task in the field **Task Name**.

2. Press [Tab]; the cursor moves to the field **Type**. (If you press [Enter ↵], the cursor will move down to the next task.)

3. Select from the task type list [Fixed Units ▼] **Fixed Duration**.

4. Enter in the **Duration** field [1 day? ⬍] the number of business days you estimate the task will take. You only need to enter the number and Project 2002 will append *days*. If the time unit is different, for example 2 hours, you have to type the time unit abbreviation as well ("m" for minutes, "h" for hours, "d" for days, "w" for weeks and "mo" for months).

5. Press [Enter ↵] and then [Home] to position the cursor for the next task.

Notice that an "m" will be interpreted as "minutes" instead of "months".

Estimating: Difficulties and Techniques

The following factors make estimating difficult:

◆ **In which time unit to estimate**
You have the choice to estimate the number of calendar days (elapsed time), business days or person days (hours). Sometimes you know the time frame in which the activity has to be ready (calendar days: deadline date), and sometimes you know first how much effort it will take (person days: work). Each situation is different.

◆ **What to include**
What do your resources include in their estimates? Do they imagine being able to work full-time on the task without interruptions? Do they include personal time, like calls to their significant other? Do they include time spent in meetings to discuss or present deliverables?

◆ **Unknown events**
In any project there are always many unknown events. For example, in a project to move a company the location is often unknown when the move is planned:
◇ How easy will it be to find a location?
◇ How long will it take to prepare the new location?

◆ **Unknown resources**
During the planning phase it is often unclear whether enough resources will be available, who will be available and if they will be available at the time they are needed.

◆ **Unknown experience and skill level**
Even if you do know which resources you will have on your project, you may not know their experience and skill level. For estimating, this creates an extra challenge, because the estimator should look not only at the job but also at who will do the job in order to come up with a precise estimate. How much skill does the job require? What is the skill level the resource has?

◆ **Unknown learning curve**
Projects create products that are unique. Some say that because of the lack of repetition, the effect of the learning curve is limited in projects. Still, I think, learning plays an important role:
◇ Because the project is new, participants have to be willing to learn. R&D projects and product development projects are prime examples.
◇ There is some repetition in projects, for example status reports, quality control and time sheets. In implementation projects the same system is installed in many locations.

The learning curve theory is therefore applicable to projects and to duration estimates.

We will discuss each of these difficulties in more detail.

In Which Time Unit to Estimate

You can estimate in person days, business days or calendar days (elapsed durations). When estimating, you have to choose if you are going to express your estimate in person days, business days or calendar days.

◆ *Person days*
You can express an estimate in person months, person weeks, person days or person hours. One person day is one person working one full day. The number of person days is the amount of *work* or *effort* needed on the task. For example, if you have to write 20 pages of text and you know it takes you about 2 person hours per page, the total effort is 20 * 2 = 40 person hours. The effort needs to be entered into the field **Work** in MS Project. Person day estimates are (fairly) independent of the number of resources who are going to do the work. Once the job is defined, it just requires a certain amount of effort to finish it.
Person day estimates are needed to calculate the cost of the project. Each person hour applied needs to be multiplied by the appropriate rate to arrive at the cost.

◆ *Business days*
A business day is a working day. The working days are defined in the project calendar. The number of working days a task will take is called the **Duration** of the task, and that is the name of the field where you enter it.
You need to know the number of business days in order to calculate the calendar days needed and the start and finish dates. MS Project also needs the duration in order to create the Gantt Chart. The length of the task bars in the Gantt Chart is driven by the duration of the task (in combination with the project calendar).

◆ *Calendar days*
One calendar day is 24 hours and is simply how everybody thinks of a day, whether educated in project management or not. For example, if paint dries in 2 days, the number of calendar days is 2. The number of calendar days needed is not dependent on the working times; paint dries at night and on the weekend as well.
You need to know the number of calendar days if you are asked to commit to a delivery date. Calendar days are also known in MS Project as *elapsed durations*.

A working day has 8 hours for most of us, whereas an elapsed day has 24 hours. An elapsed day is how most people will understand "one day". Elapsed durations are used for tasks that go through the night and through the weekend and do not follow working hours, as shown in the illustration to the left.

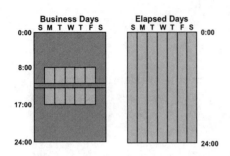

Examples are backing up a computer system or the drying of paint. At food companies, new products are shelved for months in order to find out if the food preservation procedures are adequate. These months are elapsed months because they continue over Christmas and through the summer holidays. At defense systems developers, a new monitor for a tank is kept in a shake and bake oven for, let's say, 2 days to test its ruggedness. The 2 days are elapsed days. Elapsed activities continue 24 hours around the clock.

Time unit	Enter normally as	Enter in elapsed time as
minutes	*m*	*em*
hours	*h*	*eh*
days	*d*	*ed*
weeks	*w*	*ew*
months	*mo*	*emo*

Instead of typing in "5d" to get 5 days, you have to enter "5ed" to get 5 elapsed days.

What to Include: Pure Work Time or Gross Work Time?

The term *Pure Work Time*[31] expresses an important concept very well. Pure work time is working 100% of your time with 100% focus on the task. Pure work time is 100% productive time without interruptions: crunch time!

Pure   Gross

Gross Work Time, on the other hand, includes much time spent on things other than the tasks in the task list of a project. If you look at where you spend your time during a regular workday, you will find that a lot of time is lost on things other than project tasks. It should be clear if your estimate is in pure work time or in gross work time.

Gross work time could include:

◆ Time spent on project tasks, of course

◆ Time spent on nonproject, work-related tasks, for example:
   ◇ answering e-mails that do not pertain to the project
   ◇ answering phone calls that do not pertain to the project
   ◇ professional development training (not project-related)
   ◇ providing emotional or technical support for colleagues
   ◇ introducing and training new staff
   ◇ troubleshooting
   ◇ debugging existing software
   ◇ company meetings (for example, on employee benefits)

◆ Time spent on yourself (personal time), for example:
   ◇ vacation days
   ◇ sick leave
   ◇ coffee breaks
   ◇ personal telephone calls
   ◇ visits to the restroom, water fountain and coffee pot

---

[31] I learned this term first from my former colleague Brian Petersen.

◇   TGIF,[32] farewell and anniversary lunches for colleagues
◇   daydreaming

Do you, as the project manager, estimate in pure work time or in gross work time? Do your resources estimate in pure work time or in gross work time? Is it possible that they provide you with pure work time estimates, whereas you always thought they were gross work time estimates? If that is the case, your resources will never meet their deadline dates! If, on the other hand, you receive gross estimates while using a pure work time project calendar, your project schedule will be unacceptably long.

It is important that:

◆   All team members estimate consistently in either pure work time or gross work time; you cannot use a mix of the two.
◆   The working times or resource availabilities are set accordingly in Project 2002.
◆   Time sheets are filled in with pure actual hours worked or gross actual hours worked as well.
◆   You consider whether you want the costs in your project to be calculated based upon pure work estimates or gross work estimates. The cost of pure work estimates will turn out to be lower than you may want to report and you will need a multiplication factor to correct this. That is why most people use gross estimates and gross working times.

If you ask a team member for an estimate, you should ask explicitly for an estimate in *pure work time* or *gross work time*. You can ask a question like: "*Could you tell me how many person hours this would take you in terms of gross work time?*" If you suspect that the team member is not clear on what gross work time means, you should explain it briefly and give examples from the list above to indicate the difference between pure and gross.

Only when the collected data are consistent with the project calendar can you produce reliable schedules from these estimates. Project 2002 is set up by default to receive gross work time estimates because the default working times are 8:00 AM-12:00 PM and 1:00 PM-5:00 PM. If everybody estimates in gross work time, you don't have to do anything special.

---

[32] TGIF stands for *Thank Goodness It's Friday*.

However, if you want to work with pure work time estimates, you have to do one of the following:

◆ The easiest thing to do is to decrease everybody's availability from 100% to less than 100%. If you have found that people are productive 80% of their work time, you have to enter this as their availability in the **Max.units** field in the resource sheet. More on this on page 289 under Part-Time Availability.

◆ Another option is to adjust the working times for everybody in the *project calendar*. You can simply shorten the working times.

Another issue is whether the estimates should include waiting times. Waiting time is, for example, the time you have to wait to receive a permit or approval. Many people include these waiting times in their duration estimates. We recommend entering them as lags on dependencies instead. For a definition of lag and how to enter it, see page 193.

Unknown Events: The Rolling Wave Approach

For a project to relocate the office where you have yet to find the new location, it is hard to estimate how long it will take to remodel it. Perhaps only minor remodeling will be necessary if you find a location in good shape, or maybe you will spend a long time getting the location up to par.

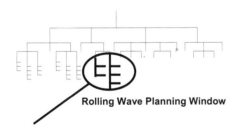

Rolling Wave Planning Window

Some project managers would keep the estimate on the safe side for this part of the project by assuming they have to remodel the new location drastically. They enter just one line item for the remodeling in the Work Breakdown Structure (WBS) and the uncertain but safe estimate. Once they have an idea what the new location needs in terms of remodeling activities, they will start listing the detail activities and create the appropriate level of detail in the WBS and schedule. Notice in the illustration that the first 8 deliverables that are within the planning window are broken down in detail, whereas the last 12 aren't yet.

This is called the *Rolling Wave* approach; you don't detail the plan until you know what to expect. Project managers will often use a *planning window* when applying the rolling wave technique. In a project of a year you could use a planning window of one quarter, for example. The planning window moves as time goes by, and as soon as a deliverable falls inside the next quarter (the planning window), you would break down the detail activities for that deliverable. This avoids having to redo large portions of the WBS. The rolling wave technique is therefore useful to handle the unknown events that are far into the future.

You can even apply the *1%-10% rule* when working with rolling wave planning to find the right level of detail for both the detail schedule and the high-level schedule. You apply the rule to the planning window period to find the right level of detail for the detailed schedule. And you take 1% and 10% of the total project duration to find the right level of detail for the high-level schedule that is farther out in the future.

Unknown Resources

If you don't know which resources you will get, you have to make assumptions just for planning purposes. If you don't make assumptions, you cannot finalize your detailed schedule. One common assumption project managers make is that the resources will be available when their project needs them. Of course, it is a good idea to discuss your resource needs with the resource manager, HR or executives as a reality check on this assumption. Make the assumption loud and clear explicitly in the project plan, so no one's lack of memory will come back to haunt you.

"C++ Programmer"   "Winston"
(C++ Programmer)

If you don't know the names of the individuals you will have on your team, you enter them as *generic resources* in terms of roles, functions or positions. The illustration shows that you don't know for sure that you will have *Winston* on your team, and you therefore enter C^{++} *Programmer* instead. This simple technique will allow you to do your estimates, enter resources and enter the assignments as well. You can now produce a detailed schedule. Once you know the names of the individuals, there are simple techniques to update your schedule to reflect this. We will discuss these techniques on page 342.

 In *Project Server* you can define generic resources in the enterprise resource pool and accumulate the workloads on these generic resources. This allows you to finalize the resource-loaded detail schedule.

You may have to formulate certain assumptions about the experience and skill levels of the generic resources.

Unknown Experience and Skill Level

Even if you do know the name of the resource that will do the job, you still may not know how much *experience* the person has and at which *skill level* he or she should be classified. This will throw your estimate off and thus your schedule.

If this is a major concern, use several resource categories such as *Junior Visual Basic Programmer* and *Senior Visual Basic Programmer*. Assign the junior resource to the easy tasks and the senior resource to the tasks that require experience or skill. Once again, you need to substitute the generic junior and senior resource with the names of the actual individuals. We will discuss these techniques on page 342.

Unknown Learning Curve

We should consider two factors:
◆ Organizations create new and unique products through projects. As a consequence there will always be a lot of on-the-job learning.
◆ The number of repetitions in projects is considerably lower than in manufacturing operations. The only repetition in projects is producing the status reports every week. *Projects are never boring.*

The amount of learning and the lack of repetition in projects combined imply that resources hired on projects have to be fast learners. The ability to learn quickly is perhaps even the most important characteristic of good project resources.

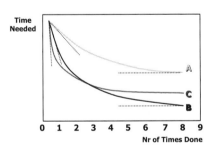

Fast learners (B and C in the illustration on the left) have a *learning curve* that has a steep slope down. The second time they repeat something, the time needed goes down fast. Fast learners can also end up with a faster time per deliverable after many repetitions than slow learners (compare the horizontal dotted lines for A and B). However, it is not a given that the fastest time possible per deliverable is eventually lower for fast learners. To see this, compare the horizontal lines for B and C. Because of the lack of repetition in projects, the initial learning rate seems to be more important than the eventual fastest time per unit. We therefore recommend you hire people with a C learning curve for your projects.

The learning curve poses difficulties, in terms of estimating. The estimator should not only look at the job, but also at who will do the job in order to produce the right estimate. How much repetition does the job have? Is the resource a slow or a fast learner? These factors complicate estimating and, again, you may have to make some assumptions as to the rate of learning of the resources. Also, don't forget to make these assumptions explicit in your project plan. Otherwise you may end up with a slow learner (and be blamed for late delivery). In addition, if you don't document how you arrived at your estimates, you will not be able to learn from the discrepancies between original plan and actual execution.

Living Document Approach

As we just saw, there are many unknowns in projects: unknown events, unknown resources, unknown experience and skill levels and unknown learning curves. A common way to deal with the unknowns is to treat the project plan as a living document.

The *living document approach* basically says that your detailed project plan is not finished and final until the project is closed. You keep revising and refining the plan during the entire project life. The project plan "lives" in a sense. You will continue to refine the task list, the estimates and assignments during project execution.

 Note that the high-level project plan does not change; the scope and quality requirements, the deadline and budget may not change at all. The baseline may not change. Changes in the high-level project plan only happen through a formal approval process that typically involves management and clients. In the living document approach, the changes happen at the lower levels of detail.

Checks on the Estimates

♦ Are the estimates reasonable given the work that needs to be performed?
   You will need some technical expertise to verify if the estimates are reasonable. If you don't have this technical expertise, you could review the schedules of previous but similar projects. You should ask your team members who have the technical knowledge, or you can ask a subject matter expert to review the estimates.

♦ Are the estimates that you collected consistent with the working hours entered in the **Standard (Project Calendar)**?
   ◇ Gross working time estimates should be entered in a schedule with gross working hours (typically 8:00 AM-5:00 PM).

◇ Pure working time estimates should be entered in a schedule with pure working hours. Note that 100% productive working hours corresponds to a shorter working day, for example, 8:00 AM-3:00 PM. For most organizations, the percentage of totally productive working time lies between 60% and 80% of the working hours.[33]

Let's say your normal workday has 8 hours. If you estimate that the productive hours are 70% of the hours worked, the working hours should be 70% * 8h = 5.6 hours, let's say 5.5 hours (68.75%). Working hours that correspond to this are, for example, 9:00 AM-12:00 PM and 1:00 PM-3:30 PM. We prefer that you set working hours like these on the project calendar. You can set other working times as long as the total number of hours adds up to 5.5. To review the steps to set working hours, see page 96.

Copying and Moving Data

Entering estimates can be a tedious job. That is the reason why we will discuss here some quick ways to enter data into MS Project.

Editing Fields of Multiple Tasks at Once

1. Select the tasks by clicking on the first task, holding down [Control] and clicking on the next ones until they are all selected.

---

[33] This range is based on answers we received in our classes in which we taught thousands of project managers.

2. Click **Task Information** 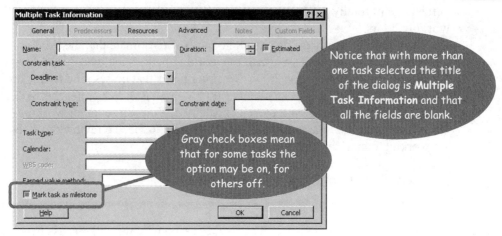 on the **Standard** toolbar, or hold down ⬚Shift and press ⬚F2; the **Multiple Task Information** dialog appears:

3. Make the changes needed on each tab.

4. Click ⬚OK.

The Multiple Task Information dialog can be used as a time saver for many purposes. Examples are:

◆ Setting the duration of all the milestones to 0 (zero) on the tab **General** and unchecking ☐ **Estimated** to make the question mark disappear.

◆ Changing the task **Type** on the **Advanced** tab in the field **Task type**. For example, you can change the type of task from **Fixed Duration** to **Fixed Work** for a series of tasks.

◆ You can assign or add a resource to many tasks at once on the tab **Resources**.

◆ Assigning *priority* numbers to groups of tasks, so they will not likely be delayed when using resource leveling. Choose the tab **General**, and enter a number between 0 and 1000 in the field **Priority**.

Copying with Fill Down

1. Enter the value that you want to copy down in the top cell.

2. Click and hold down on the top cell and drag over all adjacent cells you want to fill. OR

   Hold down ⬚Shift and press ⬚↓ to select all cells you wish to fill.

OR

Hold down Control and click on all nonadjacent cells to fill with the value.

3. Choose **Edit, Fill, Down**.
    OR
    Hold down Control and press D.

Examples in which you can use the fill down feature:

◆ Changing the constraint types for many tasks. To get rid of constraints change them to **As Soon As Possible**.
◆ Setting the **Level Assignment** field for all the detail recurring tasks to *Yes*.
◆ In the resource sheet you can fill down the department or the group for the resources.

Fill Up or Fill Down Using the Fill Handle

1. Enter the value you wish to fill into other cells in the top or the bottom cell of the area to fill into.

2. At the bottom right of the cell you will see a fill handle

3. Point to the fill handle, and when you see a crosshair mouse pointer

    drag over the cells to be filled.

You can even enter a pattern of values in adjacent cells, and when you then drag the fill handle, MS Project will copy and repeat this same pattern as many times as you drag up or down.

Copying or Moving Cells

When copying or moving cells you have to make sure that the receiving cells can accommodate the type of data you paste in. MS Project will warn you if the cells cannot receive it and will refuse the data if it does not make sense. For example, you cannot copy dates into the duration field.

Copying Cells

1. Select the cells and point to the border of the selected area. Make sure the mouse pointer changes from a plus sign ⊕ to ⬨ .

2. Hold down [Control] and drag the cells to their place.

 You cannot use copy and paste to copy one cell and paste it into many other cells, like you can in Excel. It does not work in Project 2002.

Moving Cells

1. Select the cells and point to the border of the selected area. Make sure the mouse pointer changes from a plus sign ⊕ to ⬨.

2. Click, hold down and drag the cells to their new place.

 If you classify as "mouse-challenged" or as a "careless clicker", you should consider turning this *cell drag and drop* option off. You can do so by choosing **Tools, Options,** tab **Edit** and deselecting ☐ **Allow Cell Drag and Drop**.

Clearing Cells

 The [Delete] key now clears cells in the Project 2002 release. (You can still delete entire rows with the [Delete] key if you select the entire row first by clicking on the row heading, and then pressing [Delete].)
OR
Select the cells (not the row heading — the locked first column) and choose **Edit, Clear, All**. This feature can also be used to selectively clear only the formatting, content, notes or hyperlinks of a task. A smart tag ☒ may appear to ask if you wanted to clear the entire task, but since you knew what you were doing, you can press [Esc] to make it go away.

Copying or Moving the Data in a Column

1. Select the whole column by clicking on its column heading.

2. Click **Copy Cell** 📋 on the **Standard** toolbar or choose **Edit, Copy**.

3.   Select the column in which you want to paste the data.

4.   Click **Paste** on the **Standard** toolbar to paste the contents.

Make sure the copy-to column can receive data of that type: dates can be copied into date columns, text into text and numbers into number columns. You will receive an error message from Project 2002 if it cannot paste the data.

Copying Between Projects

Copying Data Between Projects

1.   Open the project to copy from.

2.   Select the tasks or resources by dragging over their ID numbers (the first column with the gray color) to select entire tasks or resources.

3.   Choose the menu items **Edit**, **Copy** or click on the **Standard** toolbar. The data are now temporarily stored in the clipboard.

4.   Open the project to be copied to.

5.   Select the row before which to insert the data and choose the menu items **Edit**, **Paste** or click **Paste** on the **Standard** toolbar.

You can also copy certain cells between projects instead of entire rows (records). If you do this, you have to be careful to paste the data in a blank area of the sheet; otherwise existing data will be overridden. Choose **Edit, Undo Entry** or click **Undo Entry** on the **Standard** toolbar if an accident occurs.

Copying Objects Between Projects

1. Choose **Tools, Organizer**; the **Organizer** dialog appears:

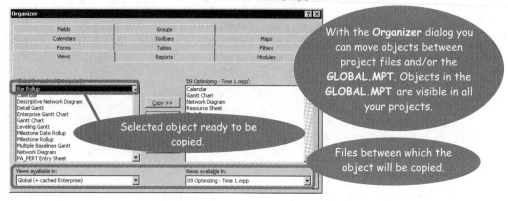

With the **Organizer** dialog you can move objects between project files and/or the GLOBAL.MPT. Objects in the GLOBAL.MPT are visible in all your projects.

Selected object ready to be copied.

Files between which the object will be copied.

2. Click on the tab of the type of objects to transfer.

3. Select from the lists at the bottom of the dialog the file from which to copy the object and the file to copy to.

4. Select the object and click Copy >> to copy from left to right or << Copy to copy from right to left.

5. Click Close or Cancel when done.

The organizer allows you to copy objects to other project files or to the *global.mpt*. Any objects you put into this global template are visible in all your projects, unless they have the same name as other objects that are part of the project file.

Using the organizer you can, for example:
◆ Make the standard project calendar available to other people.
◆ Create a standard report and make it available to colleagues.
◆ Share views, tables and filters with other people.

Exercises

Review Questions

1. Why is estimating the duration of project activities difficult?

2. Is there a need to estimate the cost of activities in MS Project? If yes, why? If not, how would you get the cost numbers?

3. You are the project manager. When you are working with your team members on estimating the tasks, somebody makes one of the following statements to you. What would you say?

Somebody's statement	Your response
Your team member says: "I can't give you an estimate because I can't predict the future! I don't possess higher powers."	
Your team member says: "Listen, we went over this already. I am not going to give you any more estimates because my estimates are always off! My estimates don't help you anyhow!"	
Your executive says: "You are one of our most experienced and best project managers. Can't you do this project in three weeks?"	

4. In your own words, what is the difference between *Duration* and *Work*?

5. What formula is working behind the screens of MS Project that relates *Duration* to *Work*?

6. Rank the following time units in terms of difficulty to estimate in (1 is easy, 3 is difficult) for project activities in a typical project for most project managers and

then for your own projects:

Time unit	Difficulty for most projects	Difficulty for your own projects
Business days		
Calendar days		
Person days		

7. What is the difference between a pure work time estimate and a gross work time estimate?

8. Somebody gives you an estimate of 100 person hours of effort for a task and says that the estimate assumes uninterrupted and fully focused work time. You just created a new project file that has all options set to the default settings in MS Project.
    a. What other fields or dialog boxes would you have to change in order to get a valid finish date forecast for this task from MS Project?
    b. In which field would you enter this estimate in MS Project?

9. What are two easy ways to change the task type to *Fixed Work* for a series of tasks that you will select in the task list by holding down the $\boxed{\text{Control}}$ key and clicking?

10. One of your fellow project managers has created a project calendar that has all the national holidays and the company holidays filled in for the next five years. You would like to use that same project calendar for your projects. How would you go about that?

Relocation Project — Entering Estimates

Continue to work with your file *Relocation.MPP* or open the file *04 Entering Estimates.MPP* that is available for download at www.jrosspub.com.

1. Insert the fields *Type*, *Duration* and *Work* in the Gantt spreadsheet in the order they appear in the column headings of the table below.

2. Check in **Tools, Options,** tab **Schedule** if the time unit for **Work is entered in** is set to **Days**.

3. Enter the data from the table below into the Relocation project file. The tasks with a zero duration will become milestones. Where no data are provided you don't enter anything; MS Project will fill in the default duration of *1 day?* and the default work of *0 days*. Leave these as they are; you cannot blank them out.

ID	Task Name	Type	Duration	Work
1.	REQUIREMENTS	Fixed Duration[34]		
2.	research staff requirements	Fixed Work		2 d
3.	summarize requirements	Fixed Work		2 d
4.	LOCATION	Fixed Duration		
5.	select the realtor	Fixed Duration	4 d	
6.	visit the sites	Fixed Duration	1 d	
7.	evaluate the sites	Fixed Duration	1 d	
8.	meet to select the location	Fixed Duration	1 d	
9.	legal review	Fixed Duration	0.5 d	
10.	location selected	Fixed Duration	0 d	
11.	REMODELING CONTRACT	Fixed Duration		
12.	select the contractor	Fixed Duration	2 d	
13.	meet to discuss contract	Fixed Duration	1 d	
14.	revise the schedule	Fixed Duration	1 d	
15.	negotiate the contract	Fixed Duration	1 d	

---

[34] Notice that you cannot change the **Type** of a summary task; it is set by MS Project to **Fixed Duration**. No **Durations** or **Work** numbers are provided for summary tasks, because these are calculated by MS Project.

ID	Task Name	Type	Duration	Work
16.	contractor contracted	Fixed Duration	0 d	
17.	REMODELED LOCATION	Fixed Duration		
18.	relocate walls	Fixed Work		100 d
19.	install electric wiring	Fixed Work		25 d
20.	paint	Fixed Work		8 d
21.	drying of paint	Fixed Duration	4ed[35]	
22.	install cabinetry	Fixed Work		40 d
23.	install LAN	Fixed Work		60 d
24.	lay carpet	Fixed Work		60 d
25.	facility remodeled	Fixed Duration	0 d	
26.	MOVE	Fixed Duration		
27.	select mover	Fixed Duration	2 d	
28.	pack	Fixed Duration	2 d	
29.	move	Fixed Work		20 d
30.	unpack	Fixed Duration	2 d	
31.	new location opened	Fixed Duration	0 d	

Compare your file with the solution file *05 Entering Dependencies.MPP* that is available for download at www.jrosspub.com.

---

[35] Notice the "*e*" in "*4ed*"; this is an elapsed duration that continues through the night and weekend.

Case Study — Escalated Estimates

Mildevices, Inc. is a manufacturer of military products. The company makes navigation and intelligence products. LCD screens and consoles are some of its major products. Mildevices has engineering and manufacturing staff. There is a project control office with 25 project management staff members, and this office reports directly to the Vice-President of Operations. The project control staff supports the engineers in delivering the projects.

Upper management typically initiates a new project. One executive becomes the project sponsor and finds an engineer that she will appoint as the project manager. The project manager puts the budget together with his team, and the budget is submitted for approval by the executives.

Executives typically cut the budget proposed by the engineers because they are concerned with the bottom line of the company. The engineers find that the cuts are applied arbitrarily and often feel they end up with impossibly tight budgets. As a consequence, they start to increase their estimates in order to end up with reasonable budgets. In subsequent projects the executives react to this in turn by cutting the proposed budgets even more. The new cuts are done in a way that makes even less sense to the engineers. As a result, the project managers now jack up their estimates even further and hide their padding in the estimates wherever they can. At this stage, the openness and the mutual trust are gone between the executives and project managers.

One of the schedulers in the project office, Debbie, says this about these developments: "The numbers the engineers receive back from senior management are so ridiculously low that they just laugh at them." Inevitably, she says, budget overruns take place.

QUESTIONS:

1. Is the estimating done in a professional manner in your opinion at Mildevices?

2. What type of problem is this? Is it predominantly an organizational problem, a cultural problem or a financial problem?

3. If a project manager asked you for advice, what would you recommend to break this escalating spiral?

4. If an executive asked you for advice, what would you recommend to break this escalating spiral?

Chapter 5 Entering Dependencies

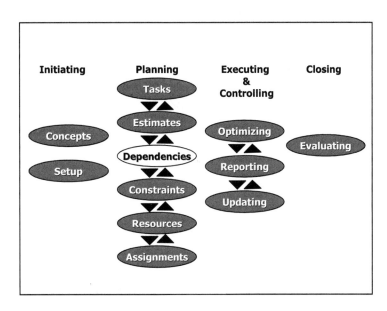

We have the tasks and the estimates entered into our project file and are ready to enter the dependencies, as the white highlight shows above. Dependencies are links between tasks.

After reading this chapter you will:

◆ know what dependencies are and think of them in terms of cause and effect
◆ realize how important dependencies are for dynamic schedules
◆ be able to enter dependencies into an MS Project schedule
◆ be able to choose the right type of dependencies
◆ be able to determine if you need a lag or lead on a dependency, expressed in absolute or relative terms
◆ be able to set multiple predecessors or successors on a task
◆ know the best practices for the network logic in project schedules
◆ be able to check the network logic of the project schedule using scheduling best practices
◆ be able to format the Network Diagram view in an attractive way

The Beauty of Logic

Bob is working away at his desk when Nob enters his office: "What'ya up to, Bob?" he says.

Bob: "I am creating the schedule for this new project that I got last week. I am trying to figure out the dependencies between the tasks. It always takes me quite a bit of time to find all of them."

Nob: "Yes, as far as I am concerned it takes too much time. I don't bother with linking everything to everything anymore. It is too much work!"

Bob: "At this time in the planning of the project, I am tempted to say that you are right. It is a lot of work and I don't get much benefit from it right now."

Nob: "So why are you always killing yourself on all those dependencies?"

Bob: "I do it because I have the time to find them during the planning phase!"

Nob: That's not a good reason ... if you are looking for some work, just ask; I can keep you very busy!"

Bob: "I was just joking ... I spend the time on dependencies because during the entire project execution phase, I benefit from them ... and that is when I don't have time for anything anymore! These dependencies keep my schedule valid and up-to-date. Whenever I enter a change or whenever I update the schedule with actual progress, they adjust the remaining schedule. I set them once when I have the time and I benefit from them when I don't have time. They allow me to be proactive...."

Dependencies

The Principle of Dynamic Schedules

A *dynamic schedule* is not just a fashionable term. A schedule is only dynamic if the schedule can easily be kept up-to-date when you are busy during project execution. Ideally, when <u>one</u> thing changes in your real-life project, you would have to change only <u>one</u> field in your MS Project model to have valid forecasts again. This ideal will only be approached if your schedule meets the following requirements:

- ◆ You find and enter all the *relationships* between the tasks that may impact your forecasts. These relationships are called "dependencies" and are discussed in this chapter.

- ◆ You minimize the number of *hard dates* in your schedule. Hard dates or *fixed dates* are called *schedule constraints* in MS Project. We will discuss constraints in the next chapter.

What Are Dependencies?

A *dependency* is a relationship between the (start or) finish of one task and the start (or finish) of another task. The dependency reflects the cause and effect between the two

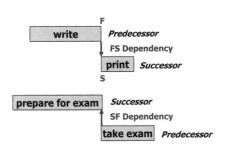

tasks. The result of the first dependency shown in the illustration is that the finish of the independent task *write* (predecessor) drives the start of the dependent task *print* (successor). When the finish date of *write* changes, the start date of *print* will move with it.

Many people think of dependencies as the chronological sequencing of tasks. If you belong to that category as well, you may get stuck on the concept of dependencies. I once met a project manager with 15 years of experience who could not establish the

difference between a successor and a predecessor. He thought the predecessor is always the task that is scheduled earlier in time. He held a chronological concept of dependencies. He became confused when he saw that successors are sometimes scheduled earlier than predecessors, like in the second example in the illustration:

prepare for exam and *take exam*. As a result he never truly understood the difference between a predecessor and a successor. It is <u>not</u> a matter of chronology! The words *predecessor* and *successor* are misleading, because they imply chronology. This project manager took the terms too literally.

Dependencies are not about chronology, but about cause and effect. Think of the predecessor as the driving task (driver) and of the successor as the driven task (follower). In order to find the predecessor, the right question to think about is *"Which task drives the other task?"* When you try to identify dependencies with your team members, we suggest you use the terms *driver* and *follower*, instead of *predecessor* and *successor*. You then enter them into the **Predecessors** and **Successors** fields in MS Project.

The whole network of dependencies is also called the *network logic*. The word "logic" provides a much better reference to the cause-and-effect character of dependencies.

Why Should I Use Dependencies?

Most people thought in terms of dates when they scheduled on paper. You may now be used to entering start and finish dates into MS Project. However, it is not necessary to

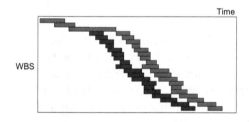

indicate start and end dates when you work with Project 2002. We even strongly recommend <u>not</u> entering start and finish dates because they create schedule constraints (hard dates). Instead, MS Project only needs to know what the cause and effect is between the tasks that have to be performed. Entering the logic between the tasks is also called *entering dependencies*. In the illustration you can see that the duration of the third task was revised and that all the dependent tasks were immediately rescheduled as a result.

The main benefit of making all the dependencies between the tasks explicit is that when the duration or start date of one task changes, Project 2002 can recalculate the entire schedule for you.

If you don't use dependencies, you have to review and perhaps redo the entire chart yourself by hand. This may seem acceptable during the planning phase when you still have the time, but it becomes impossible during the execution of the project. During execution too many things change and they change continuously. I have seen too often that early in the execution of the project the Gantt Charts were dumped in a drawer and never looked at again. Too many people abandon their schedule, and this typically happens sometime during project execution. I have come across companies that have never been able to keep even one schedule alive during project execution. And it is during project execution that you reap the greatest benefits from your schedule, such as continuous forecasts of project end date and final cost. The schedule has to be a dynamic model of your project to realize those benefits. Your schedule is only a dynamic model if it has all the dependencies set. A schedule without dependencies is just a nice chart, a one-time snapshot of your project and no more than that.

Choosing the Options

Tab	Option
Schedule	☑ **Autolink inserted or moved tasks** With Autolink on, MS Project will set or break dependencies itself inside a chain of sequential dependencies. It assumes that you want sequential dependencies for the tasks you inserted or moved inside a chain.
	Set as Default Sets the option above as the default setting for any new schedules you create. The existing schedules are not affected because this option is stored in the project files, as you can see from the label of the section: **Scheduling Options for \<file name of the project\>**.

To access the options, choose **Tools, Options**.

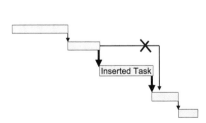

Autolink works within a series of sequentially dependent tasks. If you insert a task inside the series as shown in the illustration, Project 2002 will immediately incorporate it in the chain of dependencies. It breaks one dependency (the one crossed out) and sets two new ones (the heavy arrows).

If you move a task, it closes the chain behind the task (cutting two dependencies and creating one new one) and it incorporates the task at the destination in the chain of dependencies (cutting one dependency and creating two new ones).

This feature is very helpful during the planning phase of the project. However, during the execution of the project, it may be better to turn it off. Project 2002 makes its own decisions on which dependencies to set or break. To the uninformed scheduler they may seem arbitrary.

Types of Dependencies

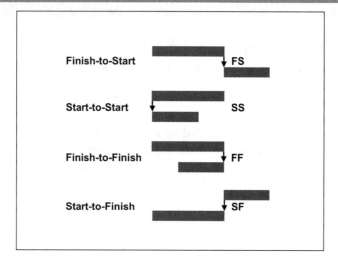

There are four types of dependencies, as shown in the illustration above and the following examples:

- *Finish-to-Start* (*FS*):
  - ◇ The foundation has to be poured before erecting the walls. Similarly, the walls need to be up before the roofing can begin.
  - ◇ A report has to be written before it can be printed. If the finish date of the writing slips, the start date of the printing slips with it. (A tough realization for me because I am trying to meet very tight deadlines while typing these words.)
- *Start-to-Start* (*SS*):
  - ◇ When you pour concrete, you want it to be leveled right away before it cures. There is an SS link between *pour concrete* and *level concrete*.
  - ◇ Two days after carpenters start to break out old drywalls and put up new ones, the electricians start (SS plus 3 days).

◆ *Finish-to-Finish (FF)*:

◇ If you train people in how to use a new software application, you would like to have the software installed when they return to their workstations. There is an FF link between *train users* and *install application*.

◇ After the writing is finished, the editing will be ready in 2 days. (FF plus 2 days).

◇ You conduct a series of workshops and only need 1 day after the end of the last workshop to complete the evaluation report for the courses (FF plus 1 day).

◆ *Start-to-Finish (SF)*:

◇ The fixed start date of the exam will force the preparation to end, whether you are ready or not.

Absolute Lead or Lag Time

When you want the follower (successor) to wait some time before it starts, you can add a *lag* to a dependency. This acts as if the dependency has a duration itself and it always keeps the two task bars apart by this amount of lag. For example, if you apply for a building permit, you often have to wait 6 weeks before you can start construction. This would be an FF dependency with a lag of 6 weeks between the tasks *apply for permit* and *dig the foundation,* as shown in the middle example in the illustration.

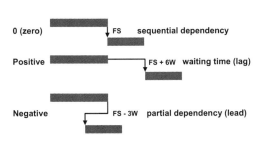

The beauty of dependencies is that the lag can be negative. A negative lag is called a *lead* since the start of the successor will be earlier than the finish of the predecessor. In such a *partial dependency* the follower (successor) is dependent upon the partial completion of its predecessor. As a result, the task bars overlap each other in time. For example, if you write a report, you could finish the entire report before you send it to the editor. You could also send the first half of the report and write and edit concurrently. This would be an FS dependency between *write report* and *edit report* with a lead of, say, 3 weeks. In Project 2002, you will enter leads as negative lags, so in this case you would enter *FS-3W*.

Note that while the lag and lead are shown here on the FS type of dependency they can be applied to the other types of dependencies as well.

You can even enter the lag as an elapsed time and MS Project will schedule the follower accordingly. You can enter an elapsed lag by entering, for example, "*2ed*" instead of "*2d*" in the **Lag** field. If the driver finishes at the end of Friday, *2ed* will cause the FS follower to start on Monday (weekend days count as elapsed days), whereas *2d* will make it start on Wednesday (Monday and Tuesday count as business days). For more details on elapsed durations, see page 167.

Relative Lead or Lag Time

You can also express the amount of lead or lag as a percentage of the duration of the driver task (predecessor), as you can see in the illustration. The task bars then take position relative to each other. With this feature it is possible to have a successor start halfway through the duration of the predecessor and to keep it at the halfway mark. This works regardless of how the duration of the driver is revised or changed later on. We need this in the *write report* example, because after the first half of the report is written we want to send it to the editor (see the second example in the illustration).

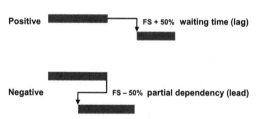

In the food sector, the shelf life of new food products has to be tested, but these tests are long. Follower tasks, like starting the marketing, are often started at 50% of the duration of these shelf-life tests when it looks as if the shelf life will be good. If the test turns unfavorable, the marketing is stopped before big expenditures are made.

In construction projects, the electrical engineering design often starts when the civil engineering design is 60% complete. This is another lag that is relative to the duration of its driver task.

Choosing the Right Type of Dependency

Sometimes when you are creating your project model, you may not be certain about the type of dependency to use. Of the examples in the illustration, the best one depends on what situation is modeled. If the situation allows you to postpone the exam if you are not prepared for it, the FS dependency is the best. An example is the PMP exam[36] or the MOS exams[37] which can be postponed if you are not ready to take them. If you cannot postpone taking the exam, as is the case for a university exam, the Start-to-Finish is the best one. When the exam starts, the preparation will have to stop, as I often experienced when I was in university. I tended to count backwards in preparing for an exam: *What is the latest date I have to start preparing for the exam so that everything will be fresh in my memory?*

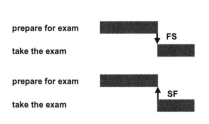

Which is the best model of the situation?

You could argue that when you schedule backward the SF dependency should be the dependency you use most often. After all, in backward scheduling, the finish date drives every task in the project. However, Project 2002 does not change the default dependency to SF when you switch to backward scheduling. In forward scheduling, you will use the FS dependency most often, which is the default in MS Project.

---

[36] PMP® stands for Project Management Professional, an accreditation by the Project Management Institute (PMI). See www.pmi.org for more information.

[37] MOS stands for Microsoft Office Specialist. See www.mous.net for more information.

Steps for Choosing the Right Type of Dependency

The following six questions will assist you in choosing the right dependency:

1. *Which task drives the other?*
   To determine which task is the predecessor, ask yourself to find the driver task: *"Which task drives the other?"* People often ask themselves: *"What should be scheduled first or earliest?"* This question asks for the chronology of tasks. Dependencies are not about chronology, but about cause and effect. We recommend you use the first question to find the predecessor.

2. *Does the start or the finish of the predecessor drive the other task?*
   This question helps to find the type of dependency you need.

3. *Does the predecessor drive the start or the finish of the successor?*
   Once you know the answer to this question, you know the type of dependency you need: FS, SS, FF or SF.

4. *Should there be a lag or a lead on the dependency?*
   A lag delays the successor in time (farther to the right in the timescale), whereas a lead schedules the successor earlier in time (farther to the left in the timescale).

5. *Do you need a positive lag or a negative lag (lead)?*
   A positive lag delays the successor; a negative lag schedules the successor earlier.

6. *Is the lag an absolute number of days (weeks), or is the lag relative to the duration of the predecessor? How much should the lag or lead be?*
   If it is absolute, you enter the number of days (or weeks), for example *"5d"* or *"3w"* (including the time unit). If it is relative, you enter a percentage in the **Lag** field, like *"50%"* (including the percentage sign).

 Often dependencies follow the flow of data, information or deliverables that are passed on between team members. So an alternative question you could ask to find the dependencies is: *What does this person need in order to do this activity?*[38] Or better yet, ask the person to identify what he or she needs from other people to do the task.

---

[38] See page 50 in the article *"Information Driven Project Management"* in *PM Network*, September 2001, PMI.

Categories of Dependencies

Different situations need different categories of dependencies:
◆ *Decision point dependencies*
◆ *Hard and soft dependencies*
◆ *External dependencies*
◆ *Resource dependencies*
We will discuss each of these in more detail.

Decision Point Dependencies

Decision points are important nodes in the network of dependencies. Decision points are also called "*gates*". Gates are to dependencies what central stations are to railroads; many tracks are coming together and springing from them, as you can see in the illustration. All the deliverables (reports) that are needed for making the right decision are drivers (predecessors) for the decision point. All activities that rely upon the decision being made are followers of the decision point (successors). What you will see in a schedule with decision points is that several networks of dependencies are linked together at the nodes, the decision points.

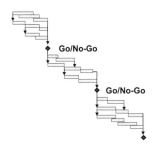

Hard and Soft Dependencies

Some tasks have to be done in an absolute sequence, while others have a preferred sequence. Hard or mandatory dependencies are dependencies that have an absolute sequence. Simple common sense dictates creating these dependencies. For example, the two activities *write* the report and *print* the report require a hard dependency. It does not make sense to schedule the printing in any other way than driven by the finish date of the writing. (If you do find another way to do this, let me know…)

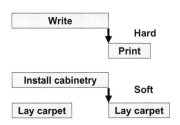

Soft or discretionary dependencies are a matter of preference from a practical or personal point of view. For example, the two tasks *installing cabinetry* and *laying the carpet* are not necessarily dependent on each other. The project manager may prefer to set a dependency to make sure that the cabinetmakers do not spill glue that damages the new carpet. However, if you are in a time crunch, you could do both tasks in parallel. You could ask the cabinetmakers to cover the new carpet with plastic and still gain time in your project.

Project 2002 does not have a special feature for creating soft dependencies. If you remember where you created the soft dependencies, it will be easier to optimize the schedule later on. You can document the soft, discretionary dependencies in the **Notes** field; click **Task Notes** 📝 on the **Standard** toolbar.

External Dependencies

External dependencies are needed when there are impacts from outside your control. You have an *external dependency* when you:
◆ Need to receive goods or materials from a supplier
◆ Require input from another department or project
In general, when you are dependent on an event that is beyond your control, you are facing an external dependency.

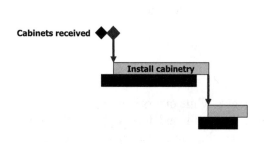

In the illustrated example on the left, you could leave the milestone out when you schedule the external dependency. If you do this and the cabinets arrive late, it would just show as a slipped start date on the task *install cabinetry*. Who will get blamed for the slip in the schedule? The installers would receive the blame. In the case of external dependencies, we recommend you insert an extra milestone for the event in your schedule with a Start-No-Earlier-Than schedule constraint. The constraint will keep the milestone diamond on the date you have agreed to. We will discuss constraints in the next chapter. Then create dependencies from the milestone into your activities.

The advantage is that if the shipment of cabinets arrives late, it is immediately clear that this was beyond your control. If the milestone were omitted, it would look like the installers started working late on their task, which would reflect badly on your performance as a project manager. It is a simple technique that keeps the fingers pointed at the right people in the case of a slippage or, worse, a contract dispute.

Resource Dependencies

Resource dependencies force tasks to be sequenced because you will have work overloads if you don't sequence them. A resource dependency occurs when two tasks compete for the same resource. If you cannot find another solution for the overload, one task has to be delayed in order to keep the workload reasonable for the resource. Of course, you could force the sequence by setting an extra *logical dependency*, but the two tasks are really independent and could be done in any order. Harry could either write the report first or read the other paper. We don't think you should model resource dependencies by setting extra logical dependencies. What happens if you reassign one of Harry's tasks to Sam? Will you remember to take the logical dependency out again? We added some question marks to the illustration for this reason.

If one of the two tasks is reassigned, the dependency should be broken as well, because it was only created to keep Harry's workload reasonable. It was not created because of any other logical reason. If you forget to break the dependency, you end up with a schedule that is suboptimal. Breaking such a soft dependency is often forgotten.

We will deal with resource dependencies in more detail in chapter 9 that starts on page 359.

Entering Logic

Project 2002 offers a variety of ways to enter dependencies into the project file. Dependencies can be entered either in the Gantt Chart or in the Network Diagram. In both views, the tools and forms work very similarly. We will discuss:

◆ Using the Link tool
◆ Using the mouse
◆ Using the Task Information dialog
◆ Using the Task Form

We will now discuss these different ways in more detail starting with the Gantt Chart view.

Entering Dependencies in the Gantt Chart

Using the Link Tool

To Set a Dependency

1. Select consecutive tasks by dragging over their names.
    OR

    Select the driver (predecessor) first and hold down ⌈Control⌉ and click on the follower (successor). You can click on the task name or on its task bar. You can click on as many tasks as you want to link. The only thing to remember is that you select the tasks in the order in which you want the tasks to be linked in the schedule. Let go of the ⌈Control⌉ key.

2. Click **Link Tasks** 🔗 on the **Standard** toolbar OR hold down ⌈Control⌉ and press ⌈F2⌉; the tasks are now Finish-to-Start dependent.

 This method allows you to set Finish-to-Start dependencies only.

To Delete a Dependency Between Two Tasks

1. Select the predecessor and the successor by dragging over their task names.
    OR

    Select the predecessor first and then hold down ⌈Control⌉ and click on the successor.

You can click on the task name or on the task bar, and you can click on as many tasks for which you want to break dependencies.

2. Click **Unlink Tasks** ⚙ on the **Standard** toolbar or hold down ⌐Control⌐ + ⌐Shift⌐ and press ⌐F2⌐.

To Delete All Dependencies on a Task

Select the task and click **Unlink Tasks** ⚙ on the **Standard** toolbar.

 You can easily delete all dependencies in the entire schedule if you select all tasks first by clicking on a column heading and then click **Unlink Tasks** ⚙ on the **Standard** toolbar. Be careful with this because it can undo tens of hours of work in a large schedule.

Using the Mouse

To Draw Dependencies

1. If necessary, click **Zoom In** 🔍 on the **Standard** toolbar to make the task bars wider/longer.

2. Point to the center of the predecessor task bar; make sure you see a four-headed arrow mouse pointer ✛ .

3. Drag vertically toward the successor task bar and make sure the mouse pointer now looks like ↔. Notice the yellow feedback pop-up window that tells you what dependency you are about to set:

Finish-to-Start Link	
From Finish Of:	Task 5
To Start Of:	Task 6

4. Release the mouse button inside the task bar of the successor. A dependency is set and shows up as an arrow. The task bar of the successor moves out to just after the finish date of the predecessor's task bar. A Finish-to-Start dependency is set:

If you drag into the edge of the screen, the screen starts scrolling very fast in the Gantt Chart. It launches like a missile even though Microsoft seems to have slowed it down a bit in this release.

 If you drag horizontally, you are rescheduling the task bar and you are setting a schedule constraint on it that you don't want, that is, if you want your schedule to be dynamic!

This method of setting dependencies allows you to set FS dependencies only, but you can change to another type of dependency with the steps below.

To Edit or Delete the Dependency

1. Point with the tip of the arrow mouse pointer precisely to the dependency arrow you want to change, as in the snapshot below:

2. Dependency arrows can overlap each other, so wait one second until the yellow feedback window pops up to confirm which dependency you have selected.

3. If you have the right dependency arrow selected, double-click and the **Task Dependency** dialog appears:

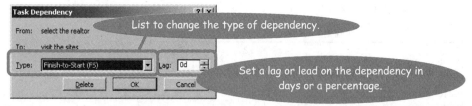

4. Select the **Type** of the dependency using the list Finish-to-Start (FS) [dropdown]
   AND
   set a positive **Lag** or a negative **Lag** (lead) time, if needed. You can also enter a percentage in the **Lag** field. The percentage will be taken from the duration of the predecessor task and then treated as the lag time.
   OR
   Click [Delete] to get rid of the dependency.

Using the Task Information Dialog

You may need this method if the predecessor and successor are a screen or more apart.

1. Select the successor task.

2. Click **Task Information** on the **Standard** toolbar or hold down ⬚Shift and press F2; the **Task Information** dialog appears.

3. Click the **Predecessors** tab; the dialog should now look like:

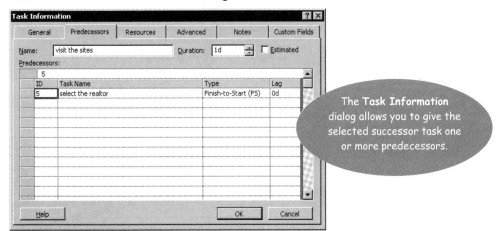

The **Task Information** dialog allows you to give the selected successor task one or more predecessors.

4. Click in the **Task Name** field and select the predecessor task from the list.

.

OR

Enter the ID number in the **ID** field.

5. Select the type of dependency in the **Type** field.

6. Enter a (negative or positive) lag in the **Lag** field. You can also enter a percentage in the **Lag** field. The percentage will be taken from the duration of the predecessor task and then treated as the lag time.

7. Click OK and the dependencies are entered into the schedule.

This method is useful if you want to give one task multiple predecessors. Unfortunately, the dialog does not have a successors tab to set successors on it at the same time. The next method allows you to set predecessors and successors at the same time.

Using the Task Form

1. In the Gantt Chart display the **Task Form** by choosing **Window, Split**; the **Task Form** appears in the bottom of the screen.

2. Click on the **Task Form** and choose **Format, Details, Predecessors & Successors** to view all dependencies of the selected task. Your screen should now look like:

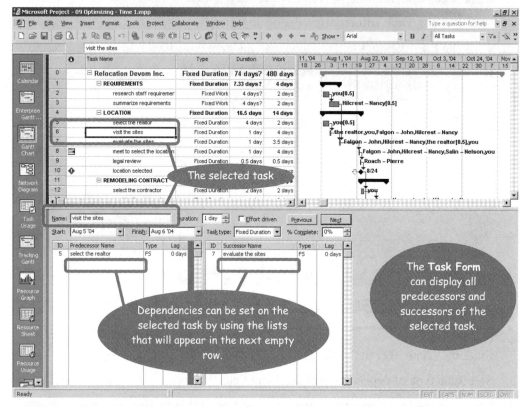

3. Click in the field **Predecessor Name** or **Successor Name** and use the list
    [_____] ▾ to create the dependency.
    OR
    Type the ID number of the predecessor or successor in the **ID** field.

4. Set the type of dependency in the **Type** field and add a positive lag or negative lag (lead) in the **Lag** field, if necessary. You can also enter a percentage in the **Lag** field. The percentage will be taken from the duration of the predecessor and treated as the lag time.

5. Click OK . The data are entered into the project database only after this button is clicked.

The **Task Form** allows you to set many dependencies on a task at the same time. You also can set predecessors and successors on it all at once. The Task Form also allows you to see exactly how dependencies run. The arrows in the Gantt timescale can run on top of one another and the Task Form can show you exactly how they run.

To delete a dependency on the Task Form, select it, and when it is highlighted press the Delete key on your keyboard. Then click OK .

Entering Dependencies in the Network Diagram

The Network Diagram

To apply the view, choose **View, Network Diagram**. The Network Diagram displays an overview of all the dependencies you have set; the dependencies are depicted as arrows.

By default, the **Network Diagram** displays the different types of tasks in differently shaped boxes:

◆ Summary tasks in a parallelogram
◆ Detail tasks in a rectangle
◆ Milestones in a hexagon

The critical tasks have a red border instead of the (default) blue. The shapes of the boxes can be changed by choosing **Format, Box Styles** (see page 223).

To navigate through the Network Diagram, the **Network Diagram** toolbar is handy.

Viewing the Network Diagram Toolbar

1. Right-click on any toolbar, and the pop-up menu appears with all available toolbars.
   OR
   Choose **View, Toolbars**.

2. Choose **Network Diagram**; the toolbar is displayed:

This toolbar makes many useful features directly accessible. Tools we recommend are:

◆ **Show Link Labels / Hide Link Labels** to display or hide little labels on the dependencies that reveal the type of the dependency and the lag, if any.

◆ **Hide Fields** to display just the ID number for each task. You now see many more boxes on your screen. The ID number may seem like too little information, but if you position your mouse pointer over a box, a pop-up window will give you the rest of the fields and values.

Displaying More Tasks on the Screen

◆ If you have the window split, remove the split window by double-clicking on the divider line between the top and bottom view when you see the mouse pointer ✦ or by choosing **Window, Remove Split**.

◆ You can also get more task boxes by using **Zoom Out** 🔍 on the **Standard** toolbar. However, the text becomes illegible when zoomed out too far. To zoom back in, click **Zoom In** 🔍 on the **Standard** toolbar. If you point the mouse pointer to a task box, a pop-up window appears that allows you to read the task data. The screen tip that pops up looks like this:

print	
Start: Thu 4/6/00	ID: 6
Finish: Fri 4/7/00	Dur: 2 days
Res:	

◆ Hide all the fields except the ID number by clicking **Hide Fields** 🔳 on the **Network Diagram** toolbar or choosing **Format, Layout...**, select ☑ **Hide all fields except ID**. To see the task names, use the screen tip that pops up when the mouse pointer is positioned for a while over the task box.
OR
Right-click and choose **Hide Fields** from the pop-up menu.

◆ Get rid of all the fields in a task box except the task name. Removing the other fields makes the box a lot smaller. See the steps on page 220.

Using the Mouse to Set Dependencies

1. Point to the center of the predecessor box and make sure the mouse pointer is a plus sign: ✛.

2. Click and hold down the left mouse button, and drag towards the box of the successor; the mouse pointer should change into a ☞. Even if the box is not visible, you can drag against the side of the screen, which will start scrolling automatically. Unlike in the Gantt Chart, the screen does not scroll too fast in the (newer) Network Diagram.

3. Release the mouse button in the center of the successor box; an arrow appears and the dependency is now set.

This method allows you to set FS dependencies only, but you can easily change the type by double-clicking on a dependency arrow.

If you release the mouse button outside of the successor box, a new task is created! For those who like to build the task list and the network at the same time, this is a great feature. If this happens inadvertently, press [Del] while the new task is still selected to get rid of it.

Using the Link Tool to Set Dependencies

When you use the Link tool, you have to select the tasks in the order in which you want to link them. In other words, you select the predecessor first, then its successor, then the successor of the successor, etc.

1. Hold down [Control] and click on all tasks to link.
   OR
   You can select multiple tasks quickly by dragging a box around them. As soon as you hold down the mouse, the mouse pointer will change to a +. When you drag, a box with a gray border appears. Any tasks that you enclose in the box will be selected upon releasing the mouse button. You can even select another set of tasks by holding down [Control] before you drag again.

2. Click **Link Tasks** 🔗 on the **Standard** toolbar.

As in the Gantt Chart, you can also set dependencies in the Network Diagram using the **Task Information** dialog or the **Task Form**. The steps are the same as for the Gantt Chart (refer to pages 203 and 204, respectively).

To Edit or Delete a Dependency in the Network Diagram

1. Point with the tip of the mouse pointer to the dependency arrow you want to delete. It should look like this:

2. Double-click and the **Task Dependency** dialog appears:

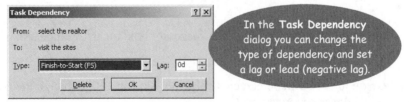

3. Change the **Type** of the dependency using the list `Finish-to-Start (FS)` ▼
   AND
   set a (negative or positive) **Lag** time, if needed. You can also enter a percentage in
   the **Lag** field. The percentage will be taken from the duration of the predecessor task
   and then treated as the lag time.
   OR
   Click `Delete` to get rid of the dependency.

When you delete an arrow, all dependent tasks are rescheduled to their
as-soon-as-possible date under forward scheduling. They may have zipped all the way to
the project start date and disappeared from your screen. We recommend you create the
new dependency first and then delete the old dependency.

Improving the Layout

The Network Diagram has an invisible grid, like a spreadsheet. When you press the
arrow keys to move the cursor they will only take you to the visible "cells," the task
boxes.

1. If you have automatic repositioning on, the boxes are rearranged with every change
   you make. It will be very difficult to check the logic in the network when the boxes
   jump all over the place. We recommend turning it off by choosing **Format,
   Layout...**; the **Layout** dialog appears:

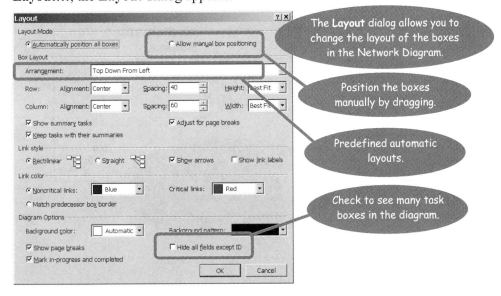

2. Select ◉ **Allow manual box positioning** and click [OK].

3. To see if the logic of the dependencies makes sense, use the arrow keys to follow a chain. Click on the first task box in a chain and press [→] to follow the chain forward. When there is a split you can press the [↓] or [↑] key to switch between the chains
OR

press [←] to go backward and press [↓] or [↑] to switch chains.

4. Use the methods discussed before to delete, add or modify dependencies, if necessary.

Logic on Summary Tasks

What are the advantages and disadvantages of setting dependencies on summary tasks?

Advantages
◆ Setting dependencies on summary tasks seems easier and quicker.
◆ Summary logic is high-level logic that executives sometimes like to see.
◆ In certain situations you can make do with one dependency on the summary task, instead of setting several dependencies on detail tasks when they start independently of each other. In the illustration below, tasks 19 to 21 are all driven by the dependency on summary task 18.

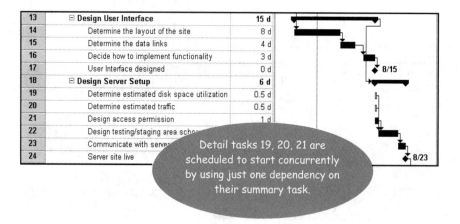

Disadvantages

◆ It is too difficult to check if the network of dependencies is complete. The check is simple if you have dependencies run over detail tasks and milestones only; you just have to find the ones without an entry in the predecessor or successor field. If you have logic on summary tasks and detail tasks in parallel, you cannot perform this simple check any longer. Checking the logic then becomes a very painstaking and laborious process. Yes, I have been there, done that and will not likely do it again!

◆ The *Critical Path* is more difficult to find when the chain runs over detail tasks and summary tasks in parallel. When you follow the Critical Path, a critical detail task may not have any successor. It looks like the Critical Path stops and you may not realize that the Critical Path continues through a dependency on the summary task. (For a discussion on the Critical Path see page 366.) In the illustration below task 17 appears to be the end of the Critical Path:

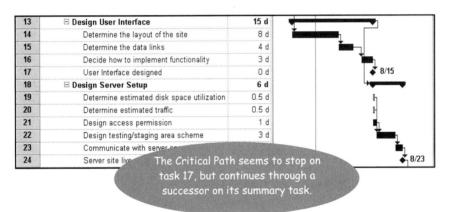

◆ On summary tasks you can only set rough, high-level logic. High-level logic often does not allow you to create the tightest schedule possible.

◆ Not all types of dependencies can be used on summary tasks; you cannot link FF or SF to summary tasks.

Even though there seem to be some advantages to setting dependencies on summary tasks, they don't measure up against the disadvantages. We therefore recommend that you keep the logic on detail tasks and milestones only.

Checks on Dependencies

We discussed the techniques to enter dependencies. All the dependencies together are called the *network* or the *logic*. Now you need to check the network to determine if it will indeed give you the benefit that you created it for in the first place. This benefit was that if you make one change, the rest of the schedule is automatically updated such that you immediately have a valid schedule of your project again: dynamic schedules.

It will only do this if the answers to the following questions are all *yes*:

◆ Does the logic of the network make sense?
You can check this best by showing only the first outline levels of the Work Breakdown Structure and checking if the timing of the deliverables (or phases) makes sense on this high level. You can use the ⟨**Show** ▾⟩ button on the **Formatting** toolbar to display **Outline level 2** or **Outline level 3**. Even though you may not be an expert in the field of this project, you can always pick up on common sense things like *design* scheduled before *construction*, *write* before *print*, etc.

◆ Are there no circular dependencies?
There should be none because a schedule with circular dependencies will not be dynamic, but entirely static. MS Project cannot recalculate the schedule if there are circular dependencies. The application will warn you if you try to create circularity in the dependencies within a single schedule. When you set dependencies across schedules, circular dependencies may still occur. They will manifest themselves in the master schedule that contains the subschedules. We are venturing out into multiple project management, which is discussed in detail in the Blue Belt course.[39]

◆ Is the network of dependencies complete?

◆ Is the network logic simple enough?

In the next section we will elaborate on the last two questions.

---

[39] Visit www.iil.com and follow the link *Microsoft Project* for more information.

Is the Network of Dependencies Complete?

The network is complete if the task bars of all detail tasks are tied up at both ends. The network can have multiple starting points, but only one ending point. Only with one ending point in the network will the Critical Path calculation be correct. The Critical Path is the most widely used technique to manage the time dimension of a project. We will explain it in more detail in Chapter 9 on optimizing.

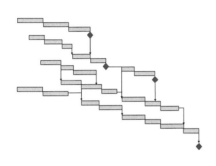

A typical network will look like the illustration. Unlike other authors, we do not require the network to start with just one starting point. We find that this makes the network unnecessarily complex and that it does not provide additional benefits. When you have multiple starting points, the only thing to check is if detail tasks that do not have a driver (predecessor) can indeed start on the project start date or if they need a Start-No-Earlier-Than constraint (under forward scheduling).

There are two reasons why you want to complete the network logic in your schedule:

◆ If you forget to set dependencies, the schedule will not update itself properly upon making a change to it. The schedule is not a dynamic schedule. Having a dynamic schedule is very important during the execution phase of the project. When you enter actual progress, you would like the schedule to update itself such that you immediately have a valid model of the project again. You need the schedule to update itself every time you update the status of the schedule. Project managers who do not check the logic of their schedule carefully typically abandon it sometime during project execution because they have to spend too much time on keeping the schedule valid. They have to check the entire schedule every time they enter actual progress. They soon find that they don't have enough time to do this at every status cycle.

◆ With an incomplete network you will most likely not have a meaningful *Critical Path*. Project managers need to see the Critical Path in order to identify the tasks that harbor possibilities for shortening the project to bring it in on time. For more on a Critical Path, see page 368.

To check if the network is complete, ask yourself the following questions:

◆ Is the logic as much as possible set on detail tasks and milestones only?
If dependencies run over summary tasks and detail tasks in parallel, it is too hard to check if the network is complete. It is also too hard to trace the Critical Path and understand it. Only with a complete network will the schedule be a fully dynamic model of the project. Therefore, we recommend that you keep the logic on the detail tasks and milestones only. You can check if there are dependencies on summary tasks by applying the filter **2 IIL Summary Tasks with Dependencies**.[40]
We discussed this point in more detail on page 210.

◆ Are all the starts of the detail tasks linked to at least one other task or milestone? Exceptions are:
◇ All tasks that can start when the project starts
◇ External delivery milestones (should have a **Start-No-Earlier-Than** date) (see page 198)
◇ Recurring tasks (see page 130)
◇ Overhead tasks (see page 132)

You can verify if all starts are linked by applying the filter
3 IIL Detail Tasks without Predecessors.[41] Note that if the project manager used SS or FF dependencies, the filter is not conclusive.
OR
Display the **AutoFilter** buttons by clicking ▼= on the **Format** toolbar. In the **Predecessors** column heading, click the button ▼ and choose the blank item in the list. Now all tasks without an entry in the predecessor field will be displayed, including summary tasks (this is where the IIL filter is better). Notice that the column label appears in blue to remind you that an AutoFilter is in effect.

◆ Are all the ends of the detail tasks linked to at least one other task or milestone? Exceptions are:
◇ The project end milestone
◇ Recurring tasks
◇ Overhead tasks

---

[40] This filter can be found in the file *Tools to check Orange Belt schedules.MPP* that is available for download at www.jrosspub.com.

[41] This filter can be found in the file *Tools to check Orange Belt schedules.MPP* that is available for download at www.jrosspub.com.

A *loose end*, *hanger* or *dangling task* is a detail task that does not have its finish tied to any other task. In any project there should be only one loose end, the project finish milestone (ignoring the summary tasks and recurring tasks).

You can verify if all ends are linked up by applying the filter **3 IIL Detail Tasks without Successors**.[42] Note that if the project manager used SS or FF dependencies, the filter is not conclusive.
OR
Display the **AutoFilter** buttons by clicking ⟨▽▪⟩ on the **Format** toolbar. In the **Successors** column heading, click the button ⟨▾⟩ and choose the blank item in the list. Now all tasks without an entry in the successor field will be displayed, including summary tasks (this is where the IIL filter is better). Notice that the column label appears in blue to remind you that an AutoFilter is in effect.

◆ Are there tasks with an unreasonably large amount of *Total Slack*?
You can check this by doing a descending sort on **Total Slack** by choosing **Project, Sort, Sort by…** and selecting **Total Slack** from the **Sort by** list. Check if the tasks with the most slack were expected to have a lot of slack. If not, you have found missing logic.[43] Even after you have given all detail tasks a successor, you should still apply this check. Having at least one successor for each detail task does not guarantee that you haven't forgotten an important link. Checking the Total Slack will actually lead you to where you forgot to set important dependencies in your model of the project. This check is very effective in catching missing logic in schedules. Remember that if you miss even just one essential dependency, your model is not dynamic and your forecasts may not be valid.

◆ When a change is entered into the schedule, does it update the rest of the schedule automatically and appropriately through dependencies?
Is the entire schedule still valid? Where the schedule is not valid, an essential dependency might be missing. If you have to check the entire schedule after each change, you don't have a dynamic model.

---

[42] This filter can be found in the file *Tools to check Orange Belt schedules.MPP* that is available for download at www.jrosspub.com.

[43] This check was contributed by Frank Walker, TWG Project Management, LLC.

Schedulers often forget to give every task one or more successors, in particular when they used SS or FF dependencies:

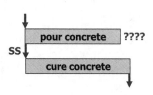

People often forget to set a dependency on the finish of the predecessor in an SS dependency (see the question marks in the illustration at the left). The finish must also be linked; otherwise the predecessor in an SS dependency could still continue even though the project is already finished. If you just checked that each detail task has a successor, you will not find these loose ends. In the illustration *pour concrete* has an SS successor, but its finish is not tied to any other task.

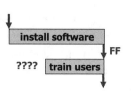

People also often forget to set a dependency on the start of the successor in an FF dependency (see the question marks in the illustration at the left). The task *train users* has an FF predecessor but its start is not linked to any other task. Alternatively, the start date can be held in place by a schedule constraint. Again, if you just checked that each detail task has a successor, you will not find these loose ends.

If you used SS or FF dependencies in your schedule, you should display all those tasks with SS and FF dependencies and check on loose ends manually. You can do this check by applying the filter **3 IIL Detail Tasks with SS or FF**.[44] Since the filter will display both the predecessor and successor involved in the SS or FF dependency, you can check if they are hooked up properly to other tasks by revealing the **Predecessors** and **Successors** fields.

---

[44] This filter can be found in the file *Tools to check Orange Belt schedules.MPP* that is available for download at www.jrosspub.com.

Some detail tasks do not need links:

◆ *Recurring detail tasks,* like status meetings
◆ *Overhead tasks*, like *project management* or *quality control*. These are also known as *hammock tasks*, because their start and end dates are driven by (hung up on) other tasks.

All other detail tasks need to have at least one successor. If you cannot find logical links to other detail tasks, you should create a link to the project end milestone. If you don't have a project end milestone, you should create one even if this only serves the purpose of hooking up your loose ends. Certain tasks can only be linked to the project end milestone. Examples are:

◆ Tasks to inform other departments or organizations (FYI tasks)
◆ Tasks that create entirely independent parts of a system, which can easily and quickly be assembled. In this case, you should perhaps consider creating a detail task for assembling the final product.

Is the Network Logic Simple Enough?

A network that is too complex to understand and maintain is not helpful in managing the project. Redundant dependencies clutter the view unnecessarily. They make the network overly complicated. If the network is complicated, team members will not try to understand or use it. Thus, the value of the network of dependencies decreases.

Many project managers fall prey to the following fallacy: *All tasks are related to each other and I have to set dependencies everywhere I notice relationships.* Yes, indeed all tasks are related to each other (that is how you arrive at a complete network of dependencies eventually). Most tasks, however, are related <u>indirectly</u> to each other, and you only have to link the tasks that have a <u>direct</u> relationship.

The following questions will help you determine if the network is simple enough:

◆ Are there dependencies that leapfrog each other?
Dependencies that skip over the back of multiple dependencies within a chain are redundant. These are the indirect relationships. Remove them.

◆ Are there dependencies that run in parallel on detail tasks and their summary tasks? If that is the case, keep the detail task dependency and remove the parallel dependency on the summary task.

◆ Can you, as the project manager, explain the network to your project team? If you cannot explain it, the network is too complex. If you can explain the network, you can immediately show a team member who else will be affected if their task slips. This is a very powerful method to facilitate communication within your team. Team members will come to you as the project manager to find out who they should talk to. This will also encourage people to stick to the plan.

A clear network also allows you to do quick analysis of impacts with executives. Imagine that your sponsor comes to you during the execution phase of a software development project and asks: *What if we waited for the latest release of this operating system?* With a simple network, you will be able to indicate the impacts very clearly by following the dependency arrows to the components that will be affected by such a change in direction.

Limitations of Dependencies

There are some technical limitations when creating dependencies:

◆ **You can set only one link between two tasks**
It is impossible to set more than one link between two tasks. Thus you cannot hook up both the start and the finish of two tasks using an SS as well as an FF dependency. For example, you may have set an SS dependency between *relocate drywall* and *wire electricity*. If relocating the walls takes longer than planned, your model may show that the electricians finish earlier than the carpenters, which is unreasonable. If you could set an FF dependency as well, the problem would be solved. What you can do, though, is insert an extra milestone and run two FF dependencies to and from the milestone. This is an easy way to work around this limitation.

◆ **You cannot set links on all parts of a split task bar**
You cannot set dependencies on all parts of a split task bar; you can only link to the start of the first part and from the finish of the last part. You cannot create very dynamic models therefore with split task bars. This is the reason why we don't recommend the use of split task bars when you are planning the project.

◆ **You cannot link to the finish of a summary task**
You cannot set an FF or SF dependency to a summary task as the successor. The finish date of a summary task is always calculated. However, you can link from the

finish of the summary task. Remember that we don't recommend logic on summary tasks.

◆ **Percentage lags only apply to the duration of the predecessor task**
You cannot set a lag that takes a percentage of the duration of the successor task; the percentages are always taken from the duration of the predecessor. So you cannot create a dependency that drives, for example, the halfway point of a successor.

Printing the Network Diagram

Printing the Network Diagram can be helpful in communicating the flow of the logic to the stakeholders. Prior to printing, you can change the appearance of the view to suit your needs.

The Layout of the Boxes

You can customize which fields are shown, the border of the boxes and the font.

Displaying Just the Task Name in Each Box

Change the layout of the fields on the task boxes in such a way that only task names will show. This will allow you to see many more boxes within one screen.

1. Choose the menu items **Format, Box Styles**.

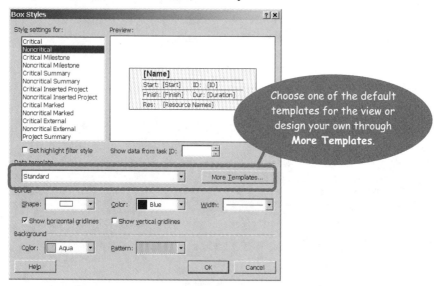

2. Click [More Templates...], and the **Data Templates** dialog opens:

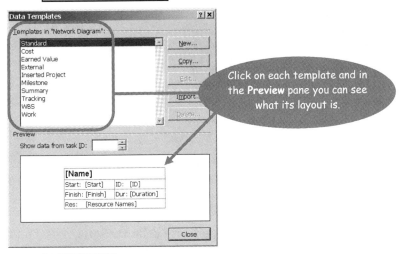

Click on each template and in the **Preview** pane you can see what its layout is.

3. Click [New...], and the **Data Template Definition** dialog opens:

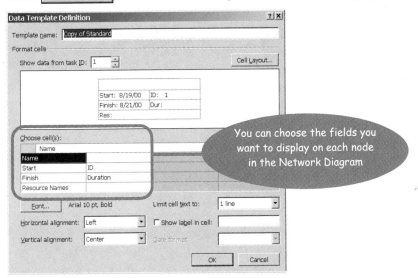

You can choose the fields you want to display on each node in the Network Diagram

4. Enter a name for this template in the field **Template Name**, for example *Task Names Only*.

5. Click [Cell Layout...], and the **Cell Layout** dialog opens:

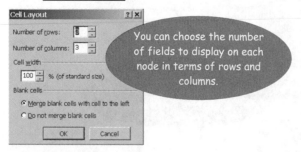

6. Set the **Number of rows** and **Number of columns**. If you have long task names, set the **Cell width** percentage to greater than 100%. All boxes will have the same width.

7. Click [OK]. You are now back in the **Data Template Definition** dialog.

8. In the table-like area below **Choose cell(s)**, click on a cell in the grid; a list button appears:

9. Select from this list the field to display. You have now created a new layout template.

10. If you have long task names, set **Limit cell text to** more than one line.

11. Click [OK], and you are now back in the **Data Templates** dialog; you can see the newly created template listed:

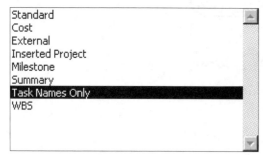

12. Click [Close], and you are now back in the **Box Styles** dialog.

13. Now we have to apply this template to the different types of tasks. Select under **Style Settings For** all the different types of tasks by dragging over them or selecting them more specifically using [Control] and click.

14. Under **Data Template** use the list to select the data template you just created.

15. Click [OK], and the **Network Diagram** view now shows boxes with only the task names; many more boxes fit on one screen.

Instead of applying a data template to all the tasks, you can use different data templates for different types of tasks. To select specific task types hold down [Control] and click in the **Format, Box Styles** dialog. If you select only the noncritical items, the list would look like:

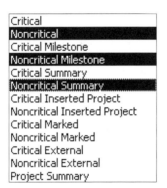

This allows you to create fancy Network Diagrams.

Changing the Border of the Boxes

You can use different border formats to indicate the status of a task, like not started, in progress, critical or completed.

1. Choose **Format, Box Styles**, and the **Box Styles** dialog appears.

2. In the list **Style Settings for** select the type of task for which to change the border. In the bottom section, **Border**, you can choose the **Shape**, **Color** and **Width**. The **Preview** area in the top right shows what it will look like. You can also choose a fill **Background Color** and even a **Pattern**.

3. If you have more than one data field inside the boxes, you can choose to:
   ☑ **Show horizontal gridlines** and/or
   ☑ **Show vertical gridlines**.

4. Click [OK].

Changing the Font

1. Choose the menu items **Format, Box Styles**, and the **Box Styles** dialog appears.

2. Click [More Templates...], and the **Data Template** dialog opens.

3. In the list **Templates in <file name>** select the data template for which to change the font.

4. Click [Edit...], and the **Data Template Definition** dialog opens.

5. Click [Font...], and select the font type and size you need.

6. Click [OK], and you are now back in the **Data Template Definition** dialog.

7. Click [OK], and you are now back in the **Data Template** dialog.

8. Click [Close], and you are now back in the **Box Styles** dialog.

9. Click [OK], and you should now see the new font applied.

The Layout of the Diagram

Showing the Type of Dependency on Each Arrow

It is often helpful to see the type of dependency displayed for each task relationship, like in the following snapshot:

Click **Show Link Labels** on the **Network Diagram** toolbar.
OR

1. Choose **Format, Layout…**, and the **Layout** dialog appears:

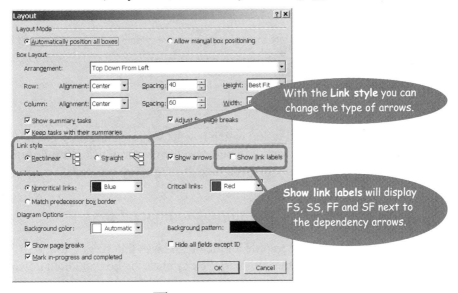

2. Under **Link style** select ☑ **Show link labels**.

3. Click [OK], and you will now see **FS** attached to each Finish-to-Start arrow, as well as **SS**, **FF** and **SF** to their respective arrows. You will also see any **Lag** (lead) displayed.

Changing the Type of Arrow

Click **Straight Links**  on the **Network Diagram** toolbar.
OR

1. Choose **Format, Layout...**, and the **Layout** dialog appears.

2. In the **Link style** section, choose the type of arrow: **Rectilinear** or **Straight**.

3. Click | OK |.

Hiding the Summary Tasks

Summary tasks look like parallelograms in the **Network Diagram** view:

Summary tasks have a collapse/expand button that will hide/display all their detail tasks.

Writing	
Start: Thu 3/30/00	ID: 1
Finish: Thu 3/30/00	Dur: 1 day;
Comp: 0%	

If you set all the logic between detail tasks, which is what we recommend, you can remove the summary tasks from the screen to decrease the clutter. Click **Hide Summary Tasks** on the **Network Diagram** toolbar to hide the summary task boxes.

Collapsing and Expanding Summary Tasks

The summary tasks can be collapsed to hide all the detail tasks that belong to the summary. Click ⊟ at the top left of the summary box or click the box and hold down [Alt] + [Shift] and press [-].

They can be expanded again by clicking ⊞ or holding down [Alt] + [Shift] and pressing [+].

Notice that if you collapse a summary task, you hide the detail tasks and also their dependencies. The network may now appear to have loose ends that may not be real loose ends. All real loose ends need to be tied up. Before checking the logic in the

Network Diagram, we recommend you expand all summary tasks, by clicking Show ▾
on the **Formatting** toolbar and selecting **All Subtasks** from the list.

Improving the Layout of the Boxes

Project 2002 attempts to arrange the boxes as well as it can. By default, the boxes are
laid out from the top left to the bottom right, but MS Project has several layout
arrangements to choose from. You can improve the layout by choosing a different
arrangement, or you can move boxes manually.

1. Choose **Format, Layout...**, and the **Layout** dialog appears:

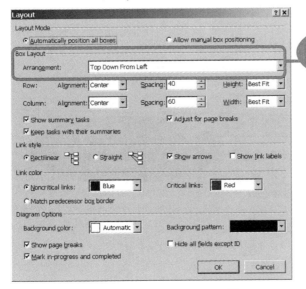

2. Make sure that under **Layout Mode,** ⦿ **Automatically position all boxes** is
    selected; otherwise you have to choose **Format, Layout Now** every time to see the
    effect of a different arrangement.

3. Under **Arrangement** use the list:

Top Down From Left ▾

    to change the layout of the boxes.

4. Click [OK], and the layout of the boxes changes according to your choice. If
    the layout is not satisfactory, try other layout arrangements.

Notice that the boxes are never positioned on the page breaks with automatic
positioning.

Improving the Layout of a Selection of Boxes

After you have selected the arrangement you prefer, you may still want to position certain boxes using a different arrangement.

1. Select the boxes by dragging a lasso around them.
    OR

    Hold down [Control] and click on them.

2. Click **Layout Selection Now** ⊞ on the **Network Diagram** toolbar. MS Project rearranges the boxes as best it can and according to the arrangement that is currently selected in the **Format, Layout...** dialog.

Laying Out Boxes Manually

1. Choose **Format, Layout...**, and the **Layout** dialog appears:

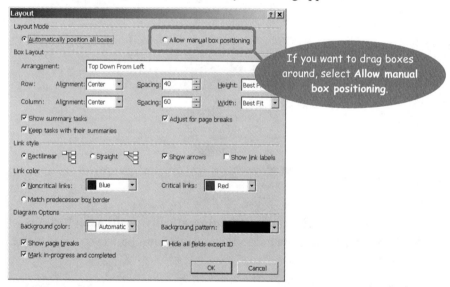

2. Select ⦿ **Allow manual box positioning**.

3. Click [OK].

4. Point to the border of the box you want to move and make sure that the mouse pointer changes to ⁺⤈.

5. Click and hold down and drag the box to its new location.

Laying Out Groups of Boxes Manually

1. First you have to select all boxes to move as a group. Click on the first box and hold down Control; then click on the other boxes. The boxes are highlighted to show they have been selected.
   OR
   Click and hold down to drag a lasso around all the task boxes to select.
   OR
   Hold down Shift and click on the border of a summary task to select it and all its detail tasks.
   OR
   Hold down Shift and click on the border of a detail task to select its entire chain of successors.

2. Click and hold down on the border of one of the selected boxes. Make sure you see the mouse pointer.

3. Click and hold down to drag the group to its new location.

 Do not choose **Format, Layout Now** after moving boxes manually; it rearranges the **Network Diagram** and undoes all your laborious manual moving. If it happened by accident, you can undo the mess by choosing **Edit, Undo Entry** or click **Undo Entry** on the **Standard** toolbar (before doing anything else). We recommend you use the tool **Layout Selection Now** on the **Network Diagram** toolbar instead of **Format, Layout Now** after you have moved boxes manually.

Aligning the Manually Moved Boxes

You can select a number of boxes and then align all boxes with the task that is the first one in the chain or the earliest one in time.

1. First you have to select all boxes to move as a group.
   Drag a lasso around all the boxes to be selected.
   OR

   Click on the first box, hold down Control and click on the other boxes; the boxes are highlighted to show they have been selected.

2. Click **Align** Align ▾ on the **Network Diagram** toolbar and choose the way to align the selected tasks. The task boxes should now be aligned.

Exercises

Review

1. Why should a project manager set all the dependencies in her schedule?

2. What are the criteria for a good and solid network of dependencies?

3. If you are dependent upon supplies to arrive for one deliverable in your project, what would you recommend in terms of scheduling this situation?

4. What are the different ways to set dependencies? There are 8 different ways discussed in this book. Please provide at least 4 ways.

5. Are the following valid entries in the lag field? Yes or no? Why?
   A. 5d
   B. –3d
   C. +30%
   D. +5ed

6. Should you allow logic on summary tasks? If yes, why? If no, why not?

7. How would you schedule *ordering materials* and *receiving materials* with an order time of 3 weeks? Would you use a Finish-to-Start dependency with a 3-week lag? Or would you split the task bar for 3 weeks? Explain your answer.

8. For each of the following situations determine:
   ◇ Which task is the predecessor and successor: A or B?
   ◇ What type of dependency do you need: FS, SS, FF or SF?
   ◇ Would you advise to add a lead or a lag to the dependency? If yes, as a relative lag or absolute lag? And how much?

	Predecessor A or B	Type of Dependency	Add Lag? Relative/absolute? How much?
You *gather requirements* (A) and then you *analyze requirements* (B).			
After you *apply for a permit* (A), you have to wait 3 weeks for *permit received* (B).			

	Predecessor A or B	Type of Dependency	Add Lag? Relative/absolute? How much?
Halfway through *perform system analysis* (A), we typically start *programming code* (B).			
You have to *pour foundation* (A) and let the concrete dry before you *lay bricks* (B) to erect the walls.			
One day after the finish of *conduct courses* (A), *write evaluation report* (B) has to be completed.			
Prepare for the PMP exam (A) and *take the PMP exam* (B).			

Relocation Project — Dependencies

Continue to work with your file *Relocation.MPP* or open the file
05 Entering Dependencies.MPP that is available for download at www.jrosspub.com.

Enter the following dependencies using the **Link** tool on the **Standard** toolbar:

1. The tasks *research staff requirements* and *summarize requirements* are sequentially dependent.

2. The tasks of the deliverable *LOCATION* are all sequentially dependent upon each other.

3. The tasks of the deliverable *REMODELING CONTRACT* are all sequentially dependent upon each other. The dependency between *select contractor* and *meet to discuss contract* has a lag of 5 days; it will take a time frame of 5 days to get the participants together to meet.

4. The tasks *relocate walls* through *install cabinetry* of the deliverable *REMODELED LOCATION* are sequentially dependent upon each other.

5. The tasks of the deliverable *MOVE* are all sequentially dependent upon each other.

Enter the following dependencies by holding down [Control] and clicking to select the tasks and using the **Link** tool:

6. In the deliverable *REMODELED LOCATION* the tasks *install cabinetry* and *install LAN* can take place concurrently after the paint dries. *Drying of paint* is the predecessor for both tasks.

7. After the tasks *install cabinetry* and *install LAN* are finished, the carpet can be put in place. *Lay carpet* is the successor for both tasks.

8. After the carpet is laid (*lay carpet*), the milestone *facility remodeled* is accomplished.

You forgot to set the dependencies between the deliverables (phases). Stay in the Gantt Chart or switch to the **Network Diagram** to enter these dependencies:

9. The task *evaluate the sites* can start after *summarize requirements* is finished.

10. The task *select the contractor* can start after the milestone *location selected* is accomplished.

11. The task *select mover* can start after *location selected*.

12. The task *relocate walls* can start after the milestone *contractor contracted*.

13. The task *pack* can start after the milestone *facility remodeled*.

Compare your file with the solution file *06 Entering Constraints and Deadlines.MPP* that is available for download at www.jrosspub.com. Use the view **Network Diagram** to make the comparison.

Case Study: CoalPower

CoalPower power station has approached you to do a 2-day introductory workshop in MS Project. CoalPower is a first-time client and it seems this 2-day contract will be its only need for training and consulting for a while, even though the organization is large and has multiple plants. The key players at CoalPower are:

◆ Andy is the plant manager. You find out that he and you share a similar cultural heritage, and you find an easy basis for conversation with him. Andy sits in on the first part of the workshop you are conducting on-site. He is only interested in the big picture of what MS Project can do for the organization. Andy is concerned about the frequent delays in the engineering projects, as you found out when you talked one-on-one during a lunch break.

◆ Norm manages the engineers, who manage repair, maintenance and construction projects in the power station. They also design the modifications that are needed. You have had difficulties in negotiating with Norm. He told you, only after you had closed your consulting contract, that you will have to travel an extra 250 miles to get to the site of the plant.

◆ Dave and Harry manage the major maintenance projects like the replacement of the $2M turbine condensers. Replacing these condensers will stop the operations in the entire plant. They have been planning their projects mostly off the top of their heads. Norm is getting increasingly anxious about this and has told them, "If you get sick, nobody knows what to do or how to do it. I need to see a detailed plan of your projects!"

◆ Art is the technical drawing expert. He designs most of the small modifications and creates the technical drawings. Art is overworked and has, at any given time, 50 projects on his plate. Norm often criticizes him for not delivering the drawings when Norm wants them.

Questions

Dave and Harry are struggling with the whole concept of scheduling and what benefits it will provide to them:

1. Do you expect them to be motivated to use the tool? Why?

2. How will they benefit from scheduling their projects with MS Project?

3. What do you think of Norm's approach of forcing them to schedule their projects?

4. How important are dependencies in their schedule?

Art approaches you during one of the breaks to talk one-on-one:

5. What is his main concern in scheduling his projects?

6. How should he model his many projects in MS Project? Address in particular whether he should use dependencies in his schedule:

   a. between the tasks within one project, and

   b. between his projects.

7. How will Art benefit from modeling his projects in MS Project?

Chapter 6 Entering Deadlines and Constraints

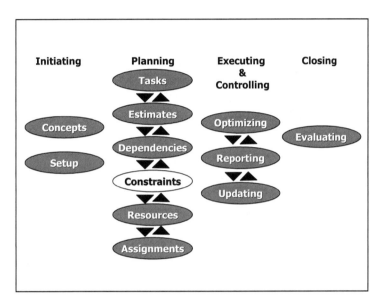

At this point we have entered the most important data into the schedule and the Gantt Chart is starting to take shape. There may be certain constraint dates that we may have to add to the model to make it stay within the boundaries of our reality. Also, we may want to capture the dates of the deadlines to monitor them. Constraints and deadlines are the topics of this chapter, as the white highlight in the illustration indicates. At the end of this chapter we will discuss formatting the Gantt Chart view for printing.

After reading this chapter you will:
- ◆ know the difference between constraints and deadlines
- ◆ know the different types of schedule constraints
- ◆ know in which situations to use constraints or deadlines
- ◆ be able to enter schedule constraints and deadlines into the project model
- ◆ know the advantages and disadvantages of entering constraints
- ◆ be able to check on deadlines and constraints in the model using scheduling best practices
- ◆ know how to format and print the Gantt Chart view

Dancing with a Rock!

Bob: "Hey Nob, did you hear about this feature of deadlines in MS Project? It is a beautiful feature! I can put all the dates that I committed to into my schedule and my schedule still floats back and forth freely. And when a deadline date is not met, a red flag appears."

Nob responds: "Why would you want your schedule to float freely; do you like it to change all the time? I don't like that!"

Bob: "Why don't you like that? The dependencies will make sure that your forecast dates are always valid!"

Nob: "When I have assigned a task to Mary to start on March 12 that task better start on March 12 or all hell will break loose and all kinds of things will start slipping!"

Bob: "Are you able to schedule so rigidly? Does it work like that for you?"

Nob: "Well ... there is no project that runs exactly according to schedule, but if we don't try to run it like that, it never happens ..."

Bob: "Well, I am probably trying as hard as you are to run projects according to their schedule, but I do expect the schedule to change constantly ... except for the tasks coming up in the next two weeks! I always receive change requests from the client and I can easily incorporate those. How do you handle change requests?"

Nob: "I reject, resist or retard them ... as much as I can!"

Bob: "As soon as I receive a change request, I enter it into my dynamic project schedule and I can see immediately what the impacts are on the project end date and on the budget. When I show it to the executives, I can often get an immediate decision from them on the change request. That works very well for me! This is partly thanks to using deadlines instead of constraints! Deadlines are life-giving, and constraints are life-sucking, as far as I am concerned! Working with a schedule that has many constraints is like trying to dance with a rock ... it does not move!"

What Are Deadlines and Schedule Constraints?

A constraint is a date that restricts MS Project in scheduling a task. A deadline is a date you commit to that does <u>not</u> restrict the scheduling of a task.

It is possible to force tasks to be scheduled on certain dates, which is necessary for certain tasks like *attend meeting, attend conference* and *monitor seminar*. Fixing dates is a matter of putting a scheduling *constraint* on the task. You could consider a Must-Start-On constraint for the aforementioned tasks. A Must-Start-On is a hard constraint, and MS Project cannot reschedule tasks with hard constraints. Constraints affect the network of dependencies. The more constraints you create, the less freely your network will flow back and forth when you enter changes. Therefore, the more constraints you have in your schedule, the more effort you will spend keeping it a valid schedule.

Deadlines, on the other hand, do not restrict the timing of task bars. Deadline dates stay visible in the timescale as down-facing green arrows ⇩. When you miss a deadline date MS Project displays a visual indicator ◆ in the ❶ **Indicators** column.

We recommend, therefore, that you enter dates that you committed to as deadline dates rather than as constraint dates. When you want to track a soft target date for a specific task, you can set a deadline date for that task. Since deadlines don't restrict the scheduling, they don't require continuous and immediate maintenance either, like scheduling conflicts caused by constraints do.

We will discuss deadlines first and then constraints (starting on page 241).

Deadlines

Entering Deadlines

1. Choose **View, Gantt Chart**.

2. Click on the task for which you want to set a deadline.

3. Click **Task Information** 📋 on the **Standard** toolbar or hold down [Shift] and press [F2]; the **Task Information** dialog appears.

4. Click the **Advanced** tab; the dialog should now look like:

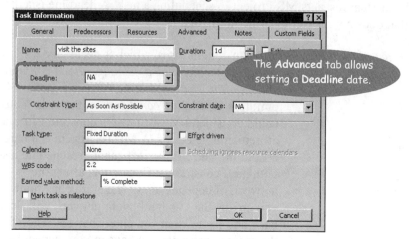

5. Under **Constrain task**, type the deadline date in the **Deadline** field or use the pull-down calendar to click on a date.

6. Click [OK], and you will now see an arrow ⇩ in the timescale that represents the deadline date you entered.

 If you have to be done before November 1, you have to enter October 31 as the deadline date. The deadline time will be at the end of the day on the date you enter. If you enter November 1 as the deadline date, the task will be done by 5:00 PM on November 1.

 You can move deadline dates by simply dragging the ⇩ in the timescale to a new date. You can start dragging as soon as you see the four-arrow mouse pointer ✛ .

 To remove a deadline, simply delete the date from the **Deadline** field on the **Advanced** tab of the **Task Information** dialog.

Managing Deadlines

You will not get automatic warning messages from Project 2002 if deadlines are not met. What you do get is an exclamation icon ◆ in the **Indicators** column. It's like raising a flag when a deadline is missed.

Also, if you use the list of filters All Tasks ▾ on the format toolbar and apply the filter **Tasks with Deadlines**, you can quickly display tasks with deadlines and see which deadlines are slipping.

Choosing the Options

To access the options, choose **Tools, Options** from the menu.

Tab	Option
Schedule	☑ **Tasks will always honor their constraint dates** This option makes tasks obey their schedule constraints. We recommend you keep this option on to make sure your schedule observes the few real and hard constraint dates that you may have in it.
	[Set as Default] Sets the option above as the default setting for any new schedules you create. The existing schedules are not affected because this option is stored in the project files, as you can see from the label of the section divider: **Scheduling Options for <file name of the project>.**

Scheduling Regimes

Before discussing the types of constraints, we need to discuss the basic scheduling regime you choose. The two choices are:

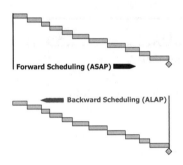

◆ *Scheduling forward* from the project start date: You do forward scheduling if you entered the project start date and want the model to tell you what the expected finish date is. Under forward scheduling tasks are scheduled as-soon-as-possible (ASAP).

◆ *Scheduling backward* from the project finish date: You schedule backward if you entered the project finish date and want to find out when you should start the project to meet this date. Under backward scheduling tasks are scheduled as-late-as-possible (ALAP).

You can see whether you are scheduling forward or backward by checking the **Project, Project Information** dialog in the list **Schedule from**. It shows there that you **Schedule from** either the **Project Start Date** (forward scheduling) or from the **Project Finish Date** (backward scheduling).

If you change from forward to backward scheduling after you have entered tasks, the constraint for these tasks will stay ASAP; new tasks will be ALAP. Combining ASAP tasks with ALAP tasks in one schedule sometimes creates unexpected results; which of the two tendencies is stronger?

Types of Constraints

The eight types of constraints can be characterized as tendencies, one-sided constraints or rigid constraints:

Tendencies
◆ *As-Soon-As-Possible* (*ASAP*; the default under forward scheduling)
◆ *As-Late-As-Possible* (*ALAP*; the default under backward scheduling)

One-sided constraints
◆ *Start-No-Earlier-Than (SNET)*
◆ *Finish-No-Earlier-Than (FNET)*
◆ *Start-No-Later-Than (SNLT)*
◆ *Finish-No-Later-Than (FNLT)*

Rigid Constraints
◆ *Must-Start-On (MSO)*
◆ *Must-Finish-On (MFO)*

Tendencies

Under *forward scheduling*, the default regime, MS Project uses **As-Soon-As-Possible** (ASAP) for the tasks. MS Project will pull the task bar in the timescale as far to the left as the network of predecessors allows. Even when the regime is ASAP, you can still schedule certain tasks **As-Late-As-Possible** (ALAP). For example, in a move project, *packing equipment* should be scheduled ALAP. ALAP task bars will tend to go to the right in the timescale as much as the network of successors and constraints allows. Note that the one ALAP task tends to be stronger than its ASAP successors, so check your schedule to make sure it looks right.

Under backward scheduling, tasks are ALAP by default, but you can still change some tasks to ASAP scheduling. Even though ALAP and ASAP do not have a **Constraint Date**, they have a tremendous impact on the schedule and are in that sense "constraining".

One-Sided Constraints

This group of one-sided constraints limits the movement of task bars to only one direction, either to the left (earlier) or to the right (later):

◆ Start-No-Earlier-Than (SNET) and Finish-No-Earlier-Than (FNET) constrain free movement of the task bars going to the left in the timescale; the start date (SNET) or finish date (FNET) cannot go to the left of the No-Earlier-Than date.

◆ Start-No-Later-Than (SNLT) and Finish-No-Later-Than (FNLT) constrain free movement of the task bars going to the right in the timescale; the start date (SNLT) or finish date (FNLT) cannot go to the right of the No-Later-Than date.

Rigid Constraints

The last group of rigid constraints, Must-Start-On (MSO) and Must-Finish-On (MFO), fix the task bar entirely to the date indicated and deny any free movement.

 Realize, though, that the task bar can still grow or shrink in size when you revise the estimate. This will make the other, unconstrained end of the task bar move.

No-Earlier-Than Constraints

An example of a Start-No-Earlier-Than (SNET) constraint is when raw materials will not be delivered until a certain date. You can start the activity no earlier than the delivery date.

An example of a Finish-No-Earlier-Than (FNET) is when you need a final approval for the deliverable. You know the approval can take place during the next board meeting planned on the first day of every month. You enter an FNET constraint on the first of the next month.

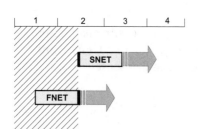

The No-Earlier-Than constraints are restricted from moving earlier in time (moving to the left in the timescale). They can be pushed to the right by the network without a limit. Under As-Soon-As-Possible (ASAP) scheduling they will not be able to cause a schedule conflict; in other words, they are soft constraints under forward scheduling.

Under backward scheduling, the project finish date is hard. As you enter dependencies you will see that the As-Late-As-Possible (ALAP) task bars will be pushed out earlier in time (moving to the left in the timescale). They can be pushed to the left as far as the No-Earlier-Than date allows. If pushed any further, Project 2002 will alert you to a schedule conflict. No-Earlier-Than constraints are therefore said to be hard constraints under backward scheduling.

No-Later-Than Constraints

An example of a Start-No-Later-Than (SNLT) constraint might be the backing up of a computer system that can be scheduled at a later time, but would have to start no later than, let's say, midnight in order to be finished on time. An example of a Finish-No-Later-Than (FNLT) constraint is when you commit to deliver a report no later than March 13, and this date is a do-or-die date.

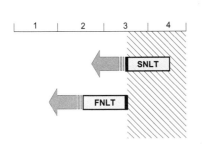

The No-Later-Than constraints are restricted from moving beyond the date specified (moving to the right in a timescale view). They can be allowed earlier by the network up to the start date of the project. Under As-Late-As-Possible (ALAP) scheduling these constraints will not be able to cause a schedule conflict. In other words, they are soft under backward scheduling.

 Under forward scheduling, the project start date is hard. As you enter dependencies, you will see that the As-Soon-As-Possible (ASAP) task bars will be pushed out to the right in the timescale (to later in time). They can be pushed out as far as the No-Later-Than constraint date allows. If pushed any further, Project 2002 will warn you that there is a schedule conflict. Therefore, No-Later-Than constraints are said to be hard constraints under forward scheduling.

Must Constraints

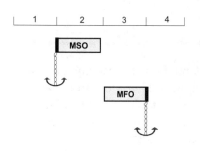

An example of a Must-Start-On (MSO) constraint is when you hold an important meeting that must start on January 9 at 9:00 AM.

An example of a Must-Finish-On (MFO) constraint is when you have a contractual date by which you must move out of an office space or pay a steep penalty.

Where you use an MSO constraint, the start will always be on the date indicated. With an MFO constraint, the finish will always be on the date specified. MSO and MFO constraints can easily cause schedule conflicts. These constraints are always hard constraints under both forward <u>and</u> backward scheduling. They should be used only when you absolutely need them to keep the schedule valid. Let's explore some situations.

In Which Situations Do You Need Constraints?

Deadlines do not need a lot of maintenance while the project is running, but constraints do. Every time you have a major change in your schedule, you may either have to update all the constraint dates downstream or you will have to solve all the schedule conflicts. If you don't solve scheduling conflicts right away, MS Project will keep nagging you with messages until you do. Constraints require immediate attention when you may not have time. If a task doesn't have any constraints, its dependencies push it into place.

 We recommend, therefore, that you enter only the constraints that are absolutely necessary. You can enter many deadlines in your schedule without any disadvantages.

 Constraints should <u>not</u> be used to model temporary availability of resources. A better place to indicate temporary availability is through availability profiles. We will discuss these on page 288.

Constraints can be set for:

◆ External dependencies
On page 198, we recommended that an external dependency be entered as an extra milestone and that the milestone can be held in place by a Start-No-Earlier-Than (SNET) constraint.

◆ Weather restrictions
For example, if you have to get road construction done before the rainy or winter season starts, a constraint can help. Constraints can also help for outdoor construction activities that can only start after the winter is over.
MS Project has another feature to schedule situations like these: Task Calendars. Task calendars create a more dynamic model than constraints (see Using Task Calendars on page 139).

◆ Meetings, presentations, training or tasks that involve a group of people in general
In order to get a group together, you have to set a date; otherwise it will not happen. When the date is agreed upon, a constraint should be set on that date so Project 2002 does not move it off its date. Often you will use Must-Start-On or Must-Finish-On here.

◆ Certain milestones (see the following section)

Types of Milestones

Milestones are used in a schedule to indicate events like decisions, approvals, target dates and ceremonies. The type of constraint needed will depend on the "*hardness*" of the milestone. The hardness of a milestone is the resistance you will experience when you try to move its date. For *soft dates* you can use the *deadline* feature instead of constraints. For *hard dates* use the feature of *schedule constraints*. The harder the date, the harder the constraint should be.

The different types of milestones used in schedules are (listed from soft to hard):

◆ *Decision points*
These are important events on which decisions about the remainder of the project are made. The decision can be:
◇ Go/No-go: A no-go decision will end the project and a go decision will authorize spending for the next phase.
◇ Go-left/Go-right: The how-to or direction is determined for the rest of the project. You will find this often in R&D type of projects where the research findings determine the direction (the deliverables) for the rest of the project.

If there is a target date or a deadline for the decision point, we recommend using the deadline feature that was discussed on page 237.

♦ **Target dates**
These are soft deadlines that are inserted to break up a long series of tasks. They focus the efforts on finishing a component of a deliverable. The project manager decides with the team where to insert these target dates. Teams need several target dates on components of their deliverable in order to meet the deadline of the deliverable. Target dates are interim evaluation points. It is like driving from Ontario to Florida and checking at the end of every day to see if you are still on schedule. Target dates function as reminders and should keep everyone focused and on track. For target dates we recommend the use of the deadline feature and no constraints.

♦ **Do-or-die dates**
These are hard deadlines and are often contractual dates by which you are committed to hand over a deliverable. There may even be a penalty clause if the date is not met. These dates should be clear in the schedule at all times. We recommend you enter these into the schedule as deadlines as much as possible in order to keep the schedule dynamic. However, if one is a very hard contractual date (with a penalty associated), you could consider a Finish-No-later-Than (FNLT) constraint. This allows it to float up to the constraint date and never pass it without notifying you.

♦ **Deliveries**
We recommend you enter the delivery dates of raw materials, supplies or client deliverables as separate milestones in the Work Breakdown Structure. We discussed these external dependencies on page 198. The delivery date you agreed upon with the vendor, supplier or client should be entered as an event milestone with a Start-No-Earlier-Than (SNET) constraint.

♦ **Ceremonies**
Ceremonies are short official events to which many people are invited. If the duration of the ceremony is negligible, it can be entered as a milestone with a zero duration. An example might be the official ribbon cutting to open a new plant. The date of a ceremony is often hard, because ceremonies are public events. The schedule needs a Must-Start-On (MSO) constraint for these events. If the ceremony has a duration, it is no longer a milestone but a task and will still need a constraint.

♦ **Project end date**
This is the delivery date for the project product. Meeting the project end date is always a challenge in project management. All the chains of dependencies come together in the project end milestone. A Must-Finish-On (MFO) or a Finish-No-Later-Than (FNLT) constraint is often set on the project end date. You will

immediately receive a scheduling conflict message when this date is in jeopardy. In many projects, a deadline date could do the trick as well. You will then only see the red exclamation icon ◆ appear in the ❶ **Indicators** column if the deadline is missed.

The **Deadlines** feature reminds you of the date agreed upon without constraining the schedule. It is a feature we strongly recommend using over schedule constraints. The more constraints you have, the more time you will spend on maintaining your schedule. And you will have to do this during project execution, when you don't have much time. The fewer constraints you have, the more dynamic your schedule will be.

Constraints

Entering Constraints

If you have to be done before November 1, you have to enter October 31 as the constraint date. The constraint time will be at the end of the day on the date you enter. If you enter November 1 as the date, the task will be done by 5:00 PM on November 1.

You can set constraint dates in a variety of ways:
- ◆ Dragging task bars: This method will allow you to set only Start-No-Earlier-Than (SNET) constraints under forward scheduling or only Finish-No-Later-Than (FNLT) constraints under backward scheduling.
- ◆ Entering dates: Under forward scheduling you can enter a start date that will set an SNET constraint, or you can enter a finish date that will set a Finish-No-Earlier-Than (FNET) constraint. Under backward scheduling, entering a start date will create a Start-No-Later-Than (SNLT) constraint; a finish date creates a FNLT constraint. This is probably too much to remember.
- ◆ Using the task fields **Constraint Type** and **Constraint Date**, where you can select the type of constraint from a list and the date from a pull-down calendar.
- ◆ Using the **Advanced** tab on the **Task Information** dialog.

As is often the case in MS Project, you can enter constraints in several different ways. The first two ways are easy and quick but do require you to know which constraints MS Project will set. We recommend using the last two ways, but we will discuss all four in more detail.

Setting Constraints by Dragging Task Bars Horizontally

1. Point to the middle of the task bar; make sure you see a four-headed arrow: ✛.

2. Click and hold down to drag the bar horizontally to where you want it scheduled. Make sure you see a horizontal two-headed arrow: ▓▓▓▓▓◄◘►▓▓[   ] .

3. Look at the yellow pop-up window to see what the new dates will be:

Task:	▓▓▓▓▓▓▓▓▓▓▓▓▓▓▓	
Start:		Tue 4/4/00
Finish:		Mon 4/10/00

4. Release the mouse when the task bar is scheduled on the date you want. It has a **Start-No-Earlier-Than** constraint on it to keep it in its new place. (Under backward scheduling it will be a **Finish-No-Later-Than** constraint.)

If you drag vertically, you will see the mouse pointer ☞ , and you are creating dependencies instead of constraints!

Setting Constraints by Entering Dates

In the field **Start** you can pick a date from the drop-down calendar. By default, this creates a Start-No-Earlier-Than (SNET) constraint on the task under forward scheduling, and it creates a Start-No-Later-Than (SNLT) constraint under backward scheduling. In the field **Finish** you can pick a date from the drop-down calendar. By default, this creates a Finish-No-Earlier-Than (FNET) constraint on the task under forward scheduling, but it creates a Finish-No-Later-Than (FNLT) constraint under backward scheduling.

Many people use the **Start** and **Finish** fields to schedule all their tasks. Most do not intend to create constraints, but are unaware that MS Project is setting them. Their schedules become rigid and require a lot of work to maintain. If dependencies are used instead, schedules require a lot less maintenance. We don't recommend using the **Start** and **Finish** fields at all for data entry. In addition, using them will require you to memorize what type of constraint will be set. We would even go as far as recommending that you eliminate those fields from the entry table. You can do this by clicking on their column heading and pressing [Delete].

Setting Constraints Using the Task Fields

1. Insert the field **Constraint Type** by clicking in the column before which you wish to insert and choosing **Insert, Column**. The **Column Definition** dialog appears:

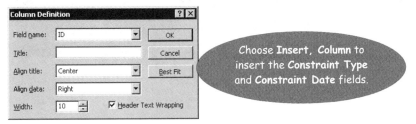

2. Select from the list **Field name:** ID the item **Constraint Type**. You can quickly get to this field name in the long list by typing the first characters of the name of the field.

3. Click OK .

4. Repeat these steps to insert the field **Constraint date** as well.

5. You can now enter any type of constraint in the Gantt spreadsheet by selecting the type from the list in the field **Constraint type** Start No Earlier Than and picking the date from the drop-down calendar in **Constraint date** Tue 4/4/00 .

Setting Constraints Using the Task Information Dialog

1. Select the task.

2. Click **Task Information** 📖 on the **Standard** toolbar or hold down Shift and press F2; the **Task Information** dialog appears.

3. Click the **Advanced** tab; the dialog should now look like:

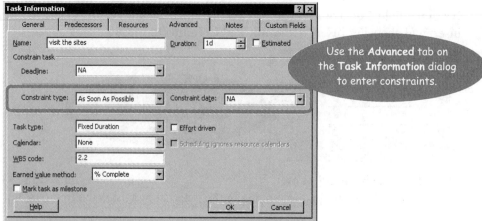

Use the **Advanced** tab on the **Task Information** dialog to enter constraints.

4. Under **Constrain task** select the type from the **Constraint type** pull-down list and select a date from the **Constraint date** drop-down calendar.

5. Click [OK].

To Check All the Scheduling Constraints

1. In the Gantt Chart choose the menu items **View, Table: <name of current table>**, **More Tables**; the **More Tables** dialog appears:

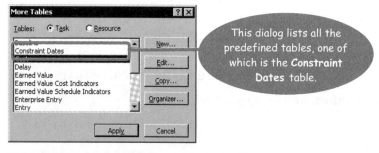

This dialog lists all the predefined tables, one of which is the **Constraint Dates** table.

2. Select the **Constraint Dates** table in the list.

3. Click [Apply]. You can now see the fields **Constraint Type** and **Constraint Dates** to check all constraints on the tasks.

4. You can apply a filter that displays all the tasks that have a constraint date. Use the [All Tasks ▼] list on the **Formatting** toolbar to apply the filter called **Tasks with Fixed Dates**.

To Remove Constraints

You can remove constraints one by one, but if you want to delete them fast, you can use the fill-down feature. This is useful if you inadvertently entered dates in the **Start** and **Finish** fields without wanting the constraints that came with them.

1. Apply the **Constraint Dates** table as per the previous series of steps.

2. Enter the constraint type you want to fill-down in the top cell. To remove the constraints, select
    As Soon As Possible under forward scheduling or
    As Late As Possible under backward scheduling.

3. Click on this top cell and hold down to drag down over all the cells into which you want to copy this new entry.

4. Choose **Edit, Fill, Down** or hold down and press D .

Make sure you don't remove real constraint dates that are necessary to keep your project schedule valid.

Limitations of Constraints

◆   You can set a maximum of one constraint per task.
    Sometimes it would be nice to set two constraints on a task when the task has to be done in a *window of opportunity*. For example, you can only do an expensive test when a specialized lab is available. You cannot model this with constraints, because you can only set one constraint on a task.
    You can use the feature of Task Calendar that allows you to create a calendar for the task that reflects the window of opportunity. You can apply it to the task using the field **Task Calendar**. We discussed this on page 139 under Using Task Calendars.

◆   You can only set SNET and FNLT constraints on summary tasks.
    MS Project does not allow other types of constraints on summary tasks because summary tasks would not be summarizing their detail tasks any longer. I try to use constraints sparsely and I have not missed the other types for summary tasks.

Checks on Deadlines and Constraints

Below you will find some checks to verify if you have applied best practices in the use of deadlines and constraints in your dynamic model of the project:

◆ Is the project deadline modeled in the schedule?
It can be set as a deadline date or as a hard constraint date on the project finish milestone.

◆ Does the schedule have as few as possible schedule constraints?
Constraints make the schedule rigid. However, constraints are allowed on:

◇ Recurring detail tasks, like *status meetings*.

◇ External dependencies, such as *delivery of supplies* or *arrival of materials*.

◇ Activities that have to take place on a certain agreed-upon date, like *deliver presentation* and *conduct training*. In general, these are activities in which a group of people is involved.

◇ Do-or-die deadlines, like the *December 31, 1999* deadline for Y2K projects.

◇ Activities affected by (winter) weather conditions, i.e., task *asphalt streets starts-no-earlier-than April 1st*. You can also use the feature of **Task Calendars** for these situations in MS Project (see page 141).

You can display all tasks that have constraints by applying the filter
4 IIL Constraints other than ASAP.[45] The filter will not display recurring detail tasks, because recurring detail tasks should have constraints.

Formatting the Gantt Chart View

In this section we will prepare the Gantt Chart view for printing.

With the **Gantt Chart Wizard** ◄💲 on the **Formatting** toolbar you can choose format options for the *Gantt Chart* by answering prompts. This wizard allows you to enjoy some of the gems hidden in the illustrious **Format, Bar Styles** dialog. Some of the things you can accomplish with this wizard are:

◆ Display the Critical Path by coloring the critical task bars red. For more information on the Critical Path, see page 377.

◆ Display text of your choice to the left of, to the right of or inside the task bars. This can also be done through the menu items **Format, Bar Styles**, tab **Text**.

---

[45] This filter can be found in the file *Tools to check Orange Belt schedules.MPP* that is available for download at www.jrosspub.com.

◆ Change the shape and color of the task bars. This can also be done through the menu items **Format, Bar Styles**, tab **Bars**.

To Adjust the Text Styles

Text styles can be applied to certain task types. The dialog is similar to the **Format, Font** dialog except that the font dialog is used for formatting only those tasks that are selected.

1. Choose **Format, Text Styles...**; the **Text Styles** dialog appears:

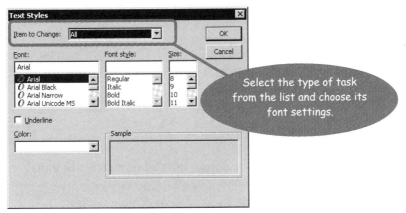

2. From the list **Item to Change:** [All ▼] at the top, select the screen element to change. Then select the format using **Font, Font style, Size** and **Color**.

3. Click [OK].

 If you select the item **All**, all the text will be affected, even the text styles you set previously.

 The Gantt Chart Wizard allowed you to color the critical task bars red. With the **Text Styles** dialog you can color the task names of the critical tasks red as well to make them appear uniformly and stand out whether you look in the spreadsheet or in the timescale.

To Wrap Task Names Around

You can double the row height of the tasks with long names (skip the first step if you want to do this) or you can double the height of all rows. The task names will wrap around automatically.

1. Select the entire spreadsheet by clicking on the table selector at the intersection of the row and column headings in the top left corner of the spreadsheet: ▢ .

2. Point to one of the row dividers in the row headings (normally the ID column); make sure you see the double-headed arrow mouse pointer ✚.

3. Drag the divider down to at least double the row height. MS Project will automatically wrap the text onto the second line. It wraps the words in the text fields **Task Name, Notes** and the extra fields (**Text1, Text2**, etc.).

 You will double the number of pages in your printout if you double the row height for all rows.

 You can now wrap the text in the column headings as well. Double-click on the column heading and check ☑ **Header Text Wrapping**. If the column width is too narrow for the title, it will start wrapping automatically.

To Adjust the Column Width

Double-click on the heading of the column to adjust; the **Column Definition** dialog shows up. Click [Best Fit]; the column width automatically takes the appropriate width for all tasks in the project, even the ones not currently visible on the screen.
OR
Point to the divider in between two column headings. Make sure you see a double-headed mouse pointer as shown below; then double click:

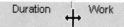

The width of the column is now wide enough to accommodate the widest text in the field for the entire project (up to a maximum of about 150 characters).

 In Project 2002, the text in the column headings will wrap automatically if the option ☑ **Header Text Wrapping** is checked in the **Column Definition** dialog. Double-click on the column heading to display this dialog.

To Position the Pane Divider on a Column Split

 Put the divider between the spreadsheet and the Gantt Chart exactly on the border of a column by double-clicking anywhere on the divider using the mouse pointer ◀▶.

To View the Whole Project Timescale

1. Choose **View, Zoom**; the **Zoom** dialog appears:

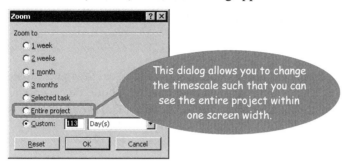

This dialog allows you to change the timescale such that you can see the entire project within one screen width.

2. Select ⊙ Entire Project.

3. Click [OK].

To Format the Timescale

Click **Zoom Out** 🔍 on the **Standard** toolbar to zoom out until you can see all the task bars. If you zoom out too far, you can use **Zoom In** 🔍 on the **Standard** toolbar to zoom back in on the details.

If you want to customize the timescale to your exact preference:

1. Double-click on the timescale itself

   Mar 26, '00
   S M T W T S .

   OR
   Choose the menu items **Format**, **Timescale**; the **Timescale** dialog appears:

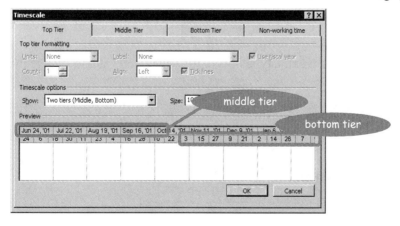

middle tier

bottom tier

2. Choose the settings for the **Top Tier** (top of the timescale), the **Middle Tier** (middle) and the **Bottom Tier** (bottom). If you want to display the third tier, you need to select **Three tiers** in the **Show** list. The **Count** is like an increment. If it is set to "*2*" in a day-by-day timescale, only every other day will be displayed.

3. Click [OK] .

Having three tiers in the timescale now allows you to show the fiscal year and calendar year next to each other so that there can be no misunderstanding about the exact dates. You can set the start month of the fiscal year in **Tools, Options, Calendar** under **Fiscal year starts in**.

To Format the Task Bars

1. Double-click anywhere in the background of the timescale area.
   OR
   Choose **Format, Bar Styles**, and the **Bar Styles** dialog appears:

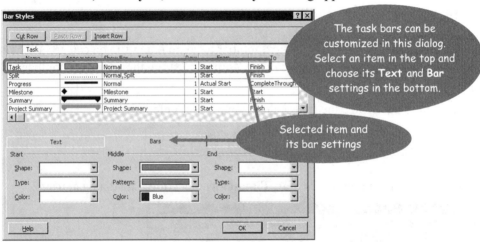

2. In the list in the top half, select the type of task for which you want to change the appearance:

Name	Appearance	Show For ... Tasks
Task		Normal
Split	....	Normal,Split
Progress	▬▬▬▬	Normal
Milestone	◆	Milestone
Summary	▬▬▬	Summary
Project Summary	▬▬▬	Project Summary

3. Choose your settings for the selected task type at the bottom of the dialog on the **Text** and **Bars** tabs.

4. Click OK .

Some remarks about this powerful, but not so intuitive dialog box:

◆ MS Project first creates in the Gantt Chart the task bar listed at the top, and then draws the second task bar on top of the first one. If they overlap, only the second bar can be seen fully. Therefore the order in which the items are listed is important. Lower ones lay on top of higher ones in the list.

◆ Under **Show For ... Tasks**:

◇ You can use the listed items. You can also type in the word **Not** in front of each item to create an exception for that type of task. "**Not Summary**" means format the task bars as specified for any task type except for summary tasks.

◇ You can specify multiple criteria separated by a comma.

◆ The lists you can display in the fields **From** and **To** have all the regular task fields in them, but also some additional ones specifically for the timescale, like the **CompleteThrough** date and **Negative Slack**. The **CompleteThrough** is used in the Tracking Gantt to display progress bars. For an application of the **Negative Slack** item, see page 373.

◆ On the **Text** tab in the bottom half of the dialog, you can add text to the left or right of or even inside the task bars. By default, you will find the following in the Gantt Chart:

◇ **Resource Names** are put to the right of the detail task bars.

◇ The **Start** dates are shown to the right of the milestone diamonds.

 If you follow our advice and remove the **Start** and **Finish** column from the spreadsheet, you could consider adding them as text next to the bars in the timescale, where you can only see them but not change them (and set constraints).

To Show Milestone Diamonds on Summary Task Bars

1. Select the milestones by holding down [Control] and clicking on each milestone in the **Task Name** column.

2. Click **Task Information** 📋 on the **Standard** toolbar, and the **Task Information** dialog appears. Click the tab **General**; the dialog now looks like:

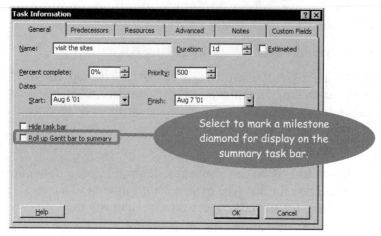

3. Select ☑ **Roll up Gantt bar to summary**

4. Click OK.

5. Select the summary task, click **Task Information** 📋 again and make sure that the option ☑ **Show rolled up Gantt bars** is selected:

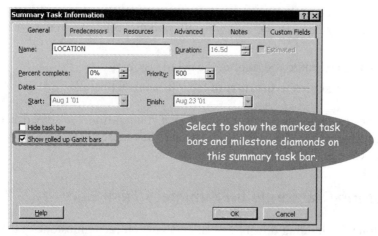

6. Click OK.

To Adjust the Page Setup

Notice that the page setup settings are view specific. For each view listed in the **View** menu you can set different settings.

Setting the Page Orientation

1. Choose **File, Page Setup**, and the **Page Setup** dialog appears. Click the tab **Page**:

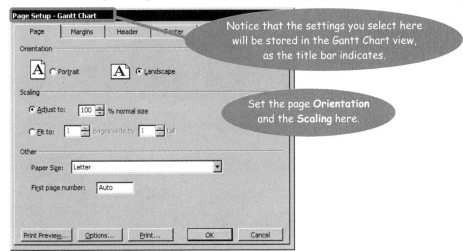

2. Select ⊙ **Portrait** or ⊙ **Landscape**.

3. Click ⬛ OK .

Setting the Margins

1. Choose **File, Page Setup**, and the **Page Setup** dialog appears. Click the tab **Margins**:

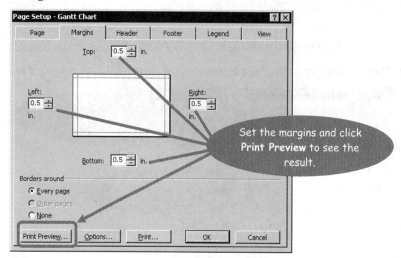

2. Set the margins you need. Click Print Preview... to check if the settings are right.

3. In print preview, click Close to return.

Creating a Header, Footer or Legend

1. Choose **File, Page Setup**, and the **Page Setup** dialog appears. Click the tab **Header, Footer** or **Legend**:

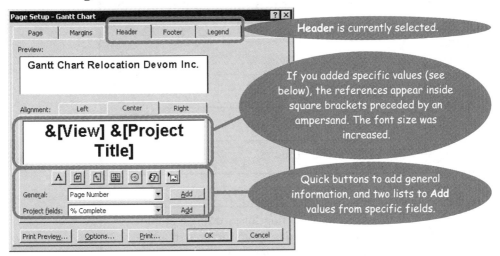

Header is currently selected.

If you added specific values (see below), the references appear inside square brackets preceded by an ampersand. The font size was increased.

Quick buttons to add general information, and two lists to **Add** values from specific fields.

2. Under **Alignment** click the tab **Left**, **Center** or **Right** and position the cursor inside the text box where you want to add a reference to project data. You can even press Enter ⏎ to create extra lines.

3. Select a reference from the **General** list at the bottom and click Add . The reference is inserted at your cursor position. Add as many text references as needed; each refers to data entered in the **File, Properties** and the **Project, Project Information** dialogs.

4. Using the list **Project fields** at the bottom, you can insert project-level information, like the **Baseline Finish** and forecast **Finish** date, or the **Baseline Cost** and forecast **Cost,** or calculated values, like the **% Complete** for the project.

5. Click one of the buttons to add information quickly:

Button	For
A	font, size and style In order to format the text in the header, select the text first and then click **A**.
[#]	page number
[+]	total number of pages
[date icon]	date: the system date
[clock icon]	time: the system time
[file icon]	the file name
[image icon]	Takes you into a dialog for inserting a graphic image into the header, footer or legend; often used to insert the project logo

6. Click [OK] or [Print Preview...].

Exercises

Review Questions

1. What is the difference between constraints and deadlines in the way MS Project treats these dates?

2. What is the main output from a project model that is scheduled forward? From one that is scheduled backward?

3. Which of the following constraints can cause a scheduling conflict? In the table below add a check mark where you foresee scheduling conflicts:

	In a forward scheduled project	In a backward scheduled project
ASAP		
ALAP		
FNET		
FNLT		
MFO		
MSO		
SNET		
SNLT		

4. Would you set a constraint in the following situations? If so, which type of constraint? In the table on the next page indicate the type if you would recommend a constraint.

Situation	Type of constraint
You have a *board meeting* coming up on January 16 in which a go/no-go decision will be taken on the next stage of your project. The board expects certain reports to be ready.	
A vendor needs to deliver custom-made computers to you that you need for testing activities in your project (*computers delivered*).	
You have planned a "*project burial*" ceremony to close off your project. You have invited senior executives and other dignitaries for this special day.	
A testing lab is only available to your project from March 1 to March 15.	

5. Why would you want to minimize the number of constraint dates in your project model?

6. Is there a way in which you can easily display the entire project duration in the timescale on your screen? If so, what are the steps in MS Project to accomplish this?

Relocation Project — Constraints and Deadlines

1. Continue to work with your file *Relocation.MPP* or open the file
   06 Entering Constraints and Deadlines.MPP that is available for download at
   www.jrosspub.com.

2. Set deadlines on the following milestones:

ID	Milestone	Deadline Date
10	location selected	August 20, 2004
16	contractor contracted	August 30, 2004
25	facility remodeled	October 25, 2004
31	new location opened	November 1, 2004

3. Enter the following constraints:

ID	Task	Constraint
8	meet to select the location	Start-No-Earlier-Than August 23, 2004
28	pack	As-Late-As-Possible

4. The CEO, *Mr. Salin,* is out of the country until *August 23,* 2004.
   The task *pack* should be scheduled *As-Late-As-Possible*; otherwise the equipment
   may be packed days before the actual move takes place over the weekend. You want
   the employees to be packed as late as possible on the Friday before the weekend.

5. Compare your file with the solution file *07 Entering Resources.MPP* that is
   available for download at www.jrosspub.com.

6. Save your file for the next exercise.

Relocation Project — Printing the Gantt Chart

With the tasks, estimates, dependencies and constraints completed, we now have entered all the data needed to print a Gantt Chart.

1. Continue to work with the file from the previous exercise.

2. Format the timescale of the Gantt Chart in the following way:

	Middle Tier	Bottom Tier
Units	Months	Days
Label	Jan '00	1, 2,...
Count	1	7
Align	Center	Center
Size	100 %	100 %

3. Format the header, footer and legend of the Gantt Chart in the following way:

Page Tab	Section	Set to	Font
Header	Center	&[View] &[Project Title]	Arial, Bold, 20
Footer	Left	&[Manager] &[Company]	Arial, Regular, 8
	Right	&[Date]	Arial, Regular, 8
Legend	Legend on	◉ None	

4. Compare your file with (a printout of) the solution file *07 Entering Resources.MPP* that is available for download at www.jrosspub.com.

Chapter 7 Entering Resources

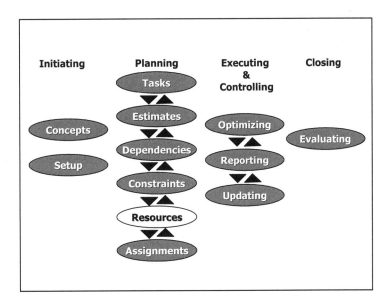

With the Tasks, Estimates, Dependencies, Constraints (and Deadlines) entered, we have a Gantt Chart that is a dynamic model of our project. You could stop here if resources, their workloads and their costs are less of a concern for you. If they are important in your schedule, you may have to add them to the model and assign them to tasks. The result is called a *resource-loaded schedule.*

After reading this chapter you will:
◆ know what resources are and when to add a resource to the project model
◆ know the different types of resources: human, facilities, machines and materials
◆ be aware of important resource-related fields
◆ be able to efficiently enter each type of resource into the project
◆ know to use generic resources if you don't know who will be on your team
◆ know how to enter temporary, part-time, full-time and overtime availability
◆ be able to create resource calendars
◆ know the cost management features of MS Project
◆ be able to check the resource list of the project using scheduling best practices
◆ know how to create a resource report

Selling the Project Manager

Joe is the sales representative for the company Bob works for. Joe deals with the clients, and when a contract is closed, he typically introduces Bob to the client as the project manager. Bob looks after the creation and delivery of the project product.

Joe enters Bob's office in a whirlwind of enthusiasm. "Hey, Bob, I got the contract!"

Bob: "Well congrats, Joe, you brought another one in. Thanks for keeping me employed."

Joe: "Yeah, I had to make some concessions though; they wanted the final prototype two weeks earlier. I thought that, with your experience, you could handle that!"

Bob: "Two weeks … that is three weeks from now! Didn't you realize that my team has at least one more week to go on our current project?"

Joe: "Oh Bob, you have pulled it off before. I am counting on you! And I am offering to help out on the weekends myself!"

Bob: "Well, no thank you. I won't commit to your deadline. I have worked enough weekends to last me a lifetime! And, by the way, what would you help us with?"

Joe: "How am I going to get the prototype done? Why don't you want to do it?"

Bob: "Well, perhaps I am not willing to work weekends because … there is no sales commission coming to me when you make ridiculous promises to clients to close the deal. You made the promise without consulting me; now it is your problem, not mine."

What Is a Resource?

Resources are people, facilities, machines or materials used to create the project product.

Each activity typically needs one or more resources. If you find an activity does not need resources, you should consider modeling it as a lag on a dependency instead of modeling it as a task in your schedule. For example, the task *drying of paint* does not need resources and would be better modeled as a lag (see page 193 for the how-to steps).

Apart from resources, there are also responsible people. A resource and responsible person differ in that:

◆ The responsible person does not necessarily spend time and effort on project activities like resources do.

◆ Resources also include material resources.

◆ Responsibilities are normally assigned on the level of deliverables, whereas resources are normally assigned to activities that are on a lower level in the Work Breakdown Structure.

Responsibilities

Responsibilities for deliverables are typically captured in a *Responsibility Assignment Matrix*[46] also called *RAM* or *Responsibility Chart*. MS Project does not have special features to create a chart like that, but responsibilities can be captured in other ways.

Each deliverable needs a responsible person. Deliverables are captured as summary tasks, and if you assign a person to summary tasks, the assignment will create work (effort) for the responsible person during the entire duration of the summary task. If you want to indicate responsibilities in your schedule without adding effort, you can accomplish this in one of three ways:

◆ You can assign the responsible people to the milestone of the deliverable. Since milestones have a zero duration and therefore no effort, there is no problem

---

[46] See the glossary of the PMBOK® Guide, 2000 Edition, Project Management Institute.

assigning responsibilities to milestones. You will find more on how to create assignments in the next chapter.

◆ You can assign the resource to the summary task if you set the **Units** to 0 (zero) to prevent this assignment from adding to the work. By default, the resource name does not show up in the timescale for summary tasks, but you can change this in the **Format, Bar Styles** dialog: select **Summary**, click the tab **Text** and in the field **Right** select **Resource Names** from the list. This will make the name of the resource appear for example as *Andrea [0]* next to the task bar in the timescale. The extra *[0]* for the zero units does not look all that great.

◆ MS Project has enough text fields to capture responsibilities. Use the extra **Text1** field, for example, and rename it *Responsible Person* by choosing **Tools, Customize, Fields**. If you click <kbd>Value List...</kbd>, you can even create a pick list for this field. You can also display names of the responsible people to the right or left of task bars in the timescale. This method has the fewest complications and may thus be the best method.

Project 2002 accommodates defining resources in the **Resource Sheet** and assigning resources in the **Gantt Chart** view. We will discuss assigning in the next chapter; here we will discuss defining the resources.

When to Add a Resource?

A resource should only be entered as a resource in the model of the project if you expect that the resource may affect the quality, duration or cost of the project significantly. If the resource will not have an impact on quality, duration or cost, you can keep your model leaner by leaving the resource out. If you add resources and assign them to the tasks, you have created a *resource-loaded schedule*.

A resource that is easy to replace will not likely affect the schedule. In fact, in construction, contractors rarely allow their schedule to be driven by a lack of resources. Generally, it is easy to find carpenters and electricians. Resources that are scarce could increase the duration of the project. Resources will increase the duration of your project:

◆ If they are not available when you need them. If you need a sign-off and the busy executives are out of the country, it may affect the duration of your project. Materials that have to come from afar can also affect the schedule.

◆ If human resources are assigned to many tasks and become over-allocated. Their workloads need to be leveled, which often leads to longer projects. Experts are an example.

If you over-allocated resources, they may affect the duration of the project. Sometimes over-allocations can be solved within the project duration, and sometimes they will extend the project duration. If you find that resource availability affects the scheduling of tasks, you have a *resource-limited schedule*,[47] also known as a *resource-constrained schedule*.

To manage the cost of the project, you have to define all the people, facilities, machines and materials that have a significant cost associated with them in the resource sheet. For example, if you need outside legal advice, you will pay high hourly rates that you need to capture in your project budget. You do not have to enter small expenses into your MS Project model. MS Project is not meant to be accounting software. There are several reasons for this:

◆ MS Project is a modeling tool with which you deliberately simplify the reality. Accountants cannot afford themselves to simplify. Accountants need to reflect the reality as precisely as they (humanly) can. Project managers should focus on the big picture from a 10,000-foot distance.

◆ Project managers use averaging when they model their project. Project managers may average levels of effort, for example. Averaging makes accountants cringe. Accountants want facts and nothing else.

◆ Project managers can afford to ignore dollars and cents. They can leave details out, but accountants cannot. Project managers would group small expenses into bigger categories and manage them as a category. Project managers have to stay away from the details to keep their sanity, or they risk letting their schedule get out-of-date.

◆ Accountants are obsessed with the past, whereas project managers are obsessed with the future. In a sense, accountants are the historians of the company whereas the project managers are the "futurologists" of the company. The future has no facts, but the past has only facts.

◆ Project managers need only be concerned with expenses that have to be paid from the project budget. Accountants have to be concerned about any expenses within the

---

[47] See the glossary of the PMBOK® Guide, 2000 Edition, Project Management Institute.

company. Resources you won't pay for from your budget can be left out of the schedule. If you use a boardroom that is paid for by the corporation, you would not add it as a resource to the resource sheet from a cost perspective. On the other hand, if you will be paying the rental on a training room from your project budget, you should add the training room as a resource to the resource sheet in MS Project.

In general, accountants do not necessarily make good project managers, as you can see. However, project managers do need some people with an accounting orientation on their team. And they will have to work well together to be successful! Project managers need to collect actual values to learn from the projects they have completed.

Choosing the Options

Choose **Tools, Options** and click on the tab where you want to change settings.

Tab	Option
General	☑ **Automatically add new resources and tasks** This allows entering a new resource, on the fly, wherever and whenever you need a new resource, without having to answer a prompt asking if you really want to create the new resource. In Project 2002 Professional with Project Server, you probably don't have the proper access rights to create new resources in the enterprise resource pool as a project manager, and we recommend the option be turned off to prevent accidentally creating many local resources.
	Default standard rate By entering a rate you can reduce the amount of typing you have to do. If the standard rate is set to $50/hr, you don't need to enter a rate for any resource that is $50/hr.
	Default overtime rate By entering a rate you can reduce the amount of typing you have to do.
	Set as Default This sets the options above as the default setting for any new schedules you create. The existing schedules are not affected because the options are stored in the project file (as indicated in the section divider label **General Options for <current file name>**).

Tab	Option
Schedule	**Show assignment units as a: Percentage** or **Decimals**
	Units of resources can be expressed as a percentage or in decimals in the **Max. Units** field (availability) and in the assignment **Units** field (workload). This option is generic and applies to all your projects, existing or new.
	For example, you have a resource that is available half-time to your project. This option gives you the choice of entering this as *50%* (percentage) or as *0.5* (decimal) in the **Max. Units** field. For part-time resources, **Percentages** seem to make the most sense.
	Let's consider a situation in which you have 3 carpenters available to your project. You could enter them as a group and enter *300%* (percentage) or as *3* (decimal). For consolidated resources the **Decimals** seem easier to understand.
	You can switch this option at any time; it is entirely your preference.

Types of Resources

MS Project knows only two types of resources: **Work** resources and **Material** resources. These are the two choices given in the resource field **Type**. In practice, you will come across four types of resources: human, facility, machine and material.

Important questions for each type are:
◆ Should the resource add to the total amount of effort in the project?
◆ Should the resource be included in workload leveling?
◆ Does the resource have a time-related or a unit-related cost?

We will discuss these questions for each resource:

◆ *Human resources* are people whose efforts should add up in the *Work* field. The total amount of work should be reasonable, which means it is within or close to their availability. If there are over-allocations, their workloads should be leveled. Human effort costs money, and human resources should be given a standard rate and an overtime rate and cost-per-use rate, if applicable. They have a time-related cost and the rate needs to be appended with "/h" (per hour), "/w" (per week), "/mo" (per month) or "/y" (per year). Human resources need to be entered as **Work** resources.

◆ *Material* resources are consumable resources. They should not add to the amount of effort (**Work**) of the project. Materials do not have a capacity like humans or facilities do and do not need to be leveled. Materials do cost money and typically have a unit-related cost only. Materials should be entered as a **Material** resource. The cost per unit should be entered in the **Std. Rate** field without a time unit.

◆ *Facilities* should not add to the total amount of effort of the project (**Work**). We, therefore, have to make them **Material** resources. The cost of facilities is typically time-related, like monthly rent, for example. Facilities therefore need a standard rate per time unit, and perhaps a cost-per-use rate. Only **Work** resources can have a time-related rate unfortunately. If you want to calculate time-related cost, you could use a workaround, which we will discuss on page 300.

If you enter facilities as material resources, MS Project cannot prevent double reservations by leveling their "workload"; you would not want two different meetings held in one room at the same time. You have to keep an eye on the reservation of the facility yourself. You could choose to enter the facility as a **Work** resource to level its "workload", but this will start adding its "effort" to the amount of **Work** in the project as well, which is not desirable.

◆ *Machines* are similar to facilities in terms of points made above. Machines should not add to the effort of the project and should be entered as **Material** resources. Machines typically have a time-related cost and thus need a standard rate per time unit, but only **Work** resources can have a rate like that, unless you use our workaround, which we will discuss on page 300.

If you enter a machine as a material resource, MS Project cannot monitor whether the machine is in use already. You will have to keep an eye on that yourself, the same as for facilities.

In MS Project, there are only two types of resources that can be seen in the field *Type*: *Work* and *Material* resources. However, there are four fundamentally different types of resources in practice. *Human resources* are typically work resources with effort, leveling and time-related cost. *Material resources* typically do not have effort or leveling and have a per-unit cost. So far, so good. *Facility resources* should not add to the effort, but their capacity should be leveled and they often have time-related cost. We have found a way to enter time-related cost for material resources which we will discuss in detail on page 300; therefore we recommend that they be entered as **Material** resources. The same is true for *machine resources*.

What If You Don't Know Who You Will Get

In the planning phase, you often don't know exactly who is going to do the task. If you know you are going to need a programmer, you can enter this resource, for the time being, under the generic name *programmer* in the resource sheet. If you need more precision in your model, you can create junior and senior generic resources, such as *junior programmer* and *senior programmer*.

 In Project 2002 Professional with *Project Server*, the enterprise resource pool will be set up by your project office. The project office will have added the generic resources that you may need. If you cannot find the resource you need, you would ask your project office to add the resource needed. You need the proper access right to edit the enterprise resource pool. If you are the one designated to maintain the enterprise resource pool, you can open it by choosing **Tools, Enterprise Options, Open Enterprise Resource Pool**. From there the steps are similar to entering resources into MS Project standalone as explained below.

 Not knowing the exact names of the individuals should not stop you from creating a resource-loaded schedule. Once you know who you will get on your team, you can reassign the tasks from the generic resources to the real individuals. There are several easy ways to accomplish this and we will discuss these ways on page 342.

Change the View to Enter Resources

1. Choose **View, Resource Sheet**.
2. Check if the table **Entry** is active. Choose **View, Table: <name of current table>, Entry**.

Resource Fields

You will find the following fields in the Resource Sheet:

Indicator — enumerated field
This field will display indicators for a variety of situations. If a resource is over-allocated, this column will show an ◈ icon.

Resource Name (note that the name of the field is *Name*) — required field
This is where you enter the name of the resource. We recommend using a standard naming convention to prevent duplicating resources inadvertently. The convention should allow you to sort the resource names. We recommend the convention *last name-first name*. Notice the use of a hyphen (-) instead of the comma (,) because the comma

is used to separate multiple entries in a field (also called the *list separator*, which is set in the *Control Panel*). MS Project thinks you are trying to enter multiple resources in one cell if you use the comma and will reject this.

What you type in this field will show up in the lists used for assigning resources, like the **Assign Resources** dialog. Only the names entered in this field will show in lists like that. It is therefore imperative that you:

♦ Make the resource names easy to recognize.

♦ Make each resource name in this field unique. If you have more than one *John Smith*, you can look at other fields like **Group** in the Resource Sheet to find out who is who. In the Gantt Chart you cannot distinguish between one *John Smith* and the other.

♦ Sort the resource list alphabetically. You can do this by choosing **Project, Sort, Sort by** and in the **Sort** dialog selecting **Name** in the **Sort by** list and checking  ☑ **Permanently renumber resources**. The **Assign Resources** dialog sorts its resources automatically in Project 2002.

Type — required field

The type of resource can be **Work** (default) or **Material**. Work resources are people. Material resources are facilities, equipment and materials. An example of a material resource is *desktop computers*.

Material Label — optional field

The label you type in (for a material resource only!) will show up in several other views and reports. For example, the label *desktop computers* will show on the y-axis in the Resource Graph view to indicate the number of units needed over time. In the timescale of the Gantt Chart, it will show up to the right of the task bars. The label is particularly important for bulk resources to indicate the unit of measurement. For example:

♦ concrete in *cubic feet, cubic meters* or *80-pound bags of mix*

♦ cable in *yards* or *meters*

When *500* units of the bulk resource *concrete* are assigned, the material label will show up in the Gantt timescale as *500 cubic feet*. The material label defines what one unit is for the bulk resource.

Initials — optional field

In previous versions of MS Project this field was very useful because you could assign resources to tasks by typing their initials, but nowadays you can point and click to assign. Initials may still be of use for reporting purposes.

Group — optional field
The group is the name of the department to which the resource belongs. If you fill in these group names, you can filter all the tasks for a department. Better still, with the group feature you can group resources together in their respective departments and see totals for work and cost. Note that the **Group** field and the group feature (**Project, Group by**) are two different things.

Max. Units (*Maximum Units*) — required field for **Work** resources
This is the maximum availability of the resource to the project. A resource that is available full-time to the project needs 100% in the **Max. Units** field, and 50% for a resource available half-time. For a consolidated resource the **Max. Units** is the total number of team members on the team. You don't need to enter availability for material resources.

Std. Rate (*Standard Rate*) — optional field
Enter the standard rate for regular work in this field. For example, if you enter "10.50/h", it means the person earns $10.50 per hour. You don't need a time unit for material resources; the rate will be calculated per unit of material you assign to the task.

If you type	you will see	which means
m	min	minutes
h	hr	hours
d	day	days
w	wk	weeks
mo	mon	months
y	yr	years

Ovt. Rate (*Overtime Rate*) — optional field
Enter the rate for overtime work in this field. Do this only if you will pay overtime instead of compensating with time off. Project 2002 expects you to indicate separately how many overtime hours are worked on each assignment; those hours will be charged against the overtime rate. Material resources cannot have an overtime rate.

Cost/Use (*Cost-per-Use* or *Per-Use-Cost*) — optional field
Enter in this field the rate that has to be paid every time the resource is used, which

means each time it is assigned. It can be an up-front fee. For example, if you need a bulldozer transported to your site, this may cost $200 up front before it does any work. The cost per use will be incurred on every task to which the resource is assigned. The cost is calculated as the Cost/Use rate times the number of units assigned.

Accrue At — optional field
Select **Start**, **End**, or **Prorated** to indicate when the costs are incurred. Tab to the **Accrue at** field and a pull-down button ![▼] appears. Select one of the following options from the list:

Accrue at	Incurs the Cost	Example
Start	As soon as the task starts.	actors
Prorated	The cost is incurred as the task progresses; the cost goes up with the **% Complete**.	employees
End	As soon as the task finishes.	consultants

The accrual options only pertain to the standard rate and overtime rate; the cost per use is always accrued at the start of the task.

Base Calendar — optional field
Select a calendar from the list. The *base calendar* specifies the general working hours and working days for the resource. You can override the base calendar and set individual working hours in the resource calendar. Material resources cannot have a base calendar.

Code — optional field
Type an alphanumeric code, such as an accounting code. This is used to charge the expenses for the resource to a particular cost account. It can be useful for the finance department. Often the tasks, and not the resources, will be coded to charge to the cost accounts.

Generic — optional field
The yes/no field *generic* which can be inserted in the resource sheet allows you to mark a resource as a generic resource. This is usually done by the *Project Server* administrator. Generic resources are roles, positions or function labels (like *carpenter* or *system analyst*); they are not names of individuals (like *Mary Cameron* or *Lucas Benning*). Project managers will use generic resources in their initial planning and will replace them with the names of the individuals as soon as they find out whom they will get on their team. Generic resources are very useful for longer term planning. Your

human resources department will be delighted if you present them with long-term resource needs instead of what you need next week.

Inactive — optional field

The resource attribute *inactive* indicates if the resource is still active in the enterprise resource pool or is inactive and kept for historical purposes only.

Entering Resources

You can enter the resources into the resource sheet in three ways:
◆ Download the resources from your address book.
◆ Key in the resources manually.

◆ Use the enterprise-wide *shared resource pool*, called *Enterprise Resource Global*.

The **Resources** Project Guide will provide all these options to enter resources. Display the Project Guide toolbar by right-clicking on any toolbar and choosing **Project Guide**. Click Resources , then click the hyperlink **Specify people and equipment for the project** and you will be presented with the three ways to enter resources.

Downloading the Resources from Your Address Book

If you are using MS Outlook for your contact information and address list, you may be able to download the resource names easily from that list. This means you don't have to retype all of them. MS Outlook even has powerful import features in the menu items **File, Import and Export …**. If you keep your addresses in another contact management application or database, you should be able to import them into MS Outlook. Then you can use the following steps to transfer the resource names into MS Project.

1. Display the toolbar by right-clicking on any toolbar and clicking on **Resource Management.** The Resource Management toolbar is displayed:

The **Address Book** and the **Windows User Account** from **Address Book** tools

2. Click **Address Book** on the **Resource Management** toolbar.

3. The **Choose Profile** dialog may appear, in which case you have to indicate which user profile you want to use on the computer system. User profiles make it possible for more than one person to use the same computer by enabling each to use their own desktop, preferences and setup.

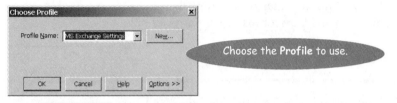

Choose the **Profile** to use.

4. Click [OK]; the **Select Resources** dialog appears:

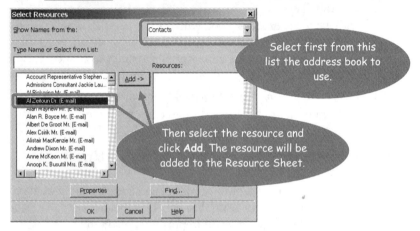

Select first from this list the address book to use.

Then select the resource and click **Add**. The resource will be added to the Resource Sheet.

5. Select the address list from the **Show Names from the:** [Contacts ▼], and the names of the resources are now shown in the list on the left. (If no address lists are shown, you have to add the **Personal Address Book** or the **Outlook Address Book** to the profile. In MS Outlook you can do this by choosing **Tools, Services**.)

6. Type in the first character(s) of the name of the person to add in the field **Type name or select from list**; the list scrolls immediately to the person. Press the arrow keys [↓] or [↑] to highlight the resource.

7. Press [Enter ↵] or click [Add ->]; the resource is now added to the list of **Resources** on the right. This list of people will be transferred into the resource sheet in MS Project.

8. Repeat the last two steps for all resources you would like to add.

9. Click | OK |; the resources are now added to the end of the resource list. You can always go back into the address list to pick up more resource names.

10. If you want to add the Windows user account information, click **Windows User Account from Address Book** on the **Resource Management** toolbar to pick up Windows user account information from your address book for the resource. It is important to have the Windows user account information when you work with *Project Server* using Windows authentication.

11. You will still have to add the other types of resources: facility, machine and material. You can do this with the next steps.

Keying in the Resources Manually

1. Customize the table first:
   ◇ Delete all columns you will not need by clicking on their column headings and pressing [Del].
   ◇ Insert new fields you will need by right-clicking on the column heading to the left of which you want to insert a new column; a pop-up menu appears. Choose **Insert Column**; the **Column Definition** dialog appears:

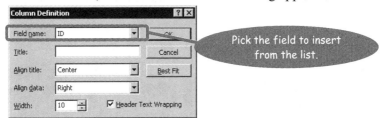

Pick the field to insert from the list.

   ◇ Select the field from the **Field Name** list |ID| and click | OK |. Repeat these bulleted steps for all fields you need.

2. Enter the name of the resource in the field **Resource Name** and press:
   [Enter ↵] to go down (to the next row), or
   [Tab] to go to the right (to the next column).

3. If the resource is a material resource (facilities, machines or materials), change the **Type** from **Work** to **Material** and enter the base unit of the material in the field **Material Label**, for example *brick*.

4. If you change the type of the resource, you will lose any rates you may have typed in for the resource. This is because **Work** resources require a time-related rate, like $50/h, whereas **Material** resources need a per-unit cost, like $150/door.

5. For **Work** resources only, enter the availability in the field **Max. Units**.

6. Enter the cost rates in the fields **Std. Rate, Ovt. Rate** and **Cost/Use** and determine when the cost will be accrued by choosing **Start**, **Prorated** or **End** in **Accrue at**.

7. Enter the **Base Calendar** field and a list button will appear. Select the appropriate base calendar for the resource from this list.

8. You can create other base calendars by choosing **Tools, Change Working Time...** and clicking the button ⎢ **New...** ⎥. This button is not available in the Professional edition when you use Project Server, because base calendars are supposed to be prepared centrally. You may have to ask your project management office to make another base calendar available.

Another easy way to enter data is to drag over all cells in which you want to enter resource information. Multiple cells are selected with one cell still white, the input cell. Enter the data in this input cell and use the ⎢Tab⎥ key to make it move to the next cell until you have filled them all. You can even select a nonadjacent series of cells by holding down the ⎢Control⎥ key while dragging.

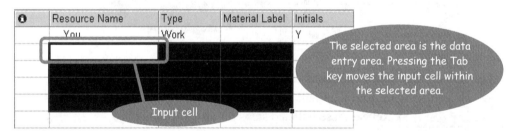

Input cell

The selected area is the data entry area. Pressing the Tab key moves the input cell within the selected area.

Using the Enterprise Resource Pool

The enterprise resource pool can only be used if *Project Server* has been set up. One of the steps in configuring Project Server is setting up the resource pool, called *Enterprise Resource Global*. If you want to do skills-based scheduling, this will take a lot of advance thinking and planning since it is not just a matter of entering the names of the resources. Your Project Server administrator needs to do the following:

1. Enter a proper *Resource Breakdown Structure (RBS)*. An RBS is similar to the organizational chart of the organization. It can be a part of the organization if you, for example, only intend to model the projects of the IT department in the Project Server database. The RBS needs to be developed and entered in the field *Enterprise Resource Outline Code 30* that has permanently been renamed *RBS*.

2. Give all resources an RBS code (*RBS-code*) using the field RBS (*Enterprise Resource Outline Code 30*).

3. Identify strategic *resource skills* and perhaps even *skill sets*. Each skill needs to be coded. If you want to work with skill sets, you need to do this for each type of skill. You may find for example in a multinational company that it is important to capture the language skills as well as the technical skills for each person. Also, each resource can have multiple technical skills, like C++ programming skills and Visual Basic programming skills. In such a case you have to use two fields to capture this: a *primary skill* field and a *secondary skill* field.

4. Identify the generic resources you need for longer term resource planning and for use in project templates.

5. Code all individual and generic resources with the skills or skill sets they possess.

 Step 3, 4 and 5 are necessary if you also want to use the skills-based scheduling features in Project Server. These features can be very beneficial and can save a lot of time for a variety of people:

♦ *Team Building*
When *project managers* are faced with a resource that leaves the project, they need to quickly find a new resource that is available and has the right skill set.

♦ *Resource Substitution*
When *project managers* first open a project template, they typically will find that only generic resources are assigned to the tasks. The *Resource Substitution Wizard* allows them to quickly find available resources with the right skill set to replace the generic resources. The result is a fully *resource-loaded schedule* with warm bodies instead of generic resources (which I often call zombies).

♦ *Resource Modeling*
Resource managers can list and sort all resources and analyze their availability across all projects they are involved in. They can edit their resource information. They can group the resources by department, location or skills. If generic resources are added to the enterprise resource pool, resource managers can even do longer term resource planning by aggregating the need for the different resource categories months in advance.

◆ *Portfolio Modeling*
Executives can develop scenarios to analyze the impact on meeting deadlines, for example, if they are considering taking on an extra project. To develop these scenarios, you can allow resources to be reassigned in certain projects, whereas assignments in other projects are not affected. If you want Project Server to develop these scenarios, you have to code the required and available skills.

 As you can see, the skills-based scheduling features of *Project Server* rely heavily on properly coded skills and skill sets in the enterprise resource pool. In other words, you have to do your homework before you can take advantage of these features.

At this point, we have reviewed three different ways to enter resources. We will now explore how to enter their working times and vacations.

Resource Calendars

A resource calendar is a calendar that is specific for an individual. You can enter individual working times and vacations in a resource calendar. There is a resource calendar available for each resource, but you do not need to modify one unless you expect it to have a significant impact. All resource calendars will have the settings that you entered in the project calendar (see page 96). Apart from the project calendar, there can be one or more base calendars on which resource calendars can be based (see the illustration). You will need base calendars if your team members are in different countries; you would create a base calendar for each country and then base each resource on his country calendar. If resources belong to different companies, you may also need multiple base calendars.

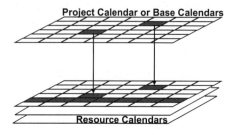

Project Calendar or Base Calendars

Resource Calendars

 If someone takes an individual holiday, the assignments will be delayed until the resource returns from the holiday. The duration of the project increases, and the resource has an impact on the schedule. It is important to model vacations in Project 2002. A poorly timed vacation can easily jeopardize precious deadlines. Entering vacations is not a lot of work, so there is no good reason not to.

To edit a resource calendar follow these steps:

1. Choose **Tools, Change Working Time…**; the **Change Working Time** dialog appears:

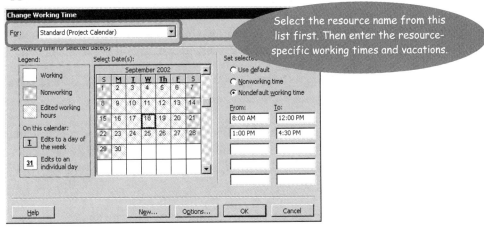

Select the resource name from this list first. Then enter the resource-specific working times and vacations.

2. Select the resource for which to set the calendar in the list
   For: Standard (Project Calendar)

3. Change the work hours by selecting the day(s) M T W Th F , selecting ⊙ **Nondefault working time** and typing the working time in the boxes:
   From: To:

4. To set an individual holiday, highlight the days (you can select multiple days by holding down Control and clicking or dragging) and select ⊙ **Nonworking time**.

5. Select the next resource from the list **For** at the top to enter another resource calendar or click OK when you are done with all resources.

You can even change days that were marked as holidays or weekend days on the **Standard (Project Calendar)** back to working days for a resource. If you want to change a day back to its original setting in the project calendar, you have to select ⊙ **Use Default**.

You can create new base calendars and new task calendars by choosing **Tools, Change Working Time…** and clicking New… . This button may not available in the professional edition since task calendars are supposed to be created centrally, likely by your project office.

 The task-related field **Ignore Resource Calendar** is by default set to *No* for all tasks. This field determines if Project 2002 will use the *resource calendar* when scheduling assignments. The field is useful when the task also has a *task calendar*. With the new field you can resolve conflicts between the resource calendar and the task calendar. If you leave it set to *No*, the resource calendar takes effect. If you change it to *Yes*, the task calendar will take effect. You can toggle the field from *No* to *Yes* when you assign a task calendar to the task.

 In earlier versions of MS Project, Fixed Duration tasks ignored the resource calendars completely. In Project 2002, the Fixed Duration tasks will look at the resource calendars, but may split the task bar when one of the assigned resources is not available. This surprises many people.

The working hours in resource calendars can become very intricate and require a lot of data entry, such as resources working day or night shifts in alternating weeks. You have to ask yourself if you would prefer to manage these shift resources as a consolidated resource instead of as individual resources. If you choose the latter option, your schedule might become very maintenance-hungry. Fortunately, shift work is less prevalent in projects than in the ongoing operations of manufacturing companies.

The Max. Units of a Resource

The maximum units of resources determine what percentage of one's work hours is available to the project. In the illustration you can see that Tom works 8 hours per day and if the **Max. Units** is 50% there would be a steep over-allocation (dark gray). If the

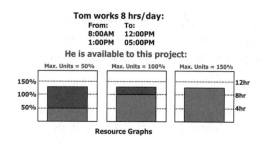

Max. Units is 100%, there is a small over-allocation. If it is 150% there is remaining availability. You can see that the percentage in the **Max. Units** field determines what constitutes an over-allocation for the resource. Note that the **Max. Units** percentage is relative to the working hours entered on the resource calendar. The working hours can change from week to week.

Resource Availability

The availability of resources varies from one resource to another. The different types of availability are:

◆ *Temporary*
Somebody can be "loaned" to a project for only one month.

◆ *Varying availability*
This is a resource that is, for example, available full-time one month, but half-time the next month.

◆ *Part-time*
This is a person who works fewer hours a day or fewer days a week than the *full-time-equivalent* resource as defined in the **Tools, Options, Calendar, Hours per Day** setting.

◆ *Full-time*
Project 2002 considers a full-time person to be someone who works 40 hours a week and 5 days a week. Microsoft has designated this as the default workweek, and any diversions from this are called *exceptions*.

◆ *Compressed workweeks*:

◇ *4-40 workweek* or *every Friday off*
A person works only 4 days per week, but 10 hours per day.

◇ *9-80 workweek* or *alternating Fridays off*
This type of workweek means that a person works for 9 days a total of 80 hours and then takes 1 day off, normally a Friday.

◆ *Overtime*
If the deadline is in jeopardy, resources can be asked to start working overtime to compensate for the lack of progress.

◆ *Consolidated resources*
Consolidated resources are multiple resources that are entered into the schedule as one group instead of as individuals.

On the next pages we will discuss how each of these resource availabilities can be entered into Project 2002. In many cases you will have to edit the resource calendar.

In Project 2002 Professional with *Project Server* you may not have the proper access rights to add or change resource availability in the enterprise resource pool as a project manager. You still need to know how to do this for the resources private to your project, called *local resources*.

Temporary and Varying Availability

If a resource is available only during a certain period, you can enter this *availability* in the **Resource Information** dialog box. Click **Resource Information** 📇 on the **Standard** toolbar, and click the tab **General**. An example of temporary availability is when a specialized test lab is only available in the month of May for a project team.

In Project 2002 you can easily model varying availability. You can set up an entire profile of availability, such as 80% in April, 50% in May, 100% in June, etc. On the same **General** tab under **Resource Availability,** you can enter the availability profile:

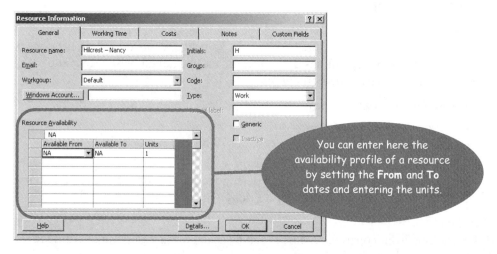

In an availability profile, you only need to enter the **Available to** dates and MS Project will enter the corresponding **Available from** dates in (next day).

The **Max. Units** field can only display one percentage of all percentages entered in the availability profile. The one number displayed in the **Max. Units** field will be the availability percentage as per the current date. You can find the current date in the **Project, Project Information** dialog. As time goes by, the field **Max. Units** will display the different values from the availability profile.

Part-Time Availability

Part-time resources can be:

◆ People who work, for example, 4 hours each workday. They should be entered in the resource sheet with the **Max. Units** set to 4h/8h x 100% = 50%.
OR
The working-time hours in the resource calendar should be set to only 4 hours per day. For example, the working hours could be set to 1:00 PM-5:00 PM.

◆ People who work 4 out of 5 weekdays; enter them in the schedule by changing a weekday to a nonworking day in their resource calendar
(**Tools, Change Working Time**).

 Someone who is working on multiple projects may only be available part-time to your project. The remaining availability is automatically calculated and displayed within your project if you use Project 2002 Professional with *Project Server*.

A resource can also be assigned to work part-time on a task, which we will discuss on page 319.

Full-Time Availability

People who work full-time need to have their **Max. Units** set to 100%.

Their working hours as set in the resource calendar should correspond with the number of **Hours per Day** and **Hours per Week** settings in the **Tools, Options, Calendar**. For example, if the hours per day in **Tools, Options** is set to 7.5 hours/day, the calendar should show, for example, 8:00 AM-12:00 PM and 1:00 PM-4:30 PM (double-click on the resource and click on the tab **Working Time** to check this).

Compressed Workweeks

4-40 Workweek or Every Friday Off

One example of a compressed workweek is when a person works 10 hours per day but only 4 days per week. This is often the case for people who have to travel a long distance to work.

The compressed workweek can be entered by increasing the working hours.

1. In the **Resource Sheet** view, double-click on a resource and the **Resource Information** dialog appears.

2. Click the tab **Working Time**; the dialog should now look like:

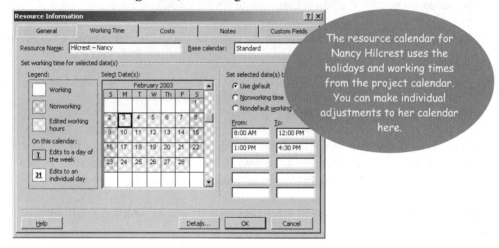

3. Select the working days for this resource by dragging over them:
M	T	W	Th	F
    .

4. Select ⊙ **Nondefault working time**.

5. Enter the longer working hours in the **From** and **To** fields.

6. When done, click   OK   .

9-80 Workweek or Alternating Fridays Off

Another example of a compressed workweek is if a person works a total of 80 hours over 9 consecutive business days and then takes 1 day off, normally a Friday. This base calendar would have to be created in MS Project before you can use it:

1. Choose **Tools, Change Working Time**; the **Change Working Time** dialog appears.

2. Click   New...   to create a new base calendar. This button may not available if you are using Project 2002 Professional with *Project Server*; only the person with access privileges to the **Enterprise Global** file can create new base calendars. In

that case you have to request that the 9-80 calendar be created for you. If you can create your own base calendars, you can now mark every other Friday off as ⦿ **Nonworking time** and increase the working hours on the remaining days.

3. To use the 9-80 workweek for a resource, switch to the **Resource Sheet** view.

4. Select the field **Base Calendar**, which is the second-last column in the resource **Entry** table; a list button 🔽 appears. Click 🔽 and select **9-80** from the list.
   OR
   Double-click on a resource and the **Resource Information** dialog appears. Click the tab **Working Time**, and in **Base Calendar** select **9-80** from the list.

Notice that there should be two 9-80 calendars: one for this week's Friday off and one for next week's. However, using only one 9-80 calendar is often precise enough in terms of the big picture. At least it makes sure that you have incorporated the impact of regular Fridays off work, regardless on which dates these Fridays fall exactly. Sometime you will loose a day, sometimes you gain a day and the law of averages is going to work for you. Again, project managers should focus on the big picture. If you are in a short project, you might consider adding the second and complementary 9-80 calendar.

Note that for a 10-day task with a 9-80 resource assigned, MS Project will only use 9 business days in the timescale for *Fixed Units* and *Fixed Work* tasks. For *Fixed Duration* tasks, it will use 10 business days in the timescale. Again, there is a difference in the way MS Project treats Fixed Duration tasks.

Overtime Availability

Overtime work is work done outside the regular work hours as indicated in the Project Calendar.

In the initial planning phase of the project, you would normally not plan overtime, unless the project is extremely time-constrained right off the bat. Normally the overtime feature is used during the execution phase, when we may try to compensate for slippages.

Overtime can be entered in several different ways depending on whether you pay and what you pay the resource for overtime:

◆ If the resource is not paid for overtime, but instead is compensated with extra time off, there are several ways in which you can model this:

◇ You can enter the overtime by increasing the **Max. Units** in the resource sheet to greater than 100%. This is the quick and easy way to enter overtime, and the resource will be working overtime during the entire project.
OR

◇ To be somewhat more precise you can use the **Resource Information** dialog 📖 , tab **General**; in **Resource Availability** you could specify overtime for a period in which the resource works more than 100%.
OR

◇ Increase the working time in the resource calendar. For example, somebody works 10 hours overtime in one week, and in the second week the overtime is compensated for with time off.
OR

◇ Enter the overtime by changing holidays or weekend days in the resource calendar to working days. Later on, weekdays are set to nonworking days to compensate in time.

◆ If the resource is paid for overtime hours at the regular rate, you only need to accept a certain level of over-allocated hours. All the hours worked are charged at the same standard rate.

◆ If the resource is paid for overtime hours at a higher rate, you have to enter all the hours worked in overtime separately. You enter them on the Task Form in the Gantt Chart (see below).

Entering Overtime Hours at the Overtime Rate

1. Choose **View, Resource Sheet** and enter the overtime rate in the field **Ovt. Rate**.

2. Choose **View, Gantt Chart**.

3. Choose **Window, Split** to display the **Task Form**.

4. Click on the **Task Form** to make it active.

5. Choose **Format, Details, Resource Work** to display the field **Ovt. Work**. The view should now look like:

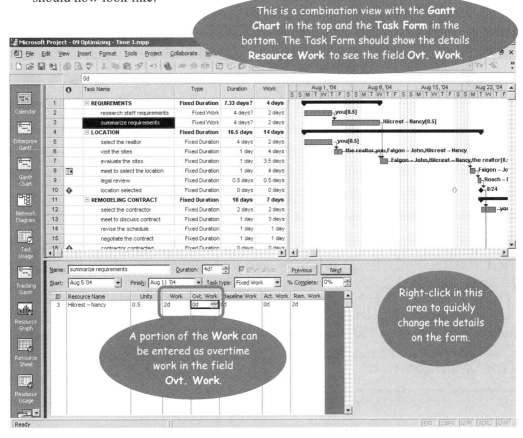

This is a combination view with the **Gantt Chart** in the top and the **Task Form** in the bottom. The Task Form should show the details **Resource Work** to see the field **Ovt. Work**.

A portion of the **Work** can be entered as overtime work in the field **Ovt. Work**.

Right-click in this area to quickly change the details on the form.

6. For each assignment you now indicate in the **Ovt. Work** field how many of the hours shown in the field **Work** will be worked in overtime.

7. Click OK when done with an assignment.

 The number of overtime hours has to be reasonable relative to the total number of hours **Work**. If an assignment is 10 hours, you could ask for 2 hours in overtime and finish the task in 1 business day. If the assignment is 20 hours, you cannot expect a resource to work 8 hours and then 12 hours in overtime to finish within 1 day. Project 2002 would schedule this as one 20-hour workday, which is asking a little too much … for most of us.

Consolidated Resources

A consolidated resource is a group of pooled individuals, not separate individuals. A group of people is entered as one consolidated resource. The maximum units are set to the number of *full-time equivalent* individuals who are part of the consolidated resource. Full-time equivalency is defined in the **Tools, Options**, tab **Calendar**, **Hours per Day** setting. For example, if you have 2 full-timers and 2 half-timers on a team, the maximum units for that consolidated resource should be set to 2 x 1 + 2 x 0.5 = 3 resources.

Consolidating resources is a beautiful way to keep the devilish details out of your schedule. You basically make an agreement with the 3 resources that you will not give them more work as a group than up to 3 full-time equivalent resources. They will have to determine who will do which task, and because they know each other's expertise best, resources tend to be very good at that. As a project manager you will spend a lot less time maintaining detailed resource data and keeping the individual workloads leveled.

Consolidating resources only makes sense though if the resources can substitute for each other. If you have experienced and novice resources, you can create two consolidated resources: junior and senior. For example, if you find that the experience level among programmers varies widely, create a group of junior and a group of senior programmers. As you can see, MS Project is a modeling tool in which you only capture the most significant parameters of the reality of your project.

Cost Management

Cost Situations

Economists distinguish between variable cost and fixed cost. Variable cost can vary with time needed, units consumed or number of uses.

Labor cost is a time-related human resource cost. Facilities can also have time-related costs, like rent or lease expenses. Machines can have:
◆ time-related cost such as rent,
◆ unit-related cost such as a newspaper printing machine for which the cost is per roll of paper, or
◆ use-related cost such as the setup cost of the printing machine

Fixed costs can be related to resources or to tasks. Resource-related fixed cost can be entered in the **Cost/Use** field if the cost is incurred on every use of the resource. An example of a resource-related fixed cost is the up-front cost to transport a bulldozer to the construction site. Examples of task-related fixed costs are expenses for licenses, patents and any fixed-price contracts.

The following table provides an overview and examples of the different types of costs as well as the way these costs are typically entered in MS Project:

Cost Type	Example	Type	Rate Field	Accrue at
Time related	3 days of work @ 300/d	Work	Std. Rate	Prorated
	2 months rent @ 400/mo	Material[48]	Std. Rate	Prorated
Unit related	3 doors @ 150/door	Material	Std. Rate	Start
Use related	$200 Up front for bulldozer	Material	Cost/Use	Start (by default)
Varying rate	Work @ $300/d, after January 1st $350/d	Work	Cost Rate Table	Prorated
Fixed cost	Fixed price contract painting the house: $8,500	—	Gantt Chart: Fixed Cost	Gantt Chart: Fixed Cost Accrual[49]

The first thing we have to determine for the expense is what **Type** of resource we should make it: **Work** or **Material**. Then the rate needs to be entered in the appropriate rate field; MS Project has many resource-related rate fields: **Std. Rate, Ovt. Rate, Cost/Use** and **Cost rate tables**. In the field **Accrue At** you determine when the cost will take place. Material costs are often accrued at the start, whereas facility and machines costs are often accrued as prorated. For human resource costs, employees are typically prorated, whereas cost for consultants is often incurred at the end. The **Cost/Use** is

---

[48] If you make the facility a **Material** resource, you have to enter the number of "*units*" used per time unit in the assignment **Units** field (see Entering Facility and Machine Cost on page 300).

[49] The task-related field **Fixed Cost Accrual** has the same options as the resource-related field **Accrue At: Start, Prorated or End**.

always incurred at the start of the task and cannot be changed. MS Project also has task-related cost fields: **Fixed Cost** and **Fixed Cost Accrual**. These are useful for entering firm fixed-price contracts.

In practice, you will find more variations:

◆ A resource can have more than one type of cost associated with it. For example, a maintenance man can have a per-use fee of $50 for travel in addition to an hourly rate of $100. In this case you would enter the per-use fee in the **Cost/Use** field and the hourly rate in the **Std. Rate** (standard rate) field.

◆ The cost rates themselves can change over time; this is known as *varying cost rates* or *rate profile*. In MS Project you can capture a rate profile in the feature *Cost Rate Table*. You can access the cost rate tables for a resource by double-clicking on the resource and clicking the tab **Costs**.

◆ You can have multiple cost rate tables per resource. MS Project allows you to use up to five different rate profiles for each resource. If you have a jack-of-all-trades resource that does systems analysis, programming and occasionally some testing as well, you could specify three different rate profiles (A, B and C) for each of these different activities. This is important if the effort is billed to clients with agreed upon rates for each type of work. When you assign the resource, you have to indicate per assignment which rate profile you would like to use. We will discuss this on page 301.

 ◆ Materials may have a *consumption rate*. The consumption rate of materials is how many units of the material are used per time unit. For example, you pour concrete that costs $1 per cubic foot and you know that you typically pour 2000 cubic feet a day with the crew you have. This consumption rate can be entered in the assignment-related **Units** field when you assign the resource to the task. In the **Assign Resources** dialog you would enter *2000/day* in the field **Units**. If the duration of the task is 3 days, the cost will be:
3 days * 2000/day * $1/cubic foot = $6000.
The duration of the task will determine the total cost for the task, and if the duration expands, more units of material will be consumed, which will increase the cost of the task. Essentially you have now entered a time-related cost for material resources.

◆ You may need to attribute capital cost to a project. For example, you may need to buy expensive test equipment that will be used in future projects as well. You only want part of this capital expense charged to your project, the part that your project should carry as an expense. MS Project does not have features to accommodate that.

◆ You may encounter discounts when purchasing large volumes; you would need to enter a table with all rate segments. This is something MS Project cannot easily handle.

◆ You may need to charge taxes to the cost amounts. Again, MS Project does not have features for this.

What you could do to address these last three situations is calculate the cost in MS Excel. Then copy the resulting cost value and paste it into the **Fixed Cost** field of your MS Project schedule. The steps to do this are:

1. Save the Excel file (this step is essential if you paste link the number in step 3 instead of paste). Select the cell with the cost to be charged to the project in the Excel worksheet. Click **Copy** .

2. Switch to MS Project and display the field **Fixed Cost**. Select the cell into which you want to paste the cost.

3. Click **Paste** .
   OR
   If you expect the number to change several times, choose **Edit, Paste Special**, select
   ⦿ **Paste Link** and select **Text Data** in the list and click [OK]. The number is now dynamically linked to the spreadsheet. Upon opening the file, MS Project will always ask you if you want to update the linked data if **Tools, Options**, tab **Edit**, ☑ **Ask to update automatic links** is checked. If it is unchecked, the update will be automatic without a prompt.

 In Project 2002 Professional with *Project Server* you may not have the proper access privileges to add or change resource rates in the enterprise resource pool as a project manager. You still need to know how to do this for the resources private to your project, called *local resources*.

Entering Human Resource Costs

If you hire, for example, a programmer at $300/day, you can enter this in the resource sheet with the following steps:

1. Choose **View, Resource Sheet**.

2. Enter the name of the resource in **Resource Name**.

3. Leave the **Type** of the resource set to the default setting of **Work**.

4. Enter the rate in the field **Std. Rate**; for the programmer you would enter *$300/d*.

5. Enter the other cost rates **Ovt. Rate** and **Cost/Use**, if applicable.

6. Enter the **Accrue At**, for which you choose **Start**, **Prorated** or **End**. The accrual determines when the cost will be incurred. **Prorated** is accrued as the task progresses, for which Project 2002 will look at the **% Complete**. The **End** is the finish date of the task when the costs will be incurred. The **Cost/Use** expenses are always incurred at the start of the task.

7. Assign the human resources to the tasks, which we will discuss in the next chapter.

In the **Task Usage** snapshot below you can see how the prorated accrual is incurred proportionally to the **% Work Complete**:

> The total Cost is $1,200. The % **Work Complete** of 50% creates $600 Actual Cost spent (time-phased $300 + $300).

❶	Task Name	% Work Complete	Cost	Actual Cost	Details	Feb 16, '03 S	1	T	W	T	F
	⊟ code module	50%	$1,200.00	$600.00	Work		8h	8h	8h	8h	
					Cum. % Complete		25%	50%			
					Act. Work		8h	8h			
					Act. Cost		$300.00	$300.00			
	programmer	50%	$1,200.00	$600.00	Work		8h	8h	8h	8h	
					Cum. % Complete						
					Act. Work		8h	8h			
					Act. Cost		$300.00	$300.00			
					Work						

If you want MS Project to automatically calculate these costs, keep the option ☑ **Actual costs are always calculated by Microsoft Project** checked in **Tools, Options**, tab **Calculation**.

The time-related cost for facilities, like rental and lease, should be entered as material costs.

Entering Material Costs

The cost of material should be incorporated into the project model if it is significant enough to keep track of and if it will be paid from your project budget.

1. Choose **View, Resource Sheet**.

2. Enter the name of the resource in the field **Resource Name**.

3. Select the field **Type**, and a list button appears Work ▼; select **Material** from the list.

4. Enter a **Material Label**, which will show up in the Resource Graph and other views to remind users that this resource is a material resource. Enter the label in plural, for example *bricks* instead of *brick*, because you typically assign more than one unit. You can even enter *thousand bricks* if you entered the cost of 1000 bricks in the **Std. Rate** field instead of the cost of one brick. For bulk resources, you have to enter the unit of measurement; for example, for concrete this would be *cubic yards* or *cubic meters*, and for cables it would be *feet* or *meters*.

5. In the **Std. Rate** field enter the cost per unit for this resource. Notice that you don't need to enter the time unit (*/h* or */d*) for material resources. For the bricks we could enter *$2.00,* for example. You can fill in a **Cost/Use** as well; for the bricks this could be the cost of transportation to the site, let's say *$400.00*. The overtime rate field is neither available nor needed for material resources.

6. Select the **Accrue At** method to determine when the cost will show up in a time-phased view. You can choose **Start**, **Prorated** or **End.** Prorated is accrued as the task progresses. Project 2002 will look at the **% Complete** to calculate the time-phased cost accrual. Materials are often accrued at the start. The **Cost/Use** is always incurred at the start of the task and cannot be changed.

The **Resource Usage** snapshot below shows how the accrual for material costs works. The 1000 bricks cost $2 each and are accrued at the start of the task. The training room rental costs $400 and is accrued and paid at the end of the task.

	Resource Name	Accrue At	Work	Details	Apr 9, 00 S	M	T	W	T
1	⊟ bricks	Start	1,000	Cost		$2,000.00	$0.00	$0.00	$0.00
				Act. Cost					
	lay bricks		1,000	Cost		$2,000.00	$0.00	$0.00	$0.00
				Act. Cost					
2	⊟ training room	End	1	Cost		$0.00	$400.00		
				Act. Cost					
	train students		1	Cost		$0.00	$400.00		
				Act. Cost					

A material cost accrued at the start of the task.

A facility cost of $400 accrued at the end of the task.

We still need to assign the number of material resources to the tasks. We will discuss assigning on page 331.

Entering Facility and Machine Costs

This is the most difficult resource situation to enter into Project 2002. The use of facilities and machines should not add to the **Work** (effort) of the project. This would lead to the conclusion that they have to be entered as **Material** resources. But you cannot have a **Standard Rate** for material resources that acts as a time-related rate, like we did for labor cost. You can only enter unit- or use-related cost. If you pay a fixed amount for every use of a training room, you enter that cost in the **Cost/Use** field.

The best way to model time-related cost for facility and machine resources in Project 2002 is to enter the resource as a **Material** resource and use the *consumption rate* to model its time-related cost for the task. The consumption rate is entered into the assignment **Units** field, which is found in the Assign Resources dialog or the Task Form. For example, you organize training and the training room costs your project $600/day. You enter the resource *training room* as a **Material** resource in the Resource Sheet. You enter *600* as the **Std. Rate**. Then you create the *training* task and you assign the training room as the resource, and you enter *1/d* as the **Units** for the assignment, which means that you will use one room per day (as the consumption rate).

This will appear in the Gantt Chart as follows:

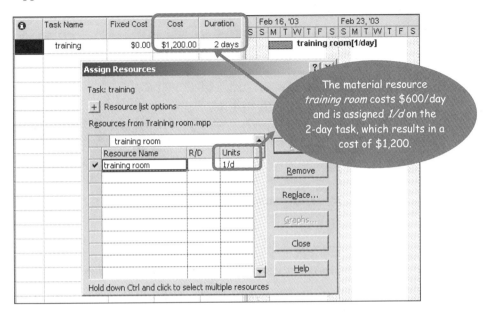

As you can see, we have used the consumption rate feature in MS Project to work around the lack of specific resource types for facilities. This same workaround can be used to model time-related cost for machines that you will need when you rent equipment, for example. Facility and machine costs are often accrued as prorated or at the end of a task.

Entering Varying Cost Rates

1. Varying cost rates can be entered in the cost rate table in the **Resource Information** dialog.

2. Select a resource and click 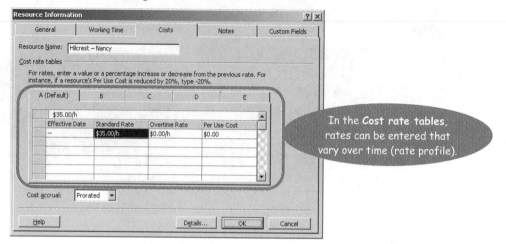; the **Resource Information** dialog appears. Click the tab **Costs** and the dialog will look like:

3. Enter the **Effective Date** and enter the rates that will apply after that date.

4. Repeat the previous step as many times as the rate will change over time.

5. Click [OK]. Project 2002 will calculate using the appropriate rate, which depends on when the task is scheduled over time.

In MS Project you can create rate profiles for all the different types of costs: **Standard Rate**, **Overtime Rate** and **Per Use Cost (Cost/Use)**.

Entering Fixed Cost in the Gantt Chart

The fixed cost has to be filled in as a task-related cost in the Gantt Chart in the column **Fixed Cost.**

1. Switch to the Gantt Chart view and insert the column **Fixed Cost** or apply the table **Cost**.

2. Enter the fixed cost value in the field **Fixed Cost**. Also indicate when the fixed cost will be accrued in the field **Fixed Cost Accrual.** Your choices are at the **Start** of the task, **Prorated** (during the task) or at the **End** (finish date).

3. MS Project will then calculate the total cost for the task in the field **Cost** as:
    Cost = Fixed Cost + (material costs) + (labor costs).
    The next snapshot shows the **Task Usage** view to illustrate this formula. The total

cost of $3,800 for the task *lay bricks* consists of *$600 fixed cost*, *$2,000* material cost for the bricks and *$1,200* labor cost for the bricklayers:

	Task Name	Fixed Cost	Cost	Duration	Work
1	⊟ lay bricks	$600.00	$3,800.00	5 days	40 hrs
	bricks		$2,000.00		1,000
	brick layers		$1,200.00		40 hrs

The **Cost** for the task is the total of **Fixed Cost**, material cost and labor cost.

Notice that if you enter any cost directly into the **Cost** field for a task, the cost is immediately interpreted as **Fixed Cost** by MS Project and transferred into that field.

Checks on the Resources

Resources and assignments should be entered for projects where it can be expected that limited resource availability or huge workloads will influence the project end date. The following checks need to be performed to verify whether the resources have been modeled well:

◆ Are all resources identified in the Resource Sheet?
This is the case if all resources that could have a potential impact on the scope, quality, duration or cost of the project are entered into the Resource Sheet.

◆ Are there no overlaps between the resources or duplication of resources?
If there are overlaps or duplications, the project manager cannot check the workloads of the individual resources. The workloads that will show up in the Resource Graph and in the Resource Usage can appear to be smaller than they really are when duplicate resources exist.

◆ Is the availability of the resources appropriately modeled?
This can be assessed by asking yourself the following questions:
◇ Does the availability of individuals not exceed 120% as captured in the resource field **Max. Units** and in the availability profile in **Resource Information**, tab **General**?
At the International Institute for Learning we had to set an arbitrary limit for schedule certification purposes and we choose this maximum of 120%. We think it is unreasonable to ask resources for more than 120% availability for periods longer than one week. In your organization the actual threshold may be lower than 120%.

◊   If the **Max. Units** are less than 100%, is there a valid reason for this?
Valid reasons are that the project manager works with pure work time estimates
(see page 169) or that the resources have other ongoing work or other concurrent
projects.

◊   Are the vacations of individual resources captured in their resource calendar?
To check this, choose the report **View, Reports, Assignments…**, **Who does
what**, click [Edit…], click tab **Details**, select ☑ **Calendar**, and
click [OK]. In print preview, you will now see individual vacations listed
under **Exceptions**. You can copy this changed report back into your
GLOBAL.MPT using **Tools, Organizer** to have it ready to go for future
schedule analysis.

◆   Are the costs of the resources appropriately modeled?
The following guidelines will help determine this:

◊   Are human resources entered as **Work** resources in the resource field **Type**? Are
facilities, machines and materials entered as **Material** resources?

◊   Do **Material** resources have an appropriate **Material Label** to indicate their unit
of measurement?

◊   Are the rates entered in the appropriate fields?

▪   Time-related costs for **Work** resources in the **Std. Rate** field

▪   Unit-related cost for **Material** resources in the **Std. Rate** field

▪   Time-related cost for facilities and machines as **Material** resources using a
combination of the **Std. Rate** field, where you enter the per-unit cost, and
the assignment-related **Units** field, where you indicate the number of units
used per time unit, for example *$1000/day* (see page 300)

▪   Use-related costs in the **Cost/Use** field

▪   Overtime costs in the **Ovt. Rate** field, but only if the overtime is paid at a
higher rate than the standard rate

▪   Rates that vary over time in the **Cost Rate Tables**

▪   Multiple rates in the **Cost Rate Tables** and the appropriate cost rate table
selected for each assignment

▪   Fixed costs in the task-related **Fixed Cost** field

◊   Is the cost scheduled appropriately?

▪   Does the resource-related **Accrue At** field reflect when the cost occurs: at
the **Start** or at the **End**, or **Prorated** with the **% Complete**?

- Does the task-related **Fixed Cost Accrual** field reflect when the fixed cost will be incurred?

Printing the Resource Sheet

Customizing the Table

1. Choose **View, Table: Entry, More Tables**; the **More Tables** dialog box appears:

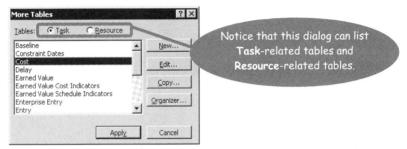

2. Select ⊙ **Resource** to display the list of resource-related tables. Select a table that is close to what you need and click Copy...; the **Table Definition** dialog appears:

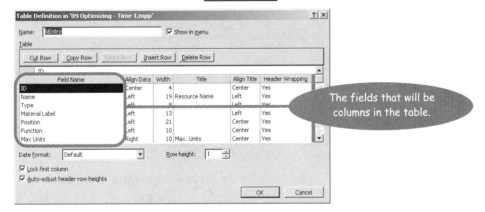

3. Change the name for the new table to a more descriptive name.

4. To add this table to the menu, check ☑ **Show in Menu**.

5. To delete a field from the table, select it and click Delete Row or press Delete.

6. To add a field to the table, click on the row before which to insert it and click Insert Row or press [Ins]. Then select the field from the list [_____▾].

7. Click [OK], then click [Apply].

 Extra columns you may have used (**Text1, Text2, … Number1, … Flag1, …**) can be permanently renamed by choosing **Tools, Customize, Fields**. This feature allows you to create new fields for resources like *Position* or *Telephone Number*. You can permanently rename these fields in the project database with [Rename…].

Sorting Resources Alphabetically

Choose **Project, Sort** and pick one of the predefined sorting orders, such as **By Cost, By Name** or **By ID**.
OR
To sort on other fields:

1. Choose **Project, Sort, Sort By…**. The **Sort** dialog appears:

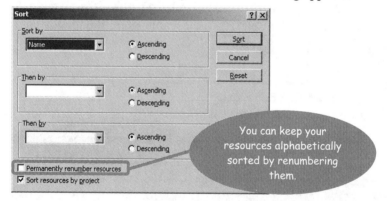

2. Then choose the first sort key in the **Sort By** list and the sorting order ⦿ **Ascending** or ⦿ **Descending**. If necessary, set a second key under **Then By** to break ties that may occur.

3. You can check the ☑ **Permanently Renumber** option to keep the resources sorted in the chosen order. This will ensure that the resources in all lists where resource names are shown are listed alphabetically.

4. Click [Sort] to effect the sorting.

Formatting the Text

1. Click on the menu items **Format**, **Text Styles**; the **Text Styles** dialog appears:

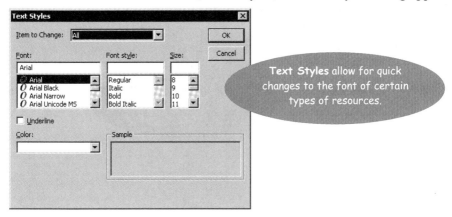

Text Styles allow for quick changes to the font of certain types of resources.

2. Choose from the list **Item to Change** the **Over-allocated resources** and notice that by default these critical resources are displayed in red.

3. Choose a color, font and appearance for the items and click [OK].

Formatting the Gridlines

1. Choose **Format, Gridlines…**. The **Gridlines** dialog appears:

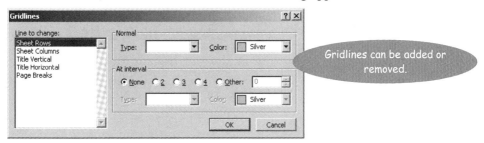

Gridlines can be added or removed.

2. Select an item in the list **Line to change** first, then select the **Type** of line for this item, its **Color** and **At Interval**.

3. Click [OK].

Choosing the Page Setup

1. Choose **File, Page Setup...**; the **Page Setup** dialog appears. Any changes you make in this dialog are stored in the current view, in our case the Resource Sheet, as the title of the dialog already suggests.

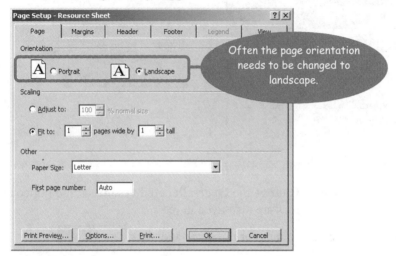

2. On the tab **Page** you can change the page orientation from **Portrait** to **Landscape**.

3. You can select the **Scaling** option to fit the report on a certain number of pages.

4. To insert headers, footers or a legend, review the instructions on page 261.

5. Choose the other options needed and click ⌗Print Preview...⌗ or ⌗Print...⌗ to see the results.

Previewing the Resource Spreadsheet

Choose **File**, **Print Preview** or click **Print Preview** on the **Standard** toolbar; the **Print Preview** screen appears:

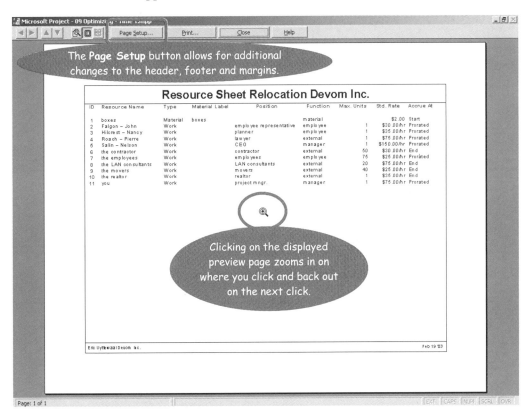

Exercises

Review A

Is it possible to model the following cost situations in MS Project? If so, how? If not, do you know a workaround?

1. Up-front fee of $500 for a bulldozer at a rate of $1000/d for onsite work

2. A consultant who charges $400/d until January 1, then $450/d

3. Car rental with free mileage for the first 100 miles, then a fee of $0.45/mile

4. Penalty of $1000/d for delivering late

5. Harry, who works as a business analyst at $500/d and as a systems analyst for $400/d

6. Volume discount for materials (for example, if you buy one door, it costs $150; if you buy 10 doors or more, they cost $90 each)

7. Pay an invoice within 30 days or pay a late charge of 10%

8. Overtime hours accumulated throughout the year and paid at the end of the year

9. Courier costs for packages

10. Low and high season hotel room rates (for example, in New York the hotel rates double in December)

Review B

Is it possible to model the following availability situations in MS Project? If so, how?

1. Movers who only work during the weekends

2. A freelancer who typically works on the weekend and delivers the work on Monday

3. Somebody who works a compressed workweek of 10 hours per day for 4 days

4. An expert resource that will be available to your project for 10% in March, 20% in April and 50% in May; after that she is unavailable

5. A part-time resource that only works mornings on Tuesdays and Thursdays

Review C

Which of the following resources should have its workload leveled in MS Project? (Enter a check mark in the appropriate cell.) Why?

Resource	Always Leveled	Never Leveled
1. expert		
2. computer		
3. mortar		
4. boardroom		

Relocation Project — Entering Resources

Continue to work with your file *Relocation.MPP* or open the file
07 Entering Resources.MPP that is available for download at www.jrosspub.com.
Below you will find the resources that will be needed in the relocation project. Notice
that there are generic resources in the list, like *movers*. You found their rates by
telephoning around. There is no **Cost/Use** for these resources.

Resource Name	Type	Material Label	Position	Function	Max. Units	Std. Rate	Accrue at
you [50]	*Work*		*project mngr.*	*manager*	*1*	*$75/h*	*Pro-rated*
Salin – Nelson	*Work*		*CEO*	*manager*	*1*	*$150/h*	*Pro-rated*
Falgon – John	*Work*		*employee representative*	*employee*	*1*	*$30/h*	*Pro-rated*
Hilcrest – Nancy	*Work*		*planner*	*employee*	*1*	*$35/h*	*Pro-rated*
Roach – Pierre	*Work*		*lawyer*	*external*	*1*	*$75/h*	*Pro-rated*
the employees	*Work*		*employees*	*employee*	*75*	*$25/h*	*Pro-rated*
the contractor	*Work*		*contrac-tor*	*external*	*50*	*$30/h*	*End*
the realtor	*Work*		*realtor*	*external*	*1*	*$35/h*	*End*
the movers	*Work*		*movers*	*external*	*40*	*$25/h*	*End*
the LAN consultants	*Work*		*LAN consul-tants*	*external*	*20*	*$75/h*	*End*
boxes	*mat-erial*	*boxes*		*material*		*$2*	*Start*

---

[50] Fill in your own name instead of "*you*".

1. Customize the table for the resource sheet view as shown in the table above. The fields *Position* and *Function* are not standard fields in MS Project. You can use the fields **Text1** and **Text2** and permanently rename them *Position* and *Function* respectively using the feature **Tools, Customize, Fields**.

2. Enter the resources in the table above. Use the **Fill Down** feature for the columns *Function* and *Accrue at*.

3. Sort the list of resources on resource *Name* as the first sorting key. Select the option to permanently renumber the resources.

4. You decided that you yourself are going to work regular working hours.
You are pressured to jump-start the project by working longer hours, but you decided to resist that pressure. The rest of the team will keep regular working hours as well.

5. *Nancy Hilcrest* will go on a 1-week holiday in the third full week of August 2004.

6. You realize that due to the project requirement that the disruption to normal company operations should be minimal, the move will have to take place over the weekend. For the *Movers* set all the weekdays to nonworking days and the weekend days to working days, so the move will take place on a weekend. The *Movers* will work 8 hours per day.

7. Compare your file with the solution file *08 Entering Assignments.MPP* that is available for download at www.jrosspub.com. Save your file for the next exercise.

Relocation Project — Printing the Resource Sheet

1. Continue to work with the file from the previous exercise.

2. Apply the following **Format, Text Styles**:

Item to Change	Font	Font Style	Size
All	*Arial*	*Regular*	*10*
Row & Column Titles	*Arial*	*Bold*	*10*

3. Enter the following **File, Page Setup** settings:

Tab	Section	Set to	Font
Page	Orientation	Landscape	
	Scaling	Fit to: 1 pages wide by 1 tall	
Margins	Top, Bottom, Left, Right	1 Inch	
	Borders Around	Every page	
Header	Center	&[View] &[Project Title]	Arial Bold 20
Footer	Left	&[Manager] &[Company]	
	Right	&[Date]	Arial Regular 8

4. Apply the following **Format, Gridlines**:

Line to Change	Normal – Type
Sheet Rows	blank (at top of list)
Sheet Columns	blank (at top of list
Title Vertical	blank (at top of list)
Title Horizontal	blank (at top of list)

5. Compare your file with a printout of the solution file *08 Entering Assignments.MPP* that is available for download at www.jrosspub.com.

Troubleshooting

1. Open the file *Last Name First Name.MPP* that is available for download at www.jrosspub.com. Enter your first name in the resource sheet, and then enter your last name. Questions:

   ◇ Why does the first name show up in two fields?

   ◇ Why does the second entry override the first one?

2. Create a new project file and try entering the resource *Smith, Harry*. Why does Project 2002 not allow you to do that?

Chapter 8 Entering Assignments

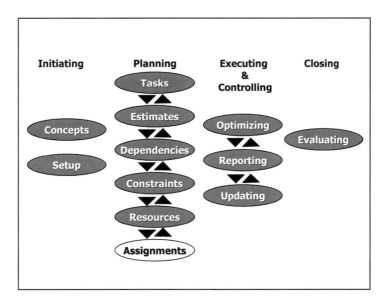

The assignments are the last type of data to enter into our project model (see the white highlight in the illustration above). After completing this chapter we will have a complete model of our project, but most likely the model will not meet all the time and budgetary constraints. We will address that in the next chapter on optimizing.

After reading this chapter you will:
◆ know what an assignment is as well as part-time and full-time assignments
◆ know the difference between Fixed Duration, Fixed Units and Fixed Work tasks
◆ be able to enter each type of task into MS Project
◆ know how to assign resources to tasks using the Assign Resources dialog or the Task Form
◆ be able to enter part-time, full-time, overtime and multiple assignments
◆ know how to make changes to assignments and predict the resulting calculations by MS Project
◆ be able to check the assignments of the project schedule using scheduling best practices
◆ know how to create a report of the assignments

Mr. Ambiguity and Friends

Nob is making the rounds in his office. He greets Mary, the system analyst on his project, and gestures her to sit down with him. "Have you started the system analysis on the web-enabling feature?" he asks.

Mary responds: "No, I haven't actually ... perhaps Richard has. Ask him."

Nob walks off to find Richard. He soon finds him: "Hey, Rich, did you start the systems analysis for my project?" Richard replies: "I was actually waiting for Lisa to call a short meeting so we can split up the responsibilities; did you ask her?"

Nob wobbles off to find Lisa. When he finds her, she tells him that she thought Mary was the lead and that she should take the initiative.

Nob: "Mary didn't say she is the lead. I can't believe the miscommunication that is happening to me ... again!"

He complains about it to Bob, who asks to see his project plan. Bob only needs one glance and says: "I see what's wrong! You have all three people assigned against this big task 32: *perform system analysis*."

Nob says: "Yes, all three are responsible for making it happen. They will have to work together on it." "But nobody is taking the initiative, are they?" Bob reacts. Nob: "I just told Lisa to get them organized." Bob fires back immediately: "So you have solved this one, but look at your schedule; you have assigned two or more people to most of your tasks. You will be running around coordinating these people all the time!" Nob: "Well, on the other hand, I kept my task list nice and short, didn't I? Only 100 tasks for this huge project, that is not bad!" Bob wonders out loud: "Yes, but does your schedule work as a delegation instrument? I always assign only one person to a detail activity, except for meetings of course. I may end up with more activities than you do, but I never have to deal with Mr. Ambiguity and his friends!"

What Is an Assignment?

An assignment is a combination of one task and one resource. An assignment reflects who works on the task. In the illustration below, *Mary* is assigned to *write report, edit report* and *print report*. Assigning the resource is also called *resource loading*, and the result is a *resource-loaded schedule*.

Each of the three data entities, tasks, resources and assignments, has its own specific fields. Some fields may be called the same but contain different information depending on the entity to which they belong. I will discuss three examples in more detail:
- Start and Finish dates
- Max. Units (resource-related) and Units (assignment-related)
- Work

Tasks, resources and assignments all have **Start** and **Finish** dates. The start date of a task is not necessarily the same as the start date of its assignments. The start date of an assignment is when one of the resources starts working on the task. If Mary only works the last 2 days of the 5-day task, the start date of her assignment is different from the start date of the task. The start date of a resource is when her earliest assignment starts on the project.

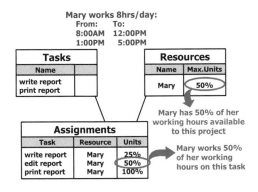

The second example is the resource field **Max. Units** and the assignment field **Units**. The **Max. Units** field of a resource reflects the maximum availability of the resource to the project. For example, the **Max. Units** would be 100% for a person who is entirely available to the project and 50% for a resource who is available half of her working hours. In the illustration, *Mary* has **Max. Units** of 50%; she has only *50%* of her working hours available to this project. We discussed resource availability on page 287. The assignment-related field **Units** is the percentage of her working hours (set in the resource calendar) the resource is working on the task. In the illustration Mary works a regular workweek, and a 50% assignment means for her 50% * 8 hours = 4 hours of effort on the task per day. If Burke works a compressed workweek of 4 days a week and 10 hours per day, a 50% assignment means 5 hours of effort on the task per day.

The assignment-related field **Units** reflects:

◆ whether a person works full-time or part-time on the task, or

◆ how many individuals of a consolidated resource are needed on the task (see page 294 for a definition of a consolidated resource).

In other words, **Max. Units** represents availability, whereas assignment **Units** represents involvement in a task.

If you want a resource to work all her working hours on the task, enter 100% in the field **Units** on the Task Form. If you enter less than 100%, you are asking the resource to work part of her available time on the task. You have assigned the resource to the task *part-time*. To create a part-time assignment, enter a percentage as the units on the assignment. In the illustration on the previous page, *Mary* will work *50%* of her working hours on the task *edit report*, which happens to equal her maximum availability to the project. The assignment units can be changed quickly in the **Assign Resources** dialog.

The third and last example of how a task-related field is different from its assignment-related field is the field **Work**. The field **Work** for tasks in the Gantt spreadsheet is not the same as the field **Work** in the Resource Sheet, nor is it the same as

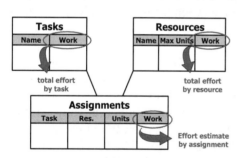

the assignment-related field **Work** on the Task Form. They are all called the same: **Work**. In the Gantt Chart **Work** is the total effort of all resources working on the task. In the Resource Sheet, **Work** is the total effort for the resource in the entire project. (For material resources, it is the total number of units used in the project.) On the Task Form, you can see the assignment-related **Work** field, which displays the effort of one resource on a particular task.

Assignments can be found in either the **Task Usage** view, where they show up as resource names indented below the task name, or in the **Resource Usage** view, where they show up as tasks indented below the resource name. You can easily recognize them because they have no ID number, their text is in italics and their timescale data have a lighter yellow background.

Double-click on an assignment and the **Assignment Information** dialog will appear with only assignment-related fields.

Full-Time or Part-Time Assignment

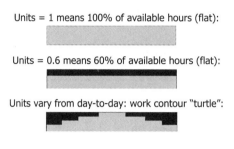

Units = 1 means 100% of available hours (flat):

Units = 0.6 means 60% of available hours (flat):

Units vary from day-to-day: work contour "turtle":

In both the 100% and 60% assignment in the illustration, the work of the resource will be spread evenly across the duration of the task. The work (effort) is spread in a flat pattern. You can spread the work over the task duration in different, predefined patterns; Project 2002 calls these *work contours*. There are eight predefined work contours, but you can also spread the work over the task duration yourself.

Some remarks about work contours:

◆ You can apply one of the predefined work contours using the **Assignment Information** dialog. If you double-click on an assignment in either the **Task Usage** or the **Resource Usage** view, the **Assignment Information** dialog will be displayed. You can then select a predefined contour from the list **Work contour**. MS Project will maintain the pattern of the contour when the duration or the work is changed, even when the task is already started.

◆ You can even fill in, on a day-by-day basis, how many hours you need from the resource over the duration of the task. You can enter the needed hours directly into the **Work** field in the timescale of the **Task Usage** view. This level of detail is seldom needed in the planning of projects.

If you do decide to enter numbers in the timescale yourself, you will spend a lot of time maintaining your schedule. In particular, if you enter the required hours on a day-by-day basis, you will have a lot of data to maintain. We do not recommend it because the chance is real that you will abandon your schedule during project execution when you are simply too busy to maintain the amount of data.

Choosing the Options

The assignment-related options are shown in the following table. Before creating assignments consider the most appropriate settings for these options. Choose **Tools, Options** to change them.

Tab	Option
Schedule	**Show assignment units as a:** `Percentage` ▼ **Percentage** is the best choice when you have part-time resources; if there are consolidated resources, **Decimal** is better. This option is a generic option; if you change it to **decimal** in one project, all your projects will use decimal numbers.
	Duration is entered in: `Days` ▼ Choose the default time unit to avoid having to key in the "*d*" of "*5d*" in the field **Duration** if set to **Days**.
	Work is entered in: `Hours` ▼ Choose the default time unit to avoid having to key in the "*h*" of "*5h*" in the field **Work** if set to **Hours**.
	Default task type: `Fixed Units` ▼ Choose the type of task for any new tasks you create. This option is meant to be a time-saver. See the next section titled *Types of Detail Tasks* for more explanation.
	☐ **New Tasks are effort driven** This option can lead to Project 2002 changing assignment units for you. For now, we recommend you turn it off. See the next section titled *Types of Detail Tasks* for more explanation.
	`Set as Default` Sets the options above (except the first one) as the default settings for any new projects you create. Existing projects are not affected because these options (except the first one) are stored in the project file. You can read this from the label of the section divider: **Scheduling Options for <file name of the project>**.

Types of Detail Tasks

For each assignment there are three variables:

◆ *Duration* is the length of a task expressed in *business days*.

◆ *Units* reflect the percentage of one resource assigned to a task, or the number of people assigned from a pooled resource. For a resource working half his available hours it would be 50%, for a resource working all available hours 100% and for two resources working all available hours 200%. You can change it to **Decimal** numbers via **Tools, Options,** tab **Schedule** in the field **Show assignments as a**. The **Units** field would then display 0.5, 1 and 2 respectively.

◆ *Work* is the amount of effort expressed in person hours or person days. A *person day* is one person working one day full-time.

MS Project uses the following *formula* for these variables: *Duration * Units = Work*

	Duration	* Units	= Work
Fixed Duration meeting	2 h	8	.....
Fixed Units budget	.....	1	6 h
Fixed Work write report	.....	2	10 h

There are three kinds of detail tasks: *Fixed Duration*, *Fixed Units* and *Fixed Work*. It is not a coincidence that each type relates to one of the variables in the formula. As their names indicate, each of the three fixes one of the three variables in the formula. If you set a task to be Fixed Duration, MS Project will never change this duration on its own. That is a comforting thought, particularly if you have been haunted in the past by numbers being changed by MS Project that you did not want changed.

If you then enter the second value, MS Project will calculate the third one for you with the formula. For example, if you have a task *meeting* with a fixed duration of 2 business hours, and you invite 8 people to the meeting, Project 2002 will calculate 16 person hours of work. Another example: a task *write report* with 10 person hours fixed work could be worked on by two people and Project 2002 will calculate a duration of 5 business hours. When entering the data the first time, most of your tasks will be either Fixed Duration or Fixed Work. The Fixed Units task type is useful when you start making changes to the assignment and you want to keep the number of resources that are working on it the same.

 Of course, you could ask yourself at this point: *Why is MS Project recalculating all these values constantly?* The answer is that if it did not calculate them, you would definitely need your calculator when you enter data and make many calculations yourself.

MS Project tries to help you, and it uses the assumption that every resource is equally efficient, which is not true of course. However, in 90% of the cases, this assumption is accurate enough for modeling purposes. Remember that we are deliberately simplifying the reality when we model projects. We try to approach reality as closely as possible but with as little effort as possible. We are not trying to recreate reality in all its complexity in our computer when we schedule. Many project managers seem to forget this when they get going with MS Project.

The following table suggests the best use for each task type:

Type of task	Use in situations like:
Fixed Duration	♦ If the duration does not decrease when human resources are added, such as when backing up a computer system. ♦ Tasks that always have more than one resource assigned, such as meetings and training. ♦ When the deadline is so tight that it is the primary driver for the duration of the task. You have to make it work within that time frame. ♦ When the workload is not your problem, e.g., for external resources, such as subcontractors and consultants.
Fixed Units (default)	♦ When you cannot get more resources to do the work, for example, you only have two internal resources. ♦ When you want to change the duration or the work on a task while keeping the number of people working on the task the same (assignment units). We will discuss this on page 341. ♦ When you want to keep the resource working on a task at a certain percentage of his available hours.
Fixed Work	♦ When the effort required is the first thing you estimate. ♦ When the effort required is the easiest thing to estimate. This is often the case. For example, you estimate that painting a home takes 12 person days of effort. A software project manager may estimate that coding a module in an application will take 20 person hours. Estimating effort is easier than estimating duration because you don't need to take resource availability and holidays into account.

The formula does not apply to tasks that have assignments with a *work contour* (that spreads the effort in a certain pattern over the duration of the task). Nor does it apply to tasks with multiple assignments where one assignment is longer than the others (*multiple, uneven assignments*). In the last situation you would find that the formula still applies on the level of each individual assignment.

Three Rules to Make MS Project a Tool for You

We would like to suggest three rules to follow when you start entering or changing assignments. If you do so, MS Project will become your obedient servant instead of *an obnoxious piece of software with an attitude*. If you don't look at the task *Type* when working with MS Project, it will inevitably recalculate values that you did not want to change. You can even end up in an endless loop with MS Project, if you keep changing the value that MS Project just recalculated.

The rules for working pleasantly with MS Project are:

1. Enter the original duration or work estimate and fix that number by setting the task **Type** accordingly. Fixing it prevents MS Project from changing it.
   ◇ If you enter a **Duration** estimate, set the task **Type** to **Fixed Duration**.
   ◇ If you enter a **Work** estimate, set the task **Type** to **Fixed Work**.

2. Provide the second value in the formula *Duration * Units = Work* and let MS Project calculate the third value.
   If you created a fixed duration task, assign the resources you need and let MS Project calculate the work. If you created a fixed work task, assign the resources and let MS Project calculate the duration. If you entered the duration and the work, MS Project only needs to know who will do the task and it will calculate the number of resources needed.

3. Before making a change to any of the three values in the formula, you ask yourself: *What type of task do I need for this particular change?* More on this below.

Changing an Assignment

 Before you change any of the three values in the formula $D * U = W$, you should always first think about the task type you need for that change. With every change, Project 2002 will recalculate one other value, and it may not recalculate the one you want if you don't think about the task type first.

Changes that will trigger a recalculation are, among others:
- Changing the duration (D) of a task by editing the value or by stretching the task bar with the mouse
- Adding a resource to a task, or removing a resource, changes the units (U)
- Changing the work (W) of a task or of one of its assignments

The **Type** of the task and the **Effort Driven** attribute determine how MS Project will react. We suggest these steps to change an assignment:

1. Choose and set the task **Type** first.
    You can determine the appropriate task type by asking yourself: *Which value do I want to keep the same?* The answer to this question will tell you which task type you need. For example, if you want to keep the assigned units the same while you change the work, you should set the **Type** to **Fixed Units**. If you want to keep the total amount of work on the task the same while you change the duration or units, you need **Fixed Work**.

2. Ensure **Effort Driven** is set to *Yes* only for **Fixed Work** tasks; for **Fixed Duration** or **Fixed Units** tasks it should be *No*.

3. Then make the change that you wanted to make on the assignment.
    MS Project will recalculate the third value. For example, if you change the **Work** on a **Fixed Units** task, MS Project will recalculate the **Duration**.

 4. Note that you never change the value that you fixed with the task type. For example, you never change the duration when the task type is Fixed Duration. If you do this, you are not controlling what MS Project recalculates. You have to change the task type first before making the change.

 The task **Type** is not something you set once and never look at again. You continue to monitor it in order to control how Project 2002 calculates. If you reconsider the type of task first, you will always be able to predict what MS Project will do.

Here is an example of how this works. Assume you have a Fixed Units task *write* of 4 days in duration with one resource assigned and you want to add a second resource.

This will show in Project 2002 as:

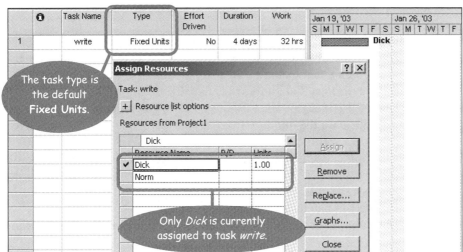

Let's say you want Project 2002 to keep the **Duration** the same when you add the resource. First, you change the task **Type** to *Fixed Duration*, **Effort Driven** to *No*, then you add the second resource, which doubles the Work (*32 hrs* to *64 hrs*):

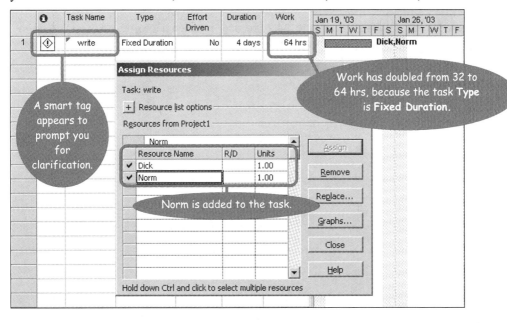

If you want to add a resource to a **Fixed Duration** task, the work goes up. Alternatively, if you add a resource to a **Fixed Work** task, the duration will go down.

Often you will find that you want to keep the assigned units the same on a task while changing the duration or the work. In this case you will need the **Fixed Units** task type. This task type is most common when making changes. For example, if you change the work on a **Fixed Units** task, Project 2002 will recalculate the duration. If the Duration = 10 days, Units = 1 (fixed), Work = 10 days and you change the work to 5 days, Project 2002 will decrease the duration from 10 to 5 days; one person can deliver 5 person days of effort (work) within 5 business days (duration). We will also use this task type when we update our schedule (see chapter 11 on page 539).

When there are multiple assignments, one (or more) of the assignments can drive the duration of the task. Before you can make a change, you should find out which assignment(s) drives the duration of the task. Consider changing that assignment instead of the task.

Notice that when you apply the task type **Fixed Work** the attribute *Effort Driven* is automatically turned on by Project 2002. When you change to a different task type again, the **Effort Driven** attribute stays on. If you leave it set to *Yes,* it may create unexpected recalculations. You can display the task-related field **Effort Driven** and quickly toggle it to *No*. Effort-driven tasks act very similar to Fixed Work tasks and seem redundant.

To replace a resource with another one, MS Project provides a shortcut. Use the **Assign Resources** dialog , select the assigned resource and click Replace... . Select the new one and click OK .

Assigning and the Types of Tasks

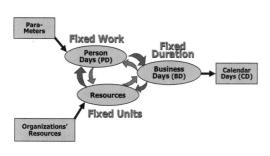

On page 160 we discussed the process of estimating, which is shown in the illustration. We recommended using Fixed Duration or Fixed Work tasks when first entering estimates. It is important to be aware of the task type when you assign resources, because each type of task makes Project 2002 calculate differently. For example, Project 2002 will never recalculate the duration on a fixed duration task (without prompting), and if you add a second resource, it will double the total work on the task following the formula *Duration * Units = Work*. We will therefore insert the column **Type**, so we can see at any point what type of task we are working with.

You may also want to insert the field *Effort Driven* because you want to keep this field set to *No* (except for Fixed Work tasks, which are always effort driven). The Effort Driven attribute works similar to the Fixed Work task type as is clear from the fact that Fixed Work tasks are always effort driven.

We recommend keeping **Effort Driven** off to keep things simple. Insert the field **Work** as well, and the layout of columns we recommend is as follows:

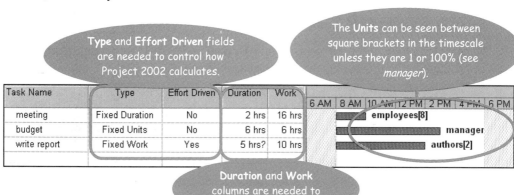

We can now see all three variables of the formula *Duration * Units = Work*
with the *Units* visible in the timescale to the right of the task bars between square
brackets following the resource name (unless the units are 1 or 100%). You could also
insert the column **Resource Names**. This field displays the number of resources as well,
but the column is often too narrow.

If there are multiple resources assigned to a task, you have to sum the units to arrive at
the number used in the formula.

Designing the View for Assigning Resources

1. Choose **View, Gantt Chart**.

2. Choose **View, Table <current table name>, Entry**; the **Entry** table is applied that
   has the columns: ❶ , **Task Name, Duration, Start, Finish, Predecessors** and
   Resource Names respectively.

3. We will insert the column **Type** before the column **Duration**. Right-click on the
   column **Duration** and choose **Insert Column...** from the pop-up menu; the
   Column Definition dialog appears:

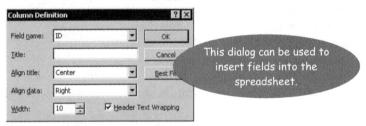

4. Select from the list **Field Name** the column **Type** and click [OK].

5. Repeat steps 3 and 4 for the fields **Effort Driven** and **Work**; we recommend you
   insert them in the order indicated in the snapshot below:

Task Name	Type	Effort Driven	Duration	Work	6 AM	8 AM	10 AM	12 PM	2 PM	4 PM	6 PM
meeting	Fixed Duration	No	2 hrs	16 hrs		employees[8]					
budget	Fixed Units	No	6 hrs	6 hrs				manager			
write report	Fixed Work	Yes	5 hrs?	10 hrs		authors[2]					

Entering a Fixed Duration Task

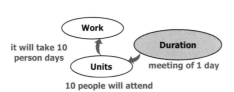

When the duration is fixed, changes in assignments or total work will not affect it. Examples of *fixed duration tasks* are *training session* and *meeting*. The duration of a training session or meeting is typically set and will not vary (much) with the number of participants, a perfect candidate for fixed duration. In the illustration, we see a training with a 1 day fixed duration. If 10 people attend, the total work will be calculated as 10 person days.

1. In the Gantt spreadsheet enter the task name and set the task **Type** to **Fixed Duration**. Enter the duration.

2. Enter the work estimate in the field **Work** or assign the resources in the required number of units. We will discuss this on page 335.

3. MS Project will have calculated the third variable in the formula $D * U = W$ (where D = Duration, U = Assignment Units and W = Work).

 MS Project schedules fixed duration tasks with more than one person assigned sometimes with a split task bar when one of the resources is not available when the others are working. This looks strange for a task such as a *meeting*, because the split task bar suggests that there will be two meetings. You can solve this by removing the resource from one of the two tasks.

Entering a Fixed Work Task

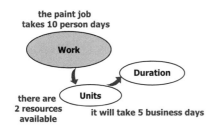

Fixed work tasks are very common. A task is a fixed work task if the first thing you estimate is the amount of effort (work). Once you fix the work, MS Project will calculate either the duration or the necessary number of resources. In the illustration to the left, we see the paint job is estimated to take 10 person days of work. If 2 people do this job, it will take 5 business days of duration.

1. In the Gantt spreadsheet, enter the task name and set the task **Type** to **Fixed Work**. Enter the total work on the task in the field **Work**.

2. Enter the available duration or assign the resources in the number of units required; we will discuss how to do this on the next pages.

3. MS Project will have calculated the third variable in the formula $D * U = W$ (where D = Duration, U = Units and W = Work).

Entering a Fixed Units Task

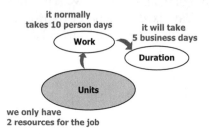

For fixed units tasks you know the number of resources available for the task. You want the duration or total work to be calculated by Project 2002. The illustration on the left shows an example in which there are 2 resources available for the job (*Units*). You know it normally takes 10 person days of *Work*. The *Duration* MS Project will calculate is 5 business days. You entered two values and MS Project calculated the third.

The **Fixed Units** task type is mostly used when you want to make changes to the task or its assignments. The Fixed Units task type allows you to keep the assigned units the same when you change the work or the duration.

1. In the Gantt spreadsheet set the task **Type** to **Fixed Units**.

2. Change the duration, or the work of the task.

3. MS Project will have calculated the third variable in the formula $D * U = W$ (where D = Duration, U = Units and W = Work).

Overview of Assigning

The following are the many different ways you can assign resources to tasks. The methods are listed from simple (and quick) to sophisticated (and cumbersome):

◆ **Task Sheet** view
   ◇ Assigning multiple resources is not easy.
   ◇ Adjusting the **Units** of resources is not easy.

◆ **Assign Resources** dialog box
   ◇ You can assign or replace resources.
   ◇ You can specify units or work by assignment.

◆ **Task Information** dialog box
   ◇ You can assign units or work.
   ◇ You can enter multiple assignments simultaneously.
   ◇ You have to display the dialog for every task.

◆ **Task Form** view
   ◇ You can assign units and work.
   ◇ You can enter multiple assignments simultaneously.
   ◇ The form stays on the screen.

◆ **Task Usage** or **Resource Usage** view
   You can assign work "day-by-day" and create varying workloads. Only in the **Task Usage** or **Resource Usage** view can you enter workloads that vary over the duration of the task. In all other situations, you create a flat workload when assigning. Generally, a flat workload is a good enough approximation of the true workload. If it isn't, you should consider breaking up the tasks into smaller tasks or using the work contour feature. Predefined *work contours* allow you to spread the work across the task duration in a certain pattern. See pages 319 and 339 for more on work contours.

 There are many ways to assign resources to tasks. The more sophisticated the method, the more detail it allows you to enter about the assignment. It is important to enter only as much detail as you need, because all data need to be maintained for the life of the project. During project execution, you will have little time to maintain the schedule.

We will discuss two methods in more detail: **Assign Resources** dialog and the **Task Form** view. The Assign Resources dialog allows you to drag resources onto tasks and is fast. The Task Form allows you to enter the units and the work for one or more resources at a time and is flexible. Together these two methods will give you the speed and the flexibility you may need.

 Project 2002 has a **Resources** project guide that helps you with assigning resources to tasks. Display the project guide toolbar by right-clicking on any toolbar and choosing **Project Guide**. Click Resources and then the hyperlink **Assign people and equipment to tasks**. It will make use of the Assign Resources dialog and the Task Form where needed; and you will need to know how to work with those, as we will now explain.

Assign Using the Assign Resources Dialog

 The assign resources dialog was nicely improved in that:

◆ It lists all the resources that are assigned to the task at the top of the list. Every time you click on a task you can now always immediately see which resources are assigned.

◆ It sorts the rest of the list alphabetically regardless what the sort order is in the resource sheet.

◆ It provides filtering options to determine who is available.

Assigning Resources by Dragging

1. Click ; the **Assign Resources** floating dialog appears:

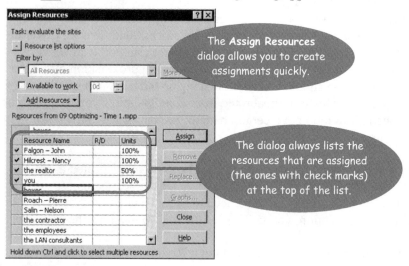

2. Click on the resource to assign.

3. Point to the resource selector ▨ in front of the resource name; the mouse pointer now has a person's (decapitated!) head attached:

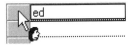

4. Hold down, drag and drop the resource onto the task you want to assign to. The resource is now assigned; it has a check mark in front of its name. It also shows in the field **Resource Names** and to the right of the task bar in the timescale.

When you drag resources onto tasks, Project 2002 assigns:

◆ the maximum availability (**Max. Units**) of individual resources
◆ only one unit of consolidated resources

You may need to edit the number of units.

Assigning Multiple Resources to Multiple Tasks

1. Click 🖼; the **Assign Resources** floating dialog appears.

2. Select the tasks to assign by dragging over them.
   OR

   Select them by holding down [Control] and clicking, if you want to randomly select tasks.

3. Select the resource you want to assign or select multiple resources to assign by holding down [Control] and clicking on their resource selector ▨ in the **Assign Resources** dialog:

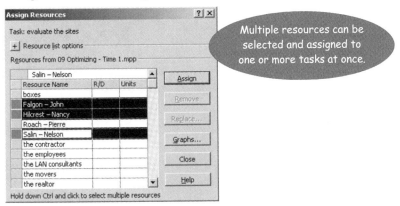

4. Click [Assign]; a check mark appears in the resource selector: [✓].

Checking Availability before Assigning

 In Project 2002, you can check if the resource is available while you are making the assignments. We recommend you use this feature to prevent over-allocations from occurring in the first place rather than sorting them out later.

1. Select the task to assign resources to. This is an important step because MS Project checks the availability of resources between the start and finish date of the task that is currently selected.

2. Insert the column **Work** by right-clicking on a column heading and choosing **Insert column**. Select **Work** from the list **Field name** and click [OK]. In this field you can see how much effort is required in total on the task.

3. Click [ ]; the **Assign Resources** dialog appears.

4. Check ☑ **Available to work** and enter the amount of effort that you need from the resource in the field to the right of it. MS Project will immediately list only the resources with enough availability (between the start and finish date of the selected task). This prevents you from having to switch to the Resource Usage view and back to make one assignment.

   OR

   Select the resource(s) in the list and click [Graphs...]; a chart will appear with the **Work** charted. In the list **Select Graph**, you can change **Work** to **Remaining Availability** to check availability.

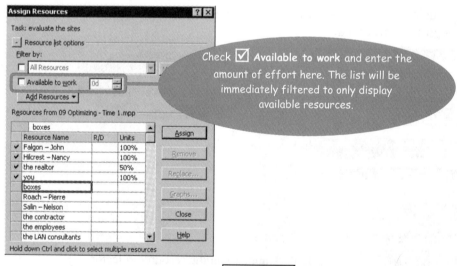

5. Select the resource to assign and click [Assign].

6. Make sure you uncheck ☐ **Available to work** again so that you see the entire list of resources again for the next task.

To Enter the Units on an Assignment

1. Select the task.

2. Click ; the **Assign Resources** dialog appears.

3. Enter the percentage of the resource's available working hours or the number of resources you need in the field **Units**. Units should be entered as a percentage or as decimals, depending on the setting in **Tools, Options,** tab **Schedule,** field **Show assignments units as**.

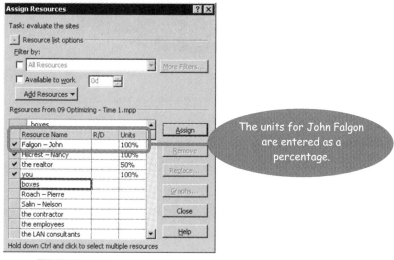

4. Click | Assign |.

5. In the field **R/D** you can indicate whether the assignment is a **Request** or a **Demand**, i.e., if the resource is requested to work on the task or must work on the task to complete it successfully. This is only relevant when your executives use the *Portfolio Modeler* in *Project Server*. You don't need to click | Assign | again.

If you change the units on an assignment or add or remove a resource, Project 2002 may (re)calculate the work if it is a **Fixed Duration** task, or the duration if it is a **Fixed Work** task.

The **Units** field asks for units to be entered, but you can even enter the work in this field and Project 2002 will calculate the units required. If you want to do so, you have to make sure you include the time unit, as in *5d*, to make it clear that Project 2002 should interpret your entry as person days of work instead of as units.

To Delete an Assignment in the Assign Resources Dialog

1. Display the **Assign Resources** dialog by clicking 🔲.

2. Look at the check marks 🔲 in front of the resource names that indicate which resources are assigned to the selected task(s).

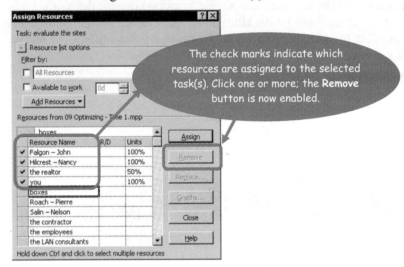

3. Select the resource to be removed.

4. Click [Remove].

Assign Using the Task Form

Fields in the Task Form

◆ *Name*
A descriptive title for the task.

◆ *Duration*
How long the task will take. Type a number followed by an abbreviation indicating the time unit. For example, *4d* means *4 business days* (of 8 hours). By default, duration is working time only, but it can also be entered as elapsed time, which includes holidays, weekends, vacations and nights (if you enter *4ed* it means *4 days of 24 hours*).

◆ *Effort Driven*
Effort driven will keep the total amount of work constant while adding or removing resources. This option only kicks in after entering the assignments the first time. It will redistribute the work among the resources when adding or removing resources (keeping the relative workloads the same). Fixed work tasks are always effort driven.

◆ *Start*
MS Project automatically calculates the start date based on task dependencies. If you enter a date, MS Project sets a Start-No-Earlier-Than constraint date for the task under *forward scheduling*, which forces the program to schedule the task on or after that date. We don't recommend entering dates because the constraints make the model less dynamic.

◆ *Finish*
MS Project calculates the finish date based on the start date plus the total duration. If you type a date, MS Project sets a Finish-No-Earlier-Than constraint for the task under *forward scheduling*. We don't recommend entering dates.

◆ *Task Type*
Detail tasks come in three kinds: Fixed Duration tasks, Fixed Units tasks, and Fixed Work tasks.

◆ *% Complete*
This percentage shows how much of the task duration is completed. We will discuss this in chapter 11 on updating schedules (see page 539).

To Assign with the Task Form

1. In the Gantt Chart, choose **Window, Split**.
   OR
   Double-click on the sliding window handle at the bottom right of the screen to display the Task Form:

The sliding window handle

2. On the Task Form we need to see at least the fields **Resource Name**, **Units** and **Work**. To display these click on the Task Form and choose **Format**, **Details**, **Resource Work**.
OR
Right-click on the Task Form and choose **Resource Work**. The Task Form now looks like:

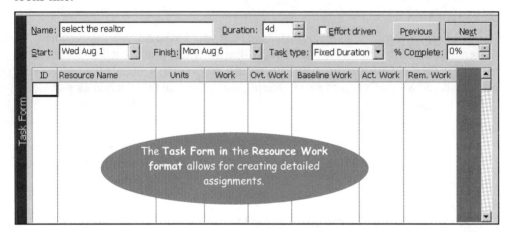

3. On the Task Form click in the field **Resource Name** and a list button will appear:

4. Click the list button and select a resource from the list that appears. Enter the **Units** (the percentage of the available working hours) and/or the **Work** (person hours of effort needed). You can assign more than one resource at a time, which is easy to do with this form.

5. Click [OK] once all resources are assigned. All new assignments are entered into the project model simultaneously upon clicking it. This makes this method better for assigning multiple resources with specific **Units** or **Work** values; you are not triggering a recalculation with every assignment you add, unlike the **Assign Resources** dialog.

To Delete an Assignment in the Task Form

Display the **Task Form**, select the resource, press [Delete] and click [OK].

Assigning to Recurring Tasks

If you assign a resource on the summary *recurring task* with the **Assign Resources** dialog, the assignments are immediately transferred to the detail tasks. This is done automatically, compliments of Project 2002.

3 Status Meeting   ⊠   ⊠   ⊠ Team
    3.1 Status meeting 1 ⊠ Team
    3.2 Status meeting 2   ⊠ Team
    3.3 Status meeting 3   ⊠ Team

In the illustration on the left, the resource *Team* is assigned to the recurring summary task *3 Status Meeting* and is transferred by MS Project to the recurring detail tasks. That is where you want the assignments.

You can assign to recurring tasks in situations such as:

◆ Long meetings: They tend to be lengthy and therefore require considerable effort (work) from the resources.

◆ Short meetings: You require attendance at short meetings and you want to show them as assignments in the to-do lists of team members.

You should only assign to recurring tasks, such as status meetings, if the efforts for these meetings are not included in the work estimates that your team members provided to you.

Assigning to recurring detail tasks can easily result in over-allocations that MS Project's leveling features will not resolve. The reason is that MS Project excludes recurring tasks from the leveling process by setting the field **Level Assignments** to **No** for the recurring detail tasks. You could switch it to **Yes** but then your recurring tasks may be rescheduled, which is probably not what you want. We recommend you keep the meetings short and ignore the over-allocations.

Entering Multiple, Uneven Assignments

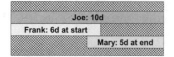

If there are multiple assignments on a task, often one of the assignments drives the duration of the task. The assignment that takes the longest to complete will drive the duration of the task. The illustration on the left shows that three painters, *Joe*, *Frank* and *Mary*, are assigned to paint a house. *Joe* will work 10 days, *Frank* only the first 6 days and *Mary* only the last 5 days, so the duration will be 10 days. *Joe* determines or "drives" the duration of the paint job.

To create *multiple, uneven assignments* on a task you need to:

1. Display the Task Form in the Gantt Chart by choosing **Window, Split**.

2. Change the details in the Task Form to show assignment start dates by clicking on the Task Form and choosing **Format, Details, Resource Schedule**
   OR
   right-clicking in the gray area of the Task Form and choosing **Resource Schedule**.

3. To enter multiple uneven assignments, set the task **Type** to **Fixed Units** in the Task Form. Click OK.

4. Click in the field **Resource Name** and select a resource to assign from the list that appears. Repeat this for all resources to assign and enter different amounts of **Work** for each assigned resource. Enter a specific **Start** date OR enter a **Delay** for each assignment.

5. Click OK; you can see the result of the uneven assignments by choosing **View, Task Usage**. The result of the example above would look like:

Task Name	Details	Dec 31, 00							Jan 7, 01					
		S	M	T	W	T	F	S	S	M	T	W	T	F
⊟ write	Work		16h	16h	16h	16h	16h			24h	16h	16h	16h	16h
Joe	Work		8h	8h	8h	8h	8h			8h	8h	8h	8h	8h
Frank	Work		8h	8h	8h	8h	8h			8h				
Mary	Work		0h	0h	0h	0h	0h			8h	8h	8h	8h	8h

Mary's assignment is scheduled on the last 5 days of the task duration.

Typically, the resources with the least work finish early, unless you change the start date of their assignment. In our example, *Mary* drives the task finish date as much as *Joe*.

The formula $D * U = W$ does not apply to a task with multiple, uneven assignments, but it does apply to individual assignments.

We generally don't recommend creating more than one assignment with different start dates on a task. The project schedule will stay simpler if you split the task into more tasks, one task for each resource. Where people need to get together as a group, you can create a short one-day meeting task. In the example shown in the screenshot, the meeting would take place on Monday, January 8. Also, recall the misery that Nob experienced by assigning multiple resources to tasks in the story at the start of this chapter.

Changing Assignment Attributes

1. Switch to a usage view, either **Task Usage** or **Resource Usage**.

2. Double-click on an assignment. Assignments have italics text, no number and a light yellow background in the timescale. The **Assignment Information** dialog appears:

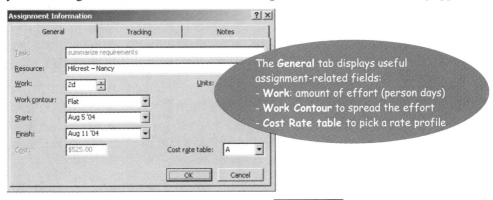

3. Make the changes to the assignment and click `OK`.

You can change many attributes of assignments. Assignments have about 50 purely assignment-related fields. Some useful examples are:

◆ **Start** and **Finish**: These fields allow you to have one or more resources start later or finish earlier on a task than the rest.

◆ **Delay**: Instead of entering start or finish dates, you could enter a number of days delay for the assignment.

◆ **Work contour**: This allows you to spread the effort on a task in a pattern you choose.

◆ **Cost rate table**: This allows you to select a specific rate profile for each assignment. This is useful for jacks-of-all-trades in small consulting firms that are billed differently for each job.

◆ **Note**: You can document actual findings and lessons learned by assignment. This allows you to create a project archive as you go along.

Replacing Generic Resources with Individuals

There are several ways in which you can replace generic resources (I call them "clones") with real flesh-and-blood individuals:

◆ In the Resource Sheet you type over the generic resource name with the name of the individual. Of course, this operation will replace the individual on all assignments of the generic resource, so you only want to do this when you have a one-to-one correspondence between generic resources and individuals.

◆ In the Resource Usage view, drag the assignment from the generic resource to a real person. This method allows you to create just one generic resource for each role, function or position you need on your team and do long-term resource planning where you accumulate workload far into the future onto generic resources.

◆ You can use the Replace... button in the Assign Resources dialog. First you select the assigned generic resource to replace, then click Replace... and select the substitute resource from the list presented. You can narrow the list of tasks down by first selecting the tasks for which you want the resource to be replaced and then using the steps above to replace the resource on only the selected tasks.

 ◆ In Project 2002 with Project Server you can use the *Team Builder* to replace generic resources. Choose **Tools, Build Team from Enterprise** and select the generic **Team Resource** in the list on the right and the substitute resource in the list **Enterprise Resource** on the left; then click Replace > . All assignments will be replaced.

 ◆ In Project 2002 with *Project Server*, you can use the *Resource Substitution Wizard* to replace all generic resources quickly with real people. This method assumes that you have coded the skills of all resources (including the generic resources) in such a way that the wizard can determine if a person has the right qualifications for the job. The Resource Substitution Wizard only looks at the availability of the people as the second most important factor. So the result can be that a person becomes over-allocated by the wizard, and you would still have to apply workload leveling after running the wizard.

Using the Resource Substitution Wizard

 This wizard is typically used with project templates. Project templates normally have generic resources assigned to tasks. The generic resources should have codes that reflect their skills. If that is the case, the Substitution Wizard can figure out what individual has a matching set of skills.

The Substitution Wizard has a broader function. It can also reallocate resources across any number of projects, thus optimizing the utilization of your resources. We will not discuss this function here; it is content for the Blue Belt course. However, it is good to be aware of this alternative use because the options in the dialog boxes of the wizard might otherwise be confusing.

1. Choose **Tools, Substitute Resources**; the **Resource Substitution Wizard** appears with its **Welcome** screen.

2. Click [Next >] and the **Step 1** dialog appears:

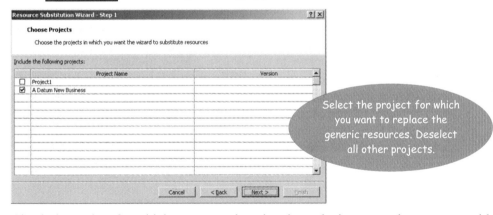

Select the project for which you want to replace the generic resources. Deselect all other projects.

3. Check the project for which you want the wizard to substitute generic resources with real ones, and uncheck any other projects listed. Selecting other projects is necessary when you want to reallocate resources across projects.

4. Click [Next >] ; the **Step 2** dialog appears:

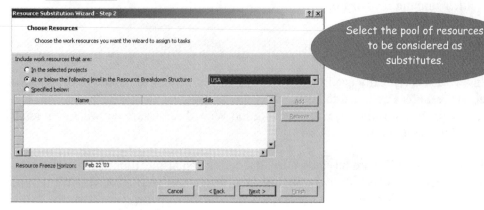

5. Choose the resources that you want the wizard to consider as substitutes. You can choose one of the options:

◉ **In the selected projects**: This option is meant for reallocating resources across multiple projects. Do not use it for replacing generic resources with real ones.

◉ **At or below the following level in the Resource Breakdown structure**: Here you can select a geographical region if you want the resources to live close to where the project is, for example.

◉ **Specified below**: You have to click the [Add] button to select all individual resources to consider for substitution. This will give you a lot of control over the end result but may not give the tightest schedule possible if you narrow down the resource pool too much. This option also allows you to make the wizard more intelligent by manually selecting those resources that have enough remaining availability for their tasks in the new project such that you are not overloading them.

6. Click [Next >]; the **Step 3** dialog appears:

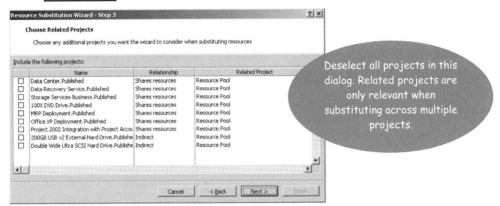

7. Choose the related projects. Related projects are projects that have cross-project links with this project or projects that share one or more of the same resources. Since the template will not have cross-project links and will only have generic resources, you will typically find that there are no or very few related projects. Click [Next >]; the **Step 4** dialog appears:

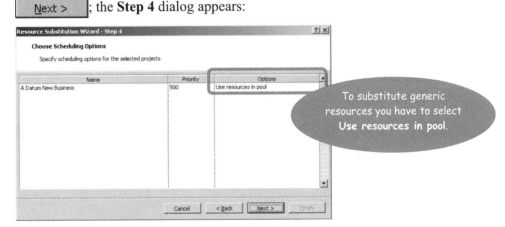

8. Choose the scheduling options. Your options are:

◇ Set the **Priority** level with a number from 0 to 1000. The higher the number, the higher priority the project will have when it competes for resources with other projects. Project 2002 will assign resources to the highest priority projects first.

◇ Under **Options,** you can specify for each project whether Project 2002 should keep the same resource in a project and only reassign within that project or should consider all resources in the enterprise pool that meet the criteria specified in the **Step 2** dialog. To replace generic resources, you would typically choose **Use resources in pool** here. If you choose **Use resources in project**,

MS Project will not propose any substitutes because it is only allowed to consider the generic resources that are already in the project.

9. Click Next > ; the **Step 5** dialog appears:

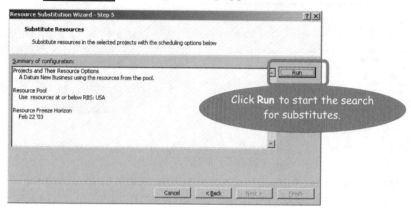

10. This dialog summarizes the settings you chose in the previous steps. Click Run to initiate the process of finding suitable substitutes. Watch the status line at the bottom of the screen because once it stops flashing, the substitution is done.

11. Click Next > ; the **Step 6** dialog appears, showing the results of the resource substitution.

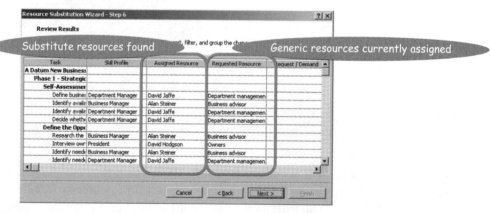

12. You can review the substitutions that Project Server proposes. The fields are as follows:

◇ **Task** contains the detail task name.

◇ **Skill profile** contains the skill profile required for the task. With generic resources assigned, it is the skill set of that generic resource.

◇ **Assigned Resource** is the resource that Project 2002 recommends as a substitute for the generic resource.

◇ **Requested resource** is the resource originally assigned, in this case the generic resource.

◇ **Request/Demand** indicates whether the resource was just requested or was demanded for the task. The generic resources typically should not have this field filled in for their assignments. Only when real people are assigned can the project manager indicate for some of the resources that they are demanded on the job to be successful. Demanded resources are never proposed to be substituted by MS Project.

13. Click [Next >]; the **Step 7** dialog appears:

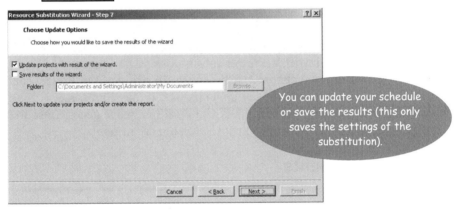

14. Select one or both options:
    ☑ **Update project with results of wizard**
    AND/OR
    ☑ **Save results of the wizard** in a separate report file. Click [Browse...] to indicate in which subdirectory.
    To replace generic resources, you would normally select the first option.

15. The report does not contain the detailed substitution suggestions by task as shown in the **Step 6** dialog of the wizard. The report does contain the date on which you created it, the settings you chose (so that you can reproduce the suggested substitutions) and the suggested team members for the project (the highest level result of the wizard). If the report did contain all suggested details, selecting both options would be useful for creating a change log. The report would then register what changes were made at what time, and could also be used as a discussion piece with your team.

16. Click [Next >] ; the **Step 8** dialog appears; this is the last dialog.
    Click [Finish] and the result will appear in the project file.

Project 2002 may not have replaced all generic resources if you set the parameters too narrow. In particular, the following parameters could decrease the number of suggestions:

◆ Choosing a Resource Breakdown Structure level that is too low in the organization makes the pool of resources too narrow (**Step 2** of the wizard).

◆ If you only allow resources to be considered if they live in the same city or state but nobody with a certain skill set lives in the area, MS Project can't find substitutes and the generic resource will stay on the task (at least, for now).

◆ The more related projects you select in **Step 3** of the wizard, the more substitutions will be suggested to you. The wizard will start substituting across all selected projects.

◆ The lower the priority level you give to the project for which to substitute the resources (**Step 4** of the wizard), the fewer substitutes will be suggested.

◆ If in **Step 4** of the wizard you choose **Use resources in project**, MS Project can only swap the resources that are already in the project. It may find some improvements, but that is not guaranteed. If you want to replace generic resources with real people, you have to always select **Use resources in pool**.

Checks on Assignments

Below you will find checks to verify if you have applied best practices to the assignments in your schedule:

◆ Is the appropriate **Type** of task chosen for each detail task?
  (**Fixed Duration**, **Fixed Units** or **Fixed Work**)

◆ Does each detail task have at least one human resource assigned?
  If there are detail tasks without human resources assigned, you have not captured all the workloads in your project. If workloads are missing, the schedule may not forecast finish dates that are feasible. In the **Resource Usage** view there should be no detail tasks listed under the first category **Unassigned**. You can also apply the filter **5 IIL Detail tasks without Resources Assigned**.[51] The filter allows you to easily copy the tasks including their ID number to provide detailed feedback to the

---

[51] This filter can be found in the file *Tools to check Orange Belt schedules.MPP* that is available for download at www.jrosspub.com.

project manager. Note that there may still be detail tasks with only material resources assigned if you check the **Unassigned** category or apply the filter. An exception to this last rule is that recurring detail tasks do not need resources assigned to them.

Printing the Assignments

Choose **View, Task Usage** to apply the **Task Usage** view, which shows all assignments in detail. The assignments appear in this view as resource names since the task names are indented below their task:

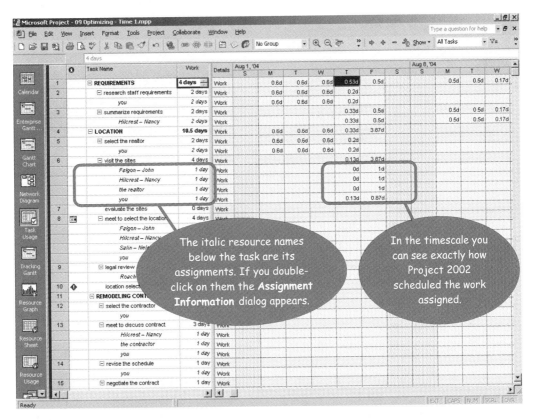

The italic resource names below the task are its assignments. If you double-click on them the **Assignment Information** dialog appears.

In the timescale you can see exactly how Project 2002 scheduled the work assigned.

To show the assignments below each resource, choose **View**, **Resource Usage**. Assignments appear in this view as task names since the resource names are already listed.

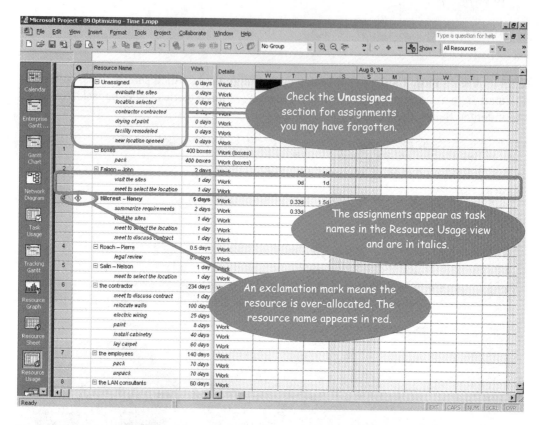

If you don't see the numbers in the timescale, select a resource and click **Go to selected task** (I guess Microsoft forgot to adjust this screen tip!). To change the time unit, use the **Zoom In** 🔍 or the **Zoom Out** 🔍 tool.

(2002) You can now print row totals and column totals in the timescale of the usage views. In the Task Usage or Resource Usage view, you can select these totals by choosing **File**, **Page Setup**, tab **View** and checking ☑ **Print row totals for values within print date range** and ☑ **Print column totals**.

Alternatively, there are assignment reports available.

1. Choose **View, Reports**; the **Reports** dialog appears:

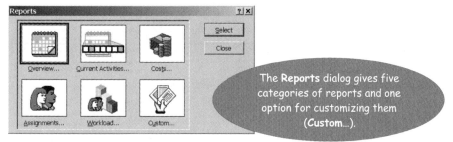

The **Reports** dialog gives five categories of reports and one option for customizing them (**Custom**...).

2. Double-click the button **Assignments...**; the **Assignment Reports** dialog appears:

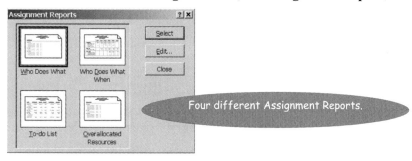

Four different Assignment Reports.

3. You can choose from:

   ◇ **Who Does What**
   This report is similar to the Resource Usage view; the assignments are listed below the tasks.

   ◇ **Who Does What When**
   The work on each task is shown spread over time.

   ◇ **To-do List**
   You will be prompted to select a resource and the report will show all the tasks by week with their start and finish times. You can change this report to show the tasks by month by selecting it and then clicking Edit.... Note that for each week (or month) the total duration of the task is repeated and the data are not truly time-phased.

   ◇ **Overallocated Resources**
   This report shows only the resources that are over-allocated with all their assignments (including the ones that cause the over-allocation).

Here is an example of a **To-do List** report:

```
                              To Do List as of Sat Dec 23
                                Relocation Devom Inc.
                                   Eric Uyttewaal

        ID        ℹ      Task Name                        Type              Duration
   ─────────────────────────────────────────────────────────────────────────────────
   Week of July 29
         2                research staff requirements      Fixed Work        4 days?
         5                select the realtor               Fixed Duration    4 days

   Week of August 5
         2                research staff requirements      Fixed Work        4 days?
         5                select the realtor               Fixed Duration    4 days
         6                visit the sites                  Fixed Duration    1 day
         7                evaluate the sites               Fixed Duration    1 day

   Week of August 12
         7                evaluate the sites               Fixed Duration    1 day

   Week of August 19
         8        📅      meet to select the location      Fixed Duration    1 day
        12                select the contractor            Fixed Duration    2 days
        27                select mover                     Fixed Duration    2 days

   Week of August 26
        12                select the contractor            Fixed Duration    2 days
        27                select mover                     Fixed Duration    2 days

   Week of September 2
        13                meet to discuss contract         Fixed Duration    1 day
        14                revise the schedule              Fixed Duration    1 day
        15                negotiate the contract           Fixed Duration    1 day
```

If you want to produce to-do lists across multiple projects, we recommend you use Project 2002 Professional with *Project Server*. Team members will see their entire task list from multiple projects brought together on one web page.

Exercises

Review A

1. What is the definition of an *assignment*?

2. In your own words, describe what the following fields represent:

    a. **Units** field in the Task Form

    b. **Units** field in the Resource Information dialog, tab **General**

    c. **Max. Units** field in the Resource Sheet

    d. **Work** field in the Gantt Chart

    e. **Work** field in the Task Form

    f. **Work** field in the Resource Sheet

3. In your own words, what is a *Work Contour*?

4. A project manager realizes that she wants to model her project on a high level. She will only enter consolidated resources (pooled resources) in her Resource Sheet. What setting would you recommend to her for **Tools, Options**, tab **Schedule**, field **Show assignment units as**?

5. What are the three task types? How does each task type function?

6. In your own words, what are the three rules that will help you control MS Project entirely when creating or changing assignments?

7. Before you make a change on an assignment, what question should you ask yourself and what field(s) should you check?

8. Describe two different ways of assigning resources to tasks in MS Project. Describe them in terms of mouse clicks or menu items to choose. What are the differences between these two methods in terms of options you have?

9. Would you recommend making multiple, uneven assignments to many tasks? Justify your answer in terms of pros and cons.

10. When you assign a resource to a recurring summary task with the **Assign Resources** dialog, what will MS Project do automatically?

Review B

Read the following situations and determine if you will make the first estimate in person days work (PD), in business day duration (BD) or in elapsed day duration (ED). Explain why and indicate which type of task you recommend: Fixed Duration (FD), Fixed Units (FU) or Fixed Work (FW).

1. Writing a 10 page report that normally takes a person 4 hours per page to produce

2. One load to be transported over a distance of 4000 miles with one driver

3. One package that has to be flown a distance of over 4000 miles and has to arrive in 2 working days

4. A house painter who is asked for a fixed price quote and the earliest end date for painting a family home

5. A contractor gives a painter a maximum of 2 weeks to finish painting a building

6. Backing up a computer system before the conversion to a new operating system, where the backing up requires little supervision once started

7. A meeting with a presentation to all team members

Review C

A resource is writing two different documents concurrently and you cannot plan or predict when he will be working on one or the other. How would you model this situation in Project 2002 and, in particular, what assignments would you make?

Relocation Project — Entering Assignments

Continue to work with your file *Relocation.MPP* or open the file
08 Entering Assignments.MPP that is available for download at www.jrosspub.com.

Enter the assignments as shown in the table below. First, add the fields **Type, Duration**
and **Work** to the view Gantt Chart in such a way that the view matches the *task fields*
column headings in the table below. Notice that you cannot add the *assignment fields*
shown in the table; you have to enter the assignment information in the **Assign
Resources** dialog or in the **Task Form**.

Remember that MS Project uses the formula *Duration * Units = Work* and will calculate
for each detail task the third value that is not provided in the table below.

Think about the easiest way to enter each assignment; decide if you should use the
Assign Resources dialog or the **Task Form**. The Task Form is best when you want to
assign multiple resources with specific numbers for units and/or work.

Only the **Fixed Work** tasks are **Effort Driven**.

TASK FIELDS				ASSIGNMENT FIELDS	
Task Name	**Type**	**Dur.**	**Work**	**Resources**	**Units**
REQUIREMENTS	*Fixed Duration*				
research staff requirements	*Fixed Work*		*2d*	*you*	*0.5*
summarize requirements	*Fixed Work*		*2d*	*Hilcrest*	*0.5*
LOCATION	*Fixed Duration*				
select the realtor	*Fixed Duration*	*4 d*		*you*	*0.5*
visit the sites	*Fixed Duration*	*1 d*		*Falgon* *Hilcrest* *the realtor* *you*	*1* *1* *1* *1*
evaluate the sites	*Fixed Duration*	*1 d*		*Falgon* *Hilcrest* *the realtor* *you*	*1* *1* *0.5* *1*

TASK FIELDS				ASSIGNMENT FIELDS	
Task Name	**Type**	**Dur.**	**Work**	**Resources**	**Units**
meet to select the location	*Fixed Duration*	*1 d*		*Falgon* *Hilcrest* *Salin* *you*	*1* *1* *1* *1*
legal review	*Fixed Duration*	*0.5 d*		*Roach*	*1*
REMODELING CONTRACT	*Fixed Duration*				
select the contractor	*Fixed Duration*	*2 d*		*you*	*1*
meet to discuss contract	*Fixed Duration*	*1 d*		*the contractor* *Hilcrest* *you*	*1* *1* *1*
revise the schedule	*Fixed Duration*	*1 d*		*you*	*1*
negotiate the contract	*Fixed Duration*	*1 d*		*you*	*1*
REMODELED LOCATION	*Fixed Duration*				
relocate walls	*Fixed Work*		*100 d*	*the contractor*	*10*
install electric wiring	*Fixed Work*		*25 d*	*the contractor*	*5*
paint	*Fixed Work*		*8 d*	*the contractor*	*4*
drying of paint	*Fixed Duration*	*4 ed*			
install cabinetry	*Fixed Work*		*40 d*	*the contractor*	*8*
install LAN	*Fixed Work*		*60 d*	*the LAN consultants*	*5*
lay carpet	*Fixed Work*		*60 d*	*the contractor*	*6*
MOVE	*Fixed Duration*				
select mover	*Fixed Duration*	*2 d*		*you*	*1*
pack	*Fixed Duration*	*2 d*		*the employees* *boxes*	*35* *400*
move	*Fixed Work*		*20 d*	*the movers*	*10*
unpack	*Fixed Duration*	*2 d*		*the employees*	*35*

Compare your file with the solution file *09 Optimizing – Time 1.MPP* that is available for download at www.jrosspub.com. Notice that the project is missing its November 1 deadline. We will need to optimize the schedule in the next chapter.

Relocation Project — Changing Assignments

Continue to work with your file *Relocation.MPP* or open the file *09 Optimizing – Time 1.MPP* that is available for download at www.jrosspub.com.

How should you go about making the following changes to the assignments? You may need to change the **Type** of the task first. The task *install LAN* currently has a duration of 12 days, 5 consultants working on it and 60 days of work.

1. You would like to know how long the task *install LAN* would take if there were 10 *LAN consultants* instead of 5? What task type do you need before you make this change?
   You should get a duration of 6 days. Keep this change.

2. You want to know how many consultants are needed if you want the task *install LAN* done in 3 days? What task type do you need before you make this change?
   You should find that 20 *LAN consultants* are needed. Keep this change.

3. You think you over-estimated the work; you will need only 30 days instead of 60 days and you want to keep the duration to 3 days. What is the number of consultants needed now? What task type do you need before you make this change?
   You should find that 10 consultants are needed. Keep this change.

4. You want to keep the number of consultants to 10, but you want to change the duration from 3 to 12 days. How much work is now on the task? What task type do you need before you make this change?
   You should end up with 120 days of work. Keep this change.

5. You want to bring the number of consultants down to 5 while keeping the 12-day duration. How much work is now on the task? What task type do you need before you make this change?
   This brings us back to where we were at the start of this exercise after exploring several scenarios.

Chapter 9 Optimizing the Schedule

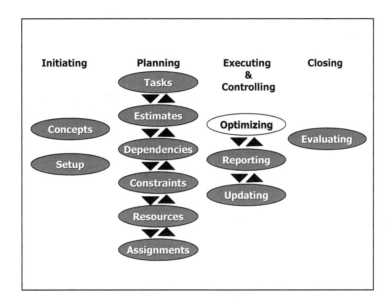

After entering the schedule data we now have a dynamic model of our project that tells us whether the project is feasible as we envisioned it. In most situations the schedule will show that the duration is too long, the cost is too high or the workloads are unreasonable. In some cases, all are off. With a dynamic model we can easily develop and explore different scenarios to find the best solution. We can optimize for time, for time and cost or for time, cost and resource availability.

After reading this chapter you will:

◆ be able to choose the appropriate approach for optimizing
◆ be able to optimize the project for time (including scope and quality)
◆ be able to display the Critical Path
◆ be able to solve a fragmented Critical Path
◆ understand the difference between Free Slack and Total Slack
◆ be able to apply several techniques to shorten the project
◆ be aware of the assumptions/shortcomings of the Critical Path Method (CPM)
◆ know what Monte Carlo simulation is and why you would use it
◆ be able to optimize the project for time and cost
◆ be able to optimize the project for time, cost and resource availability
◆ be able to make workloads and over-allocations visible in MS Project
◆ know how to level the workloads of the resources yourself
◆ know how to level the workloads of the resources automatically
◆ know what the Resource-Critical Path is and when it is important
◆ be able to find and shorten the Resource-Critical Path
◆ be able to evaluate the impacts of a change to the schedule
◆ be able to check if the schedule is properly optimized using scheduling best practices

Key Resources, The Key to Success

Nob: "Bob, what did you do to meet that deadline? It looked pretty close to impossible to meet it. Everybody was saying that this time you bit off more than you could chew... People made bets against you."

Bob: "You want to know my secrets, don't you?"

Nob: "Oh come on, I share all my secrets with you, don't I?"

Bob: "Well, I am not going to comment on that... but this time, we really got behind. We had to sort out all this new technology stuff ... and it never works the way they advertise it."

Nob: "Yeah, we heard that at one point you were four weeks behind schedule ..."

Bob: "That's right and we almost brought it in on time, mostly because our team really put in the best they had."

Nob: "Oh come on ... you have some kind of trick up your sleeve ... and you are not willing to share it with me."

Bob: "Well, what we did wasn't rocket science. We just made sure the very best resources were always working on the most critical tasks that drove our project end date. It meant that we sometimes reassigned people when progress shifted among the components. Fortunately, we established a clear understanding with the team up front that we wanted to be able to do that and they allowed us to."

Nob: "Yeah, we heard some people complain that they had to clean up other people's mess."

Bob: "Our key resources were indeed the key to our success."

The Pulling Forces

Optimizing a schedule is the true art of scheduling. When optimizing you have to consider the project in all its aspects. The Project Management Institute has identified the dimensions by which projects need to be optimized in its Guide to the Project Management Body of Knowledge (PMBOK® Guide).[52] These areas are shown with arrows in the illustration. A change in one area often impacts another. Eight forces are at work on each project, and project managers have to consider all of them in an integrated fashion. The PMBOK® Guide 2000 calls this *Project Integration Management*, the ninth knowledge area. Project 2002 provides sufficient features to manage most, but not all, areas:

◆ **Quality**
The quality of deliverables must correspond to the specifications and expectations of the client. You can schedule quality activities in Project 2002, but the tool does not provide a full-fledged quality management system. For software development projects, we recommend you complement MS Project with a requirements tracking system. However, quality can and should always be considered while optimizing.

◆ **Scope**
The scope of a project can be captured using the Work Breakdown Structure. It contains the deliverables to be produced and the activities can be derived from them. Project 2002 is an excellent tool for managing scope.

◆ **Time**
Deadlines can be scheduled and managed very well in Project 2002.

◆ **Cost**
You can manage work and material expenses with Project 2002 so they stay within the restrictions of your budget.

---

[52] See the PMBOK® Guide, 2000 edition, published by the PMI.

◆ **Resources**

The workloads have to stay within the availability of the human resources. You can do resource leveling with Project 2002. One issue we will have to deal with is that when you level resource workloads, the Critical Path can become fragmented. We will therefore introduce a new concept: the Resource-Critical Path.

In Project 2002 Professional with *Project Server*, you can now better model the resource needs in the longer term if you use an enterprise resource pool that contains generic resources. Project Server also allows you to develop *scenarios* like: *What if we allowed resource substitution between projects; could we then meet the deadlines?* or *What if we added another project to the portfolio; how would this impact deadline accomplishment?*

◆ **Risk**

Project 2002 does allow you to introduce some probability into the schedule with PERT analysis, but does not provide Monte Carlo simulation capabilities. Simulation is the superior technique, and we will discuss this in more detail. There are add-on tools that complement Project 2002 in performing simulation.

Risk management activities can be scheduled in Project 2002, but it does not have features for Risk Management Planning, Risk Identification, Qualitative Risk Analysis, Quantitative Risk Analysis, Risk Response Planning and Risk Monitoring and Control.[53]

In Project Server you can now collect and manage issues. Issue management is the start of what inevitably will grow into features in Project Server to perform *qualitative* and *quantitative risk analysis*. In this type of analysis, you identify the risk events, you qualify or quantify them and assign owners to look after them.

◆ **Communications**

You can create a variety of paper-based or online reports with Project 2002. The application, by itself, is not a complete document configuration management system. Such a system is needed for project communication management in large or complex projects.

Project Server enhances the communication features of Project 2002 tremendously because it allows you to interact with just about any project stakeholder wherever they may be as long as there is a connection to the Internet. *Project Server* also has features that allow you to store several versions of the schedule and designate one version as the official one, which is called the *published version*.

---

[53] This is the new breakdown of the Project Risk Management knowledge area in the PMBOK® Guide, 2000 edition.

◆ **Procurement**

Project 2002 is not a contract management system; a separate system is needed for managing procurement in projects.

Improving one dimension of the project often impacts the others. When the impact is negative, you are trading off among the dimensions. For example, if you hire more resources to meet a tight deadline, the impact may be positive on time, but negative on cost. Sometimes, you can find methods that are positive in more than one respect and neutral in others. These are the methods to identify and apply first. We will make several suggestions of such methods.

Three Approaches for Optimizing Schedules

We will present to you three different approaches for optimizing schedules. In all three we include consideration of quality and scope as well. Because these two dimensions do not differentiate the approaches, we have not included the words quality or scope in the name of each approach. These are the different approaches:

◆ *Optimizing for Time*
This approach is also known as *optimizing under the assumption of unlimited resources*. The other approaches will not assume that you have access to unlimited resources. You have access to unlimited resources if you can hire and fire any resource you need when you need it. Instead of firing, being able to release your resources to other projects within the company also puts you in the position of having access to unlimited resources. *Unlimited resources* also assumes that cost is not of primary concern to you and that you only need to consider the forces quality, scope and time. The common technique used in this situation is the Critical Path Method (CPM). Many industries have been using CPM for decades. Typically, the construction and consulting industries apply CPM. Many others find this optimization too narrow, particularly when cost is a concern or resource availability is a problem.

◆ *Optimizing for Time and Cost*
If cost is your concern you should apply this approach. It also is applicable if you can find more money to solve quality, scope or time problems. You could use money to buy better raw materials, rent better equipment or pay penalties for late delivery. However, if you use the extra money to increase capacity, you should use the next approach instead of just focusing on time and cost since you are now increasing the resource availability. You increase availability when you hire more people, subcontract to free-lancers, or rent more facilities or equipment.

◆ *Optimizing for Time, Cost and Resources*
If you must also consider the availability and the capacity of the resources in order to derive a feasible schedule for your project, you should use this approach. You are making trade-off decisions among quality, scope, time, cost and *resource availability*. An example of optimizing for time, cost and resources is when you consider paying extra to get more overtime from your team. If you regard your resources to be scarce, you will have to look at their availability and their workload. You will have to level the resource workloads. Leveling often disjoints the Critical Path and we cannot expect that CPM will help us any longer. The approach we will suggest is called the *Resource-Critical Path.*

As you can see, we are adding a dimension with each approach to optimization. The optimizations will become more complex as we go along. Including five out of the eight dimensions is the most complex optimization we will discuss in this book. It also is the most complex one MS Project can assist you with.

Choosing the Options

Choose **Tools, Options** to access the following options that are relevant for all optimizing approaches:

Tab	Option
View	☑ **Show summary tasks** and ☑ **Show project summary task** The project summary task is inserted at the top of the task list and summarizes the entire project, with everything indented beneath it. It has ID number 0 (zero). The project summary task is useful when optimizing because it displays the total duration, effort and cost of the project. Other schedules are not affected when you (un)check the above two options because they are stored in the project file; see the label of this section **Outline Options for <file name of the project>**.
Calculation	☐ **Calculate multiple critical paths** We recommend you keep this option off since a single project should only have one ending point in the network logic. If there are multiple ending points, there are multiple critical paths.

Tab	Option
	Tasks are Critical if Slack is less than or equal to `0` ⬍ **days**
	This field creates a threshold for marking tasks as critical or not. Normally, this option is set to zero, which means that Project 2002 displays tasks with zero or negative slack as critical and shows them in red. This option is also stored in the project file.

Optimizing for Time

The dimensions that we will consider in this type of optimization are quality, scope and time, as indicated by the solid black arrows in the illustration. When you use the *Critical Path* you are essentially doing an optimization on the dimension of time. The technique for this type of optimization is the Critical Path Method (CPM). Many project managers have gotten used to considering cost and resource availability while crashing the Critical Path, but we will not do that. We will discuss the CPM here in its original form and discuss including cost on page 404 (Optimizing for Time and Cost) and resources on page 410 (Optimizing for Time, Cost and Resources).

Techniques

◆ **The Critical Path Method (CPM)**
The CPM is a beautiful product of human logic. The beauty lies in the fact that it really helps project managers meet their deadlines by highlighting the tasks that are most likely to affect the project deadline.
Finding and highlighting the Critical Path in your schedule is known as the *Critical Path Method*. A critical task does not have buffer time, or slack, and any delay experienced on a critical task means your project end date will slip. The CPM uses one duration estimate for each task.

◆ **The PERT Method**
The *Program Evaluation and Review Technique* (*PERT*) technique is a more sophisticated application of the CPM. Instead of using one duration estimate for each task, PERT uses three estimates for each task: optimistic (O), most likely (ML)

and pessimistic (P). These durations are converted to an expected duration with the following formula: Expected Duration = (O + 4 * ML + P) / 6. After the expected durations have been calculated, CPM can again be applied to the schedule. PERT incorporates probability into the Critical Path.

MS Project has a toolbar **PERT Analysis** that enables you to apply the PERT-method to your schedule. Right-click on a toolbar and choose **PERT Analysis**. Click the tool **PERT Entry Sheet** 🔲 and enter the estimates. You can even choose the weights for each estimate by clicking **Set PERT Weights** 🔲. Then click the **Calculate PERT** 🔲 to have Project 2002 calculate the expected durations in the **Duration** field. The PERT calculation often results in durations with decimals. This is one of the reasons why PERT is used less and less. Another reason is that simulation is a more powerful technique that captures different probability issues better.

◆ **Simulation of the Schedule**
Another way to make probability visible is by subjecting the schedule to Monte Carlo simulation. This type of simulation creates many versions of the same schedule based on the probability ranges you provide for certain estimates. The simulation software then averages over all the versions to arrive at the probability for each finish date. Simulation is more powerful than PERT because it quantifies the compounding effect of parallel paths as well. For more on Monte Carlo Simulation, see page 398.

We will further elaborate on CPM and simulation in this book, but leave PERT behind us.

The Critical Path Method (CPM)

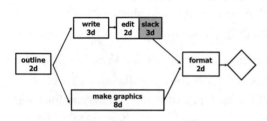

Finding the Critical Path in your network of dependencies determines how long your project will take. The concept of the Critical Path is fairly simple. The illustration depicts a simple authoring project: *outline* the document, *write* the text, *edit* the text, while somebody else does *make graphics*. When the text and the graphics are ready, the *format* can be created and the project is finished. All arrows are finish-to-start dependencies.

Before we discuss the Critical Path theory, you should ask yourself: *What is the minimum duration for this project?*

It does not take a rocket scientist to find that the duration for this project is 12 days. If you came up with the correct answer, you understand the Critical Path concept intuitively. You can find the Critical Path by comparing two parallel paths. Add the durations and the lags on each path and compare the totals. The longest one is the Critical Path. Continue comparing parallel paths until you have checked them all and found the longest path, the Critical Path, for the project.

Parallel chains make a network, of which all but one chain has slack. Sometimes a few chains are equally critical. Slack exists on each chain of tasks when it is performed in parallel with another chain that takes more time. The longest chain in the network is the Critical Path. The Critical Path determines the minimum duration of the project. I call it the minimum duration of the project because the real duration may be longer when resources are over-allocated. Over-allocations may force tasks to be delayed past the minimum duration. Finding the Critical Path is challenging:

◆ When there are many parallel paths
◆ When different types of dependencies (Finish-to-Start, Start-to-Start, Finish-to-Finish, Start-to-Finish) are used with lags or leads

In these cases it is nice to have the help of a tool that will identify the Critical Path for you.

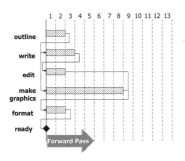

Let's look at how Project 2002 goes about finding the Critical Path. MS Project starts with all tasks cuddled up to the project start date, as shown in the illustration. Then it schedules them out to the earliest possible dates. MS Project then performs the forward pass calculation to determine the *earliest possible dates* (*early dates*). Then it schedules all tasks as late as possible for the backward pass and calculates the *latest allowable dates* (*late dates*).

Forward Pass

Project 2002 starts with the first task (*outline*), looks at its duration (*2 days*) and calculates the earliest date it can be ready. This is the **Early Finish** date. The *outline* will be ready at the end of day 2. MS Project will then continue determining the **Early Start** date of the successor(s). *Write* and *make graphics* are the successors; they can start on day 3. The early start date of the successors will be the same as the early finish date of *outline*, unless other dependencies on the successors cause them to start later. Project 2002 continues to calculate the early finish for *write* and *make graphics*.

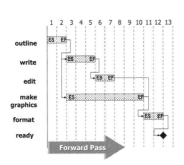

On the forward pass MS Project calculates two dates for each task: the *early start* (ES) and the *early finish* (EF) date. The result of this forward pass is shown in the illustration. *Format* cannot start until both *edit* and *make graphics* are finished, and the earliest start date for *format* is therefore day 11 even though *format* could start on day 8 if it depended solely on *edit*.

Project 2002 continues through the last task in the chain. The software now knows what the earliest finish date is for the project — day 12 in our example.

Backward Pass

Project 2002 then goes backward through the network starting at the project end date to calculate the late finish dates for the tasks, as shown in the illustration. The **Late Finish** date is the latest date a task should be finished in order to meet the project end date. By subtracting the duration of the task from the finish date, MS Project then calculates the late start date. The **Late Start** date is the latest date you can start working on the task to finish by its late finish date. For *format,* this is day 11, the same as its early finish date. We then continue with the late finish dates of the predecessors. *Edit* can finish on day 10 at the latest and the project will still end on day 12. *Edit* has a late finish date (day 10) that is 3 days later than its early finish date (day 7); therefore, *edit* has slack and is not a critical task.

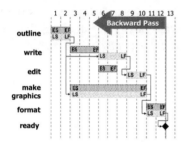

If a task has more than one successor, like *outline*, Project 2002 takes all successors into consideration to determine the late dates. The start date of the earliest successor determines the late finish date of the task, in this case day 2 (*make graphics*), not day 5 (*write*). So, the latest finish for creating the *outline* is determined by the late start date of *make graphics*, and not the late start date of *write*. As a result, the early and the late dates for *outline* are the same; *outline* does not have slack and is a critical task.

Calculating Total Slack

Total slack is the amount of time you can delay a task without affecting the project end date. The total slack (TS) of a task is the *late finish* (LF) date minus the *early finish* (EF) date:[54]

$$TS = LF - EF$$

It tells you how much a task can slip before delaying the whole project (or other hard, constraint dates in the schedule). For example, the illustration shows that the task *Write* has 3 days of total slack (*TS = 8 – 5 = 3*). If the author calls you and tells you he fell ill, you would ask, "*When do you think you might be better?*" If the answer is more than 3 days, you know you should find somebody else if you can't permit the project to slip. If the answer is less than 3 days, you may still have a problem because the editor will now receive the text later, which might cause conflicts in her planning. You need to communicate!

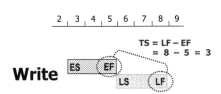

The *total slack* of tasks can be:

♦ Greater than zero: *positive slack*
These tasks have slack. They can be delayed for as much total slack as they have. More than that will delay the project as a whole. You can often level some workloads by using the total slack of a task.

♦ Equal to zero: *zero slack*
Where the late finish date is equal to the early finish date, there is no slack. Tasks without slack are by definition on the *Critical Path*.

♦ Less than zero: *negative slack*
Tasks with a negative slack are tasks that don't meet the project deadline or constraint dates set in the schedule. Slack can only be negative if there are constraints, deadlines or other forces in the schedule that inhibit MS Project from calculating and displaying a feasible schedule.

---

[54] In fact, MS Project also calculates total slack on the start dates: $TS = LS - ES$; the lesser of the two total slacks will be the total slack displayed on the task.

Calculating Free Slack

The *free slack* (FS) of a task is the **Early Start** date of the task's successor minus the **Early Finish** date of the task itself. If there is more than one successor, you should take the **Early Start** date of the earliest successor: $FS = ES_{earliest\ successor} - EF$.

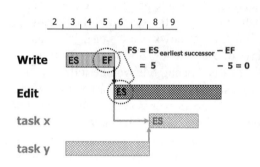

In the illustration the earliest successor of task *Write* is *Edit* instead of *task x*. The free slack tells you how much you can let the task slip before it affects any of its successors. *Write* does not have free slack since the successor *Edit* starts right after the task. The free slack of a task is always less than or equal to its total slack.

The difference between total slack and free slack manifests itself in the task *Write*; it has no free slack but 3 days of total slack. It can use the free slack of its successor *Edit*. That is the beauty of the concept of total slack; it tells you immediately when the project finish date or other constraint dates are in jeopardy.

Project 2002 generates all the dates discussed, and you can find these dates in the task fields **Early Start**, **Early Finish**, **Late Start** and **Late Finish**. The slack fields are **Total Slack** and **Free Slack**.

The Critical Path

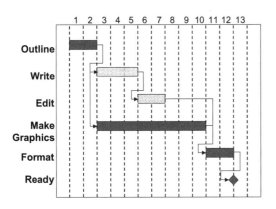

The Critical Path can now be found by finding the tasks that do not have total slack. In our example the tasks *Outline, Make Graphics* and *Format* do not have total slack and are the tasks on the Critical Path. They are the dark task bars in the illustration. Project 2002 can easily highlight the Critical Path for us displaying it in red. When you apply the **Tracking Gantt** view you will see the Critical Path highlighted in red. We need to see the Critical Path to find the tasks with which we can shorten our schedule and finish on time.

Constraints and Negative Slack

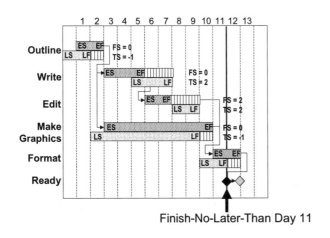

Finish-No-Later-Than Day 11

When you enter constraints into the schedule, all amounts of slack will change. The backward pass is calculated from the Finish-No-Later-Than constraint date instead of the earliest possible project finish date. As a result the late dates and total slack numbers change when you insert such a constraint. In our sample project we will introduce a hard constraint that is 1 day before the earliest possible finish date of the project. The illustration shows how this constraint changes the total slack of the project.

The backward pass takes constraints like Finish-No-Later-Than into account. The forward pass determines the early dates, regardless of constraints.

You can see that the slack turns negative when the latest allowable dates (LF) are earlier than the earliest possible dates (EF). The critical tasks now have –1 day total slack, called *negative slack*. Project 2002 identifies this as a *scheduling conflict* and warns you with a dialog:

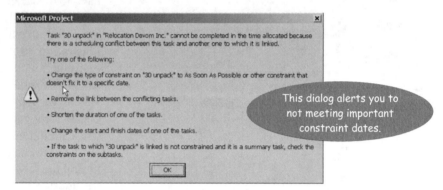

As you can see, Project 2002 gives concrete advice as to how to solve conflicts. The constraints that can cause scheduling conflicts, or negative slack, under *forward scheduling* are:

◆ Must-Finish-On
◆ Must-Start-On
◆ Finish-No-Later-Than
◆ Start-No-Later-Than

These are the constraints that can put pressure on the network of dependencies under forward scheduling.

In *backward scheduling*, the following constraints can cause negative slack:

◆ Must-Finish-On
◆ Must-Start-On
◆ Start-No-Earlier-Than
◆ Finish-No-Earlier-Than

Because constraints affect the calculation of slack, you should use them as sparingly as possible without compromising the quality of the model of the project. We recommend entering constraints for very *hard deadlines* only, the do-or-die dates. If the deadline dates are *soft deadlines* or *target dates*, we recommend you use the Deadlines feature instead, as discussed on page 237. Also, if you have constraints in the middle of your schedule, you will not see by how much the project end date is missed overall, because constraints prevent tasks from floating past them.

 Notice that if you do use the deadline feature, you will not get warning messages that alert you to conflicts in your schedule. Instead, a red flag will be raised in the **Indicators** column. Deadlines give silent alerts. Deadlines also allow you to see what the true total slippage is on the project end date.

You can display a line in the timescale for the amount of negative slack a task has. The **Format, Bar Styles** dialog has an item called **Negative Slack** in the list under **From** and **To**. It allows you to display a line in front of the task bars that represents the amount of time a task slipped past its latest allowable finish date (**Late Finish**). To use this, choose the following settings:

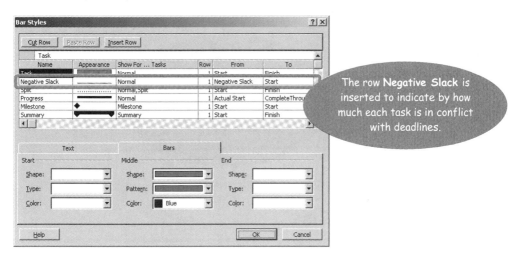

The row **Negative Slack** is inserted to indicate by how much each task is in conflict with deadlines.

The result would look like this screenshot:

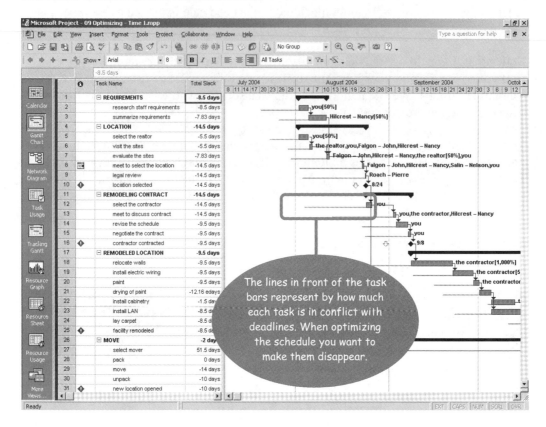

Steps to Optimize for Time

1. Highlight the Critical Path
2. Sort the tasks based on duration
3. Find the longest critical task
4. Make a change on it
5. Consider impacts on quality, scope and time
6. Decide whether you want to keep the change
7. Repeat steps 3 - 7

The rationale behind the steps as shown in the process chart is that you first have to find the critical tasks to determine which tasks drive the project duration. You should have MS Project highlight the Critical Path in red so you can easily see whether a task is critical or not. If the Critical Path switches to another chain while you are optimizing, MS Project will immediately highlight the new Critical Path in red; thus, MS Project continues to show you dynamically what tasks are critical.

Then you find out what critical tasks have the longest durations by sorting the tasks. The critical tasks with the longest durations hold the greatest opportunity for saving time. In other words: *Don't sweat the small stuff!* Focus on the long durations first that allow you to achieve the largest gains.

After that, you have to come up with a way to do the work faster. We will suggest methods and explain them. Before you decide to go on to the next longest critical task, you have to establish whether the change helped you enough, or if the trade-offs on quality or scope were too high a price to pay.

1. *Highlight the Critical Path*
2. Sort the tasks based on duration
3. Find the longest critical task
4. Make a change on it
5. Consider impacts on quality, scope and time
6. Decide whether you want to keep the change
7. Repeat steps 3 - 7

The explanation of all the steps will take quite a few pages. To show where we are, we will use the process chart. It indicates in bold italic type that we will now discuss the first step: *Highlight the Critical Path*.

Highlighting the Critical Path

Switch to the Tracking Gantt view that colors the critical tasks in red by default. Choose **View, Tracking Gantt**.
OR

1. Click the **Gantt Chart Wizard** on the **Formatting** toolbar, and a series of dialog boxes follow.

2. Press Next > and select ● **Critical Path**; the sample box on the left now shows some task bars in red.

3. Click Finish , Format It and Exit Wizard and the task bars of the critical tasks on the Critical Path are now displayed in red.

You can show the text of the task names in red for critical tasks as well:

1. Choose **Format, Text Styles**.

2. Select from the list **Item to Change** All ▼ the item **Critical Tasks**.

3. From the list **Color**, select red.

4. Click OK .

Displaying the Field Total Slack

1. Insert the column *total slack* in the Gantt spreadsheet by right-clicking on the column heading before which you would like to insert the total slack column. Choose **Insert Column** from the pop-up menu; the **Column Definition** dialog appears:

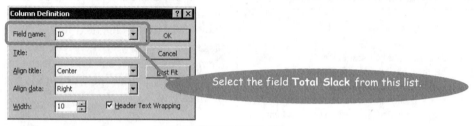

Select the field **Total Slack** from this list.

2. From the list **Field name** ID ▼ select the item **Total Slack.**

3. Click OK .

4. In Project 2002 Professional you may get the following prompt if you try to change an enterprise view. Click OK to acknowledge.

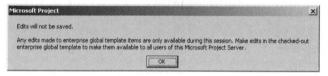

5. The field will now be displayed in the Gantt spreadsheet You can drag the sliding door bar ▶◀ (the divider between the spreadsheet and the timescale) to the right to accommodate the new field in the view. To position it exactly between two spreadsheet columns, double-click on the divider.

The total slack explains why some tasks are critical (total slack less than or equal to zero) and other ones are not (total slack greater than zero). If the total slack is negative, you are missing the project *deadline* or one or more *hard constraint dates* in your schedule.

By default, Project 2002 shows tasks as critical if their *total slack* is less than or equal to zero. This threshold for being critical can be changed in the **Tools, Options**, tab **Calculation**, if necessary.

What you will often see is that the Critical Path is not a complete chain of tasks that stretches from the project start date to the project end date. Project managers expect and need to see a Critical Path that explains the entire project duration. You will often see a fragmented Critical Path. Therefore, we will explore the possible causes of fragmentation.

A Fragmented Critical Path: Possible Causes

Normally, the Critical Path provides a complete explanation of what happens between the project start and finish dates. However, the Critical Path looks fragmented more often than not, as shown in the illustration. The Critical Path may not provide a complete

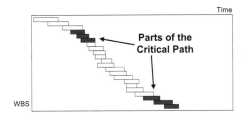 explanation of the duration of the project. Only if you shorten the duration of a critical task will the project duration shorten. If you cannot see the complete Critical Path, optimizing becomes a painful process of trial and error. Therefore, we recommend you address the causes of fragmentation first to display a complete Critical Path of tasks from the start date to the finish date of the project. This sequence of tasks explains the project duration. We will explore how to reveal the complete chain of critical tasks.

The Critical Path can become fragmented for several reasons:
- *Unavailability of resources*
- *Schedule constraints and deadlines*
- *Elapsed durations*
- *Task calendars*
- *External predecessors*
- *Workload leveling*

We will discuss each of these reasons and what to do about them in more detail.

Unavailability of Resources

In the example illustrated below, the move has to take place on a weekend, and the workweek of the movers is changed such that only Saturday and Sunday are working days. The result is that Project 2002 will always schedule the *Move* on the weekend, as shown in the illustration. Depending on when the predecessors of the move are done, this could cause slack to be created. When slack is created before the task *Move*, the Critical Path will only start with the task *Move* and, therefore, be fragmented.

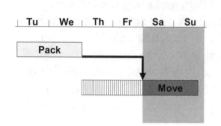

Is this real slack? Real slack is time that can be used as a buffer to compensate for slippages. In this case, the slack is real because *Pack* slipping to Friday does not impact the project.

In this particular situation, slippage would even be desirable because people may not be productive after they are all packed up and ready to go. This could be accomplished by making the schedule constraint As-Late-As-Possible for the task *Pack* in the **Task Information** 🗒 dialog on the **Standard** toolbar. If we were to do this, the slack just moves over to the predecessors of *Pack*.

Because slack now exists on the most critical tasks, we have to raise the threshold for critical tasks in order to display a complete Critical Path.

Raising the Threshold for Critical Tasks

1. Choose **View, Tracking Gantt**.

2. Insert the column **Total Slack** by right-clicking on a column heading and choosing **Insert Column**. Select **Total Slack** from the list
   Field Name | ID ⬛ ▾ | and click | OK |. The column should now be displayed in the view.

3. Check to see if you have tasks similar to the task *Move* in your project that are scheduled when the resource is available (again). Look at what the total slack is for their predecessors. Take the lowest number shown on their predecessors. In our example there is only one predecessor that has 2 days of slack and we would raise the threshold for critical tasks to 2 days in that case.

4. Choose **Tools, Options,** tab **Calculation**. Increase the field **Tasks are Critical if Slack is less than or equal to:** `0` ⇅ to the value you found in step 3.

5. Click ⟨ OK ⟩; the Critical Path has probably now extended to a more complete Critical Path. It still may not explain the entire project duration and you may have to check on the other possible causes for a fragmented Critical Path.

Schedule Constraints and Deadlines

We have already seen that constraints can cause negative slack, but they can also cause positive slack on tasks, also called *buffers*. Deadlines also affect the slack calculation in a fashion similar to constraints.

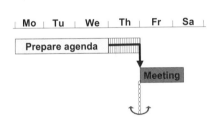

The illustration has two tasks, *Prepare agenda* and *Meeting*. Typically, official meetings, presentations and gatherings occur on a specific date and should be entered with a Must-Start-On constraint. As soon as you enter these fixed dates, slack can be created on the predecessors of that task. The Critical Path starts to look disjointed; only the task *Meeting* will be indicated as critical, because *Prepare agenda* now has slack.

This is another reason why we recommend using as few schedule constraints as possible without compromising the validity of the model of your project. In this situation, constraints make it more difficult to find the Critical Path because they tend to break it. The *constraints* that can cause positive slack in *forward scheduling* are:
◆ Must-Finish-On
◆ Must-Start-On
◆ Start-No-Earlier-Than
◆ Finish-No-Earlier-Than

In *backward scheduling* these constraints are:
◆ Must-Finish-On
◆ Must-Start-On
◆ Start-No-Later-Than
◆ Finish-No-Later-Than

The other types of constraints will not fragment a Critical Path. Again, we have to ask ourselves: *Is this real slack?* In this case the slack is real because slippage on the task

Prepare agenda does not impact the end date, unless it slips more than a day. We have to solve this by raising the threshold for critical tasks again, as discussed on page 380.

Deadlines can also fragment the Critical Path under certain circumstances, for example when there is a tight deadline halfway through the project and a time buffer at the end of the project. In this case you will only see a Critical Path up to the deadline date. This may be a reason to not use too many deadline dates in your project schedule. However, if you must set either a constraint or a deadline, we recommend using a deadline.

Elapsed Durations

An elapsed duration is expressed in calendar days as opposed to business days. A task with an elapsed duration can end during nonworking time, and when it does so, it creates slack if its successor starts on the next business day. In the illustration, the task *Lay Carpet* is scheduled to start on Monday because it has a regular duration. *Drying of Paint* can slip until 8:00 AM Monday morning without affecting *Lay Carpet*. This creates 1 day of slack on *Drying of Paint*, which has a duration of 3 elapsed days (*3ed*).

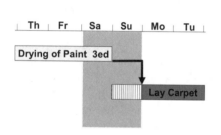

Once more we have to ask ourselves: *Is this real slack?* The slack is real here, because the *Drying of Paint* could continue for another day without impacting the project. Again, we can resolve this by raising the threshold for critical tasks, as discussed on page 380 under Raising the Threshold for Critical Tasks.

Task Calendars

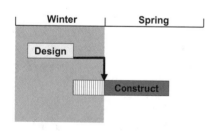

Task calendars can fragment the Critical Path. If the task *Design* can be ready long before the weather is good enough to start construction, it will have slack and therefore will not be seen as critical. The task *Construct* and its successors will be critical, as shown in the illustration. Just as in the previous examples, the slack is real slack and the only way to find a complete path of the most critical tasks is by raising the threshold for criticality (see page 380). If you do this, the

Critical Path extends in your schedule and it will explain more of the project duration.

External Predecessors

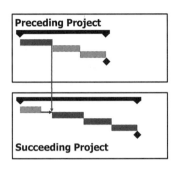

An external predecessor is a task from another project schedule that drives a task in the schedule you are working with (see the illustration). If a task has an external predecessor, this predecessor could very well drive the task farther out than the other predecessors. If it does, it creates slack on the other predecessors within the schedule. This slack is real slack, and can again be taken care of by raising the threshold for criticality in **Tools, Options**, tab **Calculation**, as discussed before.

Workload Leveling

The illustration below shows two tasks, *Print* one document and *Write* another document. The tasks can be done independently of each other; there is no logical dependency between the two tasks. You have assigned one resource that is over-loaded and decide to level the workload to make the schedule more realistic. In some instances you cannot solve the over-allocation in any other way than by delaying a task. As you delay one task, you create slack on the other task that competes for the same resource. As a result, the slack makes critical tasks noncritical, and the Critical Path evaporates before your eyes.

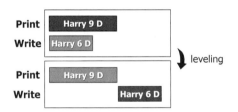

One last time, we have to ask ourselves: *Is this slack real?* In this case, the answer is *no*, unlike all previous examples. The slack is <u>not</u> real slack because any delay in either one <u>does</u> impact the project end date. If Harry needs more time for *Print*, his other task, *Write*, will slip. How are we going to solve this one?

Harry is assigned full-time to both tasks. Clearly, he cannot do both at the same time. Cloning Harry is not an accepted project management practice yet (hopefully, it never will be, even though it would make our profession of project manager much easier).

Reassigning one of the tasks to other resources is not an option either when there are no other resources. Therefore, we often have to delay one of the two tasks, but when we delay one, we create slack on the other task. This slack is not real, because if you use it, the project end date will slip. If the task *Print* slips, it will drive the task *Write* farther out, because there is a *resource dependency* between the tasks. Normally, you can use slack to buffer the impact of unforeseen events, but not in this case. Both tasks are resource-critical even though the current Critical Path algorithm suggests that only the task *Write* is critical. The CPM algorithm only looks at dependencies, not the resource dependencies, when it calculates the early and late dates. CPM does not take resource workloads into account.

We may have conveniently forgotten that CPM assumes that resources are available in unlimited quantities. However, this is applicable in only a few organizations that can easily and quickly hire (and release) extra resources, thus rendering them unlimited.

Should We Add Logical Dependencies?

Some people suggest adding dependencies to level out the workloads of the resources. Of course, you could model resource dependencies as soft, logical dependencies. This works well until you start changing the assignments. If you substitute the resource on one of the two tasks, your schedule could look shorter than it actually is, because of a dependency that has now become obsolete! Adding logic to level workloads in order to keep your Critical Path intact is a static solution that has a short life. That's why we added some question marks to the Critical Path in the illustration. We recommend keeping your schedule dynamic. We will explain a different method for optimizing in this situation on page 410 under Optimizing for Time, Cost and Resources.

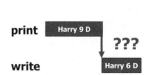

 Many schedulers apply Critical Path theory in such a way that they keep the resource workloads reasonable by creating extra dependencies. They know the schedule would not be feasible if they didn't use these extra dependencies. If you are in this category, I invite you to consider a new method instead of setting extra dependencies. We will discuss the Resource-Critical Path method in the section on Optimizing for Time, Cost and Resources starting on page 410.

Sorting on Duration

1. Highlight the Critical Path
2. *Sort the tasks based on duration*
3. *Find the longest critical task*
4. Make a change on it
5. Consider impacts on quality, scope and time
6. Decide whether you want to keep the change
7. Repeat steps 3 - 7

Now that we have highlighted the Critical Path, the next thing to do is find those tasks where we can gain the most time. We can find them by sorting on duration. The sort is just meant to find the long-duration critical tasks. We will reset the sort order as soon as we have found them. You may have to sort again after you have made changes and want to find the next longest critical tasks. You can see in the process graphic on the left that we will do steps 2 and 3 together.

1. In the Gantt Chart, choose **Project, Sort, Sort by...**; the **Sort** dialog appears:

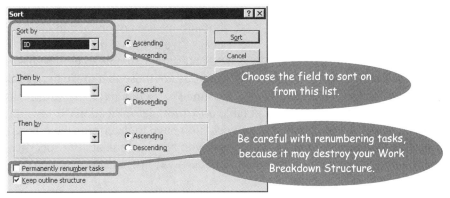

Choose the field to sort on from this list.

Be careful with renumbering tasks, because it may destroy your Work Breakdown Structure.

2. Select from the list **Sort by** ID ▼ the item **Duration** and set the sort order to ⦿ **Descending**.

3. Do not renumber the tasks by unchecking ☐ **Permanently renumber tasks**. If all tasks are renumbered, you will likely have a catastrophe on your hands, because you have lost the structure of the Work Breakdown Structure. Undo and closing without saving are your last resort!

4. Make sure you sort the detail tasks and not the summary task families by unchecking ☐ **Keep outline structure**.

5. Click [Sort]. The longest tasks are now at the top of the screen. The ones that are long and critical (in red) are the prime candidates for optimization, because that is where you can realize the biggest gains.

After you have identified the first tasks to focus on, you can revert to the original sort order by choosing **Project, Sort, by ID**.

Shortening the Duration of the Project

Shortening the Critical Path

1. Highlight the Critical Path
2. Sort the tasks based on duration
3. Find the longest critical task
4. *Make a change on it*
5. Consider impacts on quality, scope and time
6. Decide whether you want to keep the change
7. Repeat steps 3 - 7

When the project has to finish earlier than the schedule shows, the Critical Path has to be shortened. At this point in the process we will make a change to the schedule. Any change has to be evaluated in terms of the impact on at least the three driving forces: quality, scope and duration of the project. We could even consider the cost, although we are not obliged to do so, because we assumed that unlimited resources are available to us. The best solutions are those that make the quality (Q) go up (↑), the scope (S) go up (↑) and the time (T) go down (↓). Unfortunately, there are no such ideal solutions. The next table only provides indications as to what the effect of each action could be in a typical project. You have to determine the effects on your own project. If a question mark (?) is shown, you have to look at your specific situation to determine the effect of the measurement. A zero (0) means that there is no expected impact.

The table provides ideas on how to improve the schedule. The actions are ranked by overall effectiveness, with the most effective ones first. The first two methods are called *fast-tracking* and they overlap activities. Fast-tracking is working smarter instead of harder. If you choose to add resources instead, you will be working harder. Adding resources is called *crashing*. You will find this method at the bottom of the list because it often increases the cost of the project. Crashing is trading off money for time.

We recommend you start by finding the critical tasks with the longest duration. Then explore whether the first two methods of fast-tracking can be applied to those long tasks, then focus on the next-longest task, etc. After exhausting the fast-tracking on all tasks, go to the next action in the table. This is the quickest way to find the most time in your project schedule. (Q=Quality, S=Scope and T=Time)

	Action	For	Q	S	T
1.	Change sequential dependencies into partial dependencies (fast-tracking)	critical tasks	0	0	↓
2.	Create parallel paths from a sequential path (fast-tracking)	critical tasks	?	0	↓
3.	Split long tasks into shorter ones	critical tasks	0	0	↓
4.	Change schedule constraints	critical tasks	0	0	↓
5.	Shorten lags (waiting periods)	critical tasks	0	0	↓
6.	Split task bars around Must-Start-On tasks	critical tasks	0	0	↓
7.	Decrease estimates	critical tasks	↓	?	↓
8.	Reduce the scope or delete tasks	critical tasks	↓	↓	↓
9.	Add resources (*crashing*)	critical tasks	?	?	?

 It may not be clear why we ranked adding resources at the bottom of the list as the least preferred method since for many people it is the obvious thing to do. If the resources you add are second-best, they may not do as good a job as the original resources and quality (Q) may suffer. Also, the new resources need to be trained, and you want to set the right example for them, so typically you would take your best resources off the task to train the new ones. As a consequence, your progress will slow down (T) in the hope that it will pick up again later.

Before making any change, you should check what the total duration of the project is currently. You can find this by choosing **Project, Project Information** and clicking Statistics... OR **Project Statistics** -⋀- on the **Tracking** toolbar. In the row **Current** and the column **Duration** you will find the project duration.

Changing Sequential into Partial Dependencies

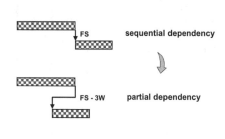

There are four types of dependencies that can be combined with a positive lag time (waiting time/gap) or negative lag time (overlap/lead). The illustration on the left shows a Finish-to-Start dependency changed into an overlap of 3 weeks (*lead* or negative *lag* of –3w): FS – 3w. The overlap can be entered in an absolute number of days or weeks, like –3w. It can also be entered as a percentage of the duration of the predecessor. Since the start of the successor is dependent upon the partial completion of the predecessor, one could also speak of a *partial dependency*.

1. In the timescale of the Gantt Chart, point with the tip of the mouse pointer to the arrow of the dependency.

2. Wait for one second until the yellow screen tip appears. Check to see if you are pointing to the dependency between the right tasks, because the dependency arrows can overlap one another.

3. Double-click if you have the right one; the **Task Dependency** box appears:

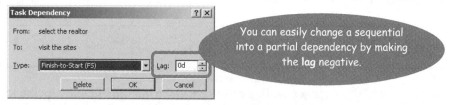

You can easily change a sequential into a partial dependency by making the **lag** negative.

4. Select from the list **Type:** Finish-to-Start (FS) ▼ the kind of dependency. Choose **Start-to-Start** or **Finish-to-Finish** to overlap tasks, or leave the type **Finish-to-Start** and enter a negative **lag** (lead).

5. Type in the **Lag** in absolute time units, like *-3W*, or in a percentage of the duration of the predecessor, like *-50%*. If you type a negative number, the tasks will move to the left in the timescale of the Gantt Chart; a positive lag moves task bars to the right. In a **Finish-to-Start** dependency, you will overlap the predecessor for the lag

you specify. For **Start-to-Start** or **Finish-to-Finish** dependencies, enter zero or a positive lag to create partial dependencies.

6. Click [OK]; you should now see the overlap you wanted between the two task bars in the timescale.

 If you can't select the right dependency with the mouse, you can use the Task Form to create the overlap. Click on the successor task in the Gantt spreadsheet. Choose **Window, Split** to display the Task Form, and you can make the lag negative in the **Predecessors** field.

Creating Parallel Paths

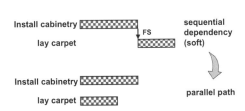

You can cut soft dependencies. Hard, mandatory dependencies should not be cut. If the tasks are critical, the time gain can be large. In the top scenario in the illustration, there is no risk of damaging the new carpet because it is laid after the cabinets have been installed (*sequential dependency*). In the bottom scenario, the carpet layers will have to work neatly and put plastic over the new carpet that has been laid because the two tasks are scheduled concurrently (*parallel path*).

1. In the Gantt Chart point with the tip of the mouse pointer to the arrow of the dependency and double-click on it; the **Task Dependency** dialog appears:

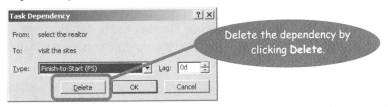
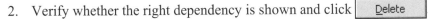

2. Verify whether the right dependency is shown and click [Delete].

3. Click [OK]; the dependency is removed. You may need a new link coming from the predecessor, because it could be a loose end in the network now. You may also need a new link to the successor, because it may have jumped all the way back to the project start date.

 Before breaking the soft dependency it is a good idea to create the new dependency on the successor because then the successor task bar will not fly off your screen to the left.

Split Tasks with a Long Duration

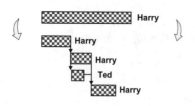

Breaking a long task into smaller tasks gives Project 2002 more possibilities to optimize, as depicted in the illustration. The benefit is immediate if you can assign portions of the task to other noncritical and perhaps cheaper resources. The easiest way to break up a long task is by adding detail tasks below it and changing it into a summary task. The advantage is that only the lower level of detail of your schedule has changed, which will not be very visible in status reports.

Changing Schedule Constraints

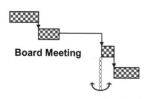

Your project may need authorization for certain matters to proceed. If these decisions are made in board meetings or steering group meetings held on the last Thursday of each month for example, this slows down the progress on the project immensely.

If you lobby hard, you might get more expedient authorization and take some "anchors" out of your schedule. The anchor in the illustration represents a constraint date on the last Thursday of the month.

1. Select the task with the constraint.

2. Click **Task Information** 📖 on the **Standard** toolbar or hold down ⌨Shift and press ⌨F2; the **Task Information** dialog appears.

3. Click the **Advanced** tab and the dialog should now look like:

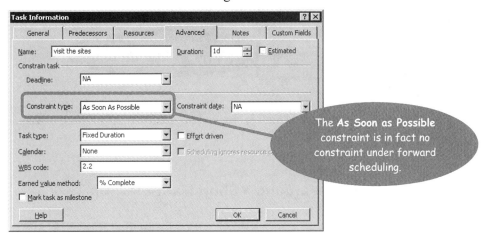

4. Under **Constrain task** change the **Constraint type** to **As Soon As Possible**.
    OR
    Change the **Constraint date** to an earlier date.

5. Click [OK].

Shorten Lag

If you find any lag between critical tasks, you might be able to reduce it now that you are armed with the argument that the lag is on the Critical Path. In the example in the illustration you have to wait for the board's decision, and you typically have to wait 3 weeks before the board convenes. You might be able to lobby for an executive decision instead of a full board decision, which would save a few weeks in this case and be a significant gain.

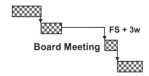

If the wait is for receipt of supplies from a vendor, you can often work miracles by offering your supplier extra money for faster delivery.

1. In the Gantt Chart, point with the tip of the mouse pointer to the arrow of the dependency.

2. Double-click on the arrow. The **Task Dependency** dialog appears:

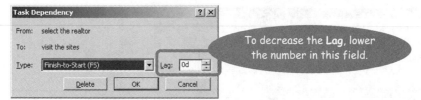

3. Verify whether the right dependency is shown and decrease the amount of **Lag**.

4. Click [OK] .

Split Task Bars around a Short Must-Start-On Task

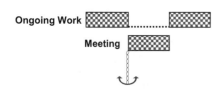

If you have a meeting or training to attend, you have to drop your regular work. The meeting or training takes place on an agreed upon, fixed date. You can model this by using schedule constraints, like Must-Start-On. In the illustration on the left, your ongoing task cannot be completed before the meeting, and could be scheduled entirely after the meeting, but splitting it around the meeting gives the tightest schedule.

To split a task bar:

1. Click **Split Task** ⬚ on the **Standard** toolbar. A yellow pop-up window appears and the mouse pointer now looks like: ⊩

2. Point to a task bar and click and drag to where you want the split to occur. A part of the task bar splits off and in the yellow pop-up you are shown what the new start and finish dates of the part will be when you release the mouse:

Task:	
Start:	Wed 4/5/00
Finish:	Sat 4/8/00

3. Drag it to where you want to schedule it and release the mouse button; the task bar is now split into two parts. Notice that the two parts are connected by dots:

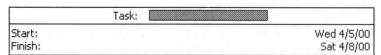

Even though this feature appears to work well at first glance, we do not recommend using it during the planning phase of the project. The predecessors may reschedule the task, and the split inside the task bar should move accordingly to keep it scheduled around the short task. The problem is that it does not move automatically. You will have to adjust your schedule manually every time a change occurs. That's why we don't recommend using this feature.

There are better approaches:

◆ You can split the task into multiple subtasks instead. For example, electricians wire a building, but after the inspection they have to come back to install the switch plates. You could show this as one task with a split task bar, but it would be better to split it into two tasks: *pull cables* and *install switch plates.* Now you can set dependencies between these tasks and keep your model entirely dynamic. If you have a choice between task splitting and bar splitting, we recommend you split the task rather than its bar.

◆ Create a task calendar for those tasks that might be affected. In the task calendar you indicate nonworking time for the duration of the short must-start-on task. As long as the must-start-on date does not change, the calendar will do a fine job. To find out how to do this, see page 140: Creating a New Task Calendar.

◆ Alternatively, you could allow the over-allocation of the resource to occur and then level the workloads using the **Tools, Level Resources…,** option ☑ **Leveling can create splits in remaining work**. In this case the resource leveling will create a split, and when you level again, it will move the split as needed.

◆ Lastly, you could ignore the over-allocation, assuming that the resources will work overtime.

Decrease Estimates

Often when you get closer to the tasks at hand you can provide a more precise estimate. Sometimes, you will find you overestimated and can do a task faster. Sometimes, you find a better and quicker way to do it. In both cases you can sharpen the estimate and cut off some of the duration. This may happen at the expense of the quality or the scope of the project, and any trade-off will have to be closely examined.

Reduce the Scope or Delete Tasks

Reducing the scope is a matter of deleting deliverables. If you delete deliverables that are on the Critical Path, you will reduce the duration of the project. Perhaps you are thinking at this point that you cannot delete deliverables that are critical. However, a critical deliverable does not necessarily mean it is an important deliverable; the word critical means in project management only that it drives the project end date. If there were critical deliverables qualified as nice-to-have, these would be good candidates. However, not delivering on what you promised may be dangerous from a contractual point of view, not to mention your reputation.

Alternatively, you could focus on the level below deliverables and find critical tasks to delete, as shown in the illustration. Sometimes you can find activities in the realm of nice-if-we-get-around-to-it. These are the candidates to cut. This may happen at the expense of the quality of the deliverables. If the quality requirement is a nice-to-have, you could cut the task. Deleting tasks is as easy as clicking on their row heading (ID number) and pressing $\boxed{\text{Delete}}$.

However, if you have set the baseline already, you should consider keeping the task and its baseline data and only deleting the dependencies, **Work, Cost**, **Fixed Cost**, as well as the assignments. Leave the fields **Baseline Work** and **Baseline Cost** alone to maintain the integrity of the baseline. For more on this, see chapter 11 on updating schedules (page 539).

Add Resources

Often people start asking for more resources when they start to feel the heat of their deadlines. In the illustrated example, the project manager asked for and got Ed to help out. If you add resources, you choose to work harder instead of smarter and it may cost you more money. I have often observed that when new resources arrive, the best resources are taken off their jobs to train them. This causes the slippage to increase at first instead of decrease.

How many people can you add to tasks? When optimizing for time only, we could in theory add an unlimited number. In practice there are, of course, limits. If you add too many people, eventually nothing will get done. People will be in each other's way and keep each other from being productive. The *law of diminishing returns* is applicable when adding resources. How many carpenters can work in one 10-by-15-foot room? The best example: adding another mother to carry the child does not shorten the pregnancy. There are simple practical limits. Even though we have assumed we have access to unlimited resources, it definitely does not seem reasonable to add more than the maximum units that are filled in on the resource sheet.

Make sure you change the task type to **Fixed Work** before adding resources. This will ensure that the duration decreases when you add them.

Considering Impacts on Quality, Scope and Time

1. Highlight the Critical Path
2. Sort the tasks based on duration
3. Find the longest critical task
4. Make a change on it
5. *Consider impacts on quality, scope and time*
6. *Decide whether you want to keep the change*
7. Repeat steps 3 - 7

As the next step, you have to evaluate the impact on quality, scope and time of the change you made. You can see the new duration of the project in one of two ways:

◆ View the **Duration** of the *project summary task*.

◆ View the **Current Duration** in the project statistics dialog.

We will discuss the steps for both in the next two sections. From the new project duration, you can see how much time you have gained, and whether it is worth the sacrifices you made on the scope of the project or the quality of the deliverables. If you find that the change did not yield the result expected, simply click undo ↰ to get rid of it.

You then continue to repeat steps 3 to 7 in the process of optimizing until you have solved the scheduling conflict.

Inserting a Project Summary Task

The project summary task is task number 0 and summarizes the entire project because everything is indented beneath it. MS Project will summarize the whole project in its fields **Start, Finish, Duration, Work** and **Cost**. It will show us the duration of the project before we make a change. To see the project summary task you have to jump to the top of the project every time. In order to make what-if analyses, you need to see the possible impact of any idea you try out. Take note of the duration of the project before making a change, then compare afterward.

1. Choose **Tools, Options**; the **Options** dialog appears.

2.   Click the **View** tab; the dialog should now look like:

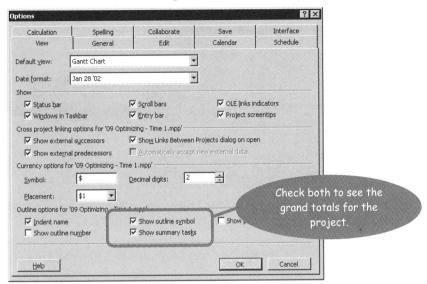

3.   Under **Outline Options** check both ☑ **Show Summary Tasks** and
     ☑ **Show Project Summary Task**.

4.   Click [OK]; the project summary task now shows the duration, total cost and
     work for the project. The task name of the project summary task is the **Title** of the
     project and can be found in **File, Properties**, tab **Summary**. If no title is filled in,
     the file name will stand in for it. We recommend, however, using the project title; it
     makes a better name for the project.

To View the Project Statistics Dialog

1.   Right-click on any toolbar and choose **Tracking** from the pop-up menu. The
     tracking toolbar is displayed:

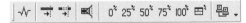

2. The dialog is now available by clicking on **Project Statistics** ⎍ on the **Tracking** toolbar. The dialog looks like:

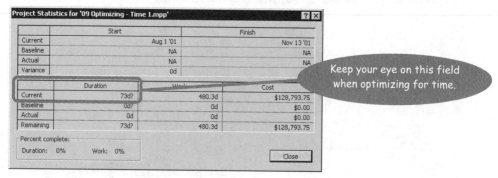

Keep your eye on this field when optimizing for time.

3. In the intersection of the **Current** row and the **Duration** column, you can see what the new duration of the project is.

The **Project Statistics** dialog seems like the best way to go because you can view it from wherever you are in your project without having to jump to the top of the project every time. It also is just one click away with the toolbar displayed.

This concludes our discussion of the Critical Path Method. And we will continue with simulation, as promised.

Monte Carlo Simulation

Once you have optimized the Critical Path you should ask yourself: *How much time contingency should I reserve in my schedule in order to protect the project deadline?* Monte Carlo simulation can help you determine that. Without simulation you will have to guess what the size of the buffer should be. One thing is certain: unforeseen events will happen and you will need a time buffer to compensate for those events.

What Is Monte Carlo Simulation?

The best-known simulation technique is *Monte Carlo simulation*. For tasks that are hard to predict (or for each task, if you have enough time) you specify the lower and upper

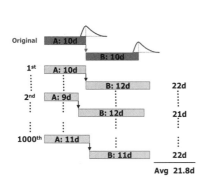

limits of an estimate and choose a probability curve between those limits. Some tasks are renowned for their wide range between the lower and upper limit, for example *debug code* in a *software development* project. The simulating software generates estimates for all the tasks using these parameters. It uses number generators that produce estimates that comply with the range and the distribution curve you have chosen for the estimate. It creates the first version of the entire schedule and calculates the Critical Path. In the illustration on the left, the *original* schedule is shown as well as the *1st*, the *2nd* and the *1000th* version created by the simulation software.

Simulation continues to create versions of the schedule and will create as many as you want. Simulations often create up to a thousand versions of the schedule. In each version the Critical Path of the schedule is calculated. The simulation software will then calculate averages and forecast end dates. It calculates the probabilities for a range of finish dates.

Output of Monte Carlo Simulation

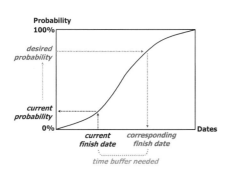

Simulation software creates an s-curve from the many versions of the schedule. An s-curve shows projected finish dates charted against the probability of meeting those dates. The illustration shows such an s-curve. The benefit of the s-curve is that you can see the chance of completing your project by the date that MS Project indicates as the project finish date in your schedule (see *current finish date* in the illustration and its *current probability*).

Alternatively, you can choose the level of probability you feel comfortable with and derive the project finish date, or you can let executives choose it for you (see *desired probability* in the illustration). With the desired probability you can find the *corresponding finish date*. You can quote this date to the client while knowing the degree of confidence that it can be met. There may still be other risks that you do not know about (*unforeseen unforeseens*), but at least you have quantified the *foreseen unforeseens* that we will discuss in the next section.

You can also calculate the size of the time buffer you need in your project. If you read from the s-curve that you need to add 3 weeks as a buffer to your current MS Project schedule for a 90% probability, you should insert this as a *buffer "task"* just before the *project finish milestone* and have it push out the milestone. Alternatively, you could hide the buffer in your schedule if you need to, but this is the least preferred way. For more on that, see page 475.

Project 2002 does not have simulation capabilities, but there are good add-ons on the market with which you can simulate MS Project schedules. One add-on is *Risk+*[55] and another is *@Risk* for MS Project.[56]

Why Do We Need Simulation?

Let me try to convince you why using Monte Carlo simulation is necessary. It is necessary because of two reasons:
- Forecasts from one-point estimates tend to be too optimistic.
- Converging paths compound the time risks.
We will discuss both in more detail.

---

[55] C/S Solutions (www.cs-solutions.com).

[56] Palisade Corporation (www.palisade.com). Note that @Risk also exists as a standalone tool and that you have to buy the *@Risk for MS Project* to simulate schedules.

One-Point Estimates

If you ask many different people for an estimate on one task, you can plot the estimated duration on the x-axis against the number of times you hear each estimate on the y-axis. The result will be a distribution curve that depicts the probability of a range of finish dates. It will look like the curve in the illustration below. The estimate that you hear most often is the mode, which is why the mode is shown under the top of the curve. The median divides the surface under the curve into two equal parts; there are as many estimates to the left as there are to the right of it. The mean is the mathematical average of all estimates you collect.

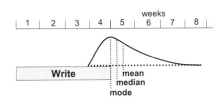

If you do this a few times, you will find that the resulting curve is often skewed to the right. In other words, durations tend to stretch rather than shrink. You probably knew that already if you have been a project manager for some time. Even if you don't have project management experience, it probably makes sense. What the skewed curve means is that the duration of the task is more likely to increase 1 week than decrease 1 week. In other words, tasks more often take longer than they shrink by the same amount.

However, the Critical Path consists of many tasks. It could be that you overran a task duration early in the schedule. This overrun can be compensated for by later underruns. The overall effect of the skewing of estimates is therefore not that dramatic. Nevertheless, you can safely state that schedules made with single estimates per task are optimistic. The PERT technique captures the cumulative effect of the skewed estimates along the critical path. However, converging paths have a more dramatic impact.

Converging Paths

It can be proven that converging paths decrease the probability of meeting the project end date. Where paths come together, the chance decreases that the milestone will be achieved with every path that is added leading into the milestone. In the illustration, the chance of delivering on time is exactly 81%. If one path is early, the other may be late and vice versa. When two paths both have to be finished, you therefore have to multiply the chances: 90% * 90% = 81%.

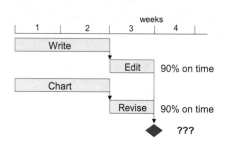

The more parallel paths you have in your schedule, the greater the time risk. This phenomenon is known as *path convergence* or *merge bias*. The aggregated effect of many merging paths of different lengths is very difficult to predict; simulation is the only way to find out. The more parallel paths you see in your schedule, the more you will need to simulate the schedule. This need is even greater if those paths have similar durations.

The paths make it unlikely that your end date, as shown by your MS Project schedule, will be met. That is why project managers developed the habit of padding their schedules. You need to do simulation in order to find the aggregated effect of the parallel paths. You can use simulation to quantify how much padding you will need in your schedule.

Assumptions of the Critical Path Method

In summary, Critical Path theory is based on three assumptions:
◆   Assumption 1: Task *estimates* are *normally distributed.*
◆   Assumption 2: There is no *merge bias* or *path convergence.*
◆   Assumption 3: You have *unlimited resources* available.

We saw on page 401 that assumption 1 does not hold true, but we can determine the magnitude of its effect by applying PERT or simulation.

As for assumption 2, we proved above that merge bias (path convergence) does exist. This effect often causes the largest slippages in projects. Simulation is the only technique that can make the compounded effect of converging paths visible. Applying the Critical Path Method (CPM) is good as long as you simulate it as well. Many overruns can be foreseen and quantified when simulation is applied to schedules.

Assumption 3 is more difficult to deal with. Both the CPM and the PERT techniques assume that resources are available in unlimited quantities. This assumption holds true, if workload is not your problem. For example:

◆ If resources are readily available, workload is not an issue.
◆ If you intend to subcontract the work, workload is not your issue. Resource allocation is the contractor's problem.
◆ For a consulting firm that can hire free-lance resources easily in the quantity and with the expertise needed, workload is not a problem either.

In these cases, the assumption can stand.

However, many project managers do not have access to unlimited resources in this day and age. In this era of global competition, many organizations cannot afford to supply unlimited resources to projects; neither can they afford not to track the usage of their resources. Today in the global market, a 1% change in return on investment (*ROI*) can be the difference between a viable and a nonviable company.

If you are managing the workload of your own scarce, internal resources, workload is your concern. In that case, both the CPM and the PERT techniques are of limited value. You need a new technique to optimize your schedule. For example, if you are managing IT resources, you probably are in a *resource-limited* situation.

Extra resources can be bought with money. We will therefore first introduce cost into the optimization (optimizing for time and cost), and then we will add the limited availability of resources (optimizing for time, cost and resources).

Optimizing for Time and Cost

When you optimize for time and cost, you should consider the dimensions scope, and quality as well. In the illustration we are adding the cost dimension in our quest for the optimal schedule. We will discuss this dimension before the resource dimension because most resource decisions impact the cost side of our model. So the logical progression in our view is optimizing for time (see page 366), then time and cost (see below), then time, cost and resources (see page 410).

Steps to Optimize for Time and Cost

Any project manager who has a budget in dollars or in person hours should at least apply this type of optimization. The steps for optimizing for time and cost are very similar to

1. Highlight the Critical Path
2. Sort the tasks on **Cost**
3. Find the **most expensive** task
4. Make a change on it
5. Consider impacts on quality, scope, time and **cost**
6. Decide whether you want to keep the change
7. Repeat steps 3 - 7

the steps for optimizing for time. The differences are highlighted in bold in the illustration. Because you should not lose sight of the time dimension of the project, you still have to find the Critical Path as well. If you want to bring the duration of the project down, you should also apply the optimizing for time methods discussed in the previous section. Keeping the duration of a project as short as possible will also keep the cost of overhead expenses down. To keep the discussion on the process for optimizing for cost simple, we will focus only on cost in the text that follows.

If you find that the restricted availability of resources is driving your finish date out, you will need to optimize for time, cost and resources, which is the third approach of optimizing (see page 410). In that case, you should read this section as well because in the next approach we will not discuss any other methods to reduce cost.

After you have highlighted the Critical Path, you sort on cost to find the most expensive tasks. You develop ideas for how you might bring down the cost with no or minimal compromise on time, scope or quality. Enter the change and check the results to see whether you want to keep the change. We will discuss how to accomplish some of these steps in Project 2002.

Sorting on Cost

To find the tasks on which we can make significant savings, we should sort the tasks on cost.

1. Choose **View, Gantt Chart**.

2. Choose **Project, Sort, Sort by...**; the **Sort** dialog appears:

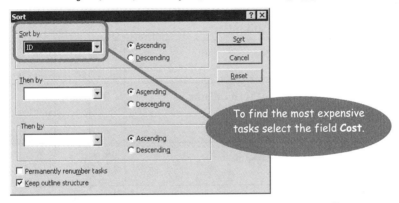

3. In the **Sort by** list, select **Cost** and set the sort order to ⦿ **Descending**.

4. Do not renumber the tasks; uncheck:
   ☐ **Permanently renumber tasks** and
   ☐ **Keep outline structure**.

5. Click [Sort]; the tasks are now fully sorted and you can easily find the ones where you can make significant savings.

6. You can reset the original sort order by choosing **Project, Sort, Sort by ID**

Lowering the Cost of a Project

The best measurements are those that make the quality (Q) go up (↑), the scope (S) go up (↑), the time (T) go down (↓) and the cost (C) go down (↓). Unfortunately, there are no such ideal measurements. However, we will give you ideas about what you can do. The following table shows actions to lower the cost (C) and their likely impact on quality (Q), scope (S) and time (T). A question mark (?) indicates that you need to look at your specific situation to determine the effect of the measurement. A zero (0) means that there is no expected impact.

	Action	For	Q	S	T	C
1	Find cheaper contracts	External contractors, consultants	?	?	?	↓
2	Reassign to cheaper resources	Expensive resources	?	?	?	↓
3	Break up a long task and reassign portions to cheaper resources	Long (critical) tasks	0	0	↓	↓
4	Shorten the project duration to decrease overhead cost	Critical tasks	?	?	↓	↓
5	Prevent overtime work	Resources with a higher overtime rate	0	0	↑	↓
6	Smooth the workloads	Resources with erratic workloads	?	?	?	↓
7	Decrease the estimate	Any tasks with labor costs	↓	0	↓	↓
8	Reduce the scope or delete tasks	Any tasks with costs involved	↓	↓	↓	↓

The actions are listed in order of overall effectiveness. You should start at the top of the table and work your way down. If you need to bring down the duration of your project as well, use the optimizing for time methods as discussed on page 386. Make sure you select those methods that do not increase the cost again. If you shorten the project duration, the overhead costs will also decrease (see method 4). You will save on expenses for project management, facilities, support staff and other overhead costs.

If you are to manage the cash flow of your project as well, another measure might be to renegotiate when the costs accrue and change the resource field **Accrue at** accordingly. Delaying the accrual of expenses will improve your cash flow.

Finding Cheaper Contracts

The question you should ask yourself is: *Do I always solicit more than one bid or proposal?* If the answer is *no*, then this method may create significant savings for you. After all, contractors and consultants are quick to find out whether or not they are in a competitive situation and will quote accordingly. Another option is to research whether there are specialized firms that are quicker or better at their trade than other suppliers. If a specialized firm is using better technology, techniques, equipment or resources, it may be cheaper, even at a higher hourly rate.

1. Create the new resource in the resource sheet. For the how-to, see page 279: Entering Resources.

2. Choose **View, Gantt Chart** where we will change the assignments to the new resource.

3. Select the task, and click **Assign Resources** on the **Standard** toolbar; the **Assign Resources** dialog appears:

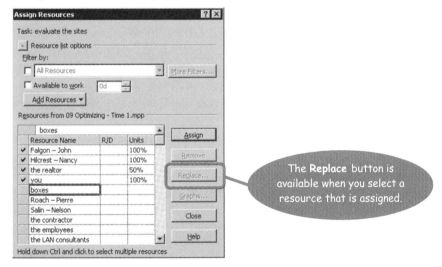

The **Replace** button is available when you select a resource that is assigned.

4. Resources that are assigned have a check mark in front of their name in the list. Click on the assigned resource to replace. In Project 2002, these resources will always appear at the top of the list.

5. Click [Replace...] ; the **Replace Resource** dialog appears on top of the **Assign Resources** dialog:

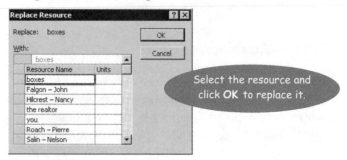

6. Click on the substitute resource and click [OK] ; the resource is now replaced on the task.

Reassigning to Cheaper Resources

We just discussed how to replace one resource with another. You can find the resource rates in the Resource Sheet.

Breaking Up a Long Task and Reassigning Portions

If you decide to break up a long task, perhaps the best way to do so is to insert subtasks below it, thereby promoting it to a summary task. Then you assign the cheaper resources to these subtasks and remove the expensive resource from the summary task. The cost should decrease as a result. Don't forget to set appropriate dependencies, so as not to leave any *loose ends* in the network logic.

Shortening the Project Duration

If you decrease the project duration, the overhead costs will decrease. The longer a project takes, the longer the project manager and team leaders need to stick around, and the longer support, facilities and equipment have to stay available. The shorter a project is, the less overhead costs you will incur. To save cost you therefore have to maintain or bring down the time as well. We discussed the methods to shorten the project duration on page 386.

Preventing Overtime Work

Preventing overtime work will only bring down the cost if you are actually paying a higher rate for overtime. For the how-to steps for decreasing overtime, refer to the section on how to create it in the first place, see page 448. Of course, if you reduce overtime, you may be extending your project duration, which is a simple trade-off against the time dimension. You can only do that if saving cost is more important than finishing as early as possible.

Smoothing the Workloads

In the illustrated example below, the total workload before and after smoothing is the same 100 person days, but you could raise the question: *Would the eventual cost for an erratic workload be more or less than the eventual cost for a smooth workload?* If a resource has an erratic workload, there may be days or weeks when the resource is not needed. The resource may have other employment during those valleys for which he is paid from funds other than the project budget. If this is not the case, the project manager will likely keep the resource around, particularly if his skill set is scarce. The project manager then assumes the cost for the idle time. The answer to the question raised, then, is that without smoothing, the actual cost is higher. The project budget does not show this cost, because it only shows the cost of the planned assignments. The extra cost of an erratic workload is hidden cost in the plan. If you smooth the workload, you will decrease this hidden cost of the project. You will therefore not see the cost of the project decrease while you are smoothing the workload. This hidden cost is difficult to quantify during the planning phase, but, in general, you can say that the more erratic the workload, the higher the hidden cost in the project plan.

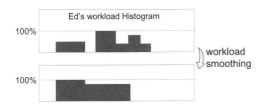

An intriguing paradox is that the scarcer a resource is, the more the resource should be shared between projects from the organization's point of view, but the less likely that project managers actually will share this scarce resource.

Reducing the Scope or Deleting Tasks

We discussed this method on page 394. Remember that the integrity of the original baseline may be compromised when you rebaseline after deleting tasks.

Optimizing for Time, Cost and Resources

The next black arrow in the illustration is the dimension *resources*. We add it to the ones we already monitor: Quality, Scope, Time and Cost. Inclusion of the resources means that we will monitor the workload of the resources relative to their availability. If you find that the limited availability (or unavailability) of resources affects the forecasted dates, you are in a *resource-constrained or resource-limited* situation. In this case you need to include resources in your optimization.

The resource dimension may make trade-offs with:
♦ Cost, when you have to pay for extra resources
♦ Time, when you cannot solve over-allocations in any other way than delaying tasks

In this section, we will only discuss how to trade off between time and resources to keep the discussion simple. If you also need to bring down the cost of your project at the same time, you should consider the methods discussed in optimizing for time and cost (see Optimizing for Time and Cost on page 404).

The optimization becomes more complex, but if we manage to handle this complexity, we will have confidence that the project is feasible as far as the resources are concerned. This will increase the validity of our forecasts.

Steps to Optimize for Time, Cost and Resources

1. **Check the workloads and level them**
2. Highlight the **Resource Critical Path (RCP)**
3. Find the **most critical resource**
4. Make a change on it
5. Consider impacts on quality, scope, time, cost and **resources**
6. Decide whether you want to keep the change
7. Repeat steps 3 - 7

As the steps in the process chart show, the first thing we have to do is *resource workload leveling*, also known as *resource leveling* or *workload leveling*. We have to check:

◆ whether the workloads are within the availability of the human resources,

◆ whether the work is within the availability of the facilities and

◆ whether the work is within the capacity of the equipment.

When resources are scarce, you will often find that the schedule extends when you level the workloads. This renders the *Critical Path* fragmented and we will need to find the *Resource-Critical Path* (*RCP*). The differences between this method of optimization and the optimizations previously discussed (see page 376) appear in bold type in the process box. There are quite a few pages on this approach to optimizing so we will show our progress using this process chart. Once you have found the RCP, optimization is very similar to the methods we used with the *Critical Path Method*.

Workload Leveling

The first step in optimizing for time, cost and resources is checking the workloads. If there are over-allocations, the workloads need to be leveled. Ideally, you will have prevented over-allocations in the first place since they are always painful to solve, particularly when you are sharing resources with other project managers. We explained how you can prevent over-allocations when you use the **Assign Resources** dialog on page 334.

We will discuss how to level workloads by making manual changes to the schedule (see page 413) or letting MS Project solve all over-allocations for you automatically (see page 420). If you level your schedule, you will often insert delays for certain tasks. These delays will influence the calculation of the Critical Path, which we will discuss.

Checking the Workloads: Resource Graph

1. Choose **View**, **Resource Graph** OR click **Resource Graph** 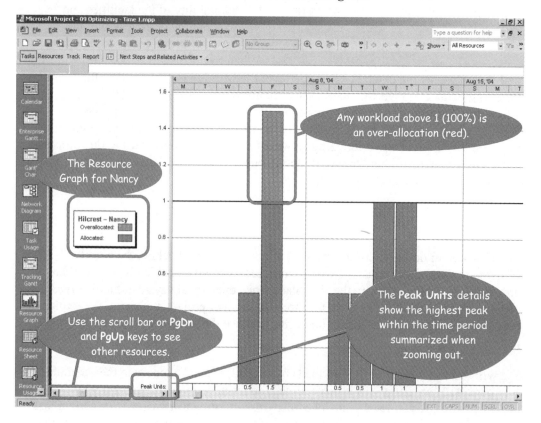 on the view bar.

2. Hold down [Alt] and press [Home] to make the timescale jump to the start of the project.

3. Use **Zoom Out** [Q] and **Zoom In** [Q] on the **Standard** toolbar to adjust the timescale.

4. Press [Page Dn] to go to the next resource OR press [Page Up] to go to a previous resource.

The *Resource Graph* is also known as the *resource histogram.*[57]

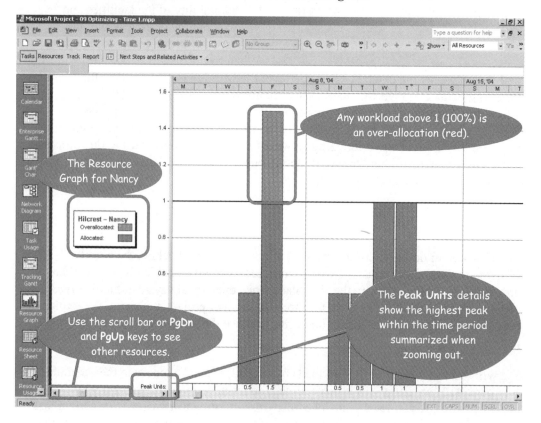

---

[57] See the PMBOK® Guide, 2000 Edition, published by the PMI.

The Resource Graph shows, by default, the **Peak Units**. **Peak Units** presents an inflated picture of the real work when you zoom out, because it shows the highest bar during the time period summarized. Choose **Format, Details, Work** to get a more realistic view of the workloads.

Level the Workloads Yourself

There are many ways in which you can level the workloads by hand without using the **Automatic Leveling** or **Level Now** feature of Project 2002. The methods are listed below in order of perceived effectiveness. The ones at the top are most effective.

1.	Allocate the best resources to the critical tasks first and only to the critical tasks. Matching people to the tasks such that the best person does the task also results in time gained.
2.	Reassign tasks from critical resources to noncritical resources. You can do this quickly in MS Project by switching to the Resource Usage view, where you can simply drag assignments (without ID number, italic text) from one resource to another.
3.	Take the critical resource off a task. Sometimes you can do this when more than one person is working on the task, or you do this as soon as you know who will really pull the cart. Remember that the word *critical* does not mean the resource is an important resource on the task; it just means the resource is driving the task and project duration. That sometimes makes it possible to simply remove the resource from the task to bring the workload down.
4.	Hire extra resources. If you hire extra resources, you can reassign the tasks from your critical resources to the new resources. This works well if the new resources have skills similar to or better than your existing resources.
5.	Contract work out to subcontractors. One definition of a subcontractor is someone who solves your workload problems in exchange for money.
6.	Negotiate more resources from subcontractors. If you can get more resources from subcontractors, the workload of existing resources can be reduced.

7.	Fine-tune the number of units assigned to the tasks involved in the over-allocation. For example, you could keep two tasks scheduled in parallel if you decrease the involvement of the resource to 50%. Make sure you keep the resource working 100% on critical tasks.
8.	Split long tasks into many shorter ones and reassign them to noncritical resources. Splitting tasks increases the number of scheduling possibilities.
9.	Delay vacations until after the deadline.
10.	Work during the weekend. If an over-allocation occurs on a Friday, you can easily solve such a situation by asking the resource to work some hours over the weekend.
11.	Assign overtime. Even though this does not solve the over-allocation, it shows that it has been dealt with.
12.	Change dependencies. Decrease overlaps between tasks that are done by the same resource. In the special case in which you have a team of people going from one city to another to install a system, consider setting extra soft dependencies. This solidifies the order in which locations are rolled out and keeps the workloads of the teams reasonable.
13.	Lower quality standards and lower work estimates, which decrease the workload. You can often cut corners in the category of nice-to-have requirements.
14.	Split task bars when multiple resources are assigned to move the workloads of the individual resources to where they fit into their availability.
15.	Delay tasks Slip one of the tasks that compete for the same resource. If you decide to delay one task, choose the task that has the most slack and the least number of resources assigned. If you delay a task with many resources assigned, you may cause many new over-allocations. Through the dependencies, successors may cause new over-allocations; you can never really tell what will happen when you start delaying tasks. You have to do it week by week.

MS Project cannot replace you as a manager. It can neither reassign tasks nor change the units on assignments. Reassigning is often better than delaying tasks. Project 2002 can only delay task bars (method number 15) or split task bars where multiple resources are assigned (method number 14). It can only apply the last two methods listed; it cannot handle any of the other methods to level the workloads. Therefore, we have to conclude that you will have to level the workloads by hand if you want the tightest schedule possible. Let's explore the steps to do this in the easiest way possible.

Apply the Resource Allocation View

Right-click on any toolbar and choose **Resource Management** from the pop-up menu. Click **Resource Allocation View** on the **Resource Management** toolbar to display the **Resource Allocation** view.

OR

1. Choose **View, More Views…**; the **More Views** dialog appears:

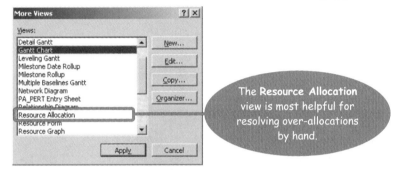

2. Select the **Resource Allocation** view and click Apply; a combination view appears with the **Resource Usage** view in the top pane and the **Leveling Gantt** in the bottom pane. The top pane shows the over-allocated resources and the bottom pane shows the conflicting tasks, which helps in resolving the over-allocation.

The Steps to Level Workloads Yourself

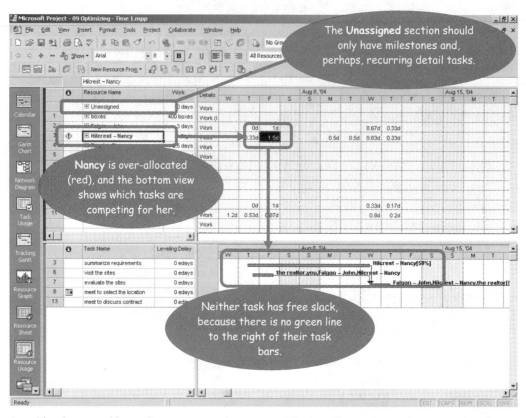

1. Check to see if you forgot any assignments. The heading ⊞ **Unassigned** at the top contains the unassigned tasks. Click on the button ⊞ to expand them, and click ⊟ to hide them again. Typically, only the milestones and recurring detail tasks should be listed in the **Unassigned** category. If you have not assigned resources to all detail tasks, you have not captured all the workloads and you should not start leveling. It will be a waste of effort.

2. Hide all assignments in the top pane by clicking ⬚ on the **Formatting** toolbar.

3. The over-allocated resources are shown in red. Position your mouse pointer over the icon ⬚ in the **Indicators ❶** column. The screen tip that pops up gives leveling advice. If you are advised to level on a day-by-day basis, then zoom in the timescale until you see the days. The over-allocations will become clear to you.

4. Scroll to the start of the project by dragging the scroll box on the horizontal scrollbar of the timescale to the far left. This step is essential since the tool will only look

forward in time for over-allocations. Unfortunately, pressing [Alt] + [Home] does not work in the Resource Usage view.

5. Go to the first over-allocation by clicking **Go To Next Overallocation** on the **Resource Management** toolbar. MS Project starts at the date you have in view and searches forward day by day to find the next over-allocation. It does not stick to the selected resource.

6. Determine if the over-allocation is serious enough that it needs resolution. MS Project tends to highlight tasks even when they overlap only 1 hour. Resolve the serious over-allocations one by one by applying one of the methods provided on page 413.

Some remarks about the tool **Go To Next Overallocation** :

◆   It often finds over-allocations that are not important. If two 1 hour tasks are scheduled concurrently, it will highlight this as an over-allocation. You can easily skip such over-allocations. Such short tasks will not affect your project end date in a significant way.

◆   It skips over-allocations that happened in the past, which is okay. You have probably already experienced a slippage in your schedule as a result of over-allocations that were left unresolved.

◆   It sometimes does not find over-allocations that are serious.

Nevertheless, we recommend this tool as the best way to go in Project 2002.

In the next illustration, you can see how the over-allocation is solved by delaying one of the tasks that was competing for the same resource:

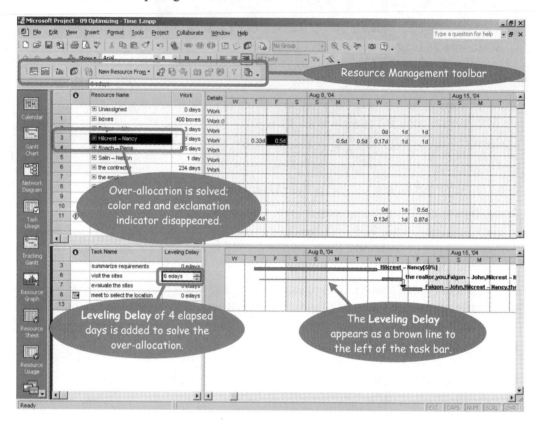

The bottom view can be improved by displaying a line for the total slack as well. If the free slack is not large enough, the total slack may provide possibilities to resolve the over-allocation. We will have to add a colored line for the total slack to each task bar. Click in the bottom pane and choose **Format, Bar Styles**.

Insert a new line above the (free) slack line. Use similar settings but change the color (use light green). Under **To**, choose **Total Slack** from the list.

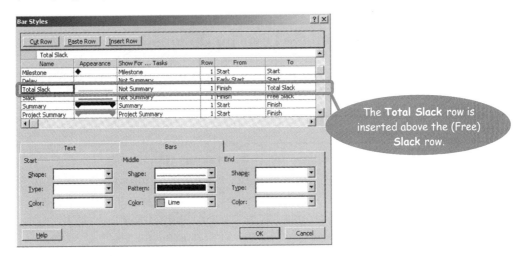

The **Total Slack** row is inserted above the (Free) Slack row.

If you insert the total slack item above the free slack item, the shorter free slack line will be superimposed on the total slack line. MS Project creates the items in the order they are listed. Now you can see how far you can delay tasks without affecting the next constraint date or the project end date.

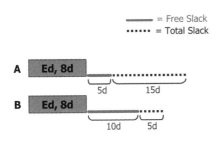

= Free Slack
= Total Slack

If a task does not have enough *free slack* to solve over-allocations, you can use its *total slack* to solve the work overload. The total slack is always greater than or equal to the free slack. In the illustration, task *A* does not have enough free slack to solve the over-allocation, but it does have enough total slack. If you go beyond the total slack, you are missing a constraint date, or you are increasing the project duration. In the illustrated example, I would delay task *B* since it resolves the over-allocation within the free slack. This assures me that no other successor is affected, which is nice to know. If I delay task *A*, successors will be affected. The art of project management is to minimize turbulence.

Have MS Project Level the Workloads

Choosing the Leveling Options

Choose **Tools, Level Resources** to access the *leveling options* when you are resolving *over-allocations*:

Section	Options
Leveling calculations	We recommend you select ⊙ **Manual.** If you select *manual leveling*, you can still have MS Project level the workloads whenever you want by clicking [Level Now]. You can also delete any traces of leveling left in the task field **Leveling Delay** by choosing **Tools, Level Resources...** and clicking [Clear Leveling...]. *Automatic leveling* continuously levels the workloads and makes the task bars jump all over the place with every change you make in the schedule. MS Project levels mostly by delaying tasks. This option is a global option that takes effect in all your project files.
	In the list, **Look for overallocations on a,** you can choose the *granularity* with which MS Project combs through the data to find over-allocations. A double workload on Monday but a total workload of 16 hours in a week constitutes an overload on a day-by-day basis, but not on a week-by-week basis. The setting is about the granularity of leveling. We recommend using **Day by Day** or **Week by Week** for most projects.
	Check ☑ **Clear Leveling values before leveling** if you want to clear the field **Leveling delay** of old leveling values. Uncheck it if you want MS Project to add to the leveling delays incrementally; this often leads to unnecessarily long project durations.
Leveling range for	Select ⊙ **Level entire project**. You normally would level the entire project, but you can also indicate a date range.
Resolving overallocations	Check or uncheck **Level only within available Slack**. You can check this option to develop a scenario when you want to know how many of the over-allocations MS Project can resolve within a certain time frame.

Section	Options
	☑ **Leveling can adjust individual assignments on a task** Check this option if you want to find the shortest leveled schedule. If you have more than one person assigned to a task, this option will level the individual assignments rather than all assignments as a group. The result is that task bars are often split into multiple parts because each assignment on the task will be scheduled separately. If you use this option, you can still override it for certain tasks by entering *No* in the task field **Level Assignments**. Notice that MS Project sets this field by default to *No* for fixed duration and recurring detail tasks; for all other tasks it is set to *Yes*. If you uncheck it, MS Project will schedule the task when the whole group is available.
	☑ **Leveling can create splits in remaining work** Check this option if you want to allow MS Project to split task bars. Splitting may generate a tighter schedule, because if you allow splitting, MS Project can schedule portions around tasks that have constraint dates. The drawback is that task bars become fragmented. If you want to exclude certain tasks from being split, uncheck their task field **Leveling can split**. Fixed duration tasks have this field set to *No* and will not be split by Project 2002 because it would increase their duration.

Three Automatic Leveling Scenarios

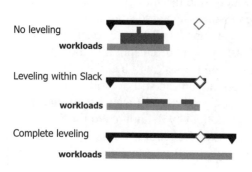

There are three scenarios you can develop with Project 2002, and you can switch back and forth among them as many times as you need to. Each scenario provides some useful information.

The illustration shows all three scenarios. The black workloads are the over-allocations. The more the workloads are leveled, the fewer over-allocations. Without doing anything, you currently have the first scenario of *No leveling*.

◆ **No leveling**
If you look at the timescale of Gantt Charts, you often see several tasks scheduled concurrently. Where two concurrent tasks have the same resource assigned, the workloads can exceed the availability of the resource. If there are no over-allocations, you will not need to level. In that case, only the task durations and dependencies drive the duration of the project. This scenario answers the question: *What is the project duration when the workloads are not leveled?* This scenario tells us the minimum duration for the project.

◆ **Leveling within the slack of the project**
If you create a milestone with a must-finish-on constraint on the proposed target date, you can level within the slack this hard date creates. This scenario answers the question: *What workload will critical resources have while meeting the project target date?* This scenario tells you how many extra resources you should hire in order to meet the target date. As you can see in the illustration, you may need an extra programmer for a few months and an extra tester for one month in a software development project, for example.

◆ **Complete leveling**
This answers: *What is the end date of the project if the workloads of all resources are entirely leveled?* This shows a comfortable deadline for the project and the team.

All three scenarios provide useful information when negotiating deadlines with upper management or clients:

◆ The no-leveling date from the first scenario is your resistance point in negotiations; you should not commit to an earlier date. You will still have to resolve all over-allocations if you commit to this date without delaying the project finish date, which can be challenging depending on how many over-allocations you have.

◆ The remaining over-allocations from the second scenario may provide the common ground in your negotiations with the client. You can ask MS Project to resolve as many over-allocations as it can while staying within a certain time frame. You can then easily find out how many extra resources you need to hire to meet the target date and calculate what that would cost. If the client is willing to pay for these extra resources, you may have a date that meets the needs of both your client and yourself.

◆ The finish date of the third scenario is the date we recommend you first quote to your client. It is a date that is nice to have, and that you will likely not get. It could be your starting position in negotiations.

For each of these scenarios it is nice to see what changes MS Project has made to the schedule, and the **Leveling Gantt** view is best suited for this purpose. To apply this view, choose **View, More Views**, select **Leveling Gantt** from the list and click Apply . The view looks like this:

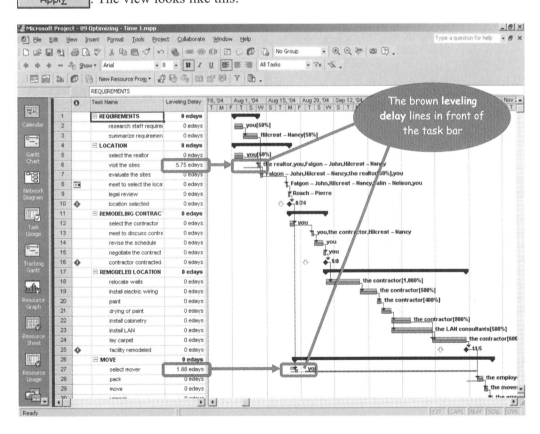

This view includes the field **Leveling Delay** as one of the columns, and it also shows the delay graphically with a brown line to the left of any task bars that were delayed.

No Leveling or Clearing the Leveling

1. If you have leveled workloads before, the field **Leveling Delay** will have entries. To check if this is the case, you can insert this field by choosing **Insert, Column**.

2. You can only clear the leveling if you are in one of the task views. Change to a task view first, if necessary.

3. To remove the leveling delay, choose **Tools, Level Resources...**; the **Resource Leveling** dialog appears:

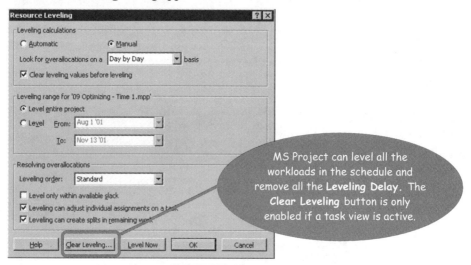

(callout) MS Project can level all the workloads in the schedule and remove all the **Leveling Delay**. The **Clear Leveling** button is only enabled if a task view is active.

4. Select ⊙ **Manual** and click Clear Leveling... ; the **Clear Leveling** dialog appears:

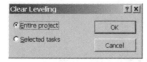

5. Select ⊙ **Entire Project** and click OK ; you are now back in the task view. The numbers in the field **Leveling Delay** should all be zero.

You now know the minimum duration for your project; there can still be over-allocations in the schedule that need to be taken care of.

Leveling within the Slack of the Project

1. Make sure you have a project finish milestone at which all dependencies come together. The project milestone should have a *must-finish-on* constraint on the proposed target date; a finish-no-later-than constraint does not work here.

2. Choose **Tools, Level Resources…**; the **Resource Leveling** dialog appears:

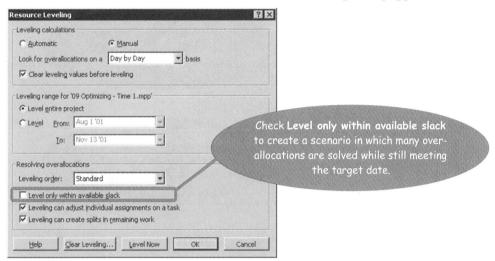

The callout in the image reads:

> Check **Level only within available slack** to create a scenario in which many over-allocations are solved while still meeting the target date.

3. Choose the granularity of the leveling by selecting from the list **Look for overallocations on a** the time unit in which MS Project should find over-allocations. We recommend **Day by Day** or **Week by Week** for most projects.

4. Check ☑ **Clear leveling values before leveling** to clear the field **Leveling delay** of old leveling values; MS Project will make a fresh start with the leveling.

5. Check ☑ **Level only within available slack**.

6. Click Level Now . MS Project may alert you that it cannot resolve certain over-allocations, which is what we expected since we gave it a fixed time frame.

7. Click OK .

8. Check the workloads of the resources; there are often some over-allocations left.

If the workloads of the resources are still too high to meet the deadline, then other methods have to be applied to make the workloads reasonable (see the methods discussed on page 416).

Complete Leveling

1. Insert the column **Leveling Delay** in the Gantt spreadsheet by right-clicking on the column heading **Duration**, choosing **Insert Column** and selecting the field **Leveling Delay** from the list. This field allows us to see the result of the leveling.

2. Choose **Tools, Level Resources…**; the **Resource Leveling** dialog appears:

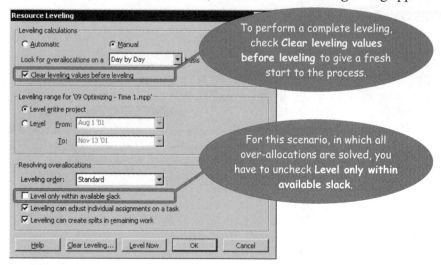

3. Choose the precision of the leveling by selecting from the list **Look for overallocations on a** the granularity with which MS Project should find over-allocations. We recommend **Day by Day** or **Week by Week** for most projects.

4. Check ☑ **Clear leveling values before leveling** if you want to clear the field **Leveling delay** of old leveling values, which we recommend.

5. Select ◉ **Level entire project**.

6. Uncheck ☐ **Level only within available slack**; otherwise Project 2002 may not solve all over-allocations.

7. Check ☑ **Leveling can adjust individual assignments on a task** if you want to find the shortest leveled schedule. MS Project schedules the assignments individually instead of as a group. You may end up with split task bars, but you can redo the leveling and uncheck the option to prevent bar splits, or you can set the task field **Level assignments** to *No* for task bars you don't want to be split.

8. Check ☑ **Leveling can create splits in remaining work** if you want to allow MS Project to split task bars. The drawback is that the task bars become fragmented.

If you want to exclude certain tasks from being split, set their task field **Leveling can split** to *No*. Fixed duration tasks have this field already set to *No*.

9. Click [Level Now]. MS Project delayed certain tasks. In the column **Leveling Delay** you can see which tasks have been delayed and by how long.

The schedule is now realistic in the sense that the resources can finish the work assigned to them without the project end date slipping further. Check the end date in the **Finish** column of the project summary task; it has likely been delayed. Only if the over-allocations are small, will MS Project be able to solve them without delaying the project finish.

Influencing MS Project's Leveling

When you ask MS Project to level your schedule, it will try to choose intelligently which tasks to delay. It looks at the amount of slack on both tasks that compete for the same resource. It will delay the one task that has the most slack. It does not always delay the task you would prefer. MS Project offers you three choices to influence which tasks are delayed. You will find these in the **Tools, Level resources…, Leveling order** list. Below are some suggestions on when to use each:

◆ **ID**
    Project 2002 will level tasks based upon their ID numbers. It will give priority to the task higher up in the list of tasks. Use this setting to prioritize projects in a consolidated file. Put your highest priority projects at the top of the list and then level your consolidated schedule using this option.

◆ **Standard**
    This is the default setting and is used for regular leveling. Under standard leveling the task with the most slack will be delayed, which makes sense.

◆ **Priority, Standard**
    When you are not entirely happy with MS Project's leveling, you can enter a priority number for each task in the field **Priority**. In this way, you can influence which task is delayed in the leveling. This involves a fair bit of work.

How can you predict which tasks will be postponed when resources are over-allocated? This is difficult unless you assign priority levels in the column **Priority** or in the view **Task Details Form**. Priority numbers can range from 0 to 1000, and the higher the number, the higher the priority. MS Project will not delay the higher priority task when you level using the leveling setting **Priority, Standard**. Another way to influence leveling is to exclude certain tasks or resources as candidates for leveling.

Excluding Tasks from MS Project Leveling

If the priority number is set to *1000*, MS Project will not delay the task, and will effectively exclude it from the leveling process. This is even the case if you use the **ID** or **Standard** setting in the **Tools, Level resources, Leveling order** list.

Excluding Resources from MS Project Leveling

Typically, you would exclude subcontractor resources from leveling because the workload of people external to your organization is normally not your problem.

You can exclude human resources by entering *No* in the resource field *Can Level*.
OR

1. In the Resource Sheet view, select the resources you want to include first, then choose **Tools, Level Resources…**; the **Resource Leveling** dialog appears.

2. Upon clicking [**Level Now**], you will see the following dialog:

3. Select the option ⊙ **Selected resources** and click [OK]. MS Project will now only level the workloads for those resources you selected. This allows you to quickly develop several scenarios.

Human resources can do more than one task at a time, which is also known as *multi-tasking*. Whether this increases or decreases productivity is a separate discussion.

	Type	Leveling
Human	Work	percentage
Facilities	Material	yes/no
Machines	Material	yes/no
Materials	Material	exclude

To level human resources, you fill the workload up to the limit of their availability. If someone is only used 80% of their time, another small part-time task could be added without causing over-allocation. I call this *percentage leveling* since you try to fill availability up to 100%. In general, facilities and machines are either occupied or not and need *yes/no leveling*. Unfortunately, Project 2002 does not consider facilities and machines as separate types of resources, nor does it have features for yes/no leveling. You will have to create a reservation system for boardrooms and training rooms outside of

Project 2002 to keep their "workload" reasonable. More importantly, you don't want unforeseen unavailability to affect the forecasts in your project model.

Materials are consumable and don't need leveling. You can exclude materials by setting the resource field **Can Level** to *No*. MS Project does this for you, in fact, for material resources.

Should I Level Myself or Have MS Project Do It for Me?

At this point we have discussed both ways of leveling workloads: doing it yourself or having MS Project do it for you. If you struggle with which to choose, here are some recommendations:

◆ If you have few over-allocations in your schedule, you could probably resolve them all yourself without puzzling for hours. We recommend you do it yourself by hand and don't use MS Project's leveling features. MS Project would likely push out your project end date unnecessarily.

◆ If there are many over-allocations in your schedule, resolving them all by hand is a lot of work, and in that case it may be easier to perform a complete leveling. This will likely push your project end date far out. You can then improve upon that by finding the Resource-Critical Path in your schedule and focusing on the resource-critical tasks. We will explain the concept of the Resource-Critical Path in the next section.

How Leveling Affects the Critical Path

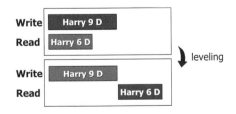

In the illustration the two tasks are *write* a report and *read* another unrelated document. The tasks are not dependent upon each other; Harry can choose to do them in any order. Before leveling, the Critical Path is the task *write*. After leveling, *read* is the only critical task. Try this out in MS Project! Don't worry, there is nothing wrong with your software; this is how the Critical Path algorithm works, is supposed to work and works in other software applications as well. The Critical Path assumes that you have access to unlimited resources.

In Project 2002 the leveled mini-schedule looks as follows:

	🛈	Task Name	Duration	Total Slack	Critical	Leveling Delay	Early Start	Late Start	Early Finish	Late Finish	Aug 31, '03	Sep 7, '03
											S S M T W T F	S S M T W
1		write	3 days	2 days	No	0 edays	Sep 1	Sep 3	Sep 3	Sep 5	▇▇▇ Harry	
2		read	2 days	0 days	Yes	3 edays	Sep 1	Sep 4	Sep 5	Sep 5	▇▇▇ Harry	

3 elapsed days of **Leveling Delay** to keep Harry's workload reasonable adds total slack to *write* and breaks the Critical Path.

Let me explain the mathematics of the algorithm in this simple example:

♦ On the forward pass, the *early start* for *write* is day 1 and the *early finish* is day 3 given the duration of 3 days. For *read* the early start is day 1; remember that there is no dependency between the tasks, and the early finish is at the end of day 5, given the delayed start date of day 4.

♦ On the backward pass, the *late finish* for *read* is also day 5; the *late start*, therefore, is day 4. *Write* has to be finished on the project finish date; the late finish date is day 5 since there is no dependency between the two. It has to start, at the latest, on day 3 to meet this date.

Total slack can be calculated by subtracting the early finish date from the late finish date. The total slack of the task *read* is 5 – 5 = 0 days; the task is critical and highlighted in red. The total slack for *write* is 5 – 3 = 2 days; the task is not seen as critical by the algorithm. However, common sense dictates that there really is no slack on the task *write*, because it competes for the same resource, *Harry*. And if the task *write* takes longer, the task *read* will be moved out. This example demonstrates the weakness of the Critical Path algorithm. The algorithm does not take resource dependencies into account because it is built on the assumption that you have access to unlimited resources.

Access to unlimited resources is not the current reality any longer for many organizations that are competing in the global marketplace. Organizations that use their resources well gain a competitive edge. Resources are often stretched to their limits and drive the project end date. An organization that does not optimize the usage of its resources will soon notice this in its bottom line. In other words, many organizations find themselves having to level the workloads of their resources, and upon doing so, the Critical Path often becomes fragmented. The leveling of tasks can make the total slack indicator of a task meaningless and thus the Critical Path as well. In fact, tasks indicated with slack may be driving the project end date, as is the case with the task *write* in the example above. If *write* slips, it will move *read* because of the resource dependency of *Harry* assigned to both tasks. The slack is false slack.

Examples of projects in which resources are scarce are pharmaceutical, IT, military R&D and biotechnology projects. In general, any project that uses expert resources tends to be a *resource-constrained* or *resource-limited* project. If you are the project manager of such a project, you should find the Resource-Critical Path in your schedule.

Critical Path or Resource-Critical Path?

We need a smarter Critical Path that takes logical dependencies as well as resource dependencies into account. Such a path is called the *Resource-Critical Path (RCP)*.

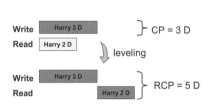

Given the example in the illustration, what should you monitor, the *Critical Path (CP)* or the *RCP*? The answer is obvious. The Critical Path in the unleveled schedule forecasts unrealistic finish dates because there is a work overload for Harry. In the leveled schedule, the Critical Path is fragmented and useless. Both tasks are resource-critical because Harry is assigned to both tasks; this is also called a *resource dependency*. One should try to find the RCP in *resource-constrained* projects. Only the RCP provides a complete explanation of the project duration. It shows what drives the project end date at any time during the project duration, just like the Critical Path used to do. The RCP is more helpful in a leveled schedule.

The Resource-Critical Path

Let us first define this new concept of the RCP. An *RCP* is the series of tasks that determines the project end date while taking logical dependencies and resource dependencies into account.[58] Notice it is not very different from the definition of the Critical Path. However, other common definitions of the Critical Path, like *the sequence of tasks without slack*, do not apply to the RCP, because resource-critical tasks can have slack. In the example we just discussed, the task *write* has slack but still drives the project end date and is therefore as critical as *read.* Both are resource-critical tasks,

---

[58] See my article in the magazine *PM Network*, December 1999, PMI: *Take the Path that is Really Critical.*

however, because the same resource does them. When two tasks compete for the same resource, those tasks have a *resource dependency*.

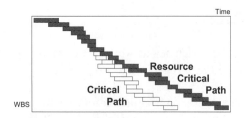

The RCP, in other words, is the chain of tasks that drives the project end date while taking into account that resources have limited availability. When you have few resources, you should focus on the RCP instead of the Critical Path. Any project manager who has experts on her team may need to find the RCP instead of the Critical Path.

You can see in the illustration that the RCP often includes some early critical tasks and then tasks that are delayed because of leveling. Those tasks now drive the project end date. *Resource-critical tasks* are tasks that, when delayed, make the project end date slip.

I would like to introduce an acronym here to help you remember this fundamental message. The acronym is **ERIC** (**E**ach **R**esource **I**mplies **C**riticality). In a leveled schedule, any resource can be so limited in availability, or needed so much, that it could drive the project finish date. Therefore **E**ach **R**esource **I**mplies **C**riticality, or **ERIC**.[59]

---

[59] Hey, that's my first name!

Finding the Resource-Critical Path

1. Check the workloads and level them
2. *Highlight the Resource Critical Path (RCP)*
3. *Find the most critical resource*
4. Make a change on it
5. Consider impacts on quality, scope, time, cost and resources
6. Decide whether you want to keep the change
7. Repeat steps 3 - 7

The next step is to find and highlight the RCP. We will discuss two methods to find the RCP: a manual process and a quick and dirty, semi-automatic process. There is no feature in Project 2002 that highlights the RCP for you, like with the Critical Path. Therefore, it will involve some effort from you to find it, but in order to optimize the schedule it is imperative that you do identify the RCP. Hopefully, we will find an RCP feature in the next release of MS Project.

◆ **Manual process**
We recommend this process for small projects. Also, this process will make you truly understand the concept of an RCP. If you can identify the RCP in a schedule by hand, you really understand this concept. When you first learned the Critical Path concept, you were also challenged to find it by hand before you started to rely on tools that could find it for you. We recommend you try this process first to enhance your understanding of RCPs.

◆ **Quick and dirty semi-automatic process**
We recommend you apply this process on large schedules. It is easy to apply but needs manual tweaking afterwards (see page 437).

Manual Process

It is easiest to identify resource-critical tasks by starting with the project end milestone and walking the path of tasks backward. You look for dependency arrows or resources that are shared between the tasks. Tasks that are resource-critical have either a logical dependency or a resource dependency with earlier tasks. A logical dependency, as you know, is shown as an arrow between the task bars in the Gantt timescale. A resource dependency occurs when two tasks are competing for the same resource. In the Gantt Chart view you can see in the timescale to the right of the task bars which resources are assigned. We recommend you use this view to identify the RCP.

Once you understand the process, you can find the RCP in a small schedule of up to 100 tasks within minutes with this manual process. If you have a large schedule, you may

have to apply the quick and dirty process, and then check and correct the RCP with this manual process.

The flowchart gives an overview of the process. You will work backward starting with the project finish milestone. This milestone is by definition resource-critical, so you mark it right away. You then ask yourself for this milestone: *Does a logical dependency drive it?* You check all the predecessors of the project milestone and determine which one is driving it to where it is scheduled. You typically find the task that has a finish date that is just before the start date of the milestone. Once you have found the driving task, you mark it as a resource-critical task. Then you go back to the top of the flowchart and start all over again with the marked task.

You start with the first question again: *Does a logical dependency drive it?* You check all its predecessors and check which predecessor finishes just before the detail task starts; this is most likely the driving predecessor. You may have to check for lags on dependencies as well. If you find a driving predecessor, you mark it and go back to the top of the chart and continue with that task. If you did not find a driving predecessor, which is often the case for detail tasks in a resource-limited, leveled schedule, you ask yourself the next question in the flowchart: *Does a resource dependency drive it?* Now you look at the resources that are assigned to the task, and you look for another task that finishes just before it that uses the same resource. Once you have found the driving task, you *Mark the task that competes for the same resource* and go back to the top of the flowchart and continue with that task. You continue until you have arrived at the project start date at which point all resource-critical tasks are marked. We recommend the view:

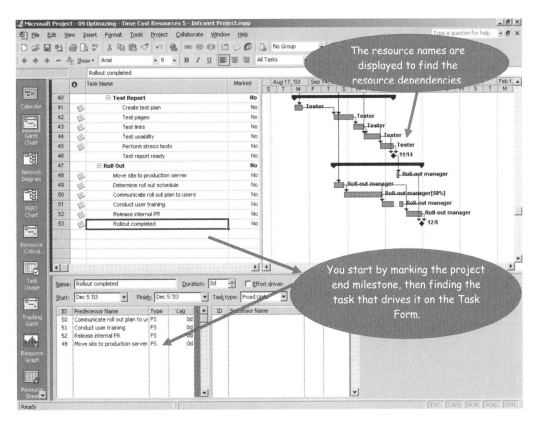

As you can see in the screenshot we recommend using the **Gantt Chart** with the **Task Form** displayed at the bottom of the view to find the RCP. Make sure you insert the task field **Marked** to tag the tasks that you find resource-critical.

The steps to identify the RCP in your schedule are:

1. Mark all resource-critical tasks as per the process explained. It is easiest to do this in the **Gantt Chart** view because the resource names are shown next to the task bars, which is useful for finding resource dependencies.

2. Switch to the **Tracking Gantt** view because it shows critical tasks in red. Choose **View, Tracking Gantt**. Notice that the Critical Path is entirely fragmented; it does not explain the entire project duration.

3. We will now make changes to the view, but we probably want to preserve the Tracking Gantt view as well. Therefore, we will copy the Tracking Gantt view first. Choose **Views, More Views**. The **More Views** dialog appears and **Tracking Gantt** is selected in the list. Click ⬚ Copy... ⬚ and enter a new name for the view, for

example *Resource-Critical Path*. Click | OK | and | Apply |. You are now back to the main screen with the new view displayed.

4. We will make the RCP look the same as our good old Critical Path. Choose **Format, Bar Styles...** We will make changes to the bars so that all normal tasks have a blue task bar, except for tasks that are marked; they will appear in red. These changes are circled in the following screenshot:

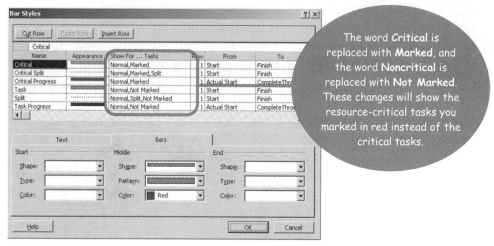

The word **Critical** is replaced with **Marked**, and the word **Noncritical** is replaced with **Not Marked**. These changes will show the resource-critical tasks you marked in red instead of the critical tasks.

5. Click | OK |; you can now color task bars red if you change their field **Marked** to **Yes**, or you can change them back to blue by entering **No** in the **Marked** field. This is useful if you need to make corrections to your RCP.

6. Click **AutoFilter** $\boxed{\text{Y=}}$, and buttons appear in the column headings. Click $\boxed{\blacktriangledown}$ in the column heading **Marked** and from the list that appears choose **Yes**. This filters and displays the resource-critical tasks only. Notice that the column heading title is now blue to remind you that an auto filter is on.

To the uninitiated the schedule now looks as if the regular Critical Path is shown, except that it really is the RCP. The RCP drives the project end date, just like the Critical Path. You could present this as your "Critical Path" to people who are not familiar with the concept of the RCP. They will not argue about the correctness of it because you can easily prove that it makes sense. After all, if any of the tasks on the RCP slips, the project will take longer. All resource-critical tasks drive the project end date.

Microsoft has yet to add an RCP feature to MS Project. It should be easy to program the logic with the flowchart presented before. For the time being, we will have to find the RCP manually, unfortunately. The concept should be automated because when you are making changes to the schedule during optimization, you need to find the new RCP over and over again, just like the good old Critical Path.[60]

Quick and Dirty Semi-Automatic Process

Here you will find a quick and dirty process that will help in identifying resource-critical tasks. The idea behind this process is that any task that is pushed beyond its *late finish* date on the Critical Path is a resource-critical task, most likely. In an unleveled schedule, we first determine and copy the late finish dates. Then we level and find the tasks that have a leveled finish date that is later than their (unleveled) late finish date.

These are the process steps:
1. Clear any leveling.
2. Copy the **Late Finish** dates into **Date1** to preserve them.
3. Level the workloads.
4. Copy the **Finish** dates into **Date2** (otherwise you cannot run filters).
5. Filter on tasks where **Date2** is greater than or equal to **Date1**.
6. Sort on **Finish** date.

The detailed steps in Project 2002 are:

1. Choose **View, Gantt Chart**.

2. Clear any leveling by choosing **Tools**, **Level Resources...** and click Clear Leveling... .

3. Display the fields **Late Finish** and **Date1**. Right-click on a column heading and choose **Insert Column...**; the **Column Definition** dialog appears with which you can insert the columns **Late Finish** and **Date1**. Then copy the **Late Finish** dates into the field **Date1** by right-clicking on the **Late Finish** column heading and choosing **Copy Cell**. Then right-click on the **Date1** column heading and choose **Paste**. The **Late Finish** dates are now copied into the spare date field.

4. To level the workloads, choose **Tools, Level Resources...** Make sure you do a complete leveling and click Level Now .

5. Copy the **Finish** dates into **Date2**, similar to step 3.

---

[60] Add-on software to MS Project that has the capability to find the RCP is called *ProChain* (www.prochain.com). This application calls the RCP the *Critical Chain* since it uses the *Theory of Constraints* approach to control projects.

6. Filter on tasks where **Date2** is greater than or equal to **Date1**. Choose **Project, Filtered for <name of current filter>, More Filters**. Click [N̲ew...] and enter the settings as shown in the following screenshot:

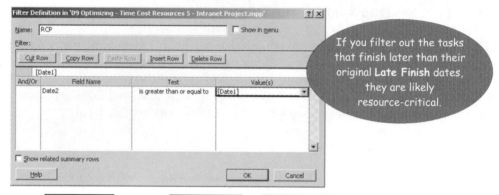

7. Click [OK] and then [Apply] or [Hi̲ghlight]; if you choose to highlight, all the resource-critical tasks will appear in blue text. If you want to change the color to red, choose **Format, Text Styles** and select the appropriate settings.

8. Sort by the **Finish** date; choose **Project, Sort, By Finish Date**. The RCP is now shown as a waterfall of task bars from the beginning to the end of the project, the same we are used to seeing as the Critical Path.

This process has some shortcomings:

◆ Often many more tasks are identified as resource-critical than really are.
◆ There are exceptional situations in which a resource-critical task is not identified as such. This will show up as a hole in the RCP. The RCP will not give a complete explanation for the project duration. It is often easy to find the missing resource-critical task since it is a matter of finding the task bar that fits in the hole.

The method previously explained provides a good approximation of the RCP, but in order to overcome the shortcomings we will have to do some tweaking. We have to get rid of the extra tasks that are displayed by the filter but aren't resource-critical and we need to mark any missing tasks to complete the RCP.

Why Should I Care About the Resource-Critical Path?

Since identifying the RCP requires some effort, I feel compelled to motivate you further so you'll start using it. There are five reasons why it is worthwhile to make the effort to find the RCP in your schedule:

◆ The RCP drives the project end date.

◆ The RCP reveals the critical resource(s).
◆ The RCP allows finding domino effects.
◆ The RCP allows workload smoothing.
◆ The RCP helps to fast-track smarter.
We will discuss each of these reasons.

The RCP Drives the Project End Date

Typically, somewhere along the Critical Path the resources start to constrain the schedule more than the logical dependencies. If the RCP stretches further, it overtakes the Critical Path. If that is the case, the RCP drives the project end date. As you can see in the illustration, the white tasks constitute the regular Critical Path, but the leveling delayed many of them. The result of the leveling is shown as black tasks. The RCP is the combination of the critical tasks early in the schedule and all the resource-dependent tasks later on. If any of these tasks slip, the project will finish later; the resource-critical tasks drive the project end date.

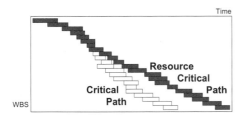

Can we give the *CPM* a well-deserved retirement? The answer is no, because critical tasks are still part of the RCP, and often at the beginning of it. At the start of the project, resources often aren't very busy and the logical sequence of tasks drives the schedule. As resources become very busy, they may start to drive the schedule instead of the logical dependencies.

The RCP Reveals the Critical Resource(s)

The RCP shows who the critical resources are. It also shows when the resources are critical. It is important for the project manager to know at any time who the resource is that determines the speed of progress in the project. Only if project managers know who is critical can they pay special attention to providing a work environment for those resources that is free of interruptions and disruptions. And they know that if those resources present an issue, they better deal with it right away.

Managers get things done through others. The RCP shows project managers which resources they should pay attention to. The RCP allows project managers to focus on people instead of tasks. The RCP puts the focus of managers back where it belongs: on people.

The RCP Allows Finding Domino Effects

Have you ever had an avalanche of changes after you made one small change? If you make one change to a schedule, you may trigger a disastrous domino effect. The illustration shows that when *John* became sick, his task slipped. Mary had planned to finish her part just before her holiday. When John was ready to hand off to *Mary* she had gone on holiday, so her part slipped even more. When she returned, finished her part and handed off to *Gord*, he was temporarily reassigned to another project and will return in 3 weeks. You decide not to wait for *Gord* and assign a new person. The new person will need 1 week of introduction and training, and so forth and so on. One little slip that seems innocuous can cause big delays because of resource dependencies.

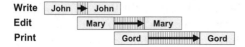

The RCP makes the most important resource dependencies visible. If you make the relationships between the resources visible, you can make changes to the schedule in a more educated fashion. If you only monitor the conventional Critical Path, you will not realize that you may be creating an avalanche of changes.

The RCP Allows Workload Smoothing

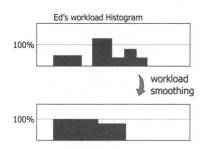

There often is a huge amount of cost involved with erratic workloads, as discussed on page 409. Refer to the illustration. How much does Ed's workload cost before and after smoothing? He has periods when he can twiddle his thumbs and other periods when he is overloaded (and may be wishing he had another job). I often see companies burn out their critical resources, especially in IT projects. If a critical resource burns out, the individual and the organization are severely hurt. For organizations, this often has expensive consequences in terms of dissatisfied employees, sick leave, demoralized work culture, deadlines missed, perhaps even lost contracts, and the cost of finding new highly specialized people.

The RCP keeps an eye on the workloads continuously, because workloads drive the RCP. Therefore, it allows you to monitor and manage workloads better. The eventual cost of a smooth workload is often less than the cost of an erratic one, as discussed on page 409.

The RCP Helps to Fast-Track Smarter

When crashing your schedule, you may create workload problems if you only focus on the Critical Path. You may work a long time to find a shorter schedule, and just when you think you have a better schedule, you may find you have exchanged time problems for workload problems. In the illustration on the left, the dependency was cut, and this created an over-allocation for Harry. The schedule is now infeasible. If you ignore the resource dependencies and just focus on logical dependencies, you may create short schedules. However, these schedules may not be feasible, because of new over-allocations.

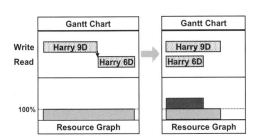

What Is the Nature of the Beast?

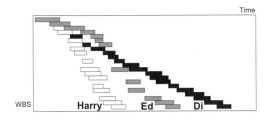

Now that we fully understand why it is important to find the RCP, we should explore the nature of the RCP a bit further. First of all, it is important to realize that each resource has its own RCP.

In the illustrated example to the left, the schedule is leveled every time for only one of the resources. This creates as many RCPs as there are resources. Harry, Ed and Di are all critical resources, but when leveled, Di pushes the end date out farther than Harry or Ed does. Di is the most critical resource. When shortening Di's RCP, you will arrive at a point after which Ed is more critical than Di. At that point, you have to shift your focus to Ed's workload instead of Di's. A similar thing can happen when crashing the Critical Path; another path can take over from the one we are working on any time. If you use the Critical Path Method in practice, you are probably familiar with that phenomenon.

What we left out of this picture is that there are hand-off points between resources. The RCP may be pushed out farther than you would expect simply based on the RCPs of individuals. These hand-off points run over a logical dependency. The logical dependencies link the chains of the resource dependencies together. The RCP has tasks that may be resource dependent on each other or logically dependent. The RCP typically reveals that multiple resources are on the RCP.

I will present three different specific situations in which finding the correct RCP can be challenging:
◆   The RCP with multiple critical resources
◆   When multiple resources are assigned
◆   *Logical dependencies* and *resource dependencies*
Scheduling software will have to find the right RCP in all three situations before one can reasonably state that a solid RCP algorithm has been found and this challenge has been met.

The RCP with Multiple Critical Resources

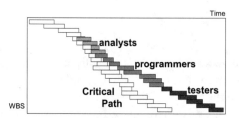

Several different resources typically work on tasks on the RCP. In the typical software development project, the analysts drive the front end of the schedule, the programmers the middle part and the testers the back end, as shown in the illustration. Every time there is a hand-off to the next resource there is a logical dependency. Again, logical dependencies connect the chains of resource-dependent tasks. The RCP shows clearly who is driving the project duration and when they are driving it.

When Multiple Resources Are Assigned

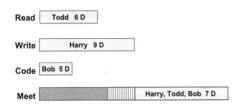

Consider another example that will pose a challenge for the algorithm that can find the RCP. The illustrated example on the left has resources assigned full-time to the tasks shown and multiple resources assigned to the last task, *Meet*. The algorithm has to pick the right resource as the critical one. In this case, *Harry* is the critical resource. Comparing this to the traditional Critical Path Method, it is similar to a task that has multiple predecessors and the algorithm has to identify the driving predecessor.

Logical Dependencies and Resource Dependencies

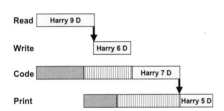

In the illustration, leveling has delayed the tasks *Code* and *Print*. The difficulty in this situation is that there is no hard dependency between *Write* and *Code*, only a resource dependency. An algorithm that identifies the RCP has to be able to handle a combination of logical dependencies and resource dependencies. In the flowchart on page 433, we therefore ask both questions. First, does a logical dependency drive the schedule? If not, does a resource dependency drive the schedule?

Methods to Optimize for Time, Cost and Resources

1. Check the workloads and level them
2. Highlight the Resource Critical Path (RCP)
3. Find the most critical resource
4. *Make a change on it*
5. Consider impacts on quality, scope, time, cost and resources
6. Decide whether you want to keep the change
7. Repeat steps 3 - 7

As you can see in the process chart we are now finally at the step to make a change. When the project has to finish earlier than the current schedule, it has to be shortened. The best measurements are those that make the quality (Q) go up (↑), the scope (S) go up (↑), the time (T) go down (↓), the cost (C) go down (↓) and the resource workload (R) go down (↓). Unfortunately, there are no such ideal measurements. The next table provides indications as to what the effect of each action could be in a typical project. Even though we indicate what the impact might be in typical project, you have to ask yourself what the possible impacts in your own project might be.

Because we now have limited resources, we should also assess each method and its impact on the resource workload in the project. Where a question mark (?) appears in the resources column (R), you have to check on new over-allocations after applying the measure. Where a zero (0) is shown, no impact is expected. The actions are ranked in order of overall effectiveness to reduce time. We recommend starting at the top of the table with the two fast-tracking methods. After exhausting the fast-tracking on all tasks, go to the next action in the table. (Q=Quality, S=Scope, T=Time, C=Cost, R=Resource workload)

	Action	For	Q	S	T	C	R
1.	Change sequential dependencies into partial dependencies (fast-tracking)	resource-critical tasks	0	0	↓	0	?
2.	Create parallel paths from a sequential path (fast-tracking)	resource-critical tasks	?	0	↓	0	?
3.	Split long tasks into many shorter ones	resource-critical tasks	0	0	↓	↓	?
4.	Change schedule constraints	resource-critical tasks	0	0	↓	0	?
5.	Shorten lags (waiting periods)	resource-critical tasks	0	0	↓	0	?
6.	Split task bars around a Must-Start-On task	resource-critical tasks	0	0	↓	0	?
7.	Decrease estimates	resource-critical tasks	↓	?	↓	↓	↓
8.	Reduce the scope or delete tasks	resource-critical tasks	↓	↓	↓	↓	↓
9.	Reallocate the best resources to the most critical tasks	resource-critical tasks	0	0	↓	?	↓
10.	Increase assignment units to full-time assignments for critical resources	resource-critical, fixed work tasks	0	0	↓	0	?
11.	Assign overtime hours to critical resources	resource-critical, fixed work tasks	↓	0	↓	?	↑
12.	Add noncritical resources	resource-critical, fixed work tasks	0	0	?	↑	?
13.	Replace critical resources with noncritical resources	resource-critical, fixed work tasks	↓	?	↓	?	↓
14.	Remove a critical resource when multiple resources are assigned	resource-critical tasks	?	0	↓	↓	↓
15.	Postpone vacation of critical resources to after the deadline	resource-critical tasks	0	0	↓	↑	0

Some remarks about optimizing an RCP:

♦ The methods discussed on page 387 are repeated in this table because they are also valid in situations with limited resources. The difference is that these methods will now only work on resource-critical tasks instead of critical tasks. The actions are ranked by overall effectiveness.

♦ Fast-tracking on the RCP is not as effective as it was on the Critical Path. However, it still is the preferred method to start with because it is quality, scope and cost neutral. Fast-tracking is less effective on the RCP because:

◇ There are fewer dependencies on a RCP, because it consists of logical dependencies and resource dependencies.

◇ You cannot fast-track two tasks if the same resource is working on both tasks and they are linked. Fast-tracking is changing the dependencies in such a way that more tasks take place concurrently. When you overlap tasks, workloads are moved as well, and you may be creating over-allocations. Fast-tracking has to be applied with greater care. The RCP will show you which tasks have the same resources assigned that will cause new over-allocations when you schedule them in parallel. You should focus your fast-tracking efforts on tasks that are done by different resources. For example, when you remodel an office, the tasks of carpenters and electricians can overlap each other as long as the carpenters start a few days ahead and finish a few days earlier.

♦ Actions 10 through 13 can shorten the durations of resource-critical tasks. These methods will work for all task types except *Fixed Duration* tasks. Before using one of these methods, you have to change its task type to *Fixed Work*, assuming the amount of effort required stays the same.

♦ Overhead tasks or support tasks should not be on the RCP. Overhead tasks support the real work and should not drive the project end date. If you see the project manager, team leaders, or technical support or administrative support people on resource-critical tasks, you may have found an easy way to shorten your project. In most cases, these people should not be on the RCP, and can easily be taken off. After all, they are managing or supporting the real critical resources (or at least that is what they are supposed to do).

We discussed the first eight measures starting on page 386. We will discuss the remainder next.

Reallocating the Best Resources to the Most Critical Tasks

This is the best and most basic principle to apply when trying to find the shortest schedule possible while keeping quality up and cost down. Only after you have created the detailed schedule and leveled the workloads, do you have a much better idea which tasks are driving your project duration. These are the resource-critical tasks. As soon as you know that, you should ask yourself: *Have I assigned my best resources to my most critical tasks?* If you review your current resource-critical tasks and see resources working on them who are not the fastest in terms of creating quality deliverables, you have an opportunity to shorten your project duration by re-allocating your best resources to these tasks. In the illustration the project manager has reassigned his best resources to the resource-critical tasks.

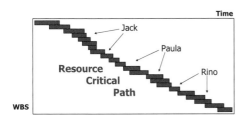

Increasing Assignment Units

When you notice that a resource is working half-time on a critical task, you can finish the task earlier if you can get the resource to temporarily work full-time. Again, the right task type has to be applied if you want to see the duration decrease. The task type has to be fixed work. If the work takes 10 person days and Harry could work full-time instead of half-time on it, he would finish the task twice as fast, as depicted in the illustration.

1. In the Gantt Chart, select a resource-critical task.

2. Choose **Window, Split** to display the **Task Form** at the bottom of the screen:

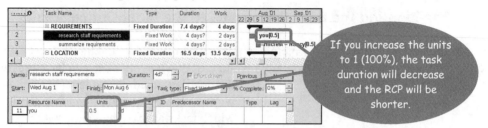

3. Determine which assignment drives the duration of the task if more than one resource is assigned to the task.

4. Select from the list **Task type** Fixed Units the type **Fixed Work** and click OK . This assures that MS Project will shorten the duration when you increase the resource units.

5. Increase the resource units on the task so the resource works full-time on the critical task. Click OK ; the duration should be decreased.

Assigning Overtime Hours

If you can get resources to put in overtime, critical tasks can often be finished earlier. In the illustration the second bar shows a shorter duration. Two situations can arise:

Harry: 40h

Harry: 30h + 10h overtime

- ◆ If overtime will not be charged to the project, then change the resource calendar of that particular resource. You can increase the working hours or change holidays to working days. You can compensate by giving the resource time off later.

- ◆ If overtime will be charged to the project at a higher overtime rate, then overtime should be entered in the overtime field (**Ovt. Work**) in the Task Form. The cost of the project will increase. The detailed steps are:

1. Select a resource-critical task.

2. Pull up the **Task Form** in the bottom pane and choose **Format, Detail, Resource Work** to display the **Ovt. Work** field. The form should now look like:

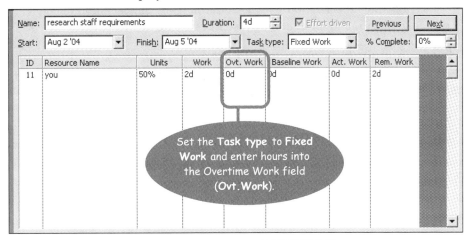

3. Set the **Task type** to **Fixed Work** and click | OK |.

4. Determine which resource drives the duration of the task, and enter the overtime hours to be worked in the field **Ovt. Work**.

5. Click | OK |; MS Project schedules the overtime hours outside regular working time and automatically recalculates the new duration.

 Do not lower the original work estimate; MS Project subtracts overtime from the original estimate before calculating the new duration.

Adding Noncritical Resources

Two resources can normally finish a task faster than one resource. When you add a resource, the duration will decrease, but it will only decrease if you have the right task type applied to the task before adding the resource. When you add a resource to a fixed work task, the same amount of work is now performed by two resources and can be done twice as fast. MS Project will calculate this for you.

Let's think about what happens in practice. When you hire new resources, you have to train them. You would typically take your best resources off their tasks to train the new ones. At first you will see a short-term decrease in the rate of progress hoping that, in the longer term, the progress accelerates. For this reason we have marked this method with a "?"for the *Time* dimension in the table. Look carefully at your situation to see if adding resources would indeed help.

1. Select a resource-critical task.

2. Choose **Window, Split** to pull up the **Task Form** in the bottom of the screen and determine which resource drives the duration of the task.

3. Select from the list **Task type** Fixed Units ▼ the type **Fixed Work**; this ensures that MS Project will shorten the duration when a resource is added. Click [OK].

4. Assign another resource and click [OK]; the duration should decrease.

Replacing Critical Resources

If you replace a critical resource with a noncritical resource, it may be possible to schedule more tasks in parallel. In the illustration, Ted replaces Harry on the second task, which can now be done in parallel with the first one. The gain in time equals the duration of the second task.

Some people argue that you cannot substitute critical resources; otherwise they would not be critical (as in *important*). Remember that the word *critical* has a different meaning in project management. *Critical* does not mean that the resource is important to the task. It merely means that the resource is driving the project duration. In fact, the resource could be a second-choice resource, and it is not a good idea to have your project duration be driven by second-choice resources if you are working against time. Your project will take long enough with first-choice resources.

1. In the Gantt Chart select a resource-critical task on which you can replace a critical resource.

2. Choose **Window, Split** to display the Task Form at the bottom of the screen.

3. Click on the name of the critical resource in the Task Form and use the list [▼] to select the substitute resource.

4. Click [OK].

If you prefer to use the **Assign Resources** dialog instead:

1. Click **Assign Resources** 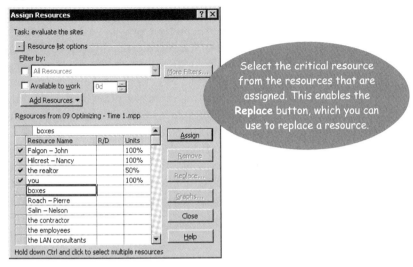 on the **Standard** toolbar, and the floating dialog appears:

2. Click on the critical resource in the **Assign Resources** dialog.

3. Click Replace... ; the **Replace Resource** dialog overlays the Assign Resources dialog.

4. Click on the resource to replace with and click OK .

Level your schedule again and keep the change if the duration of the project decreased; otherwise, return to the previous version by closing the file without saving.

Removing a Critical Resource When Multiple Are Assigned

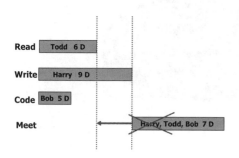

If there are multiple people working on a task, and one of them is a critical resource who has a lot of other work at the same time, you should ask yourself how important the involvement of the critical resource is on this task. If the other people could do without the critical resource, you should consider removing the critical resource from the task. Again, a *critical* resource does not mean that the resource is important for the successful completion of the task. In the illustration, Harry is removed from the task, which shortens the RCP.

Postponing Vacations to After the Deadline

If you can convince your resource to postpone a vacation until after a critical deadline, you may be able to meet the deadline. In the illustration, the deadline is depicted as a diamond. The vacation happens to have been planned for just before the deadline. If it can be moved, the deadline can be met. It is not uncommon for vacations to happen just before deadlines since projects keep shifting back and forth in time whereas vacations don't. Also, some resources seem to have a talent for planning their vacations just before deadlines. The detailed steps for moving vacations are next.

1. Choose **Tools, Change Working Time…**; the **Change Working Time** dialog appears:

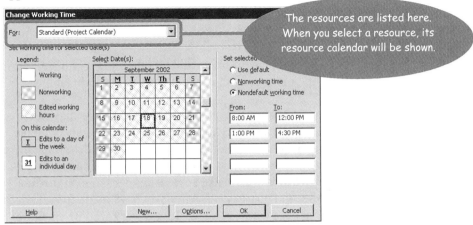

The resources are listed here. When you select a resource, its resource calendar will be shown.

2. Under **For**: [Standard (Project Calendar) ▼] select the resource.

3. Move the vacation for this resource to later dates, preferably after the deadline. Select the vacation dates by dragging over them and then select ⊙ **Use default**. Then select the new vacation dates and select ⊙ **Nonworking time**.

4. Click [OK]. The schedule should now be shorter.

Considering the Impacts

1. Check the workloads and level them
2. Highlight the Resource Critical Path (RCP)
3. Find the most critical resource
4. Make a change on it
5. *Consider impacts on quality, scope, time, cost and resources*
6. *Decide whether you want to keep the change*
7. Repeat steps 3 - 7

After making changes, you have to consider the impacts on quality, scope, time, cost and resource workload (see the process box on the left). You will have to evaluate the impact on quality and scope yourself. The impact on time and cost can be concluded from the project statistics dialog.

To display the statistics dialog choose **Project, Project Information,** [Statistics…]. You will save some mouse clicks if you display the **Tracking** toolbar, which has a tool on it to display this dialog.

Right-click on any toolbar and choose **Tracking** from the pop-up menu. The **Tracking** toolbar is displayed: ⌗. The dialog is now available with one click on **Project Statistics** ⌗, the first tool on the **Tracking** toolbar.

You can now see how much time you have gained, and whether it is worth any sacrifices you may have made on the scope of the project or the quality of the deliverables.

Whenever you make a change to a resource-critical task, the workloads may move or change. You can check to see if this created new over-allocations by displaying the Resource Usage view. You may have to level the schedule again and determine the new RCP once more. If you think at this point that it is too much work to identify the RCP after each change, you are right. You should make several changes, one in the first quarter of the RCP, one in the second quarter, etc. After you have made four changes along the RCP, you should probably identify it again. It may very well be an entirely different series of tasks now.

Before finding the RCP again, it is often easiest to unmark all resource-critical tasks first. To unmark all, enter *No* in the first cell at the very top of the field **Marked** and click on the column heading **Marked**. Choose **Edit, Fill, Down**. This will unmark all tasks. Then enter *Yes* for each task that you find to be resource-critical (see the process on page 433).

Optimizing for time, cost and resources is a lot of work, and practitioners would be greatly helped if the RCP could be found automatically.[61] Then they would not have to find it themselves after every few changes they make.

Simulation of the Resource-Critical Path

We discussed simulation of the *Critical Path* on page 398. You can also simulate Resource-Critical Paths in *resource-limited* schedules. The only thing you need to do in this case is change the leveling to automatic leveling. Choose **Tools, Level Resources...**, select ⦿ **Automatic** and deselect ☐ **Level only within available slack**. This ensures that for each scenario of the schedule the workloads are entirely

---

[61] Prochain, add-on software by Prochain Solutions Inc. (www.prochain.com), can extract the Resource-Critical Path from an MS Project schedule. This application calls the RCP the *Critical Chain* since it applies the theory of constraints.

leveled before the project duration is calculated. As you can imagine, simulating RCPs requires major computing power, so make sure you run this on the fastest computer in your office, or take a nice long coffee break…

The reasons why you should consider simulating RCPs are the same as for simulating the Critical Path:

◆ Durations are more likely to extend than shrink. Estimates do not follow a normal distribution but have a distribution that is often skewed to the pessimistic side.

◆ The more parallel paths you have, the more delays will compound at the merge points (*path convergence* or *merge bias*).

If you simulate the *RCP* you have taken care of all three assumptions that cripple the utility of the traditional *Critical Path*: the two reasons above and the fact that the Critical Path assumes access to unlimited resources.

Apart from that, there are extra factors that are quantified when you simulate resource-constrained schedules. We referred to these factors previously as *domino effects* (see page 440):

◆ The average effect of hard-date personal vacations on the project duration. It is hard to predict how much the project end date will change when some tasks are moved a little bit. The simulation software will run many scenarios and will eventually average out the effect of the hard-date vacations.

◆ The average effect on the project duration of asynchronous working hours of resources: *What overall delay will you experience from some resources working a regular workweek and some a compressed work week?* This effect is also hard to predict other than through simulation.

◆ When you identify activities that have time risk, you should also identify those activities where exact resource availability is not entirely certain. When you decide what distribution curve you need on those tasks, you can capture the likelihood of resource availability in the range and the curve you choose for these tasks.

The s-curve output from the simulation (see page 399 for an example) will indicate the probability by date for a range of project finish dates. Our experience is that most people tend to underestimate the overall effect of all the factors discussed. We prove this over and over again in classes where we ask participants to estimate the outcome of a simulation while showing them the exact inputs of the simulation. We therefore recommend you quantify the factors we discussed that can throw your schedule off its baseline by simulating your schedules. After all, as a project manager it is prudent to minimize so-called "*foreseen unforeseens*". We will still have to deal with enough "*unforeseen unforeseens*".

Checks on the Optimized Schedule

Below you will find checks to verify if you have applied best practices when optimizing your schedule.

Optimizing Workloads

◆ Is the total work within the person hour budget of the project (if a person hour or person day budget is available)?

◆ Are the workloads for the resources reasonable?

◇ For schedule certification purposes, the workload for individuals should not exceed 150% of their regular availability within any week. The workload should not exceed 120% for periods longer than a week. These upper bounds may be too high for your own organization. We have arbitrarily set them at these levels to prevent burnout, attrition and dramatic loss of productivity. These levels are cutoff points for many organizations.

◇ The workload of consolidated resources (groups) should not exceed their availability.

◇ The workloads should be fairly smooth since there are hidden costs involved with erratic workloads.

Note that it is not enough to just check if there is any red in the Resource Usage view. MS Project often highlights more resources in red than are truly over-allocated. If there is an over-allocation during only one business hour, the resource will already be shown in red. Also, assignments that are already completed are never red. Use the **Go To Next Overallocation** tool on the **Resource Management** toolbar to check the over-allocations. This tool is more selective and more reliable. However, even it does not always find all over-allocations, and it also highlights the 1-hour over-allocations. For more information, see the discussion starting on page 416.

Optimizing Costs

◆ Is the total cost within the budget of the project (if a cost budget is available)?

◆ Is the cost modeled using the right fields in the appropriate way? See page 294 for a discussion of which fields are right and their appropriate use. The following fields are available in MS Project:

◇ Resource Sheet fields: **Type, Material Label, Standard cost, Overtime cost, Cost per use** and **Accrual**. A resource can also have a **cost rate table**.

◇   Gantt Chart fields: **Fixed cost** and **Fixed cost accrual**.

Optimizing Time

◆   Are the deadline dates and other constraints met in the schedule?
You can check this by applying filter **6 IIL Deadlines or Constraints not met**.[62]
It displays tasks with a deadline or constraint that have negative slack. When
deadline or constraint dates are not met, the schedule may forecast a project end date
that is wrong.

◆   Does the schedule have a Critical Path or a Resource-Critical Path?
You can check the Critical Path by applying the **Tracking Gantt** view. This view
highlights the Critical Path in red by default.

◇   If a schedule is extended when the workloads are leveled, a Resource-Critical
Path needs to be identified. Resource-critical tasks need to be marked manually.

◇   The (Resource) Critical Path can only consist of detail tasks and milestones.
It should not contain level-of-effort tasks (overhead tasks or recurring tasks) or
summary tasks (since the logic should be kept on the detail tasks).

◇   Does the (Resource) Critical Path provide a complete explanation for the project
duration? You can check the completeness by displaying the (Resource) Critical
Path and then looking for gaps in it. Normally, there is at least one critical task
on every business day (unless there are lags on critical dependencies). If you
find gaps, the (Resource) Critical Path is fragmented and the tasks that are most
critical need to be identified in the schedule. See page 379 for possible causes of
Critical Path fragmentation and what to do about them.

◆   Are there as many parallel paths as logically possible in the network of
dependencies?
Novice schedulers tend to schedule all tasks in one long sequential chain. In that
situation there are many soft dependencies that make the duration of the project
unnecessarily long. When optimizing for time it is important to schedule in parallel
what logically can happen simultaneously.

---

[62] This filter can be found in the file *Tools to check Orange Belt schedules.MPP* that is available
for download at www.jrosspub.com.

Exercises

Review

1. We distinguished three optimization approaches in this chapter: optimizing for time, optimizing for time and cost, and optimizing for time, cost and resources.

2. What are the main differences between these optimization approaches?

3. Describe the situations in which you should apply each.

4. What are common techniques used in each approach?

5. Choose one of the four answers. Total slack is:
   a. The amount of time a task can move freely without affecting its successors.
   b. The difference between the late finish date and early finish date of the task.
   c. The amount of time in which the resource has to complete the task.
   d. The difference between the early start of the earliest successor and the early finish date of the task.

6. You receive a schedule and notice that the project finish milestone has a negative **Total Slack** of –10 days. In your own words, what does this mean?

7. There are six possible causes for fragmentation of the Critical Path; list four of those six causes.

8. When optimizing for time:
   a. What are the seven process steps for shortening the Critical Path?
   b. What are six of the nine possible methods to shorten the Critical Path?

9. One of your team leaders suggests that the duration of one of her critical tasks could be decreased if you can provide more people to do the work. What factors should you consider?

10. What is Monte Carlo simulation? What benefits can project managers derive from simulating their schedules?

11. What methods are available to decrease the cost of a project? Give at least four of the eight methods discussed.

12. Will the eventual actual cost of smooth workloads be higher or lower compared to erratic workloads? Why?

13. If you have MS Project level the workloads in your schedule, would the project duration be longer or shorter than if you leveled the workloads yourself? Why?

14. There are many ways to level workloads manually. Name at least eight ways.

15. What is the best view in MS Project to level the workloads manually?

16. What three scenarios can MS Project create for you when leveling the workloads? What is the nice-to-know thing from each scenario? Why?

17. In your own words, how does MS Project leveling affect the calculation and the display of the Critical Path?

18. Describe one of the two processes to identify the Resource-Critical Path. What is the major disadvantage of this process?

19. We discussed five reasons why finding the Resource-Critical Path might be a good idea. Name three.

20. There are 15 methods with which you can shorten the Resource-Critical Path. Name as many as you can.

21. Why is the s-curve of a simulated Resource-Critical Path the most reliable information you can present to executives about resource-constrained projects?

22. A project is experiencing a lack of progress during execution.

23. How would you determine which resources you should ask to make up the slippage by working overtime? They will not be paid a higher rate for overtime.

24. What menu items do you need to choose and what mouse-clicks do you need to make to enter overtime into MS Project?

Relocation Project — Understanding the Gantt Chart

1. Open the file *09 Optimizing — Time 1.MPP* that is available for download at www.jrosspub.com. Display the field **Total Slack** in the spreadsheet of the Gantt Chart.

2. Is the total slack expressed in calendar days, business days or person days?

3. Why does the negative slack change from task 13 *meet to discuss contract* to task 14 *revise the schedule*? Hint: Nancy is on holiday in the third full week in August.

4. Why does the negative slack change from task 20 *paint* to task 23 *install LAN*? Hint: there is a task with an elapsed duration between them.

5. Why does the negative slack change from task 25 *facility remodeled* to task 29 *move*? Hint: there is a deadline on task 25.

6. Why does the negative slack change from task 29 *move* to task 30 *unpack*? Hint: the movers only work on the weekend.

Relocation Project — Shorten the Duration

In this exercise you will use the optimizing for time approach.

1. Open the file *09 Optimizing — Time 1.MPP* that is available for download at www.jrosspub.com. Currently, the forecasted finish date is November 16, but your CEO insists that the office should be moved by November 1.

2. Display the Critical Path in your schedule. Make sure you understand all the total slack numbers on each task. If you do not understand the total slack numbers, first do the previous exercise *Relocation Project — Understanding the Gantt Chart*.

3. The objective of this exercise is to bring down the duration (time) of the project as much as is reasonably possible. Use the methods that were discussed in this chapter to get ideas. Come up with your own ways to bring down the duration of the project as much as you can. Try them out and see how much time they save. Try to:

    ◇   make the project end date as early as possible, OR

    ◇   if you have a Must-Finish-On constraint on the project end milestone, make the **Total Slack** positive and as large as possible on the project end milestone *new location opened*.

4. Try your ideas out and see if they work. If you keep a change, make a note of it, in order to compare your measures against the solution.

5. Prepare to defend the changes you made in the schedule to the other students.

6. Compare your results against the ideas we will discuss in the next exercise.

Relocation Project — Ideas for Shortening the Duration

In this exercise you will use the optimizing for time approach.

1. To illustrate how a schedule can be optimized, we will explain a complete optimization that will bring the project duration down to less than half the original duration! A similar reduction can be achieved in many projects by applying all the techniques discussed in this chapter.

2. Open the file *09 Optimizing — Time 2.MPP* that is available for download at www.jrosspub.com. The current duration of the project is 74 days.

3. When sorting the tasks on duration, it shows that the tasks *drying of paint, install LAN, relocate walls* and *lay carpet* are the longest tasks. All of these tasks are critical and seem to be a good starting point to find time in the schedule.

Enter the following changes to shorten the relocation project:

4. Create an overlap in the dependency on *relocate walls*, so that *install electric wiring* is done mostly in parallel with relocating the walls. Overlap *relocate walls* and *install electric wiring* with a finish-to-finish plus 1 day dependency. The electricians can start on a wall as soon as the carpenters have it up. What is the duration of the project now?

5. Cut the dependency between *lay carpet* and *install cabinetry* and cut the dependency between *lay carpet* and *install LAN*. Instead, make *lay carpet* dependent on *drying of paint*. Create new dependencies from *install cabinetry* and *install LAN* to *facility remodeled* to get rid of the loose ends in the network. You can lay carpet in parallel with installing cabinets and installing the LAN. What is the duration of the project now?

6. Notice that the Critical Path is fragmented at this point. We have to make sure that we continue making changes to critical tasks only. Make the necessary changes to the schedule in such a way that you see the most critical path in the schedule again. Change the type of dependency between *install electric wiring* and *paint* to finish-to-finish plus 1 day. The painters can start on a wall as soon as the electricians finish it. What is the duration of the project now? Why did the duration not come down?

7. Change the type of dependency between *paint* and *drying of paint* to finish-to-finish plus 1 day. The paint starts drying as soon as the first wall is painted. What is the duration of the project now?

8. Change the type of dependency between *facility remodeled* and *pack* into finish-to-finish. The packing should ideally be ready when the facility is ready. What is the duration of the project now?

9. Cut the dependency between *location selected* and *select the contractor*, and make *select the contractor* dependent on *evaluate the sites*. Create a new dependency between *location selected* and *meet to discuss contract*. You can select the contractor when you have an idea which location will be chosen. What is the duration of the project now?

10. Get rid of the Start-No-Earlier-Than constraint on task 8 *meet to select the location* and arrange for a conference call or internet meeting with the CEO, who is abroad. What is the duration of the project now?

11. Overlap *summarize requirements* and *research staff requirements* finish-to-finish plus 1 day. You can start summarizing as soon as you receive some completed questionnaires. What is the duration of the project now? Notice that the duration did not come down because task 13 was split even further because of Nancy's holiday.

12. Get rid of the lag on the dependency between task 12 *select the contractor* and task 13 *meet to discuss contract*. Make sure that you give advance notice of 5 days to the participants you expect at the meeting, so the 5-day time frame for calling the meeting is not needed anymore. What is the duration of the project now?

13. Change the task *install LAN* into a summary task by adding the following subtasks:
install LAN cables (20 d of Fixed Work, predecessor *relocate walls),*
install LAN hardware (20 d of Fixed Work, predecessor *install LAN cables),* and
install LAN operating system (20 d of Fixed Work, predecessor *install LAN hardware,* successor *facility remodeled).*
Cut the dependencies between *drying of paint* and *install LAN* and between *install LAN* and *facility remodeled*. Keep the resource units at 5 units for all subtasks; remove the *LAN consultants* from the summary task. The result is a more refined and shorter schedule. What is the duration of the project now?

14. Increase the resource units of the *contractor* for the task *lay carpet* from 6 to 12. This decreases the duration of *lay carpet* to 5 days, which is now done entirely in parallel with *install cabinetry*. What is the duration of the project now?

15. You decide to ask the *LAN consultants* to work with 8 consultants instead of 5. Change all assignments of the *LAN consultants* to 8 units on the subtasks of *install LAN*. This will reduce the duration of the subtasks to 2.5 days. What is the duration of the project now?

16. MS Project changed the duration of the task *meet to discuss contract* because of Nancy's vacation in the third week of August. Set its duration back to 1 day. What is the duration of the project now?

Please, answer the following questions:

17. Check the duration of the project. We have reduced it from 74 to 36 days! This is less than half of the original duration and most changes are quite defendable. You have seen here an example of how you can find time in your project schedule if you create a dynamic model of your project in the first place. Could you apply similar methods to your own project schedule?

18. Were trade-offs made against the scope or quality of this project? What are they? Would you undo some proposed changes? Why?

19. If you arrived at a different final duration, find the differences between your file and the solution file *09 Optimizing — Time 3.MPP* that is available for download at www.jrosspub.com.

Relocation Project — Lowering the Cost

In this exercise you will use the optimizing for time and cost approach.

1. Open the file *09 Optimizing — Time Cost 1.MPP* that is available for download at www.jrosspub.com.

2. The objective now is to bring down the cost of the project while maintaining or decreasing the duration. Use the methods that were discussed in this chapter to get ideas. Come up with your own ways to bring down the cost of the project as far as you can. Try them out and see how much money they save.

3. Log each change and the total cost of the project after each change you keep.

4. Prepare to defend the changes you made to the other students.

5. Compare your results against the ideas that we will discuss in the next exercise.

Relocation Project — Ideas for Lowering the Cost

In this exercise you will use the optimizing for time and cost approach. Open the file *09 Optimizing — Time Cost 2.MPP* that is available for download at www.jrosspub.com.

You found some new resources:

Name	Type	Position	Function	Max. Units	Std. Rate	Accrue at
Carpeteers	*Work*	*contractor*	*external*	*20*	*$140/d*	*End*
cablers	*Work*	*contractor*	*external*	*5*	*$40/h*	*End*
students	*Work*	*contractor*	*external*	*5*	*$80/d*	*End*

You find a specialized carpet company, *Carpeteers*, that is willing to do the job. Create this new resource. Carpeteers estimates the work will take 30 person days and they will do it with 10 employees. Reassign the task *lay carpet* to the new resource *Carpeteers*:

1. What is the current cost of the project?
   What is the current cost for the task *lay carpet*?
   What is the current duration of the project?

2. Reassign the task to Carpeteers.
   What is the new forecasted cost for *lay carpet*?
   How much did we save on this task?

3. What is the new total cost of the project?

4. What is the new total duration of the project? Why is it lower?

5. What consequences does this change have for the scope and quality of the project? Why?

6. Would you keep the reassignment to *Carpeteers*?

Enter the following additional changes to lower the cost of the relocation project:

7. Delete the task *revise the schedule;* it is a nice-to-have task. How much is the total cost now?

8. Delete the task *select the realtor* and hire the one you know. Is there a possible trade-off in doing this? How much is the total cost now?

9. Delete the task *select the contractor* and hire the one you know. Add a new dependency to keep the original logic. Is there a possible trade-off in doing this? How much is the total cost now?

10. Make the task *install LAN* a summary task by adding the following subtasks: *install LAN cables (20 d of Fixed Work,* predecessor *relocate walls), install LAN hardware (20 d of Fixed Work,* predecessor *install LAN cables),* and *install LAN operating system (20 d of Fixed Work,* predecessor *install LAN hardware,* successor *lay carpet).*
Keep the resource units at 5 units for all subtasks; remove the *LAN consultants* from the summary task. Cut the dependencies between *drying of paint* and *install LAN.* You ask the LAN consultants to use cheaper resources to do the cabling. They offer you specialized *cablers*, as shown in the table at the beginning of the question. Reassign the task *install LAN cables* to the cheaper resource *cablers.* How much is the total cost now?

11. You ask the contractor to come up with sharper estimates to save cost. He offers to provide students who can help the carpenters relocate walls. He proposes to replace half of the carpenters with *students* as per the table. Are there possible trade-offs on time, scope or quality? How much is the total cost now?

12. In your search to save cost you decide that the 35 employees should pack all their stuff in 1 day instead of 2 days. Are there possible trade-offs on time, scope or quality? How much is the total cost now?

Please, answer the following questions:

13. The cost should now be $97,950.00, down from $129,125.00. If you found a different answer, compare it with the solution file *09 Optimizing – Time Cost 3.MPP* that is available for download at www.jrosspub.com.

14. What is the forecasted duration for the project now?

15. Are there trade-offs in the scope or quality? What are they? Will you keep the proposed changes? Why?

Relocation Project — Leveling Manually

In this exercise you will use the optimizing for time, cost and resources approach and level the workloads manually.

1. Open the file *09 Optimizing — Time Cost Resources 1.MPP* that is available for download at www.jrosspub.com.

2. Set **Tools, Level Resources...** to ⦿ **Manual** leveling.

3. Which view do you recommend to check the over-allocations?

4. You find that a few resources are over-allocated: *Nancy Hilcrest* and you. What changes would you recommend to level the workloads manually for Nancy?

5. What changes would you recommend to level the workloads manually for your own over-allocation?

6. Compare your file with the solution file *09 Optimizing — Time Cost Resources 2.MPP* that is available for download at www.jrosspub.com.

Relocation Project — Leveling Automatically

In this exercise you will try the optimizing for time, cost and resources approach and level the workloads automatically.

1. Open the file *09 Optimizing — Time Cost Resources 3.MPP* that is available for download at www.jrosspub.com.

2. What is the current duration of the project?

3. Use automatic leveling to resolve all the over-allocations. Which view do you recommend for analyzing the results of automatic resource leveling?

4. Which field does MS Project change when leveling automatically?

5. Which tasks were delayed? By how much?

6. Has MS Project increased the duration of the project? Why?

7. Are there any trade-offs in scope or quality? Would you keep the solution proposed by Project 2002? Why?

8. Compare your file with the solution file *09 Optimizing — Time Cost Resources 4.MPP* that is available for download at www.jrosspub.com.

Intranet Project — Shorten the Duration

In this exercise you will use the optimizing for time, cost and resources approach using the Resource-Critical Path (RCP).

1. Open the file *09 Optimizing — Time Cost Resources 5 — Intranet Project.MPP* that is available for download at www.jrosspub.com.[63]

2. How many resources do you need by month? SA 1.5 in July, WD 2 in Aug, T and RM 2 in Sep

3. Would you level this file manually? Why?

4. What is the current duration of the project?

5. Level the workloads automatically. What is the duration now?

6. Check the Critical Path in the schedule. Does it make sense?

7. Mark the RCP by entering **Yes** in the field **Marked** for each task you identify as resource-critical.

8. While in the Gantt Chart view, choose **Format, Bar Styles** and change the settings to show a blue bar for all **Normal** tasks (critical and noncritical) and a red task bar for all **Normal, Marked** tasks (instead of for **Critical** tasks). You should now see red task bars for all tasks on the RCP in the schedule.

9. Compare your file against the file *09 Optimizing — Time Cost Resources 6 — Intranet Project.MPP* that is available for download at www.jrosspub.com; the files should look the same.

10. The objective now is to bring down the duration of the project as much as possible (time), while maintaining or lowering the cost and keeping the workload reasonable (resources). Bring down the duration by shortening the RCP. Log each change and the resulting total duration of the project for each change you decide to keep. Make a few changes before you find the new RCP.

11. Prepare to defend the changes you made to the other students.

12. Compare your results against the ideas that we will discuss in the next exercise.

_____

[63] We will use a different project here because we saw in the previous exercise that the workload leveling did not affect the project end date. In other words, the Critical Path is identical to the Resource-Critical Path.

Intranet Project — Ideas for Shortening the Duration

In this exercise you will use the Optimizing for Time, Cost and Resources approach using the Resource-Critical Path (RCP).

1. Open the file *09 Optimizing — Time Cost Resources 6 — Intranet Project.MPP* that is available for download at www.jrosspub.com.

2. What is the current duration and cost of this project schedule?

The challenge is to find methods to decrease the duration of the project that do not cost more and that do not cause new work overloads. You have to focus on the resource-critical tasks on the RCP. The following changes are examples of such measures. Enter these changes into the schedule:

3. It is somewhat peculiar that the project manager is on the RCP. We should be able to take him off the RCP. A project manager should, in general, never be on the Critical Path except in very small projects where he does tasks as a resource as well. Cut the dependency between task *9 Define specific functionality* and task *10 Develop project plan*. Give the task *10 Develop project plan* a new predecessor task *3 Define user requirements*. Give task *9 Define specific functionality* a new successor, task *11 System designed*. Is task 10 still resource-critical? Are there new work overloads? Level the workloads again. Determine the new RCP. What are the duration and cost of the project now?

4. Notice that the *Roll-out manager* is working only 50% on task: 50 *Communicate roll out plan to users.* Increase this to 100% while keeping the work on the task the same. Level the workloads in the schedule again. What is the duration and cost of the project now?

5. You see that the longest resource-critical tasks are tasks *36 Develop web pages* and 37 *Develop any custom functionality*. They take 20 days in the current schedule. If you can find an extra web designer for task 37 *Develop any custom functionality*, you can schedule those two tasks in parallel. You ask the resource manager for an extra designer and you get one for that one task. Create a new resource *Web Designer 2*, with the same rate as the first designer and assign her to task 37 *Develop any custom functionality*. Set a new dependency between task 35 *Determine development tool* and 37 *Develop any custom functionality*. Are there new work overloads? Level the workloads again. Determine the new RCP. What are the duration and cost of the project now? Are tasks 36 and 37 still resource-critical?

Please, answer the following questions:

6. We started with a schedule of 66 days that was not leveled. We then leveled and ended up with 114 days. We then shortened the schedule again to 90 days without increasing the cost and without (new) work overloads. Does the current RCP make sense? Why?

7. Compare your file with the solution file *09 Optimizing — Time Cost Resources 7 — Intranet Project.MPP* that is available for download at www.jrosspub.com.

Case Study — Multinational IT

The client is the IT department of a large multinational. Recently, the organization made the corporate decision to use MS Project for all its projects. It used Project Workbench before. The project managers still work very much as they did when they used Project Workbench; they like to enter actual hours worked and remaining hours. The organization has a separate time sheet system that reports actual hours worked by project or by category over many projects (e.g., "maintenance").

Managers in the IT department are using the MS Project schedules as checklists. Many of them become frustrated using the scheduling features of MS Project and revert to using MS Excel instead. When this was acknowledged, the client decided to organize basic training in MS Project using a local training provider. Since the training, one year ago, the situation has not improved a lot, and many people are still using Excel. The ones who use MS Project are not taking advantage of all the features of the application.

In interviews with several users you find that they experience the following problems:
◆ Double data entry of actual hours into the time sheet system and into the project scheduler.
◆ IT executives impose tight deadlines and use cost-payback arguments to successfully defend these challenging project deadlines. Your clients, the IT project managers, told you, *"We have not been able to prove that these deadlines are not feasible."*
◆ The organization has a matrix structure; many resources are working part-time on the project and are shared across several projects. There are many over-allocations, in fact so many that the project managers were advised by Project Workbench consultants to use AutoSchedule (automatic resource leveling), after which they should try to shorten the schedule.
◆ The organization experiences ripple effects between projects; a change in one project can have impacts on other schedules.
◆ Most projects are independent and do not have cross-project dependencies.

◆ The training did not teach participants how to apply MS Project to their own real-life projects.

There is a need for more guidance for the project managers to lower the threshold using the more beneficial features of MS Project.

QUESTIONS

1. Which feature of MS Project should be used to address the ripple effect across projects?

2. What optimization method do you recommend in this situation? Why?

3. Will they then be able to prove that the imposed deadlines are not feasible?

4. What would you recommend in order to:
   ◇ Get more project managers to use MS Project?
   ◇ Get project managers to use more features of MS Project?

Troubleshooting

1. Open the file *Sure Critical.MPP* that is available for download at www.jrosspub.com. Why are only tasks 3, 4, 5 and 6 shown as critical and not 1 and 2?

2. Open the file *Why Overload.MPP* that is available for download at www.jrosspub.com. Why is the resource *you* over-allocated in the week of September 2 to 9?

3. Open the file *MSF Application Development.MPP* that is available for download at www.jrosspub.com. Level the workloads completely. You may be prompted that MS Project cannot solve an over-allocation; choose **Skip All**. Why is the project duration now extended to the year 2049?

Chapter 10 Reporting

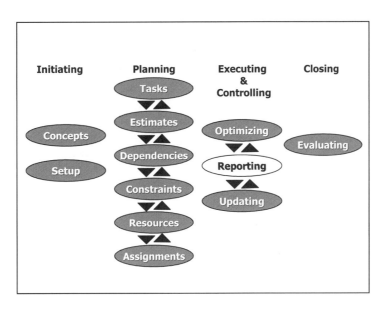

In the previous chapter we ensured that the schedule meets the project deadline and that the cost stays within the budget. We are now ready to publish the schedule to the world.

After reading this chapter you will:
- be able to determine if you need to hide the buffer in your schedule
- be able to print your schedule
- know the standard reports of MS Project
- be able to customize a standard report
- be able to customize views for reporting with a custom table, filter and grouping
- know how to create one-page reports always
- be able to check if you used scheduling best practices for project reporting
- know how to create some useful and hard-to-get-at reports
- know how to use the organizer to copy custom objects between projects

Micro-Management

Nob was in a good mood. Nob was grinning from ear to ear. He had just gotten the best project he had ever been assigned. Nob told Bob: "The project charter specifies very little oversight by executives. In fact, the charter does not specify any reporting or reporting period. It looks like I can just do what I want, and that is exactly what I am going to do."

Bob just smiled and thought to himself, "And you see that as your best project, okay..."

A few months later when Bob met Nob, Bob asked: "What happened to the project from heaven?" Nob lowered his head and voice: "Well, I'm still working on it but the project sponsor is in my office and on my back all the time! He walks in every day and wants to know what is going on. He talks to my team members as well. He is the micro-manager from hell!"

Bob asked: "How often do you submit reports to him?" Nob scoffed and said the sponsor never asked for one so he does not get any. Bob smiled: "How can the sponsor keep track of your project, if you don't provide him a written status regularly? A verbal update every day, will keep the micro-manager away!"

Project Communications Management

Hiding Your Time Buffer?

When we optimized the schedule in the previous chapter, you may have found a healthy amount of time as a buffer for deadline accomplishment. The dilemma of whether or not to hide the buffer can be one of the most difficult choices. You are in a double bind here. If you show the buffer, you may lose it. If you hide the buffer, you enter into a game of secrecy and you may have to do double bookkeeping with your schedule. We recommend you consider the following about upper management:

◆ What is the dominant pulling force in the project?
Is the project driven by time, cost, quality or availability of resources? What is the interest of upper management? If time is the dominant force, everybody will be scrutinizing your schedule to find time. The more people who look for it, the less the chance you will succeed in keeping it hidden. In many software and hardware projects, the sole focus is to be the first one to market. If that is the case, you will not likely succeed in keeping the time buffer for yourself.

◆ How mature is upper management in terms of project management?
Does management accept that, as the project manager, you should own a buffer to meet the deadlines? It is generally accepted project management practice that project managers who are responsible for meeting deadlines own a buffer in their projects. However, greedy upper management may try to confiscate it.

◆ How centralized is your organization?
Your organization may be very centralized. If that is the case, you will likely lose visible buffers. Project management thrives well in a decentralized organization. In these organizations, upper management establishes a contract with the project manager, first through a project charter and next through the project plan. These formal documents should clearly spell out the rules of the game. If your organization doesn't use these as formal project documents, you risk losing buffers you make visible.

Similar questions can be asked when it comes to the client:

◆ What is the dominant pulling force in the project?
What is the interest of the client? Does the client want the project product as soon as possible, or is high quality or low cost more important?

◆ How mature is the client in terms of project management?

◆ What is the type of contract with the client?
   In dealing with the client it is important to be aware of the type of contract that is
   established. If it is a time and materials contract, the client will be looking over your
   shoulder and you don't need a buffer. If the contract is fixed price, you will probably
   want to hide your time buffer from the client, as well as your profit margin.

The big drawback of hiding time buffers from executives is that it creates a culture of
secrecy. If levels of management stop communicating openly with each other, the
situation may worsen over time. Ideally, the time and money buffers should be on the
table instead of under it. If a project manager habitually hides time buffers and an
executive happens to find out, the executive may start cutting time off future schedules
for this project manager. In turn, the project manager will then hide bigger buffers in
harder to find places. The executive may start slashing the schedules more, making
arbitrary cuts. The situation deteriorates in a downward spiral. I have been witness to
organizations that continuously play this game, instead of conducting projects in an
open, professional manner. If you think you can defend the buffer in your project
successfully, we recommend you do that. Openness is greatly preferred over a culture of
secrecy that can create a vicious downward spiral.

Methods to Hide the Time Buffer

If you are in a situation in which it is impossible to show a time buffer explicitly, you
can hide it in your schedule. The following are methods to hide a buffer. Most of them
are the opposite of the optimizing methods we discussed in the previous chapter. They
are ranked in order of ascending sophistication. The likelihood that a buffer will stay
hidden from examining eyes increases as you move down the list:

1. **Overestimate lags**
   Lags are gaps between task bars of dependent tasks. Lags are used to model time
   that is out of your control, as when you are waiting to receive a construction permit.
   It is smart to estimate these lags on the (very) safe side. For the how-to, see page
   193. However, they can easily be noticed in the Gantt Chart.

2. **Insert extra holidays in the project calendar**
   You can insert extra common holidays in the project calendar. The task bars that
   span these days will stretch. This can be noticed in the Gantt Chart. For the how-to,
   see page 99.

3. **Decrease the working hours in the project calendar**
   This is frequently applied. Managers know that resources are not productive 8 hours
   a day even though their workday is 8 hours. In the project calendar you start the

business day later or finish it earlier. For the how-to, see page 98. This may make the calendar inconsistent with the **Hours per day** setting in **Tools, Options, Calendar**. Durations may start to show decimals. We urge caution with this method therefore.

4. **Ignore the benefits of learning curves**
   If you have repetitive activities in your schedule, you will likely benefit from the decreasing learning time with every repeat. Your estimate should be lower with every repeat. If you ignore this effect of the learning curve, you are in fact keeping a buffer in your schedule. See page 173. The cost of the project will also be overstated with this method.

5. **Introduce ramp-up and wind-down factors**
   If your resources are involved in more than one project at a time, your resources will be less productive because of setting up and closing down work on a project. You can include this time in your estimates, which will also affect the cost. See page 169.

6. **Introduce distraction factors for high-focus tasks**
   Certain tasks require your full focus, but the world around will not stop spinning. Writing a report or a book is a situation in which most people need to concentrate fully and need consecutive, uninterrupted time. Increase the estimate on these tasks with a distraction factor, which will affect the cost as well.

7. **Introduce extra revision cycles**
   Every revision cycle has two tasks: *revise* and *modify*. For writing, you could add tasks like *edit* and *rewrite*. You might even get away with another cycle of *re-edit* and *re-re-write*, but you may want to call it something else. For the how-to of inserting tasks, see page 136. Inserting extra revision cycles increases the cost as well.

8. **Keep maximum units of resources low**
   In a resource-constrained schedule you can influence the forecasted project end date by changing the availability of resources (**Max. Units**). If you are not entirely sure how many you will receive, you can create a time buffer in your schedule if you keep the maximum units on the safe and low side. For the how-to, see page 286. This will only affect the duration of the project.

9. **Assign one scarce expert to more tasks than needed**
   If one expert is in great demand, she will likely drive the project finish date. If you assign her to more tasks than strictly needed, she will drive out the forecasted finish date even further, thus creating a time buffer for you. It is hard to argue with using

the best resource on many tasks. For the how-to, see page 331. If the expert is paid at a higher rate than other resources, you are also increasing the cost.

10. **Create extra inconspicuous tasks**

    One of my students once confided that he always creates a task *Find alternative resources* in the task list wherever slightly appropriate. I won't mention his name so as not to spoil his fun. Other good ones that are hard to argue with are *Apply quality check* or *Update the project plan*. These extra tasks increase the cost as well.

11. **Pad the duration and work estimates**

    As one project manager once put it, *To pad or not to pad* is similar to the Shakespearian *To be or not to be.* You are entering into a culture of secrecy, however. Padding also increases cost.

12. **Don't use overtime yet**

    If you know you can count on your resources working some overtime, don't enter it into the schedule during the planning phase. Whenever your team members work a weekend, the 2 days will be pure gain. For the how-to, see page 448. Be careful with this method if you pay a higher rate for overtime, since the planned cost of the project may be understated because it is calculated based on regular rates.

13. **Set extra soft dependencies**

    Soft dependencies are dependencies that are not absolutely needed, but that can be defended with an argument such as: "*We prefer to do it like this, because it has the following advantage ...*" For the how-to, see page 200. This method is cost neutral.

14. **Be pessimistic about material delivery dates**

    When you are dependent upon receiving a shipment before you can do your work, create a delivery milestone on a date that is later than the date you were promised by the supplier. For the how-to, see page 198. This method is cost neutral.

15. **Insert extra holidays for your critical resources**

    Determine who the most critical resources are in your schedule and insert extra holidays in their resource calendar. For the how-to, see page 284. This cannot be easily seen in the Gantt Chart and is a very sophisticated way of hiding buffer time. This method is cost neutral.

As you may have noticed, all these methods boil down to not fully optimizing your schedule. If you don't use all the methods of optimization or if you don't apply them to their fullest, you may keep a hidden time buffer in your schedule. We recommend you try to optimize your schedule to the maximum first, to be sure about the real amount of buffer you have. Then you can hide it again in other hard to find places if you really need to.

How to Defend Visible Buffers

As we stated before, it is <u>highly preferable</u> to keep the buffer you own visible in your schedule. It is the professional thing to do, because it is generally accepted project management practice that when upper management asks project managers to commit to deadlines, project managers are allowed to own time buffers.

There are several ways for project managers to defend buffers that are explicitly visible in the schedule:

◆ Monetary budgets have reserves as a generally accepted budgeting practice. Why can't schedules have time reserves?

◆ Create a separate line item for the time buffer in the task list, instead of leaving it as an undefined, gaping hole in your schedule. Name the line item *Time Contingency Reserve*, which is a technical term that may impress some to such a degree that they let you keep it, or, if they don't understand it, they might be too afraid to ask you what it means, and you will keep it. You can assign yourself as the resource, so it becomes clear to everybody that you own it (and this also adds a buffer of effort and cost). Make sure this line item is dependent on the last tasks. Set the project end milestone as its sole successor.

◆ You can split the big buffer into smaller ones that you spread across your schedule. Visually, this will look more acceptable.

◆ Another, entirely scientific, method that will prove that you need a reasonable amount of time buffer in your schedule is Monte Carlo simulation. We discussed it on page 398. You can use simulation to create a probability curve of project end dates. When you have the curve, you can decide which probability you feel comfortable with and find out what buffered end date results. This dictates how much time you need as a buffer. Or you can ask upper management with what level of confidence they feel comfortable and quote the corresponding date from the curve. You then add the buffer as a line item that makes the schedule extend to this date.

◆ If executives still try to steal your time buffer, you may start to feel that you cannot be held responsible any longer for meeting the deadline. If that is the case, make it clear that you do not accept this responsibility any longer and, instead, you will just do the best you can. If deadline accomplishment is an item in your performance appraisal, state clearly that you don't want to see missing this particular deadline brought up in your performance appraisal, and ask for agreement on this. This will make it perfectly clear that you don't appreciate being made accountable for doing the impossible.

◆ If all else fails, you can try to provide only reports on such a high level that buffers are not visible at all. One-page milestone reports, for example, don't reveal buffers.

Choosing the Options

There are some options to be well aware of when reporting. For example, you may have noticed questions marks in the duration column. These question marks signify that you did not enter the duration yourself but had MS Project enter the default duration (*1 day?*) or a calculated duration based on the formula $D * U = W$. Project 2002 calls this *estimated durations*. You can make the question marks disappear by choosing **Tools, Options, Schedule**:

Tab	Option
Schedule	☑ **Show that tasks have estimated durations** Uncheck if you want to hide the question marks in the duration field. Executives may start asking questions if you leave question marks in your reports.
	☑ **New tasks have estimated durations** Uncheck if you don't want to see question marks for any new tasks you create.
Edit	You can change the time units for **Minutes, Hours, Days, Weeks, Months, and Years** to one character to save space on the screen.

Communication Features in Project 2002

The word *report* refers to the report feature in MS Project (menu **View, Reports**). I will therefore also use the words *printout*, *output* and *performance report*[64] to refer to what people normally call a *report*.

---

[64] See PMBOK® Guide, 2000 Edition, published by the PMI.

You can either print a report or print a view to publish your schedule. In Project 2002 you now have a third option and that is to publish your schedule on a website through Project Server.

◆ **Reports**
Several different standard reports are available in MS Project in the **View, Reports...** menu. All reports are table-like with precise, numeric information. Only the reports feature allows you to print the project calendar and resource calendars. For a detailed discussion, see page 482.

◆ **Views**
A printout of a view shows on paper whatever you created on the screen: WYSIWYG (What You See Is What You Get). MS Project is very user-friendly in this respect; rarely will you see differences between screen and paper. You can print any view from the menu except for any of the form views (Task Form, Resource Form and Relationships Diagram). You can only print the graphical charts, like the Gantt Chart, Network Diagram and Resource Graph, with views. Only in views can you apply the feature of grouping (**Project, Group by**). For a detailed discussion, see page 487.

◆ **Project Server**
Project Server is the new companion application for Project 2000 and Project 2002 Standard and Professional editions. It is a separate application that works with MS Project. It allows you to communicate with stakeholders via a website and is therefore the way of the future. Project Server is not only a communication tool; it facilitates collaboration and delegation as well. For an overview of the reporting features in Project Server, see page 509.

The following table provides a comparison of your reporting options. This may help you determine on which option you want to focus:

Reports	Views	Project Server
Paper based	Paper based	Online in real time
One-way communication	One-way communication	Two-way collaboration
No edits	Edits possible	Some edits possible
Somewhat customizable	Highly customizable	Highly customizable
Quick and easy	More effort	Most effort
Tables only	Tables & timescale charts	(Pivot) tables & all charts

In this chapter, we will discuss printing reports and views on paper in detail and give an overview of the vast online reporting possibilities with *Project Server*.

Using Reports

To print a report, first select the report category you want and then select a specific report to view in the print preview window. Choose **View, Reports**; the **Reports** dialog appears:

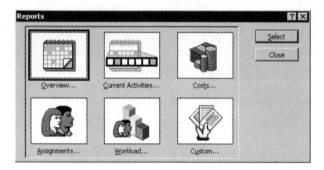

You can choose one of the standard reports from the following categories:

◆ **Overview**
Overview reports show information for the entire project duration, including summary tasks, critical tasks, project milestones, cost and schedule information.

◆ **Current Activities**
Current activity reports show a variety of task information, such as tasks that are not started, in progress, completed or behind schedule.

◆ **Costs**
Cost reports show budgets by task for the entire project duration; time-phased budget, tasks and resources that are over budget; and earned value information for all tasks.

◆ **Assignments**
Assignment reports show assignments by resource for the entire project duration, assignments for only the resources you specify, assignments displayed by week or resources that are over-allocated.

◆ **Workload**
Workload reports show task usage or resource usage information.

There is also a **Custom** category, which allows you to create a new report, customize an existing report or copy any of the reports discussed above.

Certain output can only be created if you use the report feature in MS Project:

◆ **Project Summary**: Gives statistics on the entire project. You can find it in the section **Overview**. It provides project health indicators like current **Finish** date versus **Baseline Finish** date and current **Cost** versus **Baseline Cost**. It is similar to the **Project Statistics** dialog (**Project, Project Information**, Statistics...).

◆ **Project Calendar**: Prints the holidays and working hours. You can find it in the section **Overview** listed as *Working Days*.

 ◆ **Resource Calendars**: Print the resource-specific calendars that can be included in any resource report. To include the resource calendar information, double-click on **Assignments** and select either **Who Does What** or **Overallocated Resources** and click Edit... , on the tab **Details** check ☑ **Calendar**. This is a good way to check if the vacations of the team members were captured in the schedule. Vacations require little effort to enter but can throw projects off track in a major way.

Previewing Reports

1. Choose **View, Reports...**; the **Reports** dialog appears:

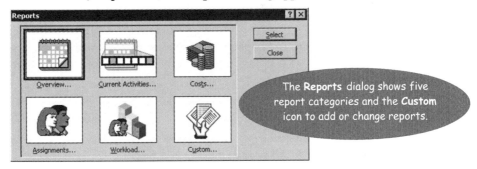

The **Reports** dialog shows five report categories and the **Custom** icon to add or change reports.

2. If you double-click on **Overview** reports, the **Overview Reports** dialog appears:

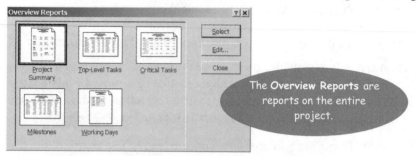

The **Overview Reports** are reports on the entire project.

3. Some performance reports cannot be produced in other ways, such as the **Project Summary** report. If you double-click on it, you will see the report in print preview:

Relocation Devom Inc.
Devom Inc.
Eric Uyttewaal
as of Jan 28 '03

The **Project Summary** report shows total **Duration, Work** and **Cost**, as well as dates relative to the baseline.

Dates

Start:	Aug 2 '04	Finish:	Nov 16 '04
Baseline Start:	NA	Baseline Finish:	NA
Actual Start:	NA	Actual Finish:	NA
Start Variance:	0 days	Finish Variance:	0 days

Duration

Scheduled:	74 days?	Remaining:	74 days?
Baseline:	0 days?	Actual:	0 days
Variance:	74 days?	Percent Complete:	0%

Work

Scheduled:	480 days	Remaining:	480 days
Baseline:	0 days	Actual:	0 days
Variance:	480 days	Percent Complete:	0%

Costs

Scheduled:	$129,125.00	Remaining:	$129,125.00
Baseline:	$0.00	Actual:	$0.00
Variance:	$129,125.00		

Task Status

		Resource Status	
Tasks not yet started:	31	Work Resources:	8
Tasks in progress:	0	Overallocated Work Resources:	2
Tasks completed:	0	Material Resources:	1
Total Tasks:	31	Total Resources:	11

4. You will get an error message when attempting to print preview if you don't have a printer set up on your computer. You can set one up through Windows, even if it is only for print preview purposes:

    ◇   In Windows XP click **start**, **Printers and Faxes, Add a Printer**.

    ◇   In Windows 2000 click **Start**, **Settings, Printers, Add Printer**.

5. When hovering over the page, the mouse pointer looks like ▇. If you click on an area of the page, you can zoom in on the details, and with another click you will zoom out again.

6. To change the margins, header or footer, click **Page Setup...** at the top of the screen.

7. To print the report, click **Print...**.
    To return without printing, click **Close**.

To Customize a Report

1. Choose **View, Reports...**; the **Reports** dialog appears:

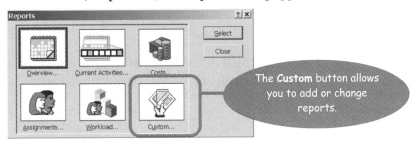

2. Double-click on **Custom...** ; the **Custom Reports** dialog appears:

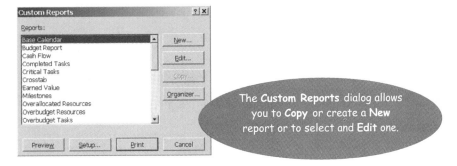

3. Select from the list a report that is closest to what you want and click Copy... to copy the report while leaving the original intact.
    OR
    Click Edit... to edit the report itself.

4. Some reports cannot be copied, for example the **Base Calendar** and the **Project Summary** report. You can only edit the font and type style in these reports.

5. If you select a task-related report, the **Task Report** dialog appears:

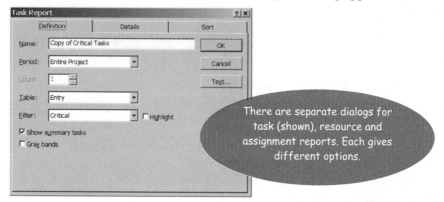

There are separate dialogs for task (shown), resource and assignment reports. Each gives different options.

6. Enter a descriptive name for your report under
    Name: [   ].
    Depending on what type of report you choose, the dialog provides the appropriate choices. For an explanation of your choices, see the next section on *Report Customization Options*.

7. Click OK when done.

8. Click Preview to display the report in print preview.

9. If it looks good, click Print... and the **Print** dialog appears.

10. Click OK to print the report.

Report Customization Options

We will discuss the most common options for customizing reports:

◆ **Definition** tab
    Choose the table and the filter.

Check ☑ **Gray bands** to print gray bands separating individual tasks or resources. This improves readability.

◆ **Details** tab
Choose the data to include in the report. If you are editing a task-related report, you can include certain task fields. In resource reports, you can include resource fields. In both resource and task reports you can include assignments.
Check ☑ **Border around details** to print borders around the details you include in the report.
Check ☑ **Show totals** for any fields that should be added up; the totals are shown at the bottom of the report.

◆ **Sort** tab
Specify a sort order for the records in the report.

On all tabs you can click | Te_x_t... |. This button opens the **Text Styles** dialog, where you can choose the font and type styles for the report.

Over the years, I have found that **Views** rather than **Reports** provide more options to create the output my clients expected. We will discuss using **Views** in the rest of the chapter.

Using MS Project Views

The view can be changed in many ways depending on the need for information. The steps to tailor views to your reporting needs are given below. It may seem like an elaborate process, but there are advantages to having custom status views only two mouse-clicks away: you will use them regularly and you may also be able to use them in other projects.

1. Customize **Fields**
   In the extra fields in MS Project (like **Text1**, **Number1**, **Flag1** among others) you can enter Excel-like formulas. You can even add graphical indicators, like red/yellow/green, to indicate status.

2. Design a new **Table**, which fields do you want?

3. Design a new **Filter**, which tasks or resources to show?

4. Create a new **Group** to categorize the tasks or resources.

5. Create a new **View** that also applies the newly created **Table, Filter** and **Group**.

6. Sort the records.

7. Apply any formats such as text styles or bar styles.

8. Choose the **Page Setup** settings.

9. Draw using the **Drawing** toolbar.

A view applies a table (with custom fields), a filter and a group. A view contains many other settings:

♦ The sorting order through the menu items **Project, Sort**.
♦ Any formats applied through the **Format** menu.
♦ All page setup settings from the **File, Page Setup** dialog.
♦ Any objects created with the **Drawing** toolbar.

Since these are stored in the **View** object, we recommend creating a new view before doing the sort, format, page setup and drawing. The **Table, Filter** and **Group** also exist as separate objects in the **Tools, Organizer**. If you want to create a new view, for example a one-page *Executive Overview*, you can create a table and call it *Executive Overview*, a filter called *Executive Overview* and a group called *Executive Overview*. When you apply the view it will apply all its *Executive Overview* components. If you name them all the same, it is clear that they belong together. This helps when you want to give the view to somebody else with the organizer; you can easily see which objects belong together.

You can start the name of certain objects with an * (asterisk) or a number to shuffle them to the top of the list. Or you can use an acronym to indicate they are customized for your organization (for example, at the International Institute for Learning, we use IIL).

New views can be created using a *single view* or a *combination view*. A combination view applies two other views, one in the top and one in the bottom pane. Combination views are useful for analyzing projects, because what you select in the top view is always shown in more detail in the bottom view.

You can now also print the row and column totals in the timescale of the **Usage** views by choosing **File, Page Setup**, tab **View**, ☑ **Print row totals for values within print date range** and ☑ **Print column totals.**

Fields

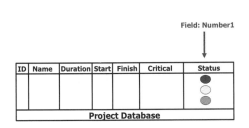

Field: Number1

Project Database

MS Project has many extra fields in the project database that are called Text1-Text30, Flag1-Flag20, or Number1-Number20. You can claim and rename these extra fields. You can even enter Excel-like formulas in them such that they calculate values of interest. You can go one step further and choose graphical indicators (red/yellow/green) to reveal the health of the project quickly. In the illustration the **Number1** field was changed to traffic light indicators.

The steps to customize fields are:

1. Choose **Tools, Customize, Fields**; the **Customize Fields** dialog appears:

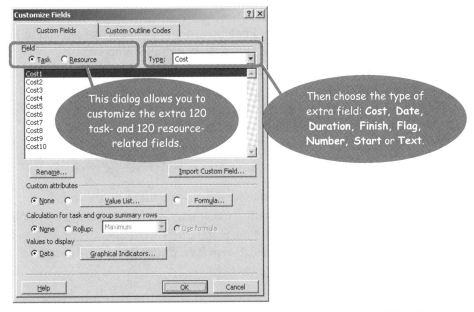

2. Click the tab **Custom Fields** or the tab **Custom Outline Codes**. With **Custom Outline Codes** you can create alternative breakdown structures than the

deliverable-oriented Work Breakdown Structure (WBS).[65] We will focus here on the **Custom Fields**. First decide if you want to customize a ⊙ **Task** or ⊙ **Resource** field.

3. Then select the **Type** of field from the list [Cost   ▼]. There are a total of 120 task-related fields and 120 resource-related fields, in addition to the extra enterprise fields that can also be customized by the project office staff:

   ◇ **Cost1 - Cost10** fields can capture extra dollar information like *committed cost*, which is useful if you have a budget to commit dollars from.

   ◇ **Date1 - Date10** fields can store dates that were used to find the Resource Critical Path (see page 433).

   ◇ **Duration1 - Duration10** fields can be used to store durations of interim plans. You have to copy them yourself since saving an interim plan (**Tools, Tracking, Save Baseline,** ⊙ **Save interim plan**) only saves the start and finish dates.

   ◇ **Finish1 - Finish10** fields are used to store finish dates in interim plans.

   ◇ **Flag1 - Flag20** fields are used to save *yes/no* type of information, for example to indicate if a resource is willing to travel.

   ◇ **Number1 - Number20** fields are often used to enter formulas that calculate with other numeric fields. For example, you could calculate the amount of *free budget*, which is the total budget minus the committed amount.

   ◇ **Start1 - Start10** fields are used to store finish dates in interim plans.

   ◇ **Text1 - Text30** fields are used to store extra textual information, like the *performing organization* for tasks or the *position* or *department* for resources. Text fields can be enriched with a pick list, known as a **Value List** in MS Project.

4. Select the field in the list that was refreshed when you chose the type.

5. Click [Rename...] to give the field a more descriptive name that reveals its purpose. Click [OK]. Eventually you will see that the field is now listed under both names in the database. If you changed the name *Cost1* to *Committed Budget*, you will see that the field is listed as *Cost1 (Committed Budget)* and *Committed Budget (Cost1)*.

---

[65] We discuss **Custom Outline Codes** in the Black Belt Professional course. For more information visit www.iil.com and follow the link *Microsoft Project*.

6. Set **Custom attributes**:
    ◇ You can create a pick list for the field. Click | **Value List...** |.
    ◇ You can enter an Excel-like formula in the field. Click | **Formula...** |.

7. Decide if you want MS Project to calculate values on summary tasks or on group headings by selecting your preferences under **Calculation for task and group summary rows**.

8. Under **Values to display** you can create | **Graphical Indicators...** | by specifying a **Test** and choosing a cute **Image** for the range of **Value(s)**. You can add more tests and images for each different range of values. By default, summary and detail tasks will use the same tests, but you can adjust tests, values and images separately for:
    ◇ **Nonsummary rows**
    ◇ **Summary rows**, if you uncheck
       ☑ **summary rows inherit criteria from Nonsummary rows**
    ◇ **Project summary**, if you uncheck
       ☑ **project summary inherits criteria from summary rows**

 MS Project has some unique functions that can be very useful when creating formulas. For example, the **ProjDateDiff** function can give you the number of business days between two dates and even base it on a particular base calendar. These functions are often better than using your own arithmetic, like *[Baseline Finish] – [Finish]*, since this will give you the number of calendar days instead of business days. Most of the data in MS Project is in terms of business days.

 When you develop formulas, you cannot put any letters in number fields, numbers in flag fields, etc.

 You can also rename the columns in the **Insert, Column, Column Definition** dialog, field **Title**. If you do this, the field will only be renamed in the active table. If you use the process described above, the field will be renamed in the entire database and will be listed under its old and new names in every table, which is a better practice.

 There are also **Enterprise fields** available for customization by the administrator of *Project Server*. Enterprise fields are fields reserved for standardization across the entire enterprise. The use of enterprise fields is typically determined centrally by the project office since they are a means to standardize data capture for enterprise reporting purposes. Organizations typically standardize on performance reports, project rollup reports and project archiving. When we discuss reporting using Project Server, we will elaborate further (see page 509).

Because the number of possibilities for customizing fields is almost without limit, a more detailed description is beyond the scope of this book.[66]

Tables

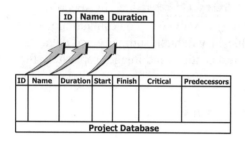

A table is a selection of fields from the project database, including their order of display. You can use the fields you may have customized in the table. A table does not contain project data; it is only a layout. MS Project is different from other applications because tables in, for example, Word or Excel contain data. In the illustration, the table at the top displays only the fields *ID, Name* and *Duration* out of all the fields present in the Project 2002 database.

Using an Existing Table

1. Make sure you are in one of the table views; a table view has a spreadsheet with columns and rows. The Network Diagram and the Resource Graph do not use tables. There are also views that are fill-in forms; they do not use tables either.

2. Choose **View, Table <name of current table>** and choose the table you want to apply. The current table (if listed) has a check mark in front of it.
OR

    Right-click on the **Select All** area ▢ where the column headings intersect with the row headings in the spreadsheet. A pop-up menu appears from which you can choose the table to apply.

3. The layout of columns is now replaced by a new layout as per the definition of the table object you applied.

---

[66] We discuss them in great detail in the Black Belt Professional course. See www.iil.com and follow the link *Microsoft Project.*

You can now rearrange the columns very quickly by clicking on a column heading, releasing the mouse and clicking and dragging the column when you see the ⁺↕⟵ mouse pointer.

Designing a New Table

Instead of constantly changing the **Entry** table for reports you want to create, there are advantages to creating a new table object for each report need. That way you will not have to reinvent the wheel every time.

1. Choose **View, Table <name of current table>, More Tables…**; the **More Tables** dialog appears:

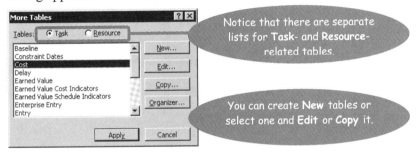

2. To list the task tables, select ⦿ **Task**; for resource tables select ⦿ **Resource**.

3. Select the table in the **Tables** box that is closest to what you want and click
   Copy… to create a duplicate with which to work. The **Table Definition** dialog appears:

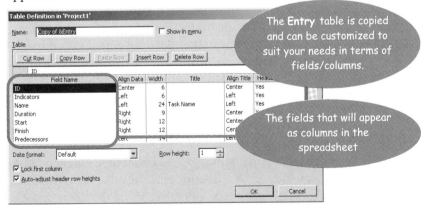

4. In the **Name** box, type a new name for the table.

5. To delete a field in the table, click the row to delete and click [Delete Row].
    To insert a new field in the table, click the row before which you want the new field
    to appear and click [Insert Row].
    To replace a field, click on its field name and select the new field from the list that
    appears.

(2002)

6. In Project 2002, you can choose to wrap the text in the column heading by setting
    Header Wrapping to **Yes**.

7. If you want to list the new table in the menu, check ☑ **Show in menu**.

8. If you want to lock the first field, check ☑ **Lock first column**. There are
    advantages to having a locked first column; it allows you to select an entire task or
    resource record in the database and the locked title will not scroll off the screen. The
    data cannot be edited in the locked column, which is just fine for ID numbers, which
    are maintained by MS Project anyway.

(2002)

9. In Project 2002, you can choose to ☑ **Auto-adjust header row heights**.

10. Click [OK]; you are now back in the **More Tables** dialog.

11. To apply the table and return to your project, click [Apply].

Filters

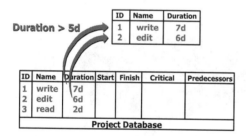

Duration > 5d

ID	Name	Duration
1	write	7d
2	edit	6d

ID	Name	Duration	Start	Finish	Critical	Predecessors
1	write	7d				
2	edit	6d				
3	read	2d				

Project Database

A *filter* selects and displays records from the project database that meet a criterion you set. You can filter tasks or resources. MS Project allows you to create a criterion that selects within any field in the database. The filter does not contain the project data, it is just the screen applied to the project database. In the illustration, the tasks with a duration greater than 5 days have been filtered from the database.

A filter does not display any detail tasks that are collapsed under their summary task, even if they meet the criterion you created. If a filter does not display the right tasks, they are probably collapsed. Expand all summary tasks first, using the [**Show ▾**] tool, before applying a filter.

The filter **All Tasks** is the default filter in task views to show all tasks; the filter **All resources** is comparable in resource views. As their names suggest, these are not real filters, because they display every record present in the project database. To get rid of a filtered view, you reapply the **All tasks** or **All resources** "filter" or press [F3].

Applying an Existing Filter

1. Choose **Project, Filtered for <name of current filter>**.
   OR
   Click the ▾ of the tool [All Tasks ▾] in task views, or [All Resources ▾] in resource views, on the standard toolbar and the list of filters appears.

2. Select a filter from the list. Only the records that meet the criterion (or criteria) you identified are now displayed.

There are some very useful filters included in MS Project. Some task filters to be aware of are:

◆ **Critical** displays all tasks that drive your project end date. Note that the word "*critical*" does not necessarily imply that the task is important. It looks for *Yes* in the calculated field **Critical**.

◆ **Cost overbudget** displays the tasks that cost more than their baseline cost.

◆ **Date range** displays tasks that fall in whole or in part within the period you indicate. This allows you to focus on the tasks in the coming weeks.

◆ **Milestones** displays all important events in your schedule. It looks for *Yes* in the calculated field **Milestone**.

◆ **Slipping tasks** displays all tasks that are forecast to finish later than their baseline.

◆ **Summary** displays all summary tasks and gives you a high-level view of the project. It looks for *Yes* in the calculated field **Summary**.

◆ **Using resource...** displays tasks assigned to a resource of your choice. This allows you to create simple to-do lists. It looks for tasks that contain the name of the resource in the **Resource Names** field.

Some useful resource filters to be aware of are:

◆ **Overallocated Resources** displays resources with too much work at certain times. Realize though that it will display resources that may only have an over-allocation during 1 hour in the project. It normally displays more resources than you need to worry about. It looks for resources with *Yes* in the calculated field **Overallocated**.

◆ **Slipping Assignments**, when applied in the Resource Usage view, displays those resources with assignments that are late.

Just as with tables, there are advantages to creating a new filter object for each reporting need. So you will not have to change or recreate your filter every time.

Designing a New Filter

1. Choose **Project, Filtered for <name of current filter>, More Filters**; the **More Filters** dialog appears:

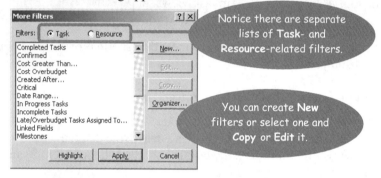

Notice there are separate lists of **Task**- and **Resource**-related filters.

You can create **New** filters or select one and **Copy** or **Edit** it.

2. Select ◉ **Task** to see a list of task-related filters or ◉ **Resource** for resource-related filters.

3. Click on a filter that is close to what you want and click $\boxed{\text{Copy...}}$; this will keep the original intact. The **Filter Definition** dialog appears:

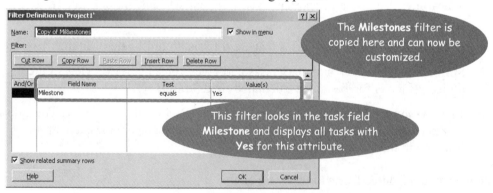

The **Milestones** filter is copied here and can now be customized.

This filter looks in the task field **Milestone** and displays all tasks with **Yes** for this attribute.

4. Enter a name for the filter; keep it the same as the table you created.

5. To list the new filter in the menu, check ☑ **Show in menu**.

6. Change the filter definition:
Select the field to filter on from the list under **Field Name**.
Select the comparison from the list under **Test**.
Enter the **Value(s)**; for an explanation of your many options in this field, see below these steps.

7. You can add more conditions by adding **And** or **Or** in the **And/Or** field and entering the second condition on the second line. **And** results in fewer records displayed, whereas **Or** results in more records displayed.

8. Click | OK |.

9. Click | Apply |.

The **Value** field in the **Filter Definition** dialog can contain:

◆ Other field names that you select from the list
This allows you to make comparisons between fields and, for example, display all tasks that slipped. The definition of such a filter would be: *Finish is greater than [Baseline Finish]*. Notice that in the field **Value** field names are enclosed in square brackets.

◆ Literal values that you type in, for example:
◇ *Yes* to filter on a flag field
◇ *$10,000* to filter on a cost field
◇ *5 days* to filter on duration or work
◇ *Jan 15, 2003* to filter on dates

◆ Prompts for the user to enter a value
You have to enter the prompt in a format similar to: "<text of the prompt>"?
where <text of the prompt> is the question to display. An example is *"Enter the minimum duration"?*. Notice that you need to include the quotation marks and the question mark at the end. As a result, the following dialog appears when you apply the filter, and after clicking | OK | the desired records are displayed:

Example of a totally customized, interactive filter

Groups

Groups allow you to rearrange the tasks (or resources) in different categories. When you apply a grouping to the task list, the original structure of the WBS will be temporarily hidden and the new grouping will be displayed. In the illustration, you can see that the tasks are categorized on the attribute *Critical* in two groups of *Yes* and *No*. The task-related field *Critical* is a calculated yes/no field indicates whether or not a task is critical. When you apply **No Group** again, the grouping will disappear and the *Work Breakdown Structure* will reappear.

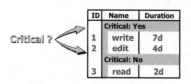

ID	Name	Duration
Critical: Yes		
1	write	7d
2	edit	4d
Critical: No		
3	read	2d

ID	Name	Duration	Start	Finish	Critical	Predecessors
1	write	7d			Yes	
2	edit	4d			Yes	
3	read	2d			No	
			Project Database			

In this way you can create alternative breakdown structures by grouping on a field. You can even create new multiple-level breakdown structures that are an alternative to the WBS. You can do so using an outline field (e.g., **Outline Code1**) in which you code the new breakdown.

For example, your finance department may request a breakdown of tasks by accounting codes for *Team member*, *Manager* and *Subcontractors*:[67]

Accounting Code	Task Name	Accounting Code	Baseline Cost	Cost	Cost Variance	Actual Cost
1	⊟ **Labour cost**	**1**	**$129,125.00**	**$135,875.00**	**$6,750.00**	**$11,025.00**
1.1	⊟ **Team member (employee)**	**1.1**	**$32,918.75**	**$32,918.75**	**$0.00**	**$4,743.75**
1.1	research staff requirements	1.1	$1,125.00	$1,125.00	$0.00	$1,125.00
1.1	summarize requirements	1.1	$525.00	$525.00	$0.00	$525.00
1.1	select the realtor	1.1	$1,125.00	$1,125.00	$0.00	$1,125.00
1.1	legal review	1.1	$281.25	$281.25	$0.00	$281.25
1.1	select the contractor	1.1	$1,125.00	$1,125.00	$0.00	$1,125.00
1.1	negotiate the contract	1.1	$562.50	$562.50	$0.00	$562.50
1.1	select mover	1.1	$1,125.00	$1,125.00	$0.00	$0.00
1.1	pack	1.1	$13,925.00	$13,925.00	$0.00	$0.00
1.1	unpack	1.1	$13,125.00	$13,125.00	$0.00	$0.00
1.2	⊟ **Manager (overhead)**	**1.2**	**$6,281.25**	**$6,281.25**	**$0.00**	**$6,281.25**
1.2	visit the sites	1.2	$1,312.50	$1,312.50	$0.00	$1,312.50
1.2	evaluate the sites	1.2	$1,181.25	$1,181.25	$0.00	$1,181.25
1.2	meet to select the location	1.2	$2,175.00	$2,175.00	$0.00	$2,175.00
1.2	meet to discuss contract	1.2	$1,050.00	$1,050.00	$0.00	$1,050.00
1.2	revise the schedule	1.2	$562.50	$562.50	$0.00	$562.50
1.3	⊟ **Subcontractor (external)**	**1.3**	**$89,925.00**	**$96,675.00**	**$6,750.00**	**$0.00**
1.3	relocate walls	1.3	$22,500.00	$29,250.00	$6,750.00	$0.00
1.3	electric wiring	1.3	$5,625.00	$5,625.00	$0.00	$0.00
1.3	paint	1.3	$1,800.00	$1,800.00	$0.00	$0.00
1.3	drying of paint	1.3	$0.00	$0.00	$0.00	$0.00
1.3	install cabinetry	1.3	$9,000.00	$9,000.00	$0.00	$0.00
1.3	install LAN	1.3	$33,750.00	$33,750.00	$0.00	$0.00
1.3	lay carpet	1.3	$13,500.00	$13,500.00	$0.00	$0.00
1.3	move	1.3	$3,750.00	$3,750.00	$0.00	$0.00

---

[67] This screenshot was created using the *Relocation Project* exercise files. We discuss custom outline codes in detail in the Black Belt Professional course. See www.iil.com and follow the link *Microsoft Project*.

This grouping feature almost gives Project 2002 the power of a relational database. An example of a grouping of resources is shown in the following screenshot. You can try to reproduce this screenshot by doing the exercise on page 538:

	Resource Name	Position	Function	Cost
	⊟ **employee**			**$28,500.00**
2	Falgon – John	employee representative	employee	$675.00
3	Hilcrest – Nancy	planner	employee	$1,575.00
7	the employees	employees	employee	$26,250.00
	⊟ **external**			**$90,825.00**
4	Roach – Pierre	lawyer	external	$281.25
6	the contractor	contractor	external	$52,650.00
8	the LAN consultants	LAN consultants	external	$33,750.00
9	the movers	movers	external	$3,750.00
10	the realtor	realtor	external	$393.75
	⊟ **manager**			**$9,000.00**
5	Salin – Nelson	CEO	manager	$1,125.00
11	you	project mngr.	manager	$7,875.00
	⊟ **material**			**$800.00**
1	boxes		material	$800.00

The resources are grouped by **Function** (resource-related field).

Notice that if an item falls in more than one group, the item is repeated. For example, if you assigned two resources to a task and then grouped the tasks by resource, the task name will show up under both resources.

Applying an Existing Grouping

1. Choose **Project, Group by: <name of current group>**; a submenu appears.
    OR
    Click ▾ on the list `No Group` ▾ on the standard toolbar; the list with different groupings appears.

2. Select a group from the list; the task or resource records are sorted and displayed within their groups.

Just as with tables and filters, there are advantages to creating a new group object for each reporting need, so you will not have to recreate your group every time.

Designing a New Grouping

1. Choose **Project, Group by: <name of current group>, More Groups…**; the
   More Groups dialog appears:

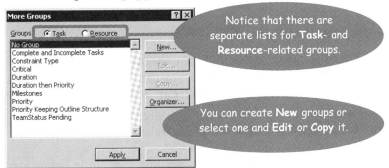

2. Select ⦿ **Task** to see a list of task-related groupings or ⦿ **Resource** for
   resource-related groupings.

3. Click on a group that is close to what you want and click [Copy…]; this will keep
   the original intact. The **Group Definition** dialog appears:

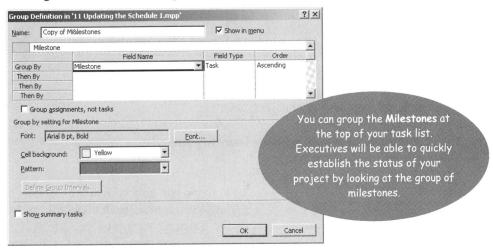

4. Enter a name for the group; keep it the same as the name of the table you created.

5. To list the new group in the menu, check ☑ **Show in menu**.

6. Change the group definition:
   Select the field to group by from the list under **Field Name**.
   Select **Descending** or **Ascending** from the list under **Order**.
   If you choose a numeric field, it is important to select the intervals as well by

clicking [Define Group Intervals…]. If you skip this, MS Project will group on each value, which is useless.

7. Click [OK]; you are now back in the **More Groups** dialog.

8. Click [Apply].

 Notice that in Project 2002 you can now also group on assignment fields. Instead of grouping on the task-related **Cost** field, for example, you can group the assignments instead. In the **Group Definition** dialog, check ☑ **Group assignments, not tasks**; this enables the list under **Field Type**. From this list select **Assignment**. The grouping will now use the assignment-related rows instead of the task-related rows.

 You can now also print the row and column totals in the timescale of the **Usage** views by choosing **File, Page Setup**, tab **View**, ☑ **Print row totals for values within print date range** and ☑ **Print column totals**.

Views

A view contains:

- ◆ A reference to the table it uses, and the table can apply custom fields
- ◆ A reference to the filter it applies
- ◆ A reference to the group by which it categorizes the records
- ◆ Any formats applied through the **Format** menu
- ◆ The sorting order applied via **Project, Sort**
- ◆ The **File, Page Setup** settings
- ◆ Any drawing objects created with the **Drawing** toolbar

The following illustration depicts this:

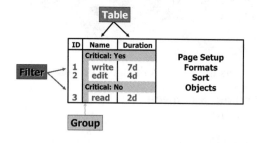

Perhaps you noticed that the **Format** menu looks different in each view. For example, the Calendar view provides different format menu items than the Gantt Chart. Also, the **File, Page Setup** dialog contains different options for each view. The fact that the menus change when you switch views can be confusing to the occasional user of MS Project. The reason for the changes is that the settings are specific to each view and are stored in the view object. Thanks to it, the view provides a steady display and printout of the project information.

It is a good idea to create a new view for each of your reporting needs. The view can also be added to the **View** menu. If you do so, the view can be accessed from then on with two simple mouse-clicks. The appearance of views can be fine-tuned using the sorting and format menus.

Creating a New View

1. Choose **View, More Views...**; the **More Views** dialog appears:

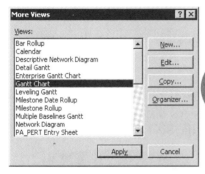

The task- and resource-related views are both listed in one list. You can create **New** views or select one and **Edit** or **Copy** it.

2. Choose the view that is closest to what you want and click `Copy...`.
    OR
    Click `New...`; the **Define New View** dialog appears, which allows you to choose between creating a *single view* or a *combination view*. We will create a single view. Click `OK`.

3. The **View Definition** dialog appears:

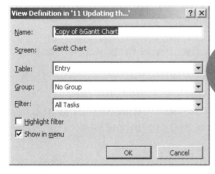

A copy of the **Gantt Chart** view is created here and the custom-made **Table, Group** and **Filter** objects can now be referred to in the lists.

4. Fill in the name of the new view and select the **Table**, the **Group** and the **Filter** from the lists provided. It helps if all the components of the view have the same

name, as we recommended before. With identical names, it is obvious they belong together. You can still return to the definition dialogs for table, group and filter to rename them.

5. If you want this view to show in the menu, check ☑ **Show in menu**; the view will be available with only two mouse-clicks.

6. Click | OK |; you are now back in the **More Views** dialog.

7. Click | Apply |.

Sort the Records

Choose **Project, Sort** and pick one of the listed sort orders; the sort will be applied immediately.
OR

1. If you want to customize the sort order, make sure you are in a *task view* to sort tasks and in a *resource view* to sort resources. In the steps that follow we will explain sorting tasks. Choose **Project, Sort, Sort by...**; the **Sort** dialog appears:

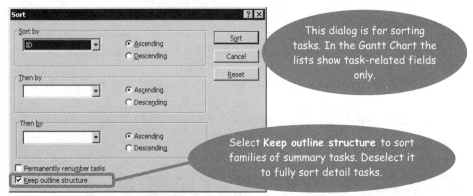

This dialog is for sorting tasks. In the Gantt Chart the lists show task-related fields only.

Select **Keep outline structure** to sort families of summary tasks. Deselect it to fully sort detail tasks.

2. Select the first sort order key from the **Sort by** list; if you think you will need a second sort key to break any ties, select it from the list **Then by**.

3. An important choice is whether you want to keep the outline structure. If you do, MS Project will only sort the families of summary tasks. If you don't keep the outline structure, MS Project will do a complete and continuous sort of detail tasks, ignoring the families.

4. Click | Sort | and the sort will be applied.

5. To reset the sort order, simply resort by ID number by choosing **Project, Sort, By ID**.

 The sort order is stored in the view object in which you applied the sort. Each view can have a different sort order.

 Be careful when using ☑ **Permanently renumber tasks**, because if you apply it, you lose your carefully crafted hierarchical structure of the WBS. You can click **Undo** ↶ to set it straight or close your file without saving.

Apply Any Formats

The **Format** menu offers many options to improve the appearance of the output. Any change you make through the format menu will be stored in the view object that you have on the screen when you make the change.

The format menu items change when you apply another view. For example, when you are in a view without a timescale, the menu item **Format, Timescale** is grayed out and inaccessible. When you realize that each view has its own format menu, you understand that MS Project is a much bigger application than it first appears to be.

We reviewed the different format options when we discussed printing each view:
◆ Gantt Chart was discussed starting on page 252.
◆ Network Diagram was discussed starting on page 220.
◆ Resource Spreadsheet was discussed starting on page 305.
◆ Resource Graph will be discussed on page 520
◆ Calendar view will be discussed on page 522
◆ Tracking Gantt view will be discussed on page 602.

I will summarize only the important choices here:

◆ What text and bar formats do you want?
You can customize the text for individual tasks you select using the menu items **Format, Font** or format the individual bar with **Format, Bar**. You can do it faster by applying a style to each type of task by choosing **Format, Text Styles** or **Format, Bar Styles**. We recommend you use the styles first before overriding the styles for single tasks using **Format, Font** or **Format, Bar**.

◆ Which date formats do you want in the spreadsheet and in the timescale?
First of all, choose the default date format for all date fields in MS Project by choosing **Tools, Options**, tab **View, Date Format**. If you want to change the date order (e.g., from mmddyy to ddmmyy), you have to go to the **Control Panel,**

Regional Options (Windows 2000) or **Regional and Language Options** (Windows XP).
To override the default date format in the spreadsheet, choose **View, Table <name of current table>, More Tables**, click [Edit...] and select the format you want from the **Date Format** list at the bottom.
To override the default date format in the timescale when you display dates next to the task bars, choose **Format, Layout** and select the date format from the list **Date Format**.

◆ Do you want to show dependencies in the Gantt Chart or Tracking Gantt?
Make your choice using the menu **Format, Layout, Links**. You can also choose between straight and hooked arrows.

◆ Do you want to roll up detail task bars into their summary task bars in the Gantt Chart?
A regular summary task bar looks like ▼━━━▼ . Rolled-up summary task bars look like ▼▓▓▯▼ with detail task bars rolled up or like ▼━◇━▼ with milestones rolled up.
You have to choose between:
◇ No rolling up (default)
◇ Rolling up certain hand-picked detail task bars
Hand-pick the task bars by selecting them, clicking the **Task Information** tool 🗎 and checking ☑ **Roll up Gantt bar to Summary**. Take similar steps for the summary task but check ☑ **Show rolled up Gantt bars**
◇ Rolling up all detail task bars when their summary tasks are collapsed
Choose **Format, Layout, ☑ Always roll up Gantt bars**. To make the rollup appear only when summary tasks are collapsed, you can then also select ☑ **Hide roll up bars when summary expanded**.

◆ What fields do you want to show in the **Task Usage** and **Resource Usage** views?
You can select fields other than the default **Work** field. Choose **Format, Details** for a quick list or **Detail Styles...** for a complete list; better yet, right-click in the yellow area of the timescale and a menu will pop up that allows you to quickly pick a field listed or other ones through the menu item **Detail Styles...** .

◆ In the Resource Graph view you can also choose to graph details other than the default **Peak Units** by choosing **Format, Details**. Notice that the peak units give an inflated impression of the workloads when you zoom out from days to weeks to months in the timescale. Workloads seem to inflate because MS Project takes the highest bar of the 4 weeks in a month to summarize the entire month. You should consider changing to the details **Work** for a more realistic depiction of the expected workload over time.

Choose the Page Setup Settings

The page setup settings are stored in the view object that you have on the screen when you choose **File, Page Setup**.

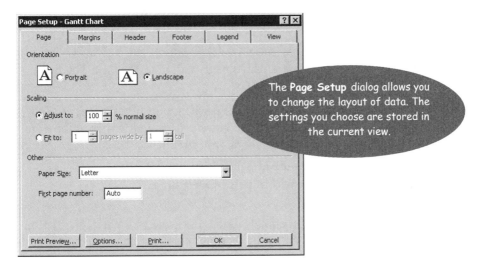

We will only summarize the important options in the **File, Page Setup** dialog, since we discussed many of them in previous chapters:

◆ **Page** tab
　◇ **Orientation**: When you print the timescale, it is often best to choose
　　⊙ Landscape. This will allow you to keep the entire timescale on one page and prevent you from having to tape pages together.
　◇ The **Scaling** option will shrink or enlarge the print image but is only available if your printer can handle scaling; the range is from 10% to 500%.

◆ **Header, Footer, Legend** tab
Choose the position first: **Left, Center** or **Right**. You can type in any header text or, better, use the lists **General** or **Project Fields** at the bottom of the dialog to select standard phrases. Select the item from the list and then click Add ; this will add a cryptic code for it in the header, footer or legend. These codes refer to entries you made in the **File, Properties** dialog. If you make changes in that dialog, all headers of all views will be updated automatically.
The font size is small by default for a header. To increase it select the text by dragging over it and clicking **A**; the **Font** dialog appears, where you can choose the font, style and size.

◆ **View** tab
The important options for *task views* (except the Calendar view) are:

◇ ☐ **Print first** `3` ⇳ **columns on all pages**: You should not have to use this option if your report is only one page wide. I have always been able to print even the largest schedules with thousands of tasks on the width of one page. You can use the landscape page orientation if you need to. The recipients of your reports will never tape multiple pages of a Gantt Chart together anyway.

◇ ☑ **Print Notes**: This will create a separate page with notes by task. The task IDs are used to relate the notes to the tasks.

◇ ☑ **Fit timescale to end of page** is only useful when your timescale does not reach the right-hand side of the page. This option will stretch it, filling the page. Note that it does not shrink the timescale; it only stretches.

◇ Available in Task Usage or Resource Usage views only:
☑ **Print row totals for values within print date range**
☑ **Print column totals**
These options allow you to add the totals to the timescale of the usage views on the right-hand side (row totals) and at the bottom (column totals by day, by week or by month).

Copying Views between Projects

Once you have created a view object, you can use it in other projects or share it with other people. You can even put it in your *global.mpt* file and use it in all your other project files.

1. Open the file that contains the object, and open the file to copy the object to.

2. Choose **Tools, Organizer...**; the **Organizer** dialog appears:

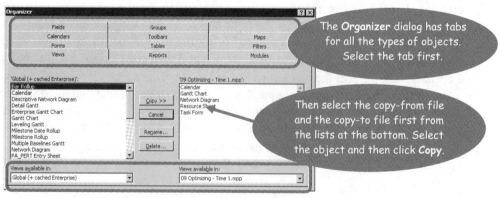

3. Activate the tab **Views** as the type of object to copy.

4. In the list on the left at the bottom of the dialog, select the file from which to copy the object and in the list on the right select the file to copy to.

5. Then select the view object to copy and click | Copy >> |.

6. Click the tab **Fields** and copy the fields the view uses in its table.

7. Click the tab **Tables** and copy the table that the view uses.

8. Click the tab **Filters** and copy the filter object that the view uses.

9. Click the tab **Groups** and copy the group object that the view uses.

10. Click | Close | when done.

It is a lot easier to see which objects are the components of one view if they all have the same name. That's why we recommended naming them the same.

The organizer allows you to copy objects into the *global.mpt* file. Any objects you put into this global template are visible in all your projects, unless there is already an object in the project file that has the same name. Give objects unique names if you want to always see them in any file you copy them to.

If you are using Project 2002 with *Project Server*, you may not have access privileges to save objects in the enterprise global (*cached Enterprise*) because this would affect all other enterprise users as well. Ask your project office to change the *Enterprise Global*.

Using Project Server Views

We discussed setting up the enterprise resource pool on page 282. The resource pool aggregates workloads across multiple projects. The *Project Server* views also aggregate data across multiple projects. In this book we focus on managing a single project and we will therefore only provide an overview of reporting with Project Server.[68]

In order to create informative views in Project Server, you have to set up enterprise fields in what is called the *Enterprise Global*. The enterprise global is a template of options, fields and views standardized across the enterprise. Only if you capture certain

---

[68] In the Blue Belt Professional and Black Belt Professional courses we focus on managing multiple projects with Project Server. See www.iil.com and follow the link *Microsoft Project*.

attributes can you report on them. You need to think about and customize the enterprise fields. Project Server has the following enterprise fields:

◆ *Project descriptors* (see the next section)
◆ *Task descriptors* (see page 511)
◆ *Resource descriptors* (see page 512)
◆ *Outline Code descriptors* for projects, tasks and resources (see page 512)

We will discuss these below. We will elaborate on questions to consider when customizing Project Server for the enterprise and we will provide some ideas on good views for the enterprise (see page 514). We will also discuss *Traffic light reporting* (see page 515).

Project Descriptors

What are important descriptors for projects on the enterprise level? You should at least think about giving each project a unique project code. But there are many more interesting characteristics to capture on each project. Only when each project is properly described (coded) can you make sorted or grouped portfolio reports on that attribute. For example, you may want to capture for each project:

◆ The *sponsor* for the project
The sponsor is typically the executive who initiated and funds the project.[69] This allows you to filter, sort or group all projects by sponsor in the project portfolio view.

◆ The *performing organization*
The performing organization is the enterprise whose employees are most directly involved in doing the work of the project.[70] This allows you to filter, sort or group all projects by performing organization in the project portfolio view.

◆ The expected percentage of *return on investment* (*ROI*)
This allows you to filter, sort or group all projects by ROI in the project portfolio view. Also, when prioritizing projects, the ROI can help determine the priority level.

◆ The financial exposure of the project for the organization (i.e., the total investment)
This can be used as a measure for risk, which can also be used when prioritizing projects.

---

[69] See page 16 of the PMBOK® Guide, 2000 Edition, published by the PMI.

[70] See page 16 of the PMBOK® Guide, 2000 Edition, published by the PMI.

◆ How well the project objective is aligned with enterprise objectives
You can capture a qualitative assessment of the strategic alignment, like *Low,*
Medium, or High, as a project descriptor. The better a project is aligned, the higher
priority it deserves.

◆ The project manager

The following screenshot shows a portfolio view for executives that has the projects
with budget and schedule traffic lights grouped by project manager:

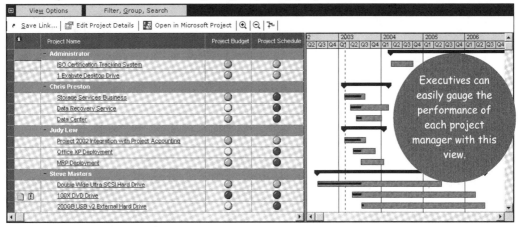

Task Descriptors

Viewing descriptors for tasks or deliverables other than those present in the default
MS Project database takes some thought. Here are some suggestions:

◆ *related deliverable* (the summary task of the activity)
This allows you to hide all summary tasks from the view or time sheet and still see
the name of the deliverable as necessary context information for each detail task.
You can even develop a macro that automatically displays and refreshes the name of
the deliverable for each detail task in an extra text field upon opening the project
file.[71]

---

[71] Visual Basic macros are the main topic of the Black Belt Standard course, see www.iil.com
and follow the link *Microsoft Project*.

◆ *responsible department* (owner) or *responsible person* (owner)
This allows you to capture the essential information of a *Responsibility Assignment Matrix (RAM)* in MS Project.

The following is an example of a view of tasks grouped by responsible department:

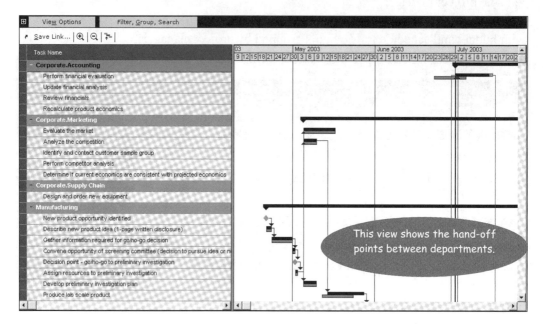

Resource Descriptors

Examples of resource descriptors are:
◆ supervisor
◆ contact information

Most resource descriptors are more complex. For example, to capture the hierarchical position, geography or skill set, you need an intricate field in which you can be specific. Such fields need to present a list with a *logical hierarchy* of items. These fields are the outline code fields.

Outline Code Descriptors

The outline code fields contain a breakdown structure in one descriptor field. For example, resources have their own spot in the organization chart. The organization chart is a hierarchy of multiple levels. With a single outline code field you can capture and uniquely describe where each resource fits in the organization's hierarchy. Without outline code fields you would need many fields to accomplish the same thing. As you can see, outline code fields are very powerful. Outline code fields for resources can also be applied to any descriptor that contains a logical breakdown structure:

◆ Location breakdown of where resources work: country, state/province, city/municipality, building

◆ Geographic breakdown of where resources are available to work

◆ Skills breakdown of the resources
Skills break down into multiple levels, for example technical, language or management skills. Technical skills break down further into programming, testing or implementing skills. Programming skills break down further into different programming languages. If you capture the need for the different skills, you can start doing long term resource planning by skill.

The following view created in *Project Server* shows the longer term workloads for a team of eight resources:

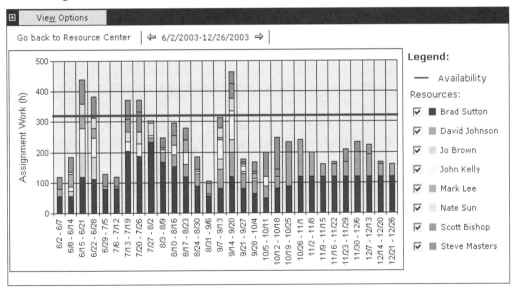

Outline code fields can also be used for tasks. They allow you to create breakdown structures that are an alternative to the WBS, the deliverable-oriented breakdown. Applications for outline code fields for tasks and deliverables are:

◆ Chart of accounts in the accounting ledger
Accountants need to categorize expenses in several categories: personnel, facility, equipment and material. Each of these can be further broken down into different

subcategories. The outline code fields would allow coding tasks (or resources) in different accounting categories.

◆ Contract breakdown of deliverables
Purchase agents need to keep track of contracts and would benefit from a contract-oriented breakdown structure.

Once these descriptor fields are created and entered by the project managers, portfolio views can be created that summarize multiple projects. Also, reporting can be standardized with enterprise views.

Enterprise Views

Enterprise views are outputs you standardize on across the enterprise. The *project office* within your organization should think carefully about what views would benefit all project managers and executives. The project office will publish these views as *Enterprise Global* views, available and similar for all projects. Only people with *Project Server* administrative privileges can change the enterprise views, typically not project managers.

Centrally designed standard views provide several benefits for your organization:

◆ They prevent project managers from having to spend time and energy developing appropriate report formats, reinventing the same wheel over and over again.

◆ They provide the capability to have all project managers create project reports in the same format. With a standard format, executives will be able to analyze faster and compare projects better.

◆ They allow help desk personnel to troubleshoot over the phone. If the technical support person asks the project manager to apply a standard enterprise view, the support person knows exactly what the project manager sees. Any other view could have been inadvertently changed by the project manager. (Of course, that never happens!)

The following sample of an enterprise view displays the progress of all projects and their baselines (Tracking view):

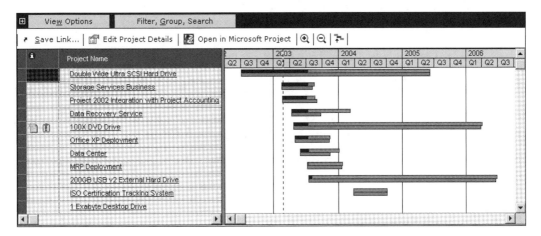

Traffic Light Reporting

If you want to do traffic light reporting with red, yellow and green indicators to give a quick impression of the health of a project or portfolio, you have to think about the business rules that determine which of the three colors will be used for projects, deliverables and tasks.

You can do this for:

◆ *Budget performance*: What are the threshold values for well within budget (green), close to the original budget (yellow) and running dangerously over budget (red)?

◆ *Schedule performance*: What are the threshold values for well within schedule (green), close to on schedule (yellow) and slipping dangerously (red)?

◆ *Quality performance*: Project Server does not have features for quality management. You will need a separate quality management system to determine or calculate the quality values. In software development projects you could develop a quality indicator that, for example, reveals if one or more must-have requirements are not met (red), one or more nice-to-have requirements are not met (yellow) and all requirements are met (green). In *Project Server*, you can definitely present these quality indicators next to schedule and budget indicators in a project portfolio view. Executives would probably be very grateful.

The *Earned Value* performance indicators are well worth exploring as a basis for budget and schedule performance.[72] No matter what you use, it should be clear to everybody what a red light means, just like driving a car. If red traffic lights weren't clearly understood by everybody, the streets wouldn't be very safe ...

The following example of a traffic light report shows projects grouped by region:

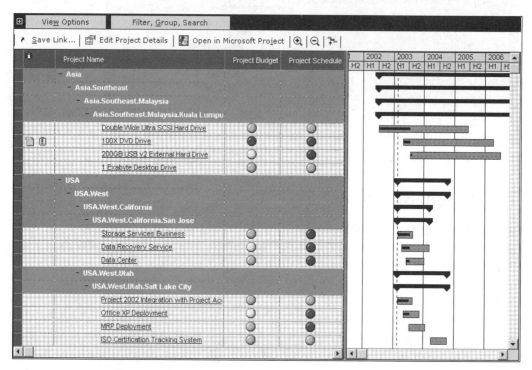

The business rules differ from organization to organization; even within an organization they can, perhaps even should, differ from business unit to business unit. It is not uncommon for them to even differ from one department to the next; the IT department can have different standards for healthy projects than the engineering department. This is particularly true if the average budget for IT projects is $50,000 and for engineering projects $1 million.

---

[72] See for more on Earned Value performance indicators:
- Guide to the PMBOK, 2000 Edition, published by the PMI.
- Earned Value Project Management, Fleming, Quentin W. and Joel Koppelman, second edition, Project Management Institute Inc., Newton Square, PA, USA, 2000.

If you created traffic light indicators on the project level, you should copy those same indicators onto the task level as well. This will allow executives to find the causes for problems using exactly the same indicators when they drill down into problem areas.

You can only customize the enterprise fields and views if you have the appropriate access privileges in the *Project Server* system. Since you may not have this as a project manager, we will not discuss the detailed how-to steps in this book.[73]

Creating One-Page Reports … Always!

This heading may seem pretentious if you are juggling a schedule with thousands of tasks. Regardless of the size of the project, you can always surprise your managers and clients with one-page performance reports. There is a simple technique to do this, and it will make your executives happy, if not euphoric. Executives typically don't have the time to dig through pages and pages of schedules. They expect you to provide concise information, i.e., one-page reports. The first one-page report should only show the major milestones. That is all you need if all the milestones are on schedule and the budgets are feasible. Where a milestone is off its baseline, you provide a second one-page report that gives an explanation for the discrepancy.

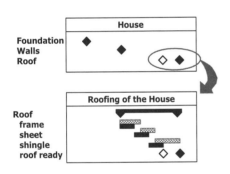

In the illustration, the milestone chart at the top shows slippage on the *Roof* milestone. In the bottom one-page report the detailed cause of the slippage is shown. With a few one-page reports you should be able to give an adequate status and forecast report for a project of any size.

In a similar fashion, you can create a one-page high-level cost report. If there are discrepancies, you can create another one-page report with the explanation for the differences.

---

[73] Our Black Belt Professional course addresses customizing Project Server views, see www.iil.com and follow the link *Microsoft Project*.

You will have to master the filters feature of MS Project to accomplish this (see page 494).

Checks on Reporting

We would like to suggest the following checks to verify if you used best practices for your projects. The checks pertain to what reporting view objects you developed in your schedule (discussed starting on page 487):

◆ Is there a one-page status report available as a **View** object in your project file that displays the *major milestones*?

   ◇ Are the major milestones filtered in this view instead of listed together in the WBS?
   Many project managers put the major milestones at the top of their schedule to create a one-page overview of the project. This makes the network of dependencies very complex in the Gantt Chart because the dependencies run up and down with long arrows. This makes it very difficult to check if the network of dependencies is complete. Instead, we advocate using a separate view that displays the milestones automatically.

   ◇ Are the appropriate milestones chosen to represent the status and to forecast the project?
   If you have many milestones, you may end up with multiple pages. Instead of reporting on all milestones, you can mark certain milestones as major milestones using a flag field (Flag1 - Flag20). The filter of the view should display these major milestones. If you use the **Flag1** field, the filter definition would be: *Flag1 equals Yes*. You then make this filter part of the view in **Views, More views**, select the view in the list and click [Edit…]. Select your newly created filter to replace the default filter in this view and click [OK]. When you switch to the view, the filter will automatically be applied. Marking the right milestones is the challenge here.

   ◇ Does the one-page view report give an appropriate impression of the health of the project?

◆ If your schedule has a *Resource-Critical Path*, is there a separate view object that displays it?
   The view should have the resource-critical tasks flagged in the field **Marked**. See page 433 for a detailed discussion of the Resource-Critical Path and how to create this view.

Examples of Useful or Hard-to-Get-At Reports

We will discuss the following special reports in more detail. Some are very useful; others are hard to get at:

◆ Responsibilities by department (see next section)
◆ Workload histogram for individuals and groups (see page 520)
◆ To-do lists in the Calendar view (see page 522)
◆ Reports that include the notes (see page 525)
◆ The time-phased budget (see page 528)

Responsibilities by Department

With the new *Group* feature, it is easy to communicate lists of responsibilities by department. For each resource you can enter the department in which each person works. Then you can create responsibility lists by department. The image below shows part of such an output:

	Resource Name	Work	Details	Aug	Sep	Oct	Nov
	⊟ **Group: No Value**	**0 days**	Work				
	⊞ Unassigned	0 days	Work				
	⊟ **Group: employee**	**148 days**	Work				
2	⊟ Falgon – John	3 days	Work	3d			
	visit the sites	1 day	Work	1d			
	evaluate the sites	1 day	Work	1d			
	meet to select the location	1 day	Work	1d			
3	⊞ Hilcrest – Nancy	5 days	Work	5d			
7	⊞ the employees	140 days	Work				140d
	⊟ **Group: external**	**316 days**	Work				
4	⊞ Roach – Pierre	0.5 days	Work	0.5d			
6	⊞ the contractor	234 days	Work	1d	133d	94d	6d
8	⊞ the LAN consultants	60 days	Work			60d	
9	⊞ the movers	20 days	Work				20d
10	⊞ the realtor	1.5 days	Work	1.5d			
	⊟ **Group: manag...**	...ays	Work				
5	⊞ Salin – Nelson	1 day	Work	1d			
11		...3 days	Work	14.43d	0.87d		
	⊟ **Group: material**		Work				
1		0 boxes	Work (				

Annotations on image: "Effort needed by department, by resource and by assignment", "Third level: assignments", "Second level: resources", "First level: departments"

1. Choose **View, Resource Sheet**.

2. Enter the department in which each person works in the field **Group**.

3. Choose **View, Resource Usage**.

4. Select from the list No Group ▾ on the **Standard** toolbar the item **Resource Group**; the result will show three outline levels:

    ◊   The first level shows the resource groups, i.e., departments.

    ◊   The second level shows all resources working in each department.

    ◊   The third level shows all the assignments for each resource.

Workload Histogram for Individuals and Groups

Workload histogram is synonymous with *Resource Graph* in MS Project. When you enter the group or department the resource works in, you can create interesting workload histograms. You can create a graph that compares the workload of an individual with the total work for that group (department). The snapshot below shows the total work of the *LAN consultants* relative to the total workload of all *external* resources (as characterized in the field **Group**) displayed using the **Group…** filter. Other resources, like *contractor*, *movers, Pierre Roach*, and *realtor* also belong to the **Group** external resources, as you can see in the exercise files for the relocation project at the end of this chapter.

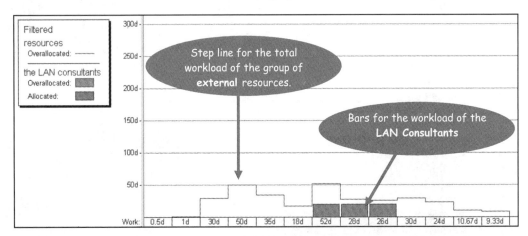

1. Enter the department in the **Group** field for each resource, as we did for the previous sample output.

2. Choose **View, Resource Graph**.

3. Press [Page Dn] until you see the graph of the individual for whom you want to compare the workload to the total workload of the department or group.

4. Choose **Format, Details, Work**; this exchanges the **Peak Units** for total **Work** numbers. **Work** provides a more accurate picture than **Peak Units**.

5. Choose **Format, Bar Styles**; the **Bar Styles** dialog appears:

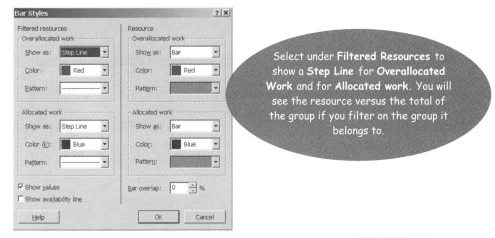

Select under **Filtered Resources** to show a **Step Line** for **Overallocated Work** and for **Allocated work**. You will see the resource versus the total of the group if you filter on the group it belongs to.

6. Select the settings as shown in the snapshot above and click [OK]; the view now shows stepped bars for the workload of the resource and a red line for the total work in the project (filter is still **All Resources**).

7. Make sure you have filled in the resource-related field *Group* in the resource sheet. Then select the filter **Group...** from the list 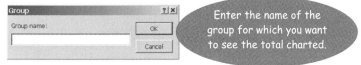 on the **Formatting** toolbar; the **Group** dialog appears:

Enter the name of the group for which you want to see the total charted.

8. Enter the name of the group the resource belongs to in the field **Group name** and click [OK]. Now you see the workload of the resource relative to the total workload of the department the person belongs to.

9. Create the header and footer in the **File, Page Setup** dialog.

10. Print the report by choosing **File, Print**.

 You can display different data in the Resource Graph more quickly by making it the bottom view, with the Resource Usage view in the top. Select in the Resource Usage the data to chart and it will immediately appear in the Resource Graph at the bottom.

Note that, unfortunately, you cannot change the y-axis; MS Project often creates a y-axis that is too long.

To-Do Lists in the Calendar View

The calendar view does not show many tasks within one day. When we first discussed this view on page 67, we stated that the calendar view is particularly suited for creating to-do lists by resource. There are several reasons for this:

◆ Typically a resource has only one or two tasks on any given day. Two tasks can easily be displayed in the calendar view, but not more.

◆ Not all people understand Gantt Charts, but most people can read calendars. To-do lists in the calendar view are often easier to understand than in the Gantt Chart.

◆ You can show the resource-specific holidays and vacation days in this view.

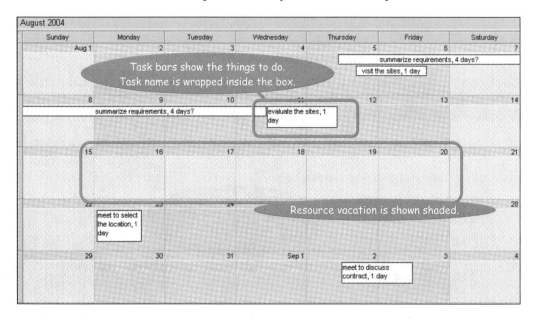

Creating a To-Do List for a Resource

1. Choose **View, Calendar**.

2. Select from the filter list  on the **Formatting** toolbar the **Using Resource...** filter; the **Using Resource** dialog appears:

The list will allow you to select a resource to filter on.

3. Select from the list **Show tasks using** the resource for which to create the to-do list. Click OK.

4. To create the shading for vacation time, choose **Format, Timescale...**; the **Timescale** dialog appears. Click the tab **Date Shading**:

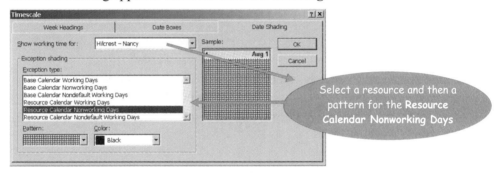

Select a resource and then a pattern for the Resource Calendar Nonworking Days

5. Under **Show working time for** select the resource of this to-do list and choose the appropriate pattern and color settings. Click OK. The view now colors or shades the nonworking days for the resource.

6. Create the header and footer in the **File, Page Setup** dialog.

7. Print the report by choosing **File, Print**.

To Adjust the Row Heights and Column Widths

Choose **View, Zoom** and select the number of weeks to display within one screen to adjust the row heights of the days.
OR
Point to the horizontal divider that separates the weeks; the mouse pointer changes to ⬍. Click and drag the divider up to decrease the height of all rows. Drag it down to increase the height.

Double-click the right-hand side of the column dividers between the days to adjust the column widths so they best fit in the entire screen. You can also drag them, but this usually takes several trial and error attempts.

To Change the Timescale

Choose **Format, Timescale** OR simply double-click on the timescale; the **Timescale** dialog appears. Click tab **Week Headings**:

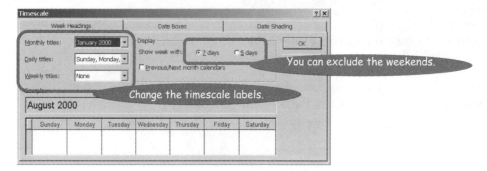

On the page tab **Week Headings** you can:

◆ Change the titles shown for the months, weeks and days.

◆ Select **Show week with** ◉ **5 days** as opposed to the default 7 days if your team never works weekend days.

To Format the View

In **Format, Bar Styles** you can:

◆ Choose the appearance of the different types of tasks.

◆ Add text labels inside the task bars by selecting the labels in the **Field(s)** dropdown list. You can even add multiple labels, like "**Name, Resource Name**", but you will find that in short task bars the text is cut off to fit inside the bar, which brings me to my next point.

◆ When task names are too long for the task bars, which they likely are for one-day tasks, use ☑ **Wrap text in bars**.

To Improve the Layout of the Task Bars

1. Choose **Format, Layout…**; the **Layout** dialog appears:

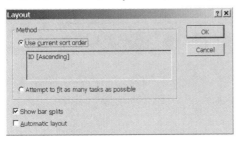

2. Under **Method** you can select different layout arrangements for the task bars:
    ◉ **Use current sort order** will list the task bars based upon the active sorting.
    ◉ **Attempt to fit as many tasks as possible** tries to optimize the use of space by displaying more than one bar horizontally.

3. If you check ☑ **Automatic layout,** the task bars will be rearranged every time the sort order changes or tasks are inserted or deleted.

Reports That Include the Notes

The **Notes** field can hold a lot of text; there is virtually no limit to it. You may need to capture a lot of text when:
◆ Creating a *WBS dictionary*, which is a narrative description of the major deliverables in the WBS
◆ Capturing *checklist items* or *reminders* to yourself

To include the notes in a report, you have two options:
◆ Print all the notes together on a separate notes page using a View
◆ Print the notes in between the tasks they relate to using a Report.

Print a View with a Separate Notes Page

The following is an example of a separate notes page using views:

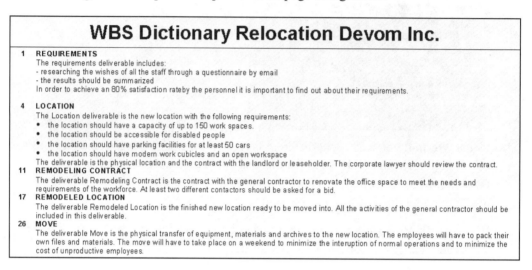

To create it, follow these steps:

1. In the Gantt Chart choose **File, Page Setup**; the **Page Setup** dialog appears:

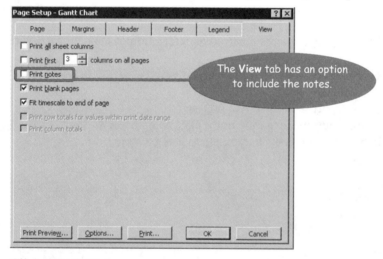

2. Click the tab **View**.

3. Check ☑ **Print notes**.

4. Click Print Preview... , Print... or OK .

Print a Report with Notes in Between the Tasks

The following report shows the notes inserted in between tasks:

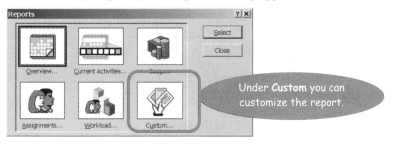

1. Choose **View, Reports**; the **Reports** dialog appears:

2. Double-click on **Custom** ; the **Custom Report** dialog appears.

3. Scroll down the list and select **Task**; the dialog should now look like:

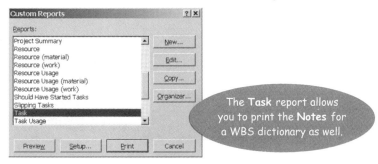

4. Click [Edit...] ; the **Task Report** dialog appears.

5. Click the tab **Definition**, if needed, and select ☑ **Show summary tasks** to include the deliverables.

6. Click the tab **Details** and check ☑ **Notes**, as in the following snapshot:

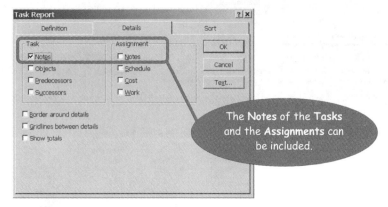

The **Notes** of the **Tasks** and the **Assignments** can be included.

7. The notes will now appear in between the tasks in the printout. Click [OK] and click [Preview] to see the report, or click [Print...].

The Time-Phased Budget

If your financial department asks you as the project manager to predict how much money your project needs over time, you can print a time-phased budget. You have two options:

◆ Time-phased budget by resource: Use the **Resource Usage** view
◆ Time-phased budget by task or deliverable: Use the **Task Usage** view

The following sample report shows expenses by deliverable by month:

	ⓘ	Task Name	Cost	Details	Qtr 3, 2004			Qtr 4, 2004		
					Jul	Aug	Sep	Oct	Nov	Dec
1		⊞ REQUIREMENTS	$1,650.00	Cost		$1,650.00				
4		⊞ LOCATION	$6,075.00	Cost		$6,075.00				
11		⊞ REMODELING CONTRAC	$3,300.00	Cost		$1,125.00	$2,175.00			
17		⊞ REMODELED LOCATION	$86,175.00	Cost			$28,125.00	$44,550.00	$13,500.00	
26		⊞ MOVE	$31,925.00	Cost		$1,125.00			$30,800.00	
				Cost						

The deliverable *remodeled location* costs *$86,175* in total that will have to be paid in *Sep, Oct* and *Nov.*

The steps to create this view are:

1. Choose **View, Task Usage** (or **Resource Usage** if you want the report by resource.)

2. Click **Go to selected Tasks** to scroll the numbers into view; you will see the details **Work** displayed by default, which is the effort required spread over time.

3. Choose **Format, Details, Cost**. Notice the check mark in front of **Work**; the work details are currently shown in the chart.
    OR
    Right-click in the yellow area of the timescale, and choose from the pop-up menu **Cost**.

4. Choose **Format, Details, Work** to turn this field off; notice that there is now a check mark in front of **Cost**.
    OR
    Right-click in the yellow area of the timescale, and choose from the pop-up menu **Work**.

5. Adjust the level of detail of the outline structure you want to show. In the Task Usage view, click on any column heading, click **Show ▾** and choose the appropriate level of detail. In the example, only deliverables are shown. In the Resource Usage view, click on any column heading and click **Collapse** ▬ on the **Format** toolbar.

6. Adjust the timescale to show the time unit your financial department would like to see by using **Zoom in** 🔍 and **Zoom out** 🔍.

7. Make sure can read all the numbers in the timescale; if the columns are too narrow, you will see ####. You can now adjust the column width of the bottom tier timescale units by dragging their right-hand border OR you can choose **Format, Timescale** and adjust the **Size** %.

8. Create the header and footer in the **File, Page Setup** dialog.

9. Print the report by choosing **File, Print**.

Printing

We will discuss some final things to do and settings to choose before sending the schedule to the printer.

Specify Columns to Spell-Check

1. To prevent MS Project from stopping on any abbreviation or code you used, choose **Tools, Options…** and click tab **Spelling**.

2. Choose or type **Yes** for those columns you want the spell-checker to check.

3. Check ☑ **Ignore words in UPPERCASE** and
   ☑ **Ignore Words with Numbers** to eliminate stopping on abbreviations or codes.

4. Click ⬜ OK ⬜.

To Check the Spelling in the Schedule

1. Choose **Tools, Spelling**.

2. When the spell-checker displays a misspelled word in the **Not In Dictionary** field, you can:

   ◇ Click ⬜ Ignore ⬜ to ignore the misspelled word, or click ⬜ Ignore All ⬜.

   ◇ Type the correction in the **Change To** field and click ⬜ Change ⬜ or click ⬜ Change All ⬜.

   ◇ Click ⬜ Add ⬜ to add the word to the user dictionary.

Inserting Page Breaks Manually

1. Select the task or resource to push onto the next page.

2. Choose **Insert, Page Break**; a dashed line will appear that represents the page break.

3. Choose **File, Print** and check ☑ **Manual page breaks** to make the breaks appear in the printout.

 The page breaks set in the table also insert breaks in other reports that are based on the same table. Therefore, use them only when really needed.

Inserting the Project Logo into the Header

1. Choose **File, Page Setup**.

2. Click the tab **Header**.

3. Click **Insert picture** 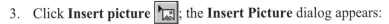; the **Insert Picture** dialog appears:

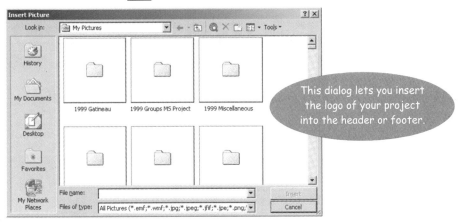

This dialog lets you insert the logo of your project into the header or footer.

4. Navigate through your directory system and select the image file with the logo of your project.

5. Click [**Insert**]; the logo is now displayed in the header.

6. If the logo image is too big, you can click on it and selection handles will appear around the image. Point to a corner selection handle and drag it to resize the picture.

The Timescale Is Too Short or Too Long

The timescale often has to be adjusted because it spills over onto the second page and you want to shorten it, or it occupies only a small part of the page and you want to stretch it.

To Shorten the Timescale

1. Choose **Format, Timescale** or double-click on the timescale; the **Timescale** dialog appears.

2. On one of the tier tabs, decrease the **Size** percentage, which will shorten the timescale. Check the sample box to see how far you can go.

 In the task and resource usage views, you can now drag the width of the time unit columns to the size you want.

To Stretch the Timescale to One Page

1. Choose **File, Page Setup**.

2. Click the tab View and check ☑ **Fit timescale to end of page**.
   This will stretch the timescale to fill the page.

Print Preview

Use print preview to check the header, footer, legend, margins and the timescale before printing or to check the position of the boxes on a Network Diagram.

1. Apply the view you want to print.

2. Click 🔍 or choose **File, Print Preview**:

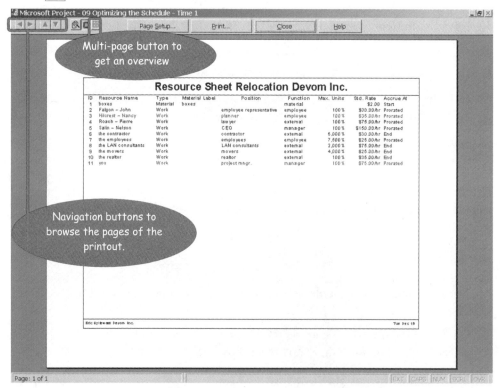

3. Use the multi-page button ⊞ to zoom out and get an overview of all the printed pages, and then click on one of the pages to zoom into that page.
   OR

Hold down [Alt], and use the arrow keys to browse through the pages of the printout.

4. On the print preview, click where you would like to zoom in to see part of a page in more detail. Click again to zoom out.

5. To change the margins, header, footer or legend text, click [Page Setup...].

6. To print the view, click [Print...].
   To exit print preview without printing, click [Close].

Printing the Current View

Click 🖶 to send the schedule directly to the default printer.
OR
Choose the print options using these steps:

1. Choose **File, Print**; the **Print** dialog appears:

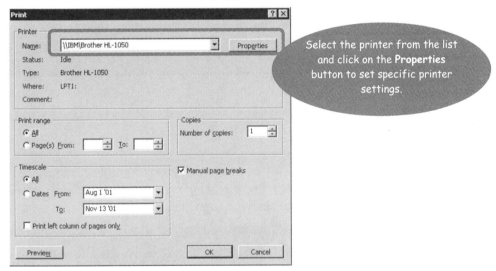

2. Select a printer in the **Name** list.

3. Click [Properties] to select the options available for the printer, such as paper source and orientation. Note that the choices you make here apply to all applications. Click [OK] when finished to go back to the **Print** dialog.

4. Select from the options available for your printer; see below for an explanation.

5. Click [OK] to start printing, or click [Close] to return to your project without printing.

Colors you may have used are automatically replaced by hatch patterns on a black-and-white printer.

Print Options

♦ **Print range**
   Select ⦿ **All** to print the entire project.
   OR
   Type the numbers of the first and last pages to print in the **Page(s) From** and **To** fields.

♦ ☑ **Manual page breaks**
   Check to use the manually set page breaks. Clear to use automatic page breaks set by MS Project.

♦ **Timescale**
   If you are printing a view with a timescale (Gantt Chart, Task Usage, Resource Graph and Resource Usage view), the **Timescale** section is active.
   To print the project from project start date to finish date use ⦿ **All**;
   for a particular period select ⦿ **Dates From To** and fill in the dates for the period you want.

Sending a Project File to Colleagues

1. Choose **File, Send To, Mail Recipient (as Attachment).** The MPP file will be attached to the e-mail. The **Choose Profile** dialog may appear: select a user profile, and click [OK]. The new e-mail message dialog appears:

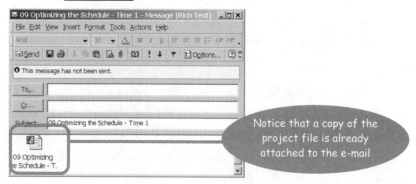

2. Fill in the **To** and the **CC** fields and send the message.

 Notice that you don't even need to save your file before sending it; the feature always sends the file as it appears on your screen.

Instead, you can use the **File, Send To, Routing Recipient** feature to send the schedule to a chain of people, each of whom will receive the schedule for review.

If you don't want your colleagues to be able to change your project file, you should create a Portable Document File (PDF) using *Adobe Acrobat*.[74] Adobe Acrobat sets itself up as if it were a printer, so you can create PDF files simply by choosing **File, Print** and then selecting as the printer either **Acrobat PDFWriter** or **Acrobat Distiller**.

---

[74] Adobe Acrobat (www.adobe.com) is not free software, although the PDF reader is.

Exercises

Review Questions

1. Is it possible to create a one-page report for a 1,000-task schedule that reflects the performance of the project? Would you recommend doing this?

2. We discussed 15 ways to hide a buffer in your schedule. Mention six ways.

3. What are the three communication features in MS Project? What are their main differences?

4. What other objects does a view object refer to and apply? What other settings are stored inside the view object?

5. How can you transfer an object to another project file?

6. Can you print the following? Would you do this through a report or through a view?

Can you print?		Yes/No	Report/View
a.	Gantt Chart		
b.	Project calendar		
c.	Resource calendar		
d.	Project statistics (as shown in the **Project, Project Information,** Statistics... dialog)		
e.	Cash outflow report		
f.	Notes		

Relocation Project — Reporting an Executive Overview

1. Open the file *10 Reporting 1.MPP* that is available for download at www.jrosspub.com. We will create a custom view that provides executives with a high-level overview of the project.

2. Create a new task table named *Executive Overview*. Use the columns **ID, Name, Duration** and **Cost**.

3. Create a new filter *Executive Overview* to display milestones and their summary tasks.

4. Create a new view *Executive Overview* that is shown in the menu. Make sure that when you apply the view *Executive Overview*, the corresponding table and filter are both applied.

5. Hide the question marks in the duration column by choosing **Tools, Options,** tab **Schedule** and unchecking the option ☐ **Show that tasks have estimated duration**.

6. Apply the following **Format, Timescale** settings:

	Middle Tier	Bottom Tier
Units	Months	Days
Label	Jan '00	1,2,...
Count	1	7
Align	Center	Center
Size	100 %	100 %

7. Format the **Header, Footer** and **Legend** of the Gantt Chart as follows:

Page Tab	Section	Set to	Font
Header	Center	&[View] &[Project Title]	Arial, Bold, 20
Footer	Left	&[Manager] &[Company]	Arial, Regular, 8
	Right	&[Date]	Arial, Regular, 8
Legend	Legend on	◉ None	

8. Compare your file with the view *Executive Overview* in the solution file *10 Reporting 2.MPP* that is available for download at www.jrosspub.com.

Relocation Project — Reporting Cost by Function

1. Open the file *10 Reporting 2.MPP* that is available for download at www.jrosspub.com.

2. Switch to the **Resource Sheet** view.

3. Create a new resource table *Cost by Function* that shows the fields **ID, Resource Name**, **Position**, **Function** and **Cost**.

4. Create a grouping *Cost by Function* such that you can easily read the total cost by function category of the project.

5. Create a new resource sheet view named *Cost by Function* that is shown in the menu. The view should apply the corresponding table and grouping.

6. Set the **Page Setup** settings as per the following:

Tab	Section	Set to
Page	*Orientation*	*Portrait*
	Scaling	*Fit to: 1 page wide by 1 tall*
Margins	*top,bottom,left,right*	*1 inch*
	Borders Around	*every page*
Header	*Center* *Arial, Bold, 20*	*&[View] &[Project Title]*
Footer	*Left*	*&[Manager] &[Company]*
	Center	*none; delete the default entry*
	Right	*&[Date]*

7. Compare your file with the solution file *11 Updating the Schedule 1.MPP* that is available for download at www.jrosspub.com

Chapter 11 Updating the Schedule

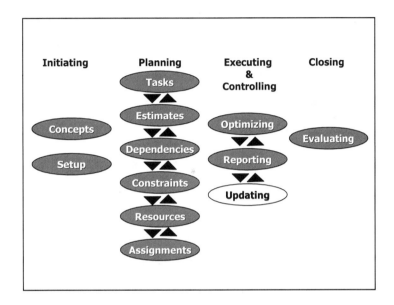

In the previous chapter on Reporting we have printed or published our optimized schedule to gain approval for it. In this chapter we will explore what you need to do after you have the go-ahead and can start the work in the project.

After this chapter you will:
- be able to set the baseline and know how to maintain it
- be able to prepare your schedule for updating
- be able to choose the appropriate way of updating your schedule:
  ◇ updating the tasks, or
  ◇ updating the assignments (time sheets)
- be able to update on the task level using actual start and finish, actual and remaining duration
- be able to update on the assignment level using paper time sheets, e-mail time sheets or web time sheets (Project Server)
- be able to handle the variety of update situations that occur in practice
- know how to communicate the status and the forecasts of the project
- be able to check if the schedule is updated properly using scheduling best practices
- be able to optimize the schedule after updating to compensate for slippages

"I am already 90% complete!"

Nob is bent over his paper schedule. "What are you doing Nob?" is Bob's question while he walks into the office.

Nob: "I am trying to figure out if I will meet the project deadline or not."

Bob: "And ... what are you finding?"

Nob: "I am not sure yet ... if Joe delivers on time I will be fine, but his percentages are going up very slowly."

Bob: "Where is he at right now?"

Nob: "Well, he tells me that he is now at 90% complete. Last week he was at 80%."

Bob: "What does 90% complete mean?"

Nob: "It means that ... he is almost done, of course!"

Bob: "Have you asked him for an estimate of how many days he still needs?"

Nob: "No, I always just ask for a % complete."

Bob: "That's why you have difficulties trying to figure out if you will meet the deadline or not. If you would ask him for the remaining duration as well, you would know! I never ask for a % complete because that number does not help me update my forecasts. Also, I find that people mean totally different things when they say it is 90% complete. Programmers often mean that they have figured out the logical puzzle at 90% complete and that they will now start programming it. When busy team members tell me it is 90% complete, they are basically telling me to get off their backs so they can do their work. Other people actually mean that they have spent 90% of the time they were supposed to spend. They may still need as much time to finish it, though. 90% complete is no information as far as I am concerned!"

Overview of Updating

Executing a project is often a more chaotic experience than anticipated in the project plan:

◆ The progress can run behind on some tasks or ahead on other tasks relative to the baseline.

◆ When a critical task slips, corrections to the schedule have to be made in order to meet the deadline.

◆ Unexpected expenses or sudden budget cuts may have to be compensated for.

◆ Tasks are completed out of sequence. Team members manage to start working on tasks they logically should not have started, at least according to your plan.

◆ People fall sick. And worse, sick people who pass deliverables on to healthy people may pass on their bugs as well…

Optimizing methods are important when you plan a project, but even more so when you execute a project.

The process steps for updating schedules can be summarized as follows:

◆ Baseline the schedule: set it once for the entire schedule and maintain its integrity.

◆ Choose the client reporting period, see page 546.

◆ Choose the update strategy, see page 548.

   ◇ Tasks update
     Updating tasks is collecting progress information on the task level. It is less effort than updating assignments, see page 551.

   ◇ Assignments update
     Updating assignments is collecting actual hours worked by day by resource. When you update assignments, you work with time sheets, see page 566.

◆ Update the schedule: enter the actual values and remaining estimates. This is discussed separately for each strategy.

◆ Check if the schedule is updated correctly, see page 599.

◆ Prepare the status and forecast report, see page 602.
   You may need to re-optimize your schedule before reporting on it.

Dynamic Scheduling with Microsoft® Project 2002

The Baseline

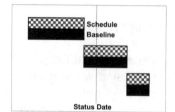

Schedule
Baseline

Status Date

The baseline is a frozen copy of the final, approved schedule. The *baseline schedule* is the target to aim for. The baseline should remain the same throughout the project as much as possible. In the illustration on the left, you can see that each task bar is split into two parts. The top part is the current schedule – the dynamic model of the project. The bottom part is the static *baseline* to compare the current schedule against. If you display the status date also as a line in the timescale, you have all you need to visually assess the status of a project.

Viewing the Baseline

1. Choose **View, Gantt Chart**.

2. Click on the menu items **View, Table <name of current table>, More Tables**.

3. Choose the table **Baseline** in the list.

4. Click [Apply]

Notice that the fields in the baseline date columns show **NA** when the baseline is not yet set for the tasks.

Setting the Baseline

1. If you want to set the baseline for certain tasks, select the tasks.

2. Choose **Tools, Tracking, Save Baseline**.

3. Select ⊙ **Save Baseline**.

4. To set the baseline for all tasks, select ⊙ **Entire Project**
    OR
    to set it for selected tasks only, select ⊙ **Selected Tasks**.

5. Click [OK]; the original schedule is copied to the **Baseline** fields for comparison.

Remarks:

◆ Note that the baseline version of the schedule contains only five fields: *baseline start* and *baseline finish* dates, *baseline duration*, *baseline work* and *baseline cost*. You can see that a baseline is not a complete version of the schedule. For example, it does not contain any information on the assignments. If what you really need is versions of the schedule, don't use baselines.

Project Server has *version control* features, like checking in and out, and one most current version: the *published* version, as well as other versions of the same schedule.

◆ You can (re)set baselines at any time. If you baseline the entire schedule for a second time, you overwrite all the values in the baseline fields: start and finish dates, duration, cost, and work. You may loose valuable (contractual) information if you do this inadvertently. There is a way to preserve baselines.

◆ Project 2002 now also has fields for ten extra baselines (Baseline1 through Baseline10), and you can copy any of these baselines back into the active **Baseline** fields. This allows you to compare against any of your ten 'steady states'. Before you copy another baseline back into the baseline fields, make sure you save your most current baseline in the next available set of baseline fields.

◆ Project 2002 now captures the date in the name of the baseline. You can see the date on which you set the baseline in **Tools, Tracking, Save baseline**.

◆ Make sure you set the baseline <u>after</u> you have substituted generic resources with real people because:

◇ You have not performed a feasibility check on your schedule from a resource availability point of view if you still have generic resources in your schedule. The schedule with only real people assigned may turn out to be not feasible. Individuals typically are less available than generic resources.

◇ The resource-related baseline fields are set back to "*0*" (zero) or "*NA*" when you use the *Resource Substitution Wizard*.

◆ Apart from the baselines, there are also ten interim plans (*Start1*/*Finish1* through *Start10*/*Finish10*), which are extra sets of only start and finish date fields. In each of these you can store a set of start and finish dates you would like to keep. You can copy a set into any other set at any time, even into the current schedule (*Start*/*Finish*). However, we don't recommend this because it affects the **Work** numbers in, perhaps, unexpected ways. Be aware that the interim plans only contain the start and finish dates, and hold no duration, work or cost data, unlike the baselines. The interim plans are useful for a quick comparison before and after a series of changes.

Maintaining the Baseline

Normally, you would set the *baseline* only once, unless:

◆ There are formal changes approved <u>after</u> the baseline has been set.
These changes could be:
  ◇ Scope changes that entail addition or removal of deliverables
  ◇ Substantial additions or deletions of tasks
  ◇ Substantial additions or losses of resources
  ◇ Substantial changes in resource rates or fixed cost

◆ When other changes are approved or imposed that force you to re-think and re-baseline your schedule, like budget increases, changes of deadline, or availability of crucial resources.

◆ When errors in the schedule turn up unexpectedly, you would need to get formal approval to re-baseline the affected tasks.

◆ There are exceptional circumstances, such as a fire, strike or a sudden economic recession. If they affect your original plan, you should submit a change request to re-baseline.

◆ There are 'acts of God' that affect your project: flood, tornado, hurricane, or earth-quake. Even if these happen elsewhere, shipments may be affected.

 In all of these cases, a change request should be submitted to the decision-makers to request approval to maintain the baseline. If you acquire approval you should only re-baseline those tasks that are affected. These are, of course, the tasks that are new and inserted but also their dependent tasks downstream (*successors*). Don't forget these last ones!

It is <u>not</u> a good idea to reset the baseline often, because comparing to a moving baseline becomes less and less meaningful. Imagine a target-seeking missile trying to catch up with a constantly moving target. Treat the baseline as a contractual agreement, even if it wasn't formalized with signatures. Insist that changes are brought forward through formal change requests. Incorporate the changes only after they were formally approved.

 Project 2002 now allows you to set up to 10 extra baselines. This makes it possible to save the different versions of the baseline when you are maintaining it. We recommend you first save the current baseline into the next available set of baseline fields for future reference. If you plan on using Earned Value this may be of particular importance. The Earned Value calculations can be based on any of these 11 baselines by choosing **Tools, Options**, tab **Calculations** and click | Earned Value... | to select the baseline from the list **Baseline for Earned Value calculations**.

Here are the steps to change the baseline:

1. To save the current baseline first, choose **Tools, Tracking, Save Baseline**; the **Save Baseline** dialog appears.

2. Select ⦿ **Save interim plan** and select under **Copy** the current **Baseline** and under **Into** the next available set of baseline fields. The first time you revise your baseline this would be **Baseline1**. In that case, the dialog should now look like:

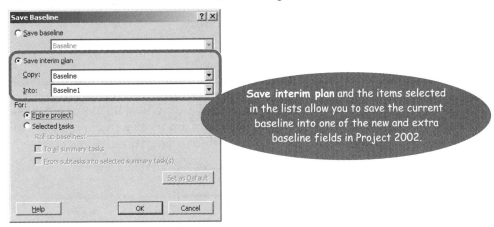

3. Click [OK]; the date on which you copied the baseline is captured in the name of the baseline in the list. This will allow you to manage multiple baselines.

4. Now we can proceed to revise the current baseline. Select the tasks affected by the change request in the Gantt spreadsheet. These can be:

    ◇ Newly inserted deliverables or tasks and any others that are dependent on the new ones that may have shifted

    ◇ Tasks affected by canceled deliverables or tasks

5. Choose **Tools, Tracking, Save Baseline**; the **Save Baseline** dialog appears again.

6. Select the option **For:** ⦿ **Selected tasks**.

7. Under **Roll up baselines**, select:
    ☑ **To all summary tasks** to update baseline information on all the higher-level summary tasks of the detail tasks selected.
    ☑ **From subtasks into selected summary tasks** to update only the summary tasks that you selected. If you had not selected the specific summary tasks in step 1, and want to use this option, cancel the dialog, include those summary tasks in your selection as well and start at step 5 again.

8. Click [OK].

If there is no formal change request, you have to be careful with deleting tasks that you don't need any longer, particularly when you do *Earned Value* performance reporting. If you simply delete these tasks, you compromise the integrity of the baseline because it decreases the *baseline work* and *baseline cost* the next time you set a baseline. Instead of deleting the task, add 'CANCELED' in capital letters to the task name and remove the assigned resources since they will not do this task any longer. You don't want to keep false workloads in your schedule. You can mark the task as 100% complete, otherwise it would create an eternal cost variance in your Earned Value report. You could consider submitting a change request to get rid of them entirely.

The Client Reporting Period

As we discussed on page 125, ten reporting periods is the minimum to give your client enough possibilities for corrective action. What does this mean for our projects? The table below shows what it means for projects of different durations.

Project Duration	Reporting Period
1 month	every other day
3 months	weekly
1 year	monthly
2 years	bi-monthly
5 years	bi-annually

You don't want too many reporting periods because each progress report takes time and effort to prepare. Each report therefore adds to the overhead cost of managing the project. With too many reporting periods, it becomes too heavy a burden for the project budget. You don't want too few reporting periods either because your project may be spinning out of control ... without the client knowing it. Clients will often prescribe the reporting period to you.

The reporting period you use for your team members to report status back to you as the project manager, should be at least as frequent as the client reporting period. In practice, team members often report much more frequently than that you report to the client as the project manager.

Showing Progress

Graphically

The progress can best be seen in the **Tracking Gantt** view. This view shows the task bars as in the illustration. The scheduled task will slowly but surely fill in with solid dark blue (*Actual*) to indicate how much progress has been made (*Actual Duration*). Notice that the actual duration represents the number of days you have worked on the task so far, even though many people only think of it as the number of days the task took once it has been completed. Ideally, the actual duration runs up to the *status date*, indicating that the task is progressing as scheduled. In the illustration

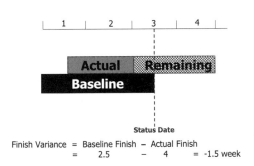

you can see that the progress has fallen behind (sickness, under-estimation, other tasks took priority). The rest of the bar in light blue (*Remaining*) represents the *Remaining Duration*. The remaining duration is how many days the task will still take from the status date on. The following formula works behind the screens as you can easily see from the illustration: *Actual Duration + Remaining Duration = Duration*
You can see that the duration is often recalculated (revised) when you update the schedule, which causes deviations from the baseline duration.

The black *Baseline* allows us to analyze slippages. In the illustration, you can see that:
◆ The task started 0.5 week later (Actual Start) than scheduled (Baseline Start).
◆ The task duration was already revised from 2.5 (Baseline Duration) to 3.5 weeks (current Duration); this is a 1-week difference.
Therefore, the total variance is 1.5 weeks (see field *Finish Variance* in MS Project). The progress is still behind; the task is also progressing 0.5 week slower, because the Actual Duration (progress) is 0.5 week behind the status date. It is likely the slippage will increase further since the remaining duration needs to be revised.

Mathematically

You can express progress in terms of the duration progress at the task level. As long as you keep revising the **Remaining Duration** with your latest estimates, the duration will be recalculated, and Project 2002 will calculate the **% Complete**. The formula is shown to the left. The *% Complete* is a calculated indicator of progress on tasks. If you want, you can even have Project 2002 calculate time sheet information based on *Actual Durations* entered. Of course, MS Project will not be as precise as when you collect time sheets yourself.

$$\% \text{ Complete} = \frac{\text{Actual Duration}}{\text{Duration}}$$

$$\% \text{ Work Complete} = \frac{\text{Actual Work}}{\text{Work}}$$

Alternatively, you can collect time sheets and enter the actual hours worked on the level of assignments from the time sheets. If you revise the **Remaining Work**, the total work will be recalculated. Just like with durations: Actual Work + Remaining Work = Work. MS Project will then calculate the **% Work Complete**, which will also be a useful progress indicator. With all of this information, Project 2002 can then calculate the Actual Duration and Remaining Duration on the task level, and update the tasks.

This shows that there are two different updating strategies you can take.

Updating Strategies

There are two different strategies to update your schedule: updating tasks or updating assignments. An assignment is always a combination of a task and a resource, as discussed on page 317. Assignments are on a more detailed level than tasks since there can be multiple resources assigned to a task.

Updating tasks means entering for each task:
◆ *Actual Start*,
◆ *Actual Duration*,
◆ *Remaining Duration*, and
◆ *Actual Finish*.

When you update assignments with time sheet information, you typically update for every assignment of a resource:

◆ *actual hours by day or by week* in the timescale field *Actual Work*
Note that there is also an assignment-related field **Actual Work** in the spreadsheet that is the total of all the timescale entries; we are not referring to that field.

◆ *remaining hours by assignment* in the field *Remaining Work* in the spreadsheet

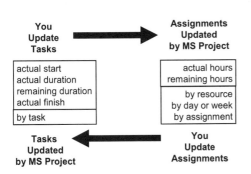

The illustration to the left summarizes the two ways of updating the schedule. If you *update tasks*, MS Project can update the assignments for you. If you update the assignments from the time sheets, MS Project can update the tasks.

The strategy of updating the tasks is quick and easy. You only have to enter actual dates and durations, and in most cases, you can do that with the mouse. MS Project can calculate and update the assignments automatically, if you want (see the option **Tools, Options**, tab **Calculation, ☑ Updating task status updates resource status**). Since you only specify the **Actual Start** date and not all the dates on which the work took place, MS Project arbitrarily spreads the actual hours in the timescale. This makes this method less precise than entering actual hours worked from time sheets when you update assignments, but in many situations it is precise enough. There are new options in **Tools, Options**, tab **Calculation** that can improve the precision of the spreading.

Updating assignments requires more numbers to process and therefore more work during the busy project execution. To illustrate this, consider the following situation. You have a schedule with 300 tasks and 10 weekly reporting periods, which means that every week you have to update an average of 30 tasks, 20 of which are typically completed in that week. If you do a task update, you would have to collect:

◆ For the 20 completed tasks, you collect actual start and actual duration, but if you are not interested in exact dates, you would only have 20 actual durations.

◆ For the 10 tasks in progress, you collect actual start, actual duration, remaining duration and actual finish. If you are not interested in exact dates, you could do with 20 pieces of information (10 actual durations, 10 remaining durations).

The grand total for updating tasks therefore is 20 + 20 = 40 pieces of data (at least).

For an assignment update, we will have to make more assumptions. We will assume that the average task duration is 4 days and the average number of resources per task is 1.5:

◆ For the 20 completed tasks: 20 tasks * 4 days * 1.5 resources = 120 pieces of data
◆ For the 10 tasks in progress: 10 tasks * 4 days * 1.5 resources = 60 pieces of data
The grand total for updating assignments is: 120 + 60 = 180 pieces of data.

As you can see, if you update assignments instead of tasks, you are processing about four times as much data during the project execution phase when you are already very busy. If you don't have an electronic time sheet system in place, we recommend you do task updates in your schedules, because paper time sheets will drown you in data. Data entry takes (too) much effort, and often project managers can't keep up, even if they only need to review the data on a weekly basis.

We have observed that too many project managers stop updating their schedules sometime during the project execution phase because they either fail to get that much information from their team members or they drown in the flood of data. If you abandon your schedule, you lose the model that provides you with up-to-date forecasts, and that allows you to do what-if scenarios to determine the best course of action. You lose your grip on the project. We recommend you consider carefully which update strategy fits your situation best.

Project 2002 with *Project Server* provides an electronic time sheet system that supports updating assignments as explained above. It will prevent double data entry and make collecting status from your team members much easier. It also makes submitting performance reports to the client much easier.

We will now discuss updating tasks in detail, and we will discuss updating assignments later on starting on page 566.

Updating Tasks

Here are the things you need to do when updating the tasks:
◆ Collect the data: actual and remaining duration by task
◆ Choose the **Tools, Options** (see page 554)
◆ Prepare the view (see page 555):
  ◇ Change the view to **Tracking Gantt**
  ◇ Apply the **Tracking** table
  ◇ Display the **Tracking** toolbar
◆ Set the **Status Date** and the **Current Date** for updating (see page 556)
◆ Set the task **Type** of the tasks you will update to **Fixed Units** (see page 557)
◆ Enter the update information (see page 559)
◆ Check whether the schedule is updated correctly (see page 599)
◆ Prepare the status and forecast report (see page 602)
  You may need to re-optimize your schedule before reporting on it.

What Data to Collect?

When we update the tasks in our project we should keep the formulas shown in the illustration in the back of our minds. They explain the values that Project 2002 calculates and displays when we enter actuals. Notice that *Actual Duration* is not only the number of days that you worked on a task after it is done. While it is still in progress, Actual Duration is also the number of days that you have worked on the task as per the status date. The *Remaining Duration* is the forecast of how many days a task will still take from the status date forward.

Actual Duration + Remaining Duration = Duration

Actual Duration / Duration = % Complete

In a tasks update, you typically enter the **Actual Duration** and allow MS Project first to calculate the **Remaining Duration** and the **% Complete** using the formulas shown in the illustration. Once resources have started working on a task they often have a much better idea how long it will take. You may find that the remaining duration calculated by MS Project may be too little or too much time left. If so, you should update the **Remaining Duration** field with a more precise estimate. MS Project will then recalculate the total **Duration** (**Actual** plus **Remaining**) and decrease or increase the **% Complete** accordingly.

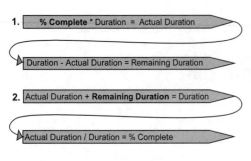

1. % Complete * Duration = Actual Duration

Duration - Actual Duration = Remaining Duration

2. Actual Duration + Remaining Duration = Duration

Actual Duration / Duration = % Complete

If you want to enter **% Complete** instead of the **Actual Duration**, it will be a longer, two-step process that follows the formulas in the illustration on the left. You can see that it is more complicated. First you enter the **% Complete** (step 1), but when you revise the **Remaining Duration** (step 2), MS Project recalculates the **% Complete** you first entered. You may not like that. Why enter a number that will change in most cases?

More importantly, you have to ask yourself what it means if a team member tells you (s)he is at *"90% complete"*. Does it mean:

◆ *I am almost finished!* (this is what it should mean, of course), or
◆ *I have spent 90% of the time I was supposed to spend on this task,* or
◆ *I have just figured out how to do this, and now I will do it*, or
◆ *I did all the easy stuff, now I will start the difficult stuff!* or
◆ *Last week it was 80% complete, so this week it must be at 90%,* or
◆ *I want you to think that I am at 90% complete!* or
◆ *Leave me alone, so I can do my work!* or
◆ *I have started to work on the task!*

I often ask groups of project managers what they have found *90% complete* means, and inevitably they indicate that *90% complete* can mean any of the above! We therefore recommend you ask for **Actual Durations** instead of **% Complete** when collecting update information; ask for facts rather than fiction. Using **% Complete** is less objective than entering the actual number of business days that people worked on a task (**Actual Duration**). The number of days somebody really worked on a task can easily be counted and is factual information. For example, if the resource worked on the task on Wednesday, Thursday and Friday the **Actual Duration** is 3 days.

If you choose to enter **% Complete** anyway instead of having it calculated by Project 2002 as we suggest, we recommend you use fairly rough percentage increments only. We suggest increments such as 0%, 25%, 50%, 75%, 100% as shown on the **Tracking** toolbar, or perhaps only 0% and 100%. In the latter case you can simply ask: *are you finished with it, or not?* This question does not leave much room for wishful thinking (or outright manipulation). However, you need to have a fairly detailed schedule in order to get good results with rough percentages. The level of detail should be near the 1% rather than the 10% in the *1%-10% rule*; see our discussion on page 121. If you create tasks that are small enough, you can get to the facts more easily.

There is an option that will influence how MS Project will spread the actual hours worked when entering **% Complete**. Choose **Tools, Options,** tab **Calculation**; the option is **Edits to total task % complete will be spread to the status date**. If you change a % complete, MS Project can calculate the actual hours and spread them out to the status date when this option is on. When it is off, the actual hours will be entered where they were scheduled or from the **Actual Start** date onward. Splits will often appear in the task bars.

Collecting the Data

In order to update your schedule with actual data you need to gather the data. You need to collect the following information for task updates from your team members. We recommend that you use the following questions:

◆ *On what date did you start on the task?* (**Actual Start**)
◆ *How many business days have been worked on the task as per the status date?* (**Actual Duration**)
◆ *How many business days do you still need to finish it from the status date?* (**Remaining Duration**) You need to ask this question only for tasks that are currently in progress.
◆ *On what date was the task finished?* (**Actual Finish**)
   This question is often not needed if you kept the remaining durations up to date in previous updates.

 Instead of collecting Actual Duration and Remaining Duration, you can also collect *Actual Work* and *Remaining Work* on the task level. If most of your tasks are based on effort (Work), this may make even more sense. This will work in a similar way as with durations, except for that you enter them into the fields **Actual Work** and **Remaining Work** of course.

There are two ways that are commonly used to collect the data for task updates:

◆ Regular status meeting
   In a short meeting of one hour at most, you quickly ask each team member for this information. You then enter it, or have it entered. Some project managers have this done immediately during the meeting to reveal new issues.
◆ To-do list turn-around reports
   You can distribute paper to-do lists to each team member that also contain empty fill-in fields for the status information. Ask the team members to enter the status information and to return it to you by the end of the week, at which time they get the next to-do list. If you report weekly, print a to-do list that covers two weeks ahead to show what is coming up, and to allow the resource to work ahead.

Choosing the Options for Updating Tasks

Choose **Tools, Options**. Here are the options we recommend for updating tasks:

Tab	Option
Calculation	☑ **Updating task status updates resource status** Updating the tasks will update the actual work of the assignments. We recommend you keep this option checked for task updates. Only uncheck it if you want to update the tasks <u>and</u> the assignments.
	☑ **Move end of completed parts after status date back to status date** This moves the actual duration bar to before the status date. Actual work done is moved into the past. We recommend you turn this on. ☑ **And move end of remaining parts before status date back to status date** The remaining duration bar will cuddle up to the status date (unless there are dependencies that keep it where it is).
	☑ **Move start of remaining parts before status date forward to status date** This moves the remaining duration bar to after the status date. Work still to be completed is moved to the future. We recommend you turn this on. ☑ **And move end of completed parts forward to status date** This moves the actual duration bar to cuddle up to the status date.
	☐ **Edits to total task % complete will be spread to the status date** If a task is falling behind, the progress entered will be evenly spread to the status date. This option is only relevant if you enter % Complete.
	☑ **Actual costs are always calculated by Microsoft Project** Updating the tasks will update the actual cost. It is up to you whether you want MS Project to do that.
	`Set as Default` Sets the options above as the default settings for any new schedules you create. The existing schedules are not affected because these options are stored in the project file as you can see in the label of the section divider **Calculation Options for <file name of the project>**.

Tab	Option
General	☐ **Automatically add new resources and tasks** Prevents a typo in a resource name from accidentally adding a new resource. Works similarly for tasks.
Edit	☐ **Allow cell drag and drop** Prevents accidentally dragging data on top of other data in your baselined schedule.
Schedule	☑ **Split in-progress tasks** Allows moving the uncompleted portion of a task to after the update date by splitting the task bar. The update date is the **Current Date** or the **Status Date** whichever is later (see **Project, Project Information**). With this option unchecked, the new options on the **Calculation** tab cannot split any task bars and will behave quite differently as a result.
	Set as Default — Sets the option above as the default setting for any new schedules you create. The existing schedules are not affected because this option is stored in the project file as you can see in the label of the section divider **Scheduling Options for <file name of the project>**.

Notice that the new options in **Tools, Options**, tab **Calculation** help to reschedule in-progress tasks but are no guarantee that your schedule will be entirely up to date. They have no effect on tasks that have not started yet but should have started since the status date is later. These tasks may have to be rescheduled to after the status date to put them back into the future where they belong.

Prepare the View for Updating

1. Choose **View, Tracking Gantt**.
   The current schedule is shown in the top half of the task bars (colored blue or red). The baseline is shown as the gray, bottom half of the task bars.

2. The tracking table has all the fields in which to enter data for task updates. To apply it, choose **View, Table <name of current table>, Tracking**. The table looks like the following snapshot and is very easy for entering actual information:

	Task Name	Act. Start	Act. Finish	% Comp.	Act. Dur.	Rem. Dur.	Act. Cost	Act. Work
1	⊟ REQUIREMENTS	NA	NA	0%	0 days	7.4 days	$0.00	0 days
2	research staff requirements	NA	NA	0%	0 days	4 days	$0.00	0 days
3	summarize requirements	NA	NA	0%	0 days	4 days	$0.00	0 days
4	⊟ LOCATION	NA	NA	0%	0 days	16.5 days	$0.00	0 days
5	select the realtor	NA	NA	0%	0 days	4 days	$0.00	0 days
6	visit the sites	NA	NA	0%	0 days	1 day	$0.00	0 days
7	evaluate the sites	NA	NA	0%	0 days	1 day	$0.00	0 days
8	meet to select the location	NA	NA	0%	0 days	1 day	$0.00	0 days
9	legal review	NA	NA	0%	0			

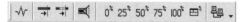

Enter actual progress into the Tracking table.

3. To display the **Tracking** toolbar: point to any toolbar and click the right mouse button. From the pop-up menu, choose **Tracking**. The tracking toolbar is displayed:

The **Tracking** toolbar has all the handy tools for updating.

Notice that all objects you need for updating the schedule have the word '*tracking*' in their name: *Tracking Gantt* view, *Tracking table* and *Tracking toolbar*. This makes it easy to remember!

Setting the Status Date for Updating

1. Change the *status date* to the date as per which you want to update tasks and compare the schedule against the baseline.

2. Choose **Project, Project Information**.

3. Change the date in the **Status Date** field to the date as per which you want to update. The status date does not yet appear as a vertical line in the timescale.

4. Set the **Current Date** to the same date as the **Status Date**. The current date does show up as a line in the timescale. The current date falls at the start of the day, and the status date falls at the end of the day. We recommend making the dates the same because some update features in Project 2002 use the later one of these two dates.

5. Choose **Format, Gridlines** and select **Status Date** in the list as the line to change. Choose a dashed line in a bright color. Click [OK]; the status line is now visible in the timescale similar to:

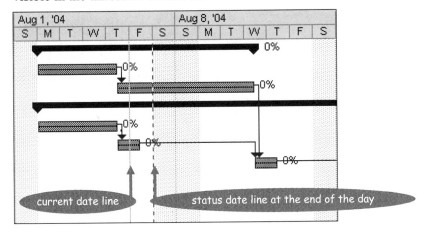

 MS Project uses the system date of your computer to continuously update the *current date*. When you open your schedule again tomorrow, you will find tomorrow's date as the current date. The *status date* stays the same since you last entered it and will refresh your memory about when your last update took place.

Set the Task Type for Tasks to Update

When you enter update information into MS Project, you will trigger recalculations in the formula D * U = W (Duration * Units of resources assigned = Work). The task **Type** has to be set in such a way that it triggers the right recalculations that are performed by MS Project unsolicited.

When we update tasks, we change the durations. Fixed duration is therefore not the right **Type** of task, because we are not controlling what MS Project recalculates. When you extend task durations, you typically want to keep the resources that work on the task the same (units), and see the total work (effort) increase. The type *Fixed Units* is appropriate for that purpose. You can also choose *Fixed Work*, if you want the number of resource units to be recalculated when the duration changes.

1. Click on any column heading in the Tracking Gantt spreadsheet to select all the tasks.
    OR
    Be more selective and select just those tasks that need to be updated.

2. Click **Task Information** 📋 on the **Standard** toolbar; the **Multiple Task Information** dialog appears. Click the **Advanced** tab; the dialog should now look like:

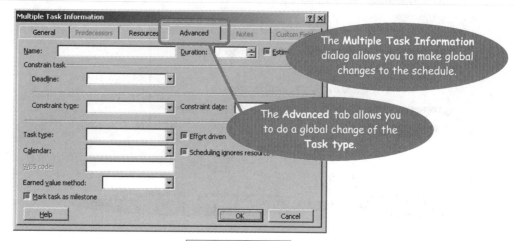

The **Multiple Task Information** dialog allows you to make global changes to the schedule.

The **Advanced** tab allows you to do a global change of the **Task type.**

3. Select from the list **Task type** [_____] ▾ the item **Fixed Units**. Changing the task type does not trigger a recalculation, only a change in a variable in the formula: *Duration x Units = Work* will do that.

4. Uncheck ☐ **Effort driven** and click [OK].

Occasionally, we have observed a slight change in the schedule when switching between task types:

◆ MS Project schedules **Fixed Duration** tasks differently. Fixed Duration tasks sometimes ignore resource calendars, which may cause a date shift when you change a Fixed Duration task to Fixed Units, or vice versa.

◆ If you have elapsed durations in your schedule, you should not switch their task type to **Fixed Units** since this changes their duration to a business day duration, which extends the task duration threefold. Exclude tasks with an elapsed duration. You can stay away from elapsed durations if you schedule a task with an elapsed duration as a lag on a dependency instead. For example, instead of inserting *drying of paint* as a task, you can add a lag on the dependency from the task *paint* to its successor.

If you want to be sure the schedule did not shift when you changed the task type, first save the dates in the **Start1** and **Finish1** fields using **Tools, Tracking, Save Baseline, ⊙ Save interim plan**. Then change the **Task type**. Now you can filter on differences between **Finish** and **Finish1** to check for unwanted shifts.

Task Updating Situations in Practice

The following six situations are all you will ever come across when updating tasks:
◆ Tasks that Ran as Scheduled
◆ Tasks that Run as Scheduled
◆ Tasks that Run Behind
◆ Tasks that Will Take Longer (or Shorter)
◆ Tasks that Started Late (or Early)
◆ Tasks that Finished Late (or Early)

You will encounter all of these situations. They each have their own best way for entering update information. We will detail how-to steps for each situation.

Tasks that Ran as Scheduled

You simply need to mark these tasks as 100% complete as shown in the illustration below.

1. In the Tracking Gantt view, select the tasks that were completed as scheduled by dragging or holding down [Control] and clicking on the tasks.

2. Click **100% Complete** on the **Tracking** toolbar
OR
Enter 100% in the **% Complete** field of the tracking table.
OR
Click **Update Tasks** on the **Tracking** toolbar and enter 100% under **% Complete**.

Tasks that Run as Scheduled

In this case you want to show actual progress up to the status date as in the illustration.

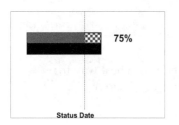

1. Select the tasks that are on schedule by dragging or by holding down ⌜Control⌟ and clicking on them.

2. Click **Update as Scheduled** 🔽 on the **Tracking** toolbar; this updates all selected tasks as if they are exactly on schedule. This tool is not very precise, but precise enough. If you get weird results, you probably have not made the *current date* the same as the *status date* in the **Project, Project Information** dialog before updating.

Tasks that Run Behind

This situation will require more updating effort. You will need to capture the actual

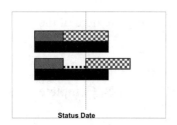

progress, but because the task is behind, you will also have to bring the incomplete portion of the task bar forward to after the *status date*. Lastly, you will have to review the forecast of the remaining duration. If the task was underestimated, you may have to increase the remaining duration.

In the illustration, you can see that the progress is falling behind because the solid color of the actual progress does not run up to the status date in the task bar at the top. The bottom task bar has a split showing the incomplete portion of work rescheduled after the status date.

1. Enter the **Actual Duration** of the task (the number of days you have worked on the task) and revise the **Remaining Duration** (the number of days still to go). MS Project will calculate the **% Complete**.

2. If there is remaining duration scheduled in the past, reschedule it to after the status date, to the future. You can do this by dragging the light blue part of the task bar. OR

Select the task and click **Reschedule Work** on the **Tracking** toolbar. This will split the task bar if the option ☑ **Split in-progress tasks** is in effect in **Tools, Options, Schedule**. Notice that this tool uses the later of the *current date* and *status date*. That is why we suggested making the current date equal to the status date.

OR

You don't need to do a thing if in **Tools, Options**, tab **Calculations**, you checked ☑ **Move start of remaining parts before status date forward to status date.**

This way of depicting lack of progress by splitting is best if there was an interruption in the work, such as a power outage, or if resources were temporarily taken off the task to do some troubleshooting elsewhere.

You still have to ask yourself if the forecasted finish date is accurate. If you look at the rate of progress in the illustration, you will notice that the rate is more or less half of what it should be (half of the work that should have been finished by the status date is accomplished). If the interruptions will continue, the eventual duration will be double the baseline duration. You can see that currently the forecasted duration is less than double the baseline duration; and the remaining duration should be increased even more (if you expect the interruptions to continue).

You have to move the remaining duration out to the future, because unfortunately you can't schedule work-to-be-done in the past. (If only we could…) Only if you move it out and revise it, will the dependent successors be rescheduled. If you forget this, you end up with a *status report* instead of a *forecast report*. A status report is like a report on yesterday's weather instead of a forecast on tomorrow's weather. As you can see, running behind goes hand in hand with taking longer.

Tasks that Will Take Longer or Shorter

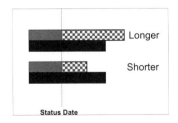

In this situation, good progress was made, but the realization sinks in that the remaining duration will not suffice. We need to increase the remaining estimate. Or, we may need to shorten it. (Hey, it has been known to happen!)

Make sure you have the **Type** of the task set such that the recalculation you trigger reflects reality. You should not leave it set to **Fixed Duration**, since we are stretching the duration. It will be hard to predict what MS Project will recalculate. If you choose **Fixed Units**, the work will increase, which is appropriate if the original estimate was too low and it turns out to take more effort. If you choose **Fixed Work**, the units on the task will decrease. You may then correct the slippage by adding people back.

1. Set the **Type** of task to *Fixed Units* tasks or *Fixed Work*. Change *Fixed Duration* tasks first to either Fixed Units or Fixed Work. If you choose Fixed Units, the work will be recalculated. If you choose Fixed Work, the units assigned will be recalculated over the remaining duration, which you can see if you reveal the field **% Allocation** in the timescale of the Task Usage view.

2. Enter the **Actual Duration** of the task.

3. Revise the **Remaining Duration**.
    OR
    Change the remaining duration with the mouse by pointing to the right side of its task bar. When you see a single-headed arrow mouse pointer ⊩ , drag to change the remaining duration to compensate for the slippage. If you cannot get it on the date you want, click **Zoom In** ⊕ on the **Standard** toolbar first.

4. You may have to use the methods to shorten your schedule as discussed in chapter 9 to compensate for the slipped finish date (see page 386).

Tasks that Started Late or Early

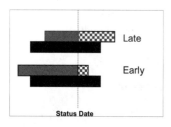

Status Date

In this situation the task did not start on the day that was planned. The illustration reveals that the top task started late, whereas the bottom task started early. If you updated your schedule regularly and if you had a dynamic schedule (with all dependencies) the start date may have moved already to the right date. If that is not the case, you have to enter it. In the illustration, you can see that in the *Late* situation, the actual start date (left side of top bar) is later than the baseline start date (the left side of the black bottom bar).

1. Point to the middle of the blue task bar, and when you see a four-headed arrow mouse pointer ⊕ , drag the task bar to its new start date. If you cannot get it on the date you want, click **Zoom In** ⊕ on the **Standard** toolbar first.
    OR
    Enter the date in the field **Act. Start** of the tracking table.
    OR

Select the task with a delayed start, click **Update Tasks** on the **Tracking** toolbar, then fill in the **Actual Start** date and click OK .

2. You may have to use the methods to shorten your schedule as discussed in chapter 9 to compensate for the slipped finish date (see page 386).

Tasks that Finished Late or Early

Late

Early

Status Date

In this situation, you need to enter the finish dates. In the illustration on the left you can see that the top task finished late, and the bottom task finished early. If you updated your schedule regularly, however, you often don't need to enter finish dates. When you revise the remaining duration, MS Project already changes the finish date to the right date, or close to it. If it still isn't the right date, you can enter that date into the project file.

The steps are:

1. Point to the right side of its blue task bar, and when you see a single-headed arrow mouse pointer ↦ , drag the finish to its new date. Set the task to 100% complete.
    OR
    Enter the date in **Act. Finish** of the tracking table.
    OR
    Select the task with a slipped finish date, and click **Update Tasks** on the **Tracking** toolbar and fill in the **Actual Finish** date and click OK .

2. You may have to use the methods to shorten your schedule as discussed in chapter 9 to compensate for the slipped finish date (see page 386).

"My Reality is More Complex..."

There are certain situations that seem more difficult to update than discussed above:

♦ Combination of situations
  For example, what to do with a task that started late, runs behind and will take longer?

♦ Updating out of sequence
  What if work has been done on a task that could not have started yet based on your dependencies?

♦ New activities on the fly
  What if you realize while working on a task that it actually consists of more tasks, or what if you decide to re-assign resources?

We will discuss each situation in more detail.

Combination of Situations

Your situation can be more complicated. No matter what, it is always a combination of the six situations we discussed before. For example, the start date is different from the baseline start and the progress is behind. Let's say, the situation on a two-day task on May 2nd 2000 at 5PM is:

♦ the Actual Start date is May 2nd with a Baseline Start of May 1st

♦ the Remaining Duration is revised from 1 day to 2 days

 In a situation like this, we recommend you start with updating the **Actual Start**, then the **Actual Duration** and the **Remaining Duration** last. Graphically speaking, you enter data going from left to right over the task bar. If you keep this in mind, you will never see unexpected results in MS Project.

The resource worked only May 2nd on the task; the Actual Duration is one day. The *% Complete* will be calculated at *50%*. Before entering the Remaining Duration, the schedule will look like:

Task Name	% Complete	Duration	Remaining Duration	Start	Apr 30, 00					
					Apr 30	May 1	May 2	May 3	May 4	May 5
write report	50%	2 days	1 day	May 2					50%	

When you enter the Remaining Duration, you trigger a recalculation of the *% Complete* and it will be *33%*; you have completed one day of what will now be a three-day task instead of a two-day task. See the schedule below:

Task Name	% Complete	Duration	Remaining Duration	Start	Apr 30, 00					
					Apr 30	May 1	May 2	May 3	May 4	May 5
write report	33%	3 days	2 days	May 2						33%

Updating Out of Sequence

Occasionally, you may need to show progress on a task that is scheduled for the future. The predecessors of the task may hold it there. If work has started on a task you need to show progress on it, regardless of the logic of the dependencies. This is known as *out-of-sequence updating*. Normally, a task can only start when its predecessors are finished.

Out-of-sequence progress often occurs in practice. For example, authors are waiting until they receive the research results before they can start writing the research report. The research takes longer and the authors decide to start already on developing the outline of the report, and on creating the format styles and layout of the document. They don't need to have the research report for this.

Updating out of sequence is simple, because actuals are stronger than any other scheduling feature in MS Project. Entering actuals overrides the logic of the dependencies, so you can go ahead and update in the same way. The option **Split in-progress tasks** (in **Tools, Options, Schedule**) will affect the result in out-of-sequence situations:

- If selected, the remaining duration is scheduled to start on the current date
- If not selected, the remaining duration may be scheduled before the current date

Notice how this option also uses the later date of the *current date* and the *status date*.

You still need to check the final result, because in some cases you want the successors of the task you updated out of sequence to keep their original dates (retain dates), and in other cases you want the successors to be rescheduled to earlier (retain logic).

New Activities on the Fly

When you are executing the project, you often realize you omitted some tasks. You may have forgotten certain activities or efforts that involve discrete effort. Or, you may find better approaches to create the deliverables. It is generally better to add new activities to show changes rather than attempting to modify existing activities. This is particularly the case if you have already reported any progress on the activities. For example, if progress is lagging, you could decide to re-assign a portion of a task to somebody else. In that case you can make this clearer if you leave the baselined activities as they are and add a new activity. The new activities end up without a baseline and are as such clearly marked as new activities that are inserted on the fly to capture how the project really unfolded. In the case of contract disputes, you need to communicate clearly what the plan was and what happened in reality. Some experts go as far as capturing all impacts with new line items.[75] This technique is particularly useful for litigation when a contract dispute erupts, but it also allows you to learn better from the projects you ran. These new line items should only be in the present or past, and not far out in the future.

Updating Assignments

An MS Project file is not accessible by multiple users at the same time. Some people want multi-user access in order to have their resources update the project file. The time sheet features in MS Project allow updating by all team members without giving access to your project file. Allowing all team members into your project file is pretty scary anyway considering how much training it requires to work with a project file without making errors.

Here are the things you need to do when updating the assignments using *time sheets*. Time sheets are sometimes called *project turn-around reports*. The steps are:
♦ Choose the options in **Tools, Options** (see page 569).
♦ Prepare the view (see page 570):
   ◇ Change the view to **Resource Usage** and customize it.
   ◇ Apply the table **Work** and customize it.
♦ Set the **Status Date** for this update.
♦ Set the task **Type** for all tasks to be updated to **Fixed Units** (see page 573).
♦ Collect the data using paper or electronic time sheets. For electronic time sheets you can use e-mail or the web (*Project Server*) (see page 578).
♦ Transfer the time sheet information into the schedule.
   The effort that you have to expend ranges from manually entering the data into MS Project (paper time sheets) to clicking a button (electronic time sheets).
♦ Check whether the schedule is updated correctly (see page 599).
♦ Prepare the status and forecast report (see page 602).
   You may need to re-optimize your schedule before reporting on it.

Time Sheet Vehicles

All the collection of data and the entry of data can be made easier if your team members have access to e-mail or to the intranet. If that is the case, you can use e-mail or Project Server to collect the actual hours worked electronically. Then you can transfer

---

[75] As suggested by Frank Walker, TWG Project Management, LLC.

the numbers automatically from the electronic time sheets into your project schedule. You can collect the data for an update of assignments in the following ways:

◆ Paper time sheets, see page 575
Distribute paper fill-in forms to all team members. For example, you can make weekly time sheets using the Resource Usage view. You will have to enter all the hours from the time sheet into your Project 2002 schedule by hand. Some people do this in fact…

◆ Electronic time sheets by Web using *Project Server*, see page 578
This establishes communication between Project 2002 and the Project Server database. The time sheets will be posted on an intranet site using Project Server. Team members can log in and enter the hours worked and revise the remaining hours.

◆ Electronic time sheets by e-mail, see page 588
This uses the e-mail system to carry custom project messages. This configuration requires less hardware and software.

◆ Any combination of the above
You can even send time sheets by Web to some people and by e-mail to other people in your project. This is useful in situations in which you work with internal employees as well as external contractors, vendors, suppliers, or client resources that do not have access to your intranet.

◆ Using third-party time sheet applications that are highly integrated with Project Server, like PSA Solution (Tenrox)[76] or TimeControl (HMS Software)[77]. One of the advantages of these third-party systems is that these systems can meet, right out of the box, other business objectives as well, such as:
◇ time and attendance tracking for the human resources department, or
◇ time and billing systems for professional services departments.

What Data to Collect?

Now that we have discussed the vehicles for collecting time sheets, we will discuss your choices on what data you can collect. The data you can collect depends on the vehicle with which you collect it. You can collect the following data from your team members:

[76] See www.tenrox.com.

[77] See www.hmssoftware.ca and in particular read the white paper *"TimeControl and MS Project 2002"*.

- **Percentage of work complete**
  (using paper and Project Server time sheets)
  Resources report the percentage of work complete between 0 and 100%. The
  % Work Complete is a weak metric to collect from team members as we argued on
  page 551. We therefore don't recommend using this first option.
- **Total actual work done and remaining work by task**
  (using paper and Project Server time sheets)
  Resources report the running total of actual work done and the work remaining to be
  done on each assignment. This option has the advantage that it requires the least
  amount of data entry, just two numbers for each assignment at every status cycle.
  The disadvantage is that these numbers are running totals that the team members
  have to calculate from memory. For example, the field may display 17 hours up to
  last week, and if the person worked for 15 hours this week, he has to enter
  17 + 15 = 32 hours. People could easily make mistakes doing this. Also, when the
  data is transferred into the schedule, MS Project has to figure out on which dates
  these hours were actually worked since you did not ask the team members when the
  15 hours were worked. Even though there are some new options in MS Project that
  allow you to control this better (**Tools, Options**, tab **Calculation**), we still find the
  third and last method preferable.
- **Hours of work done per day or per week** and **remaining work**
  (using paper, e-mail and Project Server time sheets)
  Resources report the hours worked on each assignment for each day in a weekly
  time sheet, or for each week in a monthly time sheet. This is the common and classic
  time sheet where resources enter their actual hours worked by day. The total **Actual
  Work** by assignment is calculated and the **Remaining Work** decreased accordingly.
  The resource then reviews the calculated **Remaining Work** number for the
  assignment and adjusts it if necessary. We recommend you collect these numbers;
  they are most precise, and less prone to errors. These time sheets are known as the
  traditional or 'real' time sheets.

Even though we recommend you collect the third type of data, we would like to add that
the other two types of data (or updating tasks instead) are still preferred over not
updating your schedules at all. The remainder of this chapter focuses on the
recommended third option in the list above.

 Project Server has to be configured for the type of data you chose to collect from your
team members. You need to discuss this with the Project Server administrator; otherwise
the actual work fields are grayed out and not editable in the timescale.

Choosing the Options for an Assignments Update

Choose **Tools, Options** to set the following options:

Page tab	Set to:
Calculation	☑ **Updating task Status updates Resource Status** We recommend you keep this option on so MS Project calculates the **% Complete** on the task level. If you turn it off you will not see % Complete on tasks. However, if you enter a % Complete for a task yourself, Project 2002 will calculate and override the time sheet data you entered. If you choose to do an assignments update, you should never enter *% Complete* on tasks in the Tracking Gantt chart. OR uncheck ☐ **Updating task Status updates Resource Status** if you want to update both tasks and assignments simultaneously. Doing both types of updates is a lot of work.
	☐ **Move end of completed parts after status date back to status date** This option has no effect when you work with time sheets with actual hours entered by day or week. ☐ **And move end of remaining parts before status date back to status date** This option has no effect when you work with time sheets with actual hours entered by day or week.
	☐ **Move start of remaining parts before status date forward to status date** This option has no effect when you work with time sheets with actual hours entered by day or week. ☐ **And move end of completed parts forward to status date** This option has no effect when you work with time sheets with actual hours entered by day or week.
	☑ **Actual Costs are always calculated by Microsoft Project** MS Project will calculate the actual costs based upon actual hours worked if you keep it on. If you want to enter actual cost numbers yourself you should turn it off.
Edit	☐ **Allow cell drag and drop** Prevents accidentally dragging data on top of other data in your baselined schedule. We recommend turning it off at this point.

Page tab	Set to:
General	☐ **Automatically add new resources and tasks** This prevents accidentally adding resources during updating and re-optimising.
Schedule	☑ **Split in-progress tasks** Allows you to split the task bar and move the remaining duration to after the status date.
	☐ **Autolink inserted or moved tasks** Disabling **Autolink** will prevent accidental changes to the network logic in the baselined schedule.

Notice that the new options in **Tools, Options**, tab **Calculation** have no effect when you work with time sheets on which team members fill in their actual hours worked by date as noted in the table. These options only make a difference:

◆ when you enter **Actual Durations,** like we did when updating tasks, see page 551,

◆ when you enter the total **Actual Work** on tasks or assignments in the spreadsheet (as opposed to the timescale), the second option in the list discussed on page 567. Since you don't indicate on which dates the work took place, these new options control on which dates MS Project will put the actual hours worked. The result is that the time-phased numbers are fairly rough.

Prepare the View

We will first explain in which view you can see the time sheet information. This is useful for:

◆ Entering the data by hand when you use paper time sheets.

◆ Checking the electronic time sheet information once it is transferred back into MS Project. You may need to make corrections to the time sheet information that is automatically transferred into your project file. Particularly when you did not review the data before transferring when you use automatic *rules* in *Microsoft Project Web Access*.

In case you receive updates from each resource individually, you should probably use the **Resource Usage** view. Unfortunately, the view cannot display the status date line. Instead, click on the timescale on that date; it stays selected and can act as a status date.

1. Choose **View, Resource Usage**.

2. Create a new table by choosing **View, Table: <name of current table>, More Tables**; the **More Tables** dialog appears:

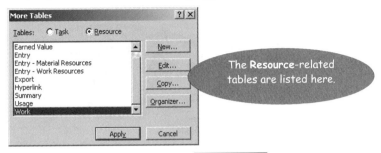

The **Resource**-related tables are listed here.

3. Select the table **Work** and click Copy... ; the **Table Definition** dialog appears:

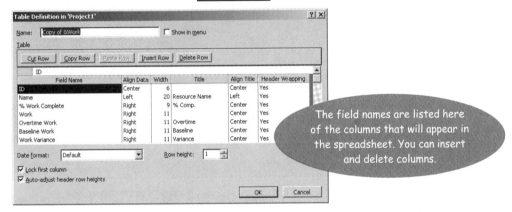

The field names are listed here of the columns that will appear in the spreadsheet. You can insert and delete columns.

4. Give the table a name, for example *Update Assignments*. After the field **Name**, insert the fields **Baseline Work, Work, Actual Work, Remaining Work** and **% Work Complete**. Abbreviate their column titles under **Title** to, for example, *Bas.Work, Work, Act.Work, Rem.Work* and *%Work Comp.* respectively to save space. Click OK and Apply.

5. Change the time to a one-character time unit label in **Tools, Options,** tab **Edit,** under **View options for time units** to save space. Click OK.

6. In the timescale, only the field **Work** is shown. Right-click anywhere in the yellow area below the timescale and select **Detail Styles...** from the pop-up menu; the **Detail Styles** dialog appears:

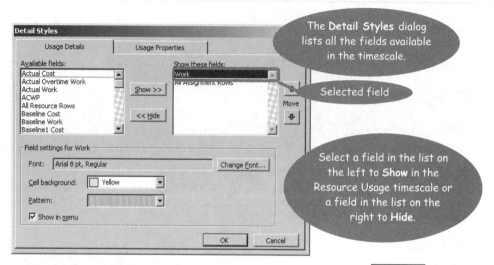

The **Detail Styles** dialog lists all the fields available in the timescale.

Selected field

Select a field in the list on the left to **Show** in the Resource Usage timescale or a field in the list on the right to **Hide**.

7. In the list **Available Fields** select **Baseline Work** and click on Show >> . Do the same for the field **Actual Work**. Rearrange the fields such that the **Baseline Work** field is at the top. Click OK .

The view should now look like:

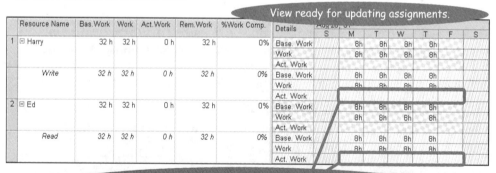

View ready for updating assignments.

Time sheet information can be entered or changed in the **Act. Work** fields of the assignments (italic) in the timescale.

Set the Task Type for All Tasks

The task **Type** has to be set in such a way that it triggers the right recalculations. When working with time sheets, we will be entering **Actual Work** values that cause the **Work** value to be recalculated as shown in the illustration. Fixed work is therefore not the right type of task because it does not control what MS Project recalculates; will it recalculate the units or the duration? When updating assignments, you typically want to see the effect on the **Duration** of the task (forecast), while keeping the **Units** of resources the same. If the task can slip, you now know by how much. If the task cannot slip, you can then still consider adding resources to it (change the units). Again, **Fixed Units** seems the most appropriate type of task for updating assignments as it was for updating tasks.

Work changes often during updates!

D * U = W

1. Switch to the Tracking Gantt view by choosing **View, Tracking Gantt**.

2. Click on a column heading in the Gantt spreadsheet to select all the tasks.

3. Click the **Task Information** tool; the **Multiple Task Information** dialog appears:

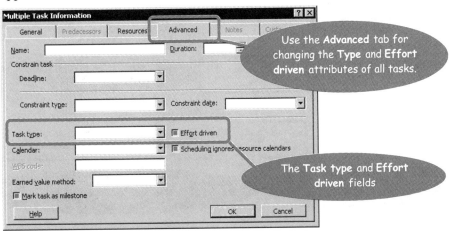

4. Click the **Advanced** tab and select from the list **Task type** the item **Fixed Units**.

5. Uncheck ☐ **Effort driven** and click [OK].

The Formulas Behind the Screens

The illustration shows the formulas that MS Project will use when updating the assignments in your project. You should keep these formulas in the back of your mind because they explain the values that MS Project calculates and displays.

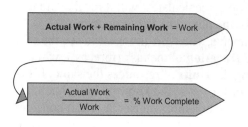

The formulas define the relationships between the four variables: *Actual Work*, *Remaining Work*, *Work* and *% Work Complete*. If you enter only two out of the four, MS Project will calculate the rest using the formulas. You should always fill in two fields and let MS Project calculate the other two values. Notice that **Work** is the total work on the assignment as shown in the spreadsheet of the Resource Usage view. In the timescale the time-phased spread of the total work is displayed.

In the following screen we show the difference between a resource and an assignment, as well as the cells where you enter the data from the time sheets:

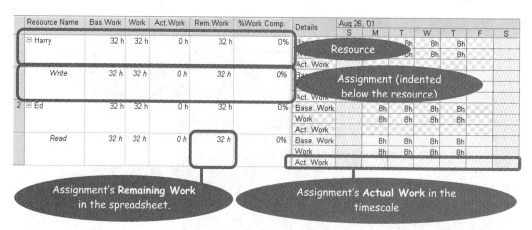

We recommend you enter time sheet data into the assignment's **Actual Work** in the timescale on a day-by-day basis and **Remaining Work** *(Rem.Work)* in the spreadsheet at the end of every week. The electronic time sheets will transfer numbers into these same fields. The **Act.Work** field in the spreadsheet will display the sum of the time-phased **Act.Work** numbers you entered.

 Notice that all fields mentioned here are assignment-related fields, not resource-related fields! You can recognize assignment rows by their lack of a row number, their indentation under a resource name, their italic font in the spreadsheet, and a lighter yellow color in the timescale.

Collecting the Data Using Paper Time Sheets

When you work with paper time sheets, you will do a lot of running around to distribute the time sheets and to chase the team members to return them in a timely manner to you. Of course, regular status meetings will make your life easier. When you receive the time sheets back you have to enter the hours worked by hand. Some administrative support may be necessary.

Assignments Update Situations

The following situations can occur when you update assignments. You will notice that these situations are similar to the task update situations:
◆ Assignments that Ran as Scheduled
◆ Assignments that Run as Scheduled
◆ Assignments that Run Behind
◆ Assignments that Will Take Longer (or Shorter)
◆ Assignments that Started Late (or Early)
◆ Assignments that Finished Late (or Early)

We will discuss all these situations, but in less detail than we did for the task update since not many people will use paper time sheets. However, you still need to know how to make corrections to the time sheet numbers in MS Project, if needed. We will use the Resource Usage view (or Task Usage).

 The tools **Update as Scheduled** and **Reschedule Work** are not available in the Resource Usage view. After we have entered the data we will still have to apply checks in the Tracking Gantt if the schedule was updated properly, and we will use the **Reschedule Work** tool there.

Assignments that Ran as Scheduled

1. Select the assignment that is completed as scheduled.

2. Enter the actual hours worked in the timescale in the field **Actual Work** or take a shortcut by entering *100%* in the **% Work Complete** field for the assignment since it ran as scheduled.

 Notice that you can't click the [100*] tool on the **Tracking** toolbar. This tool is for task updates; it would set the task and all its assignments to 100% complete instead of just one assignment.

Assignments that Run as Scheduled

1. Select the assignment that is on schedule.

2. Enter the actual hours worked in the timescale in the field **Actual Work**. Make sure the hours are entered up to the status date.
OR
In the timescale of the view, select all the days in the row **Work** up to the status date. Point to the drag-handle, and drag when you see the cross-hair mouse pointer + to copy them down into the field **Act. Work**.

the drag-handle

Assignments that Run Behind

1. Enter the actual hours worked in the timescale in the field **Actual Work**. In this situation there are typically fewer hours worked than the **Baseline Work** field displays in the timescale.

2. The remainder of the hours may have to be rescheduled to start on the status date. You can do this by selecting in the timescale the days on which no work took place in the **Work** row and press [Ins]. The hours will move over to after the status date.
OR
In the timescale, select by dragging in the row **Work** the hours that need to be rescheduled. Then point to the border of the selection (not the drag-handle) and when you see the mouse pointer ⬦ drag them to future days:

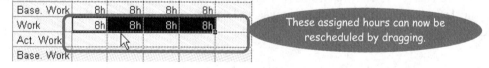
These assigned hours can now be rescheduled by dragging.

Assignments that Will Take Longer

Enter hours on the extra days you plan to do the work in the row **Work** of the timescale on dates after the status date.
OR
Fill in the first number after the status date and use the drag-handle again to enter an even series of hours quickly. Point to the drag-handle and when you see the cross-hair mouse pointer +, you can start dragging to copy the numbers.
OR
You can enter the first value, select the cells to fill into and choose the **Edit, Fill, Right** to copy the value to the extra days.
OR
You can fill in the **Remaining Work** for the assignment in the spreadsheet and MS Project will schedule this work in the timescale on extra days. They may have to be rescheduled to after the status date.

If the extension affects the fixed duration of the task you will get a prompt.

Assignments that Started Late

1. Select the assignment with a delayed start.

2. In the timescale **Work** row drag over the days on which work should have been done but wasn't, and press ⌷Ins⌷. This will shift all scheduled work out to the real start date.
    OR
    Enter an **Actual Start** date on the assignment in the spreadsheet.

Assignments that Finished Late

Enter actual hours in the timescale in the row **Actual Work** up to the date the resource finished the assignment.

Now that we have shown you how to enter data from paper time sheets, let's explore how we can make our lives easier with electronic time sheets. Sending out paper time sheets and entering the data is a lot of effort that has to be repeated many times throughout a project. You can enter the data automatically from electronic time sheets. You may still need the steps we discussed above to make corrections, when needed.

Collecting the Data Using Electronic Time Sheets by Web

Time Sheets by Web: Project Server

In this configuration there is one focal point for all stakeholders, the Project Server intranet site. The time sheet data are kept in the database that powers the site. The

database can be *SQL Server* for the enterprise, or its little brother, *MSDE* (*Microsoft Database Engine*) for workgroups of up to 15 people. The project manager publishes the assignments from within Project 2002 to the intranet site and this will populate the time sheets of the involved resources automatically. The resources can access their time sheets by browsing to the Project Server intranet site with *Internet Explorer* and logging in. They will need a *Microsoft Project Web Access Client Access License* (*CAL*) for this. When resources fill in their time sheet, they can send it back to the project manager for approval. The project manager then logs into the Project Server intranet site using *Internet Explorer* to review the time sheet information. He can then decide to reject or accept the numbers. He then transfers the accepted numbers into the Project 2002 file.

Project Server in Workgroup Mode or Enterprise Mode

MS Project now comes in two editions, Project 2002 Standard and Project 2002 Professional. Both editions can be used in combination with *Project Server*:
- Project 2002 Standard can be used with Project Server in *Workgroup mode*.

- Project 2002 Professional can be used with Project Server in *Enterprise mode*.
Both modes allow collecting time sheet information electronically.

Workgroup Mode

The *Workgroup mode* is similar to Project 2000 working with Project Central. A *workgroup* is a limited group of people involved in a project of up to 100 people. Typically a project workgroup consists of:
- Upper management
- Project manager
- Team leaders

- ◆ Team members
- ◆ Client (if different from upper management)
- ◆ Users (if different from client)

The workgroup mode facilitates the communication between the members of a workgroup. Workgroups typically should not exceed 100 people, otherwise opening and saving files slows down too much.

Enterprise Mode

Microsoft uses the word *Enterprise* to refer to an entire organization or any subset thereof, such as a division or department. The enterprise is not necessarily the same as the entire *Organization Breakdown Structure* (*OBS*) because the enterprise can also be just one division or one department. The enterprise mode of MS Project eliminates the technical limit of 100 people in the workgroup mode and allows you to model any number of people in your organization. If the (subset of the) organization that you want to model has more than 100 resources, you need the *Enterprise mode*. Choosing the entity of your organization to model depends on factors like:

- ◆ Where in the organization do you need overview reports on a series of projects? Do you need to roll up subprojects into *master projects* or view similar projects in *project portfolio* views?

- ◆ Where in the organization do projects typically have *cross-project dependencies*? Cross-project dependencies often occur between subprojects of a larger *integrated program schedule* (master project).

- ◆ Where in the organization are you *sharing resources*, which impacts deadline accomplishment in the projects? Your organization is, of course, sharing people across its entire organization to a certain degree, but that does not mean that you have to treat your entire organization as the enterprise to model. You should find out in which subset of your organization the sharing of resources occurs most often. Those subsets could then be treated as enterprises.

Any of these three factors can lead you to the right entity within your organization to model, or to the realization that the entire organization should be modeled. You are basically looking for those organizational entities that are relatively autonomous. That is where you set up *Project Server* in Enterprise mode. One organization can have multiple Project Server databases.

Notice that:
- ◆ An enterprise is not the same as a *Resource Breakdown Structure* (*RBS*) since an RBS often only contains people that are resources to the project, and not the people in upper management, clients, and users.

◆ An enterprise is not the same as the *Organization Breakdown Structure* (*OBS*) since an OBS contains everybody in the organization (receptionist, HR, accounting, etc.) whereas the enterprise resources could exclude non-project resources.

This book will not deal with the technicalities of setting up and configuring *Project Server* since that is the subject of other course offerings at the International Institute for Learning, Inc.[78]

Publishing the Assignments

In the **Collaborate, Publish** menu you will find different options. These menu items can also be accessed with a single click with the **Collaborate** toolbar. You can display the **Collaborate** toolbar by right-clicking on any toolbar and choosing **Collaborate** from the pop-up menu. The following toolbar will be displayed:

Next to the menu item references below you will find an image of the corresponding tool on the **Collaborate** toolbar:

◆ **Publish, Project Plan**
This creates the project in the database. The project will be visible in the portfolio views. It does not publish assignments.

◆ **Publish, New and changed assignments**
This publishes the assignments into the task lists of the team members. By populating their task lists, you are implicitly asking them to commit to the tasks. When the team member does not reject the assignment, a firm commitment is assumed. The assignment will have *Yes* in the assignment-related field *Confirmed*. When all assignments of a task are confirmed the task-related field **Confirmed** will be toggled to **Yes** by Project 2002. When changes happen to the assignment, such as a cancellation, a change in start date, or the amount of work, Project 2002 will immediately notice this and automatically toggle the field *Update Needed* to **Yes**. You can easily keep track of whether you communicated the change to the resources by observing this field. To communicate these changes you would choose **Publish, New and changed assignments** once more.

---

[78] See www.iil.com for a complete list of MS Project related course offerings, as well as the course catalog with cities and dates.

◆ **Request progress information**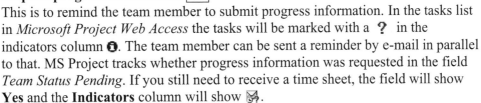
This is to remind the team member to submit progress information. In the tasks list in *Microsoft Project Web Access* the tasks will be marked with a **?** in the indicators column **❶**. The team member can be sent a reminder by e-mail in parallel to that. MS Project tracks whether progress information was requested in the field *Team Status Pending*. If you still need to receive a time sheet, the field will show **Yes** and the **Indicators** column will show 🖂.

Corresponding Assignment Fields in MS Project

1. Publish, New and changed Assignments
2. make a change to an assignment
3. Request Progress Information

Manager   Resource

1. Confirmed
2. Update Needed
3. Team Status Pending

The illustration shows the corresponding assignment fields in which Project 2002 tracks the communication. The tracking is entirely automatic even though you can make changes to certain fields.
When you publish assignments for the first time, Project 2002 toggles the field **Confirmed** for all those assignments to *Yes*. As you can see, Project 2002 assumes that the assignments will not be rejected by team members. When you make a change to an assignment, Project 2002 will toggle the field **Update Needed** to *Yes* indicating that you should **Publish New and Changed Assignments** again. When you **Request Progress Information**, Project 2002 toggles the field **Team Status Pending** to *Yes* to indicate a time sheet is outstanding.

Viewing All Commitments in MS Project

Project Server works on the assumption that a resource accepts a task unless the person undertakes action to reject it by selecting it in his time sheet and clicking 🗐 Reject.

If a resource accepts a task, this commitment is visible on the level of assignments. Project 2002 will summarize commitments received on the task level when a task has more than one assignment. Only when all resources assigned to the task have committed themselves, will Project 2002 toggle the task-related cell **Confirmed** to **Yes**.

For example, when two resources Harry and Ed are both assigned to the same task, the possibilities are:

Harry	Ed	Task field **Confirmed** will show:
Accepted	Accepted	Yes
Accepted	Rejected	No
Rejected	Accepted	No
Rejected	Rejected	No

The task-related cell summarizes its assignment cells. As you can see, Project 2002 summarizes the assignments in a pessimistic fashion. Only if all resources are committed, will **Confirmed** show **Yes** on the task level.

In the Task Usage view, you can see by assigned resource who rejected and who accepted in the **Confirmed** cells. This works in a similar fashion for the other field **TeamStatus Pending**.

If you want to see the exact commitments by assignment, view the commitments in the Task Usage view with the assignments expanded and the field **Confirmed** displayed. The following screen shows this:

ⓘ	Task Name	Duration	Confirmed	Update Needed	TeamStatus Pending
	⊟ **REQUIREMENTS**	**7.53 days**	**Yes**	**No**	**No**
	⊟ research staff requirements	4 days	Yes	No	
	you		Yes	*No*	
	⊟ summarize requirements	4 days	Yes	No	
	Hilcrest – Nancy		Yes	*No*	*No*
	⊟ **LOCATION**	**17.5 days**	**Yes**	**No**	**No**
	⊟ select the realtor	4 days	No	No	No
	you		*No*	*No*	*No*
	⊟ visit the sites	1 day	No	No	No
	Falgon – John		*No*	*No*	*No*
	Hilcrest – Nancy		*No*	*No*	
	the realtor		*No*	*No*	
	you		*No*	*No*	*No*

Assignment is published and not

Assignment still has to be published.

The **Confirmed** field can also be edited manually, but you can only edit the field in the assignment-related cells, not in the task-related cells. You can do this to make corrections.

Checking If Updates Are Needed

Project 2002 will immediately toggle the field **Update Needed** from **No** to **Yes** of accepted assignments when the start date, duration, amount of work or finish date is changed. The task field **Update Needed** will tell you if you need to publish the changed assignments again. You can see the icon ✉ in the **Indicators** column when you need to send out update messages to your team members. Point to the icon ✉ for one second and read the reminder that appears.

If the field **Update needed** shows that you need to communicate with the team member, you can choose **Collaborate, Publish new and changed assignments** to inform them of the changes. You can do this for selected tasks or for all tasks at once. Team members will find the icon ❶ in front of tasks that are updated in their time sheet.

Project 2002 will notice automatically when a resource was removed from a task or if a task was deleted entirely and will prompt you if you would like to publish this. The prompt looks like:

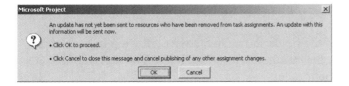

Customizing the Time Sheets

You can customize the time sheet by choosing **Tools, Customize, Published fields ….**
The **Customize Published Fields** dialog appears:

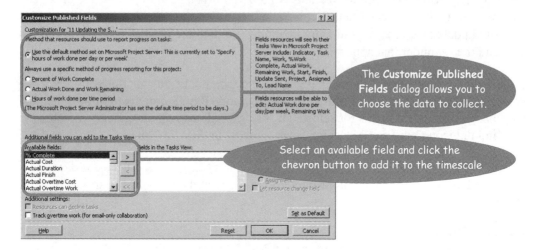

 The default time sheet view has all the fields shown in the list on the top right. These
fields cannot be removed; they are the standard time sheet fields. You can add fields to
the time sheet from the list in the bottom left.

The Resource Fills in the Time Sheet

 A resource logs into the Project Server intranet site and clicks **Tasks** to display the time sheet where actual hours can be entered. The time sheet will look similar to:

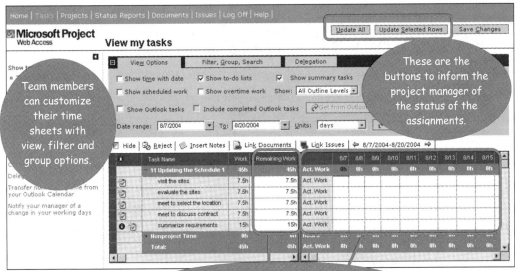

Team members can customize their time sheets with view, filter and group options.

These are the buttons to inform the project manager of the status of the assignments.

The fields **Remaining Work** and **Act.Work** are ready to be filled in.

 Resources can fill in the **Act. Work** by day (the hours the resource worked on each day of the week, if it is a weekly time sheet), or by week (for a monthly time sheet) depending on how *Project Server* is configured, see page 567. The **Remaining Work** hours are automatically decreased in Project Server every time actual hours are entered in the timescale.

After completing the time sheet, the resource has two options:

♦ The resource clicks Update All to send all numbers entered to the appropriate project manager(s).

♦ The resource selects the rows with numbers to send back to a project manager and clicks Update Selected Rows.

As an immediate result, the resource will see the icon in front of the tasks sent to the project manager for approval.

The Project Manager Checks the Time Sheets

 Time sheet information is received by the project manager as **Updates** and the page with updates looks like this:

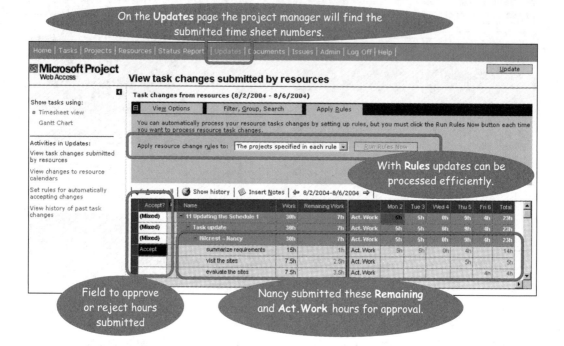

When you review the time sheets as the project manager, you have three options in the column **Accept?**:

◆ Enter **Accept** to authorize the line item. After your review you can transfer the data into your Project 2002 schedule by clicking [Update]. Project 2002 will automatically toggle the assignment-related field **Team Status Pending** back to **No** for that assignment, and the icon 🕮 will disappear from the **Indicators** column. The inserted notes will also be transferred into the project file and appear in the **Notes** field, complete with date and name of the person.

◆ Enter **Reject** to refuse the time sheet numbers. You should get in touch with the team member to sort the issue out. The team member will receive a notification by e-mail.

◆ Leave it blank to decide later.

You can speed up entering your decisions by making them:

◆ All at once: if you want to quickly approve all updates, click | ✓ Accept all |.

◆ By project: where it shows the name of the project, select **Accept** from the list in the column **Accept?**. This marks all updates in this project as accepted.

◆ By type of update message: where it shows the type of update message, select **Accept** from the list. This marks all updates in this category as accepted.

◆ Person-by-person: where you see the person's name, select **Accept** from the list. This marks all updates from that resource as accepted.

Viewing the Time Sheet Data in Project 2002

After transferring the time sheet hours, you can view the actual hours entered in the Resource Usage view with the assignments expanded. Choose **Format, Details, Actual Work** to see the exact numbers typed in by the resources as illustrated in the next screen:

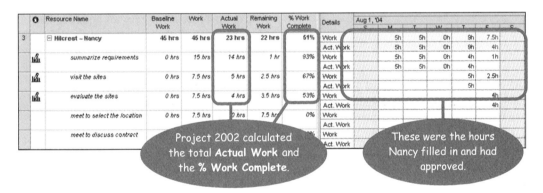

After updating the project file, Project 2002 automatically toggles the field **TeamStatus Pending** back to **No** for the time sheets received. Check this field to find out if there are still time sheets outstanding before creating status reports on the entire project. Typically you will have to chase after the resources who did not return their time sheets before you can report the status of your project.

The **TeamStatus Pending** fields can be edited manually on the level of individual assignments. This is useful for:

◆ Verbal updates

◆ Lost messages when the power goes out or the e-mail system breaks down

◆ Making corrections

The task-related cells summarize the assignment-related cells. If one of the resources assigned to the task did not submit his time sheet, the **TeamStatus Pending** will show **Yes**. Again, Project 2002 is pessimistic in summarizing on the task level.

Collecting the Data Using Electronic Time Sheets by E-mail

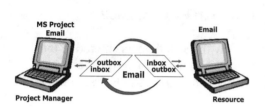

In this configuration the messages are transferred using e-mail. The illustration shows the process. The project manager sends e-mail messages to the resources. The e-mail messages arrive in the inbox of the resource. She replies and fills it in, then sends it back to the project manager. The project manager opens it from his inbox and can then accept the hours worked from the resource and update his project file. Or, the project manager can enter into a discussion with the resource by replying to the message.

As the project manager, you will need an e-mail system that can carry the MS Project-specific e-mail messages, a 32-bit MAPI-compliant e-mail system. MAPI stands for Messaging Application Programming Interface and MAPI-carriers are Lotus CC-Mail 7.0 or later, Lotus Notes 4.5a or later, MS Exchange, MS Mail (on Windows NT) or MS Outlook 97 or later.

Setting Up Time Sheets by E-mail

1. In MS Project choose **Tools, Options**, and click the **Collaborate** tab.

2. In the **Collaborate using** list, select **E-mail only**. You will get a prompt with a little advertisement for Project Server, click OK .

3. To apply the collaboration settings you selected to all new projects, click Set as Default .

4. On the **General** tab, type an identifying name for your e-mail messages in the **User name** field.

5. Click OK .

Next, we need to check and set some resource attributes:

1. Choose **View, Resource Sheet**.

2. Insert the columns **Workgroup** and **Email Address**.

3. You can change to a different collaboration system for specific resources by setting their resource-field **Workgroup** to **Microsoft Project Server**. Or you can set it to **None** to not collaborate.

4. If the **Resource Name** is identical to the name in your e-mail address list, you won't need to enter the e-mail address. Otherwise, enter the e-mail address in the resource sheet into the field **Email Address**. Choose **Insert, New resource from, Address Book**.
    OR
    On the **Resource Management** toolbar, click New Resource From ▾ and choose **Address Book...** and download all resources including their e-mail addresses.
    OR
    Click **Address Book** 📖 on the **Resource Management** toolbar.

5. The **Select Resources** dialog appears:

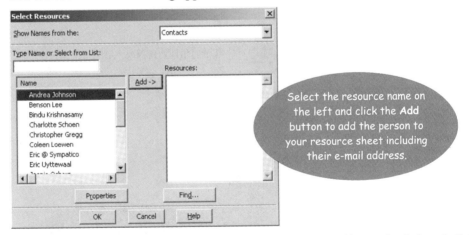

6. You can select the resources to add their e-mails from the list on the left and click Add -> to have them appended to your resource sheet. Click OK when done.

Finally, all people involved in e-mail communications need to run *WGsetup.exe* from the Project 2002 CD-ROM in the **\Files\Support\WGsetup** folder. You can also put all the files in this folder on a shared network drive or send the person all these files and run it from there. *WGsetup* will enable their e-mail systems to digest the form-like e-mail messages. *WGsetup* stands for **W**ork**G**roup **setup,** and is known as the *workgroup*

message handler. If a person did not run the message handler, the message would appear as an attachment to the e-mail instead of as a custom e-mail message.

Getting Commitments by E-mail

1. Make sure you have all assignments that you want to communicate completed in your schedule. Notice that when you assign a resource to a task, the field **Confirmed** toggles from **Yes** to **No**. A **No** means that a resource has yet to accept the assignment. Notice that e-mail works differently from Project Server. For tasks without assignments (milestones), the field shows **Yes**.

2. Select the resources in the Resource Sheet or the tasks in the Gantt chart for which you want to gain commitments.

3. Choose **Collaborate, Publish, New and Changed Assignments.**
   OR
   Click 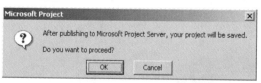 on the **Collaborate** toolbar. Project 2002 will prompt you:

4. Ignore this message and click [OK]. The **Publish New and Changed Assignments** dialog appears:

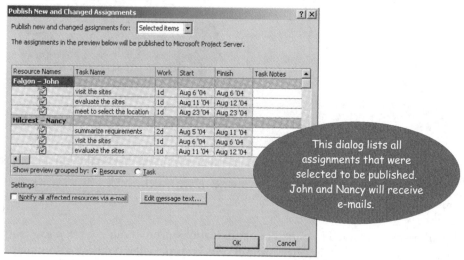

This dialog lists all assignments that were selected to be published. John and Nancy will receive e-mails.

5. In the list at the top, select to publish the assignments for:
   - ◇ **Entire project**: to publish all assignments in the project
   - ◇ **Current view**: to publish all assignments currently filtered out
   - ◇ **Selected items**: to publish the ones you selected only

6. Uncheck ☐ **notify all affected resources via e-mail** since they will already receive the message by e-mail; they don't need an extra reminder in their inbox.

7. Click ⟨ Edit message text... ⟩ to change the accompanying message.

8. In the **Task Notes** field you can even provide comments by task.

9. Click ⟨ OK ⟩ and the following dialog appears to let you know the messages were sent:

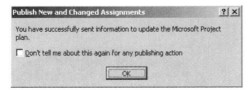

As you perhaps noticed, the steps are very similar for sending messages via e-mail or via *Project Server*.

The Resource Replies to the E-mail

Each team member should regularly check his or her e-mail inbox and reply to the messages. The **Publish New and Changed Assignments** e-mails, as the resource receives it, look like this:

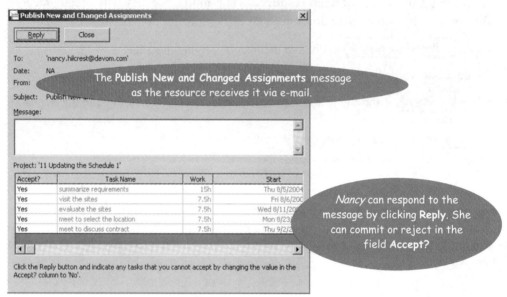

The resource can click | Reply | and indicate in the column **Accept?** whether she accepts or rejects the assignment with a simple **Yes** or **No**. In the column **Comments**, she can add any conditions or explanations. These comments will end up in the project file as permanent documentation on the assignment, another great benefit.

Checking the E-mail Replies from Your Resources

1. As the project manager, open your e-mail application and check your inbox. Responses to your messages will have **RE: Publish New and Changed Assignments** in the subject line.

2. Double-click on it to review the responses and:

    click | Reply | if you have questions or remarks for the resource, or

    click | Update Project | if you want to transfer the responses into the project file.
    The comments will be copied into the **Notes** field in Project 2002.

RE: Publish New and Changed Assignments ✕

| Reply | Update Project | Close |

To: ericu@iil.com
Date: Thu 3/6/2003 10:42 PM
From: *The response as received by the project manager*
Subject: RE: Publish New and Changed Assignments

Message:

```
----------
```

Project: '11 Updating the Schedule 1'

Accept?	Task Name	Work	Start
Yes	...mined requirements	...	Thu 8/...
Yes	visit the sites	7.5h	Fri 8/6/...
Yes	evaluate the sites	7.5h	Wed 8/11/2004
Yes	meet to select the location	7.5h	Mon 8/23/200
Yes	meet to discuss contract	7.5h	Thu 9/2/2004

Accept? and Comments will be captured in the project file.

Creating an E-mail Time Sheet

1. Select the tasks for which you want to create time sheets and click on **Request
    progress information** 🗒 on the **Collaborate** toolbar. Project 2002 will prompt
    you whether you want to save the file; click | OK |.

2. The **Request Progress Information** dialog appears:

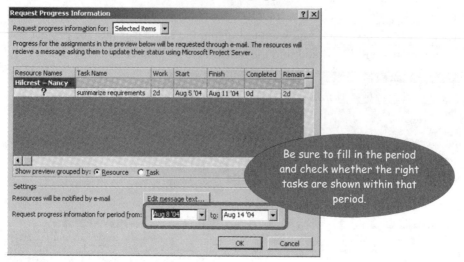

Be sure to fill in the period and check whether the right tasks are shown within that period.

3. Enter the period for which you need to collect actuals in the fields:
   Request progress information for period from: Mar 13 '00 ▼ **to:** Mar 19 '00 ▼.
   Review the data and click 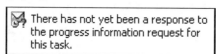; the message(s) will be sent to the recipient(s).

4. Notice that the field **TeamStatus Pending** is toggled to **Yes** for the tasks. Also the **Indicators** column has the icon 🖃 for them. If you point to the icon for one full second, you will see the pop-up:

> 🖃 There has not yet been a response to the progress information request for this task.

The Resource Fills in the E-mail Time Sheet

The resource receives the time sheet by e-mail as follows:

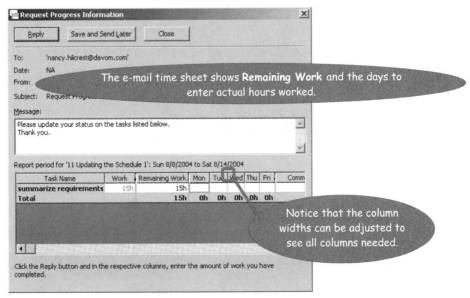

 The resource clicks **Reply** and after the resource fills in the actual hours, he should always revise the **Remaining Work**. In the e-mail system, the resource will have to decrease the remaining work herself. The resource should provide you with a new estimate, if appropriate. If needed, she can add an explanation in the **Comments** field.

After the resource has completed the time sheet, she clicks **Send** and the time sheet will be delivered to the project manager.

Reviewing the Time Sheet

In your inbox you will find the time sheets from the resources as the project manager by looking at the subject line that says **RE: Request Progress information**. The e-mail time sheet message looks like this:

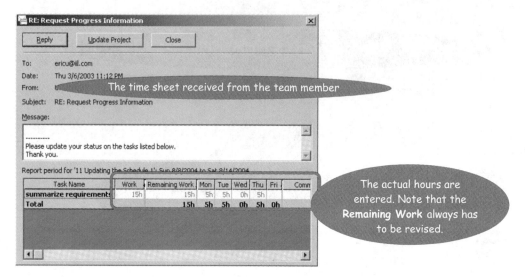

When you review the time sheets as the project manager, you have three options:

♦ Click [Reply] to ask questions or ask for clarifications.

♦ Click [Update Project] to transfer actual hours and comments into the project file.

♦ Click [Close] to decide later.

Updating the Costs

Cost Updating Strategies

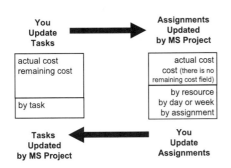

This is similar to updating the schedule:

◆ You can update the tasks and have the assignment details updated by MS Project.

◆ You can update the assignments and have the tasks updated by MS Project. If you enter the data into the time-phased assignment fields, you can model the actual cash flow very precisely. In order to do so, you have to change a default option.

Setting the Options for Assignments Cost Updates

You can enter actual costs in the time-phased **Actual Cost** fields for the assignments in Project 2002. This can be a useful way of keeping your project up to date on a daily or weekly basis, because you can enter expenses for a particular day or week in your schedule.

 In its default options, Project 2002 automatically calculates actual costs. It calculates them based on the accrual method you set and the actual time progress you enter. If you want to enter actual costs yourself, you must first turn off the automatic updating of actual costs. Then you can enter your own actual costs.

1. Choose **Tools, Options**, and then click the **Calculation** tab.

2. Uncheck ☐ **Actual costs are always calculated by Microsoft Project**.

3. Click OK .

Preparing the View for Updating Costs

1. Choose **View, Task Usage**.

2. Choose **View, Table: <name of current table>, Tracking**; the fields for updating tasks are displayed.

3. Choose **Format, Detail Styles…**, in the list **Available fields** select **Cost** and click the ⟨ <u>S</u>how >> ⟩. Do the same for **Actual Cost**. Click ⟨ OK ⟩. The **Act. Cost** field is now also displayed in the timescale:

Task Name	Baseline Cost	Cost	Actual Cost	Remaining Cost	Details	25	Aug '04 1	8	5	22
1 ⊟ REQUIREMENTS	$1,650.00	$1,650.00	$0.00	$1,650.00	Cost		$1,343.75	$306.25		
					Act. Cost					
2 ⊟ research staff requirements	$1,125.00	$1,125.00	$0.00	$1,125.00	Cost		$1,125.00			
					Act. Cost					
you	$1,125.00	$1,125.00	$0.00	$1,125.00	Cost		$1,125.00			
					Act. Cost					
3 ⊟ summarize requirements	$525.00	$525.00	$0.00	$525.00	Cost		$218.75	$306.25		
					Act. Cost					
Hilcrest – Nancy	$525.00	$525.00	$0.00	$525.00	Cost		$218.75	$306.25		
					Act. Cost					

Update the running totals in the spreadsheet.

Or update week-by-week in the timescale.

4. Update running totals: add the new cost to the running total displayed in the spreadsheet column **Act. Cost** and enter the new total actual cost.
    OR
    Update in the timescale on a week-by-week basis: enter expenditures in the **Act. Cost** row in the week you incurred those costs.

Checks on an Updated Schedule

The following checks reflect best practices on updating schedules. A schedule has to be updated if the current date is later than the project start date. The schedule needs to show actual update information and revised forecasts. Then we need to ask: *is the schedule up to date as per the Status date (or Current date)*? The following questions help determine the answer:

◆ What is the quality of the baseline in the schedule?

    ◇ Is a baseline present?
Keep in mind that projects planned far into the future that are not yet approved do not necessarily need a baseline.

    ◇ Is the baseline complete?
You can verify the presence and completeness by applying the filter **7 IIL Tasks with missing baseline info.**[79] The filter displays any tasks without entries in **Baseline Start, Baseline Finish, Baseline Duration** or **Baseline Work**. When assignments are created after the baseline is set, often the Baseline Work field is still empty. Note that the filter does not check the field **Baseline Cost**.

    ◇ Is the baseline original?
The baseline cannot be reset without formal approval of the appropriate project stakeholders.

    ◇ Is the baseline relevant?
If the project deviated too far from the baseline, a new baseline needs to be negotiated. The baseline should provide a meaningful standard of comparison for the current schedule. You can check this by looking at how far the current schedule is removed from the baseline. Does the project have a fighting chance to catch up with the baseline again, or is it a lost cause?

◆ Are the appropriate options selected in **Tools, Options, Calculation** for the chosen updating strategy?

    ◇ For task updating (revising the task-related **Actual Duration** and **Remaining Duration** fields), the following options should be selected:

        ☑ **Updating task status updates resource status**

---

[79] This filter can be found in the file *Tools to check Orange Belt schedules.MPP* that is available for download at www.jrosspub.com.

    ☑ **Split in-progress tasks**

    ◇ For assignment updating (entering numbers from the time sheets into the assignment-related **Actual Work** and **Remaining Work** fields), the following options should be selected:

    ☑ **Updating task status updates resource status**
If you keep this option selected, you should not enter **% Complete** on tasks because this will override time sheet data.

    ☑ **Split in-progress tasks**

    ◇ For updating both the tasks and the assignments, the following options should be selected:

    ☐ **Updating task status updates resource status**
Entering a **% Complete** on tasks will override the time sheet information. You cannot enter both types of information unless you de-select this option.

    ☑ **Split in-progress tasks**

◆ Is the **Status Date** set to an appropriate date?
For schedule certification purposes through our certification curriculum[80], the appropriate date is the regular reporting date that is closest to the date of submitting the schedule. Don't forget to set the **Current date** to the same date as the **Status date** in **Project, Project Information** before updating the schedule.

◆ Is the schedule up to date as per the **Status date** (or **Current date**)?

    ◇ Are all actual durations (actual work / actual hours worked) scheduled in the past?
The actuals are scheduled in the past if they are earlier than the status date. Otherwise, the schedule does not reflect up-to-date forecasts. When you bring actual durations to the past, all their dependent tasks may be rescheduled earlier as well, thus updating the forecasts. This is why rescheduling is important. You can verify this by applying the filter **8 IIL Reschedule Actual Durations...**[81]

    ◇ Are all remaining durations (remaining work) scheduled in the future?
The remaining estimates are scheduled in the future if they are later than the status date. You cannot leave unfinished work scheduled in the past. If you leave unfinished work before the status date, you are scheduling work to be done in the past. The work should be moved to the future to update the forecast dates.

---

[80] For more information see www.iil.com and follow the link *Microsoft Project*.

[81] This filter can be found in the file *Tools to check Orange belt schedules.MPP* that is available for download at www.jrosspub.com.

Otherwise, the schedule does not reflect up-to-date forecasts. If you don't do this you have created a *status report*, not a *forecast report*. You can verify this by applying the filter **8 IIL Reschedule Remaining Durations...**[82]

◇ Are the remaining durations (remaining work) revised?
Otherwise, the schedule may not reflect up-to-date forecasts. If the project manager has been revising the durations of detail tasks, these will be displayed. This filter is different from the other filters in the sense that if it displays tasks, it is good. If the filter does not display any tasks, it is an indication that the project manager is not revising his (remaining) durations while updating. If remaining durations are not revised, the forecasts are not very accurate, and may not even be reliable. You can verify this by applying the filter **9 IIL Remaining Durations revised**.[83]

---

[82] This filter can be found in the file *Tools to check Orange Belt schedules.MPP* that is available for download at www.jrosspub.com.

[83] This filter can be found in the file *Tools to check Orange Belt schedules.MPP* that is available for download at www.jrosspub.com.

Prepare the Status and Forecast Report

Regardless of whether you chose to update tasks or assignments, the Tracking Gantt Chart is good for reporting progress and new forecasts. Choose **View, Tracking Gantt** to apply this view.

Choose **View, Table <name of current table>, Variance** to see the current schedule and baseline dates. The screen should now look similar to:

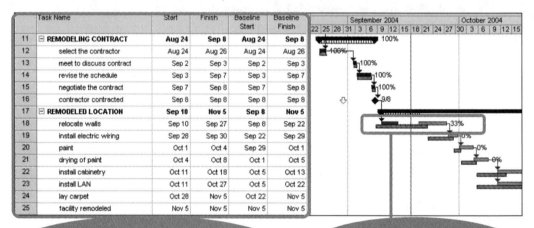

	Task Name	Start	Finish	Baseline Start	Baseline Finish
11	⊟ **REMODELING CONTRACT**	**Aug 24**	**Sep 8**	**Aug 24**	**Sep 8**
12	select the contractor	Aug 24	Aug 26	Aug 24	Aug 26
13	meet to discuss contract	Sep 2	Sep 3	Sep 2	Sep 3
14	revise the schedule	Sep 3	Sep 7	Sep 3	Sep 7
15	negotiate the contract	Sep 7	Sep 8	Sep 7	Sep 8
16	contractor contracted	Sep 8	Sep 8	Sep 8	Sep 8
17	⊟ **REMODELED LOCATION**	**Sep 10**	**Nov 5**	**Sep 8**	**Nov 5**
18	relocate walls	Sep 10	Sep 27	Sep 8	Sep 22
19	install electric wiring	Sep 28	Sep 30	Sep 22	Sep 29
20	paint	Oct 1	Oct 4	Sep 29	Oct 1
21	drying of paint	Oct 4	Oct 8	Oct 1	Oct 5
22	install cabinetry	Oct 11	Oct 18	Oct 5	Oct 13
23	install LAN	Oct 11	Oct 27	Oct 5	Oct 22
24	lay carpet	Oct 28	Nov 5	Oct 22	Nov 5
25	facility remodeled	Nov 5	Nov 5	Nov 5	Nov 5

This is the **Variance** table with **Start** and **Finish** (current schedule) and **Baseline Start** and **Finish** (baseline).

The current schedule (top half) is later than the baseline (bottom half): slippage

The Tracking Gantt depicts progress using the calculated date field **Complete Through**. You can see this field listed by choosing **Format, Bar styles** and looking under **To**. The **Complete Through** field:
- ◆ follows closely the **Actual Duration** that is entered by you, when you update tasks
- ◆ is the number of days for which actual hours are entered, when you update assignments.

 Notice that the Tracking Gantt does not show progress (**% Complete** and **Actual Durations**) if you work with time sheets and you turned the option ☑ **Updating Task Status updates Resource Status** off in **Tools, Options,** tab **Calculation**. With the option off, the **% Complete** and **Actual Duration** are not calculated. If you enter time sheet information with the option on, you have to make sure never to enter **% Complete** for tasks, because this will override the time sheet information.

In Project 2002 with *Project Server*, reporting progress is as simple as can be. As the project manager you just need to keep your schedule up to date and saved in the Project Server database. The status and forecast can at any time be viewed online by executives; even if it is on a Saturday night at 8PM. Executives will see their entire portfolio of projects in *Microsoft Project Web Access*:

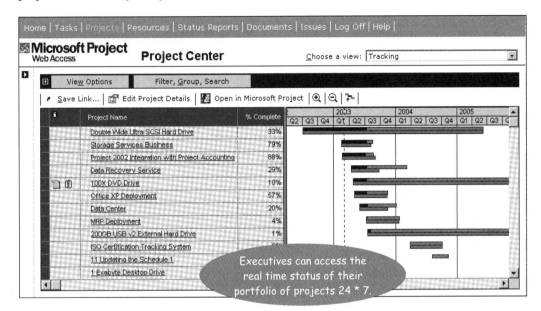

Exercises

Review

1. What are the process steps for updating schedules?

2. What benefit can you gain from a baseline in your schedule? How do you set it? How often do you set it?

3. What are the legitimate reasons to change your baseline?

4. Describe in your own words what the following indicators mean:
   ◇ Actual Duration
   ◇ Remaining Duration

5. How do the following indicators relate to each other? You could describe the relationship using formulas.
   ◇ Actual Duration
   ◇ Remaining Duration
   ◇ Duration
   ◇ % Complete

6. There are two main strategies for updating schedules. What are they and what are the main differences between them?

7. When collecting update data, you could ask for % Complete. What are the weaknesses of this metric?

8. What menu items do you need to choose to set the Status Date? Why do you need a status date?

9. What task type do you recommend when updating tasks? How can you change multiple tasks to this task type?

10. There are six different update situations in practice. Please mention four.

11. A team leader submits the following report to you as shown in the illustration below. Would you accept this report:
    ◇ as a status report? Why?
    ◇ as a forecast report? Why?
    If you would not accept it, indicate what needs to be changed.

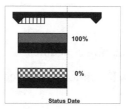

12. What are the pieces of data that you will need to collect when you want to update assignments?

13. Which vehicles are available to collect time sheets?

14. When checking whether your schedule is properly updated, what do you look at?

Relocation Project – Updating Tasks

1. Open the file *11 Updating the Schedule 1.MPP* that is available for download at www.jrosspub.com.

2. Change to the **Tracking Gantt** view and **Tracking** table. Hide the **% Complete** field. Display the **Tracking** toolbar.

3. Set the baseline for the entire project.

4. Set the **Status Date** and the **Current Date** to *September 17, 2004* and create a gridline for the status date in the Gantt timescale.

5. Set the following options in **Tools, Options, Calculation**:
    - ☑ **Updating Task status updates resource status**
    - ☑ **Actual Costs are always calculated by Microsoft Project**

6. As of *September 17, 2004* the situation is:
    All the tasks until *Remodeled Location* are done and ran as scheduled. The contractor started late because he finished his previous contract late. The contractor supplied the following update:

Task	Started	Actual Duration	Remaining Duration
relocate walls	*10 Sept.*	*3d*	*15 d*

    The rest of the tasks are not started yet.

7. Switch the task type to **Fixed Units** for those tasks you are about to update. Be careful not to switch the task *drying of paint* to fixed units since MS Project will change its duration from a *4 edays* elapsed duration to a regular duration of *12.8 days*, which distorts the schedule.

8. Enter the status of the project by updating the tasks.

9. Don't forget to check whether there are any remaining durations scheduled before the status date. Reschedule these after the status date.

10. Describe the status of the project in your own words.

11. Compare your file with the solution file *11 Updating the Schedule 2.MPP* that is available for download at www.jrosspub.com.

Relocation Project – Optimizing for Time and Cost Again

1. Open the file *11 Updating the Schedule 2.MPP* that is available for download at www.jrosspub.com.

2. You find this schedule too risky; you need to meet the new deadline date of November 16, 2004 and, on top of that, you need a time buffer to meet the project deadline. You decide to explore whether working overtime offers solutions. The overtime rates are:

Name	Std. Rate	Overtime Rate
employees	$ 25/h	$ 50/h
contractor	$ 30/h	$ 50/h
LAN consultants	$ 75/h	$ 100/h
Realtor	$ 35/h	$ 45/h

3. What is the cost of the project now?

4. Which people would you ask to work overtime first to meet the November 16 deadline? Why?

5. You want to explore whether overtime by the contractor can solve the schedule conflict.
   How many overtime person days do you propose on which tasks to meet the deadline?

6. How much does your project cost if you pay the overtime rates?

7. Could you negotiate to pay regular rates instead? Yes, Contractor was cause for slip in the first place and you negotiate paying regular rates

8. How would you enter the overtime work if you pay the regular standard rate?

9. Compare your file with the solution file *11 Updating the Schedule 3.MPP* that is available for download at www.jrosspub.com.

Chapter 12 Evaluating the Project

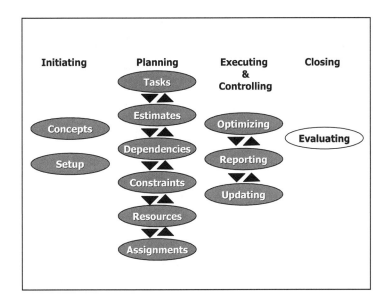

In this chapter we review how you can become a better project manager for your next projects.

After this chapter you will:

◆ Know why project evaluation is important.
◆ Have a list of questions that will help you learn from a finished project.
◆ Know what to capture in lessons learned.

"Can We Go Now …?"

Nob and his team members sit down with a pizza to look back at the project they just finished. The pizza is almost finished when Nob kicks off the meeting asking: "What did we learn from this project?"

Harry says: "Well, I learned that I am not going to work with Chris again!"

Chris fires back immediately with: "Likewise … man!"

Nob straightens his body and asks again: "Folks, we are here to learn from our mistakes and our successes … what did we learn?"

Mary: "I found out that I am always too optimistic in my estimates! Next time I will not give estimates unless I am forced to …"

Nob: "Did you ask yourself how you could get more accurate estimates?"

Mary: "I don't like estimating; it's too hard…"

Vern: "Yeah, I agree…"

Nob makes a big gesture to interrupt this exchange and summarizes: "So, what you have learned from this project is that you don't want to provide estimates anymore to the project manager?"

Vern: "That sums it up pretty well!"

Nob: "What else did we learn?"

Veronica: "I learned that filling in time sheets takes a lot of time. Particularly when we were crunching, the time sheets were a nuisance!"

Nob has grown slightly irritated by the negativity that befalls him in this meeting and remarks sarcastically: "I guess you learned you don't want to fill in time sheets anymore?"

Then Harry asks the deadly question: "Can we go now …?"

Project Evaluation

Evaluating a project when it is completed is often seen as a waste of time. The reason for this seems to be that the atmosphere during an evaluation can be loaded with animosity. When things did not run the way they should have, pointed fingers appear. These evaluations are indeed a waste of time. The little story of Nob on the previous page shows a perfect example of time wasted on an evaluation meeting.

Evaluation is useful when the focus is on, and stays on, the future. Only by learning from the past can you become better prepared for the future. Lessons learned can lead to improvements to the WBS, the accuracy of estimates, the use of dependencies, the use of resources and the appropriateness of assignments in the schedule. The meeting must be directed in such a fashion that people focus on gain for the future instead of on pain from the past. If managed well, the meeting can be a source of valuable information. Evaluating prevents running into the same troubles again.

Of course, many projects run well. Even in this case evaluating is important because it is the only way to become yet a better project manager. There is always room to deliver projects better. When you stop asking yourself the question: *What could we have done better?* you will stop learning from your experiences. In this age of constant and rapid changes, nobody can afford to stop learning. Life-long learning is the motto for success.

Evaluation Points

After the project is over you can ask some questions with your team. These are a few suggestions with respect to the schedule as a tool to manage and control the project:

1. Was the schedule clear to all stakeholders? How can it be made clearer in future projects?

2. Was the WBS complete? Was it easy to understand? Did it function as a tool for delegation? Were the deliverables clearly formulated in it, or did some deliverables cause confusion? How can the WBS be improved for similar projects in the future?

3. Were the estimates optimistic or pessimistic? What factors caused the estimates to be optimistic or pessimistic? Can these factors be better predicted in future projects?

4. Was there enough of a time buffer in the schedule to compensate for unforeseen events? Which tasks consumed most of the buffer? Why?

5. Was the schedule easy enough to maintain during project execution? Could accurate status and forecast reports be generated at each reporting period? Was the network of dependencies complete? How can the reports be produced more easily in future projects?

6. Were the right resources available at the right times? How can availability be better predicted or ensured in future projects?

To prevent learning painful lessons, you should use a checklist to ensure the quality of your schedule. We will provide a checklist in the next chapter for use in evaluating the schedule. This list can be used to check the quality of the schedule as soon as it is created. This checklist allows you to be as proactive as possibly in your next project.

Chapter 13 Summary

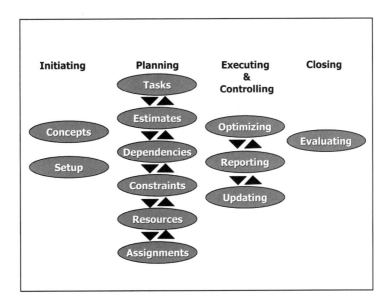

As you can see in the illustration we have discussed a project throughout its entire life cycle including updating a schedule and closing it out with lessons learned. Throughout the book we have made many recommendations that reflect best scheduling practices and we will bring these recommendations together by providing two checklists in this summary chapter:

◆ Checklist for Troubleshooting MS Project Schedules, see page 613
◆ Checklist for Dynamic Project Models, see page 614

Certificates Weather the Storm

The economy turned sour and both our friends, Bob and Nob, got laid off. When they accidentally met, they exchanged their experiences. Nob told Bob that he did not get an interview yet, but had some interest from one employer. Bob said that he had one interview coming up. He commented that prospective employers had a special interest in the certificates he had attained over the years.

"What certificates did you get?" asked Nob. "Well, I got my PMP certification from the PMI and then I also became a Black Belt in MS Project through the International Institute for Learning," Bob said with some pride in his voice. "I guess the certificates set me apart!"

Nob asked: "How did you get around to getting these certificates while you were managing your projects? I did not have time for that!"
Bob: "I don't know how I did it, but I did. I am now reaping the benefits from making it a priority at the time."

Nob looked down and said, "I guess I have enough time now to get certified, but nobody is going to pay for the training and certification. Why didn't I spare some time when I could?"

Checklist for Troubleshooting MS Project Schedules

If you don't understand why a task is scheduled on the dates it is, here are some questions to ask yourself. The questions are ranked in terms of precedence: the higher on the list, the stronger the effect. As soon as you find the reason, you don't need to go down the list further. We therefore recommend you start at the top of the list and go down when you are troubleshooting schedules:

1. Does the task have an actual start date?
    Does one of its predecessors or successors have an actual start date?
    Insert the column **Actual Start** to check this.

2. Is there a hard constraint on the task or on its predecessors or successors?
    Insert the column **Constraint Type**.

3. Is there a task calendar on the task or on its predecessors or successors?
    Insert the column **Task calendar**. To see what the task calendar has in terms of non-working days, choose **Tools, Change working time**, then select the task calendar from the list at the top under **For:**.

4. Is there leveling delay on the task (or on its predecessors)?
    Insert the column **Leveling Delay**. If the task is delayed for the purpose of leveling the workload of resources, there will be an entry in this field.

5. What predecessors does the task have?
    Insert the field **Predecessors**. Is there a lag on the dependency?
    If there is more than one predecessor, typically only one of them drives the start date of the task you are wondering about.

6. For Fixed Work/Fixed Units tasks: Are there vacation days set on the calendar of the resource who works on the task or on its predecessors or successors?

7. Fixed Duration tasks can have weird splits in their task bars if one of the resources is not available when the task is scheduled. Fixed Duration task bars can also have leading dots before the task bar or trailing dots following the task bar that are remainders of task bar splits. You can often get rid of these dots by changing the task type to Fixed Units or Fixed Work.

8. Task-specific constraint tendencies (ASAP or ALAP):
    If you have an ALAP task constraint in an ASAP schedule, it tends to move dependent ASAP tasks out to later dates.

9. Default constraint tendencies (ASAP or ALAP):
    You can check the default constraint in **Project, Project Information**. If you

Schedule from Project Start Date, the default is ASAP. **From the Project Finish Date**, the default is ALAP. Under ASAP scheduling, tasks will tend to stay close to the project start date unless one of the factors above overrides this. Under ALAP scheduling, tasks will tend to stay close to the project finish date.

Checklist for Dynamic Project Models

As a summary of this book we will provide a list of criteria for good schedules. What is a good schedule? A good schedule is a model of the project that provides valid forecasts and that is easy to maintain. Only dynamic models are easy to maintain. Let's break *valid, dynamic models* down into its components:

A schedule has to be a model of the project:
◆ A model is a simplification of the reality.
  A model should be a deliberate simplification of the complex reality. At the International Institute for Learning (IIL) we use the criterion that if you cannot explain the model to your stakeholders, the model is too complex.
◆ A model of the project provides forecasts.

A schedule has to produce forecasts that are valid. A schedule will only produce valid forecasts if:
◆ It contains all deliverables.
◆ The basis for estimates (pure work time versus gross work time) is consistent with the working times on the project calendar.
◆ The time estimates seem reasonable for the work to be done.
◆ The schedule produces accurate forecasts.
  This can only be determined after the project is over, unfortunately.

A schedule has to be dynamic. The ideal of a totally dynamic model is that if one thing changes in reality, you should have to change only one field in your MS Project model. Even though this ideal is hard to reach, you can get very close to it if you set your schedule up in the right way. A schedule is dynamic if:
◆ It has as few constraints as possible.
◆ It has a complete network of dependencies.
◆ It is easy to maintain such that it can be kept alive during project execution.
◆ It is up to date in real–time.
◆ It provides continuous forecasts.
◆ It is accessible online.

Throughout the chapters, we have made many recommendations for making your schedule a valid and dynamic model of your project. These recommendations are compiled in the checklist that follows. The list can be used to evaluate the quality of your project schedule. At the International Institute for Learning (IIL), we use this list to evaluate the quality of the schedules that are submitted to us for certification on the Orange Belt level of *Managing a Single Project with Microsoft Project.*

If your schedule meets these guidelines, you have created a valid, dynamic model of your project. You have positioned yourself well to bring the project to a successful completion. Schedules that meet the requirements not only need the least maintenance during the execution of the project, they are also ready for consolidation into master schedules on a program or department level. The next level of the IIL certification curriculum, *Managing Multiple Projects* or Blue Belt level, is targeted at people who manage more than one project. From experience we can say that managing multiple projects is a nearly impossible task if the single schedules do not meet the requirements of the checklist. You need the single schedules to meet all requirements if:

◆ You need to create an *integrated program schedule* for a large endeavor from subschedules.

◆ You want to start developing scenarios with a *portfolio* of projects using the *Portfolio Modeler* in *Microsoft Project Web Access.*

In Appendix 2 you will find a list of about one hundred examples of schedules that were certified in the curriculum. These schedules are from real-life projects and are valid and dynamic models. We recommend having a look at the schedules that are relevant for your business.

We also provide tools with the checklist to check your schedules in an efficient manner, and we will discuss these next.

Copyright of the Tools and Checklist

The tools and checklist are copyrighted material: © International Institute for Learning, Inc. This checklist is provided to you for personal purposes only, like getting certified in IIL's MS Project certification curriculum. Please feel free to use it for that purpose. If you would like to use this checklist for commercial purposes within your organization, please contact IIL and talk to one of our sales representatives about licensing these tools and the checklist, see www.iil.com or call 1-800-325-1533 (USA).

Tools to Check Schedules

At IIL, we use the following tools for evaluating the schedules submitted for Orange Belt 2002 certification: (You will find them in the file *Tools to check Orange Belt Schedules.MPP* that is available for download at www.jrosspub.com.)

◆ Small macros to avoid repetitive mouse clicks.
Use the **Tools, Organizer** to transfer the module *IIL_OrangeBeltMacros* into your project schedule. You may have to restore the shortcut keys suggested below by choosing **Tools, Macro, Macros**, select the macro, then click | Options... |:

   ◇ **CONTROL + A** to run the macro **ExpandAllSummaryTasks_A** that expands all summary tasks (A for All). Every time before you apply a filter you have to expand all summary tasks.

   ◇ **CONTROL + L** to run the macro **ListProjectSummary_L** that displays or hides the project summary task (L for List).

   ◇ **CONTROL + E** to run the macro **ZoomTimescaleToEntireProject_E** that zooms the timescale such that you can see the entire project (**View, Zoom, Entire Project**; E for Entire).

◆ Use the **Tools, Organizer** to copy the following filters into your project schedule:

   ◇ **1 IIL Level of Detail < 1% of Proj Dur...** : an interactive filter that prompts for the minimum duration for detail tasks to check the level of detail in the WBS using the *1%-10% rule*. The filter displays neither summary tasks nor recurring tasks.

   ◇ **1 IIL Level of Detail > 10% of Proj Dur...** : an interactive filter that prompts for the maximum duration for detail tasks to check the level of detail in the WBS using the *1%-10% rule*. The filter displays neither summary tasks nor recurring tasks.

   ◇ **2 IIL Summary Tasks with Dependencies**: this filter displays all summary tasks with dependencies on them. If there are many summary tasks with dependencies, it makes checking the completeness of the network logic and tracing the Critical Path too difficult. We recommend keeping the logic on detail tasks as much as possible.

   ◇ **3 IIL Detail Tasks with SS or FF**: this filter displays all tasks involved in a Start-to-Start (SS) or Finish-to-Finish (FF) dependency. SS and FF dependencies can easily have loose ends in the network of dependencies and have to be checked separately and carefully.

   ◇ **3 IIL Detail Tasks without Predecessors**: a filter that displays detail tasks without any predecessors to find the starting points of the network of dependencies. Detail tasks without predecessors may start on the project start date or will have a Start-No-Earlier-Than constraint (SNET). The network of dependencies can have multiple starting points, but only one ending point. This filter displays all starting points of the network. You can then see if there are starting points in the network that perhaps should have a predecessor. Recurring tasks are not shown by the filter. Use this filter to copy all the IDs and task names into the feedback e-mail to the project manager.

◇ **3 IIL Detail Tasks without Successors**: A filter that displays detail tasks without any successor to find tasks that are not incorporated in the network of dependencies (*loose ends*). There should be only one ending point in the network of dependencies, otherwise Critical Path and slack calculations are not likely correct. Recurring tasks are not shown. Use this filter to copy all the IDs and task names into the feedback e-mail to the project manager.

◇ **4 IIL Constraints other than ASAP**: A filter that displays any tasks with a constraint other than As-Soon-As-Possible (ASAP). A dynamic model should have as few constraints as possible. Recurring tasks are not shown, because they should have constraints.

◇ **5 IIL Detail Tasks without Resources Assigned**: This filter displays all detail tasks without any resources assigned. You can also check this by looking under **Unassigned** in the **Resource Usage** view, but this filter allows you to copy the task IDs and names into the feedback e-mail. With that information, the person can find the tasks without assignments easily. If assignments are forgotten, workloads were omitted and the forecasted dates may be too optimistic.

◇ **6 IIL Deadlines or Constraints not met**: This filter displays items with a deadline or constraint that have negative slack. These deadlines or constraint dates are not met and the schedule may forecast dates that are wrong. You can copy the task IDs and names into the feedback e-mail.

◇ **7 IIL Tasks with missing baseline info**: A filter that displays any tasks that do not have baseline information in Baseline Start, Baseline Finish, Baseline Duration or Baseline Work. When assignments are created after the baseline is set, the Baseline Work field is often empty on these tasks. Notice that the filter does not check the field Baseline Cost.

◇ **8 IIL Reschedule Actual Durations…**: An interactive filter that prompts you for the status date twice and displays tasks with an Actual Start or Actual Finish date after the status date. All actual dates should be in the past, i.e. earlier than the status date. As the status date we would enter the date on which the schedule was submitted. With this filter you can determine if there are no actuals in the future, which does not make sense. There should be no Actual Start or Actual Finish dates later than the status date. The filter shows if the schedule is updated properly and thus if the forecasted dates are accurate and reliable.

◇ **8 IIL Reschedule Remaining Durations...**: An interactive filter that prompts you for the status date twice and displays tasks with remaining durations scheduled in the past (earlier than the status date). With this filter you can determine if the schedule is updated properly and if the forecasted dates are accurate and reliable.

◇ **9 IIL Remaining Durations revised**: this filter displays all tasks for which the current duration is not equal to the baseline duration. If the filter displays any tasks, it would indicate that the project manager is revising the *Remaining Durations*. Regular revision of remaining durations is important to ensure that the forecasted dates are most accurate and reliable. Provide feedback to the project manager only if the filter does not display any tasks.

Make sure that all summary tasks are expanded before applying any of these filters since filters never display detail tasks that are collapsed under their summary tasks.

Press [Control] + [A] to expand all detail tasks with the macro. Press [F3] to stop a filter and display all tasks again.

Certification Checklist for Schedules

In the checklist we have used the words "*summary task*" and "*detail task*" very carefully. It is important that the words are interpreted correctly for the guidelines to make sense. A summary task is any task with indented subtasks listed beneath it on a lower level in the WBS. A detail task is any task without indented subtasks listed beneath it on a lower level in the WBS. These terms are always used in these meanings in the guidelines below.

The checklist has the following categories that correspond to chapters in this book. The checklist can be seen as a succinct summary of this book:

♦ Work Breakdown Structure (WBS)
♦ Estimates
♦ Dependencies
♦ Scheduling Constraints
♦ Resources
♦ Assignments
♦ Optimizing
♦ Reporting
♦ Updating

General Certification Requirements

This section may not be of practical value for you, but is needed for our certification process at IIL.

- ◆ Have you answered the following questions and included these answers in the e-mail in which you submit your schedule?
  - ◇ What is the objective or final product of the project (if not described in **File, Properties, Comments**)?
  - ◇ What is the deadline date of your project (if not shown as a deadline date in the schedule)?
  - ◇ Do you have a cost budget? If yes, how much?
  - ◇ Do you have a person hour budget (effort)? If yes, how many person hours, person days, person weeks, person months or person years?
  - ◇ Do you gather pure work time estimates or gross work time estimates? For an explanation of these terms, see page 169.
  - ◇ Do you apply the Rolling Wave approach in your planning? If so, what is the duration of your detail planning window? For an explanation of Rolling Wave, see page 171.
  - ◇ Will you do task updates (durations) or assignment updates (time sheets) or both?
  - ◇ What class did you attend? Please answer these questions:
    Did you attend a traditional, physical class? If so, in which city and on which date did it start? OR
    Did you attend an online, web-based class? If so, on which date did it start? OR
    Did you do the Orange Belt course through self-study? If so, on which date did you receive the self-study package?

- ◆ Did you create the schedule yourself?
  For the purpose of certification, you have to create the schedule yourself. You cannot use a slightly modified project template since this does not allow us to assess if you have acquired the Orange Belt scheduling skills we test on.

- ◆ Your schedule has at least 30 uncompleted tasks. Dynamic models are useful for forecasting the future. Using this checklist is meant to be an early and proactive check to see if you have created a good model of your project. Applying it is much more beneficial if there are uncompleted tasks left in your project. We feel we waste your time (and our time) if we make project models valid and dynamic, which are completed already.

Setup

◆ Does the **File, Properties**, tab **General, Comments** field contain a description of the objective or final product of the project?
The description is visible as a **Note** on the project summary task. This criterion is mostly for schedule certification purposes; we need to have some background information on the project to better evaluate the schedule.

◆ Do the working hours on the **Tools, Change Working Time, Standard (Project Calendar)** correspond to the **Tools, Options, Schedule, Hours per day** setting? For example, working times of 8AM-12PM and 1PM-5PM are consistent with 8 hours per day and 40 hours per week. If the settings are inconsistent, your forecasts are either too optimistic or too pessimistic. Also, you will often see decimals in the task durations in that case. See page 97 for a more detailed discussion.
The quickest way to check consistency is by choosing **Tools, Change Working Time**. The button ⬚ Options... ⬚ will take you directly to the **Tools, Options, Calendar** dialog. See page 93 for a way to set this straight.

WBS

◆ Is the WBS a deliverable-oriented breakdown structure? Are there deliverables in the WBS?
Deliverables should be captured using nouns (perhaps with adjectives, but without verbs). Verbs change a deliverable into an activity. If there are no nouns in the WBS, we have to conclude that there are no deliverables.
Alternatives for a deliverable-oriented breakdown are a phase-oriented breakdown or an organizational breakdown. From a project control perspective, these are less effective. See page 111 for a detailed discussion on proper breakdowns in a WBS.

◆ Is the list of deliverables complete?
◇ Are all expected deliverables explicitly included in the WBS? This should include the significant reporting items (e.g. monthly reports, test reports).
◇ Are out-of-scope deliverables that may be expected by the client explicitly excluded from the WBS? We recommend you capture exclusions in **File, Properties,** tab **General, Comments** field.
◇ There are no unnecessary deliverables in the WBS.
◇ We recommend you include the project management deliverables and activities in the WBS. See page 132 for different ways of doing that.

◆ Does the WBS have a logical hierarchy?
If you don't have a logical hierarchy, you may report the wrong cost and duration by phase or by deliverable. You can check if the WBS is a logical hierarchy by

expanding the outline structure level by level by clicking $\boxed{\textbf{Show} \blacktriangledown}$ on the **Formatting** toolbar.

◇ Is the WBS an indented list with multiple, hierarchical levels instead of one long list?

◇ Are the phases, if present, on a higher level than the deliverables?

◇ Are the tasks, if present, on a lower level than the deliverables?

◇ Does each element logically relate to its summary tasks?

◇ Do the subtasks comprise all the work of their summary task?

◇ Does each summary task have at least two detail tasks?

◇ There should be no duplication of deliverables or overlap between the deliverables.

◇ Is the feature **Tools, Options, View, Project Summary Task** used instead of a physical project summary task? MS Project's project summary task has ID number 0 (zero).

◆ Are the WBS elements properly formulated?

◇ Phases are formulated using the imperfect tense (-ing).

◇ Deliverables are formulated using a noun (perhaps with an adjective but without verb).

◇ Detail tasks are formulated using a present tense verb.

◇ Milestones are formulated using the noun of the deliverable and a verb in past or perfect tense. Instead of a verb, the words 'ready','complete' or 'sign-off' can be used.

◇ Are the names of the deliverables, tasks and milestones used consistently in the entire WBS?

◆ Are there enough milestones?
There are enough milestones when there is roughly one milestone for each deliverable. Milestone events typically center around deliverables when the deliverable is completed, approved, sent, signed off, published, or shipped, for example. You can check this by applying the standard filter **Milestones** and checking if most deliverables (summary tasks) have a milestone.

◆ Does the WBS have the right level of detail?
There may be too few detail levels in the WBS:

◇ If you cannot estimate the duration or work on the detail tasks.

◇ If you have difficulties finding the dependencies between the detail tasks.

◇ If you often assign more than one resource per task.

◇ If there are detail tasks that are longer than a reporting period.

◇ If there are detail tasks with durations longer than 10% of the project duration (*1%-10% Rule*). You can check this by applying the filter
1 IIL Level of Detail > 10% of Proj Dur.... You will be prompted to enter what 10% of the project duration is. You can find the project duration by looking at the **Duration** field of the project summary task. The filter will display all detail tasks that are longer than 10% of the project duration.
An exception to the 10% maximum is the creation of long tasks to capture overhead effort, like *project management*, or *technical support*.

There may be too many detail levels in the WBS:

◇ If you think there are too many levels, or if you think the task list is too long.

◇ If you added checklist items or reminders into the task list. Transfer these to the **Notes** field.

◇ If you can't guarantee you will be able to update all detail tasks in the schedule during project execution.

◇ If there are tasks with durations shorter than 1% of the project duration (*1%-10% Rule*). You can check this by applying the filter
1 IIL Level of Detail < 1% of Proj Dur... You will be prompted to enter what 1% of the project duration is. You can find the project duration by looking at the **Duration** field of the project summary task. The filter will display all detail tasks that are shorter than 1% of the project duration.
Recurring detail tasks will not be displayed since they typically are short. Milestones are excluded as well.

◆ Is the WBS clear to all project stakeholders?
Stakeholders like customers, suppliers, upper management, team members, and support staff need to fully understand the WBS. If you, as a reviewer, don't understand it, chances are that other stakeholders don't either.

◆ Project management overhead tasks, if present, should extend over the entire duration of the project. It does not make sense to stop managing the project halfway.

◇ Do the overhead tasks (like "*project management*") extend over the entire duration of the project?

◇ Do the status meetings, as recurring tasks, continue over the entire duration of the project?

Estimates

◆ Are the estimates reasonable given the work that needs to be performed?
This may be hard to evaluate if you are not a subject matter expert. However, we all

know that writing documents takes a long time, particularly if they are formal or contractual documents.

◆ Are the estimates collected consistent with the working hours entered on the **Standard (Project Calendar)**?

◇ Gross working time estimates should be entered in a schedule with gross working hours (typically 8AM-5PM).

◇ Pure working time estimates should be entered in a schedule with pure working hours. 100% productive working hours correspond to a shorter working day, for example, 8AM-3PM. You should change the working times to shorter **Nondefault working times** on the **Standard (Project Calendar)** in **Tools, Change Working Time**. If you do this, you should also revise the **Hours per day** and **Hours per week** conversion factors in **Tools, Options, Calendar** accordingly. This is to keep your schedule consistent.

Dependencies

◆ Does the logic of the network make sense?
You can check this by showing the highest outline levels only and checking whether the timing of the deliverables (or phases) makes sense on this high level. Even though you may not be an expert in the area of this project, you can always pick up on common sense things like *design* drives *construction*, *write* drives *print*, etc.

◆ Is the network of dependencies complete?
The network is complete if the task bars of all detail tasks are tied up at both ends. However, the network can have multiple starting points, but only one ending point. Only then will the Critical Path calculation be correct. The following questions will help determine if the network is complete:

◇ Is the logic as much as possible set on detail tasks only?
If dependencies run over summary tasks as well, it takes too much time to check if the network is complete. It is also too hard to trace the Critical Path and understand it. Only with a complete network will the schedule be a fully dynamic model of the project. You can check if there are dependencies on summary tasks by applying filter **2 IIL Summary Tasks with Dependencies**.

◇ Are all the starts of the detail tasks and milestones linked to at least one other detail task or milestone?
Exceptions are: all tasks that can start when the project starts, external delivery milestones (should have a **Start-No-Earlier-Than** date), recurring tasks, and overhead tasks. You can verify if all starts are linked by applying filter **3 IIL Detail Tasks without Predecessors.** Note that if the project manager used SS- or FF-dependencies, the filter is not conclusive, see our discussion on page

213. You can check if there are tasks with SS- or FF-dependencies by applying filter **3 IIL Detail Tasks with SS or FF.**

◇ Are all ends of the detail tasks and milestones linked to at least one other detail task or milestone?
Exceptions are the project end milestone, recurring tasks and overhead tasks. You can verify if all finish dates are linked up by applying the filter **3 IIL Detail Tasks without Successors**. Note that if the project manager used SS- or FF-dependencies, the filter is not conclusive, see our discussion on page 213. You can check whether there are tasks with SS- or FF-dependencies by applying the filter **3 IIL Detail Tasks with SS or FF.**

◇ Are there tasks with an unreasonably large amount of **Total Slack**?
You can check this by doing a descending sort on Total Slack and checking whether the tasks with the largest positive slack were expected to have a lot of slack. If not, you have found missing logic.

◇ When a change is entered into the schedule, does it update the rest of the schedule automatically through dependencies? Is the entire schedule still valid? Where the schedule is not valid, a dependency might be missing. If you have to check the entire schedule on every change, you don't have a dynamic schedule.

◆ Are there redundant dependencies that make the network too difficult to understand, explain and maintain? Project managers should be able to explain the network to their project team, otherwise the network is too complex.

◇ Are there dependencies that leapfrog each other?

◇ Are there dependencies that run in parallel on detail tasks and their summary tasks? If that is the case, keep the detail task dependencies and remove the summary task dependencies.

◆ Does the network have circular logic?
Circular logic does not make sense because it is not clear which task should be scheduled first. MS Project warns you not to set circular logic within a single schedule.

Deadlines and Constraints

◆ Is the project deadline modeled in the schedule?
It can be set as a deadline date or as a hard constraint date on the project finish milestone.

◆ Does the schedule have the fewest possible schedule constraints?
Constraints make the schedule rigid. However, constraints are allowed on:

◇ External dependencies, such as *delivery of supplies* or *arrival of materials*.

◇ Activities that have to take place on a certain agreed-upon date, like *presentations* and *training*. In general, these are activities in which a group of people is involved.

◇ Recurring detail tasks, like *status meetings*.

◇ Do-or-drop-dead deadlines, like the *Dec.31, 1999* deadline for Y2K projects.

◇ Activities affected by (winter) weather conditions i.e., task *asphalt streets starts-no-earlier-than April 1st*. You can also use the feature of **Task Calendars** for these situations in MS Project. See page 139.

You can display all tasks that have constraints by applying the filter
4 IIL Constraints other than ASAP. The filter will not display recurring detail tasks, because recurring detail tasks normally do have constraints.

Resources

Resources and assignments are important in projects in which it can be expected that limited resource availability or huge workloads will influence the project end date. They are also important if there is a budget and the cost needs to be managed.

◆ Are all resources identified in the Resource Sheet?
This is the case if all resources are entered into the Resource Sheet that could have a potential impact on the quality, duration or cost of the project.

◆ Are there no overlaps between the resources or duplication of resources?
If there are overlaps or duplications, the project manager cannot check the workloads of the resources properly. Workloads of one person will be aggregated on two different resource names in the project.

◆ Is the availability of the resources appropriately modeled?
This can be assessed by checking:

◇ Does the availability of individuals not exceed 120% as captured in the resource field **Max. Units** and the availability profile in **Resource Information**, tab **General**?
This threshold was chosen for schedule certification purposes. We think it is unreasonable to ask resources for more than 120% availability for periods longer than one week.

◇ If the **Max. Units** are less than 100%, is there a valid reason for this?
Valid reasons are that the project manager works with pure work time estimates or that the resources have other ongoing work or other projects.

◇ Are the vacations of individual resources captured on their resource calendars?
Vacations are little effort to enter, but their omission can throw projects off track

in a major way. You can check this by choosing the report **View, Reports, Assignments…, Who does what**, click [Edit…], click tab **Details**, select ☑ **Calendar**, click [OK]. In print preview, you will now see individual vacations listed under **Exceptions**. You can copy this changed report back into your GLOBAL.MPT using the organizer (**Tools, Organizer**). In this way you have it ready to go for future schedule analysis.

◆ Are the costs of the resources appropriately modeled?
   If the project manager has a cost budget, the costs of the project should be modeled in the schedule. The following guidelines will help determine this:

   ◇ Are human resources entered as **Work** resources in the resource field **Type**? Are facilities, machines and materials entered as **Material** resources?

   ◇ Do **Material** resources have an appropriate **Material Label** to indicate their unit of measurement?

   ◇ Are the rates entered in the appropriate fields?
      ▪ Time-related costs for **Work** resources in the **Std. Rate** field.
      ▪ Unit-related cost for **Material** resources in the **Std. Rate** field.
      ▪ Time-related cost for facilities and machines as **Material** resources using a combination of the **Std. Rate** field (where you enter the per-unit cost) and the assignment-related **Units** field (where you indicate the number of units used per time unit, for example *1000/day*). See page 300.
      ▪ Use-related costs in the **Cost/use** field.
      ▪ Overtime costs in the **Ovt. Rate** field, but only if the overtime is paid for and at a higher rate than the standard rate.
      ▪ Rates that vary over time in the **Cost Rate Tables**.
      ▪ Multiple rates in the **Cost Rate Tables** and the appropriate cost rate table should be selected for each assignment.
      ▪ Fixed costs in the task-related **Fixed Cost** field.

   ◇ Is the cost scheduled appropriately?
      ▪ Does the resource-related **Accrue At** field reflect when the cost occurs: at the **Start** or at the **End**, or **Prorated** with the **% Complete**?
      ▪ Does the task-related **Fixed Cost Accrual** field reflect when the fixed cost will be incurred?

Assignments

◆ Is the appropriate **Type** of task chosen for each detail task?
   (**Fixed Duration**, **Fixed Units** or **Fixed Work**)

◆ Does each detail task have at least one human resource assigned?
If there are detail tasks without human resources assigned, you have not captured all
the workloads in your project. If workloads are missing, the schedule may not
forecast finish dates that are feasible. In the **Resource Usage** view there should be
no detail tasks listed under the first category **Unassigned**. You can also apply the
filter **5 IIL Detail tasks without Resources Assigned**. The filter allows you to
easily copy the tasks including their ID-numbers to provide detailed feedback to the
project manager. Note that there could still be detail tasks with only material
resources assigned if you check the **Unassigned** category or apply the filter.
An exception to this rule is that recurring detail tasks do not need resources assigned
to them.

Optimizing Workloads

◆ Is the total work within the person-hour budget of the project (if a person-hour or
person-day budget is available)?

◆ Are the workloads for the resources reasonable?

  ◇ For schedule certification purposes, the workload for individuals should not
  exceed 150% of their regular availability on a day-by-day basis. The workload
  should not exceed 120% on a week-by-week basis. These upper bounds may be
  too high for your own organization. We have arbitrarily set them at these levels
  to prevent burnout, attrition, and dramatic loss of productivity. These levels are
  hard cut-off points for most organizations; many will use lower thresholds.

  ◇ The workload of consolidated resources (groups) should not exceed their
  availability.

  ◇ The workloads should be fairly smooth since there are hidden costs involved
  with erratic workloads.

Note that it is not enough to just check whether there is any red in the Resource Usage
view. MS Project often highlights more resources red than are truly over-allocated. If
there is an over-allocation during only one business hour, the resource will already be
colored red. Also, assignments that are already completed are never colored red. Use the
Go To Next Overallocation tool on the **Resource Management** toolbar to check the
over-allocations. This tool is more selective and more reliable. However, even that tool
does not always find all over-allocations and it also highlights the one-hour over-
allocations. See for more information the discussion starting on page 416.

Optimizing Costs

◆ Is the total cost within the budget of the project (if a cost budget is available)?

Optimizing Time

◆ Are the deadline dates and other constraints met in the schedule?
You can check this by applying the filter **6 IIL Deadlines or Constraints not met**. The filter displays tasks with a deadline or constraint that have negative slack. When deadline or constraint dates are not met, the schedule may forecast a project end date that is too optimistic.

◆ Does the schedule have a Critical Path or a Resource Critical Path?
You can check the Critical Path by applying the **Tracking Gantt** view. This view has the Critical Path highlighted in red by default.

◇ If a schedule has extended when the workloads were leveled, a Resource Critical Path needs to be identified. Resource critical tasks need to be marked manually in the field **Marked**.

◇ The (Resource) Critical Path can only consist of detail tasks and milestones. The (Resource) Critical Path should not contain level-of-effort tasks (overhead tasks or recurring tasks) or summary tasks (since the logic should be kept on the detail tasks).

◇ Does the (Resource) Critical Path provide a complete explanation for the project duration? You can check the completeness by displaying the (Resource) Critical Path and then looking for gaps in it. Normally, there is at least one critical task on every business day (unless there are lags on critical dependencies). If you find gaps, the (Resource) Critical Path is fragmented and the (resource) critical tasks that are missing need to be identified in the schedule. See page 379 for possible causes of Critical Path fragmentation and what to do about them.

◆ Are there as many parallel paths as logically possible in the network of dependencies?
Novice schedulers tend to schedule all tasks in one long sequential chain. In that situation there are many soft dependencies that make the duration of the project unnecessary long. When optimizing for time it is important to schedule in parallel what logically can be scheduled to happen simultaneously.

Reporting

◆ Is there a one-page status report available as a **View** object in your project file that displays the *major milestones*? See page 518 for more details.

◇ Are the major milestones filtered in this view instead of grouped together? Many project managers put the major milestones at the top of their schedule to create a one-page overview of the project. This makes the network of dependencies very complex in the Gantt Chart.

◇ Are the appropriate milestones chosen to represent the status of the project and to forecast the project?

◇ Does the one-page view report give an appropriate impression of the health of the project?

◆ If your schedule has a *Resource Critical Path*, is there a separate view object that displays the Resource Critical Path?
See page 431 and following for a detailed discussion on the Resource Critical Path.

Updating

The following guidelines are mandatory if the project is supposed to be started. A project is supposed to be started if today's date is later than the project start date. For schedule certification purposes this is if the date on which the schedule was submitted is later than the project start date. The schedule needs to show update information with actuals and revised forecasts. Projects planned far into the future do not necessarily need a baseline yet.

◆ What is the quality of the baseline in the schedule?

◇ Is a baseline present?
A baseline has to be present in projects that are about to start.

◇ Is the baseline complete?
You can verify the presence and completeness by applying the filter
7 IIL Tasks with missing baseline info. The filter displays any tasks without entries in **Baseline Start, Baseline Finish, Baseline Duration** or **Baseline Work**. When assignments are created after the baseline is set, often the Baseline Work field is empty. Note that the filter does not check the field **Baseline Cost**.

◇ Is the baseline original?
The baseline cannot be reset without formal approval of the appropriate project stakeholders.

◇ Is the baseline relevant?
If the project deviated too far from the baseline, a new baseline needs to be negotiated. The baseline should provide a meaningful standard of comparison for the current schedule. You can check this by looking at how far the current schedule bars are removed from the baseline bars.

◆ Are the appropriate options selected in **Tools, Options, Calculation** for the chosen updating strategy?

◇ For task updating (revising the task-related **Actual Duration** and **Remaining Duration** fields), the following options should be selected:

    ☑ **Updating task status updates resource status**

    ☑ **Split in-progress tasks**

◇ For assignment updating (entering numbers from the time sheets into the assignment-related **Actual Work** and **Remaining Work** fields), the following options should be selected:

    ☑ **Updating task status updates resource status**

    If you keep this option selected, you should not enter **% Complete** on tasks because this will override time sheet data.

    ☑ **Split in-progress tasks**

◇ For updating both the tasks and the assignments, the following options should be selected:

    ☐ **Updating task status updates resource status**

    Entering a **% Complete** on tasks will override the time sheet information. You cannot enter both types of information unless you de-select this option.

    ☑ **Split in-progress tasks**

◆ Is the **Status Date** set to an appropriate date?
For schedule certification purposes, the appropriate date is the regular reporting date that is closest to the date of submitting the schedule. Don't forget to set the **Current date** to the same date as the **Status date** in **Project, Project Information** before updating the schedule.

◆ Is the schedule up to date as per the **Status date** (or **Current date**)?
For certification purposes, we will check if the schedule is up to date per the date on which you submitted the schedule.

◇ Are all actual durations (actual work / actual hours worked) scheduled in the past?
The actuals are scheduled in the past if they are earlier than the status date. Otherwise, the schedule does not reflect up-to-date forecasts. When you bring actual durations to the past, all their dependent tasks may be rescheduled earlier as well, thus updating the forecasts. This is why rescheduling is important. You can verify this by applying the filter **8 IIL Reschedule Actual Durations...**

◇ Are all remaining durations (remaining work) scheduled in the future?
The remaining estimates are scheduled in the future if they are later than the status date. If you leave unfinished work before the status date, you are scheduling work to be done in the past. The work should be moved to the future to update the forecast dates. Otherwise, the schedule does not reflect up-to-date forecasts. If you don't do this you have created a *status report*, not a *forecast report* You can verify this by applying the filter
8 IIL Reschedule Remaining Durations...

◇ Are the remaining durations (remaining work) revised?
Otherwise, the schedule may not reflect up-to-date forecasts. If the project manager has been revising the durations of detail tasks, these will be displayed. This filter is different from the other filters in the sense that if it displays tasks, it is good. If the filter does not display any tasks, it is an indication that the project manager is not revising (remaining) durations while updating. If remaining durations are not revised, the forecasts are not very accurate, and may not even be reliable. You can verify this by applying the filter
9 IIL Remaining Durations revised.

Creating your Schedule to Submit for Certification

In order to get Orange Belt certified in our certification curriculum, you need to choose a project, create a schedule for it in MS Project and submit the schedule to your instructor for evaluation. Students doing self-study will submit to the certification administrator.

When you choose the project for your submission:
◆ The project should be preferably a real-life, work-related project. Otherwise, you can use a home- or hobby-related project.
◆ The project should be a project as per the PMBOK® Guide definition of a project.

When you create the schedule:
◆ The schedule must be created by you.
You cannot use a project template and send it in with only minor modifications. Ideally, you create the schedule yourself from the ground up.
◆ The schedule must be a valid and dynamic model of your project. You can verify this yourself by using the tools and checklist discussed in the next section.
◆ The schedule should have at least 30 uncompleted tasks.

When you submit:
◆ Submit the answers to the questions at the start of the checklist under *General Certification Requirements*.
◆ Submit the schedule of your own project (the MPP-file).
◆ The schedule must be submitted within one month after the workshop.
◆ The schedule must be submitted by e-mail and the (compressed) file size can be a maximum of 0.5MB.
◆ The schedule must be revised and resubmitted, if the instructor requests it.

The marks the instructor can give you are "*pass*" or "*revise and resubmit*". In the latter case, the instructor will provide detailed feedback as to what changes need to be made to the schedule in order to attain Orange Belt certification.

In Closing

If you have any further questions, don't hesitate to contact us. If you have any feedback on this book, please call 613-692-7778 or e-mail me at: EricU@iil.com.

This book contains the content of our first level of certification (Orange Belt). We would like to invite you to take on the challenge of becoming Orange Belt certified. You can do this through self-study, Web-based training or through traditional classes, public or onsite.

Please visit our Web site, www.iil.com, to read up on the entire certification curriculum: Orange Belt, Blue Belt and Black Belt. The Blue and Black Belts have two separate tracks:
◆ Standard: using MS Project standalone for people using Project 2002 Standard edition
◆ Professional: for people using Project 2002 Professional edition in conjunction with Project Server.
I hope to personally welcome you into one of these courses sometime.

Please visit the Web site of the publisher, www.jrosspub.com, to find the download files that accompany this book. Professors can even find a solution manual on this Web site that provides the solutions for all review exercises, relocation project exercise questions, the case study discussion questions, the troubleshooting situations and the multiple-choice questions.

Thanks for the time you spent reading this book and thank you for choosing this product from the International Institute for Learning and J.Ross Publishing. I hope you found it worth your valuable time.

Eric Uyttewaal, PMP
Vice-President, Microsoft Project Certification
International Institute for Learning
www.iil.com

Appendix 1: Certification Curriculum Sample Exam Questions

The Testing Process for Certification

In this appendix you will find exam questions that are representative of the Blue Belt exam in the certification curriculum of the International Institute for Learning (IIL). The Blue Belt exam covers the course materials of the Orange Belt workshop and the Blue Belt workshop. The Orange Belt course materials are completely covered by this book. The Blue Belt workshop has a separate course manual that is handed out to course participants when they attend the Blue Belt session. The following sample exam questions relate <u>only</u> to the text in this book, i.e. only to the Orange Belt course materials.

The exam:

◆ Tests your <u>readiness</u> to use the basic features of MS Project in practice.
In other words, it tests your active knowledge of the complete how-to steps for the basic features of MS Project. Basic features are those features most project managers need in order to model their projects, regardless of their industry.

◆ Tests your <u>practical</u> knowledge and skills.
It tests you on how to model real-life situations rather than theoretic examples. We provide real-life situations that lead into the question and ask you to make a recommendation about what the project manager should do in that situation.

◆ Tests your <u>understanding</u> of MS Project.
It tests your understanding of the behind-the-screens working of the tool. You have to understand some of the formulas that MS Project uses in the background in order to be able to predict what will happen on the screen. In order for a tool to be real tool, you have to be able to predict what it does; only then will it become a really useful tool. If you could not predict what a hammer does, the hammer would not only be a useless tool for you but even a very dangerous 'tool'. MS Project can be dangerous too, if you don't understand it.

The certification curriculum is designed such that it complies with the standards of the American Council on Education (ACE). The ACE protects the interests of American universities when auditing certification curricula from the private industry. See www.acenet.edu. The ACE has audited our curriculum and has accredited it. This means that participants should be able to get (elective) university credits with their certificate from IIL.

Each exam is carefully crafted in terms of coverage of all chapters and difficulty of the exam questions. The testing is not just an evaluation activity, but also a learning activity. It is a learning activity in the classroom in that participants mark their own exam immediately after taking it and then are given the opportunity to discuss any exam questions they would like to discuss. The participants know their score before leaving the premises, and the final score is confirmed within five business days. The passing mark is currently 60%. This passing mark will be raised to 70% in the future on recommendation from the ACE once the moving averages allow this to happen.

The test questions are subject to continuous improvement:
◆ The issues that arise from the discussions with participants are captured and, on a regular basis, used to review the exam questions.
◆ All answers given by participants are captured in the database and periodically the performance of the questions is analyzed. If a question is answered wrong all the time or never answered wrong, the question is either dropped from the database, or modified.

When a question is modified, it receives a new ID-number so it can be tracked as if it were a new question. Questions that are entirely new are introduced gradually; there will only be four or fewer entirely new questions on an exam. New questions are only used for groups of ten or more participants. This is to ensure that new questions will not jeopardize the validity of the test.

The complete certification exam consists of 40 questions on the content of the Orange Belt and the Blue Belt course. The exam is a closed-book and a closed-computer exam. The questions have to be answered within one hour. Below, you will find 40 sample exam questions. If you want to see whether you are ready to go for certification, you should be able to answer these 40 questions in 60 minutes and attain a score of 60% or higher. You should pace your work at 1.5 minutes per question. The correct answers can be found in the files available for download at www.jrosspub.com.

The answers to the questions have a good-better-best characterization. In other words, you should read all answers before picking the best one. If you don't know the answer, you have a 25% scoring chance if you just fill in any answer.

Orange Belt Sample Exam Questions

1 How can you change the contents of a project template MPT-file?
   A. You open the template file and make the changes then you choose File, Save.
   B. You cannot edit the contents of a project template; you can only replace the template file.
   C. You can change a project template using the Organizer.
   D. You open the template file in a special way that opens the original template file.

2 The summary tasks summarize their detail tasks. Which of the following fields of detail tasks do NOT necessarily add up to a total shown on the summary task?
   A. Duration
   B. Cost
   C. Work
   D. None of the fields mentioned

3 If you want to transfer a single view from one project file to another, how many objects may you have to copy at most in the Organizer?
   A. 1 view object
   B. 2 objects: 1 view object and 1 table object
   C. 4 objects: 1 view object, 1 table object, 1 group object and 1 filter object
   D. 5 objects: 1 view object, 1 table object, 1 group object, 1 filter object and 1 report object

4 What is a true statement about slack?
   A. The amount of Total Slack is always greater than or equal to the amount of Free Slack.
   B. Delaying a task and using its Total Slack will never affect its successors.
   C. Free Slack is synonymous to Float.
   D. The task bars of critical tasks are always shown in red.

5 The type of resources that is normally excluded from leveling is:
   A. Group Resources
   B. Individual Resources
   C. Facilities
   D. Materials

6   You want to create a schedule that needs the least maintenance while the project is executed, because you will be busy enough managing the project. You decide to follow these guidelines:
   A. Enter as many dependencies and schedule constraints as possible.
   B. Enter as few dependencies and schedule constraints as possible.
   C. Enter as many dependencies as needed and as few schedule constraints as possible.
   D. Enter as few dependencies as possible and as many schedule constraints as possible.

7   Which statement is true?
   A. Optimizing of the schedule should preferably be done only once.
   B. Creating a Gantt Chart should be done only once to win the bidding process.
   C. Setting the Baseline should be done only once in a project.
   D. Entering milestone constraint dates should preferably be done only once in a project.

8   .MPP-files can contain:
   A. Tasks, estimates, dependencies, constraints, resources and assignments.
   B. Schedule data (such as tasks, estimates) and objects (such as views, filters, tables, maps).
   C. Schedule data, but no objects. Objects are contained in .MPT-template files only.
   D. Schedule data (such as tasks, estimates) and generic options.

9   You want to shorten your project by creating an overlap between two tasks that are Finish-to-Start (FS) dependent on each other. How can you best accomplish this?
   A. You set a lead time on the dependency or you change the type of dependency.
   B. You set a negative lag time on the dependency or you change the type of the dependency to SS or FF.
   C. You cut the FS dependency; this will schedule both tasks in parallel
   D. You change the dependency to an SS-dependency with a 100% lag.

10 You are using forward scheduling and you have to install new computers, install software on the computers and train people in the use of the software. You want the users to be trained just before May at the latest. How would you schedule this situation?

A. The task "train people" needs an ALAP constraint and a milestone is needed with a Must-Finish-On constraint on May 1st.

B. All tasks need ALAP constraints and a milestone is needed with a Must-Finish-On constraint on May 1st.

C. The task "train people" needs an ALAP constraint and a milestone is needed with a Finish-No-Later-Than constraint on May 1st.

D. The task "train people" needs an ALAP constraint and a milestone is needed with a Finish-No-Later-Than constraint on April 30th.

11 You have a task with a Fixed Duration of 5 days. Two resources are working full-time on the task. The Work field shows 10 days. You want to change the duration while keeping the work on the task the same. How can you accomplish this?

A. You change the task type to Fixed Work, then you enter the new duration. MS Project will adjust the number of resource units working on the task.

B. You change the task type to Fixed Units, then you enter the new duration. MS Project will adjust the number of resource units working on the task.

C. You keep the task type Fixed Duration and you enter the new duration. MS Project will adjust the number of resource units working on the task and keep the Work the same.

D. The task type does not matter. You enter the new duration. MS Project will adjust the number of resource units working on the task and keep the Work the same.

12 When you have to level workloads you can do this manually or you can have MS Project do it automatically. Which of the following statements is true?

A. Automatic leveling results in tighter schedules than leveling manually.

B. With automatic leveling you can create three different scenarios: no leveling, leveled by a target date, and full leveling. You cannot go back and forth between the scenarios, but they make automatic leveling better than manual leveling.

C. Leveling manually involves more work than automatic leveling, but can lead to shorter schedules.

D. Manual leveling methods are reassigning resources, moving vacations, assigning in overtime and delaying tasks. Automatic leveling is assigning in overtime and changing non-working time into working time.

13 The differences between Views and Reports in MS Project are:
   A. The data in Views is editable, but the data in Reports is not. Views are
       customizable. Reports are not customizable.
   B. Reports always show numeric information. Views do not. The Reports are
       highly customizable. Views are less customizable.
   C. The Views are highly customizable. Reports are less so. The data in Views is
       editable. The data in Reports is not.
   D. Reports are quicker and easier for printing Gantt Charts and Time-Phased
       Budgets than Views.

14 A person complains that it always takes too much effort to create print-outs of the
    schedule regularly, such as Gantt Charts and to-do lists for each resource. What
    would you recommend?
   A. Use Reports instead of Views.
   B. Create separate views for each print-out you need. Separate the views in which
       you do the scheduling from the views you use for reporting. Use the Calendar
       view as a basis for the to-do lists in combination with the "Using Resource..."
       filter.
   C. Use Project Server to communicate to-do lists to resources. Use the Reports
       feature to create the Gantt Charts.
   D. Use the fit-to-one page feature to make the data quickly fit on one page.

15 A scheduler left some uncompleted work scheduled before the status date. The
    updated schedule shows that all the deadlines are met. What statement is appropriate
    about this status report?
   A. The report is wrong; the work should be brought forward to after the status date
       using the "Update as Scheduled" button on the Tracking toolbar.
   B. Who cares as long as the deadlines are met?
   C. The portion of work should be moved to after the status date using the
       "Reschedule Work" button, because this may affect meeting future deadlines.
   D. As long as the scheduler has entered all the Actual hours worked for each
       resource, the report is OK.

16 It is important to keep a time buffer in your program schedule. Why is this?
   A. Unforeseens
   B. Murphy's Law
   C. Path convergence
   D. Unforeseens, path convergence and the fact that task durations tend to extend
       rather than shrink

17 Which of the following statements about project calendars is TRUE?
   A. Changing the Standard Project Calendar changes all the resource calendars in
       the project.
   B. Changing the Base Calendar changes all the resource calendars in a project.
   C. You cannot create a workweek with seven work days.
   D. On the Standard Project Calendar you enter the statutory holidays and the work
       hours.

18 You are monitoring two milestones:
   "Report sent" shows a Total Slack of 2 days.
   "Test done" shows a Total Slack of -5 days.
   These figures indicate:
   A. both milestones will slip
   B. the milestone "Report sent" can be met easily, but "Test done" cannot be met
       without taking corrective action
   C. the milestone "Test done" can be met easily, but "Report sent" cannot be met
       without taking corrective action
   D. both milestones can easily be met

19 You want to update your project during project execution. Which steps should you
   follow and in which order?
   A. You set the baseline, the options and the status date in every status period. Then
       you enter actuals.
   B. You set the baseline and the options once, you enter the status date, display the
       Tracking Gantt, then you enter % Complete.
   C. You set the baseline and the options once and you maintain the baseline, if
       needed. You enter the status date, you display the Tracking toolbar and the
       Tracking Gantt view, and then you enter actuals.
   D. You set the baseline once and you never touch it again. You enter the status date
       and the options in every status period, you display the Tracking toolbar and the
       Tracking Gantt view, and then you enter actuals.

20 In which ways can you set schedule constraints?
   A. By driving a nail through a task bar on the Gantt Chart that hangs on the wall in your office.
   B. By dragging task bars to set Start-No-Later-Than constraints, or by entering start or finish dates, or by using the Advanced tab on the Task Information dialog box.
   C. By dragging task bars to set Start-No-Earlier-Than constraints, or by entering actual start or finish dates, or by using the Task Information dialog box.
   D. By dragging task bars, using the Advanced tab on the Task Information dialog box or using the task fields "Constraint Type" and "Constraint Date".

21 Two resources are working full-time on the task with 10 days of Work. You want to add an extra resource to the task, but keep the Work the same. How can you accomplish this?
   A. First you change the task type to Fixed Work, then you add the extra resource and the duration will decrease as a result.
   B. First you set the task to Fixed Duration, then you add the extra resource.
   C. First you change the task type to Fixed Units, then you set the task to non-Effort-Driven and add the extra resource.
   D. First you set the task to Fixed Duration and non-Effort-Driven, then you add the extra resource.

22 What do the "maximum units" of a resource represent?
   A. The number of part-time resources in a group resource.
   B. The percentage workload of a part-time resource.
   C. The maximum availability of the resource.
   D. The overall workload of the resource.

23 Which of the following statements is most accurate?
   A. For Summary Tasks only the task name needs to be entered. For Detail tasks the Task Name, Duration and/or Work need to be entered. For Milestones the duration needs to be set to 0.
   B. For Summary Tasks the name and the duration need to be entered. For Detail tasks the Task Name and Duration need to be entered. For Milestones the duration has to be set to 0.
   C. For Summary Tasks the task name needs to be entered. For Detail tasks the Task Name and Duration need to be entered. For Milestones the 'Mark Task as Milestone' needs to be set.
   D. For Summary Tasks the task name and the cost need to be entered. For Detail tasks the Task Name, Duration and/or Work need to be entered. For Milestones the schedule constraint needs to be set.

24 What factors should you consider, in general, when deciding whether or not to add a resource to the resource list?
   A. Whether the resource will add to the total cost of the project
   B. The impact the resource will have on the duration of the project
   C. The impact the resource will have on the workload histograms
   D. Whether the resource is available and whether the resource will have an impact on the duration or the cost of the project

25 Suppose you have several tasks to which you want to add John to the resources assigned. You can save time entering the assignments by:
   A. Selecting multiple tasks and using the Multiple Task Information dialog box.
   B. Using the Edit, Fill feature and fill John down in the field Resource Names.
   C. Copying a cell and pasting it into many other cells.
   D. Choosing the default Options appropriately.

26 Is it better to enter dependencies than to enter start and finish dates?
   A. Entering dependencies makes your schedule rigid and is worse than entering dates.
   B. If your situation allows you to enter dependencies rather than exact dates, it is better to do so because the schedule can be maintained more easily with dependencies.
   C. Dependencies are better because it is easier to enter dependencies and to explain dependencies.
   D. Entering Start and Finish dates is better because most tasks (like milestones, meetings and training) have a fixed start or finish date.

27 Which of the following statements is FALSE?
   A. A Start-No-Earlier-Than constraint will make sure that the Start and Finish date of the task will always be on or later than the date specified.
   B. A Finish-No-Later-Than constraint will make sure that the Start and Finish date of the task will always be before or on the date specified.
   C. A Finish-No-Earlier-Than constraint will make sure that the Start and Finish date of the task will always be on or after the date specified.
   D. A Start-No-Later-Than constraint will make sure that the Start date of the task will always be before or on the date specified.

28 Which of the following statements about Views is FALSE?
   A. A Gantt Chart shows tasks over time in a graphical format.
   B. The Usage views show either tasks or resources over time in a table format.
   C. The Resource Graph can show workloads in a numeric and graphical format.
   D. The Network Diagram shows the work breakdown structure clearly.

29 You contracted a painter on a fixed-price contract of $1300. In which view and in which field would you enter this cost?
   A. In the Resource Sheet in the field Fixed Cost
   B. In the Resource Sheet in the field Fixed Cost Accrual
   C. In the Gantt Chart in the field Fixed Cost
   D. In the Gantt Chart in the field Fixed Cost Accrual

30 You pay an electrician $70 per hour, and for overtime $90 per hour. In which views and in which fields would you enter these rates?
   A. In the Resource Sheet enter $70/h in the Standard Rate field. MS Project does not have features for capturing overtime.
   B. In the Resource Sheet enter $70/h in the Standard Rate field. The rate of $90/h does not need to be entered because MS Project will charge over-allocated hours automatically at the overtime rate.
   C. In the Resource Sheet enter $70/h in the Standard Rate field and enter $90/h in the Overtime Rate field.
   D. In the Resource Sheet enter $70/h in the Standard Rate field.

31 Which of the following statements is true about filtering Milestones?
   A. The Milestone filter will show all the milestones in your plan except for the milestones of summary tasks that were collapsed.
   B. The Milestone filter will show only those milestones in your plan that are marked as a milestone.
   C. Milestones cannot be filtered out.
   D. You need to create a new custom filter. You can create it through the menu items Project, Filtered For ....., More Filters. It should display tasks that have a 'Yes' in the Milestone field.

32 Which of the following statements about Work and Duration is True?
   A. Work and Duration are essentially the same.
   B. Work relates to human effort applied, whereas Duration relates to working time.
   C. The amount of Work always determines the Duration of a task.
   D. The Duration is always greater than or equal to the amount of Work.

33 Which of the following statements best characterizes the difference between pure work estimates and gross work estimates?
   A. Pure work estimates are based only on the effort necessary to perform the task. Gross work estimates include typical distractions that occur during the normal course of the day.
   B. Pure work is preferable to gross work in that gross work includes tasks like cleaning restrooms.
   C. Pure work estimates are more pessimistic in nature and, therefore, typically longer than projects based on gross work estimates.
   D. Pure work estimates are based on the effort to complete the task; whereas gross work takes into consideration the time constraints.

34 Being able to distinguish which task is the Predecessor is crucial in determining the appropriate dependency between two tasks. Which of the following guidelines will help you identify which task is the Predecessor?

A. Ask yourself: which task occurs first in time? The task that comes first, chronologically, is always the Predecessor.

B. Ask yourself: which task is driving the other one? The driving task is always the Successor.

C. Ask yourself: which task follows the other one? The follower task is always the Predecessor.

D. Ask yourself: which task is driving the other one? The driving task is always the Predecessor.

35 You have negotiated with a computer consulting firm to provide on-line technical support to your company for one month (20 working days) for a fixed fee of $5,000. What is the easiest way to capture this cost?

A. Plan on about one call per day and assign one unit of the Consultant resource to each. Set the Cost Per Use field to $250. (20 days times $250 = $5,000).

B. Assign one full-time Consultant resource to your "technical support" task and set the Standard Rate for the Consultant to $250/day (20 days times $250 = $5,000).

C. For the "technical support" task with a 20-day duration, set the task field called Fixed Cost to $5,000.

D. Set the task type to Fixed Cost and enter $5000 in the Cost field.

36 When making resource assignments, which view or dialog box listed below gives you most control over the variables that influence the resource assignment calculations?

A. Task Form view

B. Task Sheet view

C. Assign Resources dialog box

D. Gantt Chart view

37 Which of the following techniques, when applied appropriately to your project model, will typically yield the most accurate prediction of the end date of your project (assuming forward scheduling with unlimited resources)?

A. Critical Path Method (CPM) combined with Monte Carlo Simulation

B. Critical Path Method (CPM)

C. Resource Critical Path (RCP)

D. Program Evaluation and Review Technique (PERT)

38 In which of the following situations would the concept of the Resource Critical Path (RCP) be most beneficial to you?
   A. A project in which you have unlimited resources.
   B. A project in which you require several hard-to-get resources.
   C. A project in which your resources are easily replaceable.
   D. A project in which most of your resources are subcontracted out.

39 Assuming you are optimizing for time, and you've highlighted the Critical Path, which of the following methods or techniques for shortening the duration of your project is recommended as a first course of action?
   A. Breaking up long tasks into shorter tasks.
   B. Removing or softening constraints and reducing lags.
   C. Reducing scope or deleting non-value-added tasks.
   D. Changing sequential dependencies into partial dependencies or parallel paths.

40 You are using forward scheduling and you want to: 1 install new computers 2 install software on the computers 3 train people in the software while the software is installed on their computers 4 everything finishing at the latest before May. The dependencies you need are:
   A. 1 Finish-To-Start to 2, 2 Finish-To-Start to 3, 3 Finish-To-Start to 4
   B. 1 Finish-To-Finish to 2, 2 Finish-To-Start to 4, 3 Finish-To-Start to 4
   C. 1 Finish-To-Start to 2, 2 Finish-To-Finish to 3, 3 Finish-To-Start to 4
   D. 1 Finish-To-Start to 2, 2 Finish-To-Start to 4, 3 Start-To-Start to 4

Appendix 2: Certified Schedules Available for Download

J. Ross Publishing has created a resource download center on the Web site www.jrosspub.com. You will find the following files available for download:

◆ **Solutions manual for college instructors and professors** (PDF-file)
The solutions manual contains all answers to review questions and the questions in the Relocation Project exercises. It also contains the answers to the troubleshooting challenges. Finally the solutions manual contains discussions of the case studies in this book. However, this manual can only be downloaded by instructors and professors who plan on using this book in their courses.

◆ **Filters and macros to check the quality of your own schedule** (MPP-file: *Tools to check Orange Belt Schedules.MPP*)
These filters and macros are used by the instructors at the International Institute for Learning (IIL) to evaluate schedules submitted for Orange Belt certification. You can use these same filters and macros for your personal benefit to check your own schedule before submitting it for certification. Please contact IIL about licensing if you want to use these tools commercially.

◆ **Relocation Project Solution Files** (MPP-files)
This download contains the start- and finished-exercise files for the Relocation Project that is featured throughout the exercises in all the chapters in the book. The Relocation Project is taken through a complete project life cycle from inception to updating.

◆ **Troubleshooting Exercise Files** (MPP-files)
This contains files that are used for the troubleshooting exercises. Each file has a problem. The problems are representative of the kind for which technical support might be called. See the troubleshooting exercises at the ends of the chapters.

◆ **Answers to the sample exam questions of appendix 1** (PDF-file)
The multiple-choice questions in appendix one are exam questions that were really used in the certification curriculum. This download contains the right answers and brief explanations.

◆ **Quick reference tables with toolbar and keyboard shortcuts** (PDF-file)
You can print these quick reference pages and keep them close to your computer to have a personal (paper) assistant.

◆ **Certified Schedules** (about one hundred MPP-files in total)
This section contains several different files for downloading. Each file contains the certified schedules for a particular industry. Feel free to download as many as you want to explore. The files are a selection of excellent schedules that have proven valuable to the individuals that created them and to their organizations. The criteria I used to select the schedules are:

◇ The schedules meet the requirements for Orange Belt certification in the Certification Curriculum of the International Institute for Learning. The summary chapter contains an overview of all the requirements discussed throughout the book. All of them have been passed for certification and are excellent schedules.

◇ The schedules display a wide variety of projects and industries in which MS Project and our scheduling guidelines are implemented.

◇ The schedules may have value for you personally for your own projects.

I wish to extend a special thank you to all individuals and organizations that were so kind in allowing me to share their schedules with you. Their availability to you should provide insight into how the corporate world uses Project 2002 to deliver their projects successfully.

See the lists on the next pages with all the names of the individuals, the names of their organizations (if allowed) and the name of the file. They are all Project 2002 MPP-files.

CREATOR	FILE NAME
Automotive Projects	
Aytekin Bozkan	Aytekin Bozkan – TEHCM DV testing Automotive parts
Patty Amsden EPW, Inc., USA	Patty Amsden – Dew Model
Carl Koerschner Simpson Industries, Inc., USA	Carl Koerschner – Steering Knuckle Design
Steve Magee Dura Automotive, USA	Steve Magee – Recliner
Rob Miller	Rob Miller – Standard Draft Concept

CREATOR	FILE NAME
	Demonstrator
Construction Projects	
Sandra J. Perko GS XXI, Inc.	Sandy Perko – Expansion of Suite101a
Dale Dawson Central Lincoln PUD, USA	Dale Dawson – Transformer House
Alberto Alcala General Services Administration, Auburn, WA, USA	Alberto Alcala – Phased Construction
Eric Marois Algonquin College, Canada	Eric Marois – Voice and IP Installation
Hardware Projects	
Jim McCluskey	Jim McCluskey – EDI links for Pharmacies
Dick Lane WeBeGeeks, Inc.	Dick Lane – Network Installation
Wayne Broich	Wayne Broich – Install PCs
Bill Reinhart SBC/Ameritech, USA	Bill Reinhart – Router Installation
Tim Schell	Tim Schell – Install Web Hardware
Eddie Perez	Eddie Perez – Office Move
Charlie Milstead	Charlie Milstead – IT Infrastructure
Robertson Young	Rob Young – PC Deployment
Home Projects	
Nancy Tighe	Nancy Tighe – Master Bathroom
Larry Smith	Larry Smith – Landscape yard
Kenny Liss, PMP La-Z-Boy Incorporated	Kenny Liss – Building a Deck
Karel Swinnen EDS	Karel Swinnen – Garden works
Ken Taylor, PMP	Ken Taylor – Build Log Home
	Windows Restoration
Dohn Kissinger, PMP	Dohn Kissinger – Backyard Landscape Project
Ann Hardie	Ann Hardie - Summer 2001 Cleanup
Joy Barnitz	Joy Barnitz – House sale
John Rouster	John Rouster – Vacation
Tom Cappel	Tom Cappel – First Floor Remodel

CREATOR	FILE NAME
John Koepke	John Koepke – Build Fence
Kevin Gore	Kevin Gore – Build Deck
New Product Development Projects	
Chris Benson	Chris Benson – Autonomous Lawn Mower
Lisa James Pharmacia	Lisa James – Design and build air compressor
Plant Development & Maintenance Projects	
Todd A. Daily PCT Engineered Systems, LLC	Todd Daily – PCT Shop Test for Mill
	Refurbishing a Plant
	Installation Remstar equipment for comp tooling
David Peeters, PMP Alliant Energy	David Peeters – Facility Center Database
Steven Stricklin	Steven Stricklin – Heat Rolls Rebuild
Daniel Zook	Daniel Zook – Process Plant
Donald Martin Walker & Associates, Inc., USA	Donald Martin – Plant Development
Project Management	
Roy L. Ragsdale	Roy Ragsdale – Time-Keeping Project
Stephanie Ghingher AEGON USA	Stephanie Ghingher – PMO Software Selection
Kristin Horhay	Kristin Horhay – Establishing a PMO
Derek Scoble, PMP SGR Inc.	Derek Scoble – Montana State PMO
Greg Callahan	Greg Callahan – Planning Process Development
–	Project Portfolio Mgmt
Stephanie Iverson Marriott Vacation Club International, USA	Stephanie Iverson – Project Mngt System Implementation
Daniel Vitek	Daniel Vitek – HW&SW Purchase Process
Linda Lawlor Linda Lawlor Consulting, Canada	Linda Lawlor – Automated Project Office
Ann Russell	Ann Russell – Project Charters

CREATOR	FILE NAME
Software Development Projects	
Alan Bearder	Alan Bearder – W2K Active Directory SMS Schedule
Allie Darr	Allie Darr – Insurance SW development
Allie Fairfax	Allie Fairfax – AEF Data Application
Amy Schoenherr ProjectSavvy	Amy Schoenherr – Proposed Citrix Schedule
Beth Devroy Access Business Group	Beth Devroy – Skin Care System-COGS
Chas Eddingfield	Chas Eddingfield – Software Modification
Darrell Little North American Mortgage Company	Darrell Little – MERS TOSR software development
Doug Winters, PMP	Doug Winters – Data Retrieval
Frank A. Stillo, PMP OneWorld Inc.	Frank Stillo – SW Development Concert
Isabella M. Stengele Marsh	Isabella M Stengele – RMX Enhancements
James P. Crowell Marsh	James P Crowell – Detailed Analysis of Placement Repository
Joanne M. Greene-Blose Eastman Kodak Company	Joanne M Greene-Blose – ReMan release 4 Reprinted with permission from Eastman Kodak Company
	Full Flight Simulator Upgrade for Company XYZ
	Sales Forecasting Database
Carla Carter Levi,Ray & Shoup, USA	Carla Carter – Monthly checkwriting
Kathy Convery Levi,Ray & Shoup, USA	Kathy Convery – Database
–	Requirements and Specifications
–	SW Development
David Kempster Centrefile, Ltd. UK	David Kempster – Customer Database
Charlotte Mensah Centrefile, Ltd. UK	Charlotte Mensah – Develop Cube
Ron Ainsworth Centrefile, Ltd. UK	Ron Ainsworth – Software Development

CREATOR	FILE NAME
Michael Jordan Great American Insurance, USA	Michael Jordan – Claims Software
Software Implementation Projects	
Brad Jones Mount Carmel Health	Brad Jones – Software Installation
Bonnie Heinecke Fortis, Inc.	Bonnie Heinecke – Cognos suite deployment
Bob Herman	Bob Herman – Software Transition
	Beta Testing
Carol A. Ergen, PMP	Carol A Ergen – SuperMontage Implementation at NASDAQ
Dino Nosella SAP Canada Inc.	Dino Nosella – SAP Performance and Balancing
Jim Schuster, PMP Fortis, Inc.	Jim Schuster – Implementation of DB2
Larry Wentzel	Larry Wentzel – Automate Benefit Enrollment
Len Maland, PMP HP Consulting & Integration Services	Len Maland – Computer-Aided Dispatch System
Mark Cimon Cognos	Mark Cimon – Logistics Software
Nicholas Scott	Nicholas Scott – PROMPT Implementation Project Seven
R. W. Cornell, PMP The Revere Group	Randy Cornell – PepsiAmerica's IT Enterprise Infrastructure
Ronald Sonnabend	Ronald Sonnabend – SAP Upgrade Workplan
–	SW Selection and Procurement
Beth Pollard	Beth Pollard – Emulation Evaluation
Training and Organization Projects	
Tommie G. Cayton, Ph.D.	Tom Cayton – Incentive Standardization
Tara T. Miller	Tara Miller – training
Peter Avery Capital Defender Office, NY	Peter Avery – Newsclips for Capital Defender Office
	Translation Japanese
Gail Angel Cognos	Gail Angel – Document Writing

CREATOR	FILE NAME
Chris Baeten EDS	Chris Baeten – MS Project training
Caroline Robison EDS	Caroline Robison – Communications Project
Annie Nuyts EDS	Annie Nuyts – Security Organization and Governance delivery
Michael Starkey	Michael Starkey – Training Process Development
Regulation Implementation Projects	
Chetna Mathur	Chetna Mathur – Health regulation implementation

References

1. Guide to the Project Management Body of Knowledge, 2000 Edition, Project Management Institute, Inc., Newtown Square, Pennsylvania, USA.

2. Practice Standard for Work Breakdown Structures, 2001, Project Management Institute, Inc., Newtown Square, Pennsylvania, USA.

3. Work Breakdown Structure Practice Standard Project – WBS vs. Activities, Project Network, April 2000, Berg, Cindy and Kim Colenso, Project Management Institute, Inc., Newtown Square, Pennsylvania, USA.

4. Earned Value Project Management, Second Edition, 2000, Fleming, Quentin W. and Joel M. Koppelman, Project Management Institute, Inc., Newtown Square, Pennsylvania, USA.

Glossary

Activity See *task*. In this book the terms *task* and *activity* are used interchangeably.

Actuals The actuals is the set of data that represents how the project ran. It shows the real durations (*Actual Duration*), the hours that were spent (*Actual Work*), the real start (*Actual Start*) and finish dates (*Actual Finish*) of the tasks, and the final cost (*Actual Cost*).

Assignment An assignment is a combination of a task and a resource. It can be a resource scheduled to work on a particular task or a task assigned to a specific resource. Assignments have their own specific fields, such as start and finish, work, units, work contour and cost rate table.

Baseline The baseline is the original, approved schedule, plus the approved changes. The baseline schedule is meant to be compared against. The baseline schedule contains the original set of start and finish dates, durations, work and cost numbers. As soon as you have a version of the schedule that you want to use to compare progress against, you copy it into the baseline fields. The baseline values are static unless you baseline again. See *interim plan*.

Business Day A business day is a working day, normally a weekday.

Critical Path The Critical Path is the series of tasks that determines the duration of the project. The tasks on the Critical Path are often scheduled tightly; upon finishing one, the next one immediately starts. In other words, there is no slack between critical tasks. See *resource-critical path*.

Critical Path Method (CPM) The Critical Path Method is an approach for optimizing schedules that is based on identifying the Critical Path in a schedule. The method is based on the assumption that there is access to unlimited resources. See *resource-critical path*.

Critical Resource A critical resource is a resource that drives the duration of the project because of its limited availability. A critical resource is assigned to a (resource) critical task and drives the duration of the task. See also *Critical Path* and *resource-critical task*.

Critical Task A critical task is a task on the Critical Path. See also *Critical Path* and *resource-critical task*.

Delaying Delaying is rescheduling one of two tasks that compete for the same resource to a later date in order to resolve a resource over-allocation. The over-allocation is caused by the concurrent scheduling of both tasks and the use of the same resource. See also *leveling*.

Dependency A dependency is a logical cause-and-effect relationship between two tasks. A task often cannot start until another task is finished; the task is 'dependent' on completion of another task. For example, the start of printing a report is dependent on finishing the writing of it. Entering logic is called setting dependencies. See also *resource dependency*.

Detail Task A detail task is a task on the lowest outline level or any task without subtasks. Detail tasks are done by a person, and it should be possible to estimate the duration and the cost of each detail task. See also *summary tasks*.

Duration The duration is the number of business hours or business days estimated to complete a task or deliverable. See *work*.

Earned Value The earned value is the value of the completed physical work. Earned value analyses are often made during the execution of the project to evaluate the progress and to forecast the trend of the progress and cost.

Effort See *work*.

Elapsed Duration Elapsed duration is the time it takes to perform a task expressed in calendar time (which includes evenings, weekends and holidays). Elapsed time is used for tasks like *dry paint* or *back up computers*, typically tasks without human resources assigned. See *duration*.

Enterprise An enterprise can be your entire organization, or any subset thereof that you want to model the projects of using Project 2002 and *Project Server*. This word is a term used by Microsoft to position the professional edition of MS Project in the marketplace. See *workgroup*.

Filter A filter is a condition that determines whether a task or resource is displayed. A filter is an object that can be transferred between project files using the organizer. See *organizer*.

Fixed Duration Task A fixed duration task has a duration that will stay the same regardless of how many additional resources are assigned to the task. For example: *drying of paint, teaching a course*.

Fixed Units Task A fixed units task is a task that keeps the number of resources assigned the same when a change is made to the *duration* or the *work*. If the work changes the duration will change and vice versa.

Fixed Work Task A fixed work task is a task that is effort-driven; the amount of *effort* (*work*) will be the same regardless of the number of resources doing the task. For example, *coding a computer program, writing reports* and *painting walls* entail a relatively fixed amount of effort. The work can be estimated up-front.

Float See *free slack* and *total slack*.

Free Float see *free slack*.

Free Slack Free Slack is the time that a task can be delayed without influencing the start of any dependent tasks. On the *Critical Path* there is no free slack. Free slack is synonymous to *free float*.

Gantt Chart A Gantt Chart is a graphical presentation of tasks over time. Bars in a timescale represent the durations of the tasks. The chart is named after Henry L. Gantt, who invented it in the early 20th century.

Global.MPT The Global.MPT file is the default template file that is always open when MS Project is running. It contains the default objects that are accessible in new and existing project files. Each object in the Global.MPT is accessible in all project files unless there is an object with the same name in the existing project file.

Group A group is an object that categorizes task or resource records in the MS Project database. A group can be transferred between project files using the organizer. There is also a resource-related field *group* in which, typically, the department of a resource is captured. See also *organizer*.

Interim Plan An interim plan is a set of start and finish dates that is used to compare. Interim plans only contain start and finish dates and are therefore only a partial schedule. See *baseline*.

Lag Time Lag time is the duration of a dependency. In a Finish-to-Start dependency it is the time you have to wait after the independent task is finished before the dependent task can start. Lag shows as a gap between the task bars in the timescale of a Gantt Chart. Lag time pushes the dependent task to later in time.

Lead Time Lead time is the amount of time by which the independent task starts earlier than the finish of the independent task in a Finish-to-Start dependency. Lead time is like a negative duration of the dependency. The two task bars will overlap and create a partial dependency. Lead time pulls the dependent task to earlier in time. See *partial dependency*.

Leveling Leveling the workload of resources is bringing the workload of resources down within their availability. Resources can have too much work when they happen to be assigned to two tasks at the same time. Reassigning one of the tasks to another resource is one of the possible solutions. A last-resort solution is to reschedule one of the two tasks to later in time. This is called delaying a task. See *delaying*.

Logical dependency See *dependency*.

Milestone A milestone is an event with a zero-duration. A milestone is an important point in time, often an evaluation point. It can be a date on which a deliverable has to be ready or a meeting in which Go/No Go decisions are made. Events like the opening of a new facility can be milestones. Milestones appear as diamonds in the timescale of the Gantt Chart and are visual reminders of these important dates.

Network Diagram The network diagram shows all the logical dependencies between the tasks. Dependencies are shown in the network diagram as arrows between task boxes. Each arrow depicts a dependency and points from the driving task to the follower task. See *dependency*.

Object Objects are things that change the appearance of the schedule data (tables, filters, groups, views, fields, reports, maps, calendars) or components of the MS Project interface (modules, toolbars, menu bars). All objects can be seen in the **Tools, Organizer**. See *organizer*.

Open DataBase Connectivity (ODBC) ODBC is a standard set to foster the exchange of data between database applications. Databases that adhere to the ODBC standard, allow other database software to read and write the data.

Organizer The organizer is a feature in MS Project through which objects can be transferred between project files and even the *global.mpt* file. Examples of objects are: tables, filters, groups, views, calendars and toolbars. You can access the organizer by choosing **Tools, Organizer**.

Outline Structure The outline structure refers to the profile of the indented task list. Detail tasks are indented under their summary task, to form an indented list of tasks, also called the outline structure. See *work breakdown structure*.

Partial Dependency A partial dependency occurs when a task is dependent upon the partial completion of its predecessor. As a result, the tasks will overlap each other in the Gantt Chart. A Finish-to-Start dependency with lead time (negative lag) is an example of a partial dependency. See *lead* and *lag*.

Person Day A person day is one person working for one full business day. See *business day*.

PERT PERT stands for Program Evaluation and Review Technique, a technique used to analyze and optimize network logic.

PERT Chart The PERT Chart used to be a view in MS Project, but was renamed to *Network Diagram* in the Project 2000 version. The PERT Chart showed the network of dependencies between the tasks as in the current network diagram. See *network diagram*.

Predecessor The predecessor is the independent task or driver in a dependency relationship. In the example of *writing* and *printing*, the task *writing* is the predecessor of *printing* and *printing* is the successor of *writing*. See also *successor*.

Project Calendar It is the same as the *standard project calendar*. The project calendar is the calendar on which you can specify which days are working days and non-working days for everybody involved in the project. It restricts the scheduling by MS Project and is a time-saving device for creating resource calendars. You can base the *resource calendars* on the standard project calendar, which will copy all the holidays into the resource calendars. See *Standard (Project Calendar)*.

Project Database All the data that are entered in the project are stored in the project database. Data can be extracted from this database as needed for a view or a report using filters.

Project Summary Task The project summary task is the project title at the top of the task list that displays summarized totals for the entire project. Its task ID number is zero and all other tasks are indented below it, such that it summarizes the duration, work and cost for the entire project. It can be toggled on and off by choosing **Tools, Options**, tab **View**.

Project Template A project template is a standard schedule that is typical of the projects run by an organization. It contains a standard WBS with dependencies, and often generic resources assigned to the tasks. A contractor who builds houses uses the same schedule over and over again. He could use a project template as a boilerplate schedule. Template files can decrease the necessary data entry for creating similar schedules over and over again, and are protected from accidentally being changed. Project template files copy themselves when you open them.

Recalculation A recalculation is a refresh of the entire schedule based upon changes made. Whenever a task is inserted or changed, the project cost and work change, as well as the dates of other dependent tasks. All these figures have to be recalculated by MS Project.

Report A report is a tabular and numeric presentation of the project. Many reports are shipped with MS Project and are ready-to-go. Reports are customizable only to a certain degree.

Resource-Critical Path The resource-critical path is the series of tasks that determines the duration of the project given a limited availability of resources. The resource-critical path takes logical dependencies and resource dependencies into account. Unlike the Critical Path the Resource-Critical Path is not based on having access to unlimited resources. See also, *Critical Path, dependency* and *resource dependency*.

Resource-critical task A resource-critical task is a task on the resource-critical path. See also, *resource-critical path* and *critical task*.

Resource Dependency A resource dependency is a relationship between two tasks through a resource that is assigned to both tasks. If the resource needs more time to finish the task scheduled first, it will cause the other (resource-dependent) task to start later.

Resource A resource is a person, team, facility, machine or material used in a project to accomplish tasks. Anything that can influence the timing, cost or quality of tasks should be defined as a resource to the project.

Resource Leveling see *leveling*.

Responsible A responsible person is the person who is accountable for deliverables of the project. Responsible people only become resources to the project if they work on any tasks in the project. See *resource*.

Schedule A schedule is a set of start and finish dates of deliverables, tasks and milestones that will accomplish the project objective. An MS Project schedule typically contains the WBS (including tasks), the dependencies between the tasks, the estimates, the resources and assignments, based upon which it calculates the start and finish dates.

Sequential Dependency When two tasks are sequentially dependent upon each other, it means that the first task has to be finished entirely before the second can start. See *partial dependency*.

Slack see *total slack* and *free slack*.

Sort A sort is a ranking of tasks or resources based on one or more fields in the project database.

Standard (Project Calendar) It is the calendar that acts as the project calendar. See *project calendar*.

Successor The successor in a dependency is the dependent or follower task. In the example of *writing* and *printing,* the task *writing* is the predecessor of *printing* and *printing* is the successor of *writing*. See also *predecessor*.

Summary Task A summary task is a task with subtasks that shows the duration, total cost and total amount of work of its subtasks. To make a schedule easier to understand for stakeholders, you can group tasks and give each group a descriptive summary task name. Summary tasks are often deliverables. These summary tasks give the plan a logical structure. If tasks are scheduled in parallel, the summary duration is not necessarily the sum of the durations of the subtasks. See also *detail tasks*.

Table A table is a selection of task- or resource-related fields that appear as columns in the spreadsheet of a view. A table is an object that can be transferred between project files using the organizer. See *organizer*.

Task A task is a concrete piece of work that has to be done and that can be assigned to a resource. It should be possible to estimate the duration of a task.

Task bar Each task has a task bar in the timescale of the Gantt Chart that represents the duration of the task.

Total Float See *total slack*.

Total Slack Total slack is the total time a task can be delayed without influencing the end date of the project (or any earlier constraint date). There is no total slack on the Critical Path. Total slack is synonymous to *total float*.

Tracking progress Tracking progress is comparing the current schedule to the original baseline. Comparisons can be made on the dates and the duration of the tasks, the work of resources and on expenditures.

Updating Updating a project is entering what really happened in the project (*actuals*) and what you forecast for the future. Actuals are the actual start date, the actual days or hours spent on a task and the finish date.

View A view is an arrangement of project data in MS Project. A view applies a table, filter and group object, and also contains the sort order, format settings, page layout choices and drawing objects. A view is an object that can be transferred between project files with the organizer. See *organizer*, *table*, *filter* and *group*.

WBS The WBS is a deliverable-oriented grouping of project elements that organizes and defines the total scope of the project.[84] See also *outline structure*, *summary tasks* and *detail tasks*.

What If analysis This is a way of finding out by trial and error what a better schedule may be.

Work Work is the estimated number of person hours or person days a resource spends on a task or deliverable. Work is synonymous to *effort*. See *duration*.

Work Breakdown Structure See *WBS*.

Workgroup A workgroup is a limited number of people that work closely together performing projects. For MS Project a workgroup typically cannot exceed 100 people. See *enterprise*.

---

[84] See the PMBOK® Guide, 2000 Edition, published by the PMI.

Index

Z